26 –

Matsuo

Aphasiology

and other aspects of
language

Aphasiology
and other aspects of language

MACDONALD CRITCHLEY

EDWARD ARNOLD (Publishers) LTD

LONDON

SBN: 7131 4158 1

Printed in Great Britain by
William Clowes and Sons, Limited, London and Beccles

PREFACE

Like the apprentice curate who began his sermon by saying he was about to define the Indefinable, fathom the Unfathomable, and unscrew the Inscrutable, I admit to a curious caprice: a preoccupation with language. Naturally this implies an interest in impaired speech as a consequence of cerebral disorder. I have yet another quirk, as best described in Oscar Wilde's words 'everybody who is incapable of learning, has taken to teaching'.

Neurologists have traditionally been in the vanguard of what I have called 'aphasiology', but latterly many seem to have fought shy of this topic, leaving research to workers in other disciplines—phoniatrics, phonetics, psychology, logopedics, linguistics, and 'psycholinguistics'. This intervention has been fortunate, for it has filled the gap between those who deal with the pathology of speech and those who study the natural complexities of communication.

A writer can never tell how much or how little he knows until he arranges his knowledge, an axiom which may explain those who venture to record their experiences. This volume does not constitute a comprehensive account of aphasiology. Many aspects of the subject have quite deliberately been omitted, for *l'art d'être ennuyeux c'est de tout dire*, but some paralinguistic topics have been touched upon. I hope they may prove to be of interest to all who are concerned with communication and its break-down.

Many of these chapters—though not all—have already appeared in print. When preparing this volume I have resisted the temptation to make drastic alterations to the original text. True, I have in many instances expanded the original papers with additional matter in the sense of an *esprit d'escalier*. There are drawbacks to this method of colligation, for repetition inevitably occurs when one reproduces papers written over a period of twenty years. Some of the more obvious duplications have been pruned. Some I have allowed to remain at the risk of irritating readers. When an idea needs to be stressed it often requires saying over and over again. In addition, critics will discern here and there a slight shift in orientation. I do not apologise for my inconsistencies or my perseverations. 'When a point is worth sticking to, I stick to it. When not: then not.' Nonetheless, I feel that he who never changes his mind never advances in thought. Even Winston Churchill's opinions were a harmonious process which kept them in relation to the current movement of events.

I hope, therefore, that this collection of my writings upon aphasiology and other aspects of language may interest my colleagues in neurology, psychology, and linguistics, and stimulate debate.

CONTENTS

ACKNOWLEDGEMENTS

The author wishes to thank the following for permission to use copyright material:

George Allen & Unwin Ltd for an extract from *Language, Its Nature, Development and Origin* by O. Jesperson; Jonathan Cape Ltd for extracts from *Juan in China* by Eric Linklater; the Clarendon Press for eighteen letters from R. W. Chapman's edition of *The Letters of Samuel Johnson*, Vol. III; Constable & Co. Ltd for extracts from *The Virgin Soldiers* by L. Thomas; the Trustees for the Copyright of Dylan Thomas and J. M. Dent & Sons Ltd for an extract from 'From Love's First Fever to her Plague' from *Collected Poems of Dylan Thomas*; Mr Guy Endore and Victor Gollancz Ltd for extracts from *Detour through Devon*; the Literary Executor of W. Somerset Maugham and Wm Heinemann Ltd for an extract from *The Razor's Edge*; Macmillan & Co. Ltd for extracts from *Language and Intelligence* by J. Holloway and *Laughter in the Next Room* by Sir Osbert Sitwell; the New Statesman for 'Swearing' by W. L. Goodman and Routledge & Kegan Paul for Fig. 7 from *Handwriting* by K. G. Roman.

I. APHASIOLOGICAL NOMENCLATURE AND DEFINITIONS

> *If you wish to converse with me, define your terms.*
> Voltaire

> *Of all things on the face of the earth, definitions are the most cursed; for if you make a definition you may bring together under it a thousand things that have not the least connection with it.*
>
> John Hunter

The vocabulary of science is apt to follow belatedly upon the observation of data, and muddled verbiage represents both the cause and the consequence of muddled thinking. Only too often, science utilizes, borrows, or takes over the terminology of common parlance, and endeavours to fit new concepts into old terms, and *vice versa*, rather than devise a precise vocabulary of its own. Misunderstandings are only too apt to arise, merely because of the shortcomings of verbal symbols. Words are often used vaguely, and near-synonyms may be carelessly promoted to the status of true equivalents. No more useful or important preliminary consideration can be imagined than to decide upon an agreed and acceptable terminology for the benefit of our co-workers and successors in neurology.

In the first place we have to consider the students of the pathology of language; or should we say, of speech? Here at once we come up against the principal and perhaps the most important hurdle. Are 'speech' and 'language' synonymous? If not, how do they differ in connotation? Unfortunately there is a slightly different usage in different races.

The Oxford Dictionary defines *language* as the science of speech; and *speech* as the science of speaking. Here then is a terminological quibble which, although it may satisfy the non-technical student, will not be adequate for the grammarian of science.

On reflection it appears clear that the English term *language* implies certain mental operations which transcend the more mechanical faculty of articulate speech. Language is more fundamental and also more comprehensive than speech. And yet, *speech* cannot strictly be restricted to mere audible utterances, for common usage also includes the manipulation of visible symbols as in writing. *Written speech* is a perfectly correct usage, though *printed speech* strikes a less familiar note. We may with complete propriety refer to language in the context of the understanding or performance of symbolic systems other than those of a strictly verbal kind. It would be quite correct

This chapter is based upon the opening paper read at the first meeting of the Research Group on Aphasiology of the World Federation of Neurology, held in Varenna, Italy on 5th May, 1966. The lecture appears with minor alterations in *Cortex* 1967 **3** 3-25.

to refer to the language of mathematics, the language of the dance, of music, of gesture, or even of flowers. To employ phrases like the 'speech of gesture' and so on, would not make sense.

And yet the lessons of etymology may prove more misleading than helpful. *Language* stems from *lingua* or tongue, and might be expected to apply specifically to the use of vocables: while, of course, its implications go far wider and deeper.

Some of the definitions which have been devised may be quoted in illustration. Thus, *language* has been defined as 'the expression of our ideas by certain articulate sounds which are used as the signs of these ideas'. (A. Rees, 1819). Henry Sweet spoke of 'the expression of thought by means of speech-sounds'. But such definitions would equally apply to speech. The same might be argued as to Sturtevant's definition (1947): 'a system of arbitrary vocal symbols by which members of a social group cooperate and interact'. Sturtevant is preferable to Rees in that symbols are mentioned rather than signs, for a symbol is greater than a sign, since it entails a convention, explicit or implicit, between its users. The same insistence upon vocalization is contained in Whitney's definition (1870): 'the immense aggregate of the articulated signs for thought accepted by, and current among a community'; and also in J. B. Carroll's clumsier attempt: 'a structured system of arbitrary vocal sounds and sequences of sounds which is used, and can be used, in interpersonal communication by an aggregation of human beings, and which rather exhaustively catalogues the things, wants, and processes in the human environment'. But Whitney also constructed another and better description when he spoke of language as signifying 'certain instrumentalities whereby men consciously and with intention represent their thought, to the end, chiefly, of making it known to other men: it is expression for the sake of communication'. J. B. Firth (1957) defined language as 'the whole systematic background of grammar, dictionary and usage—the typology of the common elements of your speech and mine, yesterday, today and tomorrow'. Whatmough is too technical to be generally acceptable . . . 'a body of physically discreet events in which relations of similarity occur in a statistically definable pattern'. So too is the definition put forward by G. Morris (1946): 'a set of plurisituational comsigns restricted in the ways in which they may be combined'.

The broader conceptions which underlie the correct use of the word *language*, as opposed to *speech*, are better brought out in the definition suggested by Vendryes in 1925: 'the practical utilization of those physiological and psychical processes which the human being has at his disposal for speech'. Or—too terse for general approval—'a system of signs', as proffered by Leroy (1905). Another crisp definition of language is Simon Potter's 'A system of arbitrary vocal symbols'. This has a certain disadvantage in not even hinting at the possible function of language. In many ways, one of the most satisfying definitions, despite its clumsy structure, is that devised a century ago by Thomson (1860): 'a mode of expressing one's thoughts by means of motions of the body; including spoken words, cries, involuntary gestures, even painting and sculpture, together with those contrivances which replace speech in situations where it cannot be employed'. A useful, though rather cumbersome definition was suggested by Max Black: 'A system of signs (whether words or ideograms) used in regular modes of combination, in accordance with conventionally established rules, for the purpose of communication'.

A wholly satisfactory definition should call attention to the exteriorization of ideas and feelings by way of *some* symbolic system: the definition should not limit the means employed to audible speech, nor should it suggest such a restriction. Furthermore the conception of communication should not be over-stressed, for language (and for that matter speech too), may at times be quite intransitive, and play a greater part in self-expression than in transmitting information.

For such reasons Sapir's definition of *language*, made in 1921, merits particular attention: 'a purely human and non-instinctive method of communicating ideas, emotions, and desires, by means of a system of voluntarily produced symbols'. It is submitted that this would be improved still further, if the definition of language were modified to the following: 'an essentially human method of expressing ideas and feelings by way of a system of symbols'.

May I suggest then as an appropriate definition of *language*, terse yet comprehensive, *the expression and reception of ideas and feelings*? This would align the word 'language' pretty closely with what we nowadays call 'communication'. Note that it does not specify the means by which ideas and feelings are expressed or understood: coded or de-coded. Although verbal symbols are among the most obvious of these channels, they are certainly not the sole methods of communication.

Turning to definitions of *speech*, we find that there are considerably fewer for examination. Gardiner's definition (1951): 'the use between man and man of articulate sound-signs for the communication of their wishes and their views about things' possesses several important drawbacks. It needlessly raises the issue of the essentially human nature: it restricts the process to signs rather than symbols: and finally it makes no mention of the act of writing. Of greater value is the older definition made by Thomson (1860), which reads 'a system of articulate words adopted by convention to represent outwardly the internal process of thinking'. Whatmough introduced the visible symbols available when he defined speech as 'the gross physical performance of talking (including the written substitute) without reference to meaning', but many might object to the sting in the tail. Firth (1937) gave a less formal definition of speech as 'anything you say or write as an individual in a specific situation on a particular occasion; it is a personal and social activity interacting with other forces in a situation'.

It should not be impossible to devise a crisp and yet adequate definition of *speech* which would avoid the non-essential or frankly dubious aspects, and yet contain all the essential components. 'The use of verbal symbols, audible or visible, for the expression of ideas or feelings', emphasizes the necessary employment of words in one form or other. It might be objected that there is no explicit statement that verbal symbols may be perceived as well as executed. Here at once is a basis for debate. This two-way action is implicit in the expression 'the *use* of verbal symbols'. Further objection might be made that the *purpose* of speech (i.e. expression) is not a necessary part of definition, and could well be omitted. To do so however would be to imply that nonsense syllables, written, read or spoken, would also come under the category of speech, an attitude which could not readily be maintained.

Speech, therefore, should be restricted to *the expression of ideas and feelings by way of verbal symbols*, (i.e. words, or any other verbal tools which we may come to regard as units of speech). To separate in this way 'language' and 'speech', is in conformity with the usual practice in Great Britain. In the U.S.A. there is a tendency to use 'language' in a more restricted sense, that is, as synonymous with 'speech'. I think this is unfortunate, even though there are good etymological arguments in support. To the various *non-verbal* methods of communication (e.g. gesture, music, and so on) the term *paralanguage* is often used.

In England, the term 'speech' is usually restricted to the *articulate* exteriorization and comprehension of verbal units, and loss of speech would imply an inability to make one's wishes or ideas known *through the audible channels of spoken utterances*, and furthermore would doubtless entail some difficulties in receiving information of this kind. The understanding of verbal symbols by way of *reading verbal characters*, whether printed or written; or their *execution* by way of writing, printing, a typewriter, morse transmitter, stenography, stenotyping, is a matter, not of speech, but of *language*. When impaired by dint of disease as in alexia we should really speak of a limited loss of *language* rather than of *speech*.

Such then is the British custom, and despite its characteristic illogicality, I would like to recommend it.

When it comes to the problem of discussing the *use* of verbal symbols, as well as the *evolution*—ontogenetic or phylogenetic—of such symbolic systems; or their *dissolution* in advanced age or disease, then obviously the terms *language* and *speech* are often used as synonyms. On many occasions it would indeed be difficult to avoid utilizing these terms interchangeably.

Most European linguistic systems contain two terms which roughly correspond with the English *language* and *speech*. Gardiner has had some interesting comments upon this particular theme. In French we find *langue* and *parole*; in German *Sprache* and *Rede*; in Swedish *sprak* and *tal*; in Dutch *taal* and *rede*; and in Arabic *lisan* and *kalam*; and in ancient Egyptian *ro* and *nucdet*. But there are curious inconsistencies. In Rumanian there is a distinction between *vorbiri* and *limbaj*. The Swedish *tal* means *speech* but the Dutch *taal* means *language*. In French there is yet another term namely *langage* which rather vaguely embraces both speech and language; this relatively greater richness in vocabulary in French is somewhat unusual and unexpected.

Another use of the word 'language' refers to the specific linguistic system of a racial group or community. It is unfortunate that these two different meanings to the same word should co-exist, and we find only a partial benefit in the alternative word *tongue*. In English this has a faintly archaic flavour and is not often employed. It is indeed generally used in the plural. Thus we can refer to the 'tongues of men'; and to the 'tongues of primitive peoples'; or the 'tongues of the inhabitants of India', but rarely and only in a pedantic way can we speak of the 'German tongue', the 'French tongue' and so on. With slightly greater propriety we can use this word in a historical sense as when referring to the linguistic system of byegone peoples, as for example when we refer to the Latin or Greek 'tongues'. But even here, 'language' would be less mannered and more usual.

The scientific study of language was formerly spoken of as *Philology*, especially in Great Britain. On the continent of Europe, however, the word 'philology' was used in a somewhat different context and referred to a study of the specific culture of a particular nation. The study of its language was incidental. Gradually there evolved the idea of *Linguistics*, or the study of language as an end in itself, as a natural object, and not merely a part of a particular culture. There are a number of available definitions: 'The study which is concerned with language in all its aspects—language in the nascent state, and language in dissolution'. (Jakobson and Halle). 'The scientific study of the phenomenon of language.' (Whatmough). 'The scientific enterprise of investigating the languages and dialects which are in use, or have been used, by various speech communities throughout the world.' (J. B. Carroll 1953). This same writer has also put forward another definition: 'The study of languages conceived as a code or a system of distinct sound-symbols underlying the manifest speech-behaviour of the individuals comprising a speech community'.

There are modifications of this broad conception. Thus *general contrastive linguistics* has been described as 'the general comparison of the features of a language-system'. *Metalinguistics* refers to 'the study of the cultural systems of behaviour patterns, its special correspondences with language structure and language meanings'. (Trager). Or, more simply . . . 'a theory of languages about languages'. Some writers, e.g. Carroll, have preferred to speak of *exolinguistics* rather than metalinguistics.

Since about 1950 the term *psycholinguistics* has made its occasional appearance within the literature, but often without precise definition. Psycholinguistics is a sort of contemporary trend which claims to focus upon language-behaviour. This rather vague conception is said by S. Rosenberg to include studies of (1) the influence of verbal and non-verbal antecedent conditions upon verbal behaviour and verbal learning; (2) the influence of verbal stimuli upon non-verbal behaviour and learning; (3) the role of verbal mediators in behaviour; (4) interrelationships among various dimensions of verbal response; (5) relationships between verbal and non-verbal response dimensions; (6) language acquisition and language development; and (7) strictly normative studies of language behaviour. Whether enlightenment is afforded by this explanation of the term, is open to argument.

Studies restricted to certain specialized aspects of language are sometimes identified by particular titles. So we find *graphemics*, of 'the study of writing systems' (Carroll, 1953), a topic for which Hockett preferred the term *graphonomy*. *Kinesics* may be defined as the 'study of all non-vocal bodily movements which play a part in communication'. (Birdwhistell, 1952). *Phonetics* means 'the science of the vocal sounds used in language-systems' (Carroll): or, 'the study of the gross physiological and acoustic features of speech-sound' (Whatmough): or, 'the science dealing with the production, transmission and reception of speech' (Sturtevant).

Particular difficulties surround the correct use of the term *semantics* which conveys quite different meanings to different students owing to the very diverse fashions in which it has been employed. Its most general and modern connotation is to indicate 'that branch of linguistics which deals with meaning' (Whatmough). In such a context the alternative expressions *semiology* or *semiotics* are occasionally used. Pierce and C. W. Morris, however, have isolated three uses of the expression semiotics, namely (1) *syntactics*, which concerns signs and the relations between signs; (2) *semantics* —signs and their relations to *designata* or the world experience, real or imagined; and (3) *pragmatics*, i.e. signs and their relations to users. S. J. Hayakawa (1943–1953) expanded the various shades of signification which have become linked with the term semantics. Thus, to modern logicians semantics indicates 'a study of the laws and conditions under which signs and symbols, including words, may be said to be meaningful'. Used as a synonym for semiotics it may also stand for 'the study of the relation between words and things, later extended into the study of the relations between language, thought, and behaviour; that is, how human action is influenced by words, whether spoken by others or to oneself in thought'. Finally, to philologists, semantics may suggest 'the historical study of changes in the meaning of words', and in this connection it can be used synonymously with *semasiology*.

Bonfante crystallized the whole matter by tracing three distinct meanings that have been attached to the one term semantics. In the first place it was regarded as the science of signs. This was the signification given it by John Locke, and by Saussure. In this connotation it is synonymous with the terms *semiology* or *semiotics*. The second use of the word semantics is that employed by Bloomfield who applied it to 'a study of grammar or lexicon'. This was the meaning given to the term by Breal. The third has to do with problems of 'meaning'. Ordinarily this third usage is the one which is applied to the word semantics.

A considerable amount of contemporary interest in language centres around its acoustic properties, and its role as a medium of communication. The latter function may be taken to comprise 'intercourse between minds or selves whereby sensations, imagery or conceptual meanings are transferred from one to another. . . . communication includes (1) ordinary semi-mediated communication by means of speech, writing, gesture, facial expression and bodily attitudes; and (2) allegedly direct contact between minds by mental telepathy and other occult means'. (Ledger Wood).

The science of spoken speech is constituted by *phonetics* or *phonology*, subjects which are capable of considerably illuminating our knowledge of disordered speech in brain pathology. Modern phonetics, following the teaching of Courtenay, and his pupil Kruszewski, is built up on a foundation of the *phoneme* as the unit of sound. This can be defined best as the 'minimum distinctive sound-feature into which any given flow of speech can be analysed'. Phonemes may be vocalic (vowel sounds) or consonantal. There are 44 or 45 of such in the English language, 43 or 44 in Russian, and 35 or 36 in French and in German. Quite minor variations of a phoneme are spoken of as *allophones*. Thus the /k/ sound in the words 'keep calm and cool' are subtly different because of the altered positions of the tongue as determined by the vowel sounds which follow.

When quality of tone and pitch are concerned, one speaks of *prosodemes*, that is, secondary (or suprasegmental) phonemes.

Still concerned with units, phonetics isolates the smallest meaningful unit of form, and calls it a *morpheme*. These may exist in either free or bound form. Thus 'books' comprise two morphemes: viz. 'book' (a free form) and '-s' (which is a morpheme in bound form).

The principal unit of speech is almost universally regarded not as a morpheme, nor a word, but the sentence. This can be regarded, quite simply, as 'the minimum complete utterance'. Gardiner's definition is longer and fuller . . . 'those single words or combinations of words which taken as complete in themselves give satisfaction by shadowing forth the intelligible purpose of a speaker'. (The expression 'shadowing forth' is unfortunate). In logic, a sentence is defined as 'a sequence of words or symbols which expresses a proposition, or which can be used to convey an assertion'.

This takes us to the notion of 'words' which to the unthinking might possibly be looked upon as the unit of speech. Words can obviously fall into differing categories according to their reference-function. One may distinguish *full-words* (which stand for a referend), from *structure- words*. These latter are also called *operators*, a term borrowed from mathematics to stand for 'words which perform syntactic functions, linking together parts of sentences, or showing the relationships between substantives, or between substantives and verbs within sentences'. This distinction between full-words and operators is very important in a language such as Chinese, where they are described as *kenemes* and *pleremes*, respectively. They also play an important role in the structure of aphasic utterance.

We can now at last turn to the immediate purpose of our present discussions. As students of the pathology of language all of us nowadays use the term *aphasia* as suggested by Trousseau in 1864; or else its modification *dysphasia*. As a description of the science or subject itself we naturally prefer 'aphasia', while when referring to a particular patient we can say, either that he suffers from aphasia or from a dysphasia, according to our individual liking. We should not be put off by the pedantic consideration that aphasia implies a *total* loss of speech (while dysphasia does nothing of the sort), because we recall that, as a matter of practical experience, absolute speechlessness (or *aphasia totalis*) is very uncommon. Mutism, when met with in the clinic, is almost always due to some condition other than aphasia.[1]

Incidentally I would like to make a strong plea for the use of the word *aphasiac* as a noun indicating *a patient suffering from aphasia*. We can also say, if you like, a *dysphasiac*. The terms 'aphasic' or 'dysphasic' should be confined to an *adjectival usage*, so that we can properly speak of 'an aphasic patient' or refer to 'dysphasic utterances'.[2]

At this point too I also wish to urge strongly the rejection of the term 'aphasia' as applying to the occurrence of non-development of language in a child. Obviously the phenomenology of the breakdown as a consequence of disease of a mature and elaborate system of communication is logically far removed from any clinical state of failure to develop. A child who is backward in the acquisition of speech should not be described as a victim of congenital aphasia. Still less should a child with innate defective auditory perception of the meaning of verbal symbols be spoken of as a case of childhood aphasia as is often the practice in the United States. We need other terms. Perhaps *alalia* or *alogia* preceded by some such modifier as 'congenital' or 'constitutional' might be agreed as referring to these constitutional dysphasias in the realm of language. But as alalia (or more often dyslalia) is usually employed by experts in *speech*-pathology (as opposed to us who are pathologists of *language*) to indicate a special condition of disordered articulation, we might prefer to drop the term alalia in favour of *congenital alogia* to indicate what paediatricians often refer to as congenital motor aphasia. Perhaps in this context it is preferable to utilize some non-commital term such as 'developmental disturbance of language'.

Incidentally I would also like to plead for a general use of the word *aphasiology* as indicating a study of the phenomena of central disorders of language. An *aphasiologist* therefore is one who studies the pathology *of language*. I hasten to say that aphasiologists are not *speech*-pathologists, for these are the individuals who are concerned with clinical disorders of *talking*—such as stuttering, stammering, *Poltern*, dyslalia, congenital pseudo-bulbar palsy, and so on.

In pinning our standards to the masthead of aphasia we are rejecting—like neurologists of 100

[1] Members of the Symposium agreed that the terms 'dysphasia' and 'dysphasic' should be abandoned in favour of 'aphasia' and 'aphasic'.

[2] Incidentally, we might also recommend the employment of the terms *agnosiac* and *apraxiac* as substantives, and for adjectival use *agnosic* (rather than agnostic) and *apraxic* (not apractic).

years ago—the alternative terms for centrally determined and acquired speech-loss which were in use prior to Trousseau's introduction of the term 'aphasia'. These discarded terms include *aphrasia*, as well as the former usage of *alalia* and *alogia*, but in particular Broca's preferred term *aphemia*. Broca prided himself as an etymologist, but he pleaded in vain for the rejection of 'aphasia' in favour of 'aphemia'. But this expression 'aphemia' is now virtually dead in neurological literature despite Bastian's attempts in the nineteenth century to keep it in currency, and more recently Symonds' plea for its restoration. I submit that we aphasiologists here and now declare that the term aphemia is obsolete, for it has implied different things to different people, and even different things at different times to the same person, even to its instigator, Broca.

Before leaving the term 'aphasia' and turning to other definitions, I would like to mention one common linguistic ambiguity. As neurologists we often meet with speechlessness in patients who are victims not of localized damage to the dominant hemisphere, but of diffuse brain disease. I have in mind the progressive speechlessness of the dement, whether adult or child; and also the apallic syndrome, i.e. the phenomenon of mutism associated with decerebrate rigidity and paralysis. Should we, or should we not, speak of these patients as displaying 'aphasia'? And if we regard this term as inappropriate in such circumstances—as I do—then what other term should we employ? Again for want of a better word, I would put in a plea for 'alogia' as applicable to the poverty of speech, the language-disorder in fact, of the demented individual. In the case of the other type of patient I mentioned, who is to all intents and purposes a midbrain preparation, I would suggest we accept the term *akinetic mutism* originated by Cairns.

The question of disordered speech in schizophrenics is a little outside our problem today, but it certainly merits a detailed consideration at the hands of neurologists versed in aphasiology on some future occasion.

Returning to our subject of nomenclature in aphasia we find that we begin now to encroach upon problems of classification. This is a matter for discussion on some other occasion, but we cannot entirely leave this matter right away. Whichever system of classification we eventually recommend, we are likely to continue to use certain descriptive epithets and these will require precise definition. Indeed—who knows—we may decide that a logical classification of the aphasias is still a matter which is impractical at present. For some time we may still prefer to speak pragmatically of just 'aphasia', pure and simple, using however an abundance of adjectival expressions to refer to various well-organized clinical types or variants. With this possibility in mind let us proceed to indicate and define some of these principal subtypes.

As an extreme instance of aphasic severity there are those cases where speech is restricted to a solitary word (like 'yes' or 'no') or to a meaningless noise. I have referred to such a condition as *monophasia* and such patients as *monophasiacs*. If this expression is acceptable—and I do not wish to exclude other terms—I would suggest as a definition of monophasia *an extreme degree of loss of expressive language due to localized brain-disease, whereby the patient is unable to emit anything more than extremely few stereotyped utterances, either verbal or non-verbal.*

Many terms are in use by neurologists throughout the world to indicate this type of extreme limitation of vocalization. *Recurring utterance* was Hughlings Jackson's original term and it probably remains the one which is in widest currency today. Less often the adjective is changed, and one speaks of *recurrent utterance* and Jackson referred to the mathematical metaphor of the recurrent decimal. Many aphasiologists in France, notably Alajouanine, speak of *verbal stereotypy*, or *verbal automatism* which has the merit of indicating implicitly the inappropriacy, the meaninglessness, and the compulsive character of many of these recurring utterances. Some Russian neurologists speak of a *word embolus* but here the analogy is surely very strained and is apt to lead to confusion in the minds of readers not too conversant with the language. Other phrases that have been used, and I submit we should for reasons of economy, discard, are 'word rests' and also 'formula speech'.

May I suggest that we aphasiologists adopt today the terms *recurring utterance*, *recurrent utterance*, and *verbal stereotypy*, interchangeably?

Turning to another remarkable clinical type of gross aphasia we have the patient who shows among other features linguistic or otherwise, a tendency to emit a stream of utterances most of which are incomprehensible. In England we usually speak of *jargon-aphasia*. But jargon has two meanings: one refers to the esoteric and idiosignificant language of a particular sect or trade (e.g. the jargon of lawyers, or psychiatrists, or schoolboys); the other indicates sheer meaningless talk. For the latter we also have in English the synonym 'gibberish'. Strictly speaking therefore 'gibberish-aphasia' would be better than 'jargon-aphasia', were the term not so difficult to the tongue and so ugly to the ears.

For the same phenomenon German neurologists usually speak of *Wernicke's aphasia*. Nowadays however eponymous terms are out of favour, and moreover the expression does not give us any inkling as to the most striking clinical characteristic of the speech, namely its apparent incomprehensibility. I would suggest therefore that we drop the term Wernicke's aphasia from the official lexicon of our subject.

French writers when referring to this phenomenon devote less attention to the linguistic peculiarities and more to such associated features as the lack of awareness on the part of the patient regarding his verbal shortcomings. Thus we meet the term *anosognosic disintegration of the semantic qualities of language* which is indeed quite appropriate as far as it goes. But it does not readily lend itself to abbreviation, or to adjectival use, whereas we in Great Britain can easily speak of a 'jargon-aphasiac', and his jargon-aphasic utterances.

May I therefore submit that we as an aphasiological convention recommend the term *jargon-aphasia*, and that we define it as *a type of speech impairment whereby the patient emits a profusion of utterances most of which are incomprehensible to the hearer, though perhaps not to the speaker*.

This brings us to the question of malformed or distorted words emitted by an aphasiac. To some extent we may be dealing with a simple superimposed *dysarthria*. This is what the French call anarthria, i.e. a disorder in articulation, apraxic or otherwise in nature. At other times there may be a complete substitution of one word or a fragment of jargon for another word, e.g. black for white. This we may speak of as *paraphasia* defining it as *the evocation of an inappropriate sound in place of a desired word or phrase*.

We may also speak of a special type of paraphasia, namely the use of *neologism*, as when a desired word is replaced by an articulate sound which is devoid of conventional meaning.

Such neologisms may of course lend themselves to semantic analysis and prove to be an amalgam of associated ideas. The first part of one word may fuse with the last of another to form a strange hybrid. Thus wishing to speak of knives and forks the aphasiac may come out with the neologism 'norks'. Sometimes the term *portmanteau word* is used in this connection, but the metaphor is a forced one, and I propose that we do not approve this particular expression. The process whereby bits of words are fused to form a neologism is often referred to as *incapsulation*.

May we pass for a moment to those cases where the speech defect is so subtle as to elude superficial testing, but which nevertheless is there, all the same, ready to be discerned by sufficiently deep probing? Here we find those patients with a slowly expanding brain-tumour who eventually develop an aphasia. We cannot very well speak of a *pre-aphasia* as this is an etymological hybrid. Other possible terms are *inchoate aphasia* or *ingravescent aphasia* but I prefer to discard these, again for reasons of economy in vocabulary. Perhaps you will be prepared to accept the terms *latent aphasia* or *incipient aphasia*. Mindful too of the convalescent patient who has had a cerebral vascular accident with speech impairment which has almost disappeared, we can refer to *residual aphasia*. In this way residual aphasia stands in temporal contrast to incipient aphasia, and both of them represent instances of latent aphasia.

One interesting clinical feature shown by a patient with incipient aphasia, is a tendency at times to use too many words, perhaps as a reaction against an inability to find the ideal and most satisfying expression on a particular occasion. Thus in naming tests the patient may hesitate in finding the exact term, but having eventually done so he proceeds to amplify it unnecessarily. Thus shown a watch he may hesitate, and then eventually bring out the word; he then goes on to add 'and a very expensive watch too, if I may say so'. These added titbits of information, unasked for and often trivial, may be looked upon as a form of *gratuitous redundancy*. If these items possess any function at all, they may be said to serve to oil the wheels of social intercourse, rendered difficult on account of speech impairment. A definition if needed may be submitted in the following terms—*the interpolation by a patient with mild aphasia, of verbiage, comparatively low in reference function, although not wholly beside the point*. Gratuitous redundancy can be compared in some ways with the *phatic communion* so typical of the gossip or small-talk of primitive peoples. In morbid states we are reminded of the *regressive metonymy* described in lobotomized patients by Petrie.

The well-known difficulty in supplying an appropriate name to an object presented, despite a not too restricted vocabulary is a phenomenon which has been referred to in many terms. *Anomia* is one of the less attractive of these. *Nominal aphasia* is another common expression but it has the demerit of having been employed in a somewhat different sense by Henry Head who made it an important compound within his system of classification. Although the term *amnestic aphasia* is not immediately self-explanatory, it is perhaps the best available and I would like to propose that we adopt this term anomia defining it as *an aphasic difficulty in supplying the appropriate term for a particular object at a given moment in time*. This is merely a special type of difficulty which forms part of a larger 'amnestic syndrome'.

The technique of testing for anomia often brings to the fore certain other clinical phenomena. In the first place there may appear verbal *perseveration*, or the incongruous and uninhibited evocation of a word just after it has been employed in another and an appropriate context. An allied phenomenon is the inordinate cropping up of a word or phrase, appropriately or not, in the speech or writing of an aphasiac. This may be referred to as *contamination*.

We may accept, I submit, the term *de-blocking* as described by Kreindler, Weigl and others, to stand for *the technique whereby an anomic aphasiac is assisted in his search for an elusive word by showing it to him in print along with a series of other and inappropriate terms.*

A vague mental familiarity with the word which cannot be exteriorized may be shown by the *Proust-Lichtheim manoeuvre* whereby the patient though unable to evoke the particular term, can nevertheless indicate how many syllables are entailed, by dint of squeezing the examiner's hand, or by tapping the table the appropriate number of times.

Other errors which may show themselves at this stage of clinical testing are the various verbal iterations other than recurrent utterance. *When the aphasiac merely repeats the phrase spoken to him by the examiner, with or without a change in pronoun*, we may use the term *echolalia. Palilalia*, a phenomenon which straddles both dysarthria and dysphasia, being at one and the same time a disorder of talking and a disorder of language, is a sort of auto-echolalia, and refers to *that symptom whereby the patient repeats the last word or two of a verbal statement, the words tailing off in a diminuendo fashion, and with increasing rapidity.* The patient may finish by making silent articulatory movements of the lips, a phenomenon spoken of as *aphonic palilalia.*

We may now pass to the various non-articulate disorders of communication which occur in cases of aphasia. The terms *agraphia* or *dysgraphia* are self-explanatory and stand for the *difficulties experienced in self-expression by way of writing.* Of course not every instance of poor writing in cases of cerebral disease is dysgraphic, i.e. aphasic in nature, and we can recall, in passing, the errors in writing made by a patient with apraxia or by one who suffers from the so-called Gerstmann syndrome. Bay has pointed out that a clear definition of aphasic dysgraphia is needed to distinguish it from non-aphasic disorders of written language.

Difficulty in making a copy on paper from a printed or written text is often given the somewhat inelegant term *acopia.* However acopia is frequently not aphasic in character.

Perseveratory features may be demonstrable in the dysgraphic specimens of our patients. Thus we may witness both *echographia* (whereby the patient merely writes down what the examiner says), and, more often and more typically, *paligraphia* (whereby the patient continues to write a word or phrase which he already has written).

Our battery of tests might well include some other aspects of non-articulate expression, which may uncover such phenomena as, for example, a disorder in shorthand writing, or in type-setting, or in assembling letters on cards to form words, or words on cards to make up sentences. These rather specialized defects are not given any particular term. Nor do we find it necessary to manufacture a terminology here, simply contenting ourselves with a descriptive phrase.

Turning to some of the perceptual disorders met with in aphasiacs, we may discuss as the most striking among these, an inability to comprehend the meaning of written or printed verbal symbols. The terms *alexia* or *dyslexia* are today commonly employed in this connection, replacing the older expression, *word-blindness.*[1] To define alexia is not easy, for the problem is a more complex one than might appear at first sight. Alexia may be merely relative, as when an aphasiac

---

[1] It was agreed that the term 'alexia' should be restricted to those cases of acquired difficulty in reading, whereas 'dyslexia' might well be utilized to relate to those children who show a specific and constitutional difficulty in learning to read.

finds it a difficult and laborious task to ascertain the complete significance of an elaborate piece of writing (e.g. a technical text), while still quite able to comprehend the meaning of a simple printed instruction. We can also imagine a case where an aphasiac loses nothing more than the power of making an aesthetic judgement of a piece of fine writing, being no longer able to distinguish prose (or poetry) of a high order from that which is merely humdrum or second-rate. So far no term exists to describe such a condition. It would be convenient if it were possible to distinguish those dyslexic patients who can read aloud quite correctly, but without comprehension, from those who even cannot read aloud. Years ago Joffroy described this phenomenon under the term *psycholexia*, an expression which we probably will agree to reject.

In discussing dyslexia we may wish to distinguish those patients who can correctly identify individual letters of the alphabet even though they cannot interpret combinations of letters which go to form words. Others again are said to be unable to identify single letters. Thus a distinction is sometimes made between *literal alexia* (where letters are unrecognized), and *verbal alexia* (where isolated letters are identified but words are not). The distinction smacks of artificiality and we are at once confronted with the problem of the one-letter word. Thus in English 'I' may be either a letter or a word, while in Spanish the same applies to 'y', in Italian to 'e' and so on. We may also refer here to the well-known trick whereby kinaesthetic clues may be utilized in order to identify large print, by dint of movements of the eyes, or the head and neck. This is what we term the *Wilbrand manoeuvre*.

A distinction is sometimes made between an agnosic type of dyslexia and a symbolic type. In the former there is said to be an underlying disorder in spatio-constructional manipulations whereby geometrical (and other) figures, cannot either be assembled or interpreted as letters. No underlying disorder of language in the strictest sense of the word is said to exist. Standing in contrast are the more usual cases where it is the symbolic nature of the print or writing which cannot be understood. Is this subdivision of the alexias permissible or worthwhile?

Perceptual disorders in the acoustic sphere are less familiar, and less commonly encountered. The old fashioned term *word-deafness*, whereby *the patient fails to comprehend the meaning of what he hears, although he knows full well that the sounds represent speech*, has yielded to *auditory imperception*. In some cases, however, auditory imperception is merely a part of a more widely ranged difficulty in comprehending the nature of sounds within earshot, e.g. rustling of paper, ringing of bells, ticking of a clock. To this more fundamental defect the rather unsatisfactory term *auditory agnosia* is current, though one hopes it will eventually be replaced by something more appropriate.

We believe, with Luria, that one of the principal difficulties experienced by a so-called sensory aphasiac lies in the discrimination between phonemes which are somewhat alike (e.g. /d/ and /t/; /b/ and /p/). The term *paraphonemia* may be used to indicate such an *inability to distinguish between phonemes which are somewhat similar in their acoustic properties*.

To consider the merits of such terms in common use as motor and sensory aphasia, central aphasia, conduction aphasia, and so on, would be outside the scope of this paper, for the task essentially entails questions of classification. It will be of greater value to discuss and define some of the terms employed in linguistics and in information theory, and which we aphasiologists are utilizing more and more. As we have already stressed, there is general agreement that the unit of communication is not the word, but the message, the sentence,[1] or what Jackson called the *proposition*. Dorfman used the term *narreme* but this has not received general acceptance in the literature of linguistics. At the same time we must admit that a certain amount of the things we say is anything but propositional, but merely interjectional. A century ago Jackson distinguished between *superior* and *inferior speech*, placing propositionizing within the former category, and within the latter, all expletives, clichés, trite phrases, and emotionally charged utterances. Modern linguists expand this idea, and divide articulate utterance into (1) declarative (assertions); (2) interrogatory; (3) imperative (orders); (4) interjectional; and (5) aspirations (or wishes). Others speak of *mands* versus *tacts*. These are perhaps unfamiliar phrases which require definition. *Mands are self-limiting statements concerning the needs of the speaker; while tacts are comments about external stimuli.* A mand benefits the speaker; a tact benefits the listener. An alternative and perhaps better division would be to discriminate speech which is *intransitive* from that which is *transitive*. This theme could be expanded considerably, and many other interesting philological considerations might be touched upon, such as the principal purposes or functions of speech. Although this is a subject which neurologists are apt to brush aside as purely academic, this is unfortunate, for it has important bearings upon such problems as the kind of speech which suffers most, and that which is involved least in cases of aphasia. Whatmough recognized four chief purposes or uses of discourse, namely the informative, the dynamic, the emotive, and the aesthetic. According to Watts: 'Language serves to assist memory and to facilitate thought; to communicate meaning and, when necessary, to conceal it; to express feeling and, when necessary, to disguise it; to state intentions or merely to intimate their nature; to influence or control the actions of others; and sometimes to provide substitute satisfactions for those that would normally follow upon the exercise of bodily activity'. Ingraham has set out a list of at least nine functions subserved by speech, and these deserve recapitulation. (1) To dissipate superfluous and obstructive nerve-force; (2) to direct motion in others, both men and animals; (3) to communicate ideas; (4) to furnish a means of expression; (5) to make records; (6) to set matter in motion (magic); (7) to serve as an instrument of thinking; (8) to give delight merely as sound; and (most important of all) (9) to provide an occupation for philologists!

Obviously the impairment to the language-faculty imposed by brain-disease is likely to involve these individual modalities in an uneven fashion. Thus, purpose (4) might be partly intact—in so far as emotional or inferior speech is concerned. The ninth purpose of speech naturally continues in even greater force.

Breal in 1897 had something to say about the original purposes of speech, and his remarks might well apply to some aphasiacs. 'Speech was not made for the purposes of description, of narrative, or disinterested considerations. To express a desire, to intimate an order, to denote a taking possession of persons or of things—these were the first uses of a language. For many men they are still practically the only ones'.

Surely the most comprehensive of all accounts of the multitudinous functions of speech was

1 The common term *sentence* merits definition, and it may be spoken of as *a number of words arranged syntactically so as to constitute a grammatically complete sense-unit.* A *word*, on the other hand, may be explained as *the smallest speech-unit capable of functioning as a complete utterance.* (Palmer).

drawn up by Holloway, who wrote: 'Language is used to influence the actions or the feelings or the beliefs of other persons . . . it is used, more or less recited, to influence our own feelings . . . or our own beliefs . . . It is used as in polite small-talk to avoid awkward silences or to conform to certain norms of etiquette. It is used to pose questions, to make promises, requests, bids, surrenders, bets and the rest. . . . and to count and calculate. It is used to deceive and to silence those who contradict us. It is used to enter pleas to give testimony and make confessions. . . . to take oath, to pray, to give thanks, and remit sins. It is used to act, to recite, to eulogize, to mourn, to curse, to compliment, to congratulate, to celebrate, to exercise magical powers upon subjects, to conjure and exorcise spirits. It is used to indicate the time at which something occurs, or the time at which someone is to act in a certain manner. For example, to start races or announce their start or to drill a squad. It is used to draw attention to gesture, or to our own location in space. It is used to remind us of what is already familiar. It is used to train and educate. It is used to construct verbal complexes like poems which conform to certain artistic requirements or canons. It is used to tell stories and to make jokes. It is used to promulgate laws including the rules of its own use and to provide illustrative examples of how they may be kept or broken, or of any other aspect of itself. Doubtless it is used in many other ways as well'.

While we are still discussing the interdisciplinary topic of the linguistic aspect of aphasia, and the contributions of aphasiology to linguistics, we might do well to remind ourselves of some of the key terms in metalanguage, and their exact meanings.

A *word* may be regarded as a convenient subdivision of a phrase or proposition, with some claims to be looked upon as an item of syntax but of little else. Obviously to an aphasiologist just as to a linguist, the word means little *in vacuo*. Indeed in *holophrastic* terms, a word may constitute a whole sentence. Even in the monophasiac, the recurrent utterance, which may comprise a solitary lexicon 'word', ceases as a matter of fact to be a word at all. For example, the patient may be able to say nothing but 'yes', and yet his intention or desire may be to express greetings, dismissal, gratitude, or even sheer negation. The so-called word 'yes' amounts to little more than an articulated sound, often compulsive in nature.

A word is sometimes spoken of as a *semanteme* (that is, the ultimate smallest irreducible element or unit of meaning). Bloomfield preferred to speak of a *tagmene*, an expression which never achieved recognition. In the case of the single recurring utterance of a monophasiac, the stereotypy represents not a word, nor a semanteme, but a *pseudo-semanteme* or a *displaced semanteme*. These two interchangeable terms may be defined as *utterances which wear the garment of true lexicon terms, cognate to the patient's original system, but not necessarily used appropriately*.

The importance of a study of phonemes in aphasia has been already touched upon, and it is probable that a considerable field for future research lies here. Not the least important of the projects would be to determine the most satisfactory method of recording of the aphasiac's utterances in some permanent fashion, using phonetic symbols instead of letters. There are two recognized phonetic codes in use, known respectively as the *broad* and the *narrow* transcriptions (or phonemic and phonetic respectively). For aphasiological purposes, the broad international phonetic code usually suffices. To either of these scientific systems of notation one may appropriately add various *supra-segmental marks* to indicate such features, otherwise left unexpressed, as stress, pitch levels, and terminal contours.

Graphic systems of recording are now necessary if we are to have a permanent and precise record of an aphasiological interview. Perhaps the most suitable and most elaborate to date is my modification of the techniques occasionally used in psychiatric research. In order to furnish a complete account of the various paralinguistic accompaniments, including the pauses, grunts, sighs, sniffs, and diverse other *phones*, as well as the manifold alterations in the cadence, chromatic accent, or melody of the speech (Monrad-Krohn's *prosodics*), we need to resort to an elaborate system of empirical symbols. The symbols devised by Smith and by Trager are those most in use, and these have been described as *emphatics*, or, the *expressive features, emotional overtones, pauses, and non-verbal utterances which may accompany spoken speech. Prosody*, by the way, *refers merely to the fluctuations in pitch and tempo of the articulated speech*, and pays no heed to the non-verbal audible phenomena. Prosodic units are sometimes spoken of as *prosodemes*.

A faithful transcript of an aphasiological interview also requires a record of the motor activity of the aphasiac who is trying to express himself. Obviously gesture forms an important aspect of paralanguage, and this may actually be impaired to a far lesser degree than articulate speech. The gestural behaviour of the patient can be recorded in permanent fashion, either by (1) a detailed verbal description of the exact mimetic and facio-brachial-trunkal movements; or (2) by recourse to a kind of pictorial script or shorthand, as used by choreographers in the ballet; or (3) a cinematographic record on video-tape.

While still discussing the question of motor paralanguage, we should distinguish between gesture, gesticulation, pantomime and mimicry. *Gesture* (and also *gesticulation*) should be made to apply to *movements which are made in order to emphasize the verbal utterances*. As such they need not be strictly speaking volitional, or at least, not highly voluntary. They belong more to the realm of automatic, unconscious or subconscious motor activity. *Pantomime* is a word which should be confined to *movements carried out in silence and with strict deliberation in order to express an idea or feeling. Mimicry*—used in the technical sense—refers to *the facial phenomena subserved by the autonomic system which are the unwilled (and largely uncontrollable) expression of feelings and ideas*, e.g. smiling, blushing, sweating, pallor, frowning, sneering.

The whole gestural package can be included within the all-embracing term *kinesics* which may be defined as *the complex of an individual's gestural activity, conscious or unconscious, replacing speech, or merely embellishing it*. Birdwhistell's definition of this same term is 'the study of units of gestural expression'. A special type of pantomime is met with in the various sign-languages, which are examples of what is occasionally known as *pasimology*. A unit of manual expression has been called a *chereme*.

The modern study of language owes much to the lessons which we can learn from what is roughly termed *visible speech*. Two technical terms are in common currency here, namely, *sonography* and *sound spectrography*. There is good reason to believe that a study of aphasic speech along these lines will almost certainly add considerably to our understanding of aphasia.

Leaving linguistic considerations for a time it is advisable to turn for a moment to discuss some of the intellectual aspects of aphasia. The nineteenth century conception of internal or inner speech and of engrams, is one which dies hard. *Inner speech* or *endophasy* refers to *the silent processes of thought*, as opposed to *exophasy* which means *vocal, audible* language. These may or may not be wholly intact in the case of an individual aphasiac. I have always considered it worth while to distinguish between those thought-processes (in normals or in aphasiacs) which operate in silence and which are never exteriorized either in speech or in writing, and the *preverbitum*, i.e. *those pre-verbal processes of thought which take place immediately prior to speech evocation*. There is good reason to believe that the dynamics of the preverbitum differ from the phenomena of internal musing or browsing, and that a study of the preverbitum may have valuable repercussions upon our ideas as to the various clinical variants of aphasia.

The term *engram* is one of respectable antiquity. It suggests the existence of a *memory-trace, or inner conception of a word or phrase* which may however prove quite elusive when attempts at exteriorization are made by an aphasiac. If we are to believe unreservedly what many of our aphasic patients tell us, the missing word is on 'the tip of the tongue' but can neither be articulated, nor for that matter, written down. We should, I suggest, be critical of such statements, for it is probable that the aphasiac possesses only an imperfect insight into, and an understanding of, the nature of his defect. In the aphasiac's mind, nothing more than a vague notion may actually exist as to the physical properties and structure of the intangible word. Expressed differently, it can be submitted that the engram—if indeed such can be said to exist at all—is merely a shadowy ideational wraith, rather than a precise concept strangled at the moment of birth.

It is necessary to discuss two terms which have long been conspicuous in neurological writings, namely *agrammatism* and *telegrammatism*. We do not pay as much attention nowadays to these concepts, as formerly. Agrammatism is naturally a more important feature in aphasiacs whose natural language comprises one of the highly inflected tongues, and in such the defect may entail considerable errors in the employment of prefixes and suffixes. With this in mind, it would be interesting to make a comparative linguistic study of the pattern of aphasia in patients belonging to different races. Aphasia in the Chinese (where the language is virtually devoid of syntax) would be a particularly valuable object of attention. Agrammatism is a term which we shall probably continue to employ, if only for a limited period, and it may be defined as an *aphasic disorder which impairs syntax rather than vocabulary*.

Telegrammatism is a purely descriptive expression and refers to that type of aphasic speech or writing where prepositions, articles, conjunctions—the operators, or so-called 'filler words'—tend to be omitted, while the 'full words' are more or less spared, i.e. the nouns, verbs and adjectives which are usually more concrete in their nature. Telegrammatism is a feature of aphasic speech in the case of agglutinative rather than inflected tongues. The resulting diction or script is terse and abrupt, reminiscent of the poverty of language utilized in concocting telegrams. There may also be a resemblance to the various pidgin languages employed at intercultural levels as a makeshift mode of communication. Though the concept of *telegrammatism* is not an important one, there is no reason for it to be discarded, for it possesses certain descriptive merits. It may be defined as *the type of speech which results after the sacrifice of the shorter terms which are less heavily charged with reference-function, or 'meaning'*.

E. Auburtin   Paris

Jean Bouillaud   Paris

Paul Broca   Paris

A. Pitrès   Bordeaux

Plate 1

H. C. Bastian   London

Max Muller   Oxford

O. Jespersen   Copenhagen

Plate 2

E. Sapir   New Haven, Conn., U.S.A.

Henry Head   London

A. Luria   Moscow

K. Conrad   Freiburg-i-Br.

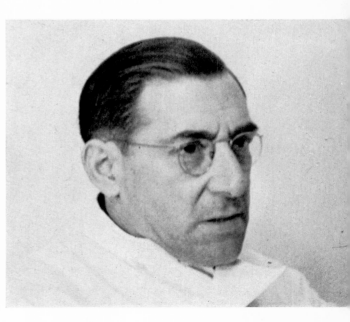

F. Grewel   Amsterdam

Plate 3

E. Bay   Düsseldorf

A. Leischner   Bonn

A. Ombredane   Geneva

Th. Alajouanine   Paris

Plate 4

II. INTRODUCTORY AND CONCLUDING REMARKS, 1961

In the beginning was the Word.
St. John 1

INTRODUCTORY REMARKS

It was most fitting that the topic of aphasia should have been selected as a principal theme for discussion at this International Congress of Neurology of 1961. The timing is peculiarly appropriate, for this year marks the centenary of the event which established speech-loss as a symptom of brain-disease. We recall that on 4th April, 1861, Dr. Ernest Auburtin, son-in-law of Dean Bouillaud, most distinguished among the supporters of Spurzheim and of Gall, delivered at the *Société d'Anthropologie de Paris*, an important paper entitled 'sur le siège de la faculté du langage'. He made an earnest plea for the anterior lobes of the brain to be regarded as the seat of language. Referring to an aphasic patient of his own named Boche, he said, '. . . if, when that man dies, I find no lesion of the anterior lobes, I shall renounce my ideas'.

Seated in the auditorium was the secretary of the Society, Dr. Paul Broca, whose interest was immediately kindled, for Auburtin's paper had appeared at the psychological moment. Just before, a speechless hemiplegic simpleton had been admitted to the surgical service of the *Bicêtre* on account of a cellulitis. After the lecture Broca invited Auburtin to examine this patient. Two days later he died, and autopsy revealed an old superficial softening in the left frontal lobe. Such was the opening of this chapter, and in honouring Broca we should not forget Auburtin, whose discourse it was that furnished the inspiration.

Furthermore, there was born in London on 5th August, 1861, Henry Head, who has surely done more than anyone else this century to orientate correctly our knowledge of aphasia.

Then again the topic 'aphasia' is a singularly happy choice. Of late there has been a tendency among neurologists to shy away from aphasia, as if the problem were too recondite, and too intangible to merit attention. Perhaps we have been smarting under the strictures of Tilney who described aphasia as a sort of touchstone upon which a neurologist tried out his skill. Certainly many a neurological reputation, like a storm-tossed ship foundering upon uncharted rocks, has been shattered by aphasia. Neurologists have latterly become only too eager to relegate research in aphasia to their colleagues in psychology, in logopaedics, and in philosophy. This is a great pity, and the prestige of neurology has suffered thereby.

From the symposium on 'Aphasia' held on the occasion of the 7th International Congress of Neurology, Rome, 14th and 15th September, 1961.

Today and tomorrow we will go a long way towards reversing this backslide, for we are to enjoy a series of important papers from neurologists who have not hesitated to grasp the nettle of that most difficult aspect of human brain-activity, and at the same time the most fundamental and the most fascinating. I refer, of course, to speech and its disorders.

SUMMING-UP

This has been an interesting and important occasion. Indeed over the century-old history of aphasiology there have been only one or two such full-dress discussions of this particularly difficult subject, the first of these being in 1868 at the annual meeting of the British Association which was held that year in Norwich. On that day there was a notable encounter between those great pioneers, Paul Broca and Hughlings Jackson. The second memorable inquiry was the three-day controversy presided over by Klippel, held in June and July 1908, at the *Société de Neurologie de Paris*, stimulated by the iconoclasm of Pierre Marie. A third took place on 11th November, 1920, when at the Neurological Section of the Royal Society of Medicine in London, Henry Head's lecture on aphasia delivered five weeks before, was debated in open forum. The latest of the great symposia upon aphasia was held in October 1960 in Bucharest, where the principal neurologists of eastern Europe forgathered to argue the present position of aphasia, particularly as viewed through Pavlovian spectacles. This meeting ended with the earnest plea for a standardization in our methods of examination, our nomenclature, and our classification of the aphasias.

The present symposium stands in direct succession, and although, alas, not a debate, it will be remembered as an important milestone in the maturation of our ideas upon this subject. It shows that the wind of change is blowing, not only through Africa, but also through aphasia.

Orthodox conceptions of aphasia rest on a tripod, the three legs of which are constituted by anatomy, physiology and psychology. This morning, Professor Hoff has retailed for us in a most eloquent fashion the bricks and mortar, or the scaffolding, of our knowledge of the morphology of aphasia. It is vitally important to build our beliefs upon solid facts. If we build upon sand, our notions of aphasia will collapse. The remarks of Hoff and Mogens Fog will go far towards constructing our edifice upon solid rock—like the Christian Church here in Rome. It is a sad commentary that it should have been still necessary for him—as indeed it rightly was—to distinguish between the localization of aphasia-producing lesions and the localization of speech. In other words we neurologists must realize that we are really handling 'centres of destruction' rather than 'centres of function'. As Alajouanine and Lhermitte put it, language is a general function, and as such, it is not to be divorced from intelligence and personality, and it cannot possibly be localized within this or that part of the brain. Today, 1961, most of us would assuredly be in full agreement, and yet in adopting this attitude we lay ourselves open to the protest 'why is it that disorders of language are correlated with disease of only the dominant half of the brain?' By admitting the lateralization of aphasiogenic lesions, we have localization already, as Kinnier Wilson said. We almost seem to be in sight of the end of the chapter on anatomy, but we still have much to explain about cerebral dominance and the tie-up between the major hemisphere and disorders of language. One of the themes for future research might well be an inquiry into the role of the minor cerebral hemisphere in language, and into those rare but important cases of disordered speech which sometimes follow disease of the right half of the brain in right-handed subjects.

The conceptions of Leischner are, I think, particularly attractive. As a secondary cerebral function, language is an accessory or even parasitic function which develops after the essential design of the brain has been completed. In other words localization of language within the brain can be only relative.

As to the physiological approach to aphasia, or *Sprachhandlung*, we have listened with great attention to what Alajouanine and Lhermitte have had to say, and also to the words of Professor Bay and Sir Russell Brain.

Of great significance is Alajouanine and Lhermitte's work upon the mechanism of jargon, of the verbal stereotypies and their recovery-stages. Let us take note of the contemporary dislike of the term 'agrammatism' which certainly never did apply so much to the English language as to the German. Alajouanine and Lhermitte are surely correct when they say that the whole conception of 'agrammatism' is unsatisfactory, in that it implies the loss of some alleged function of grammar which of course has no reality whatsoever. Several speakers have emphasized the role of auditory and muscular activity in the regulation of normal speech. An upset in the kinaesthetic control of speech is a topic which has been fully discussed by Hrbk, and—as Russell Brain said—we recognize in speech a sort of 'double feed-back' or a monitoring system which is partly auditory and partly proprioceptive. Bay put the problem of receptive difficulties in aphasia a little differently when he said that so-called sub-cortical sensory aphasia, or word-deafness, originates from an actual impairment of hearing combined with a *Funktionswandel* or lability of function in the acoustic sphere. Sensory aphasiacs, as he says, show a carefree lack of self-criticism which is by no means confined to the linguistic sphere. But nowadays of course, we have given up notions of motor versus sensory, or receptive as opposed to expressive, types of aphasia, terms which have become just as vestigial as 'word-deafness'. As Russell Brain said, speech is fundamentally a sensori-motor-sensory process, and a word is a *Gestalt* of a higher order than the sum of its constituent phonemes. Ordinarily, the comprehension of what one hears depends partly on the environmental context, partly on the framework of interest, and partly on syntax. Each one of these is a psychological process and any one—or even all—of them may be disturbed in aphasic patients.

Psychology forms the third and nowadays the most important leg of the tripod. Professor Hoff emphasized—and how right he was—that speech, written as well as articulate, reflects sharply the personality of the writer or speaker. Speech is such a personal thing that it is not going too far to declare that no two persons speak alike, just as no two persons write alike. Everyone possesses his own private idiolect. An analysis of speech, spoken or written, might well uncover a formula which is perhaps as individual as the patterning of the finger-prints. If this idea be accepted, and I think it should be, then it follows at once that the clinical picture of an aphasia largely derives its characteristics from the pre-morbid personality of the patient. This was well brought out by Professor Hoff who emphasized—and here again all experienced aphasiologists would agree with him—that in cases of polyglot aphasia the influence of affective, situational and environmental factors is at least as important as the order of acquirement of various languages. In other words the laws laid down by Ribot and by Pitres need to be drastically overhauled.

Several speakers today have touched upon the vexed problem of the status of intellect in aphasia. As to the nature of what used to be called 'inner language' or 'interior language' Alajouanine and Lhermitte rightly said that this was a sort of dynamic intermediary between thought and language, a complicated pre-linguistic organization visualized by Pick, by van Woerkom, and to some extent by Pierre Marie. The late Professor Conrad used to speak of a 'linguistic *Vorgestalt*'. In my writings I have preferred to use the term 'preverbitum' but all these expressions mean very much the same, and refer to that crystallization of thinking-processes immediately prior to the act of exteriorization in speech. It is within this pre-linguistic complex, this preverbitum, that we should be able to identify different levels of disorder in different types of aphasia, and I venture to submit that future aphasiologists will have discarded the present conventional, and eponymous methods of classifying the aphasias, in favour of a more logical one based upon levels of defect within the preverbitum or *Vorgestalt*. The interesting techniques of Weigl and Kreindler for de-blocking aphasias prove effective or ineffective, according to the depth of defect within the preverbitum.

Whether or not we believe that aphasia entails any disorder of general intelligence, we must surely admit that mentation is somehow altered, qualitatively if not quantitatively, and especially that type of thinking which concerns the silent manipulation of verbal symbols. Normally this may not be a consistent form of thinking, and it may vary from one person to another, and from one moment to another, depending upon a diversity of circumstances. But who can deny that in so far as verbal symbolic formulation and expression are concerned, thinking must be altered, or 'lame' as Hughlings Jackson used to say? Professor Bay has paid close attention, like Alajouanine in a different context, to the various non-linguistic intellectual and artistic activities which lie within the capacity of patients with aphasia. Plastic modelling has been, according to Professor Bay, a fascinating method of gauging how far concept-formation is intact or disordered in aphasiacs. All of us who have pondered the subject would probably agree that subtler modalities of language are beyond the powers of aphasiacs either to appreciate or to command. Thus, from the executive angle, inspired writing—like the highest flights of oratory—are impossible for an aphasiac. How many poets who have suffered a speech-loss have ever made such a restitution of their language-functions as to have been able once again to indulge in creative versification? Few indeed. The same holds true on the receptive side. Aphasiacs cope only very imperfectly with the less ponderable and less substantial aspects of language. The insinuation, the sly allusion, the stylistic beauties of fine writing are generally well beyond their competency to perceive. To take a humdrum example: few aphasiacs can grasp the point of a humorous drawing or cartoon, just as few aphasiacs can judge the intrinsic merits of pictorial or literary works of art. In this connection Professor Bay aptly quotes Busemann's notion of *Enfallsleere*, which may be rendered as 'lack of imagination or creative fantasy', as an important defect in an aphasiac's mode of thought.

It was especially valuable to hear the interesting remarks of Professor Luria this afternoon, for so much of the eastern European work upon aphasia lies somewhat outside the main stream of endeavour. At first blush one might have considered that Pavlovian philosophy would have proved relatively sterile in the domain of aphasia. It is not easy to visualize such a philosophy as applying to the framework of disordered language, that essentially human endowment, but Luria has shown us how wrong it would be to reject this approach. He has succeeded in combining the lessons of a Pavlovian system with a more modern, and I might almost say, an inspired approach showing us how he regards language as behaving both in evolution and dissolution. This is a refreshing way of dealing with the subject and it is one which has obviously paid dividends. Professor Luria has focussed the attention of neurologists upon the ontogeny of speech, and he has invited us to examine the steps taken by a child as he slowly acquires what Pavlov called the second system of signals. Luria has not merely *observed* what happens, but he has given us shrewd and exciting interpretations of the data. In learning to manipulate this linguistic toy, the developing child gradually uses this as a tool with which to control his own behaviour. So Luria brings us to the conception of what he calls the 'regulating, directive or pragmatic' function of language. Furthermore, Luria has suggested explicitly that in certain disease-states, types of aphasia occur wherein this directive function of speech suffers more than the other uses of language. He believes—if I understand him correctly—that after left frontal lesions there may appear a type of aphasia in which this directive function is particularly impaired. This clinical picture contrasts with the types of aphasia produced by a more posteriorly sited lesion, where phonemic auditory perception is at fault. A paradoxical state of affairs then results: the more concrete elements of a word, namely the root, are not understood while the more abstract suffixes remain intact. Luria thus offers us a novel classification of the aphasias.

Earlier I spoke of an aphasiological triad. Today it becomes obvious that we shall also have to recognize the existence of a fourth leg to the basic structure of aphasia. I refer to the lessons which we neurologists are learning from the science of linguistics and information-theory. Some of the speakers today, notably Dr. Grewel and Sir Russell Brain, have emphasized the importance of this unconventional weapon of aphasiological research. I am sure that the future of aphasiology lies very much in the judicious application by neurologists of selected fragments of linguistics and of information-theory. There will be other speakers tomorrow who will expand this belief. It is very odd that up to now linguists have been singularly blind to the help which they might have obtained had they consulted us—the specialists in the pathology of language. Few linguists have ventured into our terrain or enquired how this miracle of language which they are dissecting happens to behave when under stress from general or focal cerebral disease. Perhaps the principal exception is that doyen of linguistics Dr. Roman Jakobson who has certainly interested himself in aphasia to some extent. But I must confess, and here I agree with Dr. Grewel, that up to now linguists have not contributed very much to aphasia; less perhaps than neurologists have contributed to linguistics. Perhaps one of the reasons is that linguists have accepted too readily ideas which we neurologists have abandoned long ago. In other words the linguist's notion of aphasia is outmoded. As regards the normal faculty of speech, we can say that information-theorists are slowly revealing what we may call the 'hidden rules of speech', or its underlying statistical and syntactical framework. These are rules which we are automatically and unconsciously obeying, like M. Jourdain who did not realize that he was speaking prose. It is highly probable that in cases of aphasia, some of these hidden rules are being flaunted in a manner which we neurologists have not wholly realized. Workers at the Massachusetts Institute of Technology have shown, as we shall hear tomorrow, that the phenomenology of aphasia in many ways illustrates merely a random disturbance of the processes underlying the production of normal language. The language of the standard aphasiac operates on the same principles that govern normal language, the differences between aphasic and normal language being basically quantitative. This is an idea which can perhaps be carried too far, and it is an analogy which may not fit all the facts. However it is a novel and exciting way of looking upon our problem, and it will undoubtedly give us much food for thought and for work for many years to come.

A linguistic approach to aphasia immediately introduces the subject of non-verbal communication. Man is more than *homo sapiens, homo loquens*. In all of us there is an intense and omnipresent urge towards self-expression, something which transcends social communication. To attain this goal man will utilize whatever mechanisms happen to be available. Besides verbal symbols, which are at times unattainable, other means exist for encoding information, as well as for the expression of inner drives. We immediately recall the intriguing language of gesture. Midway between pantomime and formal articulate language lie those audible paramimic sounds, amorphous and non-verbal, which are emitted automatically rather than deliberately and are inhibited as soon as their presence is realized. Here belong the evocatives so ably described as Monrad-Krohn and by Flottorp under the term 'the third element of speech'. Their function is not so much to communicate, as to facilitate social intercourse. Like the particles 'yes' and 'no' these prosodic grunts are often interpolated within the stream of conversation as 'intimacy signals' or 'recurrent modifiers', indicating 'message received: proceed: am so far in agreement . . .' They can be compared with the particles in ancient Greek which are endowed with so little in the way of reference-function, but differ in that they are not found in the literary language but only in a slip-shod vernacular.

What we have not been told today is how this third element of speech fares in cases of aphasia. My surmise is that these prosodic grunts would be comparatively well-retained.

Finally we come to the important subject opened by Subirana of the cases of arrested maturation of the faculty of language. We are still in the dark as to their nature, and their relationship with other defects—perceptual, kinetic, spatio-temporal, or symbolic. Subirana rightly queries the propriety of the term 'aphasia' in this context. Aphasia properly speaking refers to a break-down of a fully developed linguistic endowment. We need some other term; but what? Perhaps it would be better if we were to speak of developmental 'alogia' rather than 'aphasia', or better still, 'developmental disturbance of language'.

In parenthesis, I would say that I must confess myself rather sceptical about the conception of aphasia as an ontogenetic regression; and of attempts to seek a recapitulation—phonemic, phonetic, morphemic, syntactic and semantic—in the phenomenon of acquired speech-impairment.

May I conclude by expressing the hope that when we leave Rome we neurologists do not turn our backs again upon the topic of aphasia. I believe there is scope for a very small Aphasiological Club where those few who are virtually obsessed with some of these unsolved problems could meet in amity and in comfort, and really thrash out one by one these various controversial points. Within such an international aphasiological clearing-house, we could exchange views, clear up obscurities and really make progress.

III. INTRODUCTORY AND CONCLUDING REMARKS, 1963

> *And from the first declension of the flesh*
> *I learnt man's tongue, to twist the shapes of thoughts*
> *Into the stony idiom of the brain,*
> *To shade and knit anew the patch of words*
> *Left by the dead who, in their moonless acre,*
> *Need no word's warmth.*
> *The root of tongues ends in a spentout cancer,*
> *That but a name, where maggots have their X.*
>
> *I learnt the verbs of will, and had my secrets;*
> *The code of night tapped on my tongue;*
> *What had been one was many sounding minded.*
> *Dylan Thomas*

INTRODUCTORY REMARKS

Our knowledge of the anatomy of language—or Philology as it used to be called; later Linguistics and its various allied sciences—really dates from Herder's Essay of 1772. That was a time when medical men had only the haziest notion about the nature of disordered speech resulting from brain disease. Up to the first quarter of the nineteenth century most physicians, even the experienced masters of the clinical art, tended to muddle the phenomena which followed highest-level disease of the brain with the imperfect speech of peripheral origin; and both were confused with the irrelevant mutterings of the semi-comatose patient; the hesitancies, dysphonias and mutism of the hysteric; the poverty of speech of the dement; and the secret speech of the insane. In other words, aphasia was not recognized as such, nor distinguished from dysarthria, delirium, or schizophasia. For a long time it was not realized that there could be a specific loss of memory for words alone, independent of general amnesia. Speechlessness after an apoplexy was put down to a palsy of the tongue to which stimulating blisters were applied. Not until 150 years ago was it realized that a patient whose diction was limited, also failed to express himself in writing.

Meanwhile, however, the pioneer philologists were at work, like the Schlegels, Rask, Grimm, Bopp, Rapp, Schleicher, Muller and so on.

As little as a century ago the clinico-pathological studies of Gall, Bouillaud, Auburtin, Broca,

The CIBA Foundation Symposium on Disorders of Language held in London, 21st–23rd May, 1963. The remarks are reprinted from the volume *Disorders of Language* ed. by A. V. S. de Reuck and Maeve O'Connor. Churchill, London, 1964.

and Dax, demonstrated for the first time the clear and exciting correlation between localized lesions within the dominant cerebral hemisphere, and a deficit in the realm of communication and self-expression. After this belated though dramatic start 100 years ago, our ideas about aphasia raced ahead. True, the stream of knowledge often deviated in a meandering and unprofitable fashion. Many false gods and minor prophets arose whose materialism at one time threatened to destroy the whole edifice of aphasiology. However, time sorted most things out, and for 60 or 70 years the pace of our researches into the pathology of language was far greater than that of the understanding of its normal functioning: just as a study of the insane is apt to outstrip a knowledge of the sane. But within the last few decades, the situation has altered. The tempo of linguistic advance has quickened, and the advent of that utilitarian science of information has ousted aphasiologists from the van of investigation.

The symposium at which we are about to assist, is a most important occasion, and may even be unique. If not that, it is at least one of the pioneer events in the history of language in that a free discussion is planned for linguists, philosophers, psychologists, communication theorists, and aphasiologists. Through the history of enquiry into the nature of language, its building up and its breaking down, there has been a sad lack of co-ordination between those who have devoted themselves to the faculty of speech in health, and those interested in the pathology of language.

This lack of mutual concern is regrettable, for neurologists have much to learn from contact with linguists, phoneticians and communication engineers. Few aphasiologists have availed themselves of these lessons, with such notable exceptions as Pick, Head, Grewel and Leischner. Linguists, too, have been even more remiss, and few exponents, other than Roman Jakobson, have attempted to grasp the nettle of language-impairment. True it is that Sapir did not himself show much interest in problems of aphasia but he was alive to the possibilities as shown by the oft-quoted statement that linguistics is concerned with language in all its aspects—language in operation, language in drift, language in the nascent state, and language in dissolution.

In welcoming the participants, I think I ought to emphasize that the topic of our symposium is disorders of *language*. By this is visualized the aphasias due to focal lesions of the brain, and perhaps also the dilapidation of speech associated with diffuse organic changes in the hemispheres, causing dementia. The speech peculiarities met with in such psychoses as schizophrenia are quite relevant to our theme, and also perhaps, some of the speech affections in hysteria. But entirely outside the scope of our business would be the disorders of articulation and of voice-production due to causes within the peripheral organs of speech. In other words we are not interested in the various dysarthrias, or dyslalias, or childhood speech retardations, or stammering, or cluttering. I would also point out to my neuro-psychological colleagues that today we are concerned with aphasia only in so far as we can bring our experience to bear upon the *corpus* of linguistic knowledge; or else, in so far as we can extract from the lessons of phonology, linguistics etc. something which promises to bear directly upon the pathology of speech.

To our non-medical colleagues I would stress that we seek to learn today from you only that which pertains directly to *disorders* of language. In other words linguistic data which do not have an immediate bearing upon the problem of aphasia are not strictly relevant to our present symposium.

The potential values of an inter-disciplinary meeting like this are obvious, and I hope the promise will be fulfilled. However, dangers attend all inter-disciplinary symposia, and perhaps I should mention them. Each of us, being an expert in his own field, should make great effort to avoid obscurity by undue technicality. Otherwise the target is missed, and communication is not effected. I would therefore urge my neurological colleagues to take nothing for granted, and to eschew any assumption of general familiarity with facts and beliefs which we hold and assume are held by everybody else. Likewise I would beg my co-workers in linguistics, mathematics, logic, philosophy and so on, to go out of their way to explain their ideas 'in the clear' even if this necessitates redundancy. Scientific encoders should always be very aware of their audience, and be merciful towards them. It can be done, of course. As Boileau-Despreaux truly said: '*Ce qui conçoit bien s'énonce clairement, et les mots pour le dire viennent aisément*'.

All too often obscure talk by neurologists and scientists mirrors untidy thinking, and I am sure that even the most recondite science—if enough trouble be taken—can be translated into a code which will appeal to a wide-flung communication net.

F. L. Lucas the literary critic once wrote: 'A research student may turn his life into a concentration camp; he may amass in his own field an erudition to stagger Dr. Casaubon; but he cannot communicate. And when the words are so muddled, I suspect that the mind is muddled too'.

CONCLUDING REMARKS

A few concluding remarks are perhaps called for at the termination of this very interesting symposium. As constituent members, what have we derived from our three days' endeavours? All of us, I venture to think, have learned a great deal from contacts with workers in disciplines which are allied but different. Perhaps, in modesty, some might be able to confess to having individually received more from this symposium than they were able to contribute.

One great merit in a meeting such as this has been the opportunity of seeing and hearing others previously unknown to us except through the medium of their writings. Like High Court judges we have been given the chance of assessing the credibility of witnesses. We have learned to recognize and appreciate wisdom when we meet it, as well as experience and enthusiasm. We have learned to distinguish intellectual elasticity from mental rigidity; tolerance from intolerance; and sincerity from mere over-confidence.

What of the individuals who have contributed so much by their set papers?

If, as a result of this meeting, any speaker modifies his original text, and makes some changes, if only in emphasis, or frankly erases an expression of opinion, or inserts some new idea, then indeed this symposium can be said to have achieved something very tangible. Perhaps, however, this would be to ask too much.

May I take up, quite superficially, a point here and there from those which have emerged from this discussion?

Until the third day we had heard a good deal about aphasia, but possibly not enough about aphasiacs—those poor anonymous incommunicable brain-injured individuals, whose total personality has been profoundly modified by their disability. Perhaps we did not sufficiently stress the point that language, whatever else it is, forms an all-important and integral aspect of mentation; and a very personal, highly individual and fundamental aspect of behaviour. Aphasia, therefore, must of necessity modify enormously this 'organism'. This fact accounts for the peculiar difficulties which are inherent in the clinical handling, assessment, testing and understanding of an aphasiac, and for so many of our differences of opinion about the results. The aphasiac, like so many other brain-injured persons, is struggling with whatever parts of his brain are still intact, to compensate for a lesion—which may be large or small, progressive or regressive, abrupt in onset or insidious. He is also trying hard to cope with a particular test-situation, which is often highly artificial, unfamiliar and unrealistic, under exacting and perhaps humiliating circumstances. It is not to be wondered at, therefore, that his performance should be maddeningly inconsistent. Aphasiacs perform correctly one moment, but not the next. A word which eludes him now, crops up a moment later. With one examiner he fares badly—with another he does very well. The patient is profoundly affected by such factors as fatigue, hunger, discomfort, as well as by the nature and emotional repercussions of the surrounding verbal and non-verbal situation.

We have heard a good deal about the localization of the aphasia-producing lesions and I suppose today we now have an agreed anatomical knowledge which is approaching exactitude, or at any rate promises so to do.

We have heard little or nothing, however, about the patient's pre-morbid personality, and pre-morbid verbal equipment and literary attainment, as factors which may go some way, perhaps a long way, in determining the eventual aphasic picture. Jackson's 'four factors of the insanities' need to be remembered. Questions of natural eloquence, verbosity, size of vocabulary, literacy, plurilingualism, style; aesthetic delight in words for their own sake, and the sound, shape and colour of words; the choosing, matching and combining of words in euphonious and pleasing patterns—however obsessional—these are surely most important when it comes to understanding the eventual picture of the victim who finds himself crippled in a linguistic sense.

The linkages between thought and language ordain that we must never lose sight of the inherent variation from person to person, irrespective of aphasia, and even perhaps variations between the sexes. We remember what Dean Swift said:

> The common fluency of speech in many men and most women is owing to scarcity of matter and scarcity of words; for whoever is a master of language and hath a mind full of ideas will be apt in speaking to hesitate upon the choice of both; whereas common speakers have only one set of ideas and one set of words to clothe them in; and they are always ready at the mouth. So people come faster out of a church when it is almost empty, than when a crowd is at the door.

During the symposium, many references were made to classifications of aphasia. Some of the groupings which have been put forward at various times have been physiological and traditional. Some neurologists, however, resort to eponymous epithets, as if despairing of achieving anything logical. Other groupings are frankly descriptive. A number of psychological attempts at classification have been made and more recently there have appeared one or two linguistic groupings. The average aphasiologist however is illogically inconsistent, for he tends to drag into one and the same system of classification, and at one and the same time, subgroups which are anatomical, physiological, psychological, representational, or merely patriotic.

We surely must acknowledge that no single system of classification has yet proved altogether satisfactory, and personally I do not yet see even the beginnings of such a logical approach.

But perhaps we are rather wasting our time in our quest for an ideal classification, as though classification were a sufficient end in itself.

Of course, there was a time when a rough and ready physiological distinction between the different aphasias served a useful practical purpose in guiding the surgeon's knife directly to the seat of mischief in the brain. But today this localization can be achieved more easily, more directly and more surely, by technical as opposed to clinical methods.

What then is the purpose of straining after a logical classification, unless it is to gain some knowlege of the fundamental disorder lying above or perhaps below the process of aphasia?

Did we here settle the arguments as to the role of the intellect in patients with aphasia? Is there always a defect of some degree, qualitative perhaps, if not quantitative? Or can the intellectual status of the aphasiac remain intact, depending of course upon questions of severity?

Most of the neurologists and psychologists who have directed their attention to this peculiarly difficult problem have been in the past (let's face it) evasive and elusive, or at any rate very indefinite in the expression of their view-points. This applies, I am sorry to say, to Hughlings Jackson, to Pierre Marie and to Henry Head. This indecision must of course remain, because, clinically, aphasiacs vary so considerably in the severity of their speech affliction; and furthermore, the continued lack of unanimity as to the normal bonds between thinking and speaking cannot but help colour the outlook of the psychologist and introduce some measure of prejudice.

But, as I have said elsewhere, at any time the hair-splitting of the schoolmen may be dramatically interrupted when one suddenly faces the very practical problem, occurring perhaps in one's own family, of a respected senior, who, afflicted with an aphasia, is anxious to alter his will, or to testify, or to continue to attend to his intricate business affairs. What common-sense and honest advice can we, as philosophers of language, put before the Chancery Court in such cases— advice that would appeal to the cold logic of the legal profession rather than to our less demanding neuropsychological colleagues? In such circumstances, how much weight would a High Court judge be seriously expected to put upon the matching and mating of meaningless patterns?

The question of the language disorders associated with the psychoses has aroused great interest and is likely to increase in importance. Hitherto the subject has been approached by the alienists along the lines of clinical description with attempts at psychopathological explanation. In schizophrenia there are striking points of similarity with the aphasias but at the same time there are many important distinctions. Although some clinicians were once tempted to relegate the schizophasias and schizographias to actual brain changes, this is an attitude of mind which is now out of favour. The tendency nowadays is more and more to invoke the asyndetic thinking from a primary thought disorder. Psychiatrists, however, seem still to be undecided as to whether the content of schizophrenic speech represents an enhancement of fantasy building or not.

The speech affections met with in dementia are in some ways a more difficult problem. Here, the symptomatology and the *modus operandi* probably bear a closer analogy with aphasia than does the speech of schizophrenics.

The various types of speech defect met with in cases of hysteria may well repay more detailed attention than they have had so far.

In all these speech affections—in schizophrenes, dements and hysterics—the approach hitherto has been somewhat superficial. The whole problem merits an attack from the angle of aphasiology, and still more, from the standpoint of the linguist. In this latter connection I have to mention with interest the important study of a polyglot and incoherent schizophrene studied with the utmost care by J. P. S. Robertson and S. J. Shamsie. This can be looked upon as a pioneer contribution.

From time to time the intriguing notion is put forward to the effect that the dissolution of speech in aphasia mimics the development of speech in the child. This is the notion of aphasia as a regression, and it has at one time or other been invoked to explain the phonemic changes, the disordered syntax, and the constricted vocabulary.

My own feeling is—although others may disagree—that the points of contrast far outweigh in validity the features of similarity between the two conditions. One condition represents the dilapidation of a mature endowment: the other is the arrest of a building-up of a new accomplishment or skill *de novo* without the background of a life-time of linguistic associations.

If linguistic regression is indeed ever actually met with in clinical practice, we are, I believe, more likely to discover it among the rapidly deteriorating dementias, or in the gross conversion hysterias, than ever in cases of aphasia proper.

The contributions of information theory to our knowledge of aphasia have been interesting and not inconsiderable; and obviously we have not yet come to the end of them. Perhaps the swing of the pendulum is tending to emphasize a little too much the role of speech and writing as media of communication.

This is not, or cannot be, the whole story. Much of language is not truly communicative—except in that rather strained sense of the word of merely assisting in a general milieu of communal warmth and understanding, without very much in the way of reference-function being traceable. Many of the speech-habits of our lower classes and even of our sophisticates are not far removed from the phatic communion of the savage, where meaning is grossly subordinate to sound. Much of our talk is merely self-expressive, emotive, inferior in rank, being made up of phrase-words, clichés, trite expressions, particles, which serve very little function save as 'intimacy signals'. Again much of our talk is ludic, a form of verbal play; autistic in an adult fashion, serving to satisfy the speaker rather than to inform the hearer, or even to keep him happy. As was said in a literary paper the other day, 99 per cent of conversation is not a means of communication . . . 'Watch a couple at it. Neither listens to what the other says. He is watching beadily for a momentary break in the other's talk so that he may get into his own stride. Conversation is largely a display of exhibitionism'.

In other words language is not merely communicative. It is an integral part of one's personality; it is a behavioural pattern, and as such it subtly differs from one individual to another just as facial appearances differ despite an overall similarity.

Language, whether regarded as a communicative system or as a pattern of behaviour, is so fundamental that it transcends widely the use of words. Non-verbal communicative systems and systems of self-expression therefore merit close attention, in health and in disease states.

This inborn urge to talk, to express oneself, to hold the floor, to communicate, too, at times, has been very nicely expressed by an American novelist, who also happens to be something of a linguist. In *Detour through Devon*, by Guy Endore (1959. Gollancz, London) we read:

> The desire to communicate pervades the whole body, as one can see when playing golf or billiards, how after a difficult stroke, a player will stand tensed, twisting his whole body as if he could still add the effort of his muscles to the already travelling ball. Body English, they call it in the United States. Body English. Isn't it as if the body too could speak a language, just as the tongue speaks, by muscular effort?
>
> For man is determined to express himself. He must utter. What is inside must come out. Out of his mouth, if possible, but in any case, out. On stone with signs that no one will even understand, carving pictograms, hieroglyths, Runic, Cretan, Aztec, Caribbean. All over the world and throughout all history, man speaks. On his death bed, muttering and stuttering, he still seeks to utter.
>
> And the suicide always leaves a note.

IV. THE PRESENT STATUS OF
APHASIOLOGICAL RESEARCH

Compared with what we ought to be, we are only half awake. We are making use of only a small part of our mental and physical resources. Stating the thing broadly, the human individual thus lives usually far within his limits; he possesses powers of various sorts which he habitually fails to use.

William James

The successive steps which led to the conventional or classic conception of aphasia as a symptom of brain disorder are traced in a later article, up to the year 1865. Based upon a contemporary associational psychology, speech came to be regarded as a composite faculty distinct from thought even though related thereto. The speech-complex was deemed liable to be broken down into its elementary and isolated components. Various schemata within the brain were envisaged, all of which had in common a centripetal sensory and a contrifugal motor aspect, reminiscent of a reflex arc. As Bay has put it, the one mechanism was looked upon as transforming the word heard into ideas, the other exteriorizing ideas into speech-sounds. The idea existing in between, constituted thought, and was of no interest. The traditional view further assumed that the translation of speech-sounds into ideas, and *vice versa*, takes place by the activation of mnemic material or memory-traces, deposited in the individual centres. These include acoustic word-images, word-concepts, speech-ideation, and so on. An analogy was also envisaged with apraxia and with agnosia, and certain types of motor aphasia were looked upon as an 'apraxia of articulation' while some forms of sensory aphasia were equated with a type of agnosia.

Rank and file contributors to the problems of aphasia busied themselves first with descriptions of patients' verbal defects; secondly with alleged classifications; and thirdly with anatomo-clinical correlation. But even quite early an alternative way of regarding the problem existed, modest at first and uncomprehended; but which grew steadily in influence and authority. The intermediate stage was one which Head described as 'chaos', for terms and concepts taken from a medley of disciplines—anatomy, psychology new and old, physiology and even linguistics—were employed untidily. Over the past few decades, however, the problem has gradually sorted itself out, and there is now a stricter adherence to one or other category of thinking when speech-affections are under discussion. Nowadays, most of the serious workers in the field of aphasia, represent this dynamic or organismic school.

Bay, one of the most distinguished exponents of this group, has enumerated the objections to the older views as being two-fold, stemming from holistic psychology (*Ganzheitspsychologie*) on

This paper is based upon part of the Squibb Centenary Lecture 1959.

30

the one hand, and on the other from so-called performance pathology (*Leitungspathologie*). Neurologists of today do not consider it possible to separate altogether speech from other mental processes, and in particular from thought; and to try and parcellate speech into independent individual functions is a vain pursuit. Moreover the verbal behaviour of a brain-injured subject must derive from the operation of brain-mechanisms which are intact. The modern aphasiologist is profoundly sceptical as to the status of the so-called 'pure' types of partial aphasia, believing that the stricter the clinical scrutiny the less secure is the conception of an isolated dysfuntion. Even the time-honoured antinomy of motor versus sensory aphasia has worn thin. Today we realize that types of aphasia merge one into another. We recognize that the verbal performances of aphasiacs are erratic and often inconsistent, changing from hour to hour and day to day: varying according to a great diversity of factors. Greater thoroughness of examination, although establishing a more harmonious rapport, will none the less usually reveal an increasingly elaborate type of defect. Lastly, neurologists have come to realize that an impairment in the use of verbal symbols is merely one of a complex of changes in the overall behaviour of the patient.

All aphasias comprise not only a disorder of speech but a disorder of language: by definition, this obviously also implies a disorder of thought. And in so far as the use of language is always a highly individual mode of behaviour, an aphasia will of necessity constitute an aberration of the pattern of personality. As Marcus Victoria put it 'aphasic patients do not see or hear the outer world like the rest of mankind. Their defects are deeper than the language-defects, and comprise functions correlated with the manipulation of symbols'. He proceeded to quote William Blake: 'A fool sees not the same tree that a wise man sees'.

Though most neurologists would probably subscribe to dynamic attitudes of this sort, they do not always agree about the character of the fundamental psychic disturbance which underlies an aphasic disability. Pierre Marie, one of the first to face this difficulty, envisaged a disorder of a specific aspect of intelligence. Head looked upon aphasia as affecting merely one aspect of a more fundamental faculty which he called symbolic formulation and expression. To Head, aphasia constituted a disordered facility in the manipulation of symbols, and it is tempting to align Head with Finkelnberg and his notion of 'asymboly'. Goldstein's ideas went even deeper, in that the use of symbols was viewed as being merely one aspect of an underlying concept of the human species; that is, a power of abstraction (or what the older philosophers called the idea of universals). In Goldstein's opinion abstraction requires a certain 'categorical' behaviour or attitude towards things and events. Its absence, in certain circumstances, would impair the handling of verbal symbols.

There is yet another variant of dynamic thought upon the aphasia problem, namely that which seeks to trace an identity between speech and conceptual thinking. The peculiar methodical difficulties entailed by the very nature of an aphasic defect handicap investigation, and many ingenious paraverbal testing devices have been contrived. Thus Klein was able to show, by dint of Ach's techniques, that the formation of concepts by aphasiacs lacks clarity as well as structure. Bay was able to support this view through his clinical experiences.

The attitudes towards aphasia as expressed by Conrad, working chiefly in the field on configurational psychology, are of great interest. He believed that verbal expression is inhibited or precluded by blocking mechanisms which occur during the *Vorgestalt*, or those mental processes which take place immediately prior to the exteriorization of words in speech or writing. This viewpoint tallies closely with one which I have put forward as to the existence of a 'preverbitum',[1] which may be defined as those mental activities which immediately precede speech. According to the depth at which the preverbital blockage occurs, will depend the clinical character of the aphasia. Indeed a veritable classification of aphasia according to the nature and positioning of the defect within the preverbitum, might prove of value. Even earlier, Marcus Victoria had studied aphasic patients from the angle of a *Gestalt* psychologist. Using appropriate tests, such as those of Wertheimer in the visual sphere and tapping tests in the auditory sphere, Victoria found an impaired appreciation of 'forms' (*Gestalten*). There were difficulties both in their perception and in their reproduction. Defects included undue simplification of forms; incorrect articulation of forms; and confusion of figure with background. In those types of aphasia with conspicuous 'sensory' defects, there was an apparent return to the simple speech-forms of childhood.

No reference to modern views upon aphasia should omit the role of time-relationships in the genesis of aphasia-producing lesions. This conception was expressed by Hughlings Jackson when he isolated the 'four factors of the insanities', a rather unfortunate term which embraced various cerebral symptoms including aphasia, and within this conception the factor of the rate of development of the lesion was given due importance. Von Monakow returned to this subject when he discussed the 'chronogenic factor' in the genesis of cerebral symptoms. Within our own time Walter Riese has stressed the importance of the rate of development of an aphasic disability; the slower its growth the less crippling its effects. This fact he attributed to detour-performances and compensating mechanisms, rarely achieved with rapidly advancing lesions, or with abrupt ones.

As an example of contemporary reaction against classical ideas upon clinico-anatomical correlations in aphasia we may refer to Leischner. Like some other writers, he emphasized that the acts of articulate speech and of writing are 'parasitic functions' one might say, which utilize preformed cerebral mechanisms. Vast numbers of normal persons have never learned to read or to write, and yet no one can claim that their brains are in any way deficient in 'centres' or structures which are the prerogative of literate individuals. He also made an interesting suggestion that in the remote past, not every representative of newly-evolved *homo sapiens* was endowed with speech; at one stage indeed, speech might have been the privilege of only a favoured few. Unlike hearing and vision which are primary cerebral functions with special areas of the brain allocated to them, speech is but a secondary cerebral function. Therefore it has no executive or receptive apparatus of its own. As secondary cerebral functions develop, they utilize mechanisms already in existence. Individual dispositions enter into the problem, and in this way the centre of gravity of secondary functions may shift. This fact goes a little way towards explaining some of the inconsistencies of clinical data. His idea ties up with the concept of 'functional migration' propounded by Weizsäcker. In certain conditions the faculty of speech may become metamorphosed or transposed, as for instance when a subject is long deprived of some of the ordinary means of symbol-manipulation. Examples are to be found in the sign-language of deaf-mutes; in the Braille or tactile reading of the blind; and—most impressive of all—the communicative systems of a Helen Keller or a Laura

[1] See Chapter XIX.

Bridgman, bereft of hearing, vision and articulation. In such cases, speech—or rather, language—utilizes whatever system happens to be available.

Hughlings Jackson's warning against the error of seeking to localize functions by way of local sources of disordered function, is only to often forgotten; though occasionally writers re-discover this aphorism and pay lip service to it. Anatomical brain-centres are no more than regions which when ablated cause a disturbance of function: they are not endowed with a known positive function. They should be looked upon as 'centres of destruction' and not centres of function, as Jasper put it.

Grühle stated the problem a little differently. He believed that the so-called localization of speech has been attended by partial or apparent success, but only in so far as somatic structures are concerned, the mental component of speech completely defying attempts at localization.

Leischner summed up by asserting that secondary cerebral functions are 'accessory functions' or epiphenomena, which develop only after the design of the brain is essentially complete. They possess no exclusive territory in the brain and no executive organs of their own. Both centrally and peripherally they have utilized foreign territories or alien functional systems; those indeed which are best suited for the purpose. Centrally, they are but loosely tied to definite sites, and have only a relative localization, one which is variable in place, intensity and individual type. The normal development of secondary cerebral functions depends upon a suitable educating environment: in the case of speech, upon an appropriate 'speaking environment'.

Perhaps at this point one may briefly refer to the current importance which some of us neurologists ascribe to the premorbid personal idiosyncrasies in the realm of language. Obviously this aspect of the aphasia problem is new and largely unexplored, but it promises to be immensely rewarding in future research.

Such then are the principal trends of modern aphasiology. As to the future, it can be assumed that the organismic type of approach will continue, and will yield still more fruitful results. The question may well be asked, however, whether the tempo of research is likely to continue at the same rapid rate, or whether the acme of its achievement has not perhaps been reached. In any event it is unlikely that any return to an associational or traditional attitude will take place to any serious extent.

It now becomes necessary to turn from these promising researches in order to discuss a formidable series of investigations into aphasia which lie somewhat outside of the main stream of endeavour. Here belong the eastern European studies which almost uniformly conform to an interpretation of brain-physiology along Pavlovian lines. To that extent they may be looked upon as materialistic rather than organismic, and localizational as opposed to holistic. On the face of it a mammalian or subhominid type of methodology would seem to give little promise of illuminating the faculty of speech, so specifically a human perquisite.

The work of Pavlov essentially derived its orientation from a long series of materialist philosophers, directly inspired no doubt by his teacher Sechenov. Consciousness and speech are prepared for in the animal world, but arise only in man along with the development of social forms of life based on labour. Labour, a qualitatively new form of activity, gives rise to a qualitatively new characteristic of the mind—the conscious reflection of objective reality (Brian Simon). Stalin, who himself personally dabbled in linguistics, adhered to the dialectical materialism of Marx and Engels, and asserted that language, a tool of communication between people, was also a means of struggle and development of society. According to Pavlov, an all-important addition was made to the mechanisms of nervous activity when the developing animal world reached the human stage. This addition was speech. If ideas and sensations stemming from the outer world can be looked upon as signals, then speech is to be regarded as a second system of signals, or signals of signals. (This idea can be equated with the use of 'symbols' in the more conventional philosophies). Language can be drawn into the general system of conditioned stimuli, words being reducible to the level of other simpler physical agencies. But words, by dint of man's life-experience, are connected with all the external and internal stimuli that have ever reached the cortex. Consequently they have acquired meaning: to that extent words cannot be compared with the conditional stimuli of animals. Another difference is that while the usual conditioned reflexes can be extinguished by appropriate techniques, words cannot be. As Pavlov said: '. . . human speech, once man has learned it, lasts. This means that conditioned reflexes are not the same as our words; here is a different process'. By virtue of this property, a process of generalization becomes feasible for man. Ivanov–Smolensky elaborated this idea when he spoke of 'elective irradiation'. Kapustnik formed a conditioned response experimentally in children by sounding a bell. Later it became possible to replace this conditioning stimulus by the spoken word 'bell', or even its written or printed form. In the former case the stimulus produced a direct and almost unmediated motor reaction; in the latter the response was the product of interaction between the stimulus on the one hand and the experiences impressed in the cortex by past experience on the other. These three specific stimuli can therefore be regarded as selectively generalized, by way of a faculty of elective irradiation, or 'semantic connection'. Ivanov–Smolensky concluded that a scientific explanation of human understanding is possible only on the foundation of Pavlov's theory of higher nervous activity. He claimed that this theory raises a corner of the veil covering the laws of man's thought-processes, opening the way to a genuine understanding of the whole complex and ordered work of the human brain. Such scientific material, he asserted, throws light upon certain features of the process of understanding which could in no other way be open to scientific psychological research.

Despite the bold dogmatism of this statement, Pavlovian ideas are perhaps unpromising within the realm of the investigation of speech. However, special mention must be made of the work of Luria who has utilized what is relevant or most significant in Pavlovian thought, combining it judiciously with certain items from conventional doctrine, and then embellishing both with his own stimulating contributions.

Luria has sought to equate certain broad types of disordered function with lesions near certain areas of the left cerebral hemisphere, but without seeking to trace any rigid point-to-point correspondence. Lesions of the left temporal area, though producing no loss of hearing in any part of the frequency-range, result in damage to the processes of auditory analysis and synthesis. This can be demonstrated experimentally by the fact that such patients can easily form conditioned reflexes in response to acoustic stimuli, though unable to differentiate complex groups of sounds. In such cases there exists a normal discrimination of visual complexes. The trouble lies particularly in the differentiation of phonemes of somewhat similar nature, leading to a breakdown in phonemic auditory perception. This defect is readily demonstrated if appropriate tests are used. As a secondary disorder there occurs an impairment in the pronunciation of words especially when novel words are entailed or those which are difficult phonetically. Severe difficulties occur in the act of writing, not only to dictation, but also spontaneously.

The patient, moreover, will display considerable difficulty in the comprehension of words, and an inability to isolate their meanings, not because of intellectual disorder, but through the disintegration of the complex auditory function. The upset in the phonemic structure of language leads to a break-down in its lexical structure; but not all morphological elements of a word are affected to the same degree. Luria quoted Bein to the effect that such patients may lose the power to understand the roots of words while still comprehending the suffixes. The result is a paradoxical state of affairs, whereby the patient may lose the knowledge of the concrete meanings which are attached to the root of the words, while retaining the abstract meanings inherent in such suffixes as —*ance* or—*ship* (in English);—*heit* or—*keit* (in German) and—*ost* or—*ie* (in Russian).

Following the other writers who distinguish speech-remnants after disease into superior and inferior types (or propositionizing and interjectional), Luria followed Svedelius in dividing verbal statements into 'communication of events' and 'communication of relations'. Here lies a difference not only in grammatical structure, but also in the degree of abstraction. In patients with post-parietal or parieto-occipital lesions there may occur a marked cleavage between the understanding of these two types of communication. The patient may still be able to cope with ordinary speech, but be quite unable to divine the meaning of complicated logico-grammatical sequences expressing abstract relationships. The patients moreover may find trouble in dealing with spatial relationships, mathematical categories and symbols. Luria did not think that it would be correct to ascribe such defects to a general dysfunction of either the intellect or of categorical thinking, but rather to a primary break-down of higher nervous processes. These latter include such phenomena as Wolpert's 'simultaneous agnosia', astereognosis, an inability to combine details into a coherent whole, a loss of synoptic function, a failure to see elements in a single structure, or—in Pötzl's terminology—to shift from sequential to simultaneous observation.

When parieto-occipital lesions are large enough to involve the speech-area there inevitably follows a breakdown of the more complicated mnemonic operations, connected with the abstraction of one signal and the synthesis of a series of elements in accordance with this abstracted signal. The characters of speech-affections in such cases conform to what Head termed 'semantic aphasia'. Fronto-temporal lesions produce a breakdown in the synthesis of successive elements into a single continuous series or dynamic system. The patient, although able to distinguish the phonetic elements of verbal speech and to grasp logico-grammatical relations in language, displays much difficulty in the smooth transition from subject to predicate. The easy switching off of stimuli is impeded, and there is no ready transition from one system of innervation to another. In such circumstances, one may observe a telegrammatic style of speech.

Luria has had much to say about what he called the 'regulating' function of speech. This phenomenon is observed in early childhood where the young subject uses speech not only as a form of communication but also as a means of controlling his own behaviour. Being particularly experienced in child-psychology and the development of speech, Luria not unnaturally enquired to what extent this regulating function of speech stood up to the influences of cerebral disease. He found it to be relatively resistant. Most patients with focal lesions of the brain showed a breakdown in the phonetic, lexical, semantic and syntactic aspects of speech, but they would continue to obey verbal instructions on the part of the medical and nursing staff. However he was able to determine by the use of special techniques that with frontal lobe affections a breakdown in the regulating function of speech might follow. Provided that the lesion involves the postero-inferior regions of the left frontal lobe, a special clinical type of 'frontal aphasia' may occur. This comprises a certain inactivity in speech; an impairment of 'monologue speech' with preservation of responsive or 'dialogue speech'. In severe cases, especially with bi-frontal lesions, there may be a gross upset in the regulating function of speech. Such patients may be unable to perform simple requests even though they may repeat aloud the examiner's instruction in an echolalic fashion. Or the patient may eventually be persuaded to execute an order, but be unable to stop it or to change the action, once started, to another. Defects arise which a neurologist would recognize as perseveratory, (palipraxia, paligraphia, palilalia, motor and verbal perseveration) linked to a mental state of ideational inertia. Luria and his collaborators were able to demonstrate these defects very clearly by way of the techniques of conditioned responses.

Impairment of the regulating function of speech was especially well demonstrated by means of experiments which entailed a delayed reaction (e.g. to such an order as 'When I count as far as 12, raise your hand'). It could be shown moreover that these failures were not due to impairment of memory.

Luria has shown himself convinced that the clinical patterns of speech-impairment do not necessarily recapitulate the states of development.

Even outside the U.S.S.R., Pavlovian methods of research have been applied in a study of aphasia. We may merely mention the interesting investigations now being carried out in Bucarest by Kreindler and his pupils. J. Hrbk, of Olomouc in Czechoslovakia, has utilized the techniques of language-acquirement in order to investigate the higher nervous activity of the human brain. By deliberately employing an artificial 'laboratory' language for the production of conditioned responses in subjects, adults or children, healthy or diseased, he has been able to draw conclusions of a stimulating and far-reaching character as to the nature of diverse mental activities. The influences of various factors, extraneous or personal, upon the speech as well as upon the accuracy of such functions can also be studied.

Thus, we begin to foresee the lines along which research into the problems of aphasia is likely to develop. We may, in the first place, identify a number of promising psychological techniques, entailing an accurate recording, and an analysis of the patient's utterances and creative writings. Secondly we can visualize that Pavlovian techniques, when the dead hand of rigid dogma is forgotten, may prove to be productive, especially along the lines of determining what type of conditioned responses can be evoked in aphasiacs.

There is yet a third and very promising type of approach—so far barely attempted—namely along the direction of linguistics.

This is no place for a historical recapitulation of the growth of linguistics out of the interest in language displayed by the earliest sophist philosophers; through the beginnings of philology as a science at the hands of Herder; up to the modern preoccupation with semantics, linguistics, 'general linguistics', phonology and communication theory.

One of the first of the few to seek to bring the science of language to bear upon the problems of aphasia was Pick. In his monograph upon agrammatism (1917), he repeatedly resorted to the evidence of linguistics. Maybe Pick endowed syntax with an undue importance in the role of normal speech, and thereby exaggerated the phenomenon of breakdown of grammar in the fragmentary utterances of aphasiacs.

Two contemporary workers are trying to surmount the gulf between the normal and the pathological as far as speech is concerned. One is a neuropsychiatrist, Grewel, and the other a professional linguist, Roman Jakobson. Both have realized the rich treasures which the two subjects can mutually share. Grewel (1951) enumerated in linguistic terms the various disturbances which aphasiacs may undergo, as follows:

(1) *Lexical losses:* i.e. restriction in the vocabulary. Here would also be included the naming defects in the classical anomia or amnestic aphasia. Although Grewel did not discuss this matter further, it might have been pointed out—again from the lessons of linguistics—that an individual's 'vocabulary' is a labile conception depending upon the immediate circumstances. Thus we can distinguish, in normal conditions, between a spoken vocabulary, a written vocabulary, and a passively available vocabulary. Obviously the fragmentary speech of an aphasiac may behave very differently with regard to these aspects of his linguistic store. Grewel went on to enumerate:

(2) *Phonemic disturbances:* comprising (a) *aphonemia* where a patient loses certain phonemes, not as part of a dysarthria, but as a disturbed linguistic function; and (b) *dysphonemia* where phonemes are confused from loss of knowledge of the differentiating function and value between a pair of phonemes.

(3) *Paraphonemia.* Here the aphasiac is unable to assign the phonemes their appropriate place within a word.

(4) *Paraphasia.* i.e. inability to combine syllables correctly so as to constitute the appropriate polysyllabic word; or to form compound words out of their component parts.

(5) *Agrammatism* and *paragrammatism*, as described by Pick. This heading also includes telegrammatism, nigger-speech and jargon-aphasia.

(6) *Disorder in the system of accents.* (This would correspond with Monrad-Krohn's *dysprody*).

(7) *Disturbance in non-verbal forms of communication;* e.g. gesture, pantomime, mimicry, and so on.

Turning to the work of the linguist Jakobson (1955) we find him venturing to divide the aphasias into two broad subdivisions. Thus he first of all distinguished what he called *similarity disorders*, where the principal deficiency lies in the processes of the selection and of the substitution of words. To this type he opposed a *contiguity disorder* where the chief defect entails the combining or 'contexture' of words.

The aphasiac who belongs to Jakobson's first group, i.e. a 'similarity disorder', can readily complete an unfinished phrase or sentence presented to him. He can easily carry on a conversation, though finding it difficult to start a dialogue. There is no trouble in making a reply. Monologue, or 'closed discourse', is less easy for him. The more what he has to say depends upon a context, the better he fares. He finds it difficult to make statements which do not constitute a response to an interlocutor, and also to discuss topics which have little bearing upon the actual situation. When a word depends, grammatically or otherwise, upon other words within the same sentence, it proves relatively tenacious. On the other hand, the subject of a sentence tends to be omitted, being the elusive key-word. A specific noun may be replaced by an indefinite, vague, or all embracing term (e.g. 'things'). Contextual words such as pronouns, pronominal adverbs, connectives and auxiliaries are apt to be spared. Jakobson quoted in illustration a German patient of Quensel's who said: *Ich bin doch hier unten, na wenn ich gewesen bin ich wees nicht, we das, nu wenn ich, ob das nun doch, noch, ja. Was Sie her, wenn ich, och ich wees nicht, we das dier war ja . . .*

Such patients will also experience great difficulty in naming objects before them. This, Jakobson said, is really a difficulty in *metalanguage* (or language about language). Such an aphasic patient cannot switch from a word to its synonyms, nor to its heteronyms or equivalent expressions in other languages. Having then lost his capacity for code-switching, his own 'idiolect', that is his personal and specific use of language becomes the sole linguistic reality. The utterances of such a type of aphasiac are largely governed by contiguity and hence they resort a great deal to metonymy, substituting *fork* for *knife*, *table* for *lamp*, *bread* for *butter*. Metonymies of this kind are derived from habitual contexts.

Jakobson's second class of aphasia, namely 'contiguity disorder', is characterized by a disarray in syntax and a chaotic word-order. Words endowed with purely grammatical function, e.g. conjunctions, prepositions, pronouns and articles, disappear first. The subject-word of a sentence is retained best. Often the utterances are reduced to a single sentence, phrase or even word. Or else they are made up of longer phrases which are ready-made, habitual utterances; clichés; or pre-formed tightly bound verbal automatisms. Verbal substitutions are in the nature of metaphor or quasi-metaphor rather than metonymy. Thus a patient may say *fire* for *gaslight*. He may find it impossible to disarticulate compound words into their constituent parts; or to resolve a word into its phonemic elements. For instance, a patient who could utter and understand *Thanksgiving* could neither say nor comprehend *thanks* or *giving*. Again a French aphasiac who could easily cope with the terms *café* and *pavé* could make nothing whatsoever of such nonsense-words as *féca*, *faké*; *kéfa*, *papé*.

Finally there occurs not only a disintegration in the phonetic properties but also a progressive limitation in vocabulary. The last residues of speech are one phoneme, one word, one sentence utterances; the patient lapses into the early phases of an infant's linguistic development, or even to its pre-lingual stage: he faces an *aphasia universalis*, or total inability to use or comprehend speech. Jakobson perhaps did not realize how extremely rare is a complete loss of all articulate utterance in cases of aphasia, for he was not a practising neurologist.

The relatively young science of communication, or information-theory, has up to now largely ignored the problems of aphasia. In the same way neurologists have been equally neglectful. It is obvious that the two types of thinking must and doubtless will get together.

Communication-theory is in some ways a disappointing pursuit, for it expends considerable effort in merely tracing the organization underlying the natural phenomena of speech. As Miller has said, it is rather surprising to find that one's own verbal behaviour follows statistical rules with considerable orderliness. We appear to select our words and arrange them to communicate with others, with no consideration for relative frequencies of occurrence. This apparently deliberate and conscious choice of words, actually follows statistical rules with great regularity. Most of us find it rather wonderful that our linguistic behaviour can behave so lawfully with no trouble at all.

These 'hidden rules' of speech may prove to be of value in understanding some of the phenomena of aphasia. To the communication-theorist the processes of encoding and of decoding are actually no more than parts of the same procedure. This observation tallies with the ideas of modern neurologists who are sceptical of the older division of the aphasias into motor and sensory types, preferring to believe that all aphasias are 'mixed' or sensori-motor in character. Cherry, indeed, has suggested that the perception of speech is synonymous with—or at least integrated with—the preparation to produce the same sounds. This ties up with the neurologists' notion of the preverbal processes of thought (Kussmaul, Pick, van Woerkom); the *Vorgestalt* (Conrad); or the 'preverbitum' (Critchley).

Some of the difficulties experienced by aphasiacs in the ready understanding of articulate or written speech may perhaps be illuminated by the findings of the communication-theorists and engineers. Miller has emphasized that perceiving speech is ordinarily no mere passive or automatic procedure. The perceiver contributes an active and selective process of decoding. Auditory signals can normally be identified, even though they be grossly distorted by natural or by artificial means; or if hindered by simultaneous noise. This property is normally effected by virtue of a mental process of inductive inference. The factor of context is all-important and leads to a propitious frame of expectation. The hearer soon develops an implicit knowledge of the 'probability-structure' of any given message. It may well be that much of the difficulty or delay in comprehension experienced by an aphasiac, results from a failure of the mental act of inductive inference. Time-factors too may be important, for ordinarily recognition of the meaning of spoken speech depends far less upon the actual frequencies of the encoded signal than upon the pattern of amplitudes. An aphasic disorder of chronogenic character would cause the heard-signal to be meaningless, for the significance of the melody would be lost.

Although acoustic signals withstand very well a barrier of noise and distortion, the masking of one speech sound by another is always a considerable inhibitory factor, even in normals. Indeed some would maintain that it is actually impossible to hear and interpret two different verbal messages at the same time. This constitutes the familiar 'cocktail-party phenomenon' of confusion. Ordinarily one does one's best by a process of cerebral juggling whereby one switches back and forth between the two messages, and then guesses the whole from fragmentary snatches. This gymnastic type of decoding is probably a matter of supreme difficulty for an aphasiac.

Similarly the act of reading a printed text entails the identification of words (or even word-groupings) as a whole, and not as a sum of the constituent letters. When reading aloud the eye roams ahead several words in front of the word which is actually being spoken. It is highly probable that dyslexic patients have a shrunken eye-voice span when they try to read aloud, and moreover the duration-threshold, or period of time necessary for a word to be exposed before it is identified, will probably need to be prolonged considerably.

In a later paper, I discuss the subject of the content-analysis, or what it is that an aphasiac actually talks about.[1] Communication-experts are in the habit of dividing the categories of speech-patterns into utterances which are declarative, interrogative, imperative and exclamatory. Others have divided speech into the two categories of 'mands' versus 'tacts'. A simpler classification would be transitive and intransitive utterances. In all probability the fragmented speech of an aphasiac is mainly made up of transitive items; or, using the other terminology, interrogative, imperative or exclamatory utterances to the detriment of the declarative. Communication-experts frequently analyse the written and spoken speech of an individual according to the frequency with which certain words recur. This is what they call the T.T.R. or token/type ratio, and although rarely specifically investigated in aphasiacs, it will certainly give interesting results.

In my narrative of past achievements in the field of aphasia, I have been highly selective: of the recent past I have omitted much, for it is still within the ambit of current teaching. As to the future, I will be content if I shall have stimulated the imaginative thinking of my readers. Naturally, and yet unfortunately, one has to be discriminating as to one's source-material in a review like this. As F. L. Lucas has said:

Often, the ideal of reading everything ever written on a subject seems to me a vain idol. Five centuries ago such an ambition was often possible; today it is often fantastic; tomorrow it will become still more so. Therefore it is important to develop a quick eye for fools whose books are not worth reading; and a quick power of disembowelling other books less foolish, but still of minor importance . . . In this way the reader will feel less like one of those Alpine peasants one sees scaling hillsides with haystacks on their heads.

[1] See Chapter XVIII.

V. JACKSONIAN IDEAS AND THE FUTURE,
WITH SPECIAL REFERENCE TO APHASIA

We should look for knowledge where we may expect to find it, and why should a man be despised who goes in search of it? Those who remain at home may grow richer and live more comfortably than those who wander; but I desire neither to live comfortably nor to grow rich.

Paracelsus Paragranum

You have generously forgathered to acclaim the centenary of The National Hospital, Queen Square, while we on our part rejoice in our maturity and in your good wishes. The hundred years which have passed since our modest beginnings have witnessed the emergence of neurology as an independent discipline, the offspring of general medicine and of physiology.

The art and thinking of clinical neurologists in Great Britain today stem directly from the teaching of pioneers whom few among us here ever saw. To our cradle of neurology, they brought priceless gifts. Here, I would like to focus attention upon one of these giants, namely Hughlings Jackson: to discuss Jacksonian doctrines in their formation, their present status, and their promise for the future, especially in the realm of language.

In this country we often refer to Jacksonian ideas and methods in clinical medicine. We all like to believe that consciously or unconsciously, we are incorporating his particular mental attitudes into our workaday practice. By and large all of us endeavour to emulate his tenets and his methods, even though many of us fail to live up to his model.

Just what is understood by Jacksonian ideas? To unravel the golden threads which run through the texture of his obscure writing is no easy task, but it is a rewarding one.

In the first place we owe to Jackson our realization of the need for exactitude in observation coupled with faithfulness in recording. These principles, seemingly banal, are sometimes forgotten. As an observer, Jackson was shrewd, patient and painstaking. Witness his retracing of the march of a local seizure by dint of untiring study and reportage of fit after fit. Some of this research was tinged with tragedy, as when his beloved wife herself fell a victim to Jacksonian epilepsy. To the acuity of his gaze was added the utter honesty of his documentation. He stressed the necessity for describing exactly what the patient did or said: and he pointed out the dangers of rationalizing or interpreting, which might lead to an inaccurate note, which would merely record that which the observer deemed should have taken place.

An example may be given. In an early paper, written when he was 29 years of age, Jackson commented on the common failure of a patient to protrude the tongue on request. Asserting that we

The Centennial Oration of the Institute of Neurology, 22nd June, 1960. *Brit. med. J.*

do no harm to clinical medicine if we simply record all the facts, he stated that the patient when asked to put out the tongue betrayed that he understood the request by putting his fingers into his mouth as if to help it out; and yet nothing would happen. Such would be a true statement of facts, giving the reader a basis from which to speculate. To say 'there is total paralysis of the tongue' would be to advance a theory, improbable on the face of it; and if wrong, all the more dangerous, since it might even pass for a fact. That the tongue actually is not paralysed, is revealed by the patient's ability to chew and to swallow. He may even lick his lips. As the daughter of one of his patients remarked, her father could protrude the tongue 'by accident' as it were. Jackson saw in this paradox a performance reduced to a more automatic condition.

The second splendour of Jackson's neurology lay in his reflective cast of mind. Mere noting of data was not enough. Always he was asking himself 'why?'. This imagination, restrained and disciplined, led to creative and original thinking, and marked him out from the company of his talented colleagues. Jackson owed this gift of vision to his philosophic bent, for it had been his early ambition to devote himself to philosophy. A devoted disciple of Herbert Spencer, he was rescued from medicine largely by the encouragement of Jonathan Hutchinson.

The mid-Victorian period was an era of exciting new ideas that naturally conduced to Spencerian thinking, and thence to Jacksonian hypotheses. Anticipated to some extent by Linnaeus, Buffon, Erasmus Darwin and Lamarck, the doctrine of evolution came to life in the writings of Russell Wallace and of Charles Darwin. When the 'Origin of Species' was first published, Spencer was 39 years of age and Jackson was 24. Every branch of science became profoundly influenced in one direction or another by the impact of these stimulating notions.

I had always thought it unlikely that Jackson ever met Spencer personally, but Dr. S. H. Greenblatt has kindly informed me that on one occasion at least, they dined together. This was in 1878. They corresponded and Jackson sent Spencer a reprint of one of his articles on dissolution within the nervous system. The philosopher was impressed, describing the paper as 'clearly and conclusively argued'. Spencer had first mooted his evolutionary ideas in his essay on the 'Development Hypothesis' (1852), being himself considerably influenced by the 'congruous formula' of the zoologist K. E. von Baer, or development from the homogeneous to the heterogeneous. In the 'Art of Education' (1854) the proposition was developed that the unfolding of a child's mind repeats the unfolding of the mind of the human race. Spencerian notions reached fruition, as far as Jackson was concerned, in the 'Principles of Psychology' (1855).[1] Spencer had said that progress in mental as in nervous organization is presentable in terms of evolution—and we may interpolate here that it was Spencer who first used the term 'evolution'—for in rising to the higher types of mental states characterized by definiteness, coherence, and revivability, progress takes place in integration and heterogeneity.

Jackson paraphrased Spencer, and isolated four stages in motor evolution, namely (1) increasing differentiation (i.e. greater complexity); (2) increasing specialization (i.e. greater definiteness); (3) increasing integration (i.e. greater width of representation; and (4) increasing co-operation (i.e. greater association).

[1] When, in 1896, Spencer announced that he contemplated a System of Synthetic Philosophy, Jackson added his name to the list of Guarantors.

Jackson borrowed from Spencer the term 'dissolution' to signify the opposite of evolution. By applying it to disease of the nervous system, he explained certain clinical appearances. The conception of evolution and of dissolution in neurology led logically to other bold ideas, such as the notion of levels of function within the nervous system. A contrast between positive and negative manifestations of disease became obvious, and Jackson insisted that positive clinical phenomena could not be directly due to negative lesions. For example, an aphasiac might utter wrong words like 'chair' for 'table'. But while it could be held that softening of the brain was the cause of the distorted speech, it could not have been the cause of wrong utterance. 'Softened brain is no brain; so far as function, good or bad, is concerned, it is nothing at all'. Wrong utterances occur during activity of healthy parts, not softened. The most that Jackson would concede was that the diseased brain 'permitted' wrong words to be used. Jackson would therefore equate positive clinical data with a negative state of the brain only in the legal sense of a *causa causans*, or remote mechanism.

In the same common-sense vein, Jackson stressed the uselessness of medicinal treatment for negative conditions. 'What will drugs do towards ridding the patient of his paralysis? Nothing. No drugs can do anything whatever, good or bad, for cerebral softening; softened brain is not brain at all; it is dirt in the brain . . . He who is treating by drugs hemiplegia owing to softening, or to clot, is treating a hole in the brain.'

Another principle formulated by Jackson is often forgotten today, though its validity has never been challenged. Jackson stressed the error of trying to localize a cerebral function on the grounds that a focal lesion within the brain was followed by loss of that function. This doctrine was slow in maturation. For example, early in his career, Jackson was willing to accept Broca's teaching *in toto*, first as to the position of the focus in cases of aphasia; and secondly, that a faculty of language resided within the third frontal gyrus. Later, Jackson grew more sceptical. In 1889 he confessed that at one time he had spoken of centres for Will, Memory, Reason, and Emotion; he now realized them to be elements of consciousness quite artificially distinguished. To have imagined such centres had been 'a mere artifice'. He could not now accept any abruptly demarcated centres in the cortex standing for any kind of representation. In another context Jackson admitted that he had now abandoned the words 'faculty' and 'reside' in the arbitrary manner he had used them in the past. Since speech or words enter into thought, it now seemed to him incredible that 'speech' could 'reside' in any limited spot. Nonetheless he believed that *damage* to the brain confined to the region of the corpus striatum would bring about a loss of speech. As Jasper put it, anatomical areas within the brain are not to be rated as anything more than regions which when ablated may be followed by disturbances of function. They are to be looked upon as 'centres of destruction' rather than centres of function.

Jackson protested against another example of muddled thinking, namely the employment within the same context of terminology borrowed from unrelated disciplines, e.g. anatomy, metaphysics, and physiology. Thus the word 'voluntary' was a psychological term, which could not really be used when speaking of physical processes. Classifications which were partly anatomo-physiological, and partly psychological, obscured the issues. Such confused sorting would be as scientifically improper as would be a grouping of plants into endogens, *graminaceae*, kitchen herbs, ornamental shrubs, and potatoes. He gave as an example of such mixed taxonomies, the common statement that an *idea* of a word would produce an articulatory *movement*; whereas, he argued, a psychical state, an 'idea of a word', (or simply 'a word'), could not possibly produce an articulatory movement, which is a physical state. 'In all our studies of diseases of the nervous system we must be on our guard against the fallacy that what are physical states in lower centres fine away into psychical states in higher centres.'

Like Bergson years later, Jackson was critical of the teaching that verbal memory resided within the brain. There is no such thing as memory, but only things remembered. Dealing in this vein with the common employment of the term metaphysics in a pejorative sense, Jackson declared: 'it is a mistake to suppose that those who write books on metaphysics are the more metaphysical. They have, at any rate, the knowledge that they are dealing with metaphysics. There was once a man who could conceive an abstract Lord Mayor. The conception he had, so he averred, had neither head, arms, legs nor corpulence: it was not an image of any particular Lord Mayor nor a fusion of several, but an abstract Lord Mayor. Well, we think this metaphysician was too confident in his powers of conception. But do we not imagine ourselves capable of the same kind of marvellous feats? Let us look at a case of aphasia. A man does not speak and yet can understand what we say to him, and can think, on ordinary things, at any rate. These are the facts: no one disputes them. Now comes the metaphysician, who proffers an explanation that the patient has lost words, but retains the memory or ideas of words. There are, it seems, words, and also memories or ideas of words, which latter somehow are not words. Now what is an idea of a word which is not a word? It is, like the abstract Lord Mayor, simply nothing at all'. (1882).

In the mental processes preceding articulation Jackson recognized a two-fold manoeuvre. First the mind becomes aroused in propositional form: later comes a fitting of words to the idea. These two stages, namely subject-proposition and object-proposition, together make up verbalizing. The fitting of words to the idea comprises external speech if it achieves audibility, but if the phrase takes place in silence it forms internal speech. Jackson did not believe there was any distinction other than in degree between internal and external speech. The speechless man is not wordless: he can receive propositions: he is not bereft of images. He can think, but he is lame in thinking. But if imperception is added to speechlessness, as is often the case, images will be affected, and there will be inferior comprehension.

Such were a few of Jackson's ideas relating to language. At this point it might be interesting to pause, and to enquire as to the man himself. What were the influences that bore on him and directed the stream of his intellect into the novel discipline of neurology?

John Hughlings Jackson was born in 1835 in a Yorkshire hamlet. He received his schooling first in the village, later still in Tadcaster and afterwards, in a progressive nonconformist school recently opened at Nailsworth, Glos. Formal schooling meant but little to Jackson, who always regarded himself—like the Sitwells at Eton—as largely self-taught. All his schools were bad, he said, and much of his later success was owing to his not having been over-educated. It is probable that Jackson was never an erudite man or a *conosciente*.

At 15 years Jackson became an apprentice to Dr. Anderson of York where he also joined the local medical school. After qualification, he held the post of Resident Medical Officer at the York City Dispensary from 1856 to 1859. There he came in contact with a remarkable physician, Dr. Thomas Laycock, who afterwards occupied the Chair of the Practice of Physic at Edinburgh. Laycock was a scholarly man who had been impressed by the work of Marshall Hall upon nervous reflex action. Jackson was certainly influenced by Laycock who may well have helped to orientate his attention towards the nervous system.

Moving to London in 1859, Jackson lived with his friend Jonathan Hutchinson at No. 4, Finsbury Circus. Thanks to him Jackson became employed as a fellow reporter for the *Medical Times and Gazette*. Their duties took them to medical meetings and to hospitals, where they saw selected clinical cases, and met the leaders of the medical profession. Among these was that brilliant original, Brown-Séquard, who for a few years was making London his home—the brief sojourn of an unstable eccentric. In 1859 Brown-Séquard had been invited to join J. Z. Ramskill on the staff of the projected National Hospital for the Paralysed and Epileptic, whose first patients were received in the spring of 1860 at No. 24, Queen Square. Friendship with Brown-Séquard determined Jackson's choice of career, and his decision to sublimate his philosophy into the more practical pastures of neurology. When, in 1862, a vacancy occurred at the National Hospital for an Assistant Physician, Jackson was the successful candidate. Shortly after, came further vacancies upon the senior staff. In those days there was no automatic advancement, and it was incumbent upon Jackson formally to apply. Twice in succession he was passed over in favour of others, and it was only when a third vacancy occurred in 1867 that Jackson attained the rank of full Physician. It is characteristic of Jackson's easy-going modesty that he wrote that if unsuccessful he would be happy to continue as Assistant Physician. This makes strange reading when we find him in 1900 seeking to retire from the staff under the age-rule, his colleagues, however, persuading him not to do so, but to continue on the active list another 10 years.

From his earliest days in neurology, Jackson interested himself in the principles which underlay nervous function in health and in disease. As a corollary he applied his attention to the problems of disordered speech. Here again, Brown-Séquard was to prove the instigator. At first Jackson had lightly assigned loss of speech to disease of the olives, a notion which he had derived from Laycock who in turn had adopted it from van der Kolk. But Brown-Séquard showed Jackson that the defect was often not one of talking but of language, and that some of these patients had lost all power of expression, even by way of making signs.

Stirring events had been going on in the medical circles of Paris about the time that Jackson qualified. The opinions of Gall and Spurzheim, so contrary to those of Flourens, had been received with excitement, and there were strong repercussions of sentiment either for or against. Matters came to a head in March 1861, when Auburtin delivered his thoughtful address on the relationship between loss of speech and lesions of the frontal lobes. Auburtin's role in the history of aphasia has been neglected: many neurologists today do not even know his name. And yet it was he who prompted the surgeon Broca—like himself an amateur anthropologist—to observe with particular interest the case of the speechless patient Laborgne, lately transferred to his care by reason of a septic leg. Hitherto Broca had not been concerned with problems of speech. Fortune ordained that

Broca's patient should quickly perish, and that the brain should offer up the eloquent evidence of a superficial lesion of the frontal lobe. All these happenings were topical and familiar to young Jackson, who a few years later was to meet Broca personally at a symposium in Norwich. Jackson had also heard about Broca's second patient Lelong. He was aware of Trousseau's classic demonstrations of speechless patients. He had known him reject in succession the terms *aphrasia*, *alalia*, *alogia*, and *aphemia*, and substitute them with the now traditional *aphasia*. Jackson, be it noted, used none of these terms in his earlier writings, preferring to speak of 'disorders of expression'.

Jackson must also have read about the curious intervention of Dr. Gustave Dax, nettled at the fancied slighting by Broca of his late father, who had long realized the greater importance of the left hemisphere in the genesis of aphasia.

These events were like heady wine to the young neurologist, who at Queen Square and elsewhere was now in touch with numerous hemiplegics, many with disorders of expression. One of Jackson's duties as an Assistant Physician was to visit patients in their own homes. In the drab houses within the mean streets of Holborn, Soho, and St. Pancras, bedridden survivors of an apoplexy became a cornucopia of ideas which fed Jackson's inspiration. His colleagues Brown-Séquard and Victor Bazire had collected many such disabled folk and had permitted Jackson to observe them.

But Jackson's interest in aphasia had been whetted long before he met Brown-Séquard. Boyhood impressions are often so deeply etched that they may determine the careers and vocation of later life. So it was with Jackson. When quite a child on a seaside holiday, he lodged at a house where the landlady, as he discovered to his wonderment and awe, could say nothing but 'Watty'. This unlikely disyllable was articulated with such a wide range of cadence that it could express a variety of emotions. Her laugh was merry and ringing and when anything amused her she would cry: 'Watty, watty, watty'. Years later we find Jackson making the pioneer descriptions of what he was to call the recurrent utterance of aphasiacs.

A little older he was driving to school, when his fellow-passenger, a girl of 17, daughter of the coachman, suddenly found she could not reply to a question which was put to her. With great difficulty she got out the words . . . 'I can't talk!' The coach turned back, and Jackson afterwards learned that the girl lost speech altogether for three weeks and became paralysed down the right side. Eventually she improved, but died 12 years later from eclampsia. She never regained her power of speech completely, and even to the last was apt to call things by wrong names.

These two cases encountered early, in intimate even dramatic circumstances, must surely have stamped an indelible imprint upon his eager intellect, which was to influence the direction of his life's work.

Ideas, whether they be true or false, have stupendous potentialities in human affairs. But ideas catch on slowly, as Jackson himself used to remark, especially in medicine where an innate conservatism obtains. The second half of the nineteenth century was a period in neurology when clinico-pathological correlation was winning easy prizes. The work was descriptive in character, not reflective. It was self-evident and easy to comprehend. Much of it was worthy factual bricks-

and-mortar stuff. Little wonder Jackson's ideas especially on aphasia were temporarily over-shadowed by those who made brief clinical studies high-lighting the obvious, and who sought by way of morbid anatomy a key to the understanding of the normal faculty of language.

But the seeds had fallen and in due course they germinated. Other philosophically-minded neurologists appeared whose contributions to aphasia, not necessarily deriving from Hughlings Jackson, nevertheless stand alongside Jacksonian ideas in sympathetic comity. We recall the names of Baillarger, Kussmaul, Pick, von Monakow, Freud, and particularly Bergson. The observations of the last-named upon the topic of language have been surprisingly overlooked. Bringing the story into the early twentieth century we have Pierre Marie, van Woerkoem, Goldstein, Weisen-berg, and most significant of all, Henry Head. Of contemporary English-speaking neurologists, we may enumerate Walshe, Russell Brain and Walter Riese among the most important exponents of Jacksonian ideas.

Today the forces of neurology are arrayed differently. By far and away the majority of worth-while research work into aphasia is of a dynamic quality, and harks back directly to Jackson's ideas, offering abundant promise for the future.

But the mill will not grind with the water that has passed. Let us rather project our imaginations and speculate upon how aphasiology may be expected to develop in the hundred years ahead.

Already we possess important new tools for research. In the first place we have the advantage of exact *instrumental methods for the study of aphasic utterance*. Now, under scientifically controlled test-circumstances the fragmentary speech can be faithfully recorded: played back as required, at slower or higher speeds if necessary. In this way the clinician no longer has to rely merely upon his sharp ear to interpret the distorted mumblings of the aphasiac. The clues are now caught and pre-served, and they can be transcribed and examined over and over again. The utterances can be analysed from the standpoints of phonetics, syntax and semantics. The recordings can, if required, be translated from acoustic into visual form by way of spectrography or some other technique of visible speech. Modern aphasiology is consequently furnished with evidence which is scientifically acceptable, and which can be utilized for future research.

Secondly there now exists *more satisfactory psychological testing-procedures*, including the evaluation of non-verbal performance in aphasiacs.

The third asset is a momentous one. *A link-up has taken place between academic linguists and aphasiologists.* Today, aphasia must be regarded as a problem lying within the province of linguis-tics. Language in dissolution is obviously an integral part of this stupendous topic, which no neurologist can henceforth afford to neglect. Neither can he longer avoid coming to grips with the essential nature and the purpose of the normal faculty of language. Information-theorists over-stress the role of communication. Of the many available definitions of language perhaps the most satisfying is that promulgated by Sapir, who said that language is primarily a vocal actualization of the tendency to see realities symbolically, a quality which renders it a fit instrument for com-munication; in the actual give-and-take of social intercourse it has been complicated and refined into the form which is known today. 'Language is a great force of socialization, probably the greatest that exists'. Nowadays linguistics forms a broad spectrum of endeavour ranging from philosophy at one extreme to phonetics and communication-theory at the other. Here then is a vast unexplored territory for the future. Ideas for research crop up in profusion.

Among the present-time neurologists alive to the importance of linguistics in aphasia are Grewel, Bay, Panse and Leischner. On the other hand linguists have been rather remiss at recognizing the value of the lessons of aphasia, and such meagre references they have made are usually quite out of touch with contemporary neurological thought. Roman Jakobson is a conspicuous exception.

Communication theory includes a statistical study of language. Measurement of vocabulary, and frequency of usage of individual words and clusters of words, has already been undertaken by Zipf, by Estoup, by Mandelbrot and by Herdang. It remains for future neurologists to apply these techniques to the writings and utterances of aphasiacs. A similar numerical enquiry into the ratio between the number of different words chosen and the total sum of words employed is likely to be revealing. This is the type/token ratio which clearly demonstrates that the aphasiac utilizes a very shrunken store of words, while indulging in undue or unnoticed iteration.

The subtopic of contrastive linguistics emphasizes important relationships between the syntax of a particular language and the thought-processes of those who use the language. That the association is integral, is the basis of Whorpf's principle of linguistic relativity. Hitherto the great bulk of research into aphasia has been carried out on patients speaking one of the European tongues. Little or nothing is known of the pattern of aphasic dissolution in the case of the African or Asiatic languages, where the orthodox subject-predicate system does not exist. Here then is an important subject for the future.

The fourth acquisition to the techniques of aphasia-research is an unexpected one, namely *Pavlovian ideology*. On the face of it, this might appear unpromising, being based upon an utterly materialistic philosophy moored to animal observation. But the enlightened interpretation of such workers as Luria, Bein and others, demonstrates that Pavlovian research into the evolution and dissolution of language is possible, and may indeed prove valuable.

Equipped with these new weapons of research we can now venture upon a study of many problems in aphasiology which have hitherto been obscure. Some of these questions are even now matters of debate: others have not yet been broached. The future years will surely yield answers to such queries as the following:

How far is aphasia a localizable symptom?

Already there has taken place a shift away from a preoccupation with aphasia as a static outfall-symptom of brain-disease, localizable to this or that region within the left hemisphere. Localization is not thrown overboard, however, but it has become demoted in rank or significance. The functional disturbance within the province of symbolic thinking is realized to be more complex and usually more intense than can be ascribed to the negative effect of a circumscribed lesion. Many factors are operative, some of them subtle and intangible. The role of diaschisis, and of demential epiphenomena, deriving from the 'momentum' of the causative lesion, must be reckoned with and evaluated.

Even though his name is associated with the events due to a discharging lesion of the motor cortex, Jackson was, of course, the first among neurologists to adopt a dynamic attitude towards the effects of brain-damage. As he himself said 'I am neither a universalizer nor a localizer'. Since speech and words enter into thought he deemed it incredible that 'speech' could 'reside' in any limited spot. As far as aphasia was concerned he rarely tried to track down lesions from the clues offered by the disordered speech. He did not believe in abrupt geographical localizations. Very sudden and very extensive damage to *any part* of the left cerebral hemisphere would produce *some* amount of defect of speech.

In our own time Leischner has stressed, like many others, that speech-performance is to be looked upon as an overlaid or parasitic function which utilizes pre-formed brain-mechanisms as well as pre-formed peripheral instruments.

Riese has said that there never will be a cerebral localization of productive thought, since what is really productive and creative in the human mind resists even the most generous and universal localization. Since it is a coming-into-being of what did not exist before, it cannot be correlated with existing material. Riese traced an analogy with the heel of Achilles. Although the heel was the most vulnerable region of the hero's body, and although its injury would be fatal to his life, life cannot be said to be localized at the heel; it pervades the whole body.

WHAT IS THE IDEAL SYSTEM OF CLASSIFICATION?

Jackson himself rarely tried to group his cases of disordered expression but contented himself with descriptive labels such as 'recurrent utterance', and 'occasional utterance'. A splitting into 'motor' and 'sensory' types came later, the work of others. For many years this apparent logicality served a purpose but with ever increasing inadequacy. Already, neurologists are profoundly critical of the classical Lichtheim-Wernicke classification. Head's classification was a very worthy one, based upon observed psychological data, but it was doomed to fail. Roman Jakobson, one of the few linguists to concern himself with questions of pathology, has attempted an unusual type of distinction which applies both to normal speech and to patterns of aphasia. This is based upon a contrast between metaphor and metonymy, as representing two basic methods of relation: the one is an internal relation of similarity and contrast, the other being an external relation of contiguity or remoteness. An aphasiac shows impairment in either one, but only one, of these modes of verbal behaviour, and for this reason Jakobson visualizes a 'contiguity disorder of speech' as opposed to a 'similarity disorder of speech'.

Classifications of aphasia based upon levels or functions of normal speech are unpromising, for, as Head pointed out, the types of aphasia we meet with clinically are not fragments of normal speech, and they do not directly reveal the elements out of which language is built.

We may perhaps predict that in the future there will emerge another kind of classification, clinico-psychological in nature. Attention may become directed more and more to the 'pre-verbitum', that is to say the silent processes of thinking which immediately precede the act of expression in speech or writing. This rapid but all-important fragment of mentation obviously varies widely in the normal subject according to many ever-changing circumstances, as for instance the semantic properties of the emerging words. In aphasiacs the errors or difficulties in word-finding may be the product of blockage which may occur at different levels within this preverbitum. Herein we can detect the possibility of erecting a classification based upon some such notion of levels of thought. Thus the patient who is merely at a loss to supply a word at a given moment to an article presented to him, might be deemed to have a word-block at a quite superficial level. The patient with a fluent but well-nigh incomprehensible flow of gibberish has a much deeper defect, and if such an aphasiac is also found not to comprehend the statements of others, the defect must be even more profound. Work along lines such as these will surely continue.

DOES APHASIA NECESSARILY ENTAIL A DISORDER OF INTELLECT, WHETHER QUANTITATIVE OR QUALITATIVE?

Most would expect the eventual answer to be in the affirmative. Goldstein's important dichotomy between conceptual and concrete attitudes at one time seemed to supply the solution, explaining both mild and severe cases. Latterly, however, the validity of Goldstein's hypothesis has been questioned, as by Isserlin, Bein, Luria, Bauer and Becka, Kok and others. Time will show how far these criticisms are justified. It is difficult to deny that eventually there will surely emerge proof of some affection of intellect, or of personality, or both, pervading the pattern of all aphasias.

The retrospective evidence afforded by those who have made a complete recovery from an aphasia must be regarded as suspect where the intellectual status is concerned. Organic repression, retrograde amnesia, even a veritable denial-syndrome are all too likely to intervene so as to mask the earlier deficiencies. Faulty memory puts a gloss upon the blemishes and imperfections of the spirit. As D. K. Dunlop wrote: . . . 'The mere statement that such a thing happened in a particular case under certain circumstances is inconclusive, because one can never be certain either that the description of the circumstances is sufficiently comprehensive; that is, that certain important details are not omitted from the account, or else that certain details specified in the account are not erroneously recollected. Such is the effect of the known fallibility of human testimony'.

DOES THE DISSOLUTION OF SPEECH IN DISEASE RECAPITULATE THE STAGES OF DEVELOPMENT OF SPEECH IN THE CHILD?

A. F. Watts has proclaimed that '. . . speech development in the child and in the race follows broadly the same lines, and the powers lost as a result of mental derangement disappear in the reverse order of their acquirement, just as in a stricken tree death appears in the newest twigs before it reaches the older branches'. I take leave to doubt the validity of this idea, and I believe that aphasiologists of tomorrow will examine with greater care, and, more critically, this seductive notion. Here is a facile conception which has appeared in many writings in the past and even at the present time. Some, like Jakobson, have aligned certain types of aphasia with the manner of speaking of a child. Others, like Alajouanine, and also Diamond, have sought to correlate the dysarthric defects in aphasic patients with an infantile fashion of talk. Both are believed to show a similar pattern of phonemic substitutions, the aphasiac stumbling most over consonantal sounds which a child masters comparatively late. This is what has been called the 'syndrome of phonetic disintegration'. I have never been impressed by this relationship and I am still dubious. Professor Fry of the London University Department of Phonetics has subjected one of my aphasic patients, chosen at random, to a most rigorous speech-analysis. His research completely failed to reveal any hint of a reversion to a less mature manner of articulation.

Time will show whether it is logical or appropriate to seek an analogy between the defect of speech from disease in an adult—that is to say, one who had attained linguistic maturity and then lost it—and the ontogeny of speech. At the present time it is safer to assume an attitude of scepticism and to avoid drawing parallels too freely. If we really wish to find a disease-state which recapitulates the infancy of speech we are more likely to witness it either in the halting and hesitating utterances of a dement, or better still in the baby-talk of an hysteric.

WHAT IS THE ESSENTIAL NATURE OF THE SO-CALLED CONGENITAL 'DYSPHASIAS', INCLUDING DEVELOPMENTAL DYSLEXIA AND CONGENITAL AUDITORY IMPERCEPTION?

So far we are merely at the stage of observation and recording. But already the available evidence clearly shows that some of these are not 'pure' or delimited defects as was originally imagined. To what extent they depend upon subtle inborn disorders of simple perception is a problem for the future to unravel. Whether in fact there exists an underlying structural defect is uncertain, and would appear today to be unlikely. Whether the 'dysphasia' is merely one aspect of a deeper defect of some other symbolic quality, is a matter for future neurologists. Specific developmental dyslexia may well stand apart from the other types of retarded speech in childhood.

HOW FAR IS IT CORRECT TO ALIGN SO-CALLED 'MOTOR' APHASIA WITH APRAXIA, AND 'SENSORY' APHASIA WITH AGNOSIA?

Since Liepmann's work in 1900 opinion on this subject has oscillated. Today most of us are sceptical about any isomorphism of this sort. The conception of any such pure entity as 'motor' aphasia is out of favour. Correlation of a cerebral dysarthria, that is a disorder due to a focal cortico-subcortical lesion, with an articulatory apraxia, is, however, still conceded. Further than that, modern neurologists are unwilling to go. We may re-echo the words of Bay, who, concerning apraxia and aphasia, said 'the two have as little in common as the leaping attack of a bird of prey with the strategic planning of the general staff'.

TO WHAT EXTENT ARE THE RECEPTIVE DEFECTS IN APHASIA DEPENDENT UPON AN IMPAIRMENT IN THE PERCEPTION OR UTILIZATION OF SIMPLE SENSE-DATA?

It may well be found that the reception of auditory or visual signals is imperfect, or perhaps abnormally delayed in aphasiacs. Tachistoscopic testing is likely to demonstrate such a state of affairs. Or on the other hand the defect may lie at a deeper level, namely within the patient's frame of expectation, for in normal circumstances an anticipatory state materially assists the correct reception of signals. Sensory aphasia may turn out to entail an impairment of this 'prior set'. These are straightforward questions which will assuredly be answered in the future.

HOW FAR DOES THE PROBLEM OF AN APHASIA DEPEND UPON INDIVIDUAL PRE-MORBID HABITS OF SPEECH?

Considerably more attention is due to the subject of the aphasic patient's previous educational status, with special reference to his literary attainments, habits, prejudices and predilections. The performance of an aphasic patient is now looked upon as a variable, based upon a formula entailing not only such obvious factors as the size and locus of the lesion, its nature, its chronogenic properties and its degree of abruptness, but also the make-up of the victim with particular respect to his pre-morbid literacy. The aphasiac's performance will also depend upon a complexus of immediate circumstances, both extrinsic and intrinsic. The use of language is ordinarily a very personal mode of behaviour. Aphasia must therefore constitute an aberration in the pattern of total behaviour, rather than a scotoma within the field of language-function.

Factors of age are of course of obvious importance—it is still uncertain, however, whether the sex of the patient in itself exercises any influence upon the final picture of an aphasia. This fascinating idea also ties up with the problem of the earliest appearances of speech in *homo sapiens*. While some evidence can be adduced to suggest that among our prehistoric forebears speech was a masculine prerogative, equally specious arguments are available to the effect that speech-acquisition was mainly due to the enterprise of the female sex.

Some of these considerations were envisaged long ago by Jackson when he spoke of the influence of the 'four factors of the insanities'.

According to Lenin, 'one fool can ask more questions in a minute that twelve wise men can answer in an hour'. None the less I believe I am justified in trying to trace some of the steps which aphasiologists will take in the future. The problems I have outlined are all of such a nature as would surely have intrigued Hughlings Jackson were he still with us. These questions of today and to-morrow reflect the enduring influence of Jacksonian principles, and the stimulus of his ideas continues to guide our investigations and our thinking. As far as the subject of language and its disorders is concerned, the future of neurological research is most certainly assured for yet another century.

VI. THE ORIGINS OF APHASIOLOGY

How old the new, how new the old!

History maketh a young man to be old, without either wrinkles or grey hairs; privileging him with the experience of age without either the infirmities or inconvenience thereof. Yea, it not only maketh things past present, but enableth one to make a rational conjecture of things to come.

Thomas Fuller

It is a matter for surprise that philosophers and medical scientists neglected for so long the subject of disorders of the faculty of speech. This is all the more strange in view of the speculative interest shown for well over two millennia into such recondite topics as the nature of language; the relationship between thinking and speech; communication within the animal kingdom; theories as to the manner in which human speech took origin; debates as to the rational views on the beginnings of speech as opposed to the hypothesis of divine origin; the nature of the original *lingua adamica*, and the ways by which it became transmuted into the tongues of contemporary man. There were also speculations of a theological sort, which even included discussion as to the nature of the *lingua sacra*, that is, the speech spoken in Paradise. A considerable literature is available on these and cognate topics much of which is merely of historical interest.

Thus there grew up the early science of philology—later linguistics—taking origin in the work of such philosophers as Leibniz and von Humboldt. The sparks which really set alight the philological debates were two in number. In the first place there was the appearance in 1772 of Herder's essay upon the origin of speech in man. The second great stimulus is to be found in the introduction in 1796 by Sir William Jones of the ancient Sanskrit language into the corpus of linguistic science.

But disorders of language, whatever their nature or causation, remained a neglected topic even though individuals with defective powers of communication must have been encountered not only in medical practice but even in ordinary social intercourse. The eye observed but did not perceive, while the ear heard without registering or comprehending the phenomena.

Something of this kind must, however, have faintly aroused the interest of Aristotle for we find him enquiring two or three times within his *Problemata* 'why is it that of all animals, man alone is apt to become hesitating in speech?' Merely from this question it is difficult to say whether

(Based upon the Honyman Gillespie Lecture, 1963, delivered at the University of Edinburgh, 12th December, 1963, and published in the *Scot. Med. J.*, 1964. 9, 231–242; and also upon *La Controverse de Dax et Broca*, a paper read at the Société Française de Neurologie, 4th June, 1964, and published in the *Rev. Neurol.*, 1964. 110, 553–557; as well as the *Int. J. of Neurol.*, 1964. 4, 199-206, under the title *Dax's Law*.)

Aristotle had in mind cases of stuttering, of dysarthria, or of dysphasia of one type or another. However, Aristotle went on to answer his own question by pointing out that man alone had the power of uttering words, animals merely possessing 'voices'. Those who hesitate in their speech cannot connect their words, and cannot explain their meaning continuously. These statements suggest that Aristotle was referring to a condition of dysphasia rather than a dysarthria or some other speech impediment. When warmed with wine those who hesitate in their speech are better able to put their words together. But inebriety causes a 'stumbling of the tongue' and Aristotle argued whether this might not in itself be the evidence of a stumbling of the mind. 'If the mind is in this condition, it is only natural that the tongue should suffer likewise, for the mind is the source of speech'.

An early description of one type of speechlessness—but not an aphasia—is to be found in the seventh century when the venerable Bede referred to the cure of a man who was dumb. The interesting case-report made in 1296 by Opicinus of a man whose writings became marred by inconsequential, repetitive and self-reproachful phrases probably refers to an instance of a schizophrenic disorder of language. Similarly the temporary losses in the comprehension of verbal symbols experienced by St. Teresa of Jesus (1515–1582) were probably psychotic in character and may have been associated with episodes of ecstasy.

Throughout the literature of the middle ages and indeed well into the nineteenth century it is obvious that medical writers in their references to disordered speech, were hopelessly confusing a number of conditions which are actually quite diverse. Thus they failed to distinguish sharply between the effects of focal disease or injury of the brain, i.e. what we would now call a dysphasia, and a number of general impairments. These latter would include all the dysarthrias and dyslalias; various psychotic disorders of speech including those occurring in schizophrenia, mental defect, and dementia; the hysterical aberrations of speech such as dysphonia and mutism; and the delirious utterances of those in semi-coma. Indeed the dysarthrias and the dysphasias were not clearly demarcated until the middle of the nineteenth century when Hughlings Jackson pointed out that in the former condition the patient could not swallow but he could express himself normally on paper; while the dysphasiac showed no other bulbar symptom like dysphagia, but he could not make his thoughts known either by talking or by writing.

Even when the medieval writer was obviously describing a case of true aphasia due to a circumscribed cerebral lesion, traumatic or apoplectic, in most instances the speech-defect was ascribed to a paralysis of the tongue. Hence we find that cauteries and blisters were applied to the neck to stimulate activity of the organ believed to be sluggish. It is difficult to explain how the experienced and observant physicians of the seventeenth and eighteenth centuries could have overlooked or else misinterpreted such features, so obvious to us today, as the use of wrong words; the recurrent utterances; the perseverations; the dissociation between voluntary and automatic speech; the dysgraphia; the frequent inability to read, or even to comprehend the words in use; and the striking phenomenon of a prolix torrent of gibberish. In retrospect it seems absurd to have bracketed all the foregoing as manifestations of a lingual palsy, especially when it was usually obvious that the motility of the tongue was intact.

With these points in mind let us turn back the pages of medical history in order to discern the earliest references to what we now call dysphasia, and to trace the slow and uncertain beginnings of our understanding of its true nature.

Egyptian surgery affords us the earliest clues. Thirty centuries before Christ the author of the famous Edwin Smith papyrus (who might have been Imhotep) gave a number of eloquent descriptions of the effects of wounds of the skull. Thus we read: . . . 'one having a wound in his temple, perforating his temporal bone; while he discharges blood from both his nostrils, he suffers with stiffness in the neck, *and he is speechless*. An ailment not to be treated'. Again: . . . 'one having a smash in the temple; he discharges blood from his two nostrils and from his ear; *he is speechless*, and he suffers with stiffness in the neck'.

Loss of speech was also mentioned by Hippocrates. Thus in the Epidemics he referred to a pregnant woman afflicted with fever and backache. On the third day she developed pain in the neck and head. Then . . . 'quickly she lost *her power of speech*; the right arm was paralysed with convulsion after the manner of a stroke'. Speech came back on the fourth day in an indistinct manner. Oddly enough the importance of this clinical association of a right-sided paralysis with a loss of speech was not commented upon, in the same way that the Egyptian surgeons failed to correlate the sidedness of the temporal bone fracture with the ablation of speech.

Pliny was getting closer to the essential linguistic nature of speechlessness when in his Natural History he stressed the vulnerability of the faculty of memory. He gave instances where isolated defects of memory (as opposed to a general impairment) occurred through injury. There was a man who after being struck by a stone forgot how to read and to write but nothing else. Here Pliny was anticipating by many centuries two important points which were afterwards neglected, namely the unity of writing and talking as modes of self-expression; and the notion of a memory-defect limited to words. The well-known forgetfulness of the orator-grammarian Messalla Corvinus, quoted by Pliny, which occurred a couple of years before his death might have been the expression of a dementia rather than an aphasia.

We have not succeeded in tracing any reference to speechlessness within the literature of Islamic medicine. It seems odd indeed that there is nothing in the *Paradise of Wisdom* written by Rabban in 850; nor in the *Háwí* or *Continens* of Rhazes (850–923); nor in the *Liber Regius* of Haly Abbas. And still more strange that the eleventh-century *Qánún* of Avicenna (980–1037)—the most famous medical text ever written—should be silent upon this topic. I hasten to add that these criticisms of Islamic medicine may not be wholly fair for we are in possession of still only a fraction of the literary output, and of that which is extant, much has yet to be translated into English. For a medical man who is conversant with the contemporary and classical languages of the Middle East, the subject of Islamic neurology would probably prove a rewarding though onerous pursuit.

The gap between Arabian medicine and the writings of European physicians in the seventeenth century is considerable. One or two incidents at this time are perhaps worthy of mention. Chanet (1649) described a patient with a speech-affection; and like Pliny, the author again argued that loss of words was not necessarily due to a loss of memory, an observation which remained for long unheeded.

J'ay un parent qui estant au siège de Hulst, y fut blessé à la mémoire. Il n'oublia pas seulement son non comme Messala Coruinus; mais encore toutes sortes de paroles, jusque à ne connoistre plus aucune letres de l'alphabet. Il n'oublia pourtant point à escrire: c'est à dire que lors qu'on luy donnait une example, et qu'on lui faisoit signe de la copier, et acquittoit fort bien: Mais quand on luy eust dit faires un A, ou un B, il ne l'eust scen faire, si en mesme temps on ne luy eust mis deuant les yeux: car lors il faisoit bien voir qu'il avoit autrefois appris a ecrire. Cela me confirme eu l'opinion que j'ay prounceé en mon Traité de la Connoissance des animaux, ou j'ay monstré que nous avons des habitudes inherentes aux organes exterieurs, et différéntes des idées de la Mémoire. C'est ce qui est bien clair en celuy-cy, qui ne se servant plus des Images de la Memoire, avoit neantmoins, conserue cette facilité de la main, qui est necessaire pour vien ecrire. Il apprend maintenant à lire et à parler, et y auance plus, que s'il n'aurait jamais sceu ni l'lvn ni l'autre: et on espère que son cerueau estant fortifié, il s'y fera une reminiscence générale de ce qui'il a sceu avant sa blessure.[1]

Johann Schmidt (1624–1690) described in 1673, probably for the first time in medical literature, the case of an acquired loss of the ability to read, the modern 'alexia'. In 1676, in the Philosophical Transactions, we can read of a case where a patient lost the capacity both to read and to write. Here we find:

> . . . Of a man, that upon an Apoplexy had quite forgot all reading, and knew never a letter, yet was able readily to write any of the Languages by him known before, though unable to tell any of the letters thus written by himself: *Quaere*; Whether this case might not be like that of those that can write with their eyes shut; the phancy working in the act of writing, but the memory failing in knowing and distinguishing the letters.

The name of the author is not stated. This is one of the very earliest references to dysgraphia, or to what some writers choose to call subcortical word-blindness. The author's comment anticipated by nearly 200 years the observation made by Trousseau to the effect that his patient 'wrote as though his eyes were closed'.

The invaluable writings of Thomas Willis contain at least two case-reports of an aphasia (1683). The first concerned a man of 50 who lost consciousness. 'On the next day, his Brain began a little to grow clear, so that he looked about him, and spoke a few words; he seem'd to know his Friends, but *could not utter the name of any*; and by reason of this matter sinking down more deeply into the Brain, a *Palsie seized the whole right side*. . . .' The second case was that of a man of 56 years. . . . 'he became very forgetful, and *Paralytick, in all his right side*. . . . He well understood his infirmity, knew his Friends and Relations, and others who came to visit him, but *could hardly remember the names of any of them*; and when he began to talk of any thing, *he wanted words to express his mind*'.

In 1683, too, appeared the report by Peter Rommel of what was probably a 'motor' aphasia.

---

[1] 'I have a relative who was wounded at the Siege of Hulst, his memory becoming affected. He did not only forget his own name, like Messala Corvinus, but also all sorts of words, and even the letters of the alphabet. However he had not forgotten how to write, that is if one gave him a text and told him to copy it—which he did very well. But if one said to him, write an A or a B, he could not do it—unless he could see the letter before his eyes. This confirmed the views I had expressed in my monograph upon Animal intelligence where I had shown that we possess inherent faculties in our external organs, quite apart from the ideas of the memory. That was obvious in him, who no longer employing memory-images, nevertheless had retained that skill of the hand necessary for him to write properly. He is now learning to read and to talk, and is making headway, for he could do neither of these, and one is hopeful that his brain being rested, he will regain a general recollection of what he knew before he was wounded'.

Within the eighteenth century there was an accretion of cases of acquired speechlessness, though any searching contribution to medical knowledge of the pathology of language had as yet to be made. Thus Sir Richard Blackmore (1725) stated that the tongue being benumbed and torpid, is unable to form distinct expressions. To this weakness the author ascribed the use of wrong words, despite the patient's realization of his error. R. James (1743) also referred to the current notion of a 'Hesitation of the Tongue' in explanation of a loss of speech. Two years later came an interesting description of aphasia written by the Swedish naturalist Carl Linnaeus. Regaining consciousness after an apoplexy, the patient seemed to be delirious, though this was not the case. Rather he was speaking something like a foreign language using his own names for each word. He had forgotten all nouns, and could not recall his own name nor that of his wife and children. If the appropriate name was suggested he could not repeat it but would signify assent. If he wanted to find the name of one of his colleagues he would pick it out from the official list of lecturers. Here we find an early description of what we would now recognize as the phenomena of perseveration, anomia or amnestic dysphasia and verbal contamination.

The year 1757 saw the publication of Delius's monograph *De Alalia et Aphonia* and incidentally 'alalia' now became the established term for any acquired loss of speech until eventually super-seded in 1861 by 'aphemia' (Broca) and in 1865 by 'aphasia' (Trousseau).

The first hint in the literature of what is now called 'jargon-aphasia' dates from 1770 when Johann August Philipp Gesner of Rothenburg (1738–1801) described such a case.

Perhaps the first comment upon the apparent preservation of intellectual faculties in some cases of aphasia is to be traced to the address by William Falconer before the London Medical Society in 1787. Here he asserted: 'It is not uncommon to see [paralytick] people in this condition discoursing in a manner perfectly rational, and with the memory seemingly unimpaired, but such persons are at the same time unable to read a few lines in any printed book, and still more frequently retain their own ideas tolerably clear, when they are unable to recollect the words which are proper to express them. Hence they are apt to mistake the names of objects, and to substitute wrong words while their own ideas are perfectly consistent. It, however, often happens that in the severest paralytick attacks, the faculties of the mind remain uninjured till the departure of life'.

In 1798 appeared a penetrating study of Sir Alexander Crichton, Physician to the Westminster Hospital and later to the Czar of Russia. He realized that loss of speech was neither a sign of lingual paralysis nor yet of dementia, but was the result of disturbance of memory of a specific character. Crichton's own words are worth quoting in full.

There is a very singular defect of memory, of which I myself have seen two remarkable instances. It ought to be considered a defect of that principle by which ideas and their proper expressions, are asso-ciated, than of memory; for it consists in this, that the person, although he has a distinct notion of what he means to say, cannot pronounce the words which ought to characterize his thoughts. The first case of this kind which occurred to me in practice, was that of an attorney, much respected for his integrity and talents, but who had many sad failings, to which our physical nature too often subjects us. Although nearly in his 70th year, and married to an amiable lady, much younger than himself, he kept a mistress whom he was in the habit of visiting every evening. The arms of Venus are not wielded with impunity at the age of 70. He was suddenly seized with a great prostration of strength, giddiness, forgetfulness, insensibility to all

5

concerns of life, and every symptom of approaching fatuity. . . . when he wished to ask for anything he constantly made use of some inappropriate term. Instead of asking for a piece of bread, he would probably ask for his boots; but if these were brought, he knew they did not correspond with the idea he had of the thing he wished to have, and was therefore angry; yet he would still demand some of his boots, or shoes, meaning bread. If he wanted a tumbler to drink out of, it was a thousand to one he did not call for a certain chamber utensil; and if it was the said utensil he wanted, he would call it a tumbler, or a dish. He evidently was conscious that he pronounced wrong words, for when the proper expressions were spoken by another person, and he was asked if it was not such a thing he wanted, he always seemed aware of his mistake, and corrected himself by adopting the appropriate expression. For some time I considered this a very rare case; but a few years afterwards I met with another, which came on in consequence of a paralytic affection; and other instances of it are to be met with in the writings of different medical men'.

Crichton quoted a case recorded by van Goens of a woman who though often unable to find the appropriate words to express her ideas, could nevertheless manage her household efficiently and could even demonstrate to her husband the situation of the heavens on a map.

Let us for a moment interrupt the chronological account of the steady development of our knowledge of aphasia at the end of the eighteenth century, and refer to the occasional personal account of an aphasic illness, written from the standpoint of the patient. The putative importance of the evidence has been carried forward into the nineteenth, and even into the twentieth centuries. To this data may be added the peculiarly interesting accounts of an aphasic disability encountered in the biographical study of certain famous personages.

Thus William Harvey is known to have suffered a terminal feebleness of his power of articulation before his death in 1657. It is an interesting commentary upon the ideas of that time, that, to cure the impending speechlessness the apothecary Sambroke made a little cut in the frenum of the tongue. In 1679 the philosopher Thomas Hobbes died having lost the use of his right side and of his power of speech a week previously. The last stages of Dean Swift's fatal illness (1745) were marked by a depression coupled with a curious disorder of speech. The underlying pathology may well have been a cortical venous thrombosis after a septic orbital cellulitis. In attempting to speak, Swift would often use wrong words. Sometimes he was speechless; at times merely incoherent. Occasionally Swift broke silence with an unexpected phrase, quite out of context. . . . 'I am what I am; I am a fool'. To a servant who was breaking up a lump of coal he cried. . . . 'That's a stone, you blockhead!' During his birthday celebrations he exclaimed 'It's folly, they had better leave it alone'.

In 1772 Spalding wrote an interesting description how, while writing, he suddenly realized he could not find the appropriate words or carry out the necessary movements with his pen. He went on to describe his intellectual processes at that time, in a fashion which deserves far greater recognition that it has received so far. . . . 'Under the impact of those wavy and entangled images I tried to catch basic tenets of religion, conscience, and expectation of future salvation. . . . I could not get the better of that crowding and that stir and bustle in my head. I tried to speak, to train myself as it were, and to test whether I could say something in a connected order; but much as I forced my attention and my thoughts and proceeded with the utmost slowness, I became aware very soon of monstrous shapeless words that were absolutely different from those I intended; my immortal soul was at present as little master of the inner tools of language as it has been before of my writing. . . .' Half an hour later his speech began to return. 'Those strange annoying ideas (and images) became less lively and buzzing. I was able to get through what I wanted to think, and the interruptions by those strange ideas became weaker. . . .'

In passing one may refer to the well-known case of Dr. Samuel Johnson who in 1783 sustained a transient aphasia which he described graphically and which is clearly revealed in the errors in his letters as preserved today.[1] One may also mention the last illness of Johnson's close friend Dr. Thomas Lawrence. A most intriguing insight into the patient's mentation is illustrated by the story that during his speechlessness, Dr. Lawrence wanted to procure some black drops (or tincture of laudanum). Unable to express himself he finally took up a pen with his left hand, dipped it in the inkwell, and splattering the ink upon a sheet of white paper, pointed to the blots.

Goethe has given us a first-hand description of aphasia in 1796, when he referred to his grandfather's right-sided lameness and impaired speech. 'We had to guess at everything he required'. He could not enunciate the words he wanted. Irritability and frustration were evident from his gestures. An apathy subsequently developed and was followed by death. A particularly valuable document has come down to us but it was written 50 years later. Professor Lordat of Montpellier lost his speech but eventually regained it slowly and painfully. Later, namely in 1843, he wrote a fascinating account of his 'verbal amnesia' as he called it, or alternatively, an 'incomplete alalia' which had occurred in 1825. He mentioned that he had been unable to grasp the ideas of others (in other words there was a receptive defect as well as an expressive one). It was a long time before he became fully aware of his condition (due to an initial anosognosia, or lack of awareness). Lordat insisted that his power of thought was absolutely intact, despite the realization that the inner workings of his mind had to dispense with words. Condillac's theory that verbal signs are indispensable for thought, seemed not to be the case. (This may be due to an organic repression or retrospective oblivion of the severity of the illness at the time). Although he could identify isolated letters, he could not comprehend printed or written words. Lordat then wrote about the beginnings of his improvement. 'After several weeks of deep melancholy and resignation, it dawned on me that in looking from far away an in-folio in my library I could read exactly the title *Hippocratis opera*. This discovery made tears of joy come to my eyes. I made use of this faculty to re-educate myself in speaking and in writing.' The recovery proved to be complete and Professor Lordat resumed his Chair of Medicine at Montpellier where he also acted as Dean of the Faculty, and he died in 1870 at the age of 97 years.[2]

To anticipate somewhat the record of lay accounts of aphasia, we may mention the gradual loss of memory for words as well as proper names which Ralph Waldo Emerson showed in the last years of his life. His biographers have described his frequent search for an elusive term by dint of periphrases. Once when he wanted an umbrella he said 'I can't tell you its name, but I can tell its history. Strangers take it away'. A friend asked him where he was going. 'To dine with an old and very dear friend. I know where she lives, but I hope she won't ask me her name.' He then went on

[1] See Chapter VIII. Pages 75 *et seq.*

[2] Recently Professor Bay has called attention to certain inconsistencies in this case-history, which raise the possibility of an underlying hysteria.

to describe her as 'the mother of the wife of the young man—the tall one—who speaks so well'.

For other important retrospective accounts of an aphasia we can also refer to the medical auto-biographical descriptions written by Dr. Saloz, by Professor Forel, and by Sir Frederick Andrewes, but these were made comparatively recently of course. Indeed it is possible that the last-named became mute, not because of an aphasia, but by reason of a severe though temporary dysarthria.

With the coming of the nineteenth century there was an increase in the volume of medical writings and consequently the number of references to speechlessness grew rapidly.

The posthumous work of William Heberden which appeared in 1802, contained the shrewd observation that an inability to speak is owing sometimes not to paralysis of the organs of speech, but to an utter loss of the knowledge of language.

Pinel (1809) also mentioned the possible integrity of the mind in aphasiacs, and he referred to a speechless notary who could still cope with records and contractual engagements relating to his profession.

Brief mention may be made of a series of case-records of apoplectic speechless patients collected by John Cheyne in 1812. One of these referred to an aphasia associated with a left hemiplegia. In the same year the American physician Benjamin Rush dealt in some detail with the topic of memory-loss and speech-impairment. He was the first to call attention to the dissociation of the different tongues in the case of a polyglot with disordered speech. Short case-notes were also published by Thomas Mills (1826) of Dublin. In 1831 Richard Bright published a series of cases of speechlessness, but he seems to have been out of touch with contemporary trends, for he still ascribed the disability to a paralysis either of the face, or of the tongue and larynx. What we now speak of as recurrent utterance in aphasia was reported by Samuel Solly (1836) whose patient could articulate nothing except *faut-il*?

We come now to the beginnings of the modern era in aphasiology, which stemming from the pseudo-science of Gall (1757–1828) and of Spurzheim (1776–1832), spread rapidly by way of the medical schools of Paris and of Edinburgh, and later still of London.

Mindful of a correlation between prominent eyeballs and exceptional verbal memory which he fancied he had observed as a schoolboy, Franz Joseph Gall located in due course the cerebral centre for speech within the orbital surfaces of the frontal poles. This was but one of the 37 'organs of mind' which Gall was subsequently to isolate and to localize. Assisted by Johann Gaspar Spurzheim he published an impressive atlas of the brain between 1810 and 1819. Gall left Vienna to practice in Paris. His doctrines were hotly debated, and though received coldly in England, they were acclaimed by many of the profession in Scotland. A Phrenological Society was founded in Edinburgh in 1820 and a Phrenological Journal appeared from a local publishing house from 1824 till 1847.

In this context we may refer to Alexander Hood (1824) who after describing a case of abrupt speechlessness, concluded that the brain must consist of congeries of organs, or parts, each serving to manifest a particular faculty, and that to one or more of these particular parts is appropriated the function of recollecting words or names.

John Abercrombie's monograph appeared in 1831 and quoted numerous cases of speechlessness in some of which the patient reverted to a long neglected mother tongue. One of these concerned a woman from the Highlands, a patient of Dr. Mackintosh, who, spoken to in English, would now reply only in Gaelic.

The respect accorded to Gall in Edinburgh was largely due to the influence of the Combe brothers. In 1819 George Combe (1788–1858), not himself a medical man, published his *Essays on Phrenology*, later expanded into his *System of Phrenology* 1836. Numerous cases were recorded here and also in the special Journal, of loss of speech, and in some of them, important autopsy studies came to light.

For example, he quoted the case of a man from Kilmarnock who suddenly began to speak incoherently. He had forgotten the name of each object in nature. While his memory of *things* was unimpaired the names by which they were known were entirely obliterated from his mind. 'Yes' and 'no' were his only words. He could not read. Gesture language was eloquently retained. As he recovered, the conceptions of time and space came both under the general appellation of *time*. All future events, and objects placed in front of him, were referred to as 'next time'. Past events, and objects located behind him, were designated as 'last time'. Asked his age he replied 'many times'. Combe went on to refer to the post-mortem findings in cases of speech impairment which had been observed by Inglis Nichol, by Professor Syme, and by W. A. F. Browne.

There can be no doubt but that the prestige accorded to Phrenology in Edinburgh had the important effect of stimulating attention into the faculty of speech and the loss of speech from disease. The interest which was shown went far in building up a conception of the localization of function within the brain. The pendulum of opinion had been made to swing well across from the holistic views of brain-function promulgated by Flourens. If the pendulum deviated too far and stuck too long at such an extreme, eventually the philosophy of the mid-twentieth century came along in rectification.

Even more violently than in Scotland the Gall–Spurzheim controversy continued in France. The medical community became perfervid partisans for or against the doctrine of speech as a localized faculty. One of Gall's most important protagonists was the influential Dean of Medicine, Professor Bouillaud, pioneer in both cardiology and neurology. His *credo* was to the effect that 'the principal law-giver of speech is to be found in the anterior lobes of the brain'. As evidence of his confidence Bouillaud offered to forfeit 500 francs to anyone who would produce the brain of one who had during life lost speech, and which did not show any frontal lesion. Velpeau seems to have been the only one with sufficient temerity to claim this prize. In 1843 he showed a specimen with bifrontal scirrhous tumours—the patient before his death having been not only non-aphasic, but actually talkative.

Perhaps the most important single date in the history of aphasiology is 4th April, 1861, when Ernest Auburtin, the son-in-law of Bouillaud, delivered before the Anthropological Society of Paris in the rue René Panhard, an address entitled 'on the Seat of the Faculty of Language'. This was a well-reasoned plea for correlating the anterior lobes of the brain with the faculty of speech, based upon his own clinical experience and a formidable accumulation of data from the literature.

The secretary of the Society was the brilliant young surgeon Paul Broca, who approached Auburtin after his lecture and invited him to a joint consultation at the Bicêtre hospital. There had just been admitted to his service a man named Laborgne, an old hemiplegic and speechless mental

defective with a septic infection of the leg. A day or so later, Laborgne died. At autopsy a superficial lesion was to be seen in the frontal lobe. Broca demonstrated this specimen at the next
meeting of the Society, but no great interest was aroused. A month or two later, however, another
such case cropped up in Broca's service. Once again, post-mortem inspection of the brain revealed
a lesion in the same place. This was the case Lelong.

The appearance of this second specimen created a sensation at the *Societé d'Anthropologie*. There
was sparked off an impressive series of observations, comments and controversies. The meetings
were acrimonious. Much of the opposition stemmed from Gratiolet, a fellow-townsman of Broca.
Gratiolet brought up the question of negative cases, where frank frontal lesions had not produced
speechlessness. If a faculty of speech resides in the frontal lobes how was it, he asked, that monkeys
could not speak though well endowed with these lobes. Loss of speech is not the same as loss of
language, for speechless patients could still communicate by way of gesture.

Broca mildly protested that all he had wished to do was to bring forward two pathological
specimens to illustrate a rare and curious fact which chance had brought his way. He had no wish
to take part in any debate upon the location of centres for speech. This sane and cautious attitude
was not maintained, however, especially as his collection of case-material grew, and other observers
not only in Paris entered the fray along with their pieces of evidence, and their prejudices.

In the place of 'alalia' Broca coined the word 'aphemia' to connote the type of speech-loss
which he was observing. Thus there soon grew up a notion that aphemia was a focal symptom due
to a focal lesion of the brain, and that the normal faculty of speech was actually represented within
the frontal lobes. At first Broca thought in terms of a bifrontal lesion and a bilateral speech
centre.

The arrogant Dean, Professor Bouillaud, at first looked askance at Broca, calling him 'the St.
Paul of the new doctrine' and 'one of the organizers, subinventors, augmenters, revisers, and
correctors' of Gall's pioneer and magnificent discoveries'.

Almost against his will Broca found himself proclaimed a protagonist in the matter of cerebral
localization and a pioneer in the philosophy of language and the problem of speech-loss. At that
time Broca was a busy and successful surgeon, who had contributed much to his profession. His
principal interests outside of surgery were ethnological and his papers upon this subject were very
numerous. Within ethnology his particular researches were craniometric and he was steadily
amassing a collection of skulls. His prestige and authority within the medical and scientific circles
of Paris had become considerable quite apart from his contribution to neurology.

Early in 1864 we find Broca adopting the role of an etymological purist. In an open letter to
Trousseau who had recently advocated the term 'aphasia', Broca made a strong plea for his own
invention of 'aphemia'. Even though in modern Greek the term might suggest 'infamy', as
Trousseau had pointed out, Broca asserted that the root had gradually changed its meaning, and he
invoked in his support the classic Greek. 'Aphemia' had a slightly different connotation. 'Aphasia'
implied lack of speech from lack of ideas, while 'aphemia' suggested that ideas were present but no
words were available with which to clothe them. 'Aphasia' could rightly be used to describe a
polemist who, coming to the end of his argument, had nothing left to say. Moreover, 'aphasia'
implied a speechlessness through timidity or confusion. Broca also felt warmly towards the term

'aphrasia'—indicating an inability to form sentences. The Greek word 'phraso' meant, he asserted, not merely 'I speak', but furthermore 'I speak clearly'.

Broca's plea for the rejection of 'aphasia' failed completely. 'Aphrasia' did not survive nor did 'aphemia', despite the fact that Bastian and Pierre Marie maintained the term in a state of suspended animation for a few decades.

It may be asserted that in the story of the determination of the centre of language, five names are prominent, namely Auburtin, Broca, Duval, Dax *père* and Dax *fils*.

On 3rd March in this same year 1864, M. Duval described at the same Society two children with traumatic aphemia. In each case damage to the left frontal lobe could be demonstrated. In the discussion which followed, Broca said 'I have been struck with the fact that in my first aphemics the lesion always lay, not only in the same part of the brain, but always the same side—the left. Since then, from many post-mortems, the lesion was always left-sided. One has also seen many aphemics alive, most of them hemiplegic, and always hemiplegic on the right side. Furthermore one has seen at autopsy lesions of F3 on the right side in patients who had shown *no* aphemia. It seems from all this that the faculty of articulate language is localized in the *left* hemisphere, or at least that it depends chiefly upon that hemisphere.'

At the next meeting of the Society, which was held on 21st April, Broca demonstrated yet another brain with a left-sided lesion, the patient having had a traumatic loss of speech which was restricted to *la tête, la tête* and the particle *oui*. Broca then revealed that a M. Dax, an obscure practitioner from Sommières in Provence, had complained to the *Académie de Médecine* that he (Broca) had neglected the work of his late father, who had known for a long time that lesions ablating the faculty of language always lay within the left half of the brain. Dax Senior had apparently read a paper to this effect at the *Congrès Méridional de Montpellier*. . . . 'I don't like discussions about priority', said Broca, 'but several people said that I should have quoted Dax. I erred from ignorance. The original communication was not known, not even in Montpellier. I searched the literature and I also asked the Librarian of the Montpellier Faculté to have a look, but without success.' The meeting took place between 1st and 10th July, 1836, but there is no note about the Dax paper in the *Revue de Montpellier*. At that time indeed there was no medical journal in the South of France.

Thus began the Broca-Dax controversy, which proved to be even more complex. Since a student, the younger Dax had been intensely interested in 'alalia' or speech-loss and wanted to submit a thesis upon this subject, but he was not allowed to do so. Patiently he collected case-material and evidence from the literature. He wrote a *Mémoire* which he presented to his local *confrères* in 1858 and again in 1860, entitled *Observations tendant a prouver la coincidence du dérangement de la parole avec une lésion de l'hémisphère gauche du cerveau*. Later he sent it to the *Académie de Médecine* where it was received on 24th March, 1863.

Dax *fils* was bitterly hurt by the fact that subsequent writers continued to pay no heed to his work, nor to the credit due to his father. In July 1864 Charles Richet had published in the *Revue des deux Mondes* a paper upon aphasia in which the contribution of Dax *fils* and the discovery of Dax *père* were not mentioned. This too led to another protest on the part of Dax though it did not appear until October 1865 in the *Montpellier Médical*. On 14th April, 1865, an article on aphasia was published by Falret which did mention the work of Dax *père* et *fils*, but in such terms as to infuriate the latter.

Meanwhile Dax junior had discovered in a bureau the manuscript written by his late father, and he proceeded to publish it as it stood in the *Gazette hebdomadaire de médecine et de chirurgerie* for 26th April, 1865. In 1800 Dax *père* had apparently seen a cavalry officer with impaired memory for words after a sabre wound of the left side of the head. His second patient was the naturalist Brussonet who had lost his memory for words, proved to be due to a large ulcer on the surface of the left hemisphere. Dax had now seen three such cases. As he said: 'Je fus frappé de cette identité de siège dans les trois seules observations qu'il m'eut eté donne de receuiller durant l'espace de onze ans'. He subsequently collected more than 40 comparable cases without any exceptions coming to light, and he was able to add others from his library. From all this data he concluded that 'lorseque cette mémoire (verbale) est alterée par une maladie du cerveau, il faut chercher la cause du désordre dans l'hémisphère gauche'.

He went on to say 'J'espère que mon travail ne sera pas inutile au diagnostic et à la thérapeutique des malades de ce genre. Quand l'affection cérébrale n'est pas accompagnée d'hémiplegie ou que cette dernière est tardive, il est possible de méconnaître la nature du mal, ou tout au moins le siège qu'il occupe. . . .'

Dax *fils* then took up the story in an appendix to this paper. In his discussion of speech-disorder it is obvious that he was including cases of more than one sort—dysarthrias as well as dysphasias. Thus he was repeating the error that had for centuries bedevilled medicine, and indeed was destined to confuse neurologists for many years yet to come. Like the physicians of the middle ages Dax junior was inclined to ascribe aphasia to a paresis of the tongue. He admitted that aphasiacs sometimes substituted one word for another, but Dax got round that difficulty by asserting that, unable to pronounce one word, the patient gropes (*tâtonne*) and tries another and easier one. Dax was on safer ground, however, when he went on to speculate that the same cause which provokes a dyssynergy might sometimes interfere with the memory for words; and that in the present state of our knowledge one cannot distinguish the two classes of case.

Thirteen years later Dax printed a little monograph on the topic of aphasia, and his comments upon the relative neglect of his father's discovery were bitter indeed.

Despite the support of Baillarger (1865) contemporary medicine was rather slow to accord recognition of Dax's priority in this problem. Bouillaud with all his authority as Dean obstinately ignored not only Dax, but even the notion of a unilateral speech-centre. Trousseau in his lectures kept referring to Broca's discovery of the left-sided speech-centre. This too provoked a letter of protest from Dax. Trousseau is said to have replied in two letters, generously acknowledging the debt due to the elder Dax. This correspondence, like the manuscript of the original text by Dax *père*, is missing. But in the South of France there was a greater show of loyalty towards Dax. Thus in his *Thèse de Montpellier* in 1873, due recognition was paid by Trémolet.

It was probably Grasset, however, who, in France, first acknowledged publicly the claims of the two meridional physicians, and in 1873 he spoke boldly of *la loi de Dax*.

We may now briefly return in order to examine the identity of the five men, whose names are linked with this important chapter in aphasiology and with the notion of a speech-centre.

Unfortunately but little is known of Dr. Ange Duval except that he was a Surgeon-in-Chief to the Navy, and Professor at the School of Naval Medicine in Brest.

Dr. Ernest Auburtin has actually been more neglected than Dax by historians of aphasia. Auburtin was born in Metz in 1825 where his forebears were mirror-makers. A former *Chef de Clinique* of the Faculty of Medicine, he practised in Paris at No. 16 rue Saint Benôit, near St. Germain-des-Près. He was a nephew of Professor Lallemand of Montpellier. We are not sure what aspects of medicine interested him particularly, but we know that he was doctor to the Princess Mathilde Bonaparte, the cousin of the Emperor Napoleon III. Judging from an amusing entry in the Goncourt journals, he was also the medical attendant of Popelin. His main preoccupation was with anthropology, and he was a national associate of the newly formed society. Obviously he was a deep thinker with a reflective turn of mind, and it is tempting to think that it was he who really stimulated the interest of Broca into alalia. He was intrigued with the implications of Gall's work as far as it had to do with speech. In this matter he was Gall's disciple once removed, for he aligned himself with Bouillaud, and indeed, married his daughter Elisa. Auburtin and his family inherited the Bouillaud property at Les Bergerons, near Roullet, Charente, situated between Angoulême and Bordeaux. There Auburtin died in 1895. Unfortunately there are no more Auburtins in medicine today but his grandson is the distinguished *Conseiller Municipal*, who later became *Maire* of the city of Paris.

Auburtin's original contribution has been overshadowed by that of Paul Broca, whose tremendous prestige made him a man impossible to overlook or sidestep. Paul Broca was born of Protestant stock in the little town of St. Foy-la-Grande (Gironde), on the Dordogne, just nine years after Gratiolet. Broca's father was an Army surgeon who had served through the campaigns of Napoleon. Paul Broca distinguished himself as a schoolboy, and by the time he went to Paris as a student in medicine he was already a scholar, a polyglot, a talented painter and an accomplished musician. So hard up was he that he toyed with the idea of emigrating to America, but instead he took a temporary and uncongenial job as a schoolteacher.

As a medical man Broca became well known as an anatomist and a surgeon, residing at No. 1, rue des Saints-Pères, and he worked at the Hôtel Dieu, the Bicêtre, and the Salpêtrière, among other hospitals. While an internist he took part in the 1848 revolution, turning down a commission and also the distinction of the *Légion d'Honneur*.

Throughout his career Broca had shown himself not only a man of parts, but also the possessor of that rare quality of luck. In the history of aphasiology, Broca's life-long good fortune held. Auburtin became overshadowed by the chance which brought fame to Broca. Had the crazy Laborgne sought relief for his abscess at any hospital in Paris other than the Bicêtre, we should probably never have heard of 'Broca's area' or 'Broca's aphasia' and the history of aphasiology would have been very different.

Broca's principal love was anthropology, and he was an original member and the first secretary of the *Société d'Anthropologie*. Incidentally he had some difficulty in persuading the authorities that this new term 'anthropology' had no sinister political connotation, and had nothing to do with the 'rights of man'.

Broca's contributions to aphasiology were merely incidents in the course of his remarkable career. Later in life he founded the University Department of Anthropology to accommodate his great collection of skulls, and here again he had to dispel suspicions in high places, this time the Church. During the Franco-Prussian war Broca commanded a field ambulance in the Jardin des Plantes. At the time of the Commune, he smuggled bullion to the tune of 75 million gold francs in a hay-cart out of Paris to the government exiled in Versailles. In 1880 the Republic adopted the policy of strengthening the authority of the Senate by electing a number of figures distinguished in medicine or science. Broca was so honoured, a distinction which was celebrated at a banquet at the Hotel Continental. Replying to the flattering speeches, Broca said: 'If I were superstitious I would think I were threatened with a tremendous sorrow, for never have I been so happy as now'. Six months later Broca was dead from a sudden heart attack.

Finally we come to the two doctors Dax. Dr. Marc Dax was born in 1770 in Tarascon and took his diploma in Montpellier. After fighting a cholera epidemic in the Aigues-Mortes, he settled in the little township of Sommières (Gard) on the river Vidourle as a general practitioner. Living midway between Nîmes and Montpellier, Dax was isolated from the main stream of Parisian medicine, though locally he was well respected as a family doctor. He worked on the staff of the town-hospital for 37 years, published one or two papers, but evinced no interest in neurology except for his solitary contribution in 1836. He died a year later, at the age of 66 years, and was buried in the graveyard of the hospital.

His son Dr. Gustave Dax was born in Sommières in 1815, and like his father, qualified at Montpellier and practised in his home town. Like his father he also worked at the local hospital, but after 23 years' service he was invited to resign. This extraordinary action may have been due to the fact that Marc Dax was a legitimist, in fact an *Henriquinquiste*. Boisson, one-time Mayor of Sommières and also its archivist, made no mention in his official history of the town of either Dr. Marc Dax or Dr. Gustave Dax. What could be the reason? Boisson was an *Orleanist*; his brother was the local pharmacist. Perhaps at some time or other, he fell out with Dax junior, who was obviously somewhat aggressive in temperament if not indeed an obstinate and truculent protagonist of lost causes.

Dr. Gustave Dax died in 1898. To his sorrow his son Paul did not follow in a like career, and though he became a medical student, years went by without his taking his final examinations. He was of a literary bent, a poet and a playwright of some ability. He died quite suddenly on his honeymoon, presumably from that malady of lovers, subarachnoid haemorrhage.

Today the contributions of the two Doctors Dax are no longer forgotten in the world of medicine. Until recently the quiet little town of Sommières knew little of its two distinguished oppidans. But in June 1966, through the effort of Dr. R. André the current Mayor and also of Dr. Passouant of Montpellier, an important ceremony was held in the little town. Professor Alajouanine unveiled a plaque over the house in which Dax *père* practised and his son was born, while I had the honour of unveiling a plaque in the former *Place des Marchés* now known as the *Place des deux docteurs Dax*.

VII. HEAD'S CONTRIBUTION TO APHASIA

I read so wide in my earlier years that I can never be quite certain that what I thought was a creation of my own mind may not really have been an outcome of cryptamnesia.

Freud

Henry Head first became interested in aphasia in about 1910 while he was investigating sensory effects of cortical lesions. He became aware that the responses given by the testee often betray a defect of communication as well as perception. A percentage of sensory stimuli might be missed altogether, and increasing the strength of the stimulus did not necessarily raise the patient's accuracy in scoring. One particular aphasic subject when tested with compasses for tactile discrimination could not proclaim whether he was being touched by one point or two: neither could he indicate in writing. But when Head put before him a sheet of paper upon which were printed the numerals *one* and *two*, the patient could promptly touch the appropriate symbol. Such observations caused Head to doubt the validity of current ideas about aphasia, and sent him to his library. The classical writers did not satisfy his doubts or explain his clinical findings and it became obvious to him that new tests were needed. Most physicians and surgeons, he said, unfortunately were ill-prepared to deal with the opportunities afforded by cases of aphasia. Time and energy for long-continued examination were lacking, and the methods in general use were too crude to provide satisfactory results. But among the many papers by Hughlings Jackson scattered among obscure and out-of-date journals, he found the key for which he was searching. Jackson had interpreted the problems of language-disorder along lines which appealed to him forcibly, even though they had made but little impress upon contemporary neurology. In 1914 Head also discovered Pick's monograph *die agrammatischen Störungen* which though wordy and muddled—voluminous, he called it—was almost as stimulating as Jackson's writings.

Head's role as Consultant to the Empire Hospital for Officers during the first World War brought him in touch with a number of healthy, intelligent, brain-injured young men showing a diversity of disorders in expression. This opportunity stimulated and facilitated his plans, and became the final factor determining his ultimate research. Head's intellectual make-up was peculiarly fitted for this task. His natural gusto drove him to grasp one of the thorniest problems in neurology; his obsessional traits ensured a scrupulous and minute clinical scrutiny; his erudition embraced the continental literature; his critical bent showed him the weaknesses of accepted dogma as well as the strength of Jackson's ideas. Finally his originality, disciplined by philosophy, led him to novel and exciting conceptions in aphasiology.

Being a paper read at the London Hospital on the occasion of the Henry Head centenary, 31st August, 1961. *Brain*, 1961. **84**, 551–560.

Head's first foray into this controversial subject consisted in a compilation of the most important of the relevant papers by Hughlings Jackson. In 1915 he reprinted these in a single issue of *Brain*. Though only 58 years of age, he now resigned his hospital appointment as though dedicating himself to what was to be his finest hour in neurology.

In 1920, Head delivered the Linacre and then the Hughlings Jackson Lectures, both of which dealt with the topic of aphasia. Here he ventilated the ideas which had been maturing over the previous five years. Here we can find Head's criticisms of orthodox views, his personal aphasiological credo, his technique of examination, his revision of terminologies, and the replacement of older classifications by a new psycholinguistic grouping. Ordinarily no discussion follows the Jackson Lecture, but five weeks later a special meeting of the Section of Neurology was held, in which some of his colleagues ventured their objections and observations. Collier was clever and constructive; Wilson was very Wilsonian; Purves Stewart and Barnes were not impressive, while Herbert Parsons was obscure and somewhat irrelevant.

In 1923 Head gave his Cavendish Lecture upon speech and cerebral localization. The same year, a contribution to von Monakow's *Festschrift* dealt with a case of acute verbal aphasia followed through the various degrees of recovery. Head's final exposition appeared in 1926 when he issued his two-volume monograph entitled *Aphasia and kindred disorders of Speech*. A re-statement of his personal attitudes was preceded by an intriguing survey of the history of aphasia-research. Head was critical of most authors, especially those whom he dismissed as 'diagram-makers'. Modified praise was accorded to Pierre Marie 'the iconoclast', to Kussmaul, and to Van Woerkom, while he bestowed whole-hearted approval upon only Jackson, Pick and Goldstein.

What then may we regard as Henry Head's personal contribution to the problem of disordered language?

Like Jackson, Head emphasized that speech is no more a localizable faculty than is eating. Brain-disease, however circumscribed, can never affect speech and speech only. The clinical picture of an aphasia often depends more upon the acuteness and severity of the onset of the lesion, than upon its extensity.

Any organic process which gravely impairs speech, also disturbs other functions not usually classed with the use of language; it also spares and leaves unaffected much that undoubtedly belongs to speech. The more carefully the patient is examined the less certainly does his disorder correspond with any preconceived category.

Gross injury to one half of the brain can disturb the power of speaking, reading and writing, without producing any severe loss of intellectual capacity. We have no right to be satisfied with the statement that the patient cannot speak, read or write: it is our business to discover the conditions under which he can or cannot perform any of these acts. Throughout his earlier papers Head repeatedly used the phrase 'words, numbers and pictures' to give concreteness to his ideas and to avoid dangerous generalizations. Over and over again he inveighed against the use of the terms 'aphasia', 'amnesia', 'alexia', 'agraphia', 'apraxia' and 'agnosia'. He reluctantly made use of 'aphasia' as a shortened indicative expression which saved detailed description. Internal speech plays an essential part in other acts besides writing and speaking, and hence these acts should be specifically examined in patients with aphasia.

An aphasiac's performance is inconsistent. Therefore it is necessary when examining him to present the same task two or three times, and in several different ways. The procedures should be carried out in an environment of quiet, and every remark or aside on the part of patient or examiner should be recorded. The speed of performance should be noted also.

Head then proceeded to draw up a battery of tests which was a great advance upon the current haphazard methods of investigation, and also upon the techniques suggested by Rieger and by Pierre Marie. Some of the tests were later criticized as not pertaining strictly to linguistic ability, but to Head they were indices of the state of the patient's inner speech, and were consequently relevant and important.

After unilateral lesions, not every modality of language is necessarily disturbed in any one case. The more acute and severe the lesion, the graver and more extensive will be the disorder it produces. Slighter and more localized lesions may lead clinically to dissociated manifestations, or 'types' of aphasia. There is an analogy with the sensory cortex where complete loss of all forms of discrimination may occur, or partial disturbances which involve one aspect more than another.

These dissociated forms of speech-loss are not the primary elements out of which speech has been evolved: they are not to be described in terms of reading, writing and speaking. Neither do they stem from loss of motor or sensory power; or from destruction of images; or from a diminution of general intellectual capacity. They are none of these things. They are the product of the breaking-up of one aspect of psychical activity; analogous, but on a higher level, to the sensory dissociations following a lesion of the post-central cortex.

In every one of these dissociated forms there is both a formative and an emissive aspect, and both of these are always affected.

Head thereupon advanced a new classification of verbal, nominal, syntactical and semantic types. He did not define these, but he described them at length. It is not necessary to reproduce his text but merely to state that in *verbal aphasia*, words are evoked with difficulty and tend to be abnormal in structure. *Nominal aphasia* leads to defective use and understanding of words as names or indicators. With *syntactical aphasia* the internal balance of a word as an orderly rhythmic expression is disturbed, and jargon results. *Semantic aphasia* interferes with the capacity to comprehend and retain the general significance of a word as part of a complete act of language.

Perhaps these descriptions are not entirely crystal clear, but the phraseology is Head's and Head never afforded us any simpler interpretation of his ideas.

Head had to admit that these forms of dissociation did not as a rule appear in isolated form, and that in a few cases only did the actual loss in function remain confined to any one of these clinical types. As he himself confessed. . . . 'These designations are empirical; they have no value as definitions and must not be employed to limit the extent of that loss of function to which they are assigned. Each group includes disorders of wider extent than those comprised under the name by which it is known'.

In his Cavendish Lecture Head tried to correlate his types of aphasia with the anatomical site of the brain-lesion. He adopted a careful and commendable method of reconstructing the lesion upon the basis of anatomical casts. The act of speech varies, he said, and assumes different forms according to the situation of the injury, just as a man's gait varies according to whether he has hurt his heel or his toe. Lesions of the lower part of the pre- and post-central convolutions, and the parts beneath them, lead to difficulty in finding verbal forms. Syntactical defects are associated with disease of the upper convolutions of the temporal lobe, and semantic types of aphasia with lesions around the supramarginal gyrus. Nominal aphasia though clinically distinctive, had a less firmly established morphological basis, but it seemed to centre about the angular gyrus.

Head never seemed quite happy with these efforts at localization. He said that his attempts to explain how a lesion in a certain part of the brain came to be associated with defects of symbolic formulation and expression were purely hypothetical suggestions which did not form an inherent part of his general thesis.

Anticipating Luria's conception of a loss of the regulating, directive, or pragmatic functions of speech, Head described how an aphasiac might succeed in reading a printed request but without carrying out the command. What then, he asked, really is the function which is upset in aphasia?

Head observed that aphasiacs are able to carry out any operation which does not demand formulation of symbols. When an aphasiac cannot name an article, but can describe its use by resort to a periphrasis, he is expressing a lower grade of symbolic recognition. 'Each particular variety of aphasia represents the response of the organism under the changed condition produced by physiological defects.' The dictum of Head's is strikingly akin to the principle enunciated forcefully by Goldstein, and it is difficult to determine which author merits the priority. All forms of immediate perception are intact so long as no symbols intervene; but all acts of symbolic thinking and expression are liable to be affected, more or less, in cases of disordered language. This corresponds with Hughlings Jackson's notion of the formation of propositions.

It was with the greatest reluctance that Head ventured to change Jackson's nomenclature, but he believed that under the uncouth term 'propositionizing' was included what was in his mind when he referred to 'symbolic thinking'. The question of what constituted a proposition was so disputable that Head thought it better to avoid a term which was liable to be misunderstood and to lead to controversy. He doubted moreover whether the term was strictly accurate even in the Jacksonian usage.

Head therefore suggested that the function affected in pathological conditions might be called 'symbolic thinking and expression'. Deferring to subsequent objectors, Head afterwards changed this phrase to 'symbolic *formulation* and expression'.

In no place did Head explicitly use these words as a definition either of language or of speech, though subsequent writers would often assume that such was Head's intention. Head's explicit use of this phrase was to indicate the fundamental mechanism which was impaired in cases of aphasia.

Concerning the mentation of aphasiacs Head asserted that it is not the 'general intellectual capacity' which is disturbed, but the mechanism by which certain aspects of mental activity are brought into play. Behaviour is affected in a specific manner; an action can be carried out in one way but not another. The more concrete is lower in the hierarchy of mental processes than the general and the abstract. The higher the propositional value of the mental act, the greater difficulty will it present. Somewhere on the ascending scale of difficulty the aphasiac will break down.

Regarding the ability to comprehend, Head pointed out that much of what is said by an educated person is incomprehensible to one of lowlier grade, who accepts just enough to get by, hoping it will suffice. An aphasiac of high pre-morbid intellectual stature may be the same. Recognizing his defects he jumps to conclusions without the usual logical steps. His replies are sometimes right and sometimes wrong. Moreover he may be driven to adopt childish methods like spelling out words letter by letter, or reckoning on his fingers.

'In so far as these (symbolic) processes are necessary for the perfect exercise of mental aptitudes "general intelligence" undoubtedly suffers. For a man who, in the course of general conversation, is unable to express his thoughts, or comprehend the full significance of words and phrases, cannot move freely in the general field of ideas. . . . Moreover it must not be forgotten that the intellectual life of civilized man is so greatly dependent on speaking, reading and writing, that any restriction of these powers throws him back upon himself; he shuns company and cannot occupy himself with the newspaper or social intercourse. This inevitably leads to a diminished field of thought, and many aphasiacs gradually deteriorate in mental capacity. Yet closer observation shows that this "want of intelligence" is based primarily on some distinctive defect in a definite form of behaviour.'

In some of the foregoing we perhaps detect a little inconsistency on Head's part, even a trace of contradiction. But Head was like that. His thoughts ranged widely and deeply; all were committed to paper, and self-censorship was rarely severe.

Head remarked that in some ways the manifestations of aphasia resemble the stages through which language is acquired in an individual. Thus, dissolution would seem to recapitulate evolution. But Head hastened to demonstrate the error of such an idea. The mechanism underlying speech is not a palimpsest from which an earlier and primitive text is revealed when the more recent writing is removed. The aphasiac has a mind which differs fundamentally from that of a child, even though he may react to his linguistic shortcomings in a manner somewhat resembling that adopted in childhood.

At a later stage Head introduced into his writings upon aphasia two further conceptions, namely those of 'schemata' and of 'vigilance'. The former was a carry-over from his studies upon sensation, and Head believed that models or patterns are identifiable in speech upon which subsequent patterns can be erected. The response of an organism to a stimulus depends upon an arrangement of preceding responses, already organized, but occurring outside of awareness. These responses are what he called 'schemata'. They may occur at any level of physiological response including those processes which convert thinking into speech. Head was vague upon this subject and did not elaborate these ideas. Others have since done so. This notion also ties up with Head's very speculative doctrine of vigilance. Again, Head refrained from exactly defining what he understood by this mechanism. He seems to have envisaged a sort of high-grade physiological efficiency which lies behind all types of nervous activity from the lowest to the highest. In the case of the latter, Head's 'vigilance' is very reminiscent of the orthodox notion of attention, which, whether it be an active or a passive process, is extremely sensitive to the effects of stress and disease. Perhaps today it would be equated with a species of high-level feed-back operation, acting as governor or brake upon other aspects of mentation.

Throughout the 1920s Head's opinions upon aphasia were naturally criticized, for they were disturbing; but little opposition appeared in print. In the debate which followed the Jackson Lecture, it was deemed unwise to abandon the contrasting motor and sensory types of aphasia so useful in clinical diagnosis. The new classification was not received with enthusiasm especially as Head had to admit that his types rarely existed in pure form. Kinnier Wilson urged, and continued to urge, that there were expressive and receptive types of aphasia, and that the former could be equated with an articulatory apraxia and the latter with an agnosia. When the opportunity presented, in his 1926 monograph, Head protested that those defects of language exemplified by both imperception and by apraxia were of different order from those in aphasia. Terms like 'verbal apraxia' and 'agnosia' were but descriptive of certain forms of abnormal behaviour. 'Used in any other sense they belong to that deceptive class of clinical terms which, although they explain nothing, produce a fictitious feeling that an absolute classification of the phenomena has been attained.'

In 1926 Professor Bartlett wrote a full-dress review of Head's monograph, but it reads far more like an appraisal than a critique. This is not surprising, for Head had been in intimate touch with Bartlett upon whom he had often relied for counsel and encouragement. Bartlett's main doubt was directed towards Head's conception of 'vigilance', while rating the most original and the most profoundly important aspect to be Head's doctrine and treatment of 'schemata'.

Nearly fifty years have passed since Head first opened the topic of aphasia. How do his teachings stand up to present-day attitudes? What of lasting value has resulted from his contribution? Without question, Head's intervention into aphasiology was masterly and epochal. Much of what we believe and teach today we owe to Head, possibly without realizing the magnitude of our indebtedness.

Like all other researchers, Head had to rely upon his quick ear and conscientious techniques for detecting the fragments of speech emitted by his patients. He had none of the advantages which linguists command nowadays of audible and visible methods of recording. Despite these handicaps he explored the mysterious terrain of aphasia more deeply than anyone since Jackson. Not only did he link static neurological attitudes with the dynamism of psychology—others had done this before —but he was one of the first to apply the lessons of linguistics. Others have since followed, realizing that the future of aphasiology lies in the application of a study of language itself. Linguistics too must certainly concern itself with language in all its aspects, including language in its dissolution and its drift.

Head's judgement of earlier workers in the field of aphasia must stand today before a higher court. Most of us would probably agree with the majority of his evaluations even though Head surely under-estimated Trousseau. He also probably over-praised Pick perhaps feeling warmly towards his fellow student at the University of Prague. Oddly enough Head ignored the important work upon aphasia made by Freud, by Bergson, and by Isserlin. But in his 'historical retrospect' Head frankly confessed himself to be prejudiced, and he admitted that he had selected only certain epochs and men, as representing some definite aspect of thought.

What is today's assessment of Head's battery of serial tests? That they constituted a great advance over traditional techniques is undeniable. It is no serious criticism that they are now but rarely applied. They were time-consuming and somewhat repetitive. They had the merits of being fairly rigid, and therefore suitable as a framework for the study of most aspects of disordered language. But this in itself may prove a weakness, and serial testing is apt to end in a stultifying factor-analysis with all its demerits. Head's battery of tests did not allow sufficiently for the extraordinary or unorthodox case of aphasia: the illiterate, the writer, the orator, the polyglot, the artist, the musician, and the patient of exceptional ability. Indeed it has been stated that Head obtained some of his most revealing data when he supplemented his formal tests with special *ad hoc* procedures. Head's hand-eye-ear test has come in for special criticism. Kinnier Wilson objected that it was a non-verbal manoeuvre which really explored a state of 'eupraxia'. Head countered by asserting that an inner verbalization is very much entailed, whereby such concepts take part as 'behind', 'in front', 'right' and 'left'. Later work, however, as by Quadfasel, Gordon, Fox, and others has indicated that the imitative movements concerned in this particular test do not necessarily demand a silent verbal formulation.

One particular defect of Head's battery was that, like so many other aphasiologists, he fell into the error of making no control studies. The unwisdom of this neglect is demonstrated when Pearson, Alpers and Weisenburg submitted a group of normal college students to Head's battery of tests, and found that a significant percentage scored badly.

Head's use of the phrase 'symbolic formulation and expression' was an interesting and worth-while innovation. Already it has passed out of currency, partly because nowadays we look for something shorter and more utilitarian. Head often made the mistake of not defining his terms clearly and precisely at the outset of his argument. He shrank from defining the words 'speech' 'language', and indeed he used the two of them interchangeably, like some modern American linguists. The correct employment of the term 'language' would adequately cover most if not all of the non-verbal processes which Head had in mind. It would include the manipulation of symbols, as envisaged by Head, even though nowadays the use of 'symbol' is regarded askance in some quarters. 'Communication' is perhaps the current jargon for Head's 'symbolic formulation and expression' and it is certainly crisper and more wieldy.

Head's belief in a defect of symbolic formulation and expression as the basis of aphasia has been questioned by Goldstein, by Isserlin and by von Kuenburg, though not for the same reasons. At the present time we could most satisfactorily reconcile the various objections by resorting to some such term as 'communication', or better still 'language' (in the precise sense).

Then again Head's hypothesis of 'vigilance' seems to have perished from neglect rather than by default. 'Vigilance' marked an interesting exercise in speculation, but it did not really add a great deal to our knowledge either of language or of aphasia.

With 'schemata' the case is perhaps different. Originally conceived by Head in collaboration with Gordon Holmes in a different context, its place in the aphasia-story received special commendation from Bartlett. Recently it has been employed by Russell Brain and it may well long survive in this particular framework.

What of Head's notorious classification of the aphasias? Here again it has virtually gone by the

6

board. It was doomed to extinction the moment it was admitted that it covered the clinical facts no more than the traditional subdivisions it sought to replace. Head's four types could not be defined; they could not be tersely described; they could not be squeezed into a morphological mould except as a Procrustean after-thought. Weisenburg and McBride have, I submit, correctly summed up the matter: . . . 'When Head's classification is compared with those which are more widely accepted at the present time, it seems superior to them in theory and inferior in practice. It is based on the right principle; that is, the differentiation of forms of language deterioration in terms descriptive of the pre-dominant psychological changes. It is not, however, so successful a differentiation of the types of disorder as many which employ far less justifiable terms' (1935).

In the coming and the going of Head's classification we see all too clearly the continuing need for a satisfactory method of grouping the manifold clinical expressions of language-disorder.

Like Jackson, Head did not evince much interest in speech as a localizable cerebral mechanism, or in aphasia as a focal symptom. One gets the impression that he was impelled into the subject he chose for his Cavendish Lecture with some reluctance, if not indeed against his better judgement. Even more striking was his neglect of the problem of cerebral dominance as concerning speech. As Kinnier Wilson said, once we admit that speech is a perquisite of one half of the brain, then we have the beginnings at any rate of localization. Head seemed uninterested in this question, and, in his very detailed case-reports he did not indeed always specify the patient's handedness. Head did not even follow Jackson in assigning to language some minor role in the right cerebral hemisphere.

Finally we come to Head's *magnum opus* on 'Aphasia and kindred disorders of Speech'. Henry Head was a sick man when he compiled this work, and we can perhaps detect the uncertain touch. It is prolix and repetitive, and in places even contradictory. At times Head was ambiguous or almost evasive. The work would have been the greater had it been condensed into a single volume.

These criticisms sound harsh but I think they are just. But when they have been said, Head's monograph, in my opinion, still constitutes the finest and the most significant volume in the whole literature of aphasia.

It is a strange irony. Head achieved so much in aphasia that he is remembered today more for his failings than his accomplishments. These latter have been quietly absorbed within the *corpus* of neurology. Head's faults were the demerits of a constructive and brilliant mind. After all, as Luciani has told us, a fertile error is of more value than a sterile fact. Nor should we forget the words of Vilfredo Pareto: '. . . give me a fruitful error every time, full of seeds, bursting with its own corrections. You can keep your sterile truth for yourself'.

VIII. DR. SAMUEL JOHNSON'S APHASIA

Words attracted him curiously, words rich in splendour, words rich in suggestions, and he loved a novel and a striking phrase. New words had terror and fascination for him. He could not avoid them, so he plunged into them.

H. G. Wells

Good clinical descriptions of aphasia are none too common prior to the beginning of the nineteenth century. Personal accounts written retrospectively are even rarer. Dr. Samuel Johnson's own record of his apoplectic disturbance of speech is therefore a likely subject of interest; and it seems odd that the copious literature dealing with Johnson should so lightly pass over this particular event. The same neglect even shows itself in the available studies that have been made upon Johnson's medical record.

The clinical story can be assembled from various sources. Boswell is obviously a valuable source-book, while Hawkins supplies additional material, though it is not always scrupulous in its accuracy. Most important of all are the letters which Dr. Johnson himself wrote throughout his illness, a fashion which is perhaps unique in the annals of aphasiology. The collected edition of Mrs. Thrale's correspondence throws some light from the standpoint of an onlooker.

The facts would appear to be as follows. In June 1783, Dr. Samuel Johnson, then living at Bolt Court, Fleet Street, was 73 years of age and in poorish health. Much overweight and a slave to a voracious and intemperate appetite, he was breathless, bronchitic and gouty. Some years before he had eschewed alcoholic beverages altogether, but he had not controlled his habits of gluttony. Always a hypochondriac, he kept in close touch with a number of medical men socially as well as professionally. Apothecaries too were numbered among his immediate circle and one had actually been incorporated within his own household.

On 16th June of that year the doctor had spent a fairly busy day and had in the afternoon sat for his portrait at the studio of 'Renny', that is Miss Frances Reynolds. He never liked this particular portrait, and, mindful of Percy's *Reliques*, dubbed it a 'grimly ghost'. Incidentally it has been unkindly said about Frances Reynolds that she painted pictures that made everybody laugh—and her brother, Joshua, cry. After this sitting, Dr. Johnson retired at his customary hour feeling in no way out of the ordinary, as far as we know. In the middle of the night he awoke and immediately realized that he had sustained a stroke. What precisely were the subjective sensations which befell him we can only surmise. Possibly he felt some cephalic discomfort like headache or dizziness. It is possible that he found his limbs heavy on one side. Possibly he tried to speak aloud in the solitude of his bed-chamber only to find that words eluded him. These are conjectural. We

Being the Menas S. Gregory Lecture delivered in New York 1960, and published in *Med. His.*, 1962. **6**, 27–44.

do know, however, that he proceeded to carry out an intelligence test of a most unusual type: He composed a prayer in Latin verse. The alleged text is known to us, and according to Chapman, was the following:

'Summe Pater, quodunque tuum de corpore Numen
Hoc statuat, precibus Christus adesse valit;
Ingenio parcas, nec sit mihi culpa rogasse,
Qua solum potero parte, placere tibi'.

(Almighty Father, whatever the Divine Will ordains concerning this body of mine, may Christ be willing to aid me with his prayers. And let it not be blameworthy on my part to implore that Thou spare my reason, by which faculty alone I shall be able to do Thy pleasure).

Hawkins gives a different version, alleging that Johnson attempted to repeat the Lord's Prayer, first in English, then in Latin, and after that in Greek, and that '. . . he succeeded in only the last effort'.

Mrs. Thrale in her *Anecdotes of the late Samuel Johnson, LL.D.* (2nd Ed. 1786, p. 277), reported this incident in the following terms:

Fear was a sensation to which Mr. Johnson was an utter stranger, excepting when some sudden apprehensions seized him that he was going to die; and even then he kept all his wits about him, to express the most humble and pathetic petitions to the Almighty: and when the first paralytic stroke took his speech from him he instantly set about composing a prayer in Latin, at once to deprecate God's mercy, to satisfy himself that his mental powers remained unimpaired, and to keep them in exercise, that they might not perish by permitted stagnation. This was after we parted; but he wrote me an account of it, and I intend to publish that letter with many more.

According to Fanny Burney, Dr. Johnson first of all composed this Latin prayer 'internally': next he endeavoured to speak it aloud, but found his voice was gone.

From all this evidence we are probably safe in presuming that Dr. Johnson's prayer did not entail the evocation of some well-remembered lines, but rather the execution of a spontaneous *ad hoc* composition. The task was performed with moderate success, and his awareness of any possible shortcomings was to him, correctly enough, an indication that his intellect was not too gravely disturbed.

Immediately afterwards Johnson performed another remarkable act. Hoping to loosen his tongue, as it were, he deliberately broke his habit of abstinence and drank some brandy. What effect it had upon his speech we do not know, but we learn that he at once fell asleep again.

The next morning, on awakening, or on being awakened, perhaps, his speech was still impaired. The servant, as he entered the room, was surprised to find Dr. Johnson speechless or maybe incoherent, for he put into his hands a note asking for Mr. Allen his next-door neighbour to be summoned, as well as Heberden, his physician and friend.

During the course of that day the 17th of June, Johnson continued to write letters although with some difficulty. Heberden came and prescribed a mixture containing aromatic carbonate and aloes; and ordered blisters to be applied to his head and throat. Dr. Johnson's disabilities continued throughout the ensuing days but probably in diminishing severity so that by the end of the week little or no loss in the faculty of language and no motor affection remained.

Let Dr. Johnson's own letters tell their own tale:

The original note which he thrust into the hand of his servant is not available. But during the first 24 hours of his illness he had written the following letter to Mrs. Thrale (which I have been allowed to study in holograph form, and to reproduce, through the great kindness of Mr. and Mrs. Donald Hyde).

Letter 1. First day of illness. (847 Chapman Collection)

To Edmund Allen

Dear Sir, It hath pleased almighty God this morning to deprive me of the powers of speech; and, as I do not know but that it may be his farther good pleasure to deprive me soon of my senses, I request you will, on the receipt of this note, come to me, and act for me, as the exigencies of my case may require. I am, Sincerely Yours, S. Johnson. June, 17. 1783.

The present whereabouts of this letter is not known. The following letter is reproduced through the courtesy of the New York Public Library (Berg Collection).

Letter 2. First day of illness. (848 Chapman Collection)

To the Rev. Dr. Taylor.

Dear Sir, It has pleased God by a paralytik stroke in the night to deprive me of speech.

I am very desirous of Dr. Heberdens assistance as I think my case is not past remedy. Let me see you as soon as it is possible. Bring Dr. Heberden with you if you can, but come yourself, at all events. I am glad you are so well, when (when) I am so dreadfully attacked.

I think that by a speedy application of stimulants much may be done. I question if a vomit vigorous and rough would not rouse the organs of speech to action.

As it is too early to send I will try to recollect what I can that can be suspected to have brought on this dreadful distress.

I have been accustomed to bleed frequently for an asthmatick complaint, but have forborn for some time by Dr. Pepy's persuasion, who perceived my legs beginning to swell. I sometimes alleviate a painful, or more properly an oppressive constriction of my chest, by opiates, and have lately taken opium frequently but the last, or two last times in smaller quantities. My largest dose is three grains, and last night I took but two.

You will suggest these things, and they are all that I can call to mind, to Dr. Heberden. I am &c. Sam: Johnson. June 17. 1783. Dr. Brocklesby will be with me to meet Dr. Heberden, and I shall have previously made master of the case as well as I can.

Letter 3. Second day of illness. (849 Chapman Collection)

To Mr. Thomas Davies.

Dear Sir, I have had, indeed, a very heavy blow; but God, who yet spares my life, I humbly hope will spare my understanding, and restore my speech. As I am not at all helpless, I want no particular assistance, but am strongly affected by Mrs. Davies's tenderness; and when I think she can do me good, shall be very glad to call upon her. I had ordered friends to be shut out; but one or two have found their way in; and if you come you shall be admitted: for I know not whom I can see that will bring more amusement on his tongue, or more kindness in his heart.

I am, &c. Sam. Johnson. June 18. 1783.

Letter 4. Third day of illness. (850 Chapman Collection). From the Hyde Collection.

To Mrs. Thrale, in Bath.

Dear Madam, I am setting down in no chearful solitude to write a narrative which would once have affected you with tenderness and sorrow, but which you will perhaps pass over now with the careless glance of frigid indifference. For this dimution of regard, however, I know not whether I ought to blame you, who may have reasons which I cannot know, and I do not blame myself who have for a great part of human life done You what good I could, and have never done you evil.

I have been disordered in the usual way and had been relieved by the usual methods, by opium and catharticks, but had rather lessened my dose of opium.

On Monday the 16th I sat for my picture, and walked a considerable way with little inconvenience. In the afternoon and evening I felt myself light and easy, and began to plan schemes of life. Thus I went to bed, and in a short time waked and sat up as has long been my custom, when I felt a confusion and indistinctness in my head which lasted, I supposed about half a minute: I was alarmed and prayed God, that however he might afflict my body he would spare my understanding. This prayer, that I might try the integrity of my faculties I made in Latin verse. The lines were not very good, but I know them not to be very good. I made them easily, and concluded myself to be unimpaired in my faculties.

Soon after I perceived that I had suffered a paralytick stroke, and that my Speech was taken from me. I had no pain and so little dejection in this dreadful state that I wondered at my own apathy, and considered that perhaps death itself when it should come, would excite less horrour than seems now to attend it.

In order to rouse the vocal organs I took two drams. Wine has been celebrated for the production of eloquence; I put myself into violent motion, and, I think, repeated it. But all was vain; I then went to bed, and strange as it may seem, I think, slept. When I saw light, it was time to contrive what I should do. Though God stopped my speech he left my hand, I enjoyed a mercy which was not granted to by Dear Friend Laurence, who now perhaps overlooks me as I am writing and rejoices that I have what he wanted. My first note was necessarily to my servant, who came in talking, and could not immediately comprehend why he should read what I put into his hands. (See Plate 5).

I then wrote a card to Mr. Allen, that I might have a discreet friend at hand to act as occasion should require. In penning this note I had some difficulty, my hand, I knew not how or why, made wrong letters. I then wrote to Dr. Taylor to come to me, and bring Dr. Heberden, and I sent to Dr. Broclesby, who is my neighbour. My Physicians are very friendly and very disinterested, and give me great hopes, but you may imagine my situation. I have so far recovered my vocal powers, as to repeat the Lord's Prayer with no very imperfect articulation. My memory, I hope, yet remains as it was. But such an attack produces solicitude for the safety of every faculty.

How this will be received by You I know not, I hope You will sympathise with me, but perhaps
My Mistress gracious, mild, and good,
Cries, Is he dumb? 'tis time he show'd.[1]
But can this be possible, I hope it cannot. I hope that what, when I could speak, I spoke of You, and to You, will be in a sober and serious hour remembered by You, and surely it cannot be remembered but with some degree of kindness. I have loved you with virtuous affection, I have honoured You with sincere

[1] A quotation from Swift.

and prayed God, that however he might afflict my body, he would
spare my understanding. This prayer, that I might try the integrity of my faculties, I made in Latin verse. The lines were
not very good, but I knew them not to be very good, I made them
easily, and concluded my self to be unimpaired in my faculties.

Soon after I perceived that I had suffered a paralytick Stroke, and that my Speech was taken from me.
I had no pain, and so little dejection in this dreadful State,
that I wondered at my own apathy, and considered that perhaps death itself when it should come, would excite less horrour than seems now to attend it.

In order to rouse the vocal organs I took two drams.
Wine has been celebrated for the production of eloquence; I put
myself into violent motion, and, I think, repeated it. But
all was vain; I then went to bed, and, strange as it may
seem, I think, Slept. When I saw light, it was time
to contrive what I should do. Though God stopped my Speech
he left me my hand, I enjoyed a mercy which was not granted to my Dear friend Laurence, who now perhaps looks on as
I am writing and rejoicing that I have what he wanted. My first note was necessarily to my Servant,
who came in talking, and could not immediately comprehend
why he should read what I put into his hands.

Page 2 of Dr. Johnson's letter to Mrs. Thrale, written on the third day of his
illness, June 19th 1783. (No. 850 Chapman collection.)

Plate 5

The last portrait of Dr. Johnson

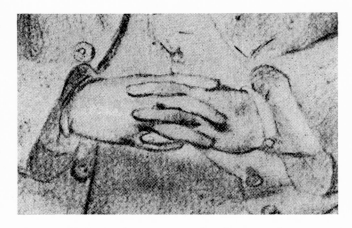

Close-up of the hands in James Roberts' portrait showing Dr. Johnson clasping them in a characteristic right-handed fashion.

Plate 6

Esteem. Let not all our endearment be forgotten, but let me have in this great distress your pity and your prayers. You see I yet turn to You with my complaints as a settled and unalienable friend, do not, do not drive me from You, for I have not deserved either neglect or hatred.

To the Girls, who do not write often, for Susy has written only once, and Miss Thrale owes me a letter, I earnestly recommend as their Guardian and Friend, that They remember their Creator in the days of their Youth.

I suppose you may wish to know how my disease is treated by the Physitians. They put a blister upon my back, and two from my ear to my throat, one on a side. The blister on my back has done little, and those on my throat have not risen. I bullied, and bounced, (it sticks to our last sand) and compelled the apothecary to make his salve according to the Edinburgh dispensatory, that it might adhere better. I have two on now of my own prescription. They likewise give me salt of hartshorn, which I take with no great confidence, but satisfied that what can be done is done for me.

O God, give me comfort and confidence in Thee, forgive my sins, and if it be thy good pleasure, relieve my diseases for Jesus Christs sake, Amen.

I am almost ashamed of this querulous letter, but now it is written, let it go.

I am, Madam, Your most humble servant. Sam: Johnson.

Bold Court Fleet Street June 19. 1783.

Letter 5. Fourth day of illness. (851 Chapman Collection)

To Mrs. Thrale in Bath.

Dearest Lady I think to send you for some time a regular diary. You will forgive the gross images which disease must necessarily present. Dr. Laurence said that medical treatises should be always in Latin.

The two vesicatories which I procured with so much trouble did not perform well, for, being applied to the lower part of the fauces a part always in motion their adhesion was continually broken. The back, I hear, is very properly played.

I have now healing application to the cheeks and have my head covered with one formidable diffusion of Cantharides, from which Dr. Heberden assures me that experience promises great effects. He told me likewise that my utterance has been improved since yesterday, of which however I was less certain. Though doubtless they who see me at interval can best judge.

I never had any distortion of the countenance, but what Dr. Brocklesby calld a little prolapsus which went away the second day.

I was this day directed to eat Flesh, and I dined very copiously upon roasted Lamb and boiled pease, I then went to sleep in a chair, and when I waked I found Dr. Broaclesby sitting by me, and fell to talking to him in such a manner as (as) made me glad, and, I hope, made me thankful. The Dr. fell to repeating Juvenal's tenth satire,[1] but I let him see that the province was mine.

I am to take wine to night, and hope it may do me good.

I am, Madam, Your humble Servant.

Sam: Johnson. London June 20 1783.

Letter 6. Fourth day of illness. (852 Chapman Collection). From the Hyde Collection.

Sir, You know, I suppose, that a sudden illness makes it impracticable to me to wait on Mr. Barry, and

---

[1] *Orandum est, ut sit mens sana in sano corpore.* Juvenal Satires X. 356.

the time is short. It if be your opinion that the end can be obtained by writing, I am very willing to write, and, perhaps, it may do as well: it is, at least, all that can be expected at present from,

Sir, your most humble servant, Sam: Johnson.

Friday, June 20th. 1783. If you would have me write, come to me: I order your admission.

Letter 7. *Fifth day of illness. (853 Chapman Collection)*

To Mrs. Thrale in Bath.

Dear Madam, I continue my Journal. When I went to Bed last night I found the new covering of my (my) head uneasy, not painful, rather too warm. I had however a comfortable and placid night. My Physicians this morning thought my amendment not inconsiderable, and my friends who visited me said that my look was spritely and cheerful. Nobody has shown more affection than Paradise. Langton and he were with me a long time today. I was almost tired.

When my friends were gone, I took another liberal dinner such as my Physicians recommended and slept after it, but without such evident advantage as was the effect of yesterday's *siesta*. Perhaps the sleep was not quite so sound, for I am harrassed by a very disagreeable operation of the cantharides which I am endeavouring to control by copious dilution.

My disorders are in other respects less than usual, my disease whatever it was seems collected into this one dreadful effect. My Breath is free, the constrictions of the chest are suspended, and my nights pass without oppression.

Today I received a letter of consolation and encouragement from an unknown hand without a name, kindly and piously, though not enthusiastically written.

I had just now from Mr. Pepys, a message enquiring in your name after my health, of this I can give no account.

I am Madam, Your most humble servant,

Sam: Johnson. London June 21. 1783.

Letter 8. *Seventh day of illness. (854 Chapman Collection)*

To Mrs. Thrale in Bath.

Dear dear Madam I thank you for your kind letter, and will continue my diary. On the night of 21st I had very little rest, being kept awake by an effect of the cantharides not indeed formidable, but very irksome and painful. On the 22 the Physicians released me from the salts of hartshorn. The Cantharides continued their persecution, but I was set free from it at night. I had however not much sleep but I hope for more to night. The vesications on my back and face are healing, and only that on my head continues to operate.

My friends tell me that my power of utterance improves daily, and Dr. Heberden declares that he hopes to find me almost well to morrow.

Palsies are more common than I thought. I have been visited by four friends who have each had a stroke, and one of them, two.

Your offer, dear Madam, of coming to me is charmingly kind, but I will lay up for future use, and then let it be considered as obsolete. A time of dereliction may come, when I have hardly any other friend, but in the present exigency, I cannot name one who has been deficient in activity or attention. What man can do for man, has been done for me.

Write to me very often. I am Madam Your most humble servant.

Sam: Johnson. June 23. 1783 London.

Letter 9. Eighth day of illness. (855 Chapman Collection). From the Prime Minister's Collection.

To Mrs. Thrale.

Dear Madam, The journal now like other journals grows very *dry*, as it is not diversified either by operations or events. Less and less is done, and, I thank God, less and less is suffered every day. The physicians seem to think that little more needs to be done. I find that they consulted today about sending me to Bath, and thought it needless. Dr. Heberden takes leave tomorrow.

This day I watered the garden and did not find the watering jobs more heavy than they have hitherto been, and my breath is more free.

Poor dear . . . has just been here with a present. If it ever falls in your way to do him good, let him have your favour.

Both Queeny's letter and yours gave me today great pleasure. Think as well and as kindly of me as you can, but do not flatter me. Good reciprocations of esteem are the great comforts of life, hyperbolical praise only corrupt the tongue of one and the ear of another.

I am, dear Madam, Your most humble servant.

Sam: Johnson London, June 24. 1783.

Your letter has no date.

Letter 10. Ninth day of illness. (856 Chapman Collection). From the Hyde Collection.

To Lucy Porter (Lichfield).

Dear Madam, Since the papers have given an account of my illness, it is proper that I should give my friends some account of it myself.

Very early in the morning of the 16th of this month, I perceived my speech taken from me. When it was light I sat down, and wrote directions as appeared proper. Dr. Heberden and Dr. Brocklesby were called. Blisters were applied, and medicines given; before night I began to speak with some freedom, which has been encreasing ever since, so that I now have very (little) impediment in my utterance. Dr. Heberden took his leave this morning.

Since I received this stroke I have in other respects been better than I was before, and hope yet to have a comfortable Summer. Let me have your prayers.

If writing is not troublesome let me know whether you are pretty well, and how you have passed the Winter and Spring.

Make my compliments to all my Friends.

I am, dear Madam, Your most humble servant, Sam: Johnson.

London. June 25. 1783.

Letter 11. Thirteenth day of illness. (858 Chapman Collection). New York Public Library, Berg Collection.
Torn. Postmark 30. VI.
Date, added by Mrs. Piozzi, 29 June 1783.

To Mrs. Thrale in Bath.

I climbed up stairs to the garret, and then up a ladder to the leads, and talked to the artist rather too long, for my voice though clear and distinct for a little while soon tires and falters. The organs of speech are yet very feeble, but will I hope be by the mercy of God finally restored, at present like any other weak limb, they can endure but little labour at once. Would you not have been very (sorry) for me when I could scarcely speak? . . .

Letter 12. Seventeenth day of illness. (861 Chapman Collection)

To James Boswell (Edinburgh)

Dear Sir, Your anxiety about my health is very friendly, and very agreeable with your general kindness. I have, indeed, had a very frightful blow. On the 17th of last month, about three in the morning, as near as I can guess, I perceived myself almost totally deprived of speech. I had no pain. My organs were so obstructed, that I could say *no*, but could scarcely say *yes*. I wrote the necessary directions, for it pleased God to spare my hand, and sent for Dr. Heberden and Dr. Brocklesby. Between the time in which I sent for the doctors, I had, I believe, in spite of my surprize and solicitude, a little sleep, and Nature began to renew its operations. They came, and gave the directions which the disease required, and from that time I have been continually improving in articulation. I can now speak, but the nerves are weak, and I cannot continue discourse long; but strength, I hope will return. The Physicians consider me as cured. . . .

July 3. 1783.

Letter 13. Nineteenth day of illness. (862 Chapman Collection). From the Hyde Collection.

To Lucy Porter (Lichfield).

Dear Madam . . . My disease affected my speech, and still continues in some degree to obstruct my utterance, my voice being distinct enough for a while, but the organs being yet weak are quickly weary. But in other respects I am, I think, rather better than I have lately been, and can let You know my state without the help of any other hand.

In the opinion of my friends, and in my own I am gradually mending. The Physicians consider me as cured, and I had leave four days ago to wash the Cantharides from my head. Last Tuesday I dined at the Club. . . .

July 5. 1783.

Letter 14. Twenty-second day of illness. (865.1 Chapman Collection)

To John Ryland (Cranbrook).

Dear Sir . . . My recovery, I think, advances, but its progress is (is) not quick. My voice has its usual tone, and a stranger in the beginning of our conversation does not perceive any depravation or obstruction. But the organs of articulation are weak, and quickly tire. I question if I could read, without pausing, a single page of a small book. . . .

July 8. 1783.

Letter 15. Twenty-ninth day of illness. (867 Chapman Collection)

To William Strahan Esq. M.P. London.

Sir . . . My breath is more free, and my nights are less disturbed. But my utterance is still impeded, and my voice soon grows weary with long sentences . . .

July 15. 1783

Letter 16. Thirty-sixth day of illness. (869 Chapman Collection).

To Mrs. Thrale in Bath.

. . . I am very well except that my voice soon falters . . .

July 23. 1783.

Letter 17. Thirty-seventh day of illness. (871 Chapman Collection)

To the Rev. Dr. John Taylor (Ashbourne)
. . . My voice in the exchange of salutations, or on other little occasions is as it was, but in a continuance of conversation it soon tires. I hope it grows stronger but it does not make very quick advance . . .

July 24. 1783

Letter 18. Thirty-seventh day of illness. (871.2 Chapman Collection) .From the Hyde Collection.

To Wm. Bowles (Heale).
Dear Sir, You will easily believe that the first seizure was alarming. I recollected three that had lost their voices, of whom two continued speechless for life, but I believe, no means were used for their recovery. When the Physicians came they seemed not to consider the attack as very formidable, I feel now no effects from it but in my voice, which I cannot sustain for more than a little time. . . .

July 24. 1783

Letter 19. Fifty-seventh day of illness. (875 Chapman Collection)

To Mrs. Thrale (Weymouth).
. . . I am now broken with disease, without the alleviation of familiar friendship, or domestick society; I have no middle state between clamour and silence, between general conversation and self-tormenting solicitude . . .

August 13. 1783

To these letters there may be added the alleged entry in Johnson's own diary, which, according to Sir John Hawkins, contained the following note:

June 16. I went to bed, and, as I conceive, about 3 in the morning, I had a stroke of the palsy.
June 17. I sent for Dr. Heberden and Dr. Brocklesby, God bless them.
June 25. Dr. Heberden took leave.[1]

The available evidence as to Dr. Johnson's illness points clearly to an apoplectic disorder of speech, not very severe, and comparatively short in duration: that the disability was not a mere articulatory disorder but a dysphasic one, is shown by defects in his written compositions. None the less the speech-difficulty seems to have included much dysarthria, a defect which continued to show itself even after the availability of words had returned to normal. His aphasia seems therefore to have belonged to the category of what used to be termed Broca's aphasia, (or aphemia), and such a diagnosis would doubtless still be applied by some neurologists uncritical in their attitude towards clinical classifications. It is of interest that, like so many aphasiacs, Johnson experienced a temporary difficulty with the particles *yes* and *no*, and found that the negative term came more readily to his lips than the affirmative.

Perusal of the manuscripts of the actual letters written by Johnson during these days, reveals first of all a general untidiness of the penmanship. In addition there are numerous instances of verbal

[1] Johnson: *Prayers and Meditations* No. 158.

corrections, and a few examples of iterations. These defects are well seen for example in Letter No. 4 (850 Chapman Collection), where we find:

1. Line 8   Two illegible words erased, and 'human life' inserted.
2. Line 10   'Had' changed to 'have' and 'been' inserted.
3. Line 18   Illegible word erased, and 'my head' inserted.
4. Line 20   'Body' inserted.
5. Line 21   'Try' inserted.
6. Line 23   'Them' inserted.
7. Line 29   'Own' inserted, 'could not' erased and 'considered' inserted.
8. Line 33   'Been' inserted.
9. Line 34   'A' changed to 'o' in 'motion'.
10. Line 37   'I' inserted; 'speech' inserted.
11. Line 38   'Not' inserted.
12. Line 39   Illegible erasure, 'perhaps' inserted.
13. Line 41   'Not' inserted.
14. Line 50   'Recovered' (corrected mis-spelling)
15. Line 58   'You' erased. 'That' inserted.
16. Line 67   Erasure of 'on each way', and 'from my ear' inserted.
17. Line 72   'Now' inserted.
18. Line 75   'Him' erased, 'me' inserted.

The later stages of his aphasia were betrayed by a sort of sthenolalia or ready fatiguability, which involved not only the volume of the voice, but probably also the task of word-finding.

Dr. Johnson was fortunate in sustaining no obvious paralysis. Nothing more than a temporary facial asymmetry developed, even though we cannot be sure whether it was the right or the left side which was impaired. A week later, Johnson was apparently himself again, for on 24th June Mrs. Thrale was writing in her diary that she had received a letter from himself . . . 'in his usual style'.

By November of the same year, that is, five months later, Johnson was exclaiming to Sir John Hawkins 'What a man am I! who have got the better of three diseases, the palsy, the gout and the asthma, and can now enjoy the conversation of my friends, without the interruptions of weakness or pain!'

Scrutiny of the clinical evidence, it must be confessed, does not give us exact information as to which cerebral hemisphere was the one involved by the presumed vascular accident. Only by assembling indirect evidence or clues, can we suspect that it was the left side of the brain which was probably at fault.

At this point some data as to the identity of Dr. Johnson's medical advisers might be interpolated.

Dr. Richard Brocklesby (1722–1797) was born in Somerset of Quaker parents, but at an early age went to live in Ireland. He studied at the Edinburgh School of Medicine, qualified at Leyden, and practised not far from Bolt Court in Norfolk Street, Strand. He was not only a friend of Edmund Burke but also the medical attendant of Samuel Wilkes, Burke's political antagonist.

Brocklesby was a close friend of Johnson's to whom he offered a home and an annual stipend of £100.

Dr. William Heberden (1710–1801) was of course one of the greatest of the eighteenth century physicians. At the time of Johnson's illness he was practising at Cecil Street, Strand, though later he went to live in what had been Nell Gwynne's house in Pall Mall. Johnson spoke of Heberden as

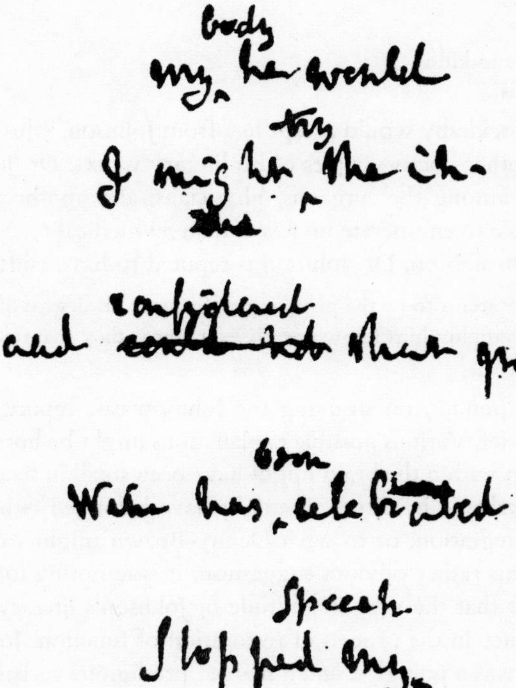

FIG. 1 Enlargement displaying the writer's emendations

(1) '. . . however he might afflict my (body) he would spare my understanding. This prayer, that I might (try) the integrity of my faculties. . . .'

(2) '. . . I wondered at my own apathy and (considered) that perhaps death . . .'

(3) '. . . Wine has (been) celebrated . . .'

(4) '. . . Though God stopped my (speech) . . .'

'the *ultimus Romanorum*; the last of our learned physicians', though in another mood he also referred to him as the '*timidorum timidissimus*'. Heberden's private case-books, now within the library of the Royal College of Physicians, unfortunately contain no certain note as to the problem of his distinguished patient. It is true that Dr. Squibb, writing in 1849, believed he discovered a mention of Johnson's case in Heberden's *Index Historiae Morborum*. Although this record has been accepted at face value by Chaplin I am by no means convinced. The date is wrong and the information meagre, and I can but regretfully conclude that Heberden made no specific mention of this important case.

Heberden was also one of London's most fashionable practitioners, as is shown by the jingle popular at the end of the eighteenth century:

'You should send, if aught should ail ye
For Willis, Heberden, or Baillie.
All exceeding skilful men
Baillie, Willis, Heberden;
Uncertain which most sure to kill is
Baillie, Heberden, or Willis'.

Neither Heberden nor Brocklesby would accept fees from Johnson, who was later to bequeath to them and to each of his other doctors copies of his literary works. Dr. Johnson had an exceptionally wide acquaintance among the surgeons, physicians, and apothecaries of London, and J. P. Warbasse (1907) was able to enumerate no fewer than 59 medical names among his friends.[1]

Concerning the medical profession, Dr. Johnson is reputed to have said:

'A Physician in a great city seems to be the plaything of fortune; his degree of reputation is, for the most part, casual: they that employ him know not his excellence; they that reject him know not his deficience.'

Neurologists might well ponder, on studying the Johnson case-report, why it was that the aphasia was so mild and so brief. Various possible explanations might be borne in mind. In the first place, the pathological lesion within the brain might have been small in size, and ischaemic rather than thrombotic or haemorrhagic in nature. It might have belonged either to the category of Pierre Marie's lacunar disintegration, or to what Denny-Brown might call a 'haemo-dynamic crisis'. But in addition to this rather obvious suggestion, it is tempting to invoke a more endogenous factor, and to argue that the very magnitude of Johnson's literary capacity might have exercised a beneficial influence in the process of restoration of function. Johnson was not only a master of language, but he was a polyglot, and a man of prodigious verbal memory, who could read and assimilate a printed text with astonishing speed. True, his literary style was ponderous, pompous, mannered, and clumsy. As Hazlitt complained: . . . 'There is no discrimination, no selection, no variety in it. He uses none but "tall, opaque words", taken from the "first row of the rubric"—words with the greatest number of syllables, or Latin phrases with merely English terminations'. His letters are quite different, being elegant and attractive. But his linguistic talents were undoubtedly shown best of all in his conversation, where his phraseology and his wit were dazzling, and of a kind which has rarely been equalled.

This personal background goes a long way to explain the nature of Johnson's dysgraphia and to indicate why the literary level continued to be so high. We recall his note to Mr. Davies written on the second day of his illness . . . 'if you come you shall be admitted: for I know not whom I can see that will bring more amusement on his tongue, or more kindness in his heart'—lines which

[1] In 1782, the year prior to Johnson's stroke, there were 149 physicians in London, 274 surgeons, and 351 apothecaries. The population of London was at that time 650,845. In other words one person in every 840 had some form of medical qualification.

anyone would take pride in composing, and few aphasiacs could emulate. We can also refer to the phrase in Letter 9. . . . 'Good reciprocations of esteem are the great comforts of life, hyperbolical praise only corrupt the tongue of the one and the ear of the other. . . .' Johnson's role as a lexicographer no doubt accounts for the vocabulary of his texts, so unusually rich for one afflicted with an aphasia. Some of the words appear in the letters written during his illness are arresting, unexpected and yet wholly appropriate. ('Exigencies', 'integrity', 'discreet', 'endearment', 'unalienable', 'salve', 'querulous', 'dereliction'). These are words which one does not expect to find in the text of the average aphasiac, but Johnson was of course not an average man, but one who was very much *hors de série*. One or two of the terms which appear in the Johnson letters strike the modern reader as so unusual as to raise the question whether they were not indeed metonymous paragraphic substitutions. For example, one can pick out the words 'disinterested' as applied to the doctors (Letter 4); 'solicitude' for the safety of every faculty (Letter 4); 'obsolete' in the sense of 'rejected' (Letter 7). Some light can be thrown upon this point by reference to Johnson's own dictionary where his personal views as to the meanings, definitions and synonyms for these unusual words can be found and where they are seen to be not quite appropriate. Certain fragments of his writings are frankly paraphasic errors as can be determined from a study of the original texts. Even as late as 4th August a letter to William Bowles (873.2 Chapman Collection) contains a word which Chapman deciphered as 'poriting', which might be a neologism, if it is not a simple misreading of 'posting').

Johnson's aphasia is also betrayed here and there in his letters by the phenomenon of 'contamination' whereby a word, evoked in one context shortly afterwards crops up in another. This phenomenon is however rare, and one indeed can but remain astonished at the amazing vocabulary which Johnson continued to employ. If we adopt a statistical analysis of his phraseology and estimate the type-token ratio of his letters we find no striking difference in those which were written before and those which were written after his aphasia. This is illustrated in the following table:

TABLE 1

Letter No.	Date	Total No. of words 'tokens'	No. of diff. words 'types'	Type-token ratio (T.T.R.)
373	20.1.75	169	90	0·53
844	4.6.83	123	80	0·65
845	5.6.83	266	170	0·64
846	13.6.83	298	185	0·62
Stroke 16/17.6.83				
847	17.6.83	69	49	0·71
848	17.6.83	253	137	0·54
849	18.6.83	117	82	0·70
850	19.6.83	887	352	0·39
851	20.6.83	255	175	0·68
852	20.6.83	80	56	0·70
853	21.6.83	232	159	0·68
854	23.6.83	232	141	0·60

Another statistical study of Johnson's writings, before and after his stroke, is possible, namely a differential punctuation-count. Chapman has said that ordinarily Johnson was rather erratic in his use of punctuational symbols. It is probably true to say that he used them freely, and for him the semi-colon was a particularly favoured technique of writing. The following table illustrates a comparison between a random sample taken from his letters before 16th June and a punctuation-count taken from the letters written shortly after he had become aphasic:

TABLE 2

Symbol	Before		After (Chapman enumeration)							
	Actual	%	847	848	849	850	851	852	853	%
Comma (,)	72	55	8	12	10	85	18	13	15	59
Full stop (.)	43	33	3	13	6	40	13	4	13	34
Semi-colon (;)	12	9	1		4	3				3
Colon (:)	3	2		1	1	1	1	3	1	3
Dash (–)										
Question mark (?)						1				
Exclamation mark (!)										
Total	130		12	26	21	130	32	20	29	

The difference, which is not great, shows itself particularly in Johnson's diminished employment of the semi-colon.

Yet another possible explanation of the transient and mild characters of Dr. Johnson's aphasia comes up for discussion. We have to consider the possibility that Dr. Johnson might have been left-handed and that no frank unilateral cerebral dominance existed. We now realize that in left-handers, cerebral lesions, whether of the left or of the right hemispheres, are apt to be followed by speech-impairment of a benign type. From a study of Johnson's upbringing it is impossible to state with confidence whether he was right-handed or left-handed. We know from Johnson's own diary that an 'issue' was cut in his left arm which was deliberately kept open and was not allowed to heal until he was 6 years of age. The purpose of this surgical intervention is not known. Probably it was a device practised to cure his defective eyesight. Whether it was of special importance that this seton—as it probably was—should have been inserted into the left arm and not the right, is conjectural. The common-sense view is that the seton was deliberately inserted into the subordinate limb, leaving the master-hand free and unimpeded. It might also be argued that perhaps the seton was a device to overcome an early sinistrality. It is indubitable that the doctor habitually wrote with his right hand, but this must not be taken as an argument for right manual preference. A scrutiny of contemporary portraits shows that Johnson usually held a book in his right hand, and also a stick. There is but one picture which would appear to argue in favour of a left-sided preference. In the well-known illustration of Johnson entertaining two pretty Methodist young ladies, a teacup lies on the table to the left-hand side. As this picture was executed many years after Johnson's death, it has no value in this present argument.

The problem of Johnson's handedness would appear, however, to be partly solved in the portrait by James Roberts, actually the last of the Johnson depictions. Here we see the doctor with his hands clasped before him in a natural posture of repose. It is clearly visible that the little finger of the right hand lies lowermost, an attitude which argues to some extent in favour of a right-handedness. However, this piece of evidence must not be over-stressed, for the hand-clasp test, taken alone, is unfortunately not an absolute index of manual preference. (See Plate 6).

Aside from the purely linguistic considerations of Johnson's aphasia, it is appropriate to consider briefly the changes in affect and personality which may have shown themselves after the stroke had occurred. A reactive depression supervening upon a preliminary period of apathy was the not unnatural change in disposition. Dr. Johnson had a particular reason for taking on an attitude of pessimism. All his life he had been of a melancholic temperament, coupled with severe obsessional and hypochondriacal preoccupations. Fears of insanity had consistently haunted him since his boyhood. Not long before his stroke his lodger, the apothecary Levitt, had suddenly died after lapsing into a final state of speechlessness. Still more disturbing was the terminal illness of his great friend Dr. Lawrence, one time President of the Royal College of Physicians. As the result of an apoplexy Lawrence sustained a right hemiplegia and a severe aphasia, and Johnson was in close touch with his friend up to the time of his death ten weeks before he himself was stricken with a cerebral vascular accident. Indeed, in a letter to Dr. Lawrence's daughter, Johnson had written: '. . . if we could have again but his mind, and his tongue in his mind, and his right hand, we should not much lament the rest.' (Chapman 802). This particular letter was despatched ten months before Dr. Lawrence's death, that is to say, ten weeks before Johnson sustained his own aphasia.

His depression lifted, however. On 1st July, Fanny Burney noted in her diary that she had called on Dr. Johnson and had found him very gay and cheerful. On 19th April, 1784, she reported that he was amazingly recovered, perfectly good-humoured and comfortable, and smilingly alive to idle chat.

The muddled state of medical ideas on aphasia which existed up till the end of the eighteenth century, needs to be recalled. It is illustrated by the treatment to which Johnson submitted, whereby blisters were applied to his head, face and pharynx in an effort to stimulate his faculty of speech. At that time, no clear distinction was ever made between mental illness producing impaired speech through delirium or confusion; hysterical affections of speech ranging from dysphonia to mutism; the various clinical types of dysarthria or faulty articulation; and aphasia proper, that is to say, a loss of the faculty of *language*. Only too often an inability to talk was attributed to a paralysis of the tongue, and desperate efforts were often made to rouse that member into activity. Only rather gradually and tardily did there grow up a conception of an incomplete disorder of language, revealing itself in a faulty performance in speaking and also in writing.

As a matter of fact, Heberden happened to be well ahead of his contemporaries in his views upon this matter. Thus we read in his *Commentaries on the History and Cure of Diseases*—a work which appeared posthumously in 1802:

When a person has been struck on the left side, and has at the same time lost his voice, there is no certainty of his being able to signify his feelings, or his wants, by writing. They . . . have sometimes been able to do it, though in a confused manner; and the same person on different days would either write intelligibly or make an illegible scrawl.

This shrewd observation was in advance of current notions of the consequence of an apoplexy. A little later we also find him writing:

The inability to speak is owing sometimes not to the paralytic state of the organs of speech only, but to the utter loss of the knowledge of language and letters; which some have quickly regained, and others have recovered by slow degrees, getting the use of the smaller words first, and being frequently unable to find the word they want, and using another for it of a quite different meaning, as if it were a language which they had once known, but by long disuse had almost forgotten. . . . One person was forced to take some pains in order to learn again to write, having lost the ideas of all the letters except the initials of his two names.

It is uncertain when exactly Heberden wrote the above. He died in 1801 at the age of 91, and his writings were not published until a year after his death. Johnson's apoplexy may well have inspired these particular paragraphs.

Johnson's autopathographic account therefore constitutes an important item in the early literature of aphasia.

It is rare for a creative writer to continue to work after an aphasia even when speech-functions have apparently been restored. Johnson lived eighteen months after his stroke, but although he regained his faculty of self-expression he continued a very sick man. During the remainder of his life his literary output did not cease altogether. As he informed Mrs. Thrale on 19th April, 1784 (Chapman 954) his nights were sleepless and he would while the time away by turning Greek epigrams into Latin. Ninety-eight of these were published by Bennet Langton in Vol. XI of *Works*, 1787. During this period Johnson also wrote a dedication to Charles Burney's *Commemoration of Handel*, which appeared in 1785. He intended to furnish a preface to the posthumous collection of the works of John Scott, but this was never completed.

In November 1784 he translated into English verse Horace's ode *Diffugere nives, redeunt, jam gramina campis*. He had also hoped to have written an epitaph in Latin verse to David Garrick but he found himself unequal to the task.

Johnson died on 13th December, 1784, from cardio-renal failure. James Wilson performed the necropsy on 15th December, 1784, and his manuscript record of the event is contained within the library of the Royal College of Physicians. An illustration of Johnson's emphysematous lung appeared in Matthew Baillie's *Morbid Anatomy* (1793–9). Dr. Johnson's right kidney was removed and preserved by the post-mortem attendant, Mr. White (subsequently Dr. White). While stitching up the body, Mr. White pricked his finger with the needle and developed later a septic infection therefrom.

So perished the gigantic but long-ailing Johnson. Let us in conclusion turn from further examination of his darker days, and carry away a recollection of what he said in a gayer heyday mood:

. . . If I had no duties, and no reference to futurity, I would spend my life in driving briskly in a post-chaise with a pretty woman; but she should be one who could understand me, and would add something to the conversation.

ACKNOWLEDGEMENTS

For facsimile reproductions of the Johnson letters quoted in the text, I am indebted to the New York Public Library (Berg Collection), the Prime Minister's library at Chequers; and to Mrs Donald Hyde in particular. To the last-named I owe an especial debt of gratitude for allowing me to reproduce the copy of Chapman No. 850 from the Hyde Collection, Sommerville, New Jersey, U.S.A. The President of the Royal College of Physicians has been very good in allowing me to reproduce the manuscript description of the Johnson autopsy. Mr. Payne, the College Librarian, has always been most courteous and helpful in his assistance.

IX. A SURVEY OF OUR CONCEPTIONS AS TO THE ORIGINS OF LANGUAGE

In the beginning was the word. The word itself, of which our works of art are fashioned, is the first art-form, older than the roughest shaping of clay or stone. A word is the carving or colouring of a thought, and gives to it permanence. We do not yet know, if ever we are able to trace, how language first began, though we may deduce that words to express love were those first used, since love is the emotion, just as speech the instrument, that even in its lowest, most primitive form, clearly distinguishes human beings from their humble cousins of the animal world . . .   Osbert Sitwell

They received the use of the five operations of the Lord, and in the sixth place he imparted them understanding, and in the seventh speech, an interpreter of the cogitations thereof.

The origin of language must have come by inspiration. A thousand, nay, a million of children could not invent a language. While the organs are pliable, there is not understanding enough to form a language: by the time that there is understanding enough, the organs are become stiff . . . when I maintain that language must have come by inspiration, I do not mean that inspiration is required for rhetoric, and all the beauties of language; for when once man has language we can conceive that he may gradually form modifications of it. I mean only that inspiration seems to me to be necessary to give man the faculty of speech; to inform him that he may have speech; which I think he could no more find out without inspiration, than cows or hogs would think of such a faculty.   Samuel Johnson

Because of their very nature, some of the problems attendant upon the origins of human language will never be solved. However, a few solutions are possible; others can be shrewdly surmised. Questions concerning the beginnings of speech; the function of speech; the distinction between animal vocalization and human utterance, and the nature of speech in eras inaccessible to historical research, are problems of a fundamental order. Von Humboldt proclaimed that 'man is man only by means of speech; but in order to invent speech he must be already man'. Unfortunately an exhaustive account of the subject in all its ramifications is not possible, for it would lead deep into the territories of philosophy, natural history, and the domain of *Gedenkpsychologie*. Therefore one might well deliberately restrict remarks and concentrate upon a mere descriptive narrative of the controversies which have arisen in the past concerning the mysterious origins of language.

Based upon a paper read at an Anglo-American Symposium held in London 15–17 July, 1957 and published in *The History and Philosophy of Knowledge of Brain and its Functions*. Ed. F. N. L. Poynter. Blackwell Scientific Publications, Oxford. 1958. 45–72.

In the first place we need to consider hypotheses which envisaged 'divine' or 'miraculous' beginnings to language. The general idea behind these concepts, irrespective of details, implied the direct intervention of an omnipotent being. Language was regarded as an essentially human faculty, bearing no discernible analogies with the cries of animals. Hebrew and Christian writers traced their authority upon this subject to the earlier chapters of Genesis. Similar doctrines of divine origins are also to be found in other religions. In most polytheistic beliefs, language was ascribed to the tutelage of one particular divinity—Brihaspati, Oannes, Hermes, Thoth, Janus, Odin-Wotan, as the case may be. In the Hindu Vedas we read that God assumed human form and danced while strumming a tambour. The resulting sounds formed the primitive vowels; later still the consonants. Grammar came later.

In the early days of the Christian era many scholastic quibbles arose as to the precise interpretation of biblical texts concerning the beginnings of speech. These include the controversies between St. Basil and Eunomius, as well as the writings upon this topic by Philo, Abelard, and later still Duns Scotus.

Somewhat later, thinkers tended rather to neglect problems of linguistic development, possibly because the literal teaching of Genesis had been tacitly accepted as incontrovertible. The philosopher was absolved from those disturbing issues which would immediately arise if one dared to question the orthodox teaching of divine bestowal. Nevertheless, difficulties were inevitable even within the framework of the 'miraculous' hypothesis. At least one query was side-tracked until well into the age of materialism. Did man acquire speech from a creator in a perfect form, complete with syntax; or *per contra*, was the original divine gift merely a handful of empirical root-forms from which man gradually developed a mature language-system over the course of time? Was it a tree with spreading branches, adorned with leaf, blossom and fruit; or was it but a seed? Most theologians at any rate were in favour of the former idea; that is, they visualized a complex language-system *ab initio*. This debate extended well into the nineteenth century. Thus Don Juan Bautista de Erro (1829) was quite emphatic that man was created 'adult' or mature, being from the start endowed with every essential quality. As to language Erro believed that God spoke to Adam as soon as he created him; the language used by God was perfect, and Adam intuitively understood this perfect language. Donaldson (1859) assumed that there must have been some nodal point from which the various languages diverged; some handle to the fan which spread out over the world; some first and primeval speech which was not of gradual growth, but which sprang like Minerva from the head of the first thinking man as a product of his intellectual conformation. Other nineteenth century writers favoured a compromise, and endeavoured to reconcile theological beliefs in a divine origin of the rudiments of speech, with contemporary ideas regarding evolution, whereby the 'first poor hoard of vocables' became elaborated and so blossomed into the tongues of mankind. Whitney, however, was highly critical, and compared such a 'childish philosophy' to the wisdom of the school-girl who asserted, 'God made me a little baby "so high" and I *grew* the rest'.

Such literal and theological beliefs found their most eloquent apologist in Süssmilch in his essay *Beweis, dass die erste Sprache ihren Ursprung allein vom Schöpfer erhalten habe*, written in 1767.

Those who advocated a divine conferment of a fully accomplished system of speech faced yet another problem, the identity, or at any rate the nature, of man's original language. A study of comparative religion reveals a recurring doctrine to the effect that all peoples of the world were originally endowed with a common tongue, or *Ursprache*, which later split into numerous un-related dialects by dint of some catastrophic happening. Witness, for example, the widely-spread myth of the Tower of Babel. According to Philo at one time all the animals shared a universal language. Eventually they sent a deputation to demand immortality and immunity from old age. They were punished for their presumption by being inflicted with a confusion of tongues. The precise identity of man's original language provoked less discussion than might be expected. It was largely taken for granted that the *lingua adamica*, as Jacob Boehme termed it, was Hebrew (St. Jerome; Origen; Bochart; Camet) despite etymological evidence to the contrary. Alternative notions were put forward, though based upon flimsy and obscure arguments. For example, Kempe (1569) asserted that God spoke to Adam in Swedish; Adam answered in Danish; while the serpent addressed Eve in French. Chardin had a different idea: according to him three languages were spoken in the Garden of Eden: Arabic by the Serpent, Persian by Adam and Eve, and Turkish by Gabriel. Erro was of the opinion that Escuran (or Basque) was the language of Noah, and also of the first man. The claims of Syriac to be the original language were supported by Theodorotus, Amira, and the Maronites of Lebanon. Others, like Forster (1859), looked upon Hamyaritic (or old Arabic) as man's primeval language. Many others favoured Welsh.

We find in Plutarch references to another prevalent belief, namely in the eventual rebuilding of the Tower of Babel, when mankind will once again share a universal tongue. *Multae terricolis linguae, coelestibus una.* Theologians, furthermore, were apt to assume that a *lingua franca* was spoken in Paradise, and though there were differences of opinion as to the nature of this celestial language it was usually equated with Hebrew. Goropius, however, opined that it was Dutch. Emanuel Swedenborg had original ideas upon this topic. 'In the whole of heaven all have one language and they understand one another . . . this language is not learned there but is natural to everyone for it flows from their very affection and thought . . . Angelic language has nothing in common with human languages, except with some words . . . the first language on our earth was in agreement with angelic language because they had it from heaven . . . the Hebrew tongue agrees with it in some things'.

The Pâli grammarian Katyâyana taught that man's fundamental and original language was Māgadhi and that this was also the tongue spoken by the Gods, by the animal kingdom, and by the damned in Hell.

Unorthodox opinions were occasionally advanced upon all these subjects and were even the topic of discussion in pseudo-scientific terminology. Thus a few scholars like John Webb (1669) were tempted to regard Chinese as man's *Ursprache*, being misled by its monosyllabic form into the mistaken idea that it was essentially a primitive language. Indeed it was not until Leibniz that the notion of an original language, and a heavenly common tongue, both identified with Hebrew, was laughed out of court. The final blow was struck by Lorenzo Hervas y Panduro.

Now and again an experimental method of study was adopted, as by Psamtek; by the Emperor Frederick II; and by King James IV of Scotland.

According to Herodotus, the Egyptian King Psamtek—or Psammetichus 1 (663–609 B.C.)—took two new-born infants and left them to grow up in isolation and silence. Eventually these children were heard to utter a certain sound, which was thought to represent the Phrygian word for bread, namely *Bekos*. Here the problem lay in an attempt to recognize the nature of those first articulate utterances which could be deemed instinctive and in some way imitative. But whereas the Egyptian experiment was believed to point to Phrygian as the natural language of man, the test-subjects observed by Frederick II and James IV perished before articulation had matured. Quintilian referred to the case of a child abandoned in a desert to fend for itself. When rescued it was found to be capable of uttering a few sounds, but it was devoid of any faculty of speech.

Opposed to the 'monogenetic' hypothesis as to the miraculous birth of a primordial system of language, was an alternative suggestion, namely that language might have arisen *de novo* in different regions at different times and among different races. This theory of polygenesis appealed both to Lord Monboddo and to von Schlegel. Such an idea, while rejecting any belief in an isolated *lingua adamica*, could still be reconciled with a supernatural origin of a specifically human faculty of speech. According to Grotius and also to de Brosses, traces of a primitive basic language might still be discerned scattered throughout the world and intermingled with other tongues.

Aside from the theological speculations as to the manner in which speech began, there were many philosophical attitudes towards this question, though varying widely in nature. Some of them were mutually exclusive theories, which, admitting of no compromise, had to be accepted or rejected as they stood. From the historical standpoint it can be said that secular theories did not come to the fore until the eighteenth and nineteenth centuries, although from time to time faint criticisms had been mooted for many years. Hellenic philosophy had already produced two rival schools of thought, termed respectively *physis* and *thesis*; or in other words 'nature' as opposed to 'convention'. Socrates and Plato may be numbered among the adherents of *physis* as contrasting with Democritus and Aristotle. The proponents of *thesis* maintained that language, whether divinely inspired or not, was no novel appearance, but the product of an operation which was deliberate and essentially human. By agreement, a vocable becomes tacked on to this or that object. 'Words', Aristotle taught, 'are but sounds which by arbitrary convention are linked with a certain meaning'. Democritus advanced four grammatical arguments to support this contention, namely the occurrence of homonyms, of synonyms, of anomalies, and of nominal change. Similar opinions were held years later by John Locke.

As a subsequent antinomy in the philosophy of language were the contrasting doctrines of 'nativism' as opposed to 'empiricism'. Here, in new dress, is the old dispute between *physis* and *thesis*. It was a problem which aligned linguistic philosophers into two opposing camps for a long time, though in a wholly artificial and unrealistic manner.

More recent writers upon the beginnings of language have made other tentative classifications. Wundt (1913) isolated three main groups of hypotheses upon this topic, namely (1) theories of invention and imitation; (2) a theory of miraculous birth; and (3) an evolutionary notion. Eisler (1930) spoke of: (1) a theological hypothesis which envisaged language as a divine endowment; (2) an empirical theory which ascribed language to the invention of certain gifted individuals; and (3) psychogenetic theories which embraced various factors and operations including gestures and interjections and the action of a 'communicative impulse'. Révész (1956) distinguished between (1) biological hypotheses which relegated the antecedent and prelinguistic stages to the animal world, with a gradual emergence from a non-linguistic to a linguistic system of communication; and (2) anthroposophical theories, which assumed language to be a product of the human mind. He went on to assert, however, that neither type of explanation was altogether satisfactory.

Whether or not speech was to be looked upon as divine in origin, there was still scope for discussion about the appearance of speech as (1) an abrupt endowment; (2) an invention of sudden origin; or (3) an evolutionary development arising out of either (1) or (2). The idea of an invention appealed to J. Grimm (1851) who considered that the imperfections of language argued against a divine handiwork. L. Geiger (1869) agreed. Herder was one of the first to speak of the action of an innate impulse towards self-expression and communication, and the idea of a continuous biological evolution proved attractive to Monboddo, Whitney, von Humboldt, Steinthal (1851–1855) and Croce (1930). Marty believed that this process was a conscious and deliberate one, governed by intention, free-will and choice; in other words, by a voluntaristic principle. Donaldson (1859), while adhering to the divine origin of speech, considered that man was originally endowed not with an actual language, but merely with an innate capacity for speaking.

At this point it may be convenient to avoid classifications, but to enumerate and discuss some of the speculative ideas which have been advanced at various times, especially since the emergence of philology as a science late in the eighteenth century.

Even earlier various important theories emerged which can be collectively deemed 'imitative' in nature, whereby language was looked upon as made up of noises which mimic animal cries or other sounds in nature. These essentially comprise an hypothesis of onomatopoeia, and must therefore imply a logical relationship in language between sound and meaning, the link being found in the source of the parent stimulus, animate or inanimate.

Among the advocates of the various imitative hypotheses were Leibniz, Steinthal, Marty, Renan, Geiger, Wedgwood, Johanneson and De Monagny. Some had been impressed by the occurrence of frank onomatopoeia in all languages and had perhaps tended to exaggerate its role in linguistic development. Their arguments would suggest that early man did little more than 'eavesdrop on the voice of nature', as Révész said. The many weighty objections to this theory are sometimes forgotten. Sound-imitation is a highly concrete activity, which cannot easily apply to concepts which are of an abstract or of a silent nature. Indeed language has been said to begin only where sound-imitation ceases.

One of the pioneers among scientific philologists advocating the doctrine of sound-imitation was Herder. In his monograph he argued that man is distinguished by his faculty of conscious reflection—his power of arresting the play of mental images; and of focusing upon a single image, identifying it and musing upon it. From that step man became able to separate and recognize the distinguishing features of an object. So . . . 'Man sees a lamb . . . the lamb stands before him, as represented in his senses, white, soft, woolly. The conscious and reflecting soul of man looks for a distinguishing mark;—the lamb bleats!—the mark is found. The bleating, which made the strongest impression, which stood apart from all other impressions of sight or touch, remains in the soul. The lamb returns—white, soft, woolly. The soul sees—touches, reflects, looks for a mark. The lamb bleats, and now the soul has recognized it. "Ah! Thou art the bleating animal", the soul says within herself; and the sound of bleating perceived as the distinguishing mark of the lamb becomes the name of the lamb. It was the comprehended mark, the word. And what is the whole of our language but a collection of such words?'

Subsequent philologists have in the main completely rejected the sound-imitative theories, although it is still admitted that some languages, like Egyptian, Manchu and Basque, are rich in onomatoepia. Even Herder was frank enough to jettison his own hypothesis at a later date. Müller asserted that onomatopoeic words, however numerous, are always self-evident and self-explanatory, being the playthings, not the tools, of speech. Words such as cuckoo or whip-poor-will are like 'artificial flowers, without a root'. They are sterile, and unfit to express anything except the one object which they imitate. 'Cuckoo' could never mean anything else but a cuckoo, so he claimed; it stands by itself like a stick in a living hedge. 'The onomatopoeic theory goes very smoothly as long as it deals with cackling hens and quacking ducks, but round that poultry yard there is a high wall, and we soon find that it is behind that wall that language really begins'.

Müller, who dubbed this particular theory of sound-imitation the 'bow-wow' hypothesis, ended his argument in powerful terms:

> The number of names which are really formed by an imitation of sound dwindle down to a very small quota, if cross-examined by the comparative philologist; and we are left in the end with the conviction that though *a* language might have been made out of the roaring, fizzing, hissing, gobbling, twittering, cracking, banging, slamming, whining and rattling sounds of nature, the tongues with which we are acquainted point to a different origin.

Another hypothesis turned for analogy to the vocalizations of the animal kingdom. It started with the assumption that two main systems of audible behaviour can be discerned in the animal world, according to whether they are transitive or intransitive in function. For the moment we may follow Révész in separating animal 'cries' from 'directed calls'; the former being mere audible overspilling of an emotional upsurge, while the latter go further and convey a message to other creatures of the same order. Here we might be tempted to discern the beginnings of communication.

Passing from the vexed and hazardous topic of animal 'language' to the problems of *homo sapiens*, we might be tempted to visualize the dawning of communication out of purely intransitive emotional utterance. In this way, interjections have at times been claimed to be the ancestors of speech, a form of speculation first put forward by Epicurus and his pupil Lecretius. Later it was supported by Vico and by Rousseau. None the less it was not difficult to adduce many important arguments inimical to this Interjectional Theory. Were the transition from cry to call in the animal world valid evidence of the beginnings of communication, somewhere among the more highly evolved mammalians there must surely have been traces of true phonetic articulation. In other words, by successive steps one would have expected to find a graduation from the cry to the call, and thence to the word. But no such steps can be confidently demonstrated in the animal kingdom. Even the talking birds with their plausible exclamations, the parrot, the mynah, and the magpie, constitute little more than instances of nature's jests.

In the case of man it can be claimed that emotional expletives are merely audible gestures. They are pantomimic acts which step over the threshold of silence, and like a cough or a sneeze, betray themselves accidentally. Of course *silent* gesture as a precursor of language is another matter altogether, and one which will be discussed later. *Audible* gestures, that is ejaculations, are mainly sounds which are emitted without deliberate intent. Though not altogether 'involuntary', to use the diction of neurology, they are only little voluntary, and much more automatic. In the realm of kinesics they correspond with a blush or a blanching of the face, or beads of sweat upon the brow, rather than with expressive movements of a limb. Man's expletives, like the cries of an animal, are often uncouth noises rather than phonemic utterances; as such they are incapable of accurate recording by way of appropriate notation. The sounds which betray scorn, disapproval, pain, amusement, surprise, are symbolized rather than transcribed by such verbal conventions as Pooh! Tut tut! Ouch! Ha-ha! and Oh! Between these non-phonetic noises and actual spellable words, yawns a wide gulf. The fact that interjections differ acoustically from one language to another argues against any instinctive properties, and suggests that they are epiphenomena rather than ancestors of speech. Interjections are but unwitting evidences of mood: words are the chosen tools of thought. Interjections are crude, self-limited oscillations of the ether: words are symbolic utterances, deliberately evoked, disciplined by phonetics and obedient to the laws of syntax. Social usage often ordains that interjections should be concealed, restricted, controlled, restrained, if not inhibited altogether: words on the other hand form the warp and woof of the fabric of human concourse and behaviour. Language, one might say, begins only when and where interjections are dispensed with, just as in the case of onomatopoeia.

Objections to any attempt to trace the origins of speech to expletives, interjectional cries and other expressive sounds were made by Descartes (1637) and by Herder (1772). Equally scornful of this interjectional notion of the origin of speech, Müller applied the nickname of the 'pooh-pooh' theory and quoted the trenchant strictures made by Horne Tooke on this subject:

> The dominion of speech is erected upon the downfall of interjections. Without the artificial contrivance of language, mankind would have had nothing but interjections with which to communicate, orally, any of their feelings. The neighing of a horse, the lowing of a cow, the barking of a dog, the purring of a cat, sneezing, coughing, groaning, shrieking, and every other involuntary convulsion with oral sound, have almost as good a title to be called parts of speech, as interjections have. Voluntary interjections are only employed when the suddenness and vehemence of some affection or passion returns men to their natural state, and makes them for a moment forget the use of speech; or when from some circumstance, the shortness of time will not permit them to exercise it.' (1798–1805)

Expressive sounds differ from semantemes first in not being communicative (or transitive), and secondly, in being involuntary. A contrast has been made between the faculties of indication and of communication, though the difference between them is somewhat artificial.

The various 'gestural' hypotheses regarding the origin of speech may now be discussed. Although diverse, all these notions agree in claiming that expressive movements, rather than sounds, form the immediate prelinguistic stage of human speech. The simplest of these speculations visualized our remote ancestors as relying at one period upon silent pantomime as a means of expressing their feelings and their primitive ideas. These gestures were looked upon as an elaboration of the crude motor and autonomic phenomena in animals which accompany, perhaps unwittingly, such emotional states as rage, fear or pleasure; or certain bodily sensations like hunger, pain and sexual arousal. The liberation of the fore-limbs from the fetters of simple locomotory function, as took place in the primates, allowed not only prehension but also a wide range of pantomimic acts. Endowed with tools for simple signalling devices and for co-ordinated motor-skills, they ceased to be quadrupeds. The more elaborate gestures replaced the global movements wherewith the sub-primate mammalia display emotion. When manual pantomime became less amorphous and more differentiated, the exercise of deliberate control became possible. In this way a form of silent communication developed. With the belief that this formed the only system of communication in early man, the conception came about of a hypothetical *homo alalus*.

This notion was so inherently unlikely that it failed to secure serious consideration. Unsupported by any real evidence, the idea of a silent communicative code perished from inanition. It was replaced, however, by a modified gestural hypothesis. This envisaged that primitive man in the course of heavy physical tasks, would throw into contraction a large number of muscles including many which were not primarily concerned as agonists. For example, the effort of lifting a heavy weight is assisted by raising the intra-thoracic pressure, brought about by fixation of the muscles of the thorax and a closure of the glottis. Partial release of the glottal stop might lead to various audible phenomena—grunts, groans and the like. Some philologists, like Noiré for instance, were tempted to regard these noises, the unconscious concomitants of muscular effort, as the precursors of speech. Thus there arose what became known as the 'Yo-heave-ho' hypothesis as to linguistic origins, a theory which Firth has also spoken of slightingly as the 'ta-ta' theory.

Some of the adherents went further. Not only did they invoke the more crude and violent physical efforts, but they even asserted that certain refined and subtle gestures were at times associated closely with vocalization. A few examples may be quoted. The forefinger placed vertically against the lips through which a hissing noise is emitted, is an almost universal signal enjoining silence. It is often graphically symbolized as 'Pst!'[1] According to the gestural theory, this was the etymological ancestor of the modern English 'hush'. The word 'no' has also been looked upon as an audible gesture, either an attenuated jerking movement dispersing the birds of ill-omen which threaten to alight upon the shoulders; or a survival of an infantile rejection of the breast; or (as in the Levantine gesture of negation) a brief movement of recoil. Similarly 'yes' has been regarded as an audible accompaniment of a curtailed obeisance.

A modification of this same hypothesis was put forward by L. Stein (1946). He believed the phylogenetic and the ontogenetic evolutionary stages of speech to be analogous. Primitive man, like the infant, utilized for the purposes of communication a repertoire of noises emitted during feeding activity, which took origin not only from the respiratory passages but also from the ali-

---

[1] Vide: *Isis, et Harpocrates digito qui significat st!*

mentary tract. The former included aspirates, soft sounds and hard, the last of which Stein ascribed to an early activity of the glottal stop. Alimentary sounds concerned in the parenthood of speech comprised audible suction and clicks. Lewis also correlated the guttural noises of infants with 'comfort sounds', associating them with Kussmaul's *Vomitiv-lauten*, or the gurgling and belching of gastric repletion. This improbable notion as to the origin of speech might well be codified in the current idiom of flippancy as the 'colly-wobble' hypothesis.

Writers upon the topic of childhood speech have often made this important assumption, and have taken it for granted that an infant recapitulates the history of the race in the steps taken to acquire speech. This bold postulate is, to say the least of it, incautious, as eventually stated explicitly by Révész among others. Where speech is concerned primitive man cannot be looked upon as a child. The newborn infant cannot speak, being still incomplete in many respects, physical as well as intellectual. But early man was not similarly 'unfinished'. And if he were unable to speak it must have been for reasons quite different from those in the case of the child. The developing infant is surrounded by a climate of linguistic maturity; primitive man is not. The child's mastery of language is preceded by a stage wherein comprehension is well ahead of execution. In other words, the way lies open for the acquisition of speech. No such chronological sequence can have existed in the early history of language. As Révész said, the understanding of speech presupposes its earlier existence; with primitive man active and passive speech-capacity must have emerged simultaneously.

There is yet another, and even more fundamental modification of the gestural hypothesis. This was an idea which focused attention upon the changes in the shape of the buccal cavity according to the precise play of activity of the articulatory musculature. It was believed that not only the acoustic properties of the issuing sounds were in this way exactly determined and ordained, but furthermore that they were endowed with specific semantic significance. Thus the claim arose that in all languages (though it happens that this particular theory has been chiefly studied as it applies to English) there exists an important bond between sound and sense. Locke, however, believed that verbal sounds were quite arbitrary. Bonfante too has said that there was no necessary connection between sound and meaning. If there were, he argued, languages would never change; and moreover we should all be speaking the same language.

This theory was discussed at length by Plato in his *Cratylus* dialogue. Much later the idea was also hinted at by von Humboldt, debated by Monboddo, strongly advocated by Davis, and referred to briefly by Gogarty. Paget has been the most enthusiastic proponent, however, and he devoted many years to collecting evidence to support this doctrine of 'echoism' as it has been called, or 'schema-topœia' as he preferred to call it. Other writers have also found merit in this hypothesis, Fabre d'Olivet, Jousse, Morlaas, Jespersen, and Whorf, believing in a natural *nexus* between sound and meaning.

To discuss this topic exhaustively, or even to afford many illustrative examples wherein sound and meaning are apparently correlated, would be outside the scope of this particular chapter. The 'click-click' hypothesis, as it has been dubbed, is mentioned merely in so far as it throws light upon the problems of the origins of human speech.

Nevertheless a few examples may be quoted where sound and meaning are correlated. According to Plato the letter *Rho* was a fine instrument expressive of motion (see *Rhein*, flow; *rhon*, current; *tromos*, trembling; *trechein*, run; *krouein*, strike; *thranein*, break; *ereikein*, send; *thruptein*, crush; *kermatizein*, crumble; *rhumbein*, whirl). The letter *iota* was used by the divine name-giver to stand for anything subtle, anything which can easily pass to other things. Hence *cenai*, go; and *iesthai*, hasten. The letter *lambda* formed by a gliding movement of the tongue is utilized in words such as *leia*, level; *olisthanein*, glide; *liparon*, sleek; *kollodes*, glutinous. Many other instances of a sound-sense correlation are to be found in the *Cratylus* dialogue which probably represents the very first discussion upon the origin of language. Van Helmont in 1667 asserted that in pronouncing the Hebrew alphabet the organs of articulation assume the shape of the Hebrew characters. According to Davis, the letter *V* carries a special quality, a cleaving incisiveness and struggle. The very shape of the letter suggests a wedge (see victory; vim; invincible; vile; vice; vivid; vigour; valour). Continuity of sound is often indicated by a stop-consonant followed by an *L* or an *R* (rattle; rumble; jangle; jingle; clutter; chatter; jabber). Words beginning with an *sl* express dislike or scorn (slight; slim; sly; sloppy; slipshod; slattern; slut). *U* sounds denote a 'dark' state of mind (glum; gluppish; grumpy; sulky; sullen; dumps). According to Gogarty, most of the ominous words in English are built about the vowel *U* (dung; lump; turd; turgescent; rum; slum). Paget went even further. He believed that the vowel sound *Ah* refers to anything which is wide open, large, spacious or flat; that *I* or *Ee* refers to things high, forward placed or little (steeple; teeny; peak); *Aw* connotes a cavity (e.g. yawn); *Oo* something enclosed, full, tubular or elongated (e.g. room; tube; loop). Regarding consonants, he alleged that sibilant sounds suggest something reaching forwards to upwards (e.g. send; sleep; gaze; stare); *L* indicates motion (e.g. length; long; leave); and *Sn* anything pertaining to the nose (snort; snout; snot; sniff; sneeze; snitch). The same climate of speculations appealed to Guy Endore who wrote:

'Word meanings are completely arbitrary. You can't feel them. No? Can't I? Then why do almost all the words beginning with *wr* involve some kind of twisting—for example, "wriggle", "wrestle", "wrench", "wring", "writhe" "wreath", "wryneck", and even "wrinkle" and of course "wrist" and also "wright", as in "wheelwright", and also "wrought" as in "wrought-iron" and "wrap" and maybe even "wrong". All twisting words . . . Doesn't that show the tongue trying to imitate a gesture of the body? Doesn't it? Otherwise why should the sound parallel the meanings over so many words? Isn't it a fact that almost all the words beginning with a *str* have to do with something being stretched from here to there? The word "stretch" to start with. And "string"? And "straight", "stride", "stream", "strut", "strain"? And you could include "strict". And "strike". And "strop". And "strip".'

Endore proceeded to give many other instances.

'Or to take another *sl* word: "slobber". Can you feel the tongue slobbering away from the "s" to the "l"? A feeling like the mouth being sluiced? A sense of slovenliness. Or slatternlike. Slothful. Sloppy. Slinky. As if the tongue had gone slack and slumped away into a slush of saliva toward the side and back of the mouth. Yes, as if the tongue had slipped on the "s" and gone sliding down into a sludge. So that you get ugly words like "slug" and "slut" and "slum" and "sleezy" and "slaver"—I mean the drool of saliva . . .'

It would be easy to argue, like Van Ginneken, that pantomime might have determined the form of the graphic symbols of *written* speech, and hence be looked upon as determining the alphabet in many tongues. But speech is something much more fundamental than writing. To look upon gesture as a parent, or at any rate a forerunner, of spoken speech, cannot be maintained without considerable reserve. In the maturation of human language, gesture and speech probably advanced together. '. . . language, even in its most primitive form was phonetic language, shot through with gestures, mimic and pantomimic movements' (Révész).

Brief reference may also be made to one or two other ideas, which though mooted, were never seriously entertained by linguists as a whole. Thus there is the supposition that speech might have evolved out of song. This unlikely conjecture was at one time put forward by Blacklock, Monboddo, Herder, Rousseau, Wundt and Jespersen. In this connection the last-named may be quoted:

> In primitive speech I hear the laughing cries of exaltation when lads and lassies vie with one another to attract the attention of the opposite sex, when everyone sang his merriest and danced his bravest to lure a pair of eyes to throw admiring glances in his direction. Language was born in the courting days of mankind; the first utterances of speech I fancy to myself like something between the nightly love-lyrics of puss upon the tiles and the melodious love-songs of the nightingale.

Donovan also argued in favour of a festal origin of human speech. The innate distractability of primitive man was arrested, he said, by dint of high-pitched, loud, or rhythmic acoustic stimuli which eventually formed sound-patterns. Ritual dances and auditory-rhythms would in time emerge as symbolic gestures. These would ultimately form the vocal evidence of a well-remembered occasion, and so constitute the beginnings of symbolic formulation.

This postulate, which we may facetiously dub the 'tarara-boom-de-ay' hypothesis, failed to survive despite the prestige of its protagonists. As was pointed out by Révész, an authority upon the psychology of music, the origins of speech must be looked for elsewhere: music stems from speech and not *vice versa*. In his essay upon the *Origin and Function of Music* written a century ago, Herbert Spencer contrived to skate all over and around the problem of speech, and to touch upon the prosodic elements of articulate utterance without ever once confronting the question of linguistic origins. He traced a clear-cut transition from pantomimic movements to interjections and thence to song, but how phonetic utterance entered into some part of this chain of events was a topic he scrupulously avoided.

The nineteenth century saw the birth of yet another surmise, an odd one which made an inconspicuous debut and soon vanished. This was a theory which, inspired by earlier writings of Heyse, Müller himself promulgated, after causticly reviewing other contemporary alternative ideas. Couched in obscure phraseology, it proclaimed that obedient to some natural law . . ., everything which is struck rings, and each substance possesses its own peculiar ring. Language was the result of an instinctive faculty peculiar to primitive man by which 'every impression from without received its vocal expression from within'. So it was with man: man responds, man rings. In addition to his power of imitation and interjection, man possesses the faculty of giving more articulate expression to the general conceptions of his mind. This faculty is instinctive, and becomes fainter as necessity wanes. Müller's colleagues, no doubt, already smarting under his critical jibes, were quick to retaliate by poking fun at this conception of man 'ringing', and to describe it as the 'ding-dong' hypothesis. Its influence upon linguistic thought was ephemeral.

In contemporary linguistics, the trend is to follow Bloomfield and to regard speech as essentially an aspect of communication, one which requires a sender, a receiver and a message. Some might well argue that this theorem has become over-stressed, to the relative neglect of those functions of language which are less utilitarian and non-communicative, being self-expressive, egocentric, autistic, ludic and aesthetic. The communicative school of thought lays emphasis upon the social properties of language, for one of man's characteristics is to live in communities or family-groups rather than in isolation.

Expanding these ideas into the realm of semantics Révész propounded his 'contact-theory' regarding the origin of speech. He traced the ancestry of language back to the animal-world, though denying that 'animal-language' can be said to exist *sensu strictu*. According to him, mammalian vocalization is made up partly of cries and partly of an assortment of more complex directed calls.

But a social instinct is by no means peculiar to *homo sapiens*. Numerous examples may be quoted from the animal-kingdom, both of small monogamous family-groupings as well as of larger gregariousness in herds or flocks. It is difficult to indicate differences between the social behaviour of, say, the lion or the elephant, and that of primitive man, save in the faculty of language. Accordingly language itself can scarcely be identified as the specific hall-mark of any instinct of 'contact', unless it can be shown that there is something quite peculiar in the case of human social behaviour. Such a difference may perhaps be found in what Révész called the 'contact-reaction'.

Every speculation which has so far been discussed, with the exception of the theory of divine endowment, presupposes a gradation from animal to human behaviour which incorporates the development of speech. The debate largely turns upon a discussion of whether between man and animals the distinction is one of kind or merely of degree. Although the nineteenth century was a materialistic era when the ideas of progressive evolutionary change were novel and exciting, many philologists continued to assert that there was a gulf separating man from animals as regards communication, which was unbridgeable. Max Müller for instance wrote in forthright terms . . .

However much the frontiers of the animal kingdom have been pushed forward, so that at one time the line of demarcation between animal and man seemed to depend on a mere fold in the brain, there is *one* barrier which no one has yet ventured to touch—the barrier of language. Even those philosophers with whom *penser c'est sentir*, who reduce all thought to feeling and maintain that we share the faculties which are the productive causes of thought in common with beasts, are bound to confess that as yet no race of animals has produced language. Lord Monboddo, for instance, admits that as yet no animal has been discovered in the possession of language, 'not even the beaver, who of all animals we know that are not, like the orang outang, of our own species, comes nearest to us in sagacity'.

At the end of the last century psychologists began to emphasize that the difference between man and animals as regards audible utterance, and the definition of the term 'language', are problems which turn around something which is much more fundamental, namely the question of the type of thinking. The problem is not so much what is the nature of so-called animal-language, as animal-thought, and in what way does it differ from mentation in *homo sapiens*. These questions will be discussed in a later chapter, when the subject of animal-communication as a whole comes under scrutiny. One very important point of distinction is man's 'time-binding faculty' to quote Korzibsky. By this expression the author referred to the ability of mankind to manipulate symbols, not only in their immediate setting, but also in the past tense and in the future. This ability man alone possesses, sharing it with no member of the animal-kingdom, however sagacious.

Pumphrey drew attention to a number of factors whereby human language differs from animal-noises and ululations, however rich they may be. He indicated three properties which are peculiar to mankind in this context, namely, (1) detachment, (2) extensibility, and (3) economy. Thus man, unlike animals, is able at will to use language to describe events in a wholly dispassionate fashion. Extensibility is another way of referring to the time-binding possibilities, whereby a proposition can be made and discussed in terms of present, past or future time. 'Economy' means that symbols enable mankind to abbreviate considerably what would otherwise be descriptive and long-winded declarations.

Sapir believed that linguistics alone would never solve the conundrum of the origin of speech. The problem is merely part of a larger question which concerns the beginnings of symbolic behaviour in man, and the specialization of such behaviour within the laryngeal region. According to Sapir, language is primarily a vocal actualization of the tendency *to see reality* symbolically, a property which renders it a fitting instrument for communication. In the later give-and-take of social intercourse it becomes complicated and refined, as we witness it today. The problem is therefore narrowed into a quest for the first indications of symbolic behaviour, rather than of articulate speech. Suzanne Langer must surely be correct in regarding the earliest sign of a tendency towards the formation of symbols simply in a sense of significance attached to certain objects, forms or sounds. This postulated tendency to see reality symbolically is vividly reminiscent of Herder, whose prize-essay written in 1772 expressed much the same attitude of mind. According to Langer, in the behaviour of the great apes, one can often detect traits which indicate that certain objects may occasionally appear to possess some modicum of meaning; to convey something; to be significant. Here then might well be the beginnings of symbolic thought; and here again we may perhaps descry the remote but none the less direct ancestry of speech. In other words, the chimpanzee has no speech; definitely none; and yet he has a rudimentary capacity for speech. Conceptually he is not far off the attainment of language, and yet an absolute barrier stands between him and man. Langer was perhaps on less secure ground when she identified the barrier with an animal's lack of instinctive urge towards babbling in babyhood. Believing that young apes never emit playful noises, she concluded that it is because every one of an ape's utterances is pragmatic and emotive, that none can acquire significance. The beginnings of human speech are anything but utilitarian: they are purposeless lalling-instincts, primitive aesthetic reactions.

The foregoing remarks depict the climate of speculation which surrounds the problem of how speech began. None of the older hypotheses is altogether satisfying, and even the recent ideas contributed by social anthropologists and communication-theorists are unconvincing. The 'rubicon' of our forebears still obtrudes itself, for we cannot escape the suspicion that some important and fundamental development may have taken place with the appearance of *homo sapiens*. This mysterious novel feature may well have been a qualitative rather than a quantitative change, and one which was abrupt; or at any rate as abrupt as the transition between the sub-hominid species and man.

Comparative psychology will no doubt eventually solve this problem, and sematicists might do better to focus their attention less upon the question of problem-solving in animals, and more upon the evolution of thinking in a wider sense.

It may well be that even neurology can contribute something to the topic of the development of speech, though up to now neglected by linguists. The clinician's intimate experience both of the dissolution and of the dysgenesis of speech, surely cannot be ignored indefinitely. Neurologists, as pathologists of language, know only too well how sensitive this essentially human faculty is to the effects of disease of the brain, and more particularly of the dominant half of the brain. This contrasts strikingly with the experience gleaned from comparative physiology, which shows that the vocalizations of animals including the highest primates, are relatively invulnerable, and cannot be silenced experimentally even by extensive ablations and resections of the cerebral cortex. This is yet another difference between the vocal behaviour of animals and man.

Pursuing further our speculations into pre-history, we may now turn from the origins of speech to the characters of man's first use of this unique endowment.

What manner of speech was utilized by early man? How would the first articulate utterances compare with the languages spoken today by civilized man? In attempting to make comparisons we must consider not only phonetic problems but also questions of syntax and of semantics. Any such pursuit is of course a purely speculative exercise, for experience obviously cannot be invoked and never will be. Discussion of the problem can never rank as a science, being little more than intelligent guess-work, aided by the use of analogy, of what is known about linguistic trends and modifications. In the first place there has been a dispute over the fundamental nature of speech in early man, that is to say whether it was an elaborate symbolic system, or, on the other hand, something primitive and immature. Langer said: . . . 'people who have not invented textiles, who live under roofs of pleated branches, need no privacy, and mind no filth, and roast their enemies for dinner, will yet converse over their bestial feasts in a tongue as grammatical as Greek and as fluent as French!' Certainly many philosophers envisaged that the *lingua adamica* was a truly 'perfect' one, implying thereby a rich vocabulary, a logical syntax, and a capacity for an extensive range of expression. Such a belief is rather too speculative, for an 'original' language must obviously have been one which was utterly devoid of etymological ancestry, and hence must have differed from all subsequent tongues of mankind. It is tempting to adopt an ethnological approach and to visualize an ancestral language bearing some analogies with 'primitive' tongues as they exist today, available for study. However, it is necessary for us to be clear in our minds as to what is meant by the expression 'contemporary primitive tongues'. We can of course only really discuss the tongues of primitive people, and not 'primitive tongues', for it may well prove that the speech of backward peoples is anything but primitive, in the sense of being simple in syntax, vocabulary and phonemic structure. Probably no such entity exists today as a 'primitive' tongue. We must therefore endeavour to be precise and we should separate our discussions of the tongues of early or

8

prehistoric man, from the tongues of contemporary but unsophisticated races. We might employ the term 'primeval speech' for the former; and for the latter, 'the speech of primitive people'. This nomenclature is clumsy, but it is more exact.

At this juncture we are once again faced with the problem of monogenesis versus polygenesis. Unless there is good anthropological evidence to suggest that *homo sapiens* first appeared within a strictly localized geographical *nidus*, it would be more reasonable to assume that the origins of language were diverse in place and possibly also in time. This idea would conform with our knowledge of the language-systems of primitive man. It is a familiar fact that inhabitants of adjacent villages may speak entirely different and unrelated tongues; and moreover that from one generation to the next a language may show remarkable alterations. This feature was emphasized by Monboddo, who instanced the Huron Indians, among whom in no two villages was the same language spoken. Indeed no two families within the same village spoke exactly the same tongue. Furthermore the Huron language underwent changes every day. The instability of language-systems within modern primitive communities suggests that in the past, parent-tongues were anything but fewer in number. This was an intrinsic tenet of Marr's Japhetic Theory which held the opinion that languages evolve, not by the splitting up of an ancestral tongue, but by the fusion of a number of unrelated ones. Hence in the past there must have been many more languages than now, and not fewer.

The topic naturally leads to the enigmatic question as to whether there is any fundamental bond between the purely linguistic characters of a language and the psychological traits of the people who use the language. In other words, does the language of a community mirror the racial idiosyncracies, and peculiarities of thought, mood and behaviour of the speakers? Agreement is still lacking. Writers like Byrne, von Humboldt, Bonfante, Jenisch, Marr, Sapir and Whorf on the one hand believed that a true correlation existed between racial singularities in thought and in language. Some indeed refer to the Sapir-Whorf 'principle of linguistic relativity' in this connection. According to Whorf, users of markedly different grammars are pointed by their grammars towards different types of observation, and different evaluations of extremely similar acts of observation. Hence they are not equivalent as observers, but must arrive at somewhat discordant views concerning the world. Whorf, who studied minutely the North American Indians and the Aztecs, stressed that their languages were anything but simple; that they were highly abstract; and that they were not founded upon the subject-predicate system common to S.A.E. (Standard Average European). Obviously there is scope for a special study of what might be called 'contrasting linguistics' which would deal with the antithesis between various tongues as regards their grammar and their logic. Other writers, however, have looked upon the complicated and unfamiliar types of syntax used by races outside the S.A.E. *bloc* as indicating no differing modalities in thinking, but merely an idiosyncratic use of metaphor.

Two centuries ago there was much debate as to the semantic nature of man's original speech, especially with regard to the priority of general ideas as opposed to particulars. According to Adam Smith the first words were nouns, which were used to stand for or apply to an object directly in view (e.g. tree, rock, man). Here then was the expression of a concrete type of thinking. At first there was no attempt to make this particular substantive apply to the other representatives of the same class, each of which would perhaps be endowed with some specific or individual term of modification. Hence to begin with there was an apparent superfluity of near-synonyms. Later appeared the humble beginnings of abstraction, as witnessed by the use of adjectives used to qualify or describe each individual substantive (e.g. green tree, large rock, strong man). This brought about a reduction in the number of nouns; the emergence of class-names; and later still of abstractions indicating the quality expressed by the adjectives (e.g. green-ness, magnitude, strength). Adam Smith's views were criticized by Archbishop Magee and by Leibniz among others, with Hamilton taking up a compromise viewpoint. Hamilton, for example, said that our developing language, like our knowledge, proceeded from that which was vague and confused to ideas which were determinate or distinct. Turning to an ontogenetic analogy, he proclaimed that at first language expressed neither the precisely general, nor the determinately individual, but only the tenuous and amorphous. Out of this, the universal is elaborated by generification, and the particular and singular by specification and individualization. So arose the classical problem of the *primum cognitum* and the *primum appellatum*. Dugald Stewart sought to explain why there should have been so much difference in opinion between such distinguished philosophers, wondering whether Leibniz had not perhaps misunderstood the term 'appellative' and had mistakenly aligned it with 'descriptive'. Müller also strove to harmonize the apparently diametrically opposite views of Adam Smith and of Leibniz. He believed, like the former, that each first name was applied to an object immediately in view, e.g. a cave. But to employ such a term, Müller agreed with Leibniz that the idea of hollowness or inwardness must have already been present, determining the choice of words. All nouns, said Müller, originally expressed merely one out of the many attributes of a thing, and such an attribute must of necessity have been a general idea. The first thing really known, the *primum cognitum* is the general. It is through it that we know individual objects and afterwards endow them with names. Later still these individual objects, now known and named, become again the representatives of whole classes, and their names and proper names become promoted to appellatives. This possession of general ideas is the hallmark of man as opposed to brutes. Whitney too made a rather similar point. It is incorrect, he said, to confuse the *primum cognitum* with the *primum appellatum* (or *denominatum*). The concepts first recognized and identified were unquestionably concrete in character. Such indeed is the case with animals. But such cognitions do not constitute, or even lead to, language. Language begins with analysis and the apprehension of characteristic qualities. The *prima appellata* were therefore expressions of quality or property; or in other words they were abstract in nature. Whitney and Adam Smith were consequently in disagreement over the nature of the *primum cognitum*, but not over the semantic nature of the earliest words employed by man.

The notional speech of early man may also be subjected to a content-analysis aimed at studying the articulate utterances from a functional standpoint. The terminology of this approach has varied since the time of Protagoras, who classified speech into prayer, question, answer and command. Nowadays one may speak of transitive versus intransitive speech. Buehler's tri-functional theory of language occupies an intermediate place. All who have given thought to this particular topic consider that questions (or interrogative utterances) materialize rather late in the development of language, and consequently might have featured only rarely in the speech of early man.

Another hallmark of sophistication or maturity in the use of speech, is the discriminating employment of silence as a communicative act. Allied to this paradoxical activity of silence, is the use of language as a purposeful means of concealing, rather than communicating, ideas or feelings. These two practices, deliberate silence and studied duplicity, are unlikely to have played an important role in the speech of early man. Nevertheless the beginnings of these practices can be descried in the magical use of words, and more particularly in the phenomenon of verbal taboo. Being important features of the speech of contemporary primitives, by analogy it would seem likely that they were also conspicuous in the case of early man.

Malinowski drew attention to another characteristic of the speech-habits of primitive communities. Among uncivilized peoples, speech scarcely serves as a medium for profound reflective thought. The same is probably true for the remote past. Early man, like the modern savage, may well have talked a lot, though having little to say. For him speech was not much more than an aspect of social comportment, a manifestation of gregariousness. Small-talk, chatter or gossip played an important role. Two conversationalists would probably talk loudly, rapidly and furthermore, simultaneously. This habit of platitudinous garrulousness was referred to by Malinowski under the term 'phatic communion'.

From the experience of ethnology, we may also suspect that the language of early man was comparatively rich in the use of metaphor. The prosodic properties of his speech were likely to have been conspicuous, leading to a certain melodious or sing-song quality. Finally, early man might be expected to have utilized very freely gesture and pantomime in order to eke out his store of available symbols.

Turning from semantic to syntactical considerations about the early speech of man, we may take up the question of the proportion of root-forms to elaborations thereof. The idea that the original language of man consisted mainly of a handful of roots, has often been mooted. This constitutes the linguistic doctrine of 'oligosynthesis'. For example, Murray believed that all languages were derived from no more than nine primitive roots. Presumably the further one delved into linguistic ancestry, the greater would appear the importance of root-forms, but whether this is actually demonstrable is uncertain. Schmidt went further and taught that all Greek words were derived from the arch-radical *E*, and all Latin words from *HI*. Not so long ago an independent attitude was adopted in Soviet Russia, where Academician J. Y. Marr promulgated his 'theory of the four elements'. Marr believed that all spoken languages were elaborations of four basic phonetic combinations, namely, *sal*, *ber*, *yon*, and *rosh*. This doctrine was sternly repudiated by Stalin in 1950, who converted it overnight from a dogma into a heresy. According to Stalin 'Marr got himself into a muddle and got linguistics into a muddle'. But a similar fate befell Stalin and today the status of Marr and his hypothesis remains obscure.

A characteristic of the speech of contemporary primitive persons lies in an unconscionable length of the words in use. This feature had also been noted by Monboddo who ascribed it to an ancestral origin in natural cries, all of which have a certain tract or extension, as heard in the lowing of an ox or the neighing of a horse. He found yet another explanation for the complexity of the words in primitive tongues: namely a paucity of consonants with a relatively high proportion of vowels. Consequently one monosyllabic word could not readily be distinguished from another.

Whether this is a valid argument is debatable, especially on the analogy of the modern Hawaiian language. Grimm also believed that the earliest consonants were relatively few in number and that even the vowels were confined to 'a' 'i' and 'u'. Certainly the proportion of quinqui- and sesquipedalia in the spoken tongues of barbaric peoples appears high, and we recall the Botocudo term for 'ocean', namely *ouatouiijipakiijouououououo*. This belief of Monboddo's is of course arguable. What is ordinarily regarded as a polysyllabic word may, in the absence of a written language, be nothing more than a chain of monosyllabic items. Inadequate lexicalization may bring about an impression of unity, by dispensing with those intervals which would have been expressed in writing by way of hyphens or punctuation marks. Grimm, it may be remembered, also believed that of man's earliest speech, all words were monosyllables.

Grammatical construction was probably more elaborate and complicated in the speech of prehistoric man, just as in the speech of so many contemporary primitive peoples. Following Bonfante, some of the grammatical changes may be enumerated as characterizing linguistic evolution: (1) loss of dual number; (2) creation of definite and indefinite articles; (3) introduction of tenses; (4) creation of a passive; (5) elimination of irregular forms; (6) loss of the nominal and verbal flexions; (7) elimination of gender, and (8) transition from a synthetic to an analytic type of grammar. Reference may also be made to the highly complex and seemingly artificial use of 'concord', which characterizes the sentences in the Bantu languages.

Word-order was perhaps fortuitous and unimportant in early speech, as contrasted with the rigidity which occurs in highly evolved tongues with a relatively simpler syntax.

Just as animal cries are virtually incapable of phonetic or phonemic transcription, so the languages of early man like those of contemporary uncivilized peoples were probably bizarre, involved and unorthodox in their acoustic properties, by our standards. Whereas spoken English comprises a mere 40 phonemes, some tongues of primitive communities can probably claim many more (and not fewer, as might perhaps have been surmised). They include phonemes which are alien to the Indo-European group of languages. Among the unusual phonetic features of some 'uncivilized' languages we can enumerate the Bantu clicks, and also the plosives frequent in African dialects. Then there are various ejectives, flaps and lingual rolls. This change in phonemic characterization ties up with what Jean Baudounin de Courtenay called a 'universal and progressive humanization of language'; that is to say a tendency towards the elimination of 'innermost articulations' in the course of evolution with a shift from gutturals towards labials and dentals.

Mention has already been made of the absence of tenses in verbs employed in the tongues of the inhabitants of underdeveloped countries. This is an important point, one which has semantic repercussions, if an analogy with the speech of early man is justified. The existence of special verbal forms to indicate past and future time can be taken as evidence of an increasing power of symbolization, and also a time-binding faculty. These are essentially human features, being quite foreign to animal-communication, however rich its pseudo-vocabulary or repertoire of sounds.

Special mention should be made of the employment in some languages of a multitude of terms for numerals. Suggestive of a bias towards concrete as opposed to abstract thinking, it might be expected that this grammatical feature was also present in the speech of early man. Even in such a highly advanced language as Japanese there are special numeral classifiers which vary according to the type of substantive qualified, and these are placed between the number and the noun. Thus the particle *hon* refers to any round or cylindrical object; *mai* refers to flat objects, *nin* to persons, *wa* to birds, *hiki* to animals, *soku* to boots, shoes and socks; *fuku* to sips of liquid; *dai* to vehicles, and *satsu* to books. Even in early English, a similar multiplicity of words was used instead of a simple generic term to denote 'many', the precise term differing according to the species, like an 'exaltation of larks'. According to Dame Julia Berners (1486), one should always speak of a

> congregation of people, a hoost of men, a felyshyppynge of yomen and a bevy of ladyes; we must also speak of a herd of herts, swannys, cranys or wrennys; a sege of herons or bytourys, a muster of peacockys, a watche of nyghtyngalys, a flyght of doves, a claterynge of choughes, a pryde of lyons, a slewthe of beerys, a gaggle of geys, a skulke of foxes, a schulle of frerys, a póntifýcalyte of prelates, a bomynable syght of monkes, a dronkenshyp of goblers and so on. Similarly game is not carved at mealtimes, for a dere is broken, a gose reryd, chekyn frusshed, a cony unlacyed, a crane dysplayed, a curlewe unioyntyd, a quayle wyndgyd, a swanne lyfted, a lamb sholderyd, a heron dysmembryd, a pecocke dysfygured, a samon shynyd, a hadoke syded, a sole loynyd and a breme splayed.

Yet another topic for discussion is the order of appearance of the various units of grammar within the earliest tongues. Herder believed that the first parts of speech were the verbs, from which much later, nouns were derived. Thus he conceived that the original term for 'sheep' was 'the bleater'. Adam Smith, Monboddo, and Dugald Stewart thought differently and ascribed priority to nouns over verbs.

Space forbids one to probe deeper into the controversies over the origins of human speech, even though other approaches to the subject are still unexplored. For example, it would be tempting to discuss the palaeo-morphological attempts to determine the stage in evolution where primitive man first began to 'speak'—in the strict sense of the word. The evidence is indirect, even flimsy; and it is based upon such clues as endocranial markings indicative of the convolutional patterning of the brain; and the anatomical signs suggesting the dawn of cerebral dominance and unimanual preference. These problems will be discussed later. Such inquiries are intriguing rather than critical, for some of the data savour more of guess-work than scientific deduction. Then, too, there is the weighty problem in natural history which as yet we have merely touched upon, concerning the nature of vocalization in animals, and the propriety of using the terms animal 'language' or 'communication'. One soon finds that the methods of observation are not enough, for the problem transcends biology and invades the domains of philosophy and of animal psychology.

We must therefore sum up with the verdict that as yet no wholly satisfactory answer to the riddle of the origins of language has been made. Maybe the answer will always elude us. Perhaps that is why, even in 1866, the *Société de Linguistique de Paris* expressly laid down in their ordinances that they would permit no papers dealing with the creation of an artificial language, and no discussion whatsoever on the topic of the origins of speech.

As was so neatly said by Suzanne Langer—that *rara avis* among women, a wit as well as philosopher '. . . the problem of linguistic origins is so baffling that it is no longer considered respectable'.

X. THE EVOLUTION OF MAN'S CAPACITY FOR LANGUAGE

. . . If you finally succeed in proving that all languages have been developed from a common root, you will indeed have effected a most valuable piece of work. . . .
Letter written by Charles Darwin 29th December, 1877, to an unknown correspondent.

The spate of criticism which followed the publication of the *Origin of Species* just over a hundred years ago often included the protest that Darwin in his arguments, had ignored man's higher mental faculties. This was perhaps true in fact though captious in spirit. A more recent critic, Leslie Paul, wrote . . . 'There is therefore through the invention of speech the entry into and the exploration of a new dimension of human activity. I think it was rather provincial and dull-witted of Darwin not to have shown a glimmer of interest in all this'. Be that as it may, the gap was filled four years after Darwin by his geological colleague, Lyell, who devoted a chapter in his classical *Antiquity of Man* to a comparison between the origin and growth of languages and of species. Schleicher, who was a botanist as well as a professional philologist, had called attention three years before ever reading Darwin's book, to the struggle for existence among words, the disappearance of primitive forms, and the immense expansion and differentiation produced by ordinary causes in a single family of speech. He looked upon languages as natural organisms, which, according to definite physical influences, and independently of human will, take origin and mature, grow old and die, and therefore manifest the series of phenomena to which are given the name of 'life'. In 1863, Schleicher issued his pamphlet *Die Darwinsche Theorie und die Sprach-wissenschaft*, which was the expansion of a letter he had written to Professor Häckel acknowledging a copy of the *Origin of Species*. Therein he argued that the inception of species is notably paralleled in the genealogy of language, and particularly of the Aryan and Semitic tongues. Analogous with the struggle for life among the more or less favoured species in the animal and vegetable kingdoms, a struggle for survival occurs among individual languages.

This analogy between the evolution of species and of language was further discussed in contemporary scientific literature. F. W. Farrar (1870) believed that comparative philology supported Darwin's hypotheses in two important respects, viz. the effect of infinitesimal modifications in gradually bringing about the great changes; and the preservation of the best and strongest elements in the struggle for existence. Just as very many primordial cells closely resembling each other, may have been the earliest rudiments of all living organisms, so in philology, different linguistic families may have sprung from multitudes of

This chapter is based upon a paper read at the University of Chicago on the occasion of the centenary of the publication of Darwin's Origin of Species. It was published in . . . *Evolution after Darwin* 3 vols. Ed. Sol Tax. Univ. Chicago Press 1960.

'speech-cells' or 'sound-cells', that is, the fundamental roots of language. Like an extinct species, a language—once extinct—can never reappear. Intermediate linguistic forms also die out. Thus external factors disturb the primitive relationship of languages, and consequently one may find radically different languages existing side by side. 'All this, as every naturalist is well aware, represents a condition of things precisely similar to that which prevails in animated nature'.

Darwin's contemporary, Max Müller, who occupied the Chair of Comparative Philology at Oxford, was also interested in this parallelism between the struggle for existence in the biological sense and in the case of different languages. He laid stress on an important difference, however. It is not on account of inherent defects that languages gradually become extinct, but rather because of external causes; that is to say, the physical, moral and political weaknesses of those who speak the languages concerned. Müller considered that a much more pertinent linguistic analogy with Darwinism lay in the struggle for survival among words and grammatical forms which is constantly going on in every language, whereby shorter and easier forms gain the upper hand.

Views of this kind were of topical interest a century ago, but since then philologists, with the possible exception of Jespersen, have been largely out of sympathy with the application of Darwinian ideas to their own subject.

In 1871 Darwin himself dealt in some detail with the human faculties which he had rightly omitted from his earlier monograph, and in his *Descent of Man* the problem of speech was specifically discussed. The faculty of articulate speech, he wrote, in itself offers no insuperable objection to the belief that man had evolved from some lower form. The mental powers in some early progenitor of man must have been more highly developed than in any existing ape, before even the most imperfect form of speech could have come about. The continued advancement of this power would have reacted on the mind itself, by enabling and encouraging it to pursue long trains of thought. Complex reflection can no more be carried on without the aid of words, whether spoken or silent, than a long abstraction without the use of figures or algebra.

Darwinian theories and ideas pervaded every aspect of scientific and philosophic thought, and Max Müller was also caught up in the current excitement. Leaving aside his purely linguistic considerations, we may examine his views upon the evolution of the speech-faculties in man. After detailing *seriatim* the characters of mind and body which are shared by man and animal, he went on to enquire . . .

"Where, then, is the difference between brute and man? What is it that man can do, and of which we find no signs, no rudiments, in the whole brute world? I answer without hesitation: the one great barrier between the brute and man is *language*. Man speaks, and no brute has ever uttered a word. Language is our Rubicon, and no brute will dare to cross it. This is our matter-of-fact answer to those who speak of development, who think they discover the rudiments at least of all human faculties in apes, and who would fain keep open the possibility that man is only a more favoured beast, the triumphant conqueror in the primeval struggle for life. Language is something more palpable than a fold of the brain or an angle of the skull. It admits of no cavilling, and no process of natural selection will ever distill significant words out of the notes of birds or the cries of beasts" (1861).

Professor Müller's views were, on the whole, opposed to those of Darwin, and their differences of opinion were discussed at length by the German linguist Noiré. Strongly critical of 'Darwinian foibles, incompleteness and one-sidedness', Noiré (1879) proclaimed that Müller was the only equal, not to say superior, antagonist, who had entered the arena against Darwin. 'Here is reason, here language, here humanity. None shall pass here; none penetrate into the sanctuary who cannot tell me first how reason, how speech, was born. And the shouting bands of the assailants were struck dumb, for they could give no answer'.

Although Müller was, in the main, out of sympathy with Darwin, nevertheless he proclaimed in 1873: 'In language, I was a Darwinian before Darwin'. As long before as 1861 he had been trying to reconcile Darwin's doctrines with linguistic phenomena. He compared Darwin with Epicurus, and he spoke of the origins of language in terms of natural selection, or as he preferred to call it, natural elimination.

Any discussion of the evolution of man's capacity for language must entail an enquiry, not only into the appropriate intellectual equipment, but also into the basic anatomical substratum. This latter is a two-fold problem. In the first place there is the question whether any physiological cerebral mechanism exists, peculiar to man. The faculty of speech also requires certain peripheral instrumentalities, comprising a complex co-ordinated activity of the lips, palate, tongue, pharynx, larynx and respiratory apparatus. Herein lies the foundation for the achievement of an audible motor-skill of the utmost delicacy. In the course of both phylogeny and ontogeny it is often possible to observe that anatomical structures are present even before they are actually utilized. Structure, in other words, antedates function. Consequently, within the animal series it may be expected that both cerebral and peripheral mechanisms will stand ready for use, though not yet productive of mature speech.

Even in the anthropoid there is no valid morphological reason at a peripheral level, why speech should not occur. At any rate, most authorities would subscribe to this opinion. The relative coarseness of the tissues would no doubt impart a certain unmusical quality to the articulation, but the phonemic range would probably be not inconsiderable, and not very inferior to that in man. As Müller said, there is no letter of the alphabet which a parrot cannot learn to pronounce, and the fact that the parrot is without a language of its own must be due to a difference between the *mental*, and not the *physical* faculties of animal and man.

It must be stressed that language is an overlaid or even parasitic function. No specific cerebral structures exist which are peculiar to the faculty of speech. It would be scarcely possible, to decide merely from a study of the brain, however meticulous, whether the subject had been a polyglot, an orator, a writer, or even indeed an illiterate or a deaf-mute. Simply by microscopical examination of the cerebral cortex it would not be easy to distinguish gorilla from man. In other words, no specific human cerebral speech-centre can yet be confidently identified as an anatomical entity. Speech likewise makes use of predetermined bucco-laryngeal structures which were primarily destined to serve for acts of feeding and respiration. Certain teleological advantages accrued when the function of communication took over structures utilized for other purposes. Man did not develop *de novo* some entirely novel means for subserving the novel faculty of language. Linguistic precursors, anatomical, physiological, psychological and cultural, must obviously have existed in the sub-human animal series. In some creatures like bees, simple communicative acts operate by dint of global movements. In birds and primates, elaborate combinations of cries, intention movements, and pantomimic displays make up a primitive sign-making or communication. Some birds possess the faculty of mimicking human utterances in a plausible and even startling fashion, but this is a learned, artificial performance; their innate instinctive calls are crude, raucous, stereotyped; indeed, anything but human in quality.

We recall Buffon's speculation as to what would have happened if the ape had been endowed with the voice of a parrot, and its faculty of speech. The talking monkey would, he said, have struck dumb with astonishment the entire human race, and would have so confounded the philosopher that he would have been hard put to prove, in the face of all these human attributes, that the monkey was still an animal. It is therefore just as well for our understanding that nature has separated and relegated into two very different categories, the mimicry of speech and the mimicry of our gestures.

Koehler has asked why it is, that if there are so many precursors of our own language in the animal kingdom, no known animal speaks like man. It is because no animal possessed all those *initia* of our language at one and the same time. They are distributed diffusely, this species having one capacity, that species another. 'We alone possess all of them, and we are the only species using words'.

Perhaps the most obvious among the prerogatives of *homo sapiens* is the faculty of speech. The animal kingdom, not excluding the higher primates, is not so endowed, however vocal may be individual representatives. By contrast it can be asserted that no race of mankind is known, however lowly, which does not possess the power of speech. Nay more, as we have already discussed, the linguistic attainments may be subtle, complex, flexible and eloquent, even though the cultural level be primitive in the extreme. How difficult it is to identify among the races of man anything which can be justly termed a 'primitive' tongue.

At the very outset it is important to be clear in what way the cries, utterances, calls and song of birds and sub-human mammals be deemed as lying outside the category of language-attainment. On enquiry, it is found that no one touchstone of distinction is entailed, but rather a combination of factors, some of which may be present in this or that animal, but which do not come together in synthesis until the stage of *homo sapiens* is achieved.

Doubtless the most weighty single criterion of human speech is the use of symbols. Animals betray abrupt fluctuations in their emotional state by emitting sounds. To this extent they may be said to utilize signs. Whether the sign be perceived and identified as such by other members of the same species, is arguable. An alarm-call may act as a signal of danger, and others in earshot take flight. This effect would be an instance of directed signalling between one bird or mammal and another. Or, possibly, the frightened creature's cry may be interjectional rather than purposeful, and others within call may thereupon be made merely partners in alarm rather than the recipients of a directed message. Be that as it may, and the possibility of both types of concerted action occurring in nature cannot be gainsaid, the animal's cry cannot strictly be looked upon either as language or as speech. At most, it is communication. The communicative act may be deliberate, willed, directed encoding; while the comprehending recipients acting upon the signal may be looked upon as decoders. Here then is communication in the accepted sense of the term. Or it may be that the communicative act is merely incidental, and no true encoding and decoding can be said to take place. (See Chapter XI).

'Animal communication' is therefore the term which carries with it the fewest drawbacks. In essence it can be said to comprise a series of signs which refer to ideas or feelings within immediate awareness. They do not and cannot apply to circumstances within past or future time. Herein lies an all-important distinction. Man's utterances entail the use of symbols or 'signs of signs', and consequently they possess the superlative advantage of applying to events in time past, present and future; and to objects *in absentia*. As we have already mentioned, this endowment has been called the 'time binding' property of human language. It also possesses the merit of initiating a process of storage of experience, a process which eventually reaches fruition with the subsequent introduction of writing.

Most of the early arguments concerning the problem of the origin of speech in man have been either theological or linguistic. In the former case the doctrine of a divine creation was taken for granted, but many controversies arose, including such questions as monogenesis versus polygenesis. The purely linguistic theories rejected altogether the idea of a special creation of a mature system of language, and while some process of transition between the communication of animals and the beginnings of speech in *homo sapiens* was assumed, there was disagreement as to the *modus operandi*. The sources of argument included the relative importance of the role of imitation, of interjectional utterances, of associated motor-vocal phenomena, of gesture and still other factors, none of which nowadays excites serious comment or concern. These problems were discussed more fully in the previous chapter.

Attention became focussed more upon the mysterious evolutionary changes which are believed to have taken place between the behavioural systems of the highest primates, and those of earliest man. The beginnings of speech, in the strict sense of the term, rank among these changes. However striking in character, and however fundamental in importance, speech cannot be looked upon as man's sole perquisite, singling him out from the rest of the animal kingdom. Several other significant developments took place at more or less the same period of evolution, any one or any combination of which may actually prove to be telling in the genesis of speech.

The principal clash of opinion revolves around the debate whether the differences between animal communication and the speech of early man entail factors which are qualitative—or merely quantitative—that is of kind or merely of degree, as far as the communicative act is concerned.

Within that stage between the most complex of animal communication, and the speech-efforts of earliest man, lies the core of our problem, Obviously this transition from animal cries to human articulation is but an item in a much bolder scheme of evolution. Instinctive responses no longer prove biologically adequate, and more and more involved vocal reactions gradually emerge. Linguistics alone can never supply the whole solution, and other realms of thought and endeavour will need exploring.

Attempts which have been made to identify these important steps in the evolution of human language, fall roughly into two classes, namely sociological versus intellectual. The former envisages some modification in behaviour, the latter implies a change in the mode of thinking as between animals and man. These two attitudes are not mutually irreconcilable, for both types of change may well have operated together.

Many would agree in relating the ancestry of language to the prehominid stages while at the same time denying the existence of anything that can be strictly termed 'animal language'.

Révész spoke of 'contact reactions' as being important in the genesis of speech in man. By this expression he understood the basic innate tendency of social animals to approach one another, establish rapport, co-operate and communicate. Contact reactions are thus a necessary precondition of linguistic communication. In a rather unconvincing fashion, Révész seems to have equated the essential differences between human speech and the cries and directed calls of the animal world, with an elaboration in the domain of articulate utterance of this 'contact reaction'.

Much earlier, Lord Monboddo realized the critical role of communal existence. To convert man into a speaking animal, he believed the factor of society to be essential. He asked which was the more important: language for the institution of society, or society for the invention of language. In his view, society came first, and perhaps existed for ages before language developed; for man is by nature a political as well as a speaking animal.

Biologists realize that communal existence is an important factor in survival which can be traced throughout the animal kingdom, even in the lowliest species. (Espinas; Kropotkin). Indeed the physiological value of co-existence can perhaps be demonstrated better in the invertebrate *phyla*. It is demonstrable in protozoa and metazoa. Among the higher ranks of mammalia, there is perhaps a greater co-ordination of group-activity, whereby a limited degree of sharing of function and a deputing of special tasks increasingly becomes the rule. Allee has shrewdly asked at what stage can an animal-group be said to have become truly social: is it at the point when animals behave in the presence of others differently from how they would behave if alone? If this is the case then we witness in an interesting fashion the first hint of ethical or moral faculties in animal behaviour.

One of the principal functions of speech is to co-ordinate the behaviour of the individual members of the group. Grace de Laguna stressed how progressively elaborate is the communal life which synchronizes with the development of speech. Planned hunting forays; the need for securing safety by night; the indoctrination of the young—all these are among the activities of early *homo sapiens*, and they must have been considerably assisted by the faculty of speech. The power of speech thus confers an important survival-value upon its owner.

Allied to this notion is the role of an increasing utilization of tools as an immediate precursor of speech. *Homo sapiens* has often been identified not only with *homo loquens* but also with *homo faber*. An animal achieves its purposes by modifying its own bodily structure, that is by making a tool out of some part of itself. Man ventures further by making use of instruments outside of his own body. As L. S. Amery said '. . . Man also began to employ a "sound-tool"; that is to say, he made use of differentiated sounds as an instrument of precision, in order to indicate not only emotions, but also specific objects, qualities, actions and judgements'. Both language and tools are instruments which man alone employs to achieve definite and concrete actions. 'Language, like the tool, and unlike the limb, is something objective to, and independent of, the individual who uses it'. (de Laguna).

We now approach a critical point in the argument. The term *homo faber* is ambiguous, for it can be interpreted in two very different ways. It can be read as signifying either the 'tool-maker'; or the 'tool-user'. This distinction is important and is not to be glossed over. Mere tool-taking or tool-utilization is quite consistent with anthropoid behaviour; tool-making is not. The higher apes are not infrequently to be seen making use of a convenient stick as an implement with which to attain a delicacy within reach. But deliberately to choose a stick and set it carefully aside, against the contingency of finding at some possible later date an edible morsel just inaccessible, is outside the capacity of the anthropoid. To select an instrument and keep it for future use, can be reckoned as analogous to fashioning a tool out of sticks or stones to accomplish a need or desire. When the species can do such things, he steps over the frontier and qualifies as *homo sapiens*. Similarly in the most primitive communal groups of man's ancestors, a sharp stone, a stick, a shell, might have been picked up and used straightway as a weapon to fell an object of prey; or as a means of self-defence; or as a tool for de-corticating a tree-trunk, or skinning a beast. This sort of activity is consistent with primate behaviour, and speech-acquisition is unnecessary. But if the ape-like creature breaks a stick in two, or pulls it out of a bush; or if he puts it aside for another occasion, he is beginning his apprenticeship for qualifying as *homo sapiens*, and here the first beginnings of speech may be detected.

With the art of knapping of flint core-tools or flake-tools, or by shaving down a stake, we witness the unmistakable evidences of attainment of man's stature, and speech can doubtless be assumed as a concomitant. For here we have the earliest mastery over purely perceptual thinking; the dawn of conceptual thought; and a release from the shackles of time-present.

Closely linked with an elaborate communal life and the construction of tools, delegation of labour can also be reckoned as a factor in the ancestry of speech. Greater efficiency in hunting and in the acquisition and preparation of food for the group, follows upon the use of speech, and leads to the beginnings of a simple form of specialization. This was an aspect of linguistics which natural-ly appealed to Soviet writers. In Russia philosophers of language believed that language first appeared when man, a particular species of animal, began to use tools and to co-operate with others in order to produce the means of subsistence. Human labour is a novel form of social activity and gives rise to an unprecedented phenomenon—articulate speech—and to a new characteristic of the mind—the conscious reflection of objective reality. Stalin, himself a dabbler in linguistics, looked upon language not only as a tool of communication but also a means of struggle, and development of society. He connected language with man's productive activity and also with every other human activity. Seppe, a Russian neurologist, went further. Work appeared to him as a main factor in the development of higher and abstract thinking of man. Speech functions are created from work. Furthermore we find Stalin declaring . . . 'In the history of mankind, a spoken language has been one of the forces which helped human beings to emerge from the animal world, unite into communities, develop their faculty of thinking, organize social production, wage a successful struggle against the forces of nature, and attain the stage of progress we have today'. (*Pravda*, 2nd August, 1950).

Such were the progressive elaborations in animal behaviour which immediately antedated and perhaps accelerated the development of speech in man.

An alternative group of hypotheses puts the emphasis more upon the elaboration of certain methods of thinking, as bridging the gap between animal communication and human speech. Since Aristotle, many philosophers have stressed man's gift of conceptual thought, enabling him to deal with general ideas as well as the particular or the concrete. This unique power of coping with 'abstractions', 'universals', 'generalizations', has been associated with his endowment of speech. Geiger, a contemporary of Darwin, was one of the most eloquent advocates of conceptual thought as a human perquisite. In his *Ursprung der Sprache*, 1869, he wrote: 'It is easy to see that blood is red and milk is white; but to abstract the redness of blood from the collective impression, to find the same notion again in a red berry, and, in spite of its other differences, to include under the same head the red berry and the red blood—or the white milk and the white snow—this is something altogether different. No animal does this, for *this, and this only, is thinking*'. Noiré (1879) enquired how man's power of abstraction came about. He attributed it to man's manual dexterity coupled with his ingenuity. More than any other creature, man has the power of making a selection from objects around him and then modifying them to suit his own purposes. Thus he became master of his environment. He learned to create things, and these creations were for him the first 'things'. Such 'things' became endowed with independent existence, and from this point to the endowment of names for the things, was quite an easy step.

Terminology readily misleads, however. We now believe that the older, narrow views as to the essentially human nature of conceptual thinking are not warranted by the facts. As Darwin showed, it is not possible to deny that in some animals, as judged by their behaviour, indications of a kind of abstract thinking can at times be traced. Although perhaps an exceptional state of affairs, it occurs often enough to cast doubts upon any notion of a Rubicon separating brute beasts from man.

Let us recall the very beginnings of philology as a science, which can be said to date from 1772, when J. G. Herder wrote his essay on the Origin of Language. Herder rejected the doctrine that language was a divine creation, and also the idea that it might be a willed invention on the part of man. Nor did he believe that the difference between man and animals was one of degree. He considered that there had taken place in man as he emerged from the sub-human state a development of all of his powers in a totally different direction. This abrupt change led to the appearance of speech. Language sprang of necessity out of man's innermost nature. Herder likened the birth of language to the irresistible strivings of the mature embryo within the egg. In particular, man possessed a keener faculty of 'attention' than any other animal, and he was thereby enabled to seize hold of isolated impressions from out of a mass of detail surrounding him. In this way man became able to identify the most arresting feature within his environment. For example, as was quoted in the previous chapter, the distinguishing property of a lamb would be its vocalization; that is, its bleating. Thereafter the lamb would be recollected, and referred to, as a 'bleater'. So, according to Herder, primitive nouns stemmed from verbs (as indeed we know to be the case in the sign-language of the deaf-and-dumb).

Herder's theory, couched in somewhat different terms by Noiré, reappeared a century later. Over sixty years later, contemporary animal psychologists are stating this theory anew. Professor E. S. Russell has warned us not to assume that an animal's perceptual world would be like our own: on the contrary, as judging from its behaviour, we must conclude that every animal has its own private perceptual world, one which is very different from ours. Animals do not ordinarily perceive their environment in the same 'articulated' fashion as we do. They perceive things only as ill-distinguished parts of a general omneity. Isolated from its habitual context, an object may not be recognized for what it is. Animals respond only to perceptual complexes and not to simple and solitary stimuli.

We have already referred to the philologist Müller as in many ways an antagonist of Darwin. This would be to do an injustice to both writers, for, as we have earlier stated, in 1861 we find Müller aligning Darwin with Epicurus. The latter believed that primitive man's uncouth instinctive ejaculations were fundamental factors in the origins of language. In addition there must have been an important second stage—whereby agreement was made in associating certain words with certain conceptions. For the 'agreement' of Epicurus, Müller would offer his doctrine of natural selection, or natural elimination. The phenomenon of the origin of language would then be visualized as follows: sensuous impressions would produce a mental image or *perception*; a number of perceptions would bring about a general notion or *conception*. A number of sensuous impressions might also occasion a corresponding vocal expression, a cry, an interjection, or an imitation of the sound in question. A number of such vocal expressions might merge with one general expression, and leave behind the root as the sign belonging to a general notion. The gradual formation of roots out of natural cries or onomatopoeia is a product of relevant control. Rational selection is natural selection, not only in nature but also in thought and language. 'Not every random perception is raised to the dignity of a general notion, but only the constant recurring, the strongest, the most useful'. Of all the multitudinous general ideas, those and only those which are essential for carrying on the work of life, survive and receive definite phonetic expression.

Some of the nineteenth century philosophers who ranged themselves against Darwin, went on to associate the origins of language in man with the beginnings of religious belief. Thus Noiré regarded the rise of mythology as a necessary and highly important stage in the development of language. Again this is looked upon as the period during which objects began to mark themselves off from the indefiniteness of the thought-process, and began to form themselves into an independent existence.

Another way of looking upon the development of human speech out of animal vocalizations, is to regard speech as the utilization of symbols. The sounds emitted by animals belong to the category of signs, while man's speech is made up of symbols. Signs *indicate* things, while symbols *represent* them. Signs are announcers of events: symbols are their reminders. In other words symbols are not restricted to the confines of immediate time and place. As 'substitute' signs, symbols can refer to things out of sight and outside present experience. When an ape emits a cry of hunger it can be looked upon as perhaps making a declaration; perhaps an imperative utterance, or even an exclamation of discomfort. No ape, however, has in the natural environment, ever uttered the word 'banana', for such a word is a concrete symbol, a tool of thought which only man can employ, and he can do so in a variety of ways, irrespective of the barriers of time and space. Man can refer to a banana in past or future tense, as well as the present. Man can talk about a banana *in absentia*. No animal can do these things, the task being far beyond its system of thought and therefore of expression. Likewise no monkey can emit a word meaning 'hunger', for this term would constitute, or refer to, an abstract or universal idea.

In Pavlovian modes of thought the use of symbols is regarded as a hallmark of a man's cerebral function even though other terminologies are used. Pavlov believed that when the developing animal world reached the human stage an extremely important accession came about, namely the functioning of speech. This signified a new principle in cerebral activity. Sensations and ideas from the outer world constitute the first system of signals (concrete signals; signals of reality). Speech, however, constitutes a second set of signals—or 'signals of signals'. These make possible the formation of generalizations, which, in turn, constitute the higher type of thinking, specific for man.

Many writers view the origins of speech as merely part of a large developing faculty, namely the beginnings of symbolic behaviour. As Sapir put it, language is primarily a vocal actualization of the tendency to see reality symbolically, a virtue which renders it a fitting medium for communication. The problem, therefore, really resolves itself into a search for the earliest indications of symbolic behaviour as the immediate precursor of speech. S. Langer believed that these beginnings of symbolic thought can be detected when an animal, the highest of the primates in fact, behaves as if significance were being attached to certain objects or sounds. This attitude may be seen in the anthropoid in captivity in its pendant to some inanimate and favoured plaything, a piece of wood, a toy, a rag, or pebble. Here then we possibly discern the dawn of symbolic thought; and here too we may perhaps descry the remote ancestry of human speech. In other words the chimpanzee, although devoid of speech, begins to show a rudimentary capacity for speech, an opinion which reminds us of Müller's uneasy feeling that the gorilla is . . . 'behind us, close on our heels'.

The intriguing question naturally arises, as to where in the evolution of primitive man, did speech, in the strictest sense of the word, first make its appearance. When did the ululations of the anthropoids give way to the use of verbal symbols, disciplined by phonetic and syntactical rules? Obviously it is impossible, nor is it ever likely to be possible, to answer this question with confidence. The evidence, such as it is, is exiguous, insubstantial and oblique. But speculation on this interesting matter is quite permissible.

Anthropological data are all important here. They comprise arguments which are of a cultural order, and which discriminate clearly between anthropoid and human communities. They also include the weighty evidence which lies within the domain of comparative anatomy. Here are to be found the impressive distinctions between ape and man, in respect of the crania, and the problems which arise from a study of the fossil skulls of man's immediate ancestors. Here too are marshalled the anatomical features in the crania which are to be regarded as specific for *homo sapiens*. The size of the cranial cavity will naturally indicate brain-volume. This is an important point in that ordinarily the human brain differs from anthropoid brain in its greater size, while the cranial capacity of prehistoric man occupies an intermediate position. But the rule is not determinate: one or two prehistoric specimens are characterized by megalencephaly. More valuable than sheer size is the question of the shape and proportions of the cranial cavity. In addition, the endocranial markings may be taken as a possible index of the convolutional pattern of the cerebral hemisphere. In assigning a fossil specimen to its evolutionary rank, the development of such specifically 'human' areas of the brain as the frontal lobes and the parietal eminences are all-important.

Obviously there are clues which should be followed when discussing the problem of when in prehistory man developed speech.

L. S. Palmer, a dental surgeon as well as palaeontologist, approached the question of the acquisition of speech in man from a somewhat unusual angle. He distinguished between human speech and animal noises, the former being regarded as being effected by delicate and deliberate variation in the size and shape of the oral cavity. The power of articulation as exemplified in human beings depends, he believed, upon a specific morphology of the jaws, and here man differs in an important manner from the ape. In man the two rami of the mandibles are splayed apart; whereas in apes they are parallel in alignment. There results a difference in the shape of the posterior ends of the mandibles as well as a wider span between the condyles at the upper ends of the rami. Consequently in man there is ample space for the free movement of the tongue, so facilitating articulate speech. Another difference between the jaws of apes and men consists in the presence of a bony ledge connecting the anterior ends of the mandibles in apes. This 'simian shelf' serves as an attachment for the genio-glossus muscles. The range of lingual movement is rather restricted. In man, however, the tongue-muscles are attached to a number of small genial tubercles, which, taking up but little room, permit freer movement of the tongue within a broader intermandibular space.

Palmer furthermore associated himself with L. A. White in believing that there was an important connection in pre-history between favourable climatic factors and cultural acceleration, which would naturally incorporate the origin of the faculty of speech. Palmer set out the chain of causes as follows:

> A rigorous ameliorating climate→appropriate gene mutation→expansion of the skull→development of brain→increased mental ability→development of articulate speech and the introduction of written words.

Thus we can surmise with some confidence that Cro-Magnon man must have been endowed with speech, even though no real evidence exists that written language was ever in use at that period. The refinement of the skeletal structure and the large cranial capacity point to a quite highly evolved type of *homo sapiens*. But the weightiest arguments are of a cultural order. The skillful cave-paintings of the Aurignacian, Solutrean, and Magdalenian periods obviously must have been perpetrated by individuals endowed with symbolic and conceptual thinking. The frequency with which hand-prints occur on the cavern walls, just as in the architecture of the Mayas, may also be taken as suggestive of individual personal awareness. Furthermore the relative preponderance of left hands over right at El Castillo (4 to 1) must indicate that cerebral dominance obtained at that period. Perhaps too, the appearance of obscure linear markings—red blobs and dots—adjacent to these hand-prints may be looked upon as the very first modest indications of written communication. In addition, the fashioning of elaborate tools, the use of fire and of clothing; the evidence of ceremonial burials, and of religious or magical practices, cannot be reconciled with a speechless state. Even that negroid variant of Cro-Magnon civilization known as the Grimaldi man, as well as the Eskimo-like Chancelate man cannot be regarded as exceptions to these arguments.

Such fragmentary clues take the story of language back to the last Ice Age of late palaeolithic times, that is to say, between 25,000 and 10,000 years B.C.

Can language be assumed in even earlier man? European *Homo Neanderthalensis* (or *Mousteriensis*) constitutes a less straightforward problem. Some anatomists are tempted to explain some of

9

the contradictory characteristics of Neanderthal skulls by suggesting that they were out on a side-line, away from the main stream of evolution. Thus the anthropoid characters of the supraciliary and occipital ridges; the massive jaw; the wide orbits and nasal apertures, contrast with the large cranial capacity which actually exceeds that of average modern man. The African Neander-thaloids including the *Homo Rhodesiensis*, and the *Homo Soloensis* of Java, present essentially the same problem.

A. Keith believed that the faculty of speech could be traced back as far as Neanderthal man, but no further. His evidence was wholly anatomical, and not very convincing. The left hemisphere was apparently more massive than the right, suggesting cerebral dominance. Tilney also believed that Neanderthal man possessed linguistic capabilities not far below the standard of *homo sapiens*. His conclusion was based upon the depth of the parietal fossae in the skulls, indicative of a well developed 'auditory area', i.e. the abutment of the parietal lobe upon the outer occipital and upper temporal lobes. This postero-inferior part of the parietal lobe is commonly regarded as a specific human perquisite. Palmer, however, was impressed by the poor temporal lobe development in the brain of Rhodesian man and he doubted very much whether this specimen of *Hominidae* ever could speak.

Cultural evidence is more convincing than the morphological. The co-existence of eoliths like sharpened flints and arrow-heads, and signs of the use of fire and the practice of cooking, all denote that Neanderthal man possessed a degree of conceptual and symbolic thinking compatible with language, just as in the case of Cro-Magnon man. If this argument be admitted, then the story of language can be taken back to about 50,000 years B.C., that is to the post-Acheulian palaeolithic period, or the last glacial era.

In the early and middle pleistocene periods, the hominid representatives were exemplified by *Pithecanthropus pekinensis* (*erectus*), or *Sinanthropus*; by *Homo heidelbergensis*; and perhaps also by *Ternifine* man. Possibly too the Swanscombe and the Steinheim skulls belong here, though admittedly they may represent a type intermediate between *Pithecanthropus* and *homo sapiens*. Later specimens belonging to this same period include the skulls associated with Ehringsdorf, Fonte-chevade, Florisbad, Krapina and Mount Carmel.

According to Tilney the left frontal area of the brain in these specimens was larger than the right, suggesting a left cerebral dominance. He also pointed out the development of the inferior frontal convolutions, a feature which led him to believe that *Pithecanthropus* could speak, though asserting . . . 'doubtless the linguistic attainments were extremely crude'. What Tilney implied by this statement is obscure, for present-day linguistics does not recognize any language-system which can be designated as 'extremely crude', even among the most uncultured communities.

Upon other grounds too there is evidence that speech was an endowment of *Pithecanthropus*. Alongside the human remains, implements of quartz have been found in the caves, obviously fabricated with some skill. There is also evidence that *Pithecanthropus* knew how to kindle fire and that he began to cook. Again it is almost useless to conjecture what manner of speech was employed by *Pithecanthropus*. Oakley was merely guessing when he surmised that the earliest mode of expression of ideas was perhaps by gesticulation, with movements of mouth and hands, accompanied by cries and grunts to attract attention.

From such *prima facie* palaeontological clues, we can refer the faculty of speech to a period at least as distant as 100,000 years B.C. that is the middle Pleistocene period. On the evidence of the Javanese and Chinese skulls (P. *soloensis and pekinensis*) the date might even be relegated as far back as the early Pleistocene era, that is perhaps 500,000 years B.C.

Few would venture to trace the pioneers of speech to any more remote period. There arises for serious discussion, however, an interesting series of fossil skulls found in South Africa, small in size and interesting in morphology. These represent an extinct series of pygmy man-apes, originally called the fossil Taung's ape, but more often nowadays as *Australopithecus*. Where these specimens rightly belong is debatable, Le Gros Clark regarding them as exceedingly primitive representatives of the family which includes both modern and extinct types of man. Leakey called them 'near-men'. There is no sure evidence that such creatures fabricated tools; consequently it is unlikely that the *Australopithecus* can be assigned to the genus *homo faber vel sapiens*, and that it was capable of speech. The recent findings of a number of crude stone implements in proximity to the bones, and the associated fractured skulls of the fossil bones, makes it possible that *Australopithecus* utilized stones as weapons even though it did not, strictly speaking, manufacture weapons.

Palmer believed, however, that *Australopithecus* was perhaps endowed with speech, basing his opinion upon the anatomical characteristics of the mandible. The absence of a simian shelf and of diastema (or gap between the incisor and the canine), and the convergence-angle of the teeth, are all features which correspond with a hominoid morphological pattern. Whether these features suffice to militate against such arguments as the small crania and the lack of sure evidence of tool-making, is doubtful.

It has been suggested that *Australopithecus* possessed the ability to make fire. If this is really the case it should be taken as an additional piece of evidence to suggest that speech might have been within its capacity. But recently the so-called embers have been identified with mere fragments of manganese. Obviously the answer to the question waits upon the production of further findings.

The date of *Australopithecus* is remote indeed; probably beyond the earliest pleistocene era, and towards the end of the pliocene. This means anything from one to fifteen million years B.C.

Australopithecus has however been regarded by Leakey and other anthropologists as lying on a side limb rather than the main stem of human development. Leakey has identified the missing link between proconsul and *Pithecanthropus* in the South African *Zinjanthropus Boisei* (the 'nutcracker man'). The proximity of crude manufactured tools would seem to relegate this creature to the rank of a remote ancestor of man, and the conformation of the hard palate is certainly consistent with the power of articulate utterance.

There is one aspect about the beginnings of speech in man which is only too often completely overlooked. Was speech a consistent and uniform endowment in the case of early man? When man first appeared on the earth in the middle and late pleistocene periods, perhaps only *some* of the newly evolved *homo sapiens* were capable of speech. In those remote times speech might have constituted an exceptional phenomenon or aptitude, one which was within the competency of only a few highly favoured individuals.

Again, in the case of hand-skills, maybe only comparatively few members of *Pithecanthropus* were able to fashion arrow-heads or flints, this capacity being a rare and no doubt highly prized accomplishment. Such a facility in handicrafts might perhaps have correlated closely with the faculty of speech. Especially gifted members of the community such as these probably also had an expectation of life above the average, and the faculty of speech combined with the art of tool-making may well have had considerable survival-value.

On re-reading these remarks, it appears that perhaps insufficient attention has been paid to the difficulties inherent in a purely Darwinian conception of the origin of language.

It was implicit in this particular hypothesis as to evolution, that differences between human and animal structure and function are matters of degree. Were this principle to be firmly established, then it would be difficult to avoid the idea that animal communication leads by insensible gradation to the faculty of speech in man. There are numerous linguistic objections to this view, however. It is important to realize moreover that language does not stand alone in this matter, and that there are other weighty considerations which lead to the well-nigh inescapable conclusion that some potent qualitative change occurs at a point somewhere between the anthropoid and *homo sapiens*.

As we shall see in the next chapter, animals may possess a limited store of vocal sounds, which are innate, instinctive, or 'natural', emitted under appropriate circumstances. Though they may happen to possess communicative effects in respect to other animals of the same species, these cries are not necessarily always communicative in intent. Ordinarily the adolescent animal does not increase its vocabulary of sounds, except in one or two strictly delimited circumstances where the vocal repertoire may be extended. Thus some animals in states of domestication may amplify their stock of cries and calls. Certain birds may elaborate their performance by dint of imitation. In this way the innate and instinctive bird-song or call is overlaid by way of learning from other birds, not necessarily of the same species. Finally, some animals, particularly a small group of birds and a few higher apes in captivity, may be taught to mimic human articulate speech, the specific cries of quadrupeds, or even inanimate noises.

The foregoing recounts the sum-total of achievement in the domain of animal sounds. Between these and human articulate speech lies a very considerable gulf. Even in the case of the most un-tutored, primitive and savage human communities, the language-system is so far removed in its complexity from the crude and simple utterances of the sagest of the primates, as to be scarcely comparable. And nowhere and at no time has there been any hint of an approximation between these two extremes. No 'missing link' between animal and human communication has yet been identified.

Can it be, therefore, that a veritable rubicon does after all exist between animals and man as Professor Müller insisted? Was a new factor abruptly introduced into the evolutionary stream at some point between the *Hominoidea* and the *Hominidea*, which we may regard as constituting a true 'barrier'? Can it be that Darwin was in error when he envisaged the differences between man and animals as differences merely in degree?

The lessons gained from comparative linguistics would certainly suggest that there are serious qualitative differences which interposed themselves at a late stage in evolution. It has been objected that the contrasting of differences in kind and in degree is in itself an outmoded attitude. Such argument is not easy to follow, and it is still tempting to doubt whether anything like a smooth gradation has occurred. Outside the domain of language there are other human endowments which are not readily within the animal series. These scarcely pertain to our present subject-matter, unless it can be shown that their very existence depends upon the presence of a language-system. Here, for example, may be placed the advent in man of what we might loosely term the various moral faculties. Darwin was not oblivious of this problem, believing that a moral sense had been evolved from pre-human ancestors. This aspect of evolution was not mediated by a process of natural selection, however, but arose from man's newly acquired power of reasoning. So then it is a mechanism of evolution outside of the ordinary natural selection. When early man became endowed with reason and when to that mental accomplishment was added the power of speech, then the way lay open for the operation of conscious purpose (de Beer), or the psychosocial factor (J. Huxley). In this way there develops, again indirectly out of the beginnings of language, the beginnings of choice as to conduct. This also implies the power of doing harm as well as the power of doing good. So arise ethical and altruistic considerations. The earlier stages of these aspects of behaviour can be visualized in the animal kingdom in the instinct of maternal solicitude. This instinct was restricted, be it noted, both in time and place. With the achievement of adult-hood, the young animal would no longer receive maternal solicitude. The instinct too was limited to the immediate family-group. Altruism extended from beyond the family-circle to the clan only with the attainment of human status; and thence with the growth of social conscience it expanded to embrace the tribe and eventually the nation. This act of stepping outside the strict family-circle, may doubtless be assisted, if not mediated, by the faculty of language.

XI. THE NATURE OF ANIMAL COMMUNICATION AND ITS RELATION TO LANGUAGE IN MAN

Man has great power of speech, but the greater part thereof is empty and deceitful. The animals have little, but that little is useful and true; and better is a small and certain thing than a great falsehood.

Leonardo da Vinci

By his zealous and inspired investigations John Hunter added enormously to the contemporary knowledge of mammalian anatomy and physiology. As a pioneer of natural history he crowded into his lifetime an amazing amount of research upon comparative structure and function. Perhaps even more fundamental problems exercised his imagination at times. What essential differences distinguish man from animals? Which faculties represent veritable human perquisites? These are among the questions which would surely have intrigued him and over which he must have often pondered. One aspect of these problems concerns language. Hunter could not have remained neutral in the controversies as to whether language is a prerogative of man. Is there a linguistic impediment which sharply divides the brute beasts from man? Or is it possible to look upon the repertoire of animal cries as a kind of language, however lowly? That Hunter was not altogether too pre-occupied with other matters to attend to such speculative topics in biology, is shown by his short personal contribution entitled *The Voice of Bees*. He observed that a bee makes one kind of sound in flight, another when about to attack, and another still when teased. He also noticed that in the evenings before they swarm bees make a kind of ringing noise, like a small trumpet. Though such remarks would be criticized by most linguists today, there has recently been some re-awakening of interest in the possible role of the humming of bees as indices of food at a distance outside the hive.

Hunter was of course conversant with the opinions of natural historians who had preceded him. Although neither a bookish man, nor a classicist, he probably knew that Aristotle assumed animals to be capable of speech of a sort, though differing in nature from human tongues. Only man has the power of uttering words, while some animals are endowed with 'voice'. On account of this difference man alone among animals is apt to show hesitation in speech or even to become dumb, hesitancy of speech or *ischaophonos* implying a failure to explain one's meaning adequately.

This section is based first of all upon the Hunterian Oration delivered at the Mansion House, London, on 17th February, 1958; and secondly on the Israel Wechsler Lecture, delivered in 1960 at the Mount Sinai Hospital, New York. The former was published in the Transactions of the Hunterian Society (London) for 1958–59, and the latter in the Journal of the Mount Sinai Hospital, 1961. **28**, 252–267.

The brief references to this topic made by Plato, and by Galen, were probably well known to him. Lucretius, he knew, believed that dumb animals utter different cries under the stress of different emotions. Possibly Hunter was also familiar with Leonardo da Vinci's manuscript entitled *Man, animals, and speech*.

From his older colleagues, Hunter must have heard about that eccentric amateur of science and of philosophy, Sir Kenelm Digby, whose monograph *Of bodies, and of man's soul*, published in 1644, may well have found a place in his library at Earls Court. Hunter might also have owned a copy of Sibscota's pamphlet on the speech of animals which was printed in 1770. Possibly he had dealings with Father Bougeant, that Jesuit priest whose monograph *A Philosophical amusement upon the Language of Beasts* (1739) led to his being thrown into jail. It was not until three years after Hunter's death that *The Dictionary of Animal Language* was compiled by Claude Charles Pierquin de Gemblout, but of course Hunter may well have been aware of the author's intentions.

Mindful of these considerations we may proceed to a brief descriptive account of the sounds in nature for which the animal kingdom is responsible. One has been at pains deliberately to avoid the expressions animal 'speech' or animal 'language' until the matter has been considered more closely. The less significant term animal 'communication' has been chosen though even this word may imply more than is perhaps justified. From description one will pass to a discussion of the nature and purpose of these sounds: their claims to be considered as linguistic in nature; and their possible bearing upon the origins of language in man.

Insects

Noises evoked by insects appear to us monotonous and repetitive. Their uniformity in pitch and in tone-quality must be noted, as well as the apparent absence of anything like reciprocation. It may be objected that, as some insect-sounds are supersonic, the human ear is not a suitable indicator of their acoustic properties. That is true, but various electrical methods can be used, including sound-spectrography, so that the physical properties of insect-song can be analysed. The differences in the time-distribution of pulses of sound can be shown. Some of the frequencies may be extremely high, even up to 50,000 vibrations per second, illustrating the tremendous *tempo* of insect metabolism.

The production of sound by insects is effected in a manner quite different from the bellows-and-reed system which obtains throughout the majority of the animal kingdom. Most insects employ a process of 'stridulation', whereby two serrated portions of the chitinous exoskeleton are rubbed together; the resulting rasping sound is intensified by the tracheal air-spaces which act like a sounding-board. The mechanism in *Cicadas* is different, in that an audible buckling of a specialized region of the skeleton on the wall of the abdomen is effected by a pair of powerful muscles. Beneath lies a large tracheal air-cavity. The rhythm of muscular contraction is determined, not by the nervous system, but by an obscure mechanism within the muscle itself.

The main purpose of insect-sound seems to be expressive of mood, especially of alarm or of sexual readiness. The relative insensitivity of the insect's own auditory apparatus must not be forgotten. Some insects are deaf to ordinary sounds in nature, but this is not an absolute rule in the

insect-world. Consequently insect-song in some instances may be not so much inter-communica-
tive in function as an attempt to frighten off an attack on the part of some species outside the
insect-world. But *Cicadas* certainly behave as if they could hear each other. Insects may well be
sensitive to high-rate supersonic vibrations which are quite outside human experience.

Many insects seem to be endowed with another form of communication at their disposal, one
which suggests a signalling system and yet is wholly silent. Maeterlinck was convinced that some
elaborate system of communication exists within a community of bees, but he could not determine
its character. He surmised that it might be a question of phonetic vocabulary; or, more probably,
some kind of tactile language or magnetic intuition, corresponding perhaps with senses and properties of matter that are wholly unknown to us. Here we may refer to the alleged pantomimic or
gestural systems peculiar to bees. Aristotle may have stumbled upon this phenomenon, for he
referred to 'curious movements' carried out by a bee after it had returned to the hive from a
foraging expedition. Spitzner, in 1788, also remarked upon these movements, but Karl von Frisch
is the name most often associated with the role of dancing activity among bees. According to this
writer, a bee returning to the community gives information to the others as to the source of food-
supply, details as to its distance, direction, and magnitude being also conveyed. This information
is ordinarily imparted within the dark interior of the hive by way of a series of rotatory and
figure-of-eight dances together with wagging movements of the abdomen. Other bees gather
round and with their feelers keep in contact with the messenger's body. In this way they interpret
the dancer's information concerning nectar outside. Von Frisch's researches have been both substantiated and elaborated by J. Lotz (1950), E. Benveniste (1952), M. Lindauer (1955), and H. Esch
(1961). It is now believed that bees can also convey information as regards the location of suitable
nesting places. Furthermore differing dialects are now detectable in the communication of bees
living in widely separated geographical territories.

Fish

Until recently, noises emitted by fish constituted a relatively little known topic, even though
specifically mentioned by Aristotle as occurring among the denizens of the River Achelous. Father
Bougeant said 'how much more is it possible that there be in the Water Noises insensible to us, and
that Fishes by that Means speak without being audible to us. At least I delight in thinking so . . .'.
Naval experience during the war brought to the notice of modern naturalists the fact that ocean-
life was anything but silent. A hydrophone lowered into the deep waters off Bermuda picked up a
remarkable medley of mewing sounds, shrieks and moans. The asdic network protecting Chesa-
peake Bay was temporarily upset by unexpected noises 'like a pneumatic drill at work'; these
proved to be emitted by croaker fish.

Some specimens are noisier than others, the loudest being the sea-robin and the trumpet-fish.
The maigre-fish possesses a fantastic repertoire of noises—bellowing, buzzing, whistling, purring;
and shoals may be audible on the surface of the ocean even when swimming at depth. In the case of
the cow-fish, the cat-fish and the toad-fish noises are emitted with a tonal quality and which are of
relatively long duration. Like insects, 'sonic' fish do not produce sounds as mammals do, and

special mechanisms are concerned. Some marine creatures, like the toad-fish, vibrate the walls of their balloon-like air-bladders. Others expel gas-like flatus. Others again stridulate like insects. Thus, the squirrel-fish grinds its gill-teeth together, the sound being amplified by the adjacent air-bladder. Others, such as the sculpins, set up a rapid vibration of muscles and so produce a noise.

The circumstances in which these marine noises arise are variable. Often they are louder in the evening than at other hours. At times the noises may appear, superficially at any rate, to be communicative, being conspicuous when and where fishes congregate, especially during the spawning season. More probably the sounds are navigational, and assist in orientation, as in the case of sea-horses. In other instances again the sounds are only incidental, as in the case of the shrimp which defends itself by noisily squirting jets of water. The snapping shrimp, makes crackling noises like fat frying or dry twigs burning, due to the clicking together of the joints of the asymmetrical giant-claw.

That these marine noises are communicative in nature and function has been doubted by some, who indeed allege that fish are devoid of a sense of hearing. John Hunter did not agree, as shown by his contribution to the Philosophical Transactions upon the *Organ of hearing in fishes*. None the less, fish may be sensitive in the tactual sphere to vibrations set up by various devices: the noise, in other words, may be merely directional and non-communicative.

Over and above these underwater noises there may also occur ultraphonic waves as emitted not only by the marine mammals to be discussed later, but also by the spiny lobster, the hermit crab and the file fish.

Amphibians

Amphibians are mainly silent as well as being deaf, though frogs are a notorious exception in this respect. The function of the sounds which these creatures emit is largely concerned with reproductive function, the males calling to the females. Many reptiles are silent, and some specimens, such as snakes, are also deaf. Some snakes produce hissing or rattling sounds which they themselves cannot hear, but none the less they serve the purpose of scaring away dangerous enemies. Reptiles often adopt grotesque postures or execute an elaborate mime, especially when alarmed. These include wide gaping attitudes of a formidable character.

Birds

Bird-sounds form an important aspect of the subject of animal communication. Their audible repertoire is elaborate, for birds compared with other vertebrates, are essentially vocal creatures.

"But birds vary as to the diversity of their song. Song proceeds from small birds rather than large; males and not females; arboreal as opposed to coastal dwellers; and birds of sober hue rather than those with bright-coloured plumage. Birds sing in the mornings and evenings, but not at noontide; and in fine weather rather than inclement weather." (Witchell)

Bird-song may be regarded as learned or imitative, while calls and cries are innate and instinctive. Song is not the only example of mimicry among birds, which often reproduce other sounds in nature including those peculiar to birds of different species, as well as those emitted by mammals and even humans. Here belong the 'talking' abilities of parrots, magpies, jackdaws, mynahs, and kuckaburras, phenomena which cannot be strictly regarded as communicative. Parrots may imitate articulate speech in a plausible even convincing fashion, but under natural conditions they emit only a few shrill cacophonous screeches.

A phenomenon of regional dialect can even at times be discerned, occurring in birds of the same species but inhabiting widely separated districts: these qualities of accent are transmitted by a process of unconscious contagion, just as in humans. This is the phenomenon which has been spoken of by Weinreich as 'synchronic dialectology'.

Many writers have stated that if it is legitimate to speak of a 'language' of birds, it is their calls rather than their song which merit this appellation. Nevertheless, field ornithology shows that an elaborate and co-ordinated combination of song with motor activity, serves something more than an autistic function. Witness the various types of 'display' which birds perform during certain important socio-physiological activities, e.g. courtship, feeding, territorial pretension, nesting and migration. Some of these displays are communicative in effect if not indeed in intention. These displays may be performed by a bird in solitude, or pairs of male and female partners may participate. In other cases other birds may look on, or even take part. Two examples may be quoted. Thus Nelson wrote (1887):

"Both birds (Alaskan cranes) joined in a series of loud rolling cries in quick succession. Suddenly the new-comer which appeared to be a male, wheeled his back towards the female and made a low bow, his head nearly touching the ground, and ending by a quick leap into the air. Another pirouette brought him facing his charmer, whom he greeted with a still deeper bow, his wings meanwhile hanging loosely by his side. She replied by an answering bow and hop, and then each tried to outdo the other in a series of spasmodic hops and starts, mixed with a set of comically grave and ceremonious bows. The pairs stood for some moments bowing right and left, when their legs appeared to become envious of the large share taken in the performance by the neck, and then would ensue a series of skilled hops and skips, which are more like the steps of a burlesque minuet than anything else I can think of. Frequently others join, and the dance keeps up until all are exhausted."

Again, in the case of the grey-cheeked thrush, O. Miller related:

". . . With body very erect and head thrown up in ecstasy, he lifted his wings high above his back, fluttering them rapidly with a sound like the soft patter of summer rain, while he moved back and forth on his perch with the daintiest of little steps and hops, now up, now down, now across the stage, with gentle noise of feet and wings. No music accompanied it, and none was needed—it was music in itself."

Some bird-displays are self-evident in character, but others are difficult for an observer to comprehend, for they may suggest an elaborate esoteric ritual. Some are of a type which seem quite inappropriate to the situation. Thus, excitement, fear, or pain may provoke a bird to burst into song: a lark which has escaped from the clutches of a hawk may trill loudly. Naturalists regard these phenomena as being the expression of a side-tracking of energy, and speak of 'substitute' or 'displacement' activity. Particularly impressive to a student of language are the

Mutual ceremony of greeting and affection in the Gannet: the young
bird is already hatched.

Plate 7

reciprocal pantomimic and vocal activities carried out by a pair of birds, like the performers of a well-rehearsed song and dance. Concerning penguins Gillespie has written 'I have seen two birds standing only a few feet from one another, trumpeting to each other in this way, and the whole affair had a delicious air of formality and correctness, each penguin being careful never to interrupt the other, but to allow his partner in the duet full time to complete his final note and fully relax before replying'.

This alliance of pantomimic display with vocalization is a phenomenon which deserves particular notice. It has an important bearing not only upon such questions as the nature of bird-communication, but also upon the more fundamental hypothesis as to the possible origin of human language out of gesture. Most writers when discussing the problem of song have tended to neglect the concomitant postures and movements. To ignore the complicated pantomimic ceremonial so characteristic of bird-life is a serious omission in this context. Bird-display does not appeal merely to an isolated special sense. It constitutes an art-form in which shape, colour, movement and sound combine to stir the spectator. At once there comes to mind an analogy with the ballet, and especially the stylized systems of oriental dancing. In the same way it would be wrong to make too sharp a distinction between bird-song, bird-calls, and bird-cries. The apparent communicative properties of all these phenomena, vocal as well as motor, led Lorenz to describe them as 'directors' or 'releasers', though Tinbergen preferred the simpler term 'signal'.

Mammalia

Among mammals the anatomy of the sound-producing mechanisms is quite different from the conformation in birds, and takes on a more human pattern. Between one mammalian species and another there are great differences in volubility though most of them lack the dramatic qualities of bird-song.

Correlation with the level of 'intelligence', whatever this word may mean, is not close, for some species are comparatively silent; some indeed seem to be mute, even though they rank comparatively high as regards sagacity. Sound-range must be distinguished from sheer noisiness, for in some animals vocalization, though loud and clamant, may be little more than an iteration of one or two sounds. Within a single species the repertoire may vary according to whether the animal is living in the wild state, in captivity, or in domestication.

The primates, by and large, may be looked upon as noisy creatures especially in their natural habitat, and they supplement their numerous cries with boisterous din-making. Some observers have been so impressed with the vocal attainments of primates that they have been tempted to read into their sounds both specificity and meaning. Vocabularies of monkey-speech have been prepared and transcribed phonetically in such a plausible fashion as almost to suggest the existence of actual primate dialects (which we might dub 'gorillic', 'chimpanzee', 'baboonese', and 'orangutani'). But these enthusiastic descriptions are not scientific. Some writers, like Yerkes and Learned, have been more cautious, and merely isolated 'food-sounds' and 'social-sounds'. Although Yerkes and Yerkes have heard chimpanzees whine, moan, groan, grunt, bark, shout, yell, hoot, and scream, never have they felt sure that the term 'speech' could fittingly be applied to these utterances. In their opinion none of the anthropoids can be said to 'speak'. Among apes mutual understanding and transfer of experience depend upon sight rather than hearing. One animal reads the mind of its fellow, interprets its attitude, and foresees its action, more like a deaf-mute than a normal person relying upon linguistic clues.

These last points are particularly important. As in the case of birds, vocalization is associated with an abundant play of pantomimic movements. Intercommunication is probably effected by the 'understanding' or reception not of individual or isolated sounds, but of a behavioural complex, wherein movement and sound are combined. The ape, in other words, appears to interpret the total situation as enacted by its companion. This belief tallies with the experience of primate-training. It is easier to teach an anthropoid to copy bodily attitudes and gestures, than to imitate sounds.

It is often said that nothing but cerebral incapacity prevents the higher primates from learning an articulate language, the peripheral equipment being ready for mental maturity to be achieved. Recent comparative anatomical studies of the larynx have thrown some doubt upon that idea however. Kelemen has shown that man-like vocalization would not be possible in apes, for their morphological equipment is not adequate. The differences between the larynges of man and the primates are all-important, and comprise a two-fold process of both increasing elaboration and increasing simplification.

Among primates, the gorillas are unusual in the way they also produce sounds by non-vocal methods, like pounding of the thorax with the fists, rattling their teeth, beating their cheeks, stamping, and striking objects. These forms of din-making connote emotional excitement, or high spirits.

Let us pass from these purely descriptive accounts of animal noises to the more basic problems of their underlying meaning and their functional role. In this connection two seemingly opposite expressions of opinion may be quoted. Thus Kroeber's contention that 'animals do not talk, because they have nothing to say' may be contrasted with the opinion of Yerkes and Yerkes about the great apes. 'These creatures' they wrote, 'have plenty to talk about, but no gift for the use of sounds to represent individual as contrasted with racial feelings or ideas'.

How far can these two opinions be reconciled?

Differences between the communicative systems of *homo sapiens* and the sub-hominids could be looked upon as matters of fundamental quality, or merely a question of degree. The former view, which implies a specificity of the human organism, has been argued by two very different schools of philosophy. On the one hand there stand the determinist views of the dialectical materialists who distinguish man from animals by the possession of a second, as opposed to a single system of signals, that is to say a system of 'signals of signals'. At the other extreme of philosophic thought, also implying a qualitative difference, stand the theists who look upon man as a special creation, who alone is endowed with a soul and with the faculty of speech. Müller was the most eloquent champion of this idea, as we have already seen. But in the other camp there is ranged a considerable body of biological opinion, even though few today would associate themselves with Garner, who argued that monkeys are endowed with a vocal system which discharges all the functions of speech. His views may be looked upon as an extreme example of anthropomorphic interpretation of animal behaviour. To attach a plausible explanation to a complicated pattern of behaviour on the part of a bird or mammal, is only too seductive, and the temptation should always be offset by applying the 'canon of the minimum antecedent'. Lloyd Morgan emphasized that an animal's activity should never be interpreted in terms of higher psychological processes if it can be fairly explained by processes which are lower in the scale of psychological evolution and development. In other words we must always seek the 'minimum' explanation of animal behaviour. This canon should also be applied to any too humanistic interpretation of sounds emitted by animals.

Is it then justifiable to assert that animals 'speak' and that there exist in nature veritable systems of animal 'speech'? The answer obviously turns upon what is understood by the term 'speech'. As we have observed in Chapter I, many definitions are available, all possessing as a common and quintessential item the use of 'articulate sound-signs' or 'articulate words' as vehicles of information. Speech, be it noted, must be articulate, and it must comprise 'words', capable of being recorded through the medium of graphic symbols. A system is demanded wherein phonemes and morphemes are combined.

But animal-sounds rarely, if ever, lend themselves to accurate phonetic transcription, and attempts to do so are but approximations which reflect rather than reproduce the sounds in nature. Consequently they are not *sensu strictu*, articulate. Still more important is the objection that words are tools of thought which can be made to stand for an idea, abstract as well as concrete, and be consistent in this usage, the same word or morpheme being employed to relate to the same notion unhampered by variations in time and in space. No animal can do this.

On these counts, to be considered more fully later, the term 'animal speech' must be deemed unjustified.

Can one then refer with propriety to an animal 'language', in contrast to animal 'speech'? It becomes apparent that definitions of language which concentrate merely on the traffic in articulate sounds, are really definitions of speech, and do not include the role of language in other contexts. Although some linguists, as we have already discussed, restrict the term language to spoken speech, this is not and has not been a universal practice. Thus one commonly talks of the language of the dance, of gesture, of painting, of mathematics, and even of flowers: are we correct in so doing? All these notions entail the idea of language as a system of symbols. If we can agree to adopt such a broad conception of language, with its inclusion of 'cries and involuntary gestures', then it would be justifiable to embrace the animal kingdom and to speak of an animal 'language'. But most linguists lay more emphasis upon the role of symbols (spoken, written, mimed, painted or hewn) as being the *sine qua non* of language, the term 'symbol' meaning an arbitrary sound or mark, used deliberately, and precisely, indicating something more than 'signs' or 'signals'. Thus if we follow Head in speaking about 'symbolic formulation and expression' it would be difficult to use the term animal 'language' except perhaps in very narrow and quite exceptional circumstances. The problem shifts to the question how far animals can utilize and manipulate symbols. On the whole, animals cannot be said to move in a climate of symbols, though again there may be times when this statement does not altogether apply, and when symbols of a vague kind come into operation. We may mention *en passant*, that certain contemporary linguists tend to avoid referring to 'symbols' even though this term has been sanctioned by psychology and philosophy, and indeed has featured conspicuously in many classical linguistic texts.

To justify the use of the term 'language', Bierens de Haan demanded six characteristics. He required the sounds to be vocal; to be articulate; to possess conventional meaning; to be indicative; and also intentional. Finally the sounds should continually be joined in varying combinations, so as to constitute phrases of differing content. Applying these criteria to animals, the author asserted that most species are dumb, or that the sounds they emit are not produced orally. Those animals which are vocal are articulate only exceptionally. Animal sounds are devoid of conventional meaning, in that they express sentiments rather than situations or objects. Sounds in the animal world are not produced with the purpose of expressing something, even though secondarily and unintentionally they may serve as a means of communication. Animals cannot emulate man in creating new words or new phrases out of a stock of existing words. 'Language' is therefore a term which cannot be applied to animals. Nor can the natural sound-systems of animals ever attain the status of a language under the influence of man or through training.

Hockett has identified 13 separate properties or characters of language under the term 'design-features'. Many of these are also to be traced in some of the animal communicative systems; others appear to be peculiar to man. The latter comprise what Hockett has called (1) displacement; (2) productivity; and (3) duality. These expressions obviously need to be interpreted. 'Displacement' is of course Pumphrey's 'extensibility'—referred to in the previous chapter—and indicates the ability while communicating, to transcend the barriers of immediacy in time and place. With the possible exception of the dancing system of communication among bees, this property is rare outside of human behaviour. 'Productivity' is the factor whereby in language new messages may be coined, and then intelligently received or decoded. This property is bound up with the availability of morphemes, which serve as elementary signalling units. Hence there obtains an 'open' semantic system which can even permit the encoding of information which is false. 'Duality of patterning' refers to the basic structure of language into morphemes made up out of phonemes. This would appear to be a human characteristic, even though Hockett cogitated whether 'significant duality', as he called it, may not perhaps also be encountered in the complex song-systems of some passerine birds. Cultural transmission, or more simply 'tradition', is another of Hockett's design-features, but it may not perhaps be altogether a perquisite of *homo sapiens* though it materially assists the development of an organized system of communication.

Obviously we would be on insecure grounds if we were to talk about the existence of 'animal language', and it would appear safer and wiser to avoid such a term altogether. Similarly the terms 'pseudo-language' and 'rudi-language' proposed by Boutan and by Wilson are unacceptable.

Since then animal 'speech' and animal 'language' are objectionable terms, would not animal 'communication' be admissible? Nowadays the communicative character of language is being emphasized more and more, and the word 'communication' certainly avoids the inference that verbalization is the sole medium. The use of this term naturally raises the question as to the nature of animal vocalization and display, and whether indeed these can logically be regarded as essentially communicative in every circumstance or context.

Révész divided the sounds emitted by animals into three main categories, viz. (1) self-expression; (2) wordless cries; and (3) directed calls. The purring of a contented cat and the trilling of a solitary caged bird exemplify the first of these, and can scarcely be rated high in the scale of communication. The other two, however, can be looked upon as potentially communicative. Although this classification is not ideal, it goes some way towards clarifying the nature of the problem. The cry— the adjective 'wordless' is distracting and unnecessary—is instinctive, non-articulated, unconcentrated and vague; it is 'directed', but not towards any definite individual. It aims at inducing the external world to co-operate in some fitting way. The communicative tendency lies in the fact that the animal seemingly senses the proximity of a creature that can free it from its state of unease. Lloyd Morgan regarded the primary purpose of animal sounds as demonstrating a comforting presence, and he spoke of '. . . the reassuring social links of sound, the grateful signs of kindred presence'. Cries may also be produced without deliberate communicative intent, but none the less they may have a communicative effect. A frightened animal does not necessarily emit a cry with the object of warning its fellows; the cry may merely instinctively express the animal's own fear, which however automatically evokes fear in others within audible range. De Laguna adopted a different nomenclature. She equated animal cries with the function of proclamation. She isolated four types though admitting that they tended to merge. Her classification was as follows; (1) proclamation of presence; (2) predicative proclamation; (3) the announcement of intention; and (4) the announcement of accomplishment.

The directed call (or better still, the 'call') differs from the cry in that it possesses individual reference. The call is explicitly addressed to some other creature. The sensible presence of a partner is required. Furthermore the call possesses an imperative character. Unlike the cry (which is instinctive by nature) the call is bound up with individual experience. Place-reference constitutes yet another characteristic of the call as opposed to the cry, for the animal indicates the place, object and person addressed. Finally there is a vocative component to the call which does not apply to the cry.

The occurrence of antiphonal singing or 'duetting' between mating birds certainly suggests a variety of communicative behaviour. According to Busnel and Bremond, only parts of bird-song are meaningful. The 'message' depends upon the alternation between high-pitched and low-pitched notes. Here lies a striking analogy with the African drum-talk, as discussed in Chapter XXVII, pages 344, 345.

It may be objected that a contrast between 'cries' and 'calls' does not really include that very individual expression of animal-behaviour, namely bird-song. A reluctance to define 'song' seems to pervade the literature of ornithology.

Between that type of vocalization which is communicative and that which seems to be purely autistic, egocentric, intransitive, ludic, there exists an intermediate group. This is what Griffin has called 'echo-ranging', 'echo-locational', or 'sonar', and consists in a sort of solopsistic 'language' or 'talking'—not to others of the same species, nor to itself—but to its own environment. Orientation sounds are emitted by the animal, and information is obtained from the echoes. No second animal is involved. Echo-location, according to Griffin, is employed to achieve precise and subtle information from various objects in the surrounding world. This kind of communication is best illustrated in the case of bats, which possess an extraordinary sensitivity and discrimination in orientating themselves in the dark, and in catching insects on the wing by means of this particular acoustic tool. Porpoises, whales and dolphins also probably navigate themselves in the dark and in turbid water by a supersonic system of echo-location, and they can avoid obstacles and locate food-stuff with uncanny accuracy and speed.

Communication is but one aspect of animal behaviour. As such, it raises the interesting *Auslöser* conception put forward by Lorenz, elaborated by Tinbergen, and studied particularly in birds and other sub-mammalians. According to these authors, animals show innate behavioural responses to certain specific attributes within their environment, such as significant shapes, colours, attitudes, movements, sounds, or scents, singly or combined. In that these attributes determine a response upon the creature's part, they have been termed *Auslöser* or 'releasers'. The reaction is believed to depend upon a special central nervous activity called the 'innate releasing mechanism'. It is clear that only certain environmental attributes act as releasers. Russell spoke of these influential stimuli as 'perceptual signs' or as 'perceptual clues', though Tinbergen preferred the term 'sign stimuli'. Since bodily postures and miming with or without audible vocalization, may serve as releasers, they can be looked upon as a modality of communication entailing an actor and a re-actor. When such a realizer evokes a response which itself is a movement-sound complex, the role of communication becomes still more evident.

Tinbergen (1951) also introduced the notion of the 'inserted link' lying between perception and the ultimate adoption response, forming a sort of signal-system. The author intimated that even human language might be capable of discussion along the lines of an 'inserted link'. As Tinbergen put it '. . . movements effect organs, innate releasing mechanisms are fitted together; they act as a wonderful, complicated system the only function of which is the construction of a means of social communication. In fact, such complicated structures are understandable; they "make sense" only in connection with their function; the coincident presence in the same species of stridulation organs, the stridulation drive, and an innate tendency to react in certain "purposive" ways can be recognized as an adaptive feature only when the releaser function is recognized'.

Reflection upon these topics raises the suspicion that no sharp demarcation exists, or can be attempted, between all these diverse vocal phenomena in nature. The gradations are so tenuous between cries, song, calls, simple expressive sounds, and the effect of releasers, that classification is difficult. Obviously there is a need for a more logical terminology. A simple all-embracing term is required to include all the sounds emanating from the respiratory apparatus which are evoked in the animal kingdom. 'Psophic communication' has been suggested, but 'vocalization' is perhaps a less objectionable term.

According to current information-theory, all communicative acts entail a sender, a receiver and a message. We have seen that in the case of animals, the aspect of 'message' may at times be slim. Often it would seem that the animal or bird gives voice without any clear 'purposes' unless to derive some satisfaction or enjoyment thereby. One cannot trace any specific difference here between the behaviour of animals and humans, for children and even adults not infrequently talk merely for 'ludic' or egocentric purposes. The receptive side of animal communication is also of different character from that in humans. As E. S. Russell has emphasized, an animal possesses its own private perceptual world—its *Umwelt*, as von Uexkuell called it. This explains a creature's apparent indifference to so much of its environmental stimuli, auditory as well as visual. At the same time animals may be uncannily responsive to apparently inconspicuous events around them. Such changes may elude our less sensitive perceptions, but nevertheless possess abundant valence for the animal. These subtle clues are more often optical than auditory.

Nevertheless, to equate animal sounds with communication would not be to fall into serious error. True, the communicative action may not always be intentional, as far as we can discern. The cry uttered by a startled bird can be best regarded as an instinctive expression of fear which happens to provoke a kindred emotion among others of its species within earshot. The original cry may not really have been a deliberate message to the others, even though it actually provoked instinctive reaction on their part. We can say that the cry was therefore communicative in effect, though not in purpose.

Much of animal vocalization does little more than express the upsurge of powerful emotion. This audible reaction may relieve tension in the animal itself. It may also interest, excite, or even influence the behaviour of other animals, but this effect (however desirable it be from a teleological standpoint) lies outside any process of volition or will.

The points of distinction between animal vocalization and man's articulate speech may now be discussed.

The verbal symbols which make up the structure of human speech are, in essence, arbitrary and conventional. Consequently they are mutable to an almost unlimited degree and can increase or change *pari passu* with maturation of ideas. The symbols are not self-evident in purport; they are conventional and need to be learned. In contrast the vocalization of animals is not made up of symbols. Animal sounds are essentially natural, innate, instinctive, spontaneous, and all-or-none in nature, even though mimicry may mask the picture. The sounds do not vary from one generation to another; in each individual member of a species they rest intact and self-sufficient.

The principal difference may therefore be summarized by stating that while an animal's sounds entail signs, man's speech is made up of symbols. Signs indicate things, while symbols *represent* them. Signs may be looked upon as announcers of events, and symbols as reminders. Symbols are 'substitute' signs, for they can take the place of things out of sight and not in present experience.

To jettison the term 'symbol' as some would have us do because it is a complex or even clumsy connotation capable of analysis into component particles, is not, I submit, justifiable. The very latitude of the term is in many circumstances an advantage.

Man's use of verbal symbols can be regarded not only as a product of his superior mentation but also as a reciprocal influence which augments, deepens, and enriches his power of thought.

Many animal vocalizations are characterized by a repetitive quality, the creature emitting the same sound from its scanty repertoire over and over again. A dog with its incessant bark; a lion roaring throughout the night; a solitary canary warbling in its cage, are all cases in point. Often it is difficult to detect any 'meaning' or purpose to these sounds, which do not appear to be cries of emotional origin, nor yet communicative calls. Possibly some of them represent yet another instance of play. There are dangers however in such anthropocentric ways of thinking. Most animal noises remain quite obscure and beyond our present powers of interpretation. As Schwidetzky has said, 'it is simpler to translate thirty pages of Cicero than to define the meaning of crocodile's grunt'.

In the case of man, however, speech may be a wholly independent form of behaviour. The words spoken need not occur merely as an element in a larger response. This fact illustrates Pumphrey's quality of detachment, which we have already referred to, and which scarcely ever applies to animal noises. Similarly human speech may be wholly devoid of emotional qualities: this is not so with animals, where cries are the true mirror of the feelings of the moment. The differences go even deeper. A man may speak with the deliberate intention of masking his feelings; or concealing thought; or deceiving the listener. Nothing like this occurs in the animal world unless we include certain audible displacement-activities. Moreover man in his communication may deliberately employ the device of *silence* as a dramatic method of expressing feelings or ideas. Such a phenomenon does not occur in the animal world, other than the sudden hush which comes over a community in circumstances of immediate danger.

Another distinction between animal and human communication derives from the intimate linkage of animal cry with immediate emotional tension. The animal's cry or call can do no more than proclaim a situation (e.g. danger, food), whereas speech can specify the situation and describe it.

The superiority of speech over animal cries as a means of social control is obvious. Co-operative behaviour among animals is instinctive; while in man, thanks to the endowment of speech, it is 'intelligent'. Possibly a few exceptions occur as in the co-ordinated chase-behaviour of such gregarious animals as lions. But here again anthropomorphism may be deceptive. A system of animal cries would not suffice to cope with novel modes of co-operative activity. Human speech evolved along with an increasingly elaborate communal life. The making and transport of tools; planned hunting expeditions; the need to secure safety at night; the indoctrination of the young by experienced elders; these are some of the activities of early *homo sapiens* which must have been materially assisted by the power of speech. Expressed differently, we can recognize that an important survival-value stems from the possession of speech.

Another difference between the vocalization of animals and speech is one which derives from neurology, and which was briefly mentioned in Chapter IV, namely the vulnerability of human speech to states of disease or injury. This property of language was noted by Aristotle even though few subsequent philosophers and biologists have referred to it. Aristotle asserted that man alone is apt to display dumbness or hesitancy in speech, implying a failure to explain one's meaning adequately. It is true that nothing comparable with an aphasia in the strict sense of the word occurs in animals even after extensive ablations of the cerebral cortex.

A fundamental question concerns the nature of the mechanisms whereby the most elaborate types of animal communication merge into the speech of *homo sapiens*. One uses the word 'merge' because the belief in a sudden appearance of some quite novel acquisition is, rightly or wrongly, out of scientific favour today. An all-important role in this transition is believed to be played by a marked elaboration of the social organization of early man. This was the basis of Révész's 'contact theory' of the origins of speech in man. However the biological axiom must not be over-looked, namely that group-existence is characteristic of all animal life, from the lowest to the highest. But with the appearance of *homo sapiens* a number of elaborations occur in which linguistic development plays a vital role. What are the social features which characterize human communal life? Some believe that division of labour is all-important. Others would point to the phenomenon whereby individual members behave differently in the presence of others from their comportment when alone.

The first manufacture of tools marks a critical point in evolution, and *homo sapiens* is at one and the same time, *homo faber* and *homo loquens*. Both language and tools are instruments which humans alone employ to achieve definite and tangible aims. 'Moreover, language, like the tool, and unlike the limb, is something objective to, and independent of, the individual who uses it. It is a factor which he finds in his psychological environment, and to which he must adapt himself. It has a structure of its own which he must learn to take account of in his use of it' (de Laguna). Even more significant than the *use* of tools and of language is the fact that man alone can devise, construct and elaborate them. To this property must be added the *carrying* of tools, though this may lie between the use and the fashioning of tools.

Hockett laid emphasis upon the possible role of what he called 'blending' during these crucial steps of transition. Two words may be accidentally confused so as to produce a neologism which contains parts of the two words in question—a familiar enough phenomenon to aphasiologists. It has been suggested that eventually one of these neologisms 'catches on' and becomes accepted within the corpus of a communicative system as a useful addition.

It has also been claimed that an ability to mimic speech-sounds is absolutely fundamental for the acquisition of language. Such powers of imitation are not ordinarily met with in sub-human mammalia owing, it has been claimed on somewhat speculative grounds, to the absence of an arcuate fasciculus from the brains of all but *homo sapiens*. Herein therefore stands a barrier between animals and man. And yet, despite the absence of a larynx, certain birds possess uncanny powers of imitating human speech. Whether the avian brain is furnished with an arcuate bundle is not known but the idea is highly improbable. It would thus appear that in some ways birds are the group which ought to have been able to evolve language in the true sense, as Thorpe put it, rather than the mammalia.

Clearly the transition from animal vocalization to speech is not entirely a problem of linguistics. We believe with Sapir and Suzanne Langer, that the origin of language is really part of a larger question which ties up with the beginning of symbolic behaviour in animals. Reference has already been made to Langer's suggestion that the earliest sign of this trend is an apparent sense of significance which an animal may attach to certain articles like stones or children's toys. In the behaviour of the anthropoids, one can at times detect clues that some objects—quite limited in number and in occurrence—may seem to possess for them a 'meaning'; to convey something; to be significant; to be valent. Here lies an analogy with the common behaviour of autistic children, or very young schizophrenes, who are apt to endow a quite unlikely article with highly personal significance.

Discussion upon animal communication naturally involves an enquiry into the nature of animal thinking. Apart from experimental studies of animal sagacity, maze-learning, and conditioned responses, little is known about the nature of an animal's mental rumination. During its waking but inactive moments, an animal obviously does not utilize an imagery made up of verbal symbols. But an imaginal type of thinking probably exists and may well take the form of perceptual complexes of a vague character. Abstractions are largely beyond the capacity of an animal, though it may be trained to utilize or act upon abstractions. When Thorndike said that animals 'think things, but do not think about things', he was indicating the concrete nature of their imagery.

The limitations of animal intelligence and powers of communication make it difficult for us to conceive of them planning or thinking ahead except in rare and special circumstances. Of course animals sometimes anticipate events, as in the rituals of nest-building, migration or pre-hibernation activity, but these are almost certainly instinctive proleptic drives, and not premeditated acts. Without words an animal cannot achieve much in the way of complicated planning, as in the corporate action of man. An animal's inability to employ spatial and temporal orientations in its mental processes is reflected in the poverty of its vocal utterances. Man's power of explicit mental differentiation brought language into being, as R. A. Wilson said.

To what extent do animals, particularly those in domestication 'comprehend' the speech of man? Exaggerated claims are often made, but it is doubtful how far they can be scientifically sustained. Samuel Butler must not be taken too seriously when he wrote: 'It is idle to say that a cat does not know what the cat's-meat man means when he says "meat". The cat knows just as well, neither better nor worse than the cat's-meat man does, and a great deal better than I myself understand much that is said by some very clever people at Oxford or Cambridge'. As a matter of fact, a cat associates the presence of a cat's-meat man with food by dint of a veritable medley of clues, olfactory, situational, gestural. The sound of the word 'meat'—should it come into the picture at all—is a mere signal, comparable with a flashing light, or a bell in the case of a laboratory animal. There has been an amusing correspondence in the British Press about the regional differences in the noises commonly employed to attract the attention of the domestic cat. Whereas 'Puss Puss' is commonplace for most of England, there are areas where some such call as 'ch ch' is preferred. Dr. Samuel Johnson's alleged remarks upon this topic were recalled:

Boswell: 'Is it not strange that the mode of address to a cat varies with its geographical habitat?'
Johnson: 'A cat will respond to any familiar fulmination which it knows from experience is a promissory of a reward.'
Boswell: 'But is it not strange that in some districts we say "Puss" and in others "ch ch"?'
Johnson: 'No sir, it is not so strange as the fact that an Englishman says "Yes", whereas a Frenchman, for reasons no philosopher comprehends, says "oui".'

Those who fondly imagine that their domestic pets really identify and interpret the purport of items of human speech, often quote the evidence of Clever Hans the calculating horse, and the 'talking-dogs' who spell and answer questions. The famous Elberfeld horses used to signal by hoof-taps the answer to arithmetical problems involving the four primary rules, fractions, brackets, the extraction and multiplication of roots, and the solution of equations. After thorough investigation it was concluded that this was an elaborate trick. Animals, especially when in domestication, are apt to display a sensitivity to a total situation which on the face of it gives the impression of an uncanny understanding of human speech. The truth is, that it is not so much the audible morpheme which is comprehended as the paralinguistic accompaniments of tone, pitch, loudness and rate of speaking. Still more significant are the non-verbal clues, made up of the gestures of the speaker, and of other environmental circumstances perhaps too subtle to attract our notice. As Lorenz said, among social animals the apparatus of 'mood-convection' is much better developed than it is with us, and so they become responsive to minute intention-displaying movements made by humans, and also by other animals. These calculating horses of Elberfeld were merely highly trained animals which responded to minimal clues on the part of the impressario, conscious or unconscious. None of the horses could solve a problem which was beyond the competency of the trainer.

An animal's apparent but often inconsistent recognition of human speech is merely a special instance of what has already been said about the nature of perception in animals. Some items of the visual and acoustic environment are simply ignored, for they possess for the animal, no meaning, or better, no 'valence'. On the other hand, a complex of sense-data may prove valent or significant, such as the tone of voice combined with a gesture. These, placed against an appropriate background of events, may combine to form a stimulus which is far more valent than the mere phonemic structure of the words of command. We must realize that animals in general do not perceive their surroundings in such an 'articulated' way as we do. Their perceptual world is not a co-ordinated compound of clearly separate and distinct objects. Things are perceived only as ill-distinguished parts of a general complex, and always in relation to that complex, so that when a thing is isolated from its normal context it may not be recognized for what it is. Animals may react to perception-complexes comprising linkages of ill-differentiated objects. We must not assume that the features of a perceptual field which are significant to us, are necessarily those which appear significant to an animal. In the auditory sphere the same arguments hold true. A dog may act as if deaf to many sounds though they must surely reach its ear. The perception however is highly specific and the animal may react promptly to whichever noise possesses a definite valence, and to that alone.

Animals also vary considerably in their response to the sounds evoked by other animals, especially those of different species. Unless immediate danger threatens, animals are often singularly inattentive to the cries of other creatures; but here again inconsistencies occur. This may be exemplified by the effect of recorded animal noises upon pet animals when played over in their hearing. Dogs and cats sometimes appear quite uninterested: at other times they take notice: sometimes they even show excitement and frantically search for the intruder. Once again movement may prove a more efficient signalling system than sound. Thus the flight of the startled sentry birds away from their perch upon the back of a rhinoceros may serve as an adequate alarm to the host and indicate the proximity of a dangerous situation.

Two technical terms have recently appeared as newcomers to the biological sciences. Thus 'ethology' has been proposed as standing for the scientific study of animal behaviour. As a specialism of ethology we now have 'zoosemiotics' which is concerned with the scientific study of signalling behaviour in and across animal species.

At this juncture the alliance in animal communication of bodily movements with sounds needs to be re-emphasized. In so far as an animal of one species comprehends the primitive message which may be emitted by another of its kind, the perception is an 'interpretation' of—or a 'response to'—a complex of activity, wherein sound forms only a part. Natural historians look upon this as a rule throughout the animal kingdom: it is conspicuous in the case of birds and primates, which incidentally are the most vocal of all creatures. Signalling gestures, silent or otherwise, are also known to take place among such diverse species as certain spiders; the fiddler crabs; and wolves. Many biologists believe that in the chimpanzee, vocalization is an even less important means of intercommunication than pantomime. In stressing this combined motor-vocal quality of animal communication, Wundt's visualization of two distinct hierarchies of behaviour whereby oral speech arose as a modification of general movements, is not necessarily accepted.

Even in the case of bees it is now believed that the communicative dancing also requires an auxiliary sound-track. According to Sebeok, Esch has discovered that the tail-wagging dance carries no information unless accompanied by a whirring sound, the duration of which increases according to the remoteness of the source of food. The whirring is followed by short, chirping beeps emitted by the onlookers within the hive, presumably denoting reception of the code. When the beeps occur, the dancing bee stops; if not she is stung to death.

It is interesting to speculate which component of animal communication proved to be the most important step in the march towards language in man. Was it the gestural system, or the audible cries and calls? One can easily overlook the part played by the former, and assume that audible systems of communication were all-important. The gestural hypothesis as to the origin of speech once held by many, never became popular, and few believed that there ever existed a *homo alalus*, who gestured but did not speak. But throughout the vertebrate series, bodily movements have always been important, as in the rituals of display among birds. Mammals on the whole betray their feelings by a different type of movement-complex, a conspicuous part being played by horripilation, baring of the fangs, lashing of the tail, arching of the back and so on. In the case of man these latter phenomena are represented by such autonomic signs as flushing or blanching; dilatation of the pupils; and sweating. These are largely beyond the control of the will. They are communicative in effect, whether or not in intention also, just as in the case of many animal cries. Man also possesses an eloquent language of gesture of a different kind.

With the assumption of arboreal habits, the primate began to use the forelimbs for prehension as well as locomotion: man alone uses the forelimbs exclusively as tools. In man they may serve as adjuvants of speech. Mimic movements made with the arms and hands emphasize his utterance, and may even take the place of audible speech. This pantomime is a direct, though remote, descendant of the ritual displays in the bird-world. Furthermore, between these deliberate gestures and the involuntary autonomic phenomena, man utilizes, more or less automatically, a variety of facial movements which betray the feelings. Here belong tears, frowning, scowling, smiling, laughter, and many other grimaces. These may occur in silence; or they may accompany the sound-track of speech so as to give emphasis. Though automatic, they can be inhibited by a deliberate effort of will, so that what is spoken and mimed need not necessarily be the true index of thought, and opportunities arise for deceit or the issue of negative information.

Among the many anatomical modifications culminating in *homo sapiens*, linguists should note the disappearance of hair from the dorsum of the body and from the face. This facial hairlessness reveals the play of the muscles of expression, a fact which might appeal to those who support the gestural origin of speech. The differences in the sexes as far as facial hirsutism is concerned must not be overlooked, and if we were unreservedly to accept the gestural hypothesis, we might be tempted to ascribe a more important role in the genesis and maturation of speech to primitive woman rather than to primitive man. And why not indeed? For there are many imposing linguistic arguments which could be marshalled to demonstrate the significant part women play in moulding, elaborating, and even changing our language.

In conclusion it should be borne in mind that there probably exist in the animal world systems of intercommunication of which we as yet know nothing. Among bees the language of the dance may be merely one of many other elaborate codes. The supersonic methods of echo-location practised by bats, and by porpoises and whales have been mentioned. Some of these are not only exploratory but also communicative; transitive as well as intransitive. We must not imagine that all these obscure systems of animal-communication are essentially acoustic in nature. Some of them may well be tactile, chemical or olfactory.

As T. A. Sebeok wrote 'it has been pointed out that a linguist approaching a totally unknown language acts as a cryptanalyst: he receives messages not destined for him and not knowing their code. The student of animal communication also resembles a cryptanalyst, but he is faced with some problems which need not occupy the observer of speech: thus, initially, he cannot even be sure through what physical channel or channels the presumed messages are being transmitted. Since "any form of energy propagation can be exploited for communication purposes" (R. M. Fano 1961), and many forms are in fact at the disposal of animals, one of his first tasks is to specify the sense or constellation of sense employed in the message-processing situations which he is observing'. (1963).

These remarks upon this fundamental topic may be concluded by a quotation from the ornithologist Eliot Howard:

"... I seek the nature of a bird's world, not with any hope of finding it, but to know what to find. There is more joy in finding a problem than in trying to solve one, for to solve a problem is vain delusion. There is a mystery of flight; a mystery of song; a mystery of a nest; and yet, not three mysteries, but one: a bird is the mystery, for it steals our values of beauty and mingles them strangely in form no less than in feathers; in colour no less than in song; and in what we value most, devotion to its home. And no less strangely it seems to mingle the blindness of an insect with the intelligence of an ape; and because nothing is really blind and no one is likely to know what intelligence really is, mysteries will be mysteries still. I would not change it. . . ."

XII. THE DEVELOPMENT OF SPEECH IN THE CHILD

> *How quick children are to discover this wonderful inner world where they are all-powerful! Who teaches them this amazing art of manipulating symbols? So that from the tenderest age they can sit down as masters at the keyboard of the ten billion cells of their brains and tease the various microscopic nerve endings into producing endless simulacra of reality? Endless variation on whatever melody they love best?*
>
> *As soon as they know words as the symbols for things, they realize that they have a magic instrument within them by which, by their mere calling up of the right word, they can bring to their minds the image of the thing they crave. Broca's area in the brain's frontal lobe, so the anatomists tell us, is the keyboard of the magic instrument.*
>
> Guy Endore
>
> *Vaticanus they knew, the god of the Child's first cry; and Fabulinus, who watched over its first articulate word.*

The study of aphasia in the adult can be assisted by comparison with the diverse types of speech-lessness encountered in children. Of even greater interest is the development of speech in the normal infant and child. These steps in ontogeny are of importance when one comes to compare them with the exiguous utterances of speech-dissolution. They are also important when considering delayed or erratic speech-development in a child.

Up to now speech-development has been studied in Great Britain and America mainly by educational psychologists who have made an intimate investigation of a single individual, or at the most, of a small series of cases. Less profound analyses of a larger case-material are rarer. Noteworthy assistance has also materialized from certain non-medical philologists, particularly Jesperson. Dr. Mary Sheridan approached the subject more from the standpoint of the phonetician, and she has been interested in the sounds evoked in childhood talk, rather than the choice of words or the syntax employed.

Most of the published work on infant and childhood speech has been in the English language. The names of Gesell, Lewis, Watts, Darwin, Preyer, Sully, Shinn, McCarthy, Slim, Jagger, M. E. Smith, Nice, Shirley, Isaacs, are important in this connection. The pioneer study was however made in Germany by C. and W. Stern, while French contributors include Delacroix, Piaget, Descoeudres, among others. Of particular value however have been the contributions from Russia, especially Chukovsky, Luria and Yudovich.

An infant's earliest vocalizations are of course reflex manifestations which serve to enhance respiratory function, and which have no speech value at all. Later, however, the infant's cries may attain some purposive significance by betraying hunger or discomfort, which is followed by satisfying attentions. In this way speech value is achieved, constituting a crude form of communication. Throughout this period, screaming continues to serve as a beneficial physical activity.

At this early stage of development, a child not asleep may be regarded as silent only when in a state of placid indifference, for vocalization betrays discomfort. Later, however, some differentiation occurs, in that other sets of sounds appear, and connote a condition of comfort.

The earliest discomfort cries are largely vowel sounds, emitted with a certain nasal quality. Later appear the evidences of consonantal or semi-consonantal sounds, i.e. /h/, /l/, or /ng/. Stern regarded these as the audible manifestations of a glottal sphincter which acts as a protective mechanism to prevent solid particles from entering the air-passages. Comfort sounds do not strictly belong to the realm of crying sounds; they include gurglings, crowings and chucklings. So far as they have any reflex speech significance they would seem to betray a feeling-tone of pleasure or comfort, and are analogous to the purring of the domestic cat. In all probability these sounds also constitute a form of play, in which the infant indulges and takes delight. It has been claimed that deaf-mute children also utter these sounds at this age, indicating that the verbal 'play' is kinaesthetic rather than auditory.

Next in order of appearance are a number of back consonants—in so far as it is possible to distinguish in babyhood vowels from consonants. Conspicuous among them is the velar fricative /g/ and also /x/, /k/, /r/. Later come the front consonants /p/, /b/, /t/, /d/, and later still the nasals /m/, and /n/. Understandably, these comfort-sounds accompany a state of satiety after taking food, and are intimately associated with eructations of wind and the grunting and belching noises of gastric repletion. Stern spoke of some of them as 'clicks', not an altogether suitable term in this connection. Kussmaul described them as *Vomotiv-lauten*. In part at least these noises may be due to the tongue falling back against the soft palate while the child lolls relaxed in the mother's arms, or supine in its cot. Swallowing of post-prandial saliva may also play a rôle, and we recall that the blind deaf-mute Laura Bridgman used to emit similar back consonantal noises as an index of satisfaction. Yerkes and Learned's study of chimpanzee talk also suggested that /g/ and /k/ sounds were largely 'food words' or sounds associated with excitement. Front consonantal sounds are largely evoked by the same movements as occur in the act of sucking, and they may be observed when the child is about to be fed. That they are not noises made merely in imitation of a mother's crooning is shown by their occurrence in the deaf (Wundt) and also in the blind (Bean).

The infant first responds to the speech of others during the second month (Lewis). To begin with, the child smiles on hearing adult speech. Later, largely as the result of training, the child begins to discriminate sounds of pleasant from those of unpleasant connotation. At first it is the melodic pattern which is distinguished; not until the end of the sixth month does the child learn to distinguish between differing phonetic forms.

Still later, usually in the eighth or ninth month though sometimes earlier, the infant begins to recognize that the sounds and gestures of its parents or nanny possess a meaning, and the infant now listens to these sounds, watches the actions, and makes some attempt at imitating them. Hitherto the infant had been living in a world, where, as William James said, all was a 'big, blooming, buzzing confusion'. That the imitation is very imperfect is not surprising, since, quite apart from the cochlea, the organs of articulation and phonation are immature in an infant.

Highly important in speech development is the rôle of 'babbling', or the use of sound as an expression of play; that is, sound for its own sake, as shown by the child attending to and enjoying its own utterances. Babbling in the way of isolated sounds probably starts in the second month, while in the third month appear the characteristic repetitive chains of sounds. That kinaesthetic modalities as well as auditory are important is shown by the presence of babbling in infants born deaf (Kamlik), just as in the case of food words.

Lewis agreed with Freud in regarding play as a means for attaining self-mastery. He thought that the child in its babbling, relives both experience and its emotional accompaniment, because speech is also an expressive faculty. Thus an infant which has cried *Mama* when hungry, and babbles *Mama* in play, is both playing at crying, and playing at being hungry, and in Freud's opinion would thereby gain a conquest over both. Lewis also agreed with Koffka in regarding babbling as an expression of delight in an acoustic pattern, thus forming a sort of rudimentary art—the beginnings of aesthetic sensibility.

Imitation now begins to constitute an important factor. Lewis recognized three stages, viz: (1) the first 3–4 months, when the infant responds to human utterance by making sounds; (2) a pause, wherein the child's vocal reactions to sound grow less or even cease; and (3) more definite and more complex imitative phenomena dating from about 9 months. The second stage, wherein the child seems to lose ground in its speech-development, has been ascribed to the earliest begin-nings of meaning. Stage three embraces several phenomena: a richer vocabulary of sounds emitted; a more faithful imitation of intonational forms; the appearance of delayed imitation or metalalia, that is to say the imitation of sound sequences novel to the child; and the development of echolalia.

At this stage, the vocalization of a congenitally deaf child begins to fall behind that of the normal; previously the speech-pattern of the deaf and the non-deaf had kept more or less abreast.

According to whether there is any propositional significance, Stein distinguished prelinguistic from linguistic babbling. The latter also accords with Meumann's 'emotional-volitional' speech.

The meaningful use of conventional speech begins about the tenth month and constitutes Stein's linguistic babbling. Gradually this becomes modified, embellished and extended so that it loses many of its baby-talk characteristics and becomes what Jesperson called 'little speech'. The stages through which this comes about are important.

As far as it is possible to use a phonetic terminology it can be said that in these early sounds of conventional speech vowels antedate consonants. Some vowels are seemingly easier than others, and come more readily to the infant. Long and short vowels, according to Sheridan, are perceived some time before diphthongs. Mistakes are not infrequent and /e/, /u/, and /o/, may be lowered to /a/, /u/ to /o/, /i/ to /e/. Diphthongs may be interchanged, just as in the case of the cockney dialect of accepted English.

The alleged order of appearance of consonantal sounds in a growing infant differs from one author to another. It is usually said that the sounds first uttered are those which are 'easiest of enunciation'. According to most writers the first consonantal sounds are the /p/, /b/, /m/, sounds. There are many speculative ideas as to why this should be so. It has been asserted that the child watches the mother's lips emitting these sounds and imitates them. If so one might not expect the same /p/, /b/, /m/, sounds to be the earliest ones enunciated even by a blind infant; whether this is true or not is not yet known. Another suggestion is that the muscles which form these consonantal sounds are the same as those which participate in the automatic act of sucking.

A little later the 'front stops' /t/, and /d/ are audible, while the 'back stops' /k/ and /g/ seem to be more 'difficult' sounds, and are not heard until comparatively late. Where both front and back stops apply the child finds difficulty and prefers to repeat two front stops or two back stops *doddy* for 'doggie', *tat* for 'cat', *gerky goggy* for 'dirty doggie'.

Sounds represented by /r/, /l/, /w/ and /y/ are especially difficult and are often avoided or confused. Thus 'rabbit' often becomes *wabbit* or *labbit*. Sheridan described these features clearly, though she probably had in mind an older child. While still an infant, as Jesperson pointed out, sounds may actually be enunciated which will later prove quite difficult. It is as though the infant uttered automatically and in an unmeaning fashion sounds which will elude it when he comes to use them purposively. Thus the range of sounds may actually seem to diminish in passing from the infant to the childhood stage.

Some phoneticians are reluctant to speak of 'easy' as opposed to 'difficult' phonemes. And yet some of these sounds must obviously entail a greater expenditure of electrical potential. Surely it cannot be gainsaid that /r/ is a phoneme which is 'difficult', in that it is mastered late by the average English-speaking child. Indeed many children continue to display well into adolescence a 'rhotacism', or imperfect enunciation of the phoneme /r/: in fact many adults never succeed in achieving an articulatory competency in this respect. The various ways of coping with /r/ as between one language and another are of interest. The prolonged trilled /r/ of the Spaniard might be expected to afford a different problem to the developing child than, say, the phonemes /b/ or /d/. It would be interesting to note the age at which young children in Spain first master this particular phoneme, and furthermore to study the nature of their inadequate attempts, before mature articulation is attained.[1]

A like problem is raised in the case of Arabic, where several gutteral sounds are entailed which are entailed to most European languages. Such gutturals must surely be 'difficult', i.e. 'laborious' phonemes. At what age are they first correctly enunciated? Personal enquiry has yielded divergent replies. According to some, the very young Arabic child takes these complicated sounds 'in its stride': others however have asserted that these are late-comers to the articulatory repertoire. There is always a lack of precise information both as to the age when these various gutturals appear, and also what forms of speech-impairment occur in young Arabic dyslaliacs.

Irwin (1947, 1948) has tabulated in detailed fashion the diverse order of appearance of consonantal and vocalic phonemes in English-speaking Americans, and reference should be made to his careful studies.

---

[1] This subject has been specifically studied by Tomás y Tomás. He stated that in Spanish there are three types of r-like phonemes. There is the fricative /r/ which is essentially unstressed as in accepted Southern English. In addition there is a single trilled /r/ and also a doubly trilled /r/ the latter usually appearing orthographically as 'rr'. These three phonemes appear at different stages in the developing child. First of all and in the place where an /r/ might be expected is a semi-vowel /y/. Later this is replaced by a back consonant, i.e. /j/. A little later still appears a uvular /r/ a phoneme which is lacking in adult Spanish. Then comes the single trilled /r/ used in a correct context, and then the double trilled /r/ or 'rr'. Last of all, oddly enough, appears the fricative /r/.

While still in the infant phase, there is a proclivity towards reduplication of easy syllables which may again be regarded as an instance of play. Thus *dada* and *mama* appear early and probably indicate a trick or divertissement of the muscles of the lips and tongue facilitated by the act of sucking and the process of eruption of the incisors. Parents usually have their own special explanations, however, by choosing to believe that the infant is thereby recognizing its father and mother. But 'dada' and 'mama' appear early in languages where the usual diminutive terms for father and mother are different.

This argument must not be pushed too far, however. The child's awareness is largely limited to its immediate environment of parents, nurse, food, bed, and playthings. The mother is usually associated with utterances entailing the consonantal sound /m/. It has already been mentioned that this nasal phoneme when used as an expressive cry, is largely associated with hunger. The occurrence of /m/ sounds with an imitation of the act of sucking is a close one. This view is plausible enough, but does not serve to explain why the infant's father usually becomes associated with the consonantal forms /p/, /b/, /t/ or /d/. A materialistic explanation of their appearance at this age can be sought in the tip of the tongue rubbing against the alveolar ridge at the time of the eruption of the incisor teeth. As Fannie Hurst put it: '. . . Papa. A primitive phonetic word that must have had its etymology along the toothless gums of babes'.

Why there should be an association of /m/ sounds with the mother, and the front consonants with the father has been the subject of much speculation, none of it altogether satisfactory. Perhaps the sounds were basically expressive in origin, meaning being read into them later, so that the tie-up becomes firmly established.

Still in these early days the infant uses elaborate inflections, or 'tunes' in its babblings. The all-attentive parent learns to interpret these sound-sequences and invests them with a 'meaning' which may elude a stranger. At the same time the infant exaggerates the volume of sound which goes to form the utterance. Only later does control both of pitch and of intensity of speech develop.

By such gradations the infant's babblings merge slowly into the 'little speech' of a child. Here it seems safe to assume that a child's comprehension of the sounds it hears and the gestures it observes, is always ahead of its powers of vocalization. By trial and error; by imitation of adult speech; by solitary and sedulous speech-play, improvement occurs. As with the infant it must always be recalled that the child's larynx, pharynx, and buccal musculature are imperfect instruments for the faithful reproduction of adult sounds. A phonetician can discern at this stage certain rules underlying the difficulties and errors.

For example, during this period, a three-fold process of elision, substitution, and assimilation is continually at work. Thus a difficult consonantal sound is dropped; an easy one may be put in its stead; if two consonants occur in a single word, then the more difficult sound is replaced by the simpler one, which now becomes dominant for that word (e.g. French *peau-peau* instead of *chapeau*).

Just as certain phonemes may prove more difficult than others, so various combinations of sounds constitute even greater hurdles. The phonemes /h/, /z/, /zh/, /v/, /th/, (voiced and unvoiced) /s/, /sh/ and /f/, are difficult, and one of them may inappropriately surplant another. The unvoiced /th/ is probably the most difficult sound of all and the last to be mastered. Thus Sheridan found that out of 650 children under the age of 5, only 20 per cent of the girls and 9·7 per cent of the boys used it correctly. The author saw in this difficulty a confirmation of the theory of an auditory basis of speech development, for according to Harvey Fletcher, the phonetic force of the voiceless /th/ is 680 times less than the vowel-sound /aw/.

Double consonantal sounds offer special difficulty for the child, and one or other of them is usually elided. Thus *pretty* becomes *pitty*; *clean* becomes *keen*, and so on.

Attention may be drawn at this point to the composite table compiled by McCarthy (1946) indicating the development of linguistic behaviour. (See Table 1).

No study of the development of speech in the child can overlook the all-important rôle played by environmental factors. A child reared in a frigid and silent climate of indifference, will of necessity be late in attaining speech despite its innate readiness. On the other hand, if the parents or a loving nurse continually subject the infant to a linguistic barrage, even though it may be couched in baby-talk, speech maturity will appear earlier. Not only will it seemingly respond to coaxing and cosseting, and to lullabies, but it will comprehend earlier and react more readily to conversational situations.

An interesting study might be made in the development of speech in the Nigerian infant. Some mothers carry their infants in their arms; most, however, hitch them on to their hips. In the latter situation the infant is relatively deprived of sight and hearing of its mother. Whether there is a significant difference in subsequent development, especially in the linguistic sphere, is not known, but deserves specific enquiry.

G. A. Miller in an arresting fashion has summed up the interplay of extrinsic and intrinsic influences affecting language-development. 'If we tried to picture the most precocious child orator, we should think of a blind girl, the only daughter of wealthy parents. The child with the greatest handicap would be a hard-of-hearing boy, one of a pair of twins, born into a large family with poor parents who speak two or three languages'.

The exact date of the earliest beginnings of symbolic vocalization, or the use of meaningful words, varies within a month or two from one child to another. Even before the close of the first year an isolated word may have been enunciated clearly and in a correct context. M. W. Shirley (1933) studied 20 infants and found that the age of appearance of the first word varied from 46 to 66 weeks, the average age being 60 weeks. Earlier, G. Bateman (1917) had observed a series of 35 rather exceptional babies, and noted that the onset of the first word averaged 10 months. A few simple words lay within the province of three-quarters of them at the age of 12 months. Girls were found to be more forward than boys in this respect.

Seth and Guthrie were able to identify 12 to 22 meaningful words in their subject at the age of 15 months. As an example of a fuller analysis there is the record of speech-development made by W. S. Hall (1897). The child studied had 3 words at ten months, 12 in the eleventh, 24 in the twelfth, 38 in the thirteenth, 48 in the fourteenth, 106 in the fifteenth, 199 in the sixteenth, and 232 in the seventeenth. At six years it was reckoned that the child could utilize 2,688 words, apart from proper names. At the age of 2 years the child's speech entered the naming stage, or 'stage of substance' as Stern put it. About this time too, the child began to link words together in such a way as to betray both a primitive syntax, and also a word-order conventional for the language involved. By the end of the third year the vocabulary had become much expanded and the recurring question 'why' loomed largely. A third rapid increase in range of vocabulary took place between the ages of 4½ and 5½ years.

A study of the child's early attempts at the meaningful use of words brings to light many points of interest. It must always be realized that the understanding of a word or phrase ordinarily precedes the power of evoking correctly this same word or phrase. Many hurdles of magnitude have to be surmounted in the quest for adult speech. One difficulty lies in the use of concrete terms to signify group-ideas or abstractions. Thus the child who hears the word 'chair' may at first connect the symbol solely with a particular chair within its field of experience. To proceed from limitation of that sort to the categorical word 'chair', applicable to specimens of all shapes and sizes, is a big step.

TABLE 3.

STAGES IN THE DEVELOPMENT OF SPEECH IN THE INFANT FROM A STUDY OF EIGHT CASES BY MCCARTHY 1946

Behavior	Age in months					
	0	6	12	18	24	30
First noted vocalizations	XXXXXXXXX					
First responds to human voice	XXXXXX					
First cooing	XXXXX					
Vocalizes pleasure	XXXXXXXX					
Vocal play	XXXX					
Vocalizes eagerness and displeasure		XXX				
Imitates sounds		XXXXXXXXX-				
Vocalizes recognition		XX				
Listens to familiar words		XXXX				
First word		XXXXXXXXXX				
Expressive sounds and conversational jargon			XXXXXXXXXXXXXXXXXXX			
Follows simple commands			XXXXXXX			
Imitates syllables and words			XXXXXXXX			
Second word			XXXXX			
Responds to "no" and "don't"			XXXXXXXXXXXXX			
First says more than 2 words			XXXXX			
Names object or picture				XXXXXXXXXXXX		
Comprehends simple questions				XX		
Combines words in speech					XXXXXXX	
First uses pronouns					XXXXX	
First phrases and sentences					XXXX	
Understands prepositions						XXX

The next difficulty entails the correct use of such a word as 'father'. At first this may have for the child the significance of a proper name applicable only to a particular person. Later it may be realized that another child may use this same term 'father' for some other person who stands in a definite relationship to him. Still later there may be a confused application of 'father' to every other man; or to men of a particular age-group or appearance. The difficulties are enhanced when the man who is correctly regarded as 'father' by the child, is heard to be addressed as 'son' by the grandparent, or 'husband' by the mother. Even worse is the confusion if the child's mother is in the habit of addressing her husband as 'father'.

The conception of plurality and the correct use of numerals represent other hurdles. Yet another difficulty concerns the full understanding of the various meanings of the many homophones which occur not only in English but also in French and Chinese.

Jesperson emphasized another difficulty in a class of words which he spoke of as 'shifters', where meaning differs according to the situation. As examples we may quote once again 'father' and 'mother'; other instances are to be found in 'enemy', 'home', and, of course—perhaps the best examples of all—the personal pronouns. The meaning of the pronoun 'I' may at one time indicate mother or father, or someone else; or even the child itself. Parents and governesses ordinarily address the child by its proper name, in this way avoiding the use of a pronoun. This practice postpones the stage of mastery. Jesperson's comments on this problem deserve full quotation . . .

If some children soon learn to say 'I' while others speak of themselves by their name, the difference is not entirely due to the different mental powers of the children, but must be largely attributed to their elders' habit of addressing them by their name or by the pronouns. But Germans would not be Germans, and philosophers would not be philosophers, if they did not make the most of the child's use of 'I' in which they see the first sign of self-consciousness. The elder Fichte we are told, used to celebrate not his son's birthday, but the day on which he first spoke of himself as 'I'. The sober truth is, I take it, that a boy who speaks of himself as 'Jack' can have just as full and strong a perception of himself as opposed to the rest of the world as one who has learnt the linguistic trick of saying 'I'. But this does not suit some of the great psychologists, as seen from the following quotation: 'The child uses no pronouns; it speaks of itself in the third person, because it has no idea of its 'I' (ego) nor of its 'Not-I', because it knows nothing of itself nor of others'.

Pari passu with this intention of a meaningful vocabulary, there occurs an increasing practice of linking words into phrases. Herein we find the beginnings of syntax. This is a formidable undertaking which is steadily and eventually mastered by the young brain, and the magnitude of the achievement can be realized only when an adult attempts to learn a foreign tongue. Throughout this linguistic apprenticeship, the child comes up against various obstacles, some of them purely artificial. One of the most striking is shown by the interpretation by the child of what it hears, which may at times be erroneous, especially when the words are unusual, or when they constitute an oft-repeated phrase, as for example a prayer. Thus 'Our Father *chart* in heaven' is common enough. 'Hail Mary Mother of God be with us now and in the *arbardeth* (i.e. hour of our death)' is another example. Most of us have heard of the child who spoke of arithmetical sums as '*goesintos*', and in *Tom Brown's Schooldays* of the boy who thought that '*gudenuff*' was a simple word. This type of error is known as 'imperfect lexicalization', the expression 'lexicalization' meaning the power of detecting the vocal units in a flow of speech. Since, after all, a single word is rarely the natural linguistic unit, it is only to be expected that the beginner, like the student of a foreign language, should find difficulty in recognizing where one word ends and the next one begins. As Bertrand Russell said: 'At the lowest level of speech, the distinction between sentences and single words does not exist'. The English tongue is difficult enough, but the French language, by reason of its homophones and its intrinsic elisions and slurrings, adds considerably to the linguistic task. This observation is well shown by the couplet:

Gal, amant de la Reine, alla tour magnanime,
Gallament de l'Arène a la tour magne, a Nîmes.

(Gal, lover of the Queen, went, brave feat, gallantly
from the Arena to the large tower at Nîmes).

Should the developing child happen to be afflicted with a hearing-defect, even quite mild, or localized to a part only of the audiometric scale, the detrimental effect upon articulation may prove to be considerable.

The syntax of the child's 'little speech' has also been studied. Nouns appear early. At first they monopolize the vocabulary and later they predominate. Thus Stein found that nouns constituted 100% of all available words in a child of 15 months, but that by 20 months they made up only 78%, verbs comprising the remainder. At 23 months the proportion of nouns had shrunk to 63%, verbs constituting 23%, while 14% were made up of other parts of speech. To the young child all nouns are probably in the nature of proper nouns, being associated with particular persons, things or places; later some of them may become 'class-names' or collective nouns. Pronouns appear later than verbs, and are rarely used correctly before the age of two years. According to A. Gesell (1925) the ability to manipulate two pronouns with grammatical accuracy, means that the mental age of 2 has been reached; while three pronouns indicate the mental age of 3; and four or five pronouns the mental age of 4. According to Muntz, of 50 children aged 2 years, 48% used 'I', 'me' and 'you' appropriately, while 38% used none of them.

Plural forms and past tenses of verbs begin to crop up about the same time as pronouns appear, but they remain a source of difficulty until the age of 3. Of Muntz's series of 50 children aged 2 years, 54% could not utilize plurals and past tenses correctly, while 10% could use just one form of each.

According to Jesperson, most children learn to say 'no' before 'yes', negation being a stronger feeling than assent. Moreover, in the rather older child who is beginning to use phrases and sentences, negation is expressed by an affirmative statement to which a revocatory word is tacked on at the end. . . . 'just as in the speech of the deaf-mute' (Tracy), or in traffic signs in Latin America.

According to A. F. Watts (1944) the order of appearance of various parts of speech is roughly as follows: (1) proper names; (2) common nouns; (3) simple connecting words; (4) verbs and verbal forms referring to well-defined events; (5) prepositions, and simple relational words; (6) pronouns; (7) adjectives denoting qualities easily distinguished; (8) abstract nouns of increasingly higher level; and (9) adverbs.

The size and growth of vocabulary have already been mentioned as they appear in young children. With the increase in age and the expansion in vocabulary, precise estimations become increasingly difficult. One source of doubt entails the decision whether single and plural forms should be reckoned as one word or two. Should homonyms be regarded as merely one word? (e.g. bear, bare; site, sight; sun, son.) Jagger believed that during the kindergarten stage there is an increase of 800 words a year while M. E. Smith said 500–600 words. A. F. Watts concluded from a study of his own cases as well as from the literature, that the average English child entering the infant school at 5 years of age possesses a vocabulary of at least 2,000 words, and attains at 7 years or a little more at least 4,000 words. On leaving school at the age of 14 he should be in possession of some 8,000 to 10,000 words.

But it must be realized that as the child grows older, there arises an increasing disparity between his literary or passive vocabulary, and his oral or active vocabulary. That is to say, as the result of reading, the child becomes cognizant of numerous terms which it more or less understands, but which do not pass into the common currency of its spoken speech. According to Watts' estimate at 7 years the oral, active, or utilized vocabulary constitutes about only 50 per cent of the full vocabulary with its passive or literary components.

Jesperson's 'little speech' has been sympathetically studied in Russia by K. Chukovsky in his book so ably translated by Miriam Morton under the title *From Two to Five*. As the author asserted 'beginning with the age of two, every child becomes for a short period of time a linguistic genius. Later, beginning with the age of 5 to 6, this talent begins to fade'. The young child ordinarily imagines and uses words as occurring in pairs, as though each word had a twin, matched either in meaning or in sound. Rhyming, chanting and word-repetition are natural to the young child. Thus 'night-night' is easier than 'good-night'; 'bye-bye' simpler than 'goodbye'. All children are versifiers at first; learning to speak in prose comes later. Rhyming is an expression of the child's high spirits, and is often accompanied by lively motor activity, like running, jumping, and skipping. Between the ages of 2 and 5 the child is apt to compose what the author termed *ekiki* or nonsense rhymes. Certain properties are entailed, namely (1) spontaneity, or else inspiration out of merriment; (2) melodic exclamation; (3) an association with clapping or dancing; (4) a 'choreatic' mode of rhythm; (5) brevity; (6) repetitiousness; and (7) infectivity from one child to another. Chukovsky gave examples of Russian *ekiki* as in the following nonsense poem chanted and danced to by a little girl barely 2 years of age:

> Kossi minie, kossi koi
> Lieba Kussi, lieba koi.
> Kossi baba, kossi koi,
> Kussi paki, kussi moi.
> Ioka kuku, shubka koi
> Lieba kusia, shubka koi.

The author was well aware of the maternal rôle in the development of speech in the child. Often, in an upsurge of affection, the mother automatically plays a similar game. Thus a woman was observed to clutch her 4-month-old baby and rhapsodize:

> Butsiki, mutsiki, dutsiki,
> Rutsiki, putsiki, book!
> Kutsen'ki by, tarakutsen'ki,
> Putsen'ki by, marabuk!

Not one of these utterances was meaningful.

Chukovsky also dealt with the role of topsy-turvies (*pereviortyshi*) in the young child's ludic speech. Thus a child masters an idea and then makes it a verbal plaything by reversing the usual relationship of things. The function of object A is assigned to object B. An instance in English would be the nursery rhyme 'Hey diddle diddle, the cat and the fiddle ....' and so on where ludicrous activities are dreamed up and expressed in melodic form. To such items of nonsense, semi-nonsense, or familiar story-telling, the child will listen avidly, wearying the parents with his demands to 'read it again' or 'say it again' even though he knows the text by heart.

The classical monograph upon children's speech in English is the work of I. and P. Opie (1959) which should be consulted as a valuable and at the same time amusing source-book. Quoting Dylan Thomas who observed children 'tumble and rhyme' out of school, they proceeded to discuss the vast number of jingles uttered by schoolchildren, as for instance:

> 'Oh my finger, oh my thumb,
> Oh my belly, oh my bum'.

The Opies asserted 'these rhymes are more than playthings to children. They seem to be one of their means of communication with each other. Language is still new to them, and they find difficulty in expressing themselves. When on their own they burst into rhyme, of no recognizable relevancy, as a cover in unexpected situations, to pass off an awkward meeting, to fill a silence, to hide a deeply felt emotion, or in a gasp of excitement. And through these quaint ready-made formulas, the ridiculousness of life is underlined, the absurdity of the adult world and their teachers proclaimed, danger and death mocked, and the curiosity of language itself is savoured'.

Among the many phenomena of children's speech, the Opies dealt with the so-called 'truce names' which the youngster emits as a magic formula to secure respite from boisterous activity or chase. These are largely regional and according to the district may include such terms as 'barley', 'fainites', 'cree', 'keys' and many others. (See Fig. 2).

Although this chapter deals with the development of speech in the normal child it cannot avoid some reference to its delayed appearance. A certain latitude as to the time of onset of meaningful words must be conceded. Despite the suspicion of deafness, or of intellectual subnormality, or of a specific non-maturation of speech, none of these pathological conditions may actually be present. Most parents or grandparents are probably familiar with the phenomenon of a disturbingly late appearance of speech in one who in later life actually excels himself in the sphere of language, as a writer, public speaker or conversationalist.

Several unorthodox modes of development are recognizable: (1) The child may start to speak relatively late, after which his progress may be slow. His articulation is however clear, and eventually a normal level of linguistic attainment takes place. (2) The child starts to speak late; thereafter progress is slow. Articulation is abnormal, with perhaps a dyslalia; or cluttering; or stammering. These speech-defects may or may not disappear eventually. (3) The child may remain speechless for an unconscionable and disturbing length of time. Eventually however articulate speech appears, and thereafter matures with unusual rapidity. (4) Here again, the child may remain silent for an unconscionable length of time, when suddenly a quite elaborate phrase or sentence is emitted. After this somewhat startling *début*, speech advances rapidly. An even commoner but analagous phenomenon is that of 'free speech' encountered later in life. Here a young child unexpectedly gives vent to some obscenity or crudity which the shocked parents usually ascribe to the painters and decorators recently in the house.

Curious anomalies may concern the development of speech in identical twins. If the onset of speech is late, due to mental retardation for example, the eventual little speech may resemble a jargon mutually recognizable by the twins but incomprehensible to all others, as if the twins shared a secret language.

FIG. 2   Truce terms in Great Britain
(from I. and P. Opie 195)

This is exemplified in the case of the uniovular twin brothers G. whom I first saw when they were 11 years of age. They were restless phenyl pyruvic oligophrenics with a mental age of 3. In hospital they 'spoke' very little, and displayed indifference to requests or questions. Most of their time was spent in playful wrestling or fighting like a couple of high-spirited puppies.

They were re-admitted 4 years later by which time they were far less hyperkinetic. To some extent they responded to the speech of others. It was almost impossible to understand what they said and yet their sounds were certainly communicative and not merely verbal play. This was demonstrated by placing the twins in a room, with a tape-recorder concealed. Obviously one twin would articulate, while the other listened and then replied, showing that their utterances were mutually comprehensible, though not to others.

Here then was an extreme instance of speech retardation in twins who were mentally defective. But even in twins of normal intelligence speech development may be relatively late. Luria and Yudovich (1959) studied this phenomenon. Like most Soviet observers, they regarded the mental processes of the young child as products of his intercommunication with the environment. In 1929 Vigotsky asserted that every time a youngster of 4 or 5 is confronted with a problem, external speech appears, not directed to his entourage. The child would state the situation, and take from it 'verbal copy' and then utilize past experiences to help him out of present difficulties. According to these authors, this is not the same as Piaget's 'egocentric speech' but an inclusion of speech to mediate behaviour. Later Luria called this the 'regulating' function of speech and by a series of ingenious test-procedures entailing conditioned responses showed how a child's learning, and his problem-solving were assisted by audible speech. Working with Yudovich, Luria studied a pair of identical twins who like the couple already quoted, were endowed with some measure of what Eliasberg called 'autonomous' speech. Their understanding of the speech of others was imperfect: they might gather the meaning of simple statements accompanied by actions only if they were directly addressed to them. Their autonomous speech was sparse, and as in the case of the G. twins, it often ceased when in the presence of others. Much of it was 'synpraxic', i.e. accompanied by gesture. Phonetic inadequacies were present, for many sounds were not pronounced at all, while others were distorted. Often an object would receive different names on different occasions. Their 'words' did not possess a stable and precise meaning. Thus *itik* (leaf) also connoted a flower. *Makoka* (which should have been *morkovka*) referred not only to a carrot, but also to a turnip, a water-melon, and a plum. The same term might serve to indicate objects, actions, and qualities.

Removal of the twin-situation by separating the children, produced a steady improvement in their speech so that they began to articulate and to comprehend in accordance with their age.

But the researcher most often associated with the semantics of speech in childhood is Piaget. He recognized two chief categories, namely egocentric talk as opposed to socialized talk. In the former case the child does not bother to know to whom he is speaking or whether anyone is listening to him. He talks mainly to himself, If others are present the child has no desire to influence them or to tell them anything.

Egocentric speech is of 3 kinds: (1) repetition (or echolalia); (2) monologue; and (3) dual or collective monologue. Piaget believed that conversation between children entails imperfect comprehension. The effort to understand other people, and to communicate thoughts objectively does not appear in children before the age of about 7 or 7½. Socialized speech is made up of (1) adapted information; (2) criticism; (3) commands, requests, and threats; (4) questions; and (5) answers. Piaget followed Claparède in believing that young children perceive by means of general schemata, and words may be comprehended *in toto* whereas the component letters are not. Hence the terms 'syncretistic perceptions' and 'verbal syncretism'. To quote Piaget's own words . . . 'the fact that from the syncretistic point of view everything is related, everything is connected to everything else, everything is perceived through the network of general schemes built up of imagery, of analogies of detail and of contingent circumstances, makes it quite natural that idea of the accidental or the arbitrary should not exist for the syncretistic mentality, and that consequently a reason should be found for everything'.

A chapter dealing with the development of speech in the child is not complete without reference to the rare contrary phenomenon of linguistic precocity. Perhaps the best example is that of the 'Yale Prodigy'. At 4 months the child began to utter isolated words, while at 6 months he unexpectedly, but appropriately, said 'put on another record'. When 12 months of age he completed a first-grade reader. At 22 months he played by ear Liszt's Second Hungarian Rhapsody. He entered the sixth grade at school when he was 6 years of age. Two years later he had completed his first symphony. Passing top in mathematics and chemistry he entered the Western Reserve University at 10 years and when he was fourteen he graduated at Yale.

XIII. THINKING AND SPEAKING: VERBAL SYMBOLS IN THOUGHT

Language requires to be tuned like a violin: as just as too many or too few vibrations in the voice of the singer or the trembling of the string will make the note false, so too much or too little in words will spoil the message.

O. Wilde

The curse of philosophy has been the supposition that language is an exact medium. Philosophers verbalize and then suppose the idea is stated for all time.

Whitehead

I believe that the process of thought might be carried on independent and apart from spoken or written language. I do not in the least doubt that if language had been denied or withheld from man, thought would have been a process more simple, more easy, and more perfect than at present.

Samuel Taylor Coleridge

The nature of the association between thought and language has been a problem in philosophy for over two thousand years: whether, for example, thinking necessarily entails an imagery of words. Subsidiary questions also arise. For example, is the participation of verbal symbols in thought essential or accidental; universal or individual; habitual or occasional; optional or obligatory?

To the behaviourists no problem exists. For them, thought is nothing more than talking to oneself, though they would qualify this by the statement that talking comprises the use of verbal symbols or their muscular or visceral concomitants. Expressed a little differently, a behaviourist would regard thinking as largely subvocal talking, even though the use of words is not necessarily entailed.

From the earliest times there have been two opposite attitudes towards this subject. According to the 'monistic' theory thought and speech are one and indivisible (Leibniz, Schleiernicher, Schilling, Mueller, J. S. Mill, Wordsworth, Daudet, Mead, Bain, Ribot, Watson). The rival school adheres to a wholly 'dualistic' hypothesis which teaches that thought and speech are independent (Berkeley, Schopenhauer, Shelley, Galton, Binet, Hebb, Schilder, Hadamard, Einstein, Piaget, Reichenbach, Miller, Gasset and Tolman). Perhaps the majority of modern writers belong here, but with certain reservations. Thus, although thought and language are now generally regarded as being essentially independent, they are also looked upon as being in frequent co-operation and as mutually adjuvant.

In the sacred books of the East we read that the matter was definitely settled when a dispute took place between Mind and Speech as to which was the better of the two. Both Mind and Speech proclaimed their

159

own merits. Mind said: 'Surely I am better than thou, for thou dost not speak anything that is not under-stood by me; and since thou art only an imitator of what is done by me, and a follower in my wake, I am surely better than thou!' Speech replied: 'Surely I am better than thou, for what thou knowest I make known, I communicate!' They therefore appealed to Pragapati 'The Master of Life' who decided in favour of Mind, saying to Speech, 'Mind is indeed better than thou, for thou art an imitator of its deeds and a follower in its wake; and inferior surely is he who imitates his better's deeds and follows in his wake'.

Man shares with animals the function of sign-making, but he stands apart in his ability to utilize words, and these transcend the category of signs. The noise of barking in the street can be accepted as a 'sign' that there is a dog outside, but the assemblage of the four letters b.a.r.k. is not to be regarded as a sign either of barking or of a dog. It is something more. Admittedly onomato-poeic terms may be looked upon as signs, but most other classes of words are 'signs of signs' or more simply, 'symbols', in that they can refer to things *in absentia*. Thus speech becomes, in the words of Henry Head, an aspect of 'symbolic formulation and expression'. This definition may or may not be adequate for neurological purposes, but it certainly does not satisfy the logicians or epistemologists of today.

The topic has been side-tracked in the past by fluctuating notions of what is meant by the terms 'thinking' and 'thought'. These two words have been employed synonymously to cover a complex and most diverse series of mental processes, extending from a passive and intransitive state at one end of the scale, to a highly active transitive procedure at the other.

That the expressions 'thought' and 'thinking' are so often used interchangeably, testifies eloquently to the short-comings of verbal symbols as vehicles for meaning. One trouble is that these two terms are part of everyday linguistic usage. In addition they are employed in a technical or narrow sense both by philosophers and by psychologists, but possibly not quite identically. Psychologists of today have travelled a long way from Plato's definition of thinking, or . . . 'the conversation which the soul holds with herself in considering of anything . . . The soul when thinking appears just talking, asking questions of herself and answering them, affirming and denying'. The term 'thought' may well be taken as embracing every conceivable aspect of menta-tion which proceeds during a conscious state. But the level of consciousness may differ widely. 'Thought' (or 'thinking') may include such willed or deliberate activities as are entailed in literary creation; planning; scheming; problem-solving; adjudication, and polemics. The same term can also be made to apply to purely passive mental processes, like browsing, day-dreaming, the pleasurable anticipation of a meal, or gratified rumination thereafter.

The scientist's problem would be simplified if only there were words which could be used with precision to connote these diverse aspects of mentation. Compelled to accept an all-embracing pair of synonyms—thought and thinking—we find that our ideas as to their relationship with speech are needlessly complicated.

To Noiré's dogmatic assertion that thought is just as little possible without language as language without thought, it may be protested—what particular type of thought? Or did Noiré use that term, not loosely, but with studied deliberation, as a comprehensive label which could be attached to every possible type of cerebral activity? According to Buyssens, the term 'thinking' refers to any psychological activity the existence of which is assumed in order to interpret behaviour. He defined 'thought' as denoting that which this activity concerns, or what may be called the content of the mind when it is thinking that which is thought of, felt or decided. This conception supplants the dictum put forward by Titchener, who regarded thought as the verbal counterpart of active imagination. 'Active imagination is thinking in images; thinking is active imagination carried on in words'.

The whole idea of mental images as the scaffolding of thought is unfashionable nowadays, though philosophers may well have gone too far in their iconoclasm. Perhaps they have not sufficiently taken into account the nature of the mental operations of humbler minds. As Professor Price has said: '. . . it is a misfortune for a philosopher to be too clever. It is the human mind in general, and not just the minds of highly intellectual persons like himself, which he is supposed to be studying'.

Neurologists adhere to the school of Imaginists, for they still consider that most thinking takes place through the instrumentality of images, mainly in the form of verbal symbols. But during states of day-dreaming, an imagery of non-verbal character may operate. At any moment, however, by a deliberate act of introspection or of focussing of attention upon the content of the reverie, the thinking-processes may crystallize out into formal symbols of a verbal sort. This formulation not only applies to the immediate content of the thought, but it can also extend backwards into the time-past, though only for a very short period. It may also reach forwards and continue to regiment the thinking into words, though usually not for long. As attention gradually wanes or switches elsewhere, the pattern of thinking becomes less clear-cut, and definite verbal symbols may then be discarded. A primitive and rather passive type of thinking probably obtains in the case of an animal, savage or child, who awake but inactive, can be looked upon as musing, rather than indulging in creative or active thinking or problem-solving.

The extent to which verbal symbols enter into the framework of these diverse modes of thought is variable.

Some thinking processes are of a more lofty order within which verbal symbols play a minor role, if any at all. Here belongs the 'naked thought' which we identify with mathematics, physicists and chemists. Then again, freedom from the trammels of words may possibly act as a pabulum for creative and inspired thought. Perhaps the cerebration of musicians belongs within this category, especially in their productive moments. As Charles Morgan said: 'Sometimes the music composed silently is about nothing that is visible or touchable or audible; it's about something inside nature and beyond the senses, which isn't even thinkable except in music, and, I suppose, only imperfectly, even in music'.

Here we approach Bergson's dichotomy of knowledge into symbolical as opposed to intuitive. We submit that it is justifiable to correlate the terms 'knowledge' and 'thought', in that knowledge, in the sense of that which is known, is—or ought to be—communicable. Intuitive knowledge, however, must by definition be a mode of thinking which is incommunicable, for it transcends verbal symbols. It seems impossible to avoid the difficulties entailed by Bergson's ideas, except by recourse to an evasion or quibble. An intuitive experience can be made known, described and conveyed to others, only retrospectively; that is by dint of concepts framed after the intuition.

Perhaps no rigid rules can be laid down. Utilization of verbal symbols may well be a highly personal mode of thinking; but surely it is one which applies to most persons most of the time. However, there may be exceptional people who utilize verbal symbols less often. Here may belong persons within the highest intellectual or aesthetic brackets; and, conversely, some of those with lowly levels of intelligence. Révész contrasted an 'object-coherent' method of speaking with a more 'language-coherent' type, the former being typical of a scientist, the latter of a philosopher or a student of the humanities. Silent utilization of verbal symbols is not necessarily a consistent phenomenon, for an individual may switch from one mode of thinking to another according to circumstances. Some thought can be looked upon as being 'word-near', other types of thinking being 'word-free'.

Thought and speech may well be independent processes, but as we shall see, the act of speaking can influence the processes of thought in an antidromic or retrograde manner, bringing order and precision out of formless things.

'Let it be admitted then', said Whitehead, 'that language is not the essence of thought. But this conclusion must be carefully limited. Apart from language, the retention of thought; the easy recall of thought, the interweaving of thought into higher complexity, the communication of thought, are all gravely limited.'

Another argument against a narrow equation of thinking and speaking is exemplified by the polyglot who, while using a foreign tongue, hesitates in the selection of the appropriate heteronym. This act of surveillance suggests that there may exist a vigilant and detached process of super-linguistic judgement which chooses, sorts, selects, rejects and decides between rival symbols, but remains independent of actual thinking-in-words. As Buyssens said, 'the equivalents between expressions can only be established by some activity that is not language'. In the case of the mother-tongue too, there is a process which goes on during the choice of words which evaluates meaning, selects and compares. This process must entail an aspect of thinking which is both independent of words and superior to them.

Thought as the precursor of speech is one matter. But, like a reversible chemical reaction, speech certainly is capable of exercising some moulding effect upon our thought. When Oscar Wilde said that 'language is the parent, not the child of thought', he was going too far. All the same, as Francis Bacon, and as Schopenhauer clearly emphasized, we do, by the sheer act of speaking, shape and modify our thinking processes in a very significant fashion.

The act of speaking effects a sort of discipline upon thought, assisting it, and also arranging and clarifying one's ideas. There is the familiar phenomenon of the committee man or the debater who, when called upon to speak extemporaneously, starts off with quite a nebulous idea as to what he wants to say. His views may be undefined; his thoughts vague. But as he speaks, slowly to begin with, his words cause his ideas to crystallize out, to shape themselves. He proceeds in a groping and fumbling fashion at first, but gradually some regimentation results. It used to be said of Charles James Fox that during his parliamentary debates he would get himself into the middle of a sentence and would trust to Providence to get himself out again. When we give tongue, therefore, we find that the process of talking transmutes thought from an amorphous passive faculty into some kind of order. Sometimes too rigidly so, for grammar may place its cold, dead hand upon inspired creative exuberance in a deleterious fashion. The polyglot who switches from a stilted and rigidly inflected syntax (such as German) to an entirely different language-system, such as for example, Chinese, is really engaging in a sort of mental acrobatics. He actually changes his own code of thought; he virtually sheds one kind of personality and assumes another. That is why we believe that a bilingual man has two strings to his bow, both of them, however, a little slack.

The protagonists in the long drawn-out debate upon the relationship of thought to speech have strangely neglected the lessons available from medical experience. Neurologists, for instance, are familiar with not a few circumstances in which thinking and speaking are dissociated. Thus there are sundry ineffable mental events, usually short-lived, which perplex the subject especially in his faltering attempts to describe them. Here belong those experiences described by Mayer and Orth under the term 'attitudes of consciousness' (*Bewusstseinlagen*). A striking example is to be seen in the paroxysmal states associated with psychomotor or temporal lobe epilepsy. Some bizarre drug intoxications entail such psychedelic episodes. There are also those states of so-called 'ecstasy' recorded both in theological and psychiatric literature. All these phenomena might be included within the group of mystical experiences which Bergson would doubtless have correlated with intuitive knowledge.

Somerset Maugham well described the inadequacy of words in such circumstances

... I'd never known such exaltation and such a transcendent joy ... I felt as though I were suddenly released from my body and as pure spirit partook of a loveliness I had never conceived. I had a sense that a knowledge more than human possessed me, so that everything that had been confessed was clear, and that everything that had perplexed me was explained ... No words can tell the ecstasy of my bliss ... It's impossible to deny the fact of its occurrence; the only difficulty is to explain it. If I was for a moment one with the Absolute or if it was an inrush from the subconscious of an affinity with the universal spirit which is latent in all of us, I wouldn't know.

There are other occasions when language cannot adequately keep pace with thought: when it falters behind, as in such circumstances as the spell of artistic, poetic, and musical aesthetic inspiration. This is one reason why the terminology of the critic of music and of painting is often so bizarre, so very inadequate.

Most important however among the neuro-pathological dissociations between thinking and speaking is the condition of aphasia, where speech becomes more or less ablated in one who had attained maturity in the realm of language. A chronic aphasia is encountered usually in a conscious sentient adult of presumed normal intelligence, whose educational background had previously assured him an average competency in the use of words. Despite his impaired language, the victim is alert, more or less in touch with his environment, and capable of considerable range of spontaneous activity.

With due modesty, medical men may thus venture into the territory of philosophy by dint of their acquaintance with this clinical phenomenon of aphasia, whereby the aptitude of speech is undermined in a specific fashion. This side of the topic, hitherto rather neglected, promises to throw light upon the more fundamental problems of thinking and speech. It immediately raises the important rider as to the role of 'intelligence' in aphasia; whether loss of speech necessarily entails a disorder of general intellectual functions; and whether such intellectual disorder—if present—is quantitative or qualitative, or both. If it be objected after consideration that such a matter is little more than academic quibble, or mere word-spinning, we can remind ourselves that at any moment we doctors may be confronted with harsh and practical issues of a medico-legal character. In addition there is the question, not so much of the integrity of the 'intellect' in aphasiacs, but the actual nature of their thinking-processes. These are in reality two quite distinct problems which should be considered apart. There is perhaps no more difficult exercise in neurology than the decision as to whether aphasia, in general or in particular, entails a disorder in *Gesamptpsyche*.

On all counts the problem is a difficult one. Dysphasia is not a sharply demarcated clinical entity, but comprises many grades and varieties of speech-disorder. When this fact is realized, it becomes obvious that there can be no clear-cut answer to the question whether intelligence is impaired in cases of aphasia. Neurology recognizes a number of quite different clinical variants of speech-impairment. Obviously no ready formula offers itself as a simple index of the intellectual state of aphasiacs with differing types of speech-affection.

A century ago Hughlings Jackson, a disciple of Herbert Spencer, broke away from contemporary materialistic notions as to cerebral function and dysfunction. He emphasized again and again that a severe aphasiac is speechless but not wordless; that by reason of left brain-disease the power of voluntary evocation of words is lost, but that with his other hemisphere he can still understand words and evoke them automatically as images. No essential difference, he said, exists between external speech and internal speech. When people are not 'talking' they may still be 'speaking', for they may be utilizing internal speech. But thought, so he said, is not internal speech. The speechless man can think because he has in automatic form all the words he ever had. It is not a question of whether or not a 'memory' of words is lost in aphasia. The speechless patient is 'lame' in his thinking; that is, he cannot learn novel or complex things; he cannot speak to himself and tell himself about things presented or represented in unfamiliar relations. He can bring two images into co-existence within one unit of time, but he cannot organize the connection if it entails difficulty. Words are not essential for thought, but conceptual thought necessitates some sort of symbols. Lower animals think, using inferior symbols to serve their lowly mentation. In the same way man may utilize symbols other than words, that is, 'arbitrary perceptive signs', or 'arbitrary images'. The use of such symbols constitutes ideation which is akin to perception, differing only in that the images are fainter and less vivid: the images are projected in an indefinite way; and the faint images previously acquired. Many of Hughlings Jackson's beliefs are no longer held, but when they were first promulgated, they constituted the iconoclastic beginnings of a dynamic of philosophic attitude to the problem, one which is still operative.

Let us turn for a moment to the methods that have been employed by us neurologists in studying aphasia, particularly in our quest for the physiological mechanism of the underlying defect.

Hitherto we have relied chiefly upon a close examination of the patient, noting carefully not only what he cannot do or say, but also what he can. More and more ingenious and intricate tests have been devised, some of them exploring aspects of mentation and of behaviour which do not pertain very closely to the faculty of speech. In this way a stock of non-verbal tests has accumulated, and is still increasing.

To this type of research one may add the relatively scant evidence garnered by introspective probing of the difficulties experienced during aphasia, as described in retrospect by intelligent subjects who have recovered from a transient speechlessness. Some of these interesting reports have been made by medical men, such as Lordat, Saloz, Forel, Tilney, Andrewes, Tinel. Intriguing though they are, their value is limited. For various reasons it must be deemed unsafe to accept uncritically the personal conclusions reached by such writers.

Various linguistic considerations may be carried over to the problem of the aphasiac. In such states of pathology the speechless person is something more than an individual whose means of imparting information has been affected. He has become one whose total behaviour has of necessity undergone a modification, and a continually changing modification at that. It is not correct to assert, as some have done, that the aphasiac is like a tourist in a foreign country whose language he does not speak. The difficulties go far deeper. The traveller's problem arises from ignorance of the verbal symbols which are conventional to the environment; but his power of thinking about things remains intact. The aphasiac, however, has not only lost the ability to use certain symbols in intercourse, but he finds that they may also be unavailable to him at a silent level.

The nöeticists are surely closer to the truth when they describe the aphasiac as being afflicted with some measure of disorder of language in the fullest sense of the word, and hence a disorder of his thought, his behaviour, orientation and philosophy.

Speaking entails activity at many distinct levels, and persons differ widely according to the use they make of these various linguistic hierarchies. Individual habits of speech, or linguistic usages, probably play no small part in determining the final pattern of aphasia. This is a factor which deserves at least as much attention as the better known variables, namely, the size of the lesion, the exact location, and the rate of its development.

Obviously it would be too formidable a task to deal with the whole subject of thought and intellect in aphasiacs. Let us concentrate upon an extreme case, one that forms a curiously interesting, although uncommon clinical type, namely, the aphasiac with recurrent utterance. For some weeks after the onset of his stroke, the patient may be confused and unable to fend for himself; he will doubtless be confined to bed. As time goes by the sensorium may become clearer. The patient, if not actually hemiplegic can now dress, shave and bathe himself; potter around his home; eat at table and mix with others. But he can neither read nor write; he understands what is said to him provided only that the topic is simple and familiar, and does not entail a succession of ideas or the problem of a choice. It is imperative too that the conversation should be directed exclusively to himself, without the handicap of cross talk or linguistic noise. He is correctly orientated and he recognizes persons and objects. He can interpret simple representational book-illustrations and pictures. He watches television and the cinema, though without full understanding. In his social intercourse he makes excessive use of pantomimic movements and he follows the gestures of others. His speech however continues to be restricted to a solitary verbal automatism. Whether this ejaculation be a word or a phrase, or even a fragment of gibberish, it is, in any event, wholly inappropriate.

The problem here entails two matters: (1) the state of the patient's intelligence; and (2) the content and nature of his thinking-processes.

General intelligence suffers in aphasiacs, first as a straightforward epiphenomenon of an extensive destruction of cerebral tissue independent of the loss of speech. In the second place mentation is altered qualitatively in aphasiacs, in that conceptual thinking and behaviour are generally considered to be difficult if not impossible, being replaced, it is claimed, by a far more concrete attitude. And thirdly, general intelligence suffers in so far as the appropriate mental operations demand the use of verbal symbols. Clearly the total impairment will depend partly upon the premorbid personality of the victim, including his habitual type of imagery, as well as his former habits and usages of speech. It will also directly depend upon the number of available verbal symbols. An aphasiac with a solitary recurrent utterance can be looked upon as being very nearly speechless, having only a single verbal symbol available for exteriorization.

Hughlings Jackson's belief in the identity of internal and external speech is not held today. Endophasy, inner speech, internal speech, or the 'preverbitum' (as I have called it), is by no means identical with subvocal or silent speech. This statement is true both for the normal subject and the aphasiac. Inner speech is more amorphous than articulated utterance. It dispenses with grammar, being abrupt and incomplete. 'Empty' words are not used; only 'full' words. Word-order is logical rather than conventional, and may differ from that ordained by grammarians. Inner speech belongs to what Vigotsky called 'predicative speech'. Inner speech exists for oneself, outer speech for others: Inner speech is intransitive, outer speech may be transitive. Inner speech is made up of tacts; outer speech of mands as well as tacts. 'Inner speech works with semantics, not with phonetics' (Vigotsky). Inner speech is not intended for communication. It is more concerned with the sense of words than with their meanings, as Paulhan would say. There occurs a predominance of sense over meaning, sentence over word, and context over sentence.

Any patient with recurrent utterance must obviously suffer an affection of his inner speech, though to a lesser degree than of his external speech. The fact that he can receive, comprehend, and react to a few verbal symbols put to him in the way of simple commands or requests, means that he can identify and recognize these verbal symbols, even if he cannot utilize them. Perhaps in this task he is materially assisted by the interlocutor's gestures, as well as by the general climate of expectation. The difficulty which the patient displays in manipulating auditory verbal symbols is demonstrated by the serious defect in intellectual operations which require the medium of verbal symbols. Intelligence must therefore of necessity suffer, and in direct relationship to the degree of receptive rather than expressive difficulties.

During the later stages when the aphasia is established, the patient with recurrent utterance recovers at least some measure of awareness of his plight. First he learns to inhibit their compulsive evocation, by willed silence. Later he will make an effort to compensate for his single-code communication-system by varying the tones and inflections of his voice. In this way he does his best to make his sole instrument serve many purposes—assent or denial; greeting or dismissal; interrogation, assertion, or request. All these belong to the class of mands, as opposed to tacts. He is like a musician deprived of every instrument save a one-string violin upon which he feebly attempts an orchestral symphony.

Furthermore, in this chronic stage, the aphasic patient with recurrent utterance is still capable of imparting secondary information (to use the language of communication-theory), though still unable to emit primary information. Thus he can receive from an interlocutor a simple and straight-forward piece of news (e.g. 'your supper is ready'), and if he comprehends this phrase, the patient can then let the speaker know that he understands by an appropriate nodding of the head, or by smiling, or by getting up out of his chair and going to the dining-room. These signs constitute one kind of secondary information. The patient is however unable to perform the additional normal technique, and repeat back the message correctly.

What is the nature of the silent rumination of such an aphasiac? Is it in the nature of image-less thinking? This is unlikely. Yet it is probably not a type of reverie in which verbal symbols take part. In his states of contemplation, as he sits browsing or day-dreaming, the patient may well be merely a passive receptor of a series of images, mainly of a visual character. These images will be quite loosely connected, being vaguely related one with another by the freest of associations. There is nothing consistent, stable, or profound.

Such a patient resembles a primate who under experimental conditions can be observed to solve easy problems, to make use of a tool in a simple way, and to carry out straightforward and short-term planned or purposive acts. He differs from the animal in that he can in propitious circumstances recognize, identify and respond to a more considerable package of verbal commands or requests. But like the animal he cannot return the message.

Let us for a moment turn aside from the main argument in order to discuss another matter which is partly germane. This concerns the nature of speech, with particular reference to its functions. Here we may perhaps quote Holloway's catalogue of the multitudinous purposes of speech:

> Language is used to influence the actions or the feelings or the beliefs of other persons . . . It is used, more or less recited, to influence our own feelings . . . or our own beliefs . . . It is used as in polite small-talk to avoid awkward silences or to conform to certain norms of etiquette. It is used to pose questions, to make promises, requests, bids, surrenders, bets and the rest . . . and to count and calculate. It is used to deceive and to silence those who contradict us. It is used to enter pleas to give testimony and make confessions . . . to take oath, to pray, to give thanks, and remit sins. It is used to act, to recite, to eulogize, to mourn, to curse, to compliment, to congratulate, to celebrate, to exercise magical powers upon subjects, to conjure and exorcise spirits. It is used to indicate the time at which something occurs, or the time at which someone is to act in a certain manner. For example, to start races or announce their start or to drill a squad. It is used to draw attention to gesture, or to our own location in space. It is used to remind us of what is already familiar. It is used to train and educate. It is used to construct verbal complexes like poems which conform to certain artistic requirements or canons. It is used to tell stories and to make jokes. It is used to promulgate laws including the rules of its own use and to provide illustrative examples of how they may be kept or broken, or of any other aspect of itself. Doubtless it is used in many other ways as well.

The numerous definitions of speech and of language put forward at one time or another and already quoted in Chapter 1, demonstrate a preoccupation with the function of speech rather than with its essential nature. Furthermore there is a current emphasis upon the role of speech as a channel for imparting information. This represents the functionalist's attitude towards speech. The conception of speech as a means of communicating ideas and feelings lies behind most of the modern definitions. Thus speech becomes purposeful and utilitarian, being directed towards an object or goal. Every act of speech is said to entail a speaker, a message, and a recipient; the three aspects being termed: utterance (or expression); evocation; and reference (or representation). Reference may be said to straddle the expressive and evocatory aspects of speech, making communication possible and endowing it with its idiosyncratic character.

Yet there must be another side to the problem. Speech is concerned with feelings as well as ideas. It may be claimed that communication of emotions is perhaps of lesser import than the expression of emotions. Words may be emitted and even set down upon paper, less as a deliberate act of imparting information, than from an impelling and egocentric urge towards self-expression. When words are uttered in song the communicative act is subordinate; the lyric matters less than the melody. So in speech. At times words are articulated or written, largely for their own sake: as a form of play; as a mental catharsis; as an alleviation of a *cacoëthes scribendi*; as an aesthetic exercise where an audience means little. A self-expressive type of speech can be observed in the babbling of infants; the rhyming and chanting of children as we have already discussed at length; the small-talk and *tripotage* of the chatter-box; much of the verbiage of a politician's studied filibustering; and most of the versification of the poet. Nor is this the whole story. There is an intermediate type of speech half-way between communication and expression. Here belongs the declamation of the orator, and especially the prosy after-dinner speaker; here too belongs the phenomenon of wit, where the *bon mot* or the scintillating phrase achieves little communicative purpose, but gives enjoyment of itself, and more to the perpetrator than to the listener.

We are realizing more and more that the use of language in normal persons is an individual or idiosyncratic matter. No two speakers and no two writers have exactly the same habits of verbal expression. As Buffon said: '*Le style. . . . c'est l'homme même*'. Language, as a highly personal accomplishment, is much more than a utilitarian contrivance; it is also a social act, an aspect of behaviour, a 'mode of action'. When a skilled polyglot turns rapidly from one language to another, he faces the task not only of selecting alternatives and pseudo-synonyms, but of shifting from one personality to another like a play-actor.

One of the weaknesses of current linguistic philosophy (and also of the pathology of speech) lies in the fact that only a few of the world's language-systems have been under scrutiny. Most research work has been carried out upon one or other of the Indo-European languages, to the neglect of the manifold linguistic-systems of Africa, Asia, Melanesia, Polynesia, and Amerindia. This is regrettable, because there are important differences in linguistic structure which one cannot afford to overlook. A few philologists have been alive to this lacune, such as for example Abel, Byrne, Sapir and Whorf. The last-named in particular emphasized repeatedly that certain languages are built upon a plan entirely different from what he called the S.A.E. (Standard Average European) group of tongues. The former, he said, are 'oligosynthetic' languages which are built up from a small number of elements. This structure is quite different from the subject-predicate system with which we are so familiar.

A few examples may be given. The Hopi language of North America has no words and no grammatical expression which refer directly to 'time': that is, there are no indications as to past, present, or future; nor to the notions of 'enduring' or 'continuing'; nor even for the matter of that, to space. Hopi may thus be called a 'timeless language'. Plurality is expressed in an odd fashion: there are no orthodox plurals in Hopi. Instead of . . . 'they stayed 10 days', the Hopi Indian would say, 'they stayed until the eleventh day'; or else 'they left after the tenth day'. The standard European phase-terms (summer, winter, noon and so on) are used in quite a different manner. Instead of 'in the morning' a Hopi would say 'while the morning phase is occurring'. The Hopi cannot say, 'in the summer', but 'summer now' or 'summer recently'. Likewise in Chinese there is no term which stands for 'word', the nearest approximation being *tsz* which indicates a syllable rather than a word, and which never exists in free-form but always in combination.

Absence of a subject-predicate basis is well observed in Nootka, a tongue spoken in Vancouver Island, which has no grammar, and where the simplest utterance is a sentence. Long sentences are not sentences of words, but sentences of sentences, as Whorf put it. The statement 'he invites people to a feast' would be rendered in Nootka more or less as 'boiled eaters go for he does'.

Some would consider that behind all these indications of an utterly different linguistic structure lies a fundamental difference in the mode of thinking. Whorf, for instance, held that the structure of a language influences the manner of understanding reality and also behaviour. Herein lies his 'principle of linguistic relativity' which has since been commonly spoken of as the 'Sapir-Whorf hypotheses'. Whorf defined his principal linguistic relativity by saying that 'users of markedly different grammars are pointed by their grammars towards different evaluations of externally similar acts of observation, and hence are not equivalent as observers, but must arrive at somewhat different views of the world'.

This fascinating doctrine has been discussed by many authors besides Sapir and Whorf. The German philologists Vossler, Spitzer, Lerch, among others, were of this opinion; but Bonfante believed that the hypothesis originated with Croce. According to Kluckhorn and Leighton it is impossible to comprehend the Navaho way of thinking without a profound knowledge of the Navaho tongue. Hoijer correlated the passivity and fatalistic attitude of Navaho mythology with the verb-system of the language (whereby persons do not 'initiate' acts but only 'become involved' in them). Years before, James Byrne had sought to trace a parallel between language-structure and Jung's two types of personality. Like Pott who had discussed 'separate linguistics', Whorf felt that there was a need for a science of 'contrastive linguistics' as opposed to comparative linguistics, and he made the point, with which few would disagree, that there is no such thing as a 'primitive' language. Sapir had already said that the lowliest South African bushman utilizes a rich symbolic system that is in essence comparable with the speech of a cultivated Frenchman. We remind ourselves that something similar was expressed by Suzanne Langer even more picturesquely. The language spoken by primitive peoples may at times prove to be more rational, or more logical than the standard average European. Thus, reverting again to the Hopi tongue, Whorf stated that the two English phrases 'I see that it is red' and 'I see that it is new' would require in Hopi two different terms to translate the verb 'see'. Whorf put the question '. . . does the Hopi language show here a higher plane of thinking, a more rational analysis of situations than our vaunted English? Of course it does. In this field and in various others, English compared to Hopi is like a bludgeon compared to a rapier'. Whorf also stated that one of the characteristics of Hopi behaviour is fundamentally concerned with preparation. This preoccupation includes not only an announcement of the intention but also getting ready for events in very good time. Elaborate precautions are taken to ensure persistence of described conditions, with emphasis on goodwill. Hopi 'preparing behaviour' may be divided into proclamation, outer preparing, inner preparing, covert participation, and persistence. All these ideas are mirrored in their language (Whorf).

Which comes first, the mode of speaking or the mode of thought? The question even now cannot be answered dogmatically. Yet again: are the profound differences in linguistic structure really of fundamental import? Some, like Lenneberg and also Faner, have said that a general and basic similarity of thinking exists despite all linguistic differences, and that variations of verbal expression are largely questions of metaphor. But Whorf disagreed. He claimed that the background linguistic system, i.e. the grammar of each language is not merely a reproducing instrument for voicing ideas, but is in itself the shape of ideas, the programme and guide for the individual mental activity, for his analysis of impression, for the synthesis of his mental stock in trade. Formulation of ideas is not an independent process, but is part of a particular grammar, and differs in greater or lesser degree, between different grammars. 'We dissect nature along the lines laid down by our native language.'

At this point it might be wise to pause to consider again the problem of how the act of communication influences the act of thinking. As Francis Bacon said: 'Men believe that their Reason is lord over their words, but it happens too, that words exercise a reciprocal and reactionary power over our intellect'. Regarding the interaction of language and thought, Sapir stated that the instrument makes possible the product, while the product refines the instrument. The mere act of speaking exerts a disciplinary effect upon the associated thinking-process, co-ordinating ideas and clarifying them.

The same sort of frustration may affect the linguist who tries to funnel the torrent of his ideas through the narrow offices of an unfamiliar tongue.

There are many other circumstances when the use of words may unduly control thinking, stultify it and destroy it. This is unfortunately no uncommon state of affairs. It stems from the tendency to confuse the names of ideas with the ideas themselves, and the names of things with the things themselves. This is a subtle error which can insinuate itself into our system of beliefs, and before we know where we are we have erected a system of prejudices. All the more dangerous is this error, because it begins to assert itself in the early stages of the development of speech. It is particularly obtrusive in the speech of primitive communities where words are liable to become endowed with magical significance: hence arise the phenomena of verbal taboo, of verbal spells and talismans. Even within the speech of modern man there is a danger that over-indulgence in slipshod linguistic habits—recourse to the too trite phrase for example—will dominate the speaker's thought. Words which should be servants now become masters. A veritable tyranny of words develops. A *pot-pourri* of clichés may eventually usurp the place of intellectualism, beliefs and judgements. Such is one of the insidious weaknesses of the structure of modern life, threatening to be an even greater menace in the future.

Upon all counts, words must be looked upon as inadequate symbols, far less satisfactory for example than those used by mathematicians or chemists. Were communication of ideas really the sole function of speech, the mechanism would have to be rated as imperfect. Words are imprecise;

often ambiguous; at times wholly deceiving. Always they are elliptic and incomplete, and no combination of words, however many they be and however carefully chosen, can fully do justice to the underlying idea. Language can convey only a part of thought.

'Words are as moody as prima donnas and as plastic as putty. They cannnot be relied upon to mean the same thing at different times, or to different people at the same time.' (Holbrook Jackson). The properties of the same word may alter according to the speaker and the frame of reference. Professor Dougall illustrated this with the word 'power'. Ordinarily this has a connotation which might equally well be expressed by such allied terms as 'strength', 'force', 'impetus', or 'momentum'. But to a scientist, these five terms are anything but synonymous, and each has its own clear-cut definition and applicability. A poet, however, might deliberately utilize the word 'power' in an allusive, vague and imaginative fashion, as when he talks of the 'principalities and powers of darkness'.

The inadequacies of words as symbols of thought are well shown in the task of translating from one language to another. Croce declared that a work of literary art can never be translated. Some persons naïvely imagine that any logical idea can be transmitted from one tongue to another, without detriment. On this point Stuart Chase declares . . . 'a few minutes in the glass palace of the United Nations in New York will quickly disabuse one of this quaint notion'. Even such a common concept as 'democracy' may not survive translation. It is impossible to interpret a foreigner without losing thereby some semantic nuance. *Traduttore, traditore* as they say in Italy. In 1655 James Howell wrote:

> Some bold Translations not unlike to be
> The wrong side of a Turkey tapistry;
> As Wines drawn off the Lees, which filled in Flask
> Lose somewhat of their strength they had in Cask.
> 'Tis true each Language hath an Idiom
> Which in another couched, comes not so home.

We may also quote from a still earlier source:

> For it is by no means always the case that translated terms preserve the original thought; indeed, every nation has some idiomatic expressions which it is impossible to render perfectly in the language of another. (Iamblichus)

That verbal symbols are far from perfect tools of thought, has already been stressed. We have seen the way words fail to convey the entire content of what is intended to be communicated. F. C. S. Schiller has pushed this conception *ad absurdum*. 'For', he wrote, 'if a word has a perfectly fixed meaning it would be used only once, and never again; it could be applied only to the situation which originally called for it, and which it originally fitted. If, the next time it was used, it retained its original meaning, it would not designate the actual situation but would still hark back to its past use, and this would disqualify it for all future use. Thus, if the meaning of "Nero" had been tied down to a certain historical Roman Emperor, I could not call my dog "Nero".' The loop-holes for misinterpretation are consequently always present, whether the verbal communication be oral or written. When, furthermore, the task of translation arises, and communication has to switch from one linguistic code to another, then the chances of error increase.

In an attempt to obviate misunderstandings, the device is commonly adopted of increasing the length of the message. But herein lies a trap. The urge to leave nothing unsaid, nothing obscure, only too often leads to tautology. When technical topics are concerned there is an additional hazard, namely that of lapsing into 'jargon', i.e. diction which is meaningless to the uninitiated. When jargon is combined with verbiage, as it so often is, we find the grotesque phenomenon known in America as 'gobbledygook'. Examples of this are only too readily detected—civil service regulations; journalese; art-criticism. Three instances may be quoted from contemporary sources.

The first is an art review, an easy target for attack. . . .

These paintings which begin with the idea of depth and then contest it till the elusive point is reached at which space seems to have a radiant amplitude and yet be destructable. Thus it becomes infinitely precious.

In these uneasy sentences the doubt arises whether there is any underlying meaning at all. The second example is from the Civil Service:

For the purpose of this Part of this Schedule, a person over pensionable age, not being an insured person, shall be treated as an employed person if he would be an insured person were he under pensionable age and would be an employed person were he an insured person.

The third specimen is also an instance of administrative writing:

The purpose of the foundation is to foster 'across-the-board' basic research in order to enrich the substratum of our knowledge of structures and mechanisms underlying chronic disorders. The foundation does not oppose 'target' research in categorical disease areas, but believes that serendipity should be encouraged and more emphasis should be placed on 'free-wheeling' basic research to broaden the case of our knowledge. This has become the Foundation's mission, which it hopes to achieve through the award of 5-year fellowships to physicians and scientists who, standing on their merit, wish to persue their investigations free from restrictions of protocol.

Here we witness yet another dissociation between words and thought, one which is known commonly as verbalism. A surfeit of words conceals a poverty of intellectual content; reminiscent of Plato's simile of the sound emitted by an empty bronze vessel when struck.

'Gobbledygook' is not quite the same as 'waffle'. In the former, meaning is obscured: in the latter, meaning can scarcely be said to exist at all. Waffle is more often met with in spoken speech than in print: it is the hall-mark of the speaker who has little to say, and inadequate command over words with which to cloak his shortcomings.

Even though technical speakers and writers may perhaps protest, on the whole, clarity of diction can be said to be the hallmark of clear thinking, however lofty the intellectual level. As Boileau-Despreaux wrote:

Ce qui conçoit bien, s'énonce clairement,
Et les mots pour le dire viennent aisément.

A. F. Watts, writing as an educational psychologist, asserted that 'linguistic ability and general intelligence overlap to a greater extent than many of us are ready to admit'. And again . . . 'other things being equal, a person's mastery of language for general purposes is a reliable index to his intellectual powers'. A similar plea for disciplined simplicity in language has come from a litterateur, F. L. Lucas: 'A research student may turn his life into a concentration camp; he may amass in his own field an erudition to stagger Dr. Casaubon; but he cannot write. And where the words are so muddled, I suspect that the mind is muddled too . . .'

English possesses many virtues as a language, not the least being its relative freedom from the nebulosities of some other tongues. Although there is but little planned effort in the direction of language-engineering, there is a tendency, in the course of time, for languages to develop greater semantic exactitude. Basic English represented a deliberate expression of this sort. Generations hence these trends may perhaps culminate by English splitting into two parallel language-systems: one which will be mainly expressive or emotive, to be used for fine-writing in prose and poetry, and perhaps for higher literary purposes; and the other which is communicative and functional, which will be the language of business and law, and, in more debased form, of common parlance. So we approach George Orwell's conception of 'newspeak', the language of 1984:

> Don't you see that the whole aim of Newspeak is to narrow the range of thought? In the end we shall make thoughtcrime literally impossible because there will be no words in which to express it. Every concept that will be needed will be expressed by exactly *one* word, with its meaning rigidly defined and all its subsidiary meanings rubbed out and forgotten. Already . . . we are not far from that point. But the process will still be continuing long after you and I are dead. Every year fewer and fewer words, and the range of consciousness always a little smaller . . . The Revolution will be complete when the language is perfect . . . Has it ever occurred to you, Winston, that by the year 2050, at the very latest, not a single human being will be alive who could understand such a conversation as we are having now?

Be that as it may, the argument remains that words are, at the present time, inadequate symbols. As du Maurier wrote:

> Language is a poor thing. You fill your lungs with wind, and shake a little slit in your throat, and make mouths; and that shakes the air; and the air shakes a pair of little drums in my head—a very complicated arrangement with lots of bones behind—and my brain seizes your meaning in the rough. What a roundabout way, and what a waste of time![1]

[1] This masterly paragraph which from time to time appears as a quotation in linguistic manuals, has also been expressed somewhat differently by Guy Endore: 'Here is man who can do what no animal can do: speak. And for that purpose skilfully directs a faint column of air from his lungs through throat and mouth, past vocal cord, and past an arrangement of tongue to palate, to teeth or to lips, in such a way as to produce a succession of disturbances in the surrounding air, disturbances that will reach another person's ear and there transform themselves into disturbances of the tiny members of the ear apparatus, which in turn will become irritations travelling along certain nerves and awakening activity of an unknown kind in certain brain cells'.

XIV. THE INADEQUACY OF WORDS AS SYMBOLS

I am daily bothered almost beyond endurance by words, and what lies behind words, and the extraordinary difficulty of using any word about anything that won't do more harm than good.
Archbishop of Canterbury

When I use a word it means just what I choose it to mean—neither more nor less.
Alice through the looking glass

Be warned in time, and remain, as I do, incomprehensible; to be great is to be misunderstood.
Emerson

A word fitly spoken is like apples of gold in pictures of silver.
Prov. 25

Six persons take part in all conversations between a man and a woman. He, as he thinks he is; and as he thinks she thinks he is; and, as he is. And, as she thinks she is; and, as she thinks he thinks she is; and, as she is.
O. W. Holmes

John Locke, the philosopher, once attended a tedious and wordy debate among medical pundits as to whether the filaments of the nerves were traversed by a fluid substance. Finally Locke objected that perhaps the question was merely one of terminology, and that a clear definition was needed of the word 'liquor'. Somewhat taken aback, the learned men pondered and eventually realized that they were more or less in agreement that some fluid or subtle matter passed through the conduits of the nerves, but whether or not it was to be called 'liquor' was really not important. Locke was one of the first and ablest to call attention to the imperfections of words and their abuse. Today the validity of these strictures is sometimes forgotten.

The falsity and fickleness of words constitute a most serious handicap to what is surely one of the supreme attributes of man. Between the vocalizations of the most sagacious of the anthropoids and the utterances of the primitive savage, lies a tremendous gulf. The beginnings of speech in fossil man, and the first babblings in infancy and early childhood are problems beyond the scope of this paper. Nor can we discuss the ideas that have been put forward to explain how and why speech came about; just when in the evolutionary ascent these began; and the possible nature of this primordial tongue. There is reason to believe that man's first evocations were holophrases, or sentence-words, just as in infants. Fragmentation, reduplication, and coupling of sounds came later.

Being the E. H. Young Lecture entitled 'The Falsity and Fickleness of Words' delivered at the University of Bristol on 2nd March, 1965.

This forms an interesting dissociation between semantic and phonic development, the one progressing from the whole to the particular, and the other contrariwise. (Vigotsky).

Whatever the mechanism whereby animal cries developed into human language, psychobiological factors must have assisted, like the beginnings of a communal mode of existence; the organization of hunting expeditions; and mutual protection at night. Soviet scientists have always been interested in proto-linguistics, and both Engels and Stalin fancied themselves as students of language. The earliest division of labour within the herd was regarded as an important factor in determining language.

Mankind has become enthusiastic in the use of this versatile yet dangerous tool. There is a fundamental and powerful urge to utilize it, one which pervades all ages and races; a drive to communicate, on all occasions however trivial; a reluctance to reflect in quietude.

Let us realize too, that even the term 'communication' is misleading in this context. Language is something more than communication, if by this is understood merely the deliberate passing on of information, or reference-function. Speech may take place for other reasons, and in other circumstances. Much talk is social rather than sociological, and constitutes a mode of behaviour its object being nothing loftier than neighbourliness. Phatic communion is not confined to the unlettered or to the primitive. There is also ludic speech which is an intransitive, egocentric form of verbal play, indulged in by old as well as young. Indeed, as we recall, Ingraham identified as many as nine purposes of language, the ninth being to give employment to philologists.

The next theorem is really the crux of this article, namely that the small tools of language—verbal symbols, or words—are inadequate and often misleading. Linguists and philosophers of language are unanimous here. However concrete they appear, words fail to express the whole private network of significant detail. The solitary word 'dog' for instance has for one speaker a vortex of 'meanings' which cannot possibly be the same for others. If speaker and listener should have in mind an identical poodle, it is fortunate, but none the less the personal overtones of the word 'dog' remain unshared. If this imprecision can occur in discussing an object within view, how much less must be the overlap of ideas culled up by a word referring to something which is remote in place or time, or to an abstraction.

Every word we use possesses to a greater or lesser degree the properties of a generalization. Although the word 'dog' means slightly different things to different people, there also exists, or should exist, some common factor that is shared.

At this point it is necessary to grasp the nettle of terminology. To use 'meaning', 'significance', 'sense', 'connotation' and 'denotation' as though they were synonymous, was known to be unsafe even before the work of Ogden and Richards. It is unfortunate that the commonplace term 'meaning' should prove technically insufficient to apply to the linkage between a word and its interpretation. As Paulhan stressed, it is the 'sense' of a word which really stands for all that is implied in relation to the background of previous experience and association of ideas. Thus the 'sense' of a word transcends its 'meaning'. Paulhan's conception of the sense of a word embraces the sum of all the psychological events aroused in our consciousness by the word. 'It is a dynamic, fluid, complex whole, which has several zones of unequal stability. Meaning is only one of the zones of sense, the most stable and precise zone. A word acquires its sense from the context in which it appears; in different contexts, it changes its sense. Meaning remains stable throughout the changes of sense. The dictionary meaning of a word is no more than a stone in the edifice of sense, no more than a potentiality that finds diversified realization in speech.'

In the course of conversation both parties may be handling the same verbal counters, but their sense though similar is not identical. According to the degree of correspondence in the personal attitude evoked by terminology, so ideas become shared. When one person addresses another, the problem of mutual intelligibility lies, not so much in the speaker's words, as in the ability of the the listener to comprehend them with all their overtones. One device for ensuring greater mutual comprehensibility consists in lengthening the message. This practice of redundancy will be dealt with later.

Whatever means be adopted, however, no trick or technique of word-spinning ever succeeds in transmitting the idea in its entirety. The message always leaves something unexplained, unexpressed; this is the *under-text*. That which goes astray during the transmission of a piece of information is spoken of as an *entropy*. Under-text represents a hiatus: entropy a distortion. The mere fact that members of a common linguistic group speak the same tongue does not for a moment mean that they share the same ideas. Contrariwise, those who seem to understand one another do not necessarily speak the same language. (Carroll).

If every member of a race were completely sharing an identical code, differences of opinion would no longer occur in the interpretation of written or spoken texts. Holy Writ would cease to be the battle-ground of warring religious sects. Legal practitioners would be reduced by half, for those who draft our laws would no longer need to keep a watchful eye on future loopholers among their own profession. Perhaps even political parties would disappear. But seriously, we cannot afford the price these verbal inadequacies at times entail. Balaclava was lost and won through a misinterpreted signal—an entropy in fact. Roger Casement was hanged because of a comma in a statute of Edward III, so Lucas tells us.

Misunderstandings arise because each and every one uses verbal symbols in his own highly individual way. Linguistic habits develop which accord with personality and behavioural pattern, and these habits cannot be concealed. Such idiosyncrasy applies not only to what is spoken, but also to what is written. In other words, no two persons really employ exactly the same language. Each has his own idiolect, which is so personal that linguistic analysis will always reveal the authorship. The Bacon-Shakespeare controversy could be solved today by way of a computer technique.

The 'meaning'—or rather the 'sense'—of a word need not remain established, for circumstances constantly change and associations are always shifting. Word-meaning is a dynamic and not a static phenomenon. (Vigotsky). As Professor Polyani put it . . . 'since every occasion on which a word is used is in some degree different from every previous occasion, we should expect that the meaning of a word will be modified in some degree on every other occasion'.

Words, being such frail units of thought and social comportment, are vulnerable, the commonest disorders being uncritical acceptance, ambiguity and verbiage. First there is the malfunction of language wherein we see the substitution of the word for the idea, so that the symbol becomes in time the thing itself. This is one example of the so-called tyranny of words. Ambiguity is another defect. This may at times be due to the perpetuation of a childhood misconception; two words are confused because they sound alike. Polyani, for example, could never understand his early association of *buns* with *luggage* until he realized years later that he had been muddling up the two German terms *Gebäck* and *Gepäck*. Dylan Thomas as a boy could not make out why the one word 'front' should stand for the outside of his home and also for some sinister battle-ground in Flanders. Even adults are apt in writing and speaking to employ terms which are only half-understood—a pretentious and dangerous practice.

But imprecision is most often the product of woolly thinking and careless writing, with undue resort to firmly locked word-linkages, trite phrases, and to clichés. Technical writers may be to blame by fostering, deliberately it would almost seem, a cult of obscurity. Ribot spoke of 'words written in profundity' which refer to nebulous, inexact ideas, especially in metaphysics. Linguistic philosophy has come in for some very hard knocks at the hands of Professor Gellner on the score of this very fault, which he regards as a heritage from its founder Wittgenstein.

Professor Blanshard has shown how clarity and specificity go hand in hand: 'To say that Major André was hanged is clear and definite; to say that he was killed is less definite, because you do not know in what way he was killed; to say that he died is still more indefinite because you do not even know whether his death was due to violence or to natural causes. If we were to use this statement as a varying symbol by which to rank writers for clearness, we might get something like the following: Swift, Macaulay and Shaw would say that André was hanged. Bradley would say that he was killed. Bosanquet would say that he died. Kant would say that his mortal existence achieved its termination. Hegel would say that a finite determination of infinity had been further determined by its own negation.'

Verbiage and ambiguity are frequent bed-fellows. This conjunction constitutes what is called 'waffle', and—when overloaded with technical or private terminologies—jargon or pedagogese. Bafflegab or gobbledygook is a disease of American politics. Tautology in writing and speaking is an all too common symptom of language-pathology, and resembles the morbid phenomena of neoplasia or hypertrophy. Such verbalism offends against good taste, and can be corrected only by drastic surgery—like substituting within the text Anglo-Saxon for Mediterranean terms, or better still, cutting out every other word, as Sydney Smith prescribed.

The evil may on occasion be practised deliberately and with malice, as in the political device of the filibuster. A speaker may harangue the House of Commons for hours on end about nothing at all, for the sole object of obstructing business. Some parliamentarians are more addicted to this vice than others, the record being held by an Irishman who spoke for three consecutive days.

Perhaps the most serious product of the inadequacy of verbal symbols shows itself in the short-comings of translation. Despite what dictionary-writers assert, it is not possible to find a faithful and wholly satisfactory equivalent in another tongue for any term or phrase. The different language-systems are not just interchangeable modes of expressing a common idea, for as Stuart Chase said: . . . 'a few minutes in the glass palace of the United Nations in New York will quickly disabuse one of this quaint notion'.

If in any one tongue there lies a personal aura around every single term—an under-text, a dynamic and shifting word-sense—there may also exist a national one as well, not necessarily shared by other linguistic groups. Interpreters may not always be alive to these nuances of meaning. Thus a complete volume has been devoted to the topic of Soviet double-talk, pointing out that terms like *bourgeoisie*, *democracy*, and *patriotism* mean to a Russian something quite distinctive and unexpected. The German *Freund* is not quite the same as the French *ami*; *billig* represents something more than 'fair'; the Russian *krasny* (red) has a tie-up with concepts of beauty; *jil*, which is the Siamese word for 'cool' also implies 'nice and cool', just as the Welsh word for robin is really a 'dear little robin'. The Hebrew *shalom* means welfare, as well as peace. Every language also has its quota of words which are deemed to be untranslatable, like the German *gemütlich*, and the Italian *omertà* and *vilipendo*.

Winston Churchill once said that verbal ambiguity has in our own life-time led to the outbreak of two world wars. Moreover, a misreading of the difficult Japanese expression *mokusatsu* prolonged the conflict in the East and made the atomic bomb inevitable. An even simpler instance can be quoted whereby contrary meanings are attached to the same expression by two different racial groups who share a common language. Early in the second world war Anglo-American discussions were for a long while held up until it was realized that when an Englishman spoke of 'tabling a document' he meant that it was rendered available to the committee, while to an American it meant the very opposite.

Mindful of the complexities of polyglottism, students of language including aphasiologists are sceptical about the alleged existence of absolute or total bilingualism. A switch from one tongue to another, is not just a simple exercise in coding and decoding, but a manoeuvre demanding a quick-change in *Motorick*, and mental make-up, including personality and even prejudices. Aphasia in a plurilingualist is a far more complicated business than Ribot or Pitrès ever dreamed, and text-book writing would have us believe.

The bilingual who speaks one of the African, Asiatic or Amerindian languages presents an even greater problem. Every European tongue is built up on a fundamental subject-predicate basis, but this is far from being so elsewhere, and we believe that the structure of a language and the mode of thinking of the user are intimately related.

So far we have been stressing the short-comings of our verbal symbols in the role of communication. At times however the opposite seems to hold true. Instead of being achieved through redundance, rapport now seems to flourish upon a sacrifice of words. I refer to predicative speech, where the words in use are allusive and elaborately metaphorical. Syntax goes by the board. Predicative speech is an esoteric language understood only by intimates. It is the language of lovers and of privileged members of close-knit communities. Being elusive and evocative, it resembles in some ways verse rather than prose, but there is always a risk that a missed cue may shatter understanding. John Horne Burns has left us a remarkable description of predicative speech:

"This little language between a man and a woman in love is composed of elliptical references to their lives in common. The longer they live together, the richer and more obscure their little language becomes. They devise terms of endearment for each other, echolalic, rhyming, and allusive. And it is fortunate that great lovers of the past have elected not to preserve their little languages in print; for they are as personal as the bed, not to be shown the light of day or of reason. If everyone in this world were in love there would be as many little languages as there are people on the globe, divided by two. And all formal tongues would speedily become as dead as Sanskrit".

Betty Smith too had something to say upon this subject:

> When children asked questions, the parents didn't know how to answer them, for the reason that these people did not know the correct words to use. Each married couple had its own secret words for things that were whispered in bed in the quiet of the night. But there were few mothers brave enough to bring these words out into the daylight and present them to the child. When the children grew up, they in turn invented words which they couldn't tell *their* children.

We may suggest yet another instance of the unreliability of verbal symbols, namely in the employment of words intended not to inform, but to misdirect. Words may be twisted so as actually to conceal thought and furthermore to steer the minds of the audience into illogical and devious channels. Herein lies the sinister weapon of propaganda, the armoury of the advertiser. The possibilities of perverse indoctrination and the distortion of thought through the cunning mis-use of mass media, are terrifying. The unscrupulous use of what Korzybski called 'loaded words', heavily charged with feeling-tone, has long been known as a conquering force. Hume declared . . . ''tis not Reason that gains the prize, but eloquence;—The victory is not gained by the men at arms, who manage the pike and sword; but by the trumpeters, drummers, and musicians of the Army'.

Modern psycholinguists, however, hold that the power of deliberately transmitting negative or fallacious information by means of articulate speech, is more limited than one would imagine. Whatever the words upon the lips of the liar, the paralinguistic signs will betray his true intent to those who know how to read them.

This brings us to consider an anomaly: the communicative role of wordlessness or pregnant silence. How often one receives a message with all its impact, not from what the speaker has said but from his silent pauses whether deliberate or not. This is what Chesterman meant when he spoke of silence as the 'unbearable repartee'. The studied use of intervals within speech constitutes 'timing', and as such is an important feature of the stock-in-trade of the actor, orator, or lecturer. Other kinds of speech-arrest may be just as deliberate, but they are not to be looked upon as part of the prosody of an accomplished speaker, being far too prolonged. Though nothing has been said, 'meaning' is all too clear.

Of quite a different character are the gaps which may unwittingly break up a speaker's diction; or which intervene during a conversation-piece between question and answer. Dr. Goldman-Eisler has worked intensively upon this subject. A study of large tracts of spontaneous speech shows that on an average between 40 and 50 per cent of utterance-time is occupied by pauses. These hesitations are the signs of underlying thought-processes concerned with verbal planning. But we can go even further. Though these pauses are usually inadvertent and often unconscious, they nevertheless carry some reference-function, and on this account are to be reckoned as paralinguistic. Thus they may represent a word-block which in turn may denote embarrassment, or a *suppressio veri*. Jung's word-association test is actually a very practical utilization of a well-known aspect of paralanguage.

We are now approaching the various non-verbal aspects of communication which may in turn bear upon our problem of the inadequacy of words. Laughter occupies a mid-way position being a non-phonemic vocalization, sometimes deliberate, sometimes automatic. Often it may qualify as communication, but pitfalls in interpretation occur, for differing cultures betray differing purposes in laughter. To carry over an interpretation from one tradition to another may prove hazardous. Certain Africans laugh in circumstances which we, who align hilarity with amusement, would deem inappropriate. At times they seem callous or insincere, as when they chuckle at the sight of someone in pain. Actually this is their mark of profound sympathy. Again during an argument laughter may indicate intellectual appreciation though not necessarily agreement. In a minor vein we recall the conundrum of the Japanese smile which we usually look upon as inapposite or inexplicable, for smiling is laughter in miniscule, and may bedizen social intercourse in diverse ways.

The topic of kinesics or the study of gesture is a complicated one. As a buttress to communication, or a substitute thereof, it has an imposing ancestry. Suffice it to say that it comprises a silent but eloquent aspect of language which in many ways is free from the frailties and falsities of spoken words.

What of the future of communication? Will it eventually be possible to overcome the inadequacy of verbal symbols? How far will precision come about through natural evolution, or must it depend upon planned language-engineering?

We are familiar with the progressive changes in grammatical structure which can be traced over the centuries as a language matures. By projecting the curve we can predict what the future state of linguistic affairs is likely to be. But this is a matter of syntactics, and has only an indirect bearing upon the problem of semantics.

Another feature which merits discussion is the inevitable gap between the written form of a language and the vernacular. Though this discrepancy differs in degree from one tongue to another, it is always there. As time goes by, it is more likely to widen than shrink, so that the task of ensuring intelligibility will increasingly constitute two distinct issues. Indeed, many generations hence, the incidence of literacy, after an initial rise, may show a steep decline, so that fewer and fewer members of a community will be able to read and write. To attempt to close this gulf between written and spoken speech would however be a serious error.

We recall sympathetically some of the efforts of Korzybski, that eccentric pioneer of 'General Semantics', to ensure greater specificity in the printed word. A modern text, though possessing the merit of permanency, lacks the modulation and the variations of pace, the emphatics and prosodic qualities which eloquently accompany the spoken word, as well as the associated gestural play. Punctuation marks are inadequate substitutes. Max Beerbohm made this clear. . . . 'When we write we have nothing but words, words, with those little summary and meagre things whose hard office is to ape the infinitely varied pauses of the human voice'. Korzybski strove to reform and enrich our typology by a number of cunning devices. An expression of opinion or policy requires some temporal ticketing, or a subscript to indicate a time-factor. For example, we should be enabled to distinguish Harold Wilson $_{1962}$ from Harold Wilson $_{1967}$. Nor should the time-factor be withheld from more banal situations. An apple plucked from the tree is not quite the same as the shrivelled and discoloured specimen it will be six months later. We should be able to distinguish apple$_1$ from apple$_2$.

Other expedients are possible in constructive linguistics. Spoken English would be the richer and more specific if sundry ambiguous words and phrases were replaced by planned neologisms. At present the word *aunt* can refer either to mother's sister or to father's sister; we would be the better off if we had two separate words, as indeed is the case with many African tongues. The negative and affirmative particles could with advantage be elaborated by making distinct words for *perhaps-yes* and *perhaps-no*, as well as *thank you* (*yes*), and *thank you* (*no*). Furthermore the pronouns need an overhaul; we should be able to discriminate between *you* (singular) and *you-two*, *all of you here*, and *all of you* (*out of sight*). The Texan's *you-all* goes a little way in the right direction. Medical men who daily contend with Ministry certificates, are in desperate need of a word to stand for something intermediate between the verbal phrase 'I have *seen* . . .' and 'I have *examined* . . .'. We doctors have a perfectly good term for one phase of the sleep-cycle, namely 'awakening', but we lack a word like 'sleepening'. These are examples which immediately come to mind: there must be many, many others.

Quite apart from the replacement of notoriously inadequate terms, there is much to be said in favour of a restrained word-coinage. A happy creation of an arresting or crisp new word is a practice favoured by many fine writers. Max Beerbohm spoke up warmly for this indulgence and he introduced such neologisms as *pop-limbo* and *bauble-tit*. Baron Corvo was also an unashamed verbal coiner, but his too contrived handiwork was often the sheerest counterfeit. But in giving our language a 'new look' we need not emulate Lycophron who in *Cassandra*, with his iambic monologue of 3,000 words, introduced for the first time 117 completely new terms, and used 518 others in a manner which was private and peculiar to himself.

Vernacular differs from literary language in containing a profusion of particles which are almost bare of reference-function. The interlarding of small talk with an oft repeated *really; if you know what I mean; you know;* and with minor interjections like *fancy, there now, well I never,* does not transmit information. But our enthusiastic language-mechanic should not be allowed to prune our speech with these excrescences as though they were so much dead wood. Though devoid of meaning, these interpolations are anything but devoid of function. They are 'intimacy signals' which oil the wheels of social intercourse, and serve to establish a setting of cosy co-operation. Connolly called them 'collision mats' which we hand out in conversation lest we grind against each other. These little modifiers suggest mutual pleasure at seeing and hearing each other, and still more at the opportunity for giving tongue. Probably every language contains its stock of reiterated interpolations which egg-on conversation. Thus a Brazilian generously lards his discourse with the monosyllable *la*. Though the dictionary meaning is 'there', the function is really that of mere mutual encouragement.

A considerable increase in our vocabulary might be imagined as bringing about a greater precision. In theory the English language could be converted into an international medium, either by scaling down the vocabulary to the 800 items of Basic English, or by the reverse. One target would be a one-word, one-meaning system. Polyani has shown that on the basis of an alphabet of 23 letters, it would be possible to build up an artificial language consisting of 8-letter words. This would give us 50,000 million separate terms, a vast surplus for our purpose. Each term could stand, not for a word, but for every sentence needed. The result would be chaotic. Memory could not tolerate the burden. Mutual comprehension would never come about, for each word would probably be employed once, and once only, in a life-time. Words would therefore remain denuded of 'sense'.

Far from an augmentation of the stock of available words, the opposite process is more likely to represent the future of language. We recalled in the previous section George Orwell's alarming prediction of the world position in 2050. Dictionaries would have steadily shrunk, and *Newspeak* as he called it, would comprise a grammar-less handful of terms. 'Every year, fewer and fewer words; and the range of consciousness, always a little smaller'.

Perhaps in the future of language there will be a compromise. Some new words will be there, including technical terms, but perhaps the overall quantum of words will be smaller. On the other hand, understanding will be secured by a greater use of repetition—a controlled surplusage, in fact. Every message will be longer, and more words will be utilized, but fewer different words. This will be merely an extension of our present way of signalling, that is to say, transmitting information by mechanical means. It conforms indeed with Belloc's formula for a lecture . . . 'First I tell them what I am going to tell them; then I tell them; and then I tell them what I've told them'.

Imprecision is partly the fault of the receiver, for accurate reception largely depends upon the recipient being ready to accept the message. He must already be within a 'prior set', an anticipatory state, or suitable frame of expectation. This aspect of vigilance lends itself to improvement through practice. Already in the States there are 'listening clinics' where valuable results are claimed, so they say.

Much of all this is speculative, and in any event, unrealistic. But now I would like to describe recent work of a clinical character, the object of which is the extraction at an interview of the maximum information—I almost used the word Truth. This is anything but fanciful for it is proving to be functional and reliable. These newer techniques, adopted by some psychiatrists and by a few aphasiologists, aim at detecting and recording the complete package of linguistic and paralinguistic phenomena appearing during a medical interview. They are based upon the fact that articulate communication is always accompanied by elaborate non-verbal phenomena which can be perceived and assessed. These non-verbal concomitants are vital, for they constitute a far more faithful index of the speaker's thoughts and feelings than the mere words employed. The latter may lie; the former cannot. As proclaimed by its pioneers—'anything anyone ever says is true, the 'truth' of a communication being what has caused it to occur . . . people may not always say what they mean but they always mean what they say'.

The potential forensic value of such an interview-technique, is obvious, and even frightening. The utilization of paralinguistic data in psychiatric interviews arose out of the researches of Trager and his associates at the University of Buffalo. It is interesting to remember that the technique had been anticipated years before by Freud. According to Trager *et al.* paralanguage comprises the vocalizations, and voice-qualities. The former consist of the variegated noises, without the structure of language, which occur in the course of communication. Vocalizations are made up of: (1) vocal characterizers, such as laughter, crying, yelling, whispering, moaning, groaning, whining, sighing, belching and yawning; (2) vocal qualifiers, i.e. modifications in intensity, pitch-height and extent; and (3) vocal segregates. Here belong the American *uh-uh* for 'no' and *uh-huh* for 'yes'; the *um*'s and *er*'s of unpolished speakers, and the inspiratory hiss of the Japanese. The numerous voice-qualities, which constitute the other part of the paralanguage, concern pitch-range and control, control of glottis, lip, articulation and rhythm, as well as tempo and resonance. In order to record all these items of paralanguage, Trager devised a vocabulary of symbols.

In a remarkable work entitled 'The First Five Minutes', a team comprising two psychotherapists (Pittenger and Danehy), and a linguist (Hockett) made a most elaborate record of a single short medical session, using the technique and symbol-system of Trager. A specimen page from this record of the interview is shown in Fig. 3.

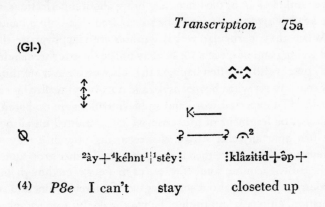

Transcription 75a

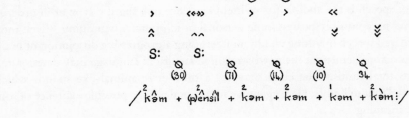

FIG. 3

For the purpose of investigating victims of aphasic speech-loss I too have adopted this system. I have elaborated it in an important fashion however by adding a 'kinesic strip', which correctly synchronized, describes the mimico-gestural behaviour of the aphasiac, and constitutes a silent but illuminating third aspect of paralanguage (see Fig. 4).[1] In this way we have a complete record of

[1] See also Chapter XV.

the total behaviour of the patient throughout the interview, comprising every aspect of communication, non-verbal as well as verbal. Researchers can scrutinize the records time after time and can thereby recapture the patient's halting efforts at self-expression. A peep is also rendered possible into the aphasiac's processes of thinking, word-finding and recall. Perhaps we could improve the kinesic strip by replacing it with a sort of printed choreographic score adapted from the ballet.

In medical practice we who are neurologists often meet with pathological instances where words are inaccurate indices of thought. The faculty of language is exquisitely sensitive to noxious influences and even mild lesions of the brain may bring about inperfections in function. In aphasia for example, the available vocabulary may be so reduced that only a handful of words remain ready to hand. When these particular verbal symbols are inappropriate the victim is at a loss, incapable both of writing and of speech. Or he may utilize these few remaining verbal counters on all occasions, and consequently it often happens that his words mean anything but what they say. A severe aphasiac may say *yes* when he means *no*, and not always realize his error. Or he may utter a neologism instead of an expected word and so his intentions are obscured. Often there is but a solitary word, phrase, or fragment of gibberish which is emitted on all occasions, like a faulty radio-record. At first after an acute stroke, this recurring utterance may resemble a tic, being compulsive and uncontrollable. Here then is an extreme and rather grotesque instance of the falsity of words. Later the patient acquires some measure of mastery even though his range of words does not extend. He contrives to bring about some degree of reference-function, and by a very deliberate play of intonation, emphasis and timing, he may make his solitary speech automatism stand for affirmation, negation, greeting, request, dismissal and so on.[1]

In mental disorder too the victim's words may have little or no validity. The curious word-salad of the schizophrene fails as a vehicle of communication between patient and physician, or even between one patient and another. His words are a truly fantastical banquet of many strange dishes. This type of speech is the audible (or written) evidence of a specific type of disordered thinking, and as such it may possibly possess some personal or idiosyncratic meaning.[2] Even more uncanny is the disordered speech in young children undergoing a progressive dissolution of brain-function. In these precocious dementias the newly-acquired faculty of language may deteriorate and before lapsing into total mutism the child may for a time utter animal-like sounds which are non-phonemic and unintelligible. Here again we must not deny the possible existence of some personal and simple meaning.

We neurologists are also familiar with another type of pathological instance of words breaking down as vehicles of communication. In certain disorders physical and mental experiences are so complex and so exquisitely subtle as to defy description. The conjunction of deep introversion, high intelligence, and a rich vocabulary may result in some attempt at communication, but the result may baffle the comprehension of the recipient. We meet this state of affairs in those rare cases in psychiatry known as ecstasy, or cosmic consciousness. St. John of the Cross spoke of 'silent music' or 'the sound of solitude'. According to the diary of H. F. Amiel (1882–1884). . . . 'we cannot find words to express this experience (i.e. glimpses of the joys of Paradise) because our

[1] See also Chapter XV.
[2] See also Chapter XXVIII.

languages can only describe particular and definite conditions of life; they have no words to express this silent contemplation, this heavenly quietness, this ocean of peace which both reflects the heavens above, and is master of its own vast depth'. Verbal descriptions are at times essayed, as when we read. . . . 'the Captain knew no terror now; he had soared to that rare level of consciousness where the mystic feels that the earth is he and that he is the earth.' (Carson McCullers). We may also find it in instances of deliria due to certain drugs, notably mescal, hashish, and lysergic acid. Commoner still are cases of temporal lobe epilepsy where the ictal experiences may be transcendental and ineffable. Stumbling efforts at portrayal may evoke such monstrous attempts as 'a smell of green thunder' where a jumble of special sense impressions provokes a synaesthetic complex which is virtually inexpressible.

My concluding remarks must serve to repair an omission. In discussing word-failure I deliberately avoided the poetic use of language. Herein exist laws all to themselves, for conventional attempts to ally words with meaning no longer apply.

Putting aside the topic of Latin verse, and indeed of poetry in many foreign languages, we may distinguish two main aspects of poesy in our own language. First there is traditional verse which for many centuries has constituted a particular art-form. Here, words are chosen less for their exactitude in meaning than for their aesthetic properties. Beauty, euphony, colour—these are the qualities that count. The full effect of such poetry falls upon the listener rather than the reader, for it should be intoned or declaimed aloud. In poetry words may also possess mental associations but they are as amorphous and flimsy as in predicative speech. Verse is evocative and not propositional. It bears closer links with song than with thought. To construct poetry of this kind usually remains beyond the powers of one who has recovered his speech after an aphasia. The aphasic poet in his convalescence, however subtle or minimal his speech-defect, has lost for ever his cunning in versification. (See Chapter XXI).

In contrast today, stands *avant-garde* verse. Here aesthetic qualities mean little—indeed they seem out of place. Such poetry is cerebral rather than emotive, but meaning is deliberately obscured and eludes the uninitiated. Logical thinking is short-circuited and intermediate steps bypassed. Ideas, however remote one from the other, become compressed so as to lie in close but bewildering proximity. The end-product is a labyrinth wherein ordinary people get lost but which seemingly presents no problem to the cognoscenti.

In a monstrous sentence of 163 words with two parenthetic clauses Henry Treece has given us a ruling upon the poetic use of language. Where sense survives strangulation, he seems to be saying that the poet uses words his own way and that it is up to us to recapture the emotional and intellectual climate of inspiration. Lucas put it better when he said that in much modern literature communication is replaced by private maundering to oneself which tries to inspire the audience to maunder privately to *themselves*—much as if the author had handed round a box of drugged cigarettes of his own concoction to stimulate each guest with his own private dreams.

It is interesting to observe that literature of this sort bears many analogies with schizophrenic writing. As a neurologist I might point out that this kind of verse is not necessarily beyond the competency of the brain-injured. One severely aphasic poet, who was a patient of mine, continued to produce *avant-garde* poetry, confessing to me he found it 'easier than prose'. (See p. 252).

Leaving poetry as something which lies outside the broad highways of communication, we can bring to a close our reflections upon the fickleness of words. How well this was summed up by Dr. Angell of Yale when he said: 'Not all my class attends my lectures. Of those who attend, only half listen to what I say. Of those who attend and listen, only half understand. Of those who attend and listen and understand, only half remember. Of those who attend and listen and understand and remember, only half agree. The damage therefore is not serious'.

XV. THE DRIFT AND DISSOLUTION
OF LANGUAGE

The predicament of a severe aphasiac was graphically discussed by Zola who wrote of Madam Raquin's 'walled-in intelligence, still alive, yet imprisoned in dead flesh. . . . She could see, hear, and doubtless she could reason quite clearly, yet she had no movement or speech to express her thoughts to the outside world. Maybe her thoughts choked her. . . . Her mind was like one of those people who are, by some mischance, buried alive, and who wake up in the middle of the night with five or six feet of earth on top of them . . .

Medicine owes to Hughlings Jackson the inceptive glimpses into the psychology of expressive disorders. His first reflections upon this subject appeared in print just a century ago (Jackson 1864). He looked upon aphasia, not so much as a focal cerebral deficit, as a 'taking apart' of a complex symbolic endowment, namely language. His dynamic thinking was decades ahead of his time, and we are still astonished at the exciting ideas he promulgated, and the way he anticipated many of our contemporary notions. I think that Jackson today would be intrigued with the opportunities opening up through the lessons of linguistics and information-theory, especially when linked with the technical refinements of speech-recording.

It has been rightly proclaimed that linguistics should concern itself with language in all its aspects: language in operation; language in drift; language in the nascent state; and language in dissolution. Although not entirely conforming with the specific use of the terms, we might proceed to examine two of these aspects, namely, the drift and the dissolution of language. I borrow these expressions to indicate the opposite poles of disordered language, the mildest and the severest types of an aphasia respectively.

Drift: minimal dysphasia

Let us first examine what we might call 'minimal dysphasia', where the linguistic imperfections are often so slight and so fine as to elude routine testing. Likewise in ordinary conversation the shortcomings pass unnoticed by both speaker and listener. These features may herald the slow encroachment of a space-occupying lesion upon the zone of language. We may therefore speak of a 'pre-aphasia', or of an 'incipient, inchoate, or ingravescent dysphasia'. . . . the harbinger of an

This communication is based upon the Hughlings Jackson Lecture 1964, originally appearing in the *Proc. Roy. Soc. Med.*, 1964. **57**, 1189–1198.

unequivocal speech-impairment. Or, these very same minimal defects may be discerned in the final recovery-stages, as a 'residual dysphasia'.

Nothing less than an extended technique of testing will uncover these slender signs. These may stand out against a background or setting of an adynamism, or lack of spontaneity, which also applies to language. This inertia may, however, be interrupted by activity which is impulsive and unrestrained, which again may extend to verbal behaviour.

The hallmarks of a pre-aphasia may be mentioned briefly. There will be a lessened facility in the choosing of words, the available vocabulary remaining intact. The number of 'types'—that is different words employed—is reduced. Less common terms are selected slowly, if at all, and with a notable inconsistency. Defect of word-finding is revealed when the patient tries to recite a catalogue of instances belonging to a particular generic class (animals, flowers); or sharing a common property (redness, sharpness).

Pari passu with the restriction of vocabulary in actual use is an over-employment of certain trite phrases and phrase-words, clichés, preformed speech-patterns, favoured word-linkages, verbal biases, and successive habits of connected speech.

An over-elaborate and unorthodox use of words may come to light during an interview. In naming articles before him, the patient may supply the correct term quite promptly, but then lapse into an odd spontaneous verbalism. Quite unasked for, he may proceed to indulge in verbose circumstantiality. Thus, shown a watch, the patient may name it but then go on to exclaim . . . 'and a very nice one too, if I may say so'. Or, '. . . my husband hasn't got one like that, and he's got everything'. This little *manie de parler* may be spoken of as 'gratuitous redundancy'. In some ways it recalls Petrie's 'regressive metonymy' described in certain leucotomized patients (Petrie 1949).

An inadequate performance of sequential tasks as opposed to isolated ones, may prove revealing. Both interpretation and recapitulation of verbally presented material may be poor, particularly when interlocking or consecutive themes are concerned, and when references are allusive or ambiguous. The patient may fail to paraphrase such commonplace slogans as 'Players please', or wise saws like 'easy come, easy go', 'still waters run deep', or 'a bird in the hand'. This failure may be due to a defect either in comprehension or in explanation (Zangwill 1964), or in both.

In attempting to repeat a couple of consecutive jokes or fables, the patient may confuse the two propositions, and contaminate his narrative with inappropriate ideas and words. The patient may likewise fail to solve arithmetical problems when posed verbally, in speech or in print. Spontaneous letter-writing, or the production of an essay upon a set theme, may also betray a minimal dysphasia, whether inchoate or residual. Such a text will in addition lend itself to linguistic analysis, and disclose aberrations in the token-type ratio, or in sentence-length, or in the verb-adjective fraction. Inadequacy may be observed in what Luria (1958, 1959) has called the regulating function of speech. For example, the patient may fail at such a sequential task as 'when I tap the table once, lift your right hand; raise you left hand when I tap twice; and if I tap three times, do nothing'. Or, directed to squeeze a rubber bulb with the right hand in response to the flashing of a red light, and with the left hand when a blue light appears, the patient may soon become confused and make stereotyped actions (Mescheryakov 1953, Ivanova 1953). Likewise the pre-aphasiac fails when given some instruction as . . . 'when I count as far as 12, raise your hand' (Luria 1958). A pre-aphasiac may be unable to supply an analogy when given a series of three items, e.g. 'lion, teeth; eagle, . . .? . . .'. He will remain perplexed even when the missing word is included among others and put to him in a multiple choice type of question.

Behind all these minor defects one may also observe a raised duration threshold, or a slowness in both the execution and reception of verbal material in the case of very mild aphasiacs. Botez's term 'inattention' in this connection is not a happy one, as the author himself realized (Botez 1961).

Dissolution: maximal speech-loss

Let us turn from these minimal cases to a consideration of massive defects of communication—the dissolution of language—for the 'method of extreme cases' is one which is often of unexpected value in studying a problem. *Aphasia totalis* is rare save as a transient phenomenon. Ordinarily the maximal speech-impairment is met with in cases of 'monophasia'. This term refers to those cases where spontaneous speech is restricted to a kind of *hapax legomenon*, that is, a solitary 'word' or holophrastic word-cluster, which is reiterated in a stereotyped fashion. Russian neurologists refer to this phenomenon as a 'word embolus'. Other terms like 'formula-speech', 'word-rests' (*Wortreste*), or 'speech automatism' have also been used at times, but in this country we usually follow Jackson and speak of 'recurring utterance'. Originally described in the eighteenth century, this phenomenon was first specifically investigated by Hughlings Jackson, inspired, I believe, by the memory of a boyhood acquaintance who was so afflicted. (See Chapter V).

Jackson's four-fold classification of these recurring decimals of speech is a little artificial. By far the commonest state of affairs is for the patient to give vent to the stereotype 'yes'—or 'no'—or sometimes both of them. Analysis of 100 cases of recurrent utterance compiled from the records made by Henschen (1922) where a solitary comprehensible word was concerned, has shown that in 63 it was a matter of 'yes' and/or 'no', the remaining 37 being made up of a great diversity of utterances. It was possible to break down these figures. Of 65 such cases out of a total of 134 patients, 36 were males and 29 females. Negative particles ('no', *nein*, etc.) alone were used by 6 (2 males and 4 females); affirmative particles ('yes', *oui*, *ja*, etc.) by 23 (11 males, 12 females); and both negative and affirmative by 36 (23 males, 13 females).

The survival of these two particles is not surprising for they constitute important as well as common units of spoken speech, as I have stressed at length in Chapter XXX. Their rank in written speech is far less exalted. However, the mere frequency of 'yes' and 'no' in normal diction cannot be the whole explanation of their important role as a recurring utterance. Though 'yes' and 'no' rank high in the Lorge-Thorndike tables of frequency of usage, they stand lower than many other words (articles, prepositions, conjunctions) which rarely if ever appear as stereotypes. Table 4 shows their place in the Lorge-Thorndike word-lists, as compared with other terms, common in normal parlance, rare in aphasia (Thorndike and Lorge 1944).

When a recurring utterance comprises some term other than 'yes' or 'no', it is often a most unusual and unexpected one. Likewise, when entailing more than a single 'word' it may show itself as a phrase, and a seemingly significative one at that. Frequently, speech automatism is duplicated—'yes, yes'; 'no, no'; 'come, come'. According to Sapir (1921), reduplication in speech indicates distribution, plurality, repetition, customary activity, increase of size, added intensity, continuance. In the context of our present problem it suggests a primitive method of enhancing meaning with verbal economy. This striving towards communication on the part of the patient may be all-important.

TABLE 4

SOME OF THE MOST COMMONLY OCCURRING WORDS IN THE ENGLISH LANGUAGE

Word	Lorge magazine count	Lorge-Thorndike semantic count
THE	236,472	Not known
AND	138,672	Not known
A, AN	131,119	Not known
I	89,489	24,250
IN	75,253	96,674
IS	33,404	43,816
WITH	32,903	38,041
ON	30,224	28,382
BUT	23,704	21,380
ME	23,364	5,818
ONE	17,569	14,860
NO	11,742	9,492
YES	2,202	593

Reprinted with the permission of the publisher from Edward L. Thorndike and Irving Lorge's *The Teacher's Word Book of 30,000 Words* (New York: Teachers College Press), copyright 1944, Teachers College, Columbia University.

A stereotyped phrase may be either banal in context (like 'Good morning', or *je ne peux pas parler* or *Ich kann nichts*), or else a wholly unexpected one ('Ace of Spades', *Boulevard de Grenelle 131*). However plausible in content, the phrase is incongruous in its setting. Each 'word' wears the garment of a semanteme but in reality it is quite devoid of reference-function. Perhaps we should speak of 'displaced semantemes' or 'pseudo-semantemes'. Terminology obviously raises difficult problems. The fact that the so-called 'word' appears on all occasions means that it actually ceases to be a word. Its method of employment precludes its habitual reference-function. When for example the aphasiac proclaims nothing but the syllable 'come' he is admittedly employing a dictionary word with a conventional connotation. But as the patient uses it there is no such attached significance; it might just as well be any other word, or a piece of nonsense, or even a grunt. The recurrent utterance 'come' does not therefore qualify as a word in the strict sense, for it is a linguistic counter that has been filched, to be used out of context in an inconsistent and highly individual manner. Since the stereotypy is not strictly speaking a word at all, the patient cannot pronounce a part only of it, any more than he can say any other word. To a particular aphasiac, his recurrent 'Battersea' meant nothing, and consequently he could emit neither 'Batter' alone, nor 'sea'. The same remarks apply to clusters of 'words' occurring as stereotypes. As Jackson (1879–80) said . . . 'these phrases, which have propositional structure, have in the mouths of speechless patients no propositional value. They are not speech, being never used as speech; they are for use only compound jargon'. Often the phrase is interjectional, with profane or obscene overtones ('My God!' 'Jesus'), sometimes curtailed or deformed (*cré nom, Mede* (= *merde*); *é nom é ieu*; *sacon*). Another compulsive manifestation sometimes observed in aphasiacs, bears a distant relationship with our subject. The patient interjects at regular intervals a tic-like phrase into the stream of talk. Moutier's (1908) patient could not speak four words on end without the exclamation *Ah merde! cré catin de casaque!* Professor Alajouanine has told me of one of his aphasiacs who would interject *tata* after every two or three words, thus: *je me porte tata très bien tata aujourd'hui tata*. A very mild variant has been encountered quite inappropriately in an aphasiac who would tack on a terminal /s/ to the final word of each phrase or sentence (e.g. 'I don't remember you*s*'). That this sibilant was not merely an attenuated 'sir' was shown by the fact that he frequently ended his speech with a 'sirs'.

Impressed no doubt by his juvenile experience, Jackson drew attention to the frequency with which a fragment of jargon forms a stereotypy. Here again, reduplication is common, if not the rule ('tan tan', 'zu zu', 'watty watty', 'taratara').

Modification of the recurrent utterance

Whether the recurrent utterance be a 'word', phrase or piece of gibberish, certain modifications may develop over the course of time. The stereotyped formula-speech is at first produced on every possible occasion, however unlikely. Hence, to begin with, it possesses the attributes of a compulsion, emitted at times when silence would be more fitting. Thus during a three-corner interview between doctor, patient and relative, the aphasiac may butt in with his inappropriate verbal automatism—like Epimarchus, incapable of speech, but unable to hold his tongue. In its role as a compulsion the stereotyped sound may be uttered in an explosive, almost violent fashion, 'released like a vigorous trumpet blast' (*wie kräftige Trompetenstösse*, von Monakow 1914).

The positive side of this problem deserves mention. It is unnecessary to discuss at length the various hypotheses which seek to explain why a particular expression should appear as a recurring utterance in an individual patient. We can be sure, however, that it is no haphazard event. Though we may not understand, meaning certainly must be there. The role of an overpowering emotion immediately prior to the stroke has been widely accepted, as suggested by Freud (1891). Whether Jackson's theory of a 'stillborn proposition' is credible, or Gowers' modification thereof (1885), depends upon one's knowledge of the immediate pre-morbid circumstances of each case. Certainly I have observed patients where Jackson's theory could well apply, but also others where that of Gowers would seem more reasonable. Again there have been many other cases where none of these hypotheses would fit. The common iteration of jargon, as well as of 'yes' and 'no', though not flatly contradicting the views of Freud, Jackson and Gowers, is rather more difficult to explain.

While remaining the sole item of communication, the recurrent utterance later loses much of its tic-like nature. The patient now becomes able to inhibit the upsurge of stereotypy, and he may remain silent for longer periods. At this stage additional speech-automatisms may develop so that the vocabulary will now comprise a handful of recurrent utterances. But this does not indicate the existence of a code. That is to say one particular stereotype does not 'stand for' any specific object or idea, with another stereotype linked with another. It bears no analogy for example with the binary principle of the drum languages of Africa. An apparent exception was Broca's patient Lelong who had several recurring utterances (Broca 1861). One of them, *tois*—a corruption of *trois* no doubt—was used solely in the context of number. Another important advance will by now have come about, leading to some measure of communicative play, despite the attenuated vocabulary. This results from the patient learning to utilize to the full the supra-segmental phonemic factors. By altering the prosodics of the recurrent utterance the aphasiac now makes his solitary 'word'—'no', for example—refer in an idiosyncratic way to a variety of concepts: greeting, dismissal, acknowledgement, affirmation, denial. The melody of speech is restored, even enhanced. The patient 'sings' his recurrent utterance, as Jackson put it. Thus the patient has learned to endow his involuntary stereotyped 'word' with his own specific significance. In this way the sound emitted takes on a meaning for the occasion like a disguise; a meaning which is not fixed or consistent, but which is elastic, expedient, and dependent upon the setting. This same meaning may or may not be shared by others, for communication depends upon the skill with which his attempts can be decoded.

This property whereby a solitary word can constitute not only a sentence-word, but can also relate to a great diversity of ideas, is well known to linguists aside from the problem of aphasia. According to Dostoievsky (1876–81) 'it is possible to express all thoughts, feelings, and even reflections, in one word', and he gave an account of a ridiculous argument between six topers, comprising merely one unmentionable word.

Such adaptability precludes any grouping of the recurrent pseudo-semantemes into syntactical classes, e.g. declarative, interrogative, interjectional, hortatory. One and the same stereotype can serve now as an exclamation, now as a question, and perhaps later as a proposition.

Non-verbal aids to communication, such as kinesics, soon become pressed into service. With his intact limb and facial musculature the patient will employ a rich pantomime in order to eke out the meaning he seeks to attach to his solitary utterance. At a later date, if and when the stereotypy becomes established as the sole articuleme, the patient may make an extraordinary adjustment. The ability of such patients to transmit information of a complicated sort is astonishing. Superficially this would appear to represent a fantastic antinomy between intellectual integrity and failure to verbalize. It would be unwise, however, to accept the clinical dissociation at its face value, for searching test-procedures will almost certainly uncover other defects.

At this stage in recovery the patient may respond to re-educational measures (Kuttner 1928, Alajouanine 1956). Half the patients with recurrent utterance improve while in the other half the stereotypy is perpetuated. In favourable cases the patient can often be made to emit a pre-formed speech pattern. Thus he may be coaxed to articulate, albeit haltingly, the days of the week, numerals, letters of the alphabet, if put into an appropriate frame of endeavour. By accurate imitation of the therapist's lip-movements, he may be prevailed upon to repeat phonemes, then words.

He may be encouraged to complete a familiar verbal automatism started by the examiner: 'Bull and (Bush)'; 'black and (white)'; 'sausage and (mash)'.

However, such accomplishments may get no further than amounting to a mere trick, or *jeu des mots*. In an ordinary setting the spontaneous utterances stay chained to the original stereotypy, with the verbal acquisitions appearing merely at the bidding of the neurological ringmaster. An all-important factor in retarding recovery is the persistence of an oral apraxia, an epiphenomenon which is often overlooked. During the stage of rehabilitation new words are as a rule articulated slowly, hesitatingly, on a staccato monotone. Such newly acquired diction is quite unlike the fluent melodious evocation of the recurring utterance.

Apart from his attempts at talking, the monoaphasiac is seriously handicapped when he tries to write. Rarely if ever can he do more than scribble, or laboriously copy a text. The recurrent utterance, be it noted, does not obtrude itself as a recurrent grapheme, a point which contradicts Jackson's view that stereotypy of speech is due to the automatic action of the opposite hemisphere. It may well be that an oral apraxia plays a part in perpetuating the initial efforts at spoken communication, a mechanism which does not affect the act of writing. Other means of expression are at times less difficult for these patients with recurrent utterance. For example a monophasic secretary may find it possible to communicate better by recourse to a typewriter than by relying on speech, writing or gesture. Thus a young woman rendered aphasic after carotid ligation, could say nothing whatsoever except 'no'. Put before a typewriter she slowly and unassisted executed the following note: 'Dear Doctor Critchley. Where are the speech therapists? I am getting fed up. Love, V. H.'.

Attention is rarely directed towards the perceptual defects in cases of recurrent utterance. In greater or lesser degree they are usually present, a point which detracts from the conventional ascription of this type of speech disorder to an extreme Broca's aphasia.

Nowadays morbid anatomy attracts less attention among aphasiologists than it did and it is unnecessary to pursue here this matter of localization of lesions in recurrent utterance. It is more tempting to turn one's back upon pathology, and to regard recurrent utterance as the clinical manifestation of severe speech-loss, brought about by a conjunction of various factors, including *inter alia* a necessary mass of brain-damage; a sufficient magnitude of speech-defect; abruptness of onset; potent emotional and intellectual circumstances operating just before the stroke; and an associated bucco-labio-lingual apraxia. More appropriately we should focus attention upon a dynamic type of ætiology rather than on a static location of a mere brain-defect. 'An insignificant spar remaining from the ship-wreck of speech' is how Alajouanine (1956) vividly described the phenomenon of recurrent utterance. Perhaps, by a close and imaginative examination of such verbal flotsam, we may learn to reconstruct some of the circumstances of the disaster.

Mental status of patients with recurring utterance

Those neurologists who have carefully observed over a long period of time patients with an established recurrent utterance can hardly refrain from trying to assess the state of mentation. How striking the contrast between the crippling failure to communicate, and the relative integrity of alertness, social behaviour, and adjustment. To what extent is the patient handicapped in his conceptual thinking? What is the nature of his silent rumination? Can he still utilize a verbal type of imagery even though he is incapable of verbal exteriorization?

Such questions naturally tie up not only with disputes as to the intellectual status of aphasiacs, but also with that still older problem, the normal relationship between Thought and Speech. For centuries, philosophers have locked horns in an uncompromising contest over this latter point. Opinionated pronouncements have been made, characterized as much by disaccord as by dogmatism. To some it would seem that no problem exists, and that the answer is obvious to all save the obtuse or the prejudiced. Unfortunately, however, philosophers answer this question now one way, now the other, but always with the utmost assurance.

In reviewing the age-old arguments, it seems astonishing to find how rarely the schoolmen have resorted to the lessons which might be learned from observing those who are speechless but still vigilant. Inter-disciplinary sectarianism has rarely been broken down, and the promising co-partnership of philosophers and aphasiologists has scarcely been broached.

Although the victim of recurrent utterance is virtually bereft of words as a tool in communication, he is not necessarily deprived of the service of words. Jackson used to say that he is speechless but not wordless. But whatever alliance exists in such a case between speech and thought it must be indeed remarkable. He can identify words when he hears them, even though complete verbal comprehension is impaired. To some extent he can 'manipulate' words at a silent level, as when he picks out and assembles letters to form a word, or when he points to an appropriate word from a list of alternatives before him. His performance may be hesitant, even halting, but the very fact that some attempt is made is important.

A patient whose speech is restricted to a stereotyped 'no', may be shown an article and asked to name it, for example a pair of scissors. Obviously its identity is recognized. Pressed for an answer, the patient may painfully emit a post-dental fricative sound but no more. With a pencil he may scrawl an 'S' and then give up. On a typewriter, or with cut-out letters, he fares better and selects an 's' and a 'c'. Shown a list of possible alternatives the patient may point to the word 'scissors' but even so fails to verbalize. Or, given a dictionary, the patient may thumb the pages until he arrives at 's' and then he may narrow his search to 'sc' and even 'sci'. Further than this he may not be able to go. Again the patient may succeed in giving some inkling that he has a knowledge of the word which he cannot exteriorize. By tapping, or by squeezing the examiner's hand, he can indicate the number of syllables in the elusive term (Proust-Lichtheim manœuvre). All these procedures serve to show that the patient still possesses an engram of the word 'scissors', vague and intangible though it be.

In the context of the Thought-Speech controversy, such experiments can only mean either that in ordinary circumstances thought remains possible in the absence of words; or else that to the monophasiac words are still available despite a powerlessness to exteriorize them.

Some measure of conceptual thinking lies therefore within the capacity of a patient with recurrent utterance. In this exercise he utilizes to some extent words at a silent level. This is one problem: the question as to the nature of his silent browsing is another. At such times, he is not in contact with an interlocutor; he is neither decoding information, nor trying to act upon it. He is merely caught up in silent reverie. Is this day-dreaming a type of imageless thinking? This is un-likely, though the images involved may not be of a verbal sort. In such circumstances this type of aphasiac may well be simply a passive agent for a series of images which are mainly of a visual character. These images will be loosely connected, being linked one with another by the freest of associations. Consistency is not there; nor is profundity.

In many ways the phenomenon of recurring utterance differs from the malperformance of most other aphasiacs. From all the clinical evidence it would seem that the patient possesses at least some measure of inner speech and conceptual thinking. Faced with a situation like putting a name to an object he appears to have some idea of what he wishes to say. So far there is little difference from other aphasiacs. But as soon as the preverbitum ends by the patient with recurrent utterance breaking silence, a fantastic travesty of verbal behaviour takes place. Irrespective of what he wants to say or tries to say, his articulatory muscles take charge and involuntarily shape themselves according to a rigid pre-determined pattern, so that one audible complex and one only becomes exteriorized. This resulting sound bears no relationship whatsoever with the idea within the pre-verbitum. As Alajouanine and Lhermitte wrote (1963): 'Thought is squeezed into a mould so as to produce the same copy or *similacrum* each time'.

The patho-physiological mechanism appears to be two-fold. First there is an imperfect selection of the necessary sound-symbol, a defective ecphoria in fact. Secondly an uncontrolled, uninhibited activity of the muscles of articulation takes place, like a severe action tremor which appears as soon as a deliberate attempt is made to execute a skilled movement.

Speech-recording in aphasiacs

Modern instrumental methods of recording constitute a considerable advance over the guess-work descriptions of the past. Furthermore such records lend themselves to unhurried and repeated analysis. Certain new points come to light with an important bearing upon the theory of speech in aphasia, the research now becoming nomothetic as well as idiographic (Allport 1942). Some of the problems of recurrent utterance may in this way become clarified.

An up-to-date mode of transcribing an aphasiac's performance can be devised by extending and elaborating the technique of recording a psychiatric interview, practised by Pittenger, Hockett and Danehy (1960). It is really a logical development of what Hughlings Jackson taught, namely that one should set down a faithful record of exactly what a patient says and does, and not a personal interpretation.

This technique has been mentioned before, but quite briefly. Its importance merits a rather more detailed consideration.

An extended transcript of a structural interview was illustrated in Fig. 4, (see p. 183). On the bottom line one reads the examiner's question and the patient's reply set out in conventional typology. Silent pauses are marked by a symbol and registered in tenths of a second. Just above, the patient's speech is translated into the broad or international phonemic script, to which have been added the approved supra-segmental notations, indicating stress, pitch levels, and terminal contours. At the top of the record is a description of the patient's gestural and mimetic behaviour as agreed by a panel of observers at the interview. Between the last two transcripts are placed the various expressive features, or 'emphatics' of speech—as Laziczius called them (Sebeok 1959)—according to the symbol-system of Smith (1952) and Trager (1958). Here we find a note as to such paralinguistic features as volume and tempo of utterance, register effects, audible overtones, drawling or clipped modes of delivery, as well as the interpolated glottal closures, breaks, nasalization, spirantization, exhalations, and so on. Some of these paralinguistic symbols are set out in Fig. 5.

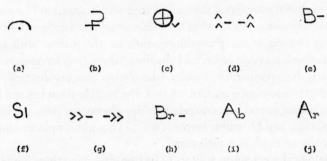

FIG. 5 Examples of some paralinguistic symbols devised by Pittenger, Smith, Trager, and others.

(*a*) slight drawl   (*f*) sloppy or slurred articulation
(*b*) glottal closure   (*g*) considerably overfast
(*c*) pharyngeal constriction   (*h*) breaking
(*d*) considerably overloud   (*i*) wide open mouth exhalation (breathed)
(*e*) breathiness   (*j*) wide open mouth exhalation (voiced)

Such a graphic record of the patient's behaviour consequently entails a detailed account of a communicative 'package', that is to say a complex set made up of mutually reinforcing signals. Though demanding much time, close attention, and experience, a record like this is invaluable, demonstrating amongst other things that throughout the interview the aphasiac is striving to communicate by one means or another, the difficulties of the task being evidenced by the delays and indecisions, and the manner in which the words appear. Every interpolated sound, every mutilated phoneme, indeed every silent period is an eloquent signal, just as it is in a psychiatric interview. The introduction of a sigh, or laugh, or yawn must not be regarded as linguistic 'noise' but rather as an integral part of the information—in aphasiacs just as in normals. The transcripts demonstrate very clearly the Smith-Trager aphorism that in speech 'nothing, never happens'. Communicative behaviour is continual; and motionless silence is a special kind of communicative act'. Within every utterance, however imperfect, there lies a meaning which can be neither disguised not concealed. This is implied in the 'law of immanent reference' which means that no matter what else human beings may be communicating about, they are always communicating about themselves, about one another, and about the immediate context of the communication (Pittenger *et al.* 1960). This law, which includes Ruesch and Bateson's notion of 'metacommunion' (1951), is obeyed by all speakers, however aphasic they may be.

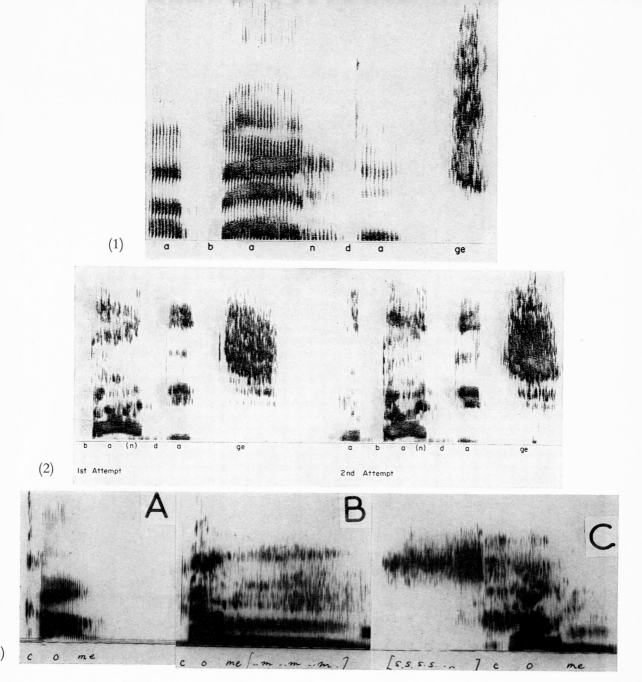

(1) Spectrogram of a normal subject saying 'a bandage'.
(2) Spectrographic record of a dysphasic patient saying the same words.
(3) Spectrograms emitted by a dysphasic patient whose recurring utterance was 'come'.

Plate 8

A study of aphasia by way of 'visible speech', i.e. sonography or spectrography, is new. The drawback of audible recording lies in the difficulties of translation into accurate printed symbols. Visible speech surmounts this problem. As Herodotus said: 'The ear is a less trustworthy witness than the eye'. Comparison of the broad band spectrograms of normal and aphasic speakers emitting the same word, shows obvious differences. The normal records are briefer, crisper, and tidier (see Plate 8). Aphasic records are longer, blurred, less defined. We can also observe the intromission within the breath-stops, of foreign elements like subvocal spirantization—the hallmark of doubt or distress—or a nasalized prolongation of a consonantal phoneme. Hence, it can be said that even at a purely phonemic level, the utterance of an aphasiac differs from that of a normal subject, though the difference may escape the ears of the untutored observer. The possible importance of these spectrographic findings is great, for they suggest that aphasia embraces a physiological disorder involving lower as well as higher nervous activity, just as in the case of so-called agnosia.

This line of research into aphasia obviously promises to prove most informative. The linguistic philosopher Whatmough (1956) has emphasized that up to now no one has attempted to match or compare the findings of speech spectrography with those of electroencephalography. 'If ever this could be done', he said, 'it may point to an answer to the old poser of whether "thought" is subvocal language'.

Indeed we can take up this last point and direct our specific attention to the silent pauses which occur during an aphasiac's efforts to talk. This is specially profitable in the case of recurrent utterance, where the victim strives in vain to emit one term and produces quite another. It has long been known that the silent preverbitum may be the seat of subvocal movements of the articulatory organs. Behaviourists have paid particular attention to this phenomenon, which they often quote in support of the identity of Thought and Language. In recent times, electromyographic studies of the tongue and lips during silent thinking have been popular in the U.S.S.R. (I. S. Iucevitch, Novikova 1955, Bassin and Bein 1955, A. M. Fonarev, N. A. Kryshova) and also in Poland (Herman and Krolikovska 1961). These techniques can be extended to aphasiacs.

Figure 6 is taken from the case of a patient with recurrent utterance whom I studied in Moscow in collaboration with Dr. H. N. Pravdina-Vinarskaya. At first the patient's sole spontaneous speech was 'nou, nou', though later a few other jargon-like automatisms developed. Later still he could be persuaded to repeat a few simple words. In the silent phase while the patient vainly endeavoured to name an object, succeeding in producing after a delay only a stereotype, electrodes in the lip muscles picked up a complex of action potentials. Such findings again illustrate that in aphasia as in normal speech, silence is only relative, and that in any event, it is potentially communicative.

SUMMARY

How can we sum up our remarks? Nothing in discourse is so hard as the ending of it. There is always something more to be said. Belloc was very clear on this: it is always difficult to turn up the splice neatly at the edges. Panurge's monograph on Conchology would never have been finished had not the publisher intervened by threatening him with the Law. And as it is, the last sentence has no verb in it.

I have tried to direct attention to the polar opposites of speech-impairment, the minimal and the maximal, which I have termed respectively the drift and the dissolution of language. In the former

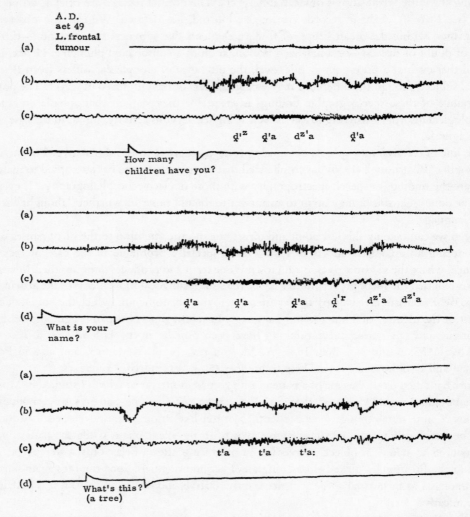

FIG. 6 Electro-myographic studies during the silent period in a patient with recurrent utterance.

there is the incipient dysphasia seen in the earliest stages of a steadily advancing syndrome which later destroys speech; and it is likewise detectable in the last surviving errors in patients recovering from aphasia. The signs are subtle and require an extended clinical examination for their discernment.

The contrasting and severest type of speech-loss is found in aphasiacs with recurrent utterance. In such cases there exists an extraordinary *mésalliance* between the content of the will to speak, and the resulting sounds. As propositions these latter are meaningless, and it signifies little whether they take the form of lexicon words or of gibberish. There is no reason to doubt that some sort of inner speech operates, in which verbal symbols are involved. The ritual strangulation which takes place at the end of the preverbitum may well be due to the unrestrained activity of a compelling buccal apraxia. What determines the pattern of the ritual in a given case is conjectural.

Newer techniques throw light upon the speech-mechanisms in aphasia, and suggest the simultaneous involvement of lower as well as higher speech centres.

'The real life of a thought only lasts until it reaches the frontier of the words. There it petrifies, is dead from then on'. This dictum of Schopenhauer's is surely a caricature of the normal physiology of speech. But it certainly applies to cases of recurrent utterance, especially when he went on to say: . . . 'thereafter it is imperishable, comparable to the fossils of prehistoric animals and plants . . .'.

XVI. ITERATIONS OF WRITTEN AND SPOKEN SPEECH: VERBAL TICS

She only answered 'ting-a-ling'
  To all that I could say.
She seemed to live on 'ting-a-ling'
  By night as well as day.
When I asked her if she'd marry me
  All that she could say
Was 'ting-a-ling a ling ting
  Ting a ling a ling ting
Ting a ling a ling ting tay'.

Late 20th century vaudeville song

Ik zag lacht in een stella straat een aardig meisje spaan
Dat meisje zong ees aardiglied, ik kon het niet verstaan.
Dat meisje zong, dat meisje zong:
Ei loeki da sjoemel la di roedel didel da,
Ei loeki da sjoemel la di roedel didel da,
Ei, ei, ei, roedel didel da,
Ha, ha, ha, sjoemel didel da,
Sjoemel di roedel
Roedel didel da.
Ha, ha, ha, ha,
Ha.

Nonsense song from Holland

Lord Francis Stilton, had once bet a hundred guineas with Colonel Carbury that he would play dice with the Canterville ghost, and was found the next morning lying on the floor of the card-room in such a helpless paralytic state that, though he lived on to a great age, he was never able to say anything again but 'Double Sixes' . . .

Oscar Wilde

There's a story that Lincoln, in the days before his Presidency, was riding on a local train with his son Todd. And the little boy, looking out of the window, observed how often he saw a certain word written on walls and fences. 'What does it mean', he asked his father. Lincoln pretended he saw nothing unusual. 'Just the name of the station.' 'But it's the name of every station', the boy argued. 'That's because more people', Lincoln said, 'get on and off at that station than any other. That's why, son.'

Guy Endore

Like a tourist abroad who rings the changes in his conversation on the few phrases of which he is the master, so in the same way we clinicians meet patients who reiterate certain words, phrases or sentences to the exclusion of all others. Thereby we are reminded not only of our traveller, but of some animal cries and infantile babbling—monotonous repetitions which constitute the whole of the subject's vocalization.

The circumstances under which these speech iterations occur are very diverse; some of the patients are frankly psychotic, others represent neurological problems. Sometimes they obviously form an aphasic disturbance, a disorder of language. In other cases the defect is one of articulation or of the act of speaking. At other times it is difficult to decide, and possibly a disorder both of

200

speech and of speaking coexists. With others again the defect is plainly the result of a thought-disorder upon a conceptual plane higher than the zone of language.

Years ago Gairdner applied the term 'barrel-organisms' to all these various kinds of speech iterations. The term is not a very satisfactory one for the recurrent vocalization is neither a melody nor a theme. More often it is merely a phrase, or maybe a single word. One might, perhaps, use the term 'ting-a-ling phenomenon', after the music-hall song which was familiar last century.

English folk music embodies a number of meaningless phrases of dubious etymology. Ranging from the old-time 'Hey nonny nonny ney' and 'Fol-de-rol', etc., we come to the 'Tick-a-tang' and the 'Tararaboomdeay' of two generations ago, the 'Yip I addy I ay I ay' and the 'Hitchy-koo' of the first war, and the various nonsense syllables of the Hill-Billy songs of a later date. Perhaps these are merely melodious phrases easy to sing; more probably they represent broken-down sense-words or dilapidated speech.

Dealing first with the simplest examples, we may mention the phenomenon of *stammering* or *stuttering*. Whatever the pathogenesis of this condition, whether it be psychogenic, or what is more likely, an organic disorder of a verbal skill, it is clearly an articulatory difficulty in which the faculty of language is not severely deranged. Possibly there is a delay in the conversion of the engrams into verbalization—a delay which may be due, as Jackson believed, to 'right-brained hurry', or to inadequate cerebral dominance, or to a hesitancy in self-expression. There often occurs in stammerers an associated impairment in the act of writing. This subject, first noted by Froeschels, has been well studied by Roman 1959. The penmanship of a stammerer tends to be untidy, messy, poorly co-ordinated, and defective in fluency and continuity. So-called 'hemmings and drawlings' occur with repetitions of words, syllables, letters, or fragments of letters. Probing dots are frequent, and the writer tends to exert heavy pressure with pen or pencil (see Fig. 7). Occasionally stammering occurs as an acquired phenomenon after a left-sided cerebral lesion, as part of an aphasic disorder. Here then is a combination of a defect in speech and defect in articulation comparable with what was said to occur in Broca's 'aphemia'.

Much more complex is the phenomenon of *palilalia*, originally described by Brissaud. This is essentially an organic manifestation associated with diffuse pallido-striatal disease. Hence it may form part of a post-encephalitic Parkinsonism or of a pseudo-bulbar syndrome. Palilalia entails the involuntary repetition two or more times of a terminal word, phrase or sentence. (Example, 'Good morning, doctor, I'm not so well today, today, today, today . . .') The words as they are repeated tend to become more and more clipped or abrupt; the voice becomes softer; while the rate of speaking accelerates. The palilalia occurs not only during spontaneous speech but also in reply to questions. But palilalia does not appear during the recital of an automatic speech-pattern, as for instance when the patient reads aloud, or recites a well-remembered verse or prayer, or when he declaims the days of the week, months of the year, the letters of the alphabet, or when he counts. Palilalia occurs not only in the course of intellectual speech or 'propositionizing', but also—at times—during emotional cries, oaths, interjections and other forms of inferior speech. But this is not always the case, and in some palilalic patients, emotional speech may be free from such repetitions.

14

When the patient's utterance consists of a number of consecutive sentences, it is only the last part of the final sentence which shows the palilalic repetitions. It is as though the stream of talk proceeds quite smoothly only so long as the patient has something to say, or information to impart, but as soon as he comes to the end of his ideas and wishes to lapse into silence, the speech runs on like a gramophone record that has stuck. Sometimes the speech reiterations amount to as many as 20 or more, the voice tailing off in a *diminuendo* manner, while the lips afterwards continue to make the tiny inaudible movements of a *palilalie aphone*.

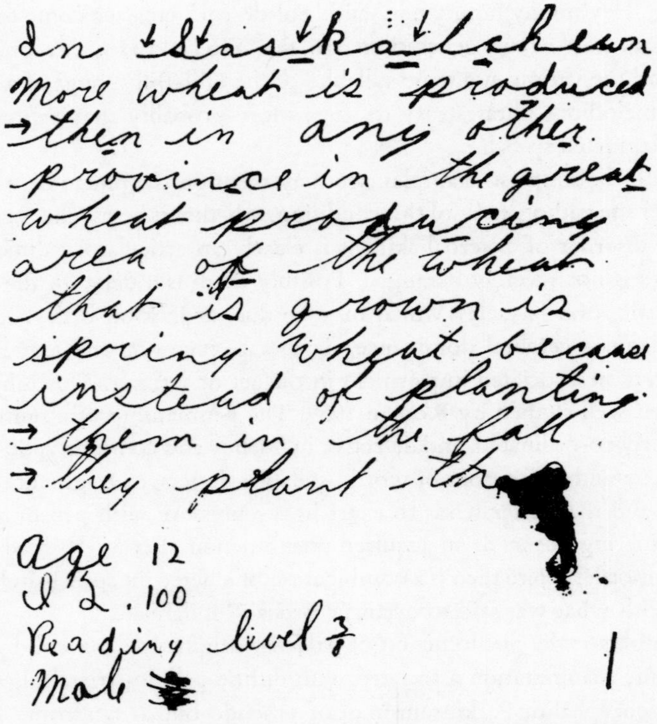

FIG. 7   Handwriting executed by a stammerer aged 12 years (from K. Roman).

What is the nature of this strange phenomenon? Clearly it is a disorder more of 'speaking' than of 'speech'. Babinksi and Mlle. Lévy pointed out that many of these patients exhibit a poverty of speech as though they were unwilling to embark upon the act of speaking. But once this reluctance is overcome, the patient becomes vocal, and the rate of utterance tends to increase. Then, as in the act of walking in Parkinsonians, the patient finds difficulty in coming to a halt, as though it were easier to go on talking than to make the effort of stopping. In other words, as Claude put it, palilalia can be regarded as a sort of verbal antepulsion and festination.

Paligraphia in a patient with palilalia, does not occur. This is natural, for palilalia is not a manifestation of aphasia or any other disorder of language. But on the other hand, palilalia may be combined with well-marked *palipraxia*. One patient, a post-encephalitic Parkinsonian with severe palilalia, compulsive thoughts and oculogyric crises, also tended to continue unduly with any repetitive act such as hammering a nail, combing his hair or brushing his teeth.

In passing, other forms of speech iterations need to be mentioned which can be distinguished without much difficulty from palilalia. First, there is *palilogia*, which is an idiosyncrasy of certain rhetoricians and public speakers who deliberately repeat a word or phrase or sentence for the sake of emphasis. Field Marshal Montgomery used to employ this trick a great deal when addressing his troops. For example: 'We have been fighting the Germans a long time now. A very long time . . . a good deal too long. It's time we finished things off. And we can do it. We can do it. No doubt about that. No doubt about that whatever . . .' and so on. Analogous to this palilogia is the irritating use of *verbal mannerisms*, whereby a person in conversation emits *ad nauseam* such trite little phrases as 'Don't you know', 'I say', 'As a matter of fact', 'Do you know what I mean?'. By gradual steps these verbal sillinesses graduate to sheer *verbal tics*, where a phrase is enunciated as an obsessional trait, without any pretence at meaning or congruity. Such tic-like exclamations are often of a scabrous nature, as in the malady of Gilles de la Tourette or the *manie blasphématoire* of Verga. Meige reported that the Marquise de Dampierre throughout her long life was in the habit of repeating certain immodest sayings even on the most solemn occasions. In a cathedral city in the South of England there dwelled a silvery haired old lady of saintly appearance who could be seen to mutter quietly to herself whenever there was a pause in the conversation. An attendant cleric was once incautious enough to ask her to repeat her observations a little louder, and was startled to hear a stream of obscenities—only a few of which he could understand.

The gradual development of a fully-fledged case of Gilles de la Tourette's disease bears an interesting analogy with one of the classical notions as to the origin of speech in man. The patient usually shows to begin with nothing more than an involuntary motor tic-like mannerism. Later, this becomes associated with some form of vocalization, a grunt, or sniff, or cough, devoid of any semantic properties. Still later, the noise which is emitted becomes articulate and identifiable as a lexicon word. This progression from a motor act to a word recalls the now discredited 'Yo-heave-ho' hypothesis as to the beginnings of speech, namely out of movement.

Allied to the verbal tics is the rare though well-known phenomenon of *echolalia*, whereby statements or questions are repeated by the patient with or without a change in pronoun. This may be found as a mannerism in schizophrenics, dements and other psychotics.

In *echographia* there occurs a slavish repetition in writing of the subject-matter which has just been executed. The phenomenon is rare except in journalism, and usually connotes a gross poverty of ideation. A striking example was seen in a patient with juvenile dementia paralytica, whose letters to his mother were almost a word-for-word transcription of what she had written to him.

Dear Ern, Just a line in answer to your most kind and welcome letter I received from you and pleased to know you are better than you were and that you will try to steady your nerves for to be home quicker. I am longing to see you as you are to see me Ern but its far better to get well now as you are in the best place for it, but cheer up you won't be long now. Its nice to know you can join in all the sports and get about Ern. Thelma Parry's husband came home this week after four years a prisoner of war. They were all excited in the street. Well, Ern, I had a letter this week from Dave and he told me he had a letter from you. Olive is still home. She did not go to Weston after and Muriel is up at Mervyns home this three weeks. She is coming home next Monday with Mervyn he will be on leave then. I don't know what she intends doing after shes gone back. Well, Ern, Mr. Humphreys and Muriel asks how you are and I told him what the doctor said and he told me to tell you to put your mind and getting well to come home on leave and he also said you promised to write to him when you went back the last time you was home. Well, Ern, I will be sending some more cigs and some bake-scones that is if you would like some later on in the week.

The patient's reply read as follows:

To my dear Mother, Just thank in answer to your most kind and welcome letter I received from you pleased to know you. Pleased I am to know you are better than you were that will try dry steady your nerves for to be home quicker. I am longing to see you as you are to see Ern, but its far better to get well now as you are in the best place for it. Just cheer up you wont be long now its nice to know you can join now in all the sports get about. Ern Thelma Parry husband came home this week after four years a prisoner of war they were all excited in the street. Well Ern I had a letter this week from Dave he told me he had a letter from me. Olive is still she didn't go to Weston after. Muriel is up at Mervyns home this three ask she is coming home next Monday she will be on leave know what she intends doing after she gone know he gone back. Well Ern Mr. Humphrey tell you to put your mind getting well do come home on leave he also said you promised to write to him when you went back the last the time you was home. Well Ern I will be sending some more cigs some bakesdonie that is the week.

A fragmentary and literal echographia, or rather an 'autoechographia' is, of course, quite common in the spontaneous writings of aphasic patients, as in the following example:

21 Westbury Park,

Dear Miss Alice Day,
   My begin with the bing with with with the the old doing into (with) into into (into) with with (with) (with) will (will) with the oldest (older) the oldest the the oldest with the oldest the (the) the oldest.

Yours sincerely,
Meggie Brown.

(N.B.—Words in brackets were elided by the patient).

In comparison here is another example of spontaneous writing littered with repetitions:

Now to eat if one cannot other one can—and if we cant the girseau O.C. Washpots prizebloom capacities—turning out—replaced by the headpatternsmyown—capacities—I was not very kind to them. Q.C. Washpots under-patterned against—bred to pattern. Animal sequestration capacities and animal sequestired capacities under leash—and animal excretions. Q.C. Washpots capacities leash back to her—inthetrain from Llanfairfechan armybarracks wishe us goodbye in Llandudno station and turned in several Q.C. Washpots capacities . . .

This specimen, full of neologisms, irrelevancies, incoherence, and verbal perseveration, was executed not by an aphasiac, but by a schizophrenic. This fact should not have been difficult to discern from the bizarrities and the obscure symbolism of the writing. The point should be made, however, that many pathological features are common to both aphasic and schizophrenic utterance, both vocal and graphic. (Chap. XXVIII.)

Kleist believed that in both conditions the speech-peculiarities are comparable, and that in schizophrenia there is a *paralogia* arising from a specific disorder in gnosic faculties. He associated speech-iterations with lesions in the caudatum and perhaps also in the midbrain. Berze, Grühle and others, however, ascribed the fantastic speech of the psychotic to an underlying schizophrenic thought-disorder. This hypothesis would place the disorder at a different level within the pre-verbal processes of speech.

Where should this third example of *paligraphia* be relegated?

This that they were not to have, they were having. They were having now and before and always and now and now and now. Oh now, now, the only now, and above all now, and there is no other now but thou now and now is thy prophet. Now and for ever now. Come now, now, for there is no now but now. Yes, now. Now, please now, only now, not anything else only this now, and where are you and where am I and where is the other one, and not why, not ever why, only this now; and on and always please then always now, always now, for now always one now; and on and always please then always now, always now, for now always one now, one, going now, rising now, sailing now, leaving now wheeling now, soaring now, away now, all the way now, all of the way now; one and one is one, is one, is one, is still one, is still one . . .

The foregoing sentences have been taken from a well-known novel[1] in which they form an isolated and unorthodox paragraph. The meaning can be guessed from the context, if not from its content. Advanced students of literary style will no doubt comprehend and appreciate this particular technique of writing, but as neuro-psychiatrists we may be satisfied in recognizing the nature and perhaps also the mechanisms of many of the prosodic unconventionalities. At this point let us also quote another and extreme instance of verbal perseveration, from a calligrammatic poem of the Dadaist school:

Persienne Persienne Persienne
Persienne Persienne Persienne
Persienne Persienne Persienne Persienne
Persienne Persienne Persienne Persienne
Persienne Persienne
Persienne Persienne Persienne
Persienne?

Echopraxia is a rare symptom which may be associated with echolalia, and it is apt to occur in circumstances of enhanced suggestibility as in a community of hysterics. During the 1939–45 war, both Anderson and I met this manifestion in torpedoed sailors days adrift in the Atlantic in a small boat. In such shipwrecked personnel, tortured by thirst, hunger and cold, the sensorium would become clouded, and mass suggestibility develop together with, at times, shared hallucinosis. One man might proclaim that he could see land, or a ship or a tree laden with ripe fruit growing out of the sea; another would assert he could see it too, then another. Then if one man were to stand up in the boat so would another. If one waved his arms others did the same. Should he bury his head in his hands that movement would be repeated by his shipmates.

[1] From Hemingway's *For Whom the Bell Tolls*, reproduced by kind permission of the publishers, Messrs. Jonathan Cape.

Verbigeration is a variety of speech-iteration which belongs frankly to the realm of psychosis. It can occur as an instance of verbal stereotypy in the schizophrenic, who in season and out may declaim an idiosignificant but otherwise meaningless utterance. 'Here I come, here I stay . . .', 'And the Lord shall prepare a niche in the Rock!', 'Don't touch me', 'Oh dear me!'. These are all examples of schizophrenic verbigeration. Then there are the exclamations of despair which may be uttered over and over again by agitated melancholics, 'Oh my God, what shall I do?' or 'Oh God, kill me!' and so on. Furthermore, in patients with dementia, hypochondriacal pre-occupations may be responsible for some such phrase as 'Please can I go to the lavatory, Mummy?' which may dominate the conversation, though not to the entire exclusion of other forms of speech.

Most interesting of all the examples of barrel-organisms are the *recurring utterances* encountered in severe aphasiacs. The patient is limited in his speech to a solitary word or phrase which he employs on all occasions, however irrelevant, however incongruous. The word or phrase which over-runs the garden of his speech like a weed, may be a most unexpected one, even quite complicated, so that it bears more the stamp of a curtailed proposition than an emotional interjection.

Thus the vocabulary of one of my monophasic patients was restricted to the solitary phrase 'on the booze', which he enunciated in reply to questions as well as spontaneously. By altering the melody of his voice, or by employing gesture he was able to utilize these three words with such success as to make them express his immediate desires or to signify assent, negation or dismissal.

From the literature other articulate stereotypes can be found which may be uttered quite out of context. These include such phrases as *As de pique*; *Bon soir, les choses d'ici bas*; *J'ai terriblement peur*; *Gerechter Gott*; *N'ya pas de danger*; *tout de même*; 'the other day'; 'that's mine'; 'list complete'.

Broca's original patient at the Bicêtre could say nothing at all except *Tan-tan*, by which nick-name he was known to all the other patients and doctors.

Other examples of recurring utterance have been recorded in such fragments of jargon as 'Da de da, do de da', 'Yabby' 'Me me comittimy pittimy', the rags and tatters of what was once the patient's speech, as Jackson put it. Such aphasic patients cannot say a part only of their recurring utterance. Thus Bazire's patient muttered *sapon, sapon*, but could not be made to say *sap* or *pon* alone. During Baudelaire's last days in the Institute of Saint-Jean and Sainte-Elizabeth, his speech was restricted to the expletive *Cré nom*, to the distress of the good sisters in attendance who regarded him as possessed by the devil. His biographer, Enid Starkie, has remarked, 'with these two words, he who had so loved conversation, was obliged to express all his feelings and thoughts, joy, sorrow, anger and impatience, and he used to fly into a rage at his inability to make clear his meaning and to answer those who spoke to him'. But his mind was clear. His friend Nadar visited him and described how he got on to the topic of immortality. 'Voyons comment peux-tu croire à Dieu, repétai-je. Baudelaire s'écarta de la barre d'appui ou nous étions accoudés et me montra le ciel. Devant nous, au dessous de nous, c'était, embrasant toute la vue, cernant d'or et de feu la silhouette puissante de l'Arc de Triomphe, la pourpre splendide du soleil couchant. Cré nom! Oh, cré nom! protestait-il encore, me rispostait-il indigné, à grands coups de poing vers le ciel.' Nadar went on to exclaim, 'Les deux seuls mots qui puissent sortir des lèvres d'ou avaient jailli des plaintes immortelles. Oh, l'horreur de cette fin lamentable, la cruanté effrayante de lui qui a frappé Baudelaire dans le verbe, ce sertisseur de gemmes de rubis, comme il avait frappé Beethove dans l'ouïe et Michel Ange dans la vue'.

Jackson suspected that the words which make up a recurring utterance were those associated with the victim's thoughts at the time of the stroke, and represented the phrase which the patient was about to utter before losing consciousness; that is to say, a sort of 'stillborn proposition'. Gowers, however, believed the words of a recurring utterance were actually the last ones which the patient had spoken before losing consciousness. On the whole the clinical evidence seems to support the belief of Gowers rather than Jackson. My patient with the recurring utterance 'on the booze' had been overcome by his apoplexy during a taproom brawl. The patient who kept saying 'list complete' was an accountant who lost consciousness just after making up his books for the half-year. Another patient sustained a head injury in a street fight; his recurring utterance was 'I want protection'. A woman who developed a stroke while riding a donkey found herself unable to say anything except 'Gee-gee'. One of Gowers' patients was taken ill in a cab. On entering the vehicle she had told the cabby to drive her to Mrs. Waters. These were the last words she spoke. Her reiterating phrase was 'Missus'. An attractive young lady of dubious marital status, after a cerebral haemorrhage, could say nothing but the revealing words, 'Not tonight, I'm tired'. A female patient whose ictus had occurred when her husband made love to her in the early hours was restricted in her speech to the iteration 'Good morning'.

In this connection the case of a war-time sailor who was one of the crew of a landing craft during the Normandy invasion of Tuesday, 6th June, 1944 can be recalled. The troops had been standing by for some days in readiness to attack, until the tension was eventually relieved and the signal for zero hour was given. The sailor sustained on the beaches a bullet wound of the skull producing a right hemiplegia and an aphasia with recurring utterance. This took the form of the statement 'Yes, today', and it is not difficult to imagine the dramatic circumstances under which that particular declaration originally arose. A woman was taken ill with a cerebral vascular accident at a dinner party celebrating the seventeenth anniversary of her marriage. In her post-apoplectic monaphasia her sole utterance was '17'.

The phenomenon of recurring utterance brings up for consideration the more profound problem of the relation between thought and speech. 'Without speech no reason, without reason no speech . . .' We recall this dictum around which philosophers have disputed for centuries. A study of aphasia has gone far to clarify the issue for we know that behind every aphasic speech-disorder there exists a special defect of mentation over and above a lesser disorder of general intelligence. The latter may be extremely slight and difficult to demonstrate. But what of the aphasics with recurrent utterance? In a long-standing case we can satisfy ourselves that thought processes are present—to some degree at any rate. Speech, too, is there, but only after a fashion. As has been discussed in a previous chapter, speech and thought are linked in a grotesque alliance, so that the plenitude of inner speech finds outlet in one sole form of vocal expression. Awareness or insight into the nature of the defect will develop and efforts at compensation later appear in the correct use of inflections in the fragmentary speech. We are reminded of a musician who is deprived of all instruments save a one-string violin on which he eventually learns to play a tune.

Again following Jackson, we may also refer to the phenomenon of *occasional utterance* in aphasiacs. It might be better to speak, in this connection, of 'isolated utterance', or 'unique utterance'. Thus a speechless patient, or one who is almost speechless, may in certain circumstances be heard to enunciate quite unexpectedly an interjection, a word, or even a comprehensible phrase. An aphasiac with recurrent utterance may very occasionally be coaxed to say something outside his ritual. A coloured aphasic patient seen in New Orleans was once noted to articulate 'cereal' when the topic of breakfast was raised: hitherto her speech had been limited to the affirmative and negative grunts traditionally represented as 'uh-uh'. The unexpected word or phrase may in turn constitute a perseveration and so a recurrent utterance, or it may be incorporated within the expanding vocabulary. A patient who could only say 'Yes, but you know', once said 'Take care', when the baby fell. A patient of Trousseau's said *Merci* when a lady picked up his handkerchief. At an interview with an aphasiac and his wife the latter suddenly sneezed. Immediately the patient interjected 'Bless you!'; hitherto his speech had been confined to 'yes' and 'no'. Thus a patient whose stereotypy was for a long period nothing but a piece of recurrent gibberish, was observed on one occasion to tack on the expletive 'Goddammit'. Another patient of mine—almost speechless—suddenly when being demonstrated to my students, who were puzzled over the problem of his cerebral dominance, cried aloud the word 'unilaterality'. Another patient, totally aphasic and in bed after her stroke, saw her daughter fiddle with her jewel-case on the dressing table, and called out 'That's mine'; thereafter the phrase 'that's mine' became a recurring utterance. A severely aphasic man was in the habit of chanting to the buxom night-nurse. 'She's my Lily of . . .' When, eventually the nurse replied 'Laguna' the patient triumphantly cried 'That's it!', an interjection which thenceforward became an established parrot-cry. One of the strangest examples, however, is an aphasic patient of Jackson's who unexpectedly demanded, 'What's all this bloody fuss about?'. A patient of Sir William Gowers was afflicted with the comment 'Tons of it' as his sole item of speech. In an unguarded moment at a clinical demonstration Gowers once asked the patient 'Tons of what, my poor man?' and received a monosyllabic reply as unexpected as it was embarrassing.

At this point might be quoted an unusual case where a speech-iteration developed. A child whose early milestones had been uneventful began, at the age of 5, to show mild disturbances in behaviour and in speech. There was no antecedent illness to account for this. Gradually his vocabulary seemed to become more limited and he spoke less and less. There was no evidence of any deafness and he seemed to understand fully all that was said to him. He ceased to take interest in picture-books, and his childish powers of reading gradually waned. After a period of some months of almost complete mutism, he became vocal again. But now, at the age of 8, his speech was restricted to the meaningless phrase 'Teezha', an utterance which he repeated over and over again, sometimes excitedly, sometimes with calm deliberation. To all questions he would reply 'teezha', the phrase apparently serving both as 'yes' and 'no'. He would approach his parents or nurse with this word 'teezha', obviously by the intonation of his voice making a request. It was clear from listening to him in these circumstances that 'teezha' had for him most of the properties of speech, both propositional and interjectional. On the other hand, when he was occupied with his toys, or in exciting games with other children, he could be heard to chatter aloud 'Teezha, teezha, teezha' in a manner reminiscent of the babbling of the contented infant or the deaf-mute. At these times the patient was obviously using these words as a form of play, exercising the so-called 'ludic function' of speech, to employ the terminology of Ombredane.

The pathological nature of this patient's syndrome was never determined. His iteration 'teezha' is unusual and important in that it combined the role of an aphasiac's recurrent utterance with the added use of truncated speech as a pleasurable exercise.

The question may now be considered of so-called *reduplications* in speech. These are linguistic phenomena which bear a remote relationship to speech-iterations in that both consist in repetitions arising out of a background of a restricted vocabulary. Re-duplications in speech are encountered in at least four circumstances:

1. In the speech of primitive peoples and particularly the Hottentot and Polynesian tongues. It is not necessary to give examples, but attention should be directed to the fact that many of these reduplicated words are onomatopœic in their nature.

2. The speech of young children. Among English speaking communities, for example, the common term in baby-talk for horse is *gee-gee*, for train *puff-puff*. Once again it is noteworthy that some of these expressions are echo-words while others are based upon interjections (*gee-gee*). Some would seek to detect in the reduplications of the children's speech an atavistic return to the kind of language in primitive communities. Such an idea is far-fetched, and Jespersen was probably correct in regarding the child's reduplications as a form of verbal play, and he referred to the pleasure always felt in repeating the same muscular act until one is tired. He also recalled that in the act of laughter the same vowel sound preceded by an aspirate is repeated over and over.

3. In some of the makeshift languages used as a *lingua franca* between whites and coloured races, reduplications may loom large. They are to be found, for example, in the *Bêche-de-mer* of the South Sea Islands, in the *Patois créole* of Mauritius, in the *Chinook* jargon of North America, but best of all in the pidgin-English of China. In the last named there occur a very large number of reduplications, for example, *chin-chin* (salutations), *fu-fu* (ordure), *chop-chop* (quickly), *man-man* (slowly), *chow-chow* (to eat), *sing-song* (a poem), and *boom-boom* (sexual intercourse).

4. Lastly we meet at times strange reduplications in the language employed by man while exhorting animals. This topic forms a fascinating chapter in philology, though its connections with neurology are remote. A good example of reduplication in man's calls to his beasts can be found in the traditional French hunting cries. To encourage the hounds to work the huntsman cries, *Ha hallé, hallé, hallé!* or *Hau, hau, hau tahaut!* or *Ha bellement la ila, la ila, haut valet*, etc. An eighteenth century treatise on the subject solemnly adds a list of exhortations for English dogs, 'for there are very many English hounds in France and it is difficult to get them to work when you speak to them in an unknown tongue!'.

XVII. ARTICULATORY DEFECTS IN APHASIA: THE PROBLEM OF BROCA'S APHEMIA

What a curious thing speech is! The tongue is so serviceable a member (taking all sorts of shapes just as it is wanted)—the teeth, the lips, the roof of the mouth, all ready to help; and so heap up the sound of the voice into the solid bits which we call consonants, and make room for the curiously shaped breathings which we call words!

Oliver Wendell Holmes

Take care of the sense, and the sounds will take care of themselves.

Lewis Carroll

Here is man who can do what no animal can do: speak. And for that purpose skillfully directs a faint column of air from his lungs through throat and mouth, past vocal cord, and past an arrangement of tongue to palate, to teeth or to lips, in such a way as to produce a succession of disturbances in the surrounding air, disturbances that will reach another person's ear and there transform themselves into disturbances of the tiny members of the ear apparatus, which in turn will become irritations travelling along certain nerves and awakening activity of an unknown kind in certain brain cells.

How this finally turns into understanding and into a return movement called a reply, no one knows. But this is speech. And no one can guess how it arose, or why all the millions of mankind, barring some few crippled members, can speak some tongue. Nor why all the thousands of different languages are all in their own way structurally complex and yet at the same time perfect, as if each were the creation of a master artist.

Guy Endore

What power can be packed into a tiny bit of air merely by forcing it through the throat and mouth of man! And especially when the usual direction of our breath is reversed and we speak by pulling air in instead of expelling it. Then we make those strange sounds that are like the last survivals of some prehistoric language. Animal sounds. Neanderthal man's first attempt at speech. The avulsives. Which somehow remain connected with our deepest emotions. The avulsive 'Oh!' or 'Ah!'. The gasp that is torn from us by shock or amazement. The fricative avulsive 'Tsk-tsk-tsk', which expresses real or mocking concern. The lateral avulsive that is used to control horses and to entice a smile from a baby.

And most of all, that word of affection, the kiss, which is a labial avulsive, in which the skin of another person's body is often used to form the vacuum which is broken by the noisy intake of air.

Guy Endore

The term 'aphemia' was coined by Broca over a century ago. Its exact connotation has since changed, and indeed the word has been and still is applied by different authors in various contexts. There are two main usages. In the first place the term 'aphemia' can be made to signify merely an impairment of speech—what most would call 'dysphasia'. So it was used originally by Broca in 1861, who applied it to the speech-affection of his two patients, Laborgne and Lelong, in preference to the term previously suggested by Frank, namely 'alalia'. A few years later Trousseau objected to the word 'aphemia', on the grounds of etymology, and with the help of a Greek scholar he proposed the expression 'aphasia'. In an open letter to the medical Press Broca, more stubborn than correct, pleaded for the rejection of 'aphasia', and continued to favour 'aphemia', or alternatively 'aphrasia'. However, Trousseau prevailed, and aphasia has been universally accepted by neurologists as the term indicating loss or defect of the endowment of mature speech through acquired disease.

However the term aphemia here and there lingered on, being used by Bastian, Henschen, Dejerine, Balett, by Pierre Marie (rather grudgingly), and in contemporary medicine by Symonds. These authors have mainly applied the term, as Broca did in later years, to a specific clinical type of dysphasia. Although there have been minor differences in the employment as between one author and another, the context has usually been a severe disorder of articulate utterance coupled with an intact intellectual equipment; perfect comprehension of words heard or read; and a retained power of self-expression by means of writing as well as pantomime. Some aphasiologists have utilized the expression 'pure sub-cortical motor aphasia' in synonymous fashion. Those authors who employ 'aphemia' in this restricted sense, expressly exclude cases of disordered articulation from disease of the nerve-supply to the muscles of the lips and tongue (in other words, dysarthria). They would differentiate aphemia from bulbar or pseudo-bulbar dysarthria by pointing out that certain words may be altogether lost, while others, e.g. oaths and interjections, are retained; that the patient may incorrectly substitute one word for another; and furthermore that some patients may repeat a phrase over and over again in an incongruous fashion. Be it noted that these are all criteria of a disorder of speech which transcends mere articulatory difficulties.

Although such a dissociated speech-loss, implying a potential parcellation of the faculty of speech, accorded well with the materialism of the nineteenth century, it was at variance with the more dynamically minded school of neurology inspired by Hughlings Jackson. To the latter, speech was a fundamental human endowment; a modality of language, and hence an aspect of cerebration and of behaviour, not to be regarded as the arithmetical sum of a set of psychophysical activities, e.g. reading, writing, talking and listening.

Modern neurologists therefore regard with the gravest reserve all claims for the existence of aphemia; that is to say, of an isolated aphasic disorder involving nothing except the act of talking. They would feel sympathetic with Hughlings Jackson when he wrote: 'To say that he cannot speak and yet can express himself in writing is equivalent, I think, to saying he cannot speak and yet he can speak'. Most neurologists today would look upon an alleged case of aphemia as an aphasia which has been inadequately studied and imperfectly evaluated; they would suspect, moreover, that the conception implies an underlying view of the nature of normal speech which is far too simple and mechanistic. It is significant that those neurologists who have embarked upon the most intensive and at the same time extensive study of cases of aphasia (like Head, and Weisenburg and McBride) seem never to have encountered these so-called 'pure' forms of dissociated speech-loss including aphemia.

Yet it would be unwise and indeed illogical to shrug off the question of aphemia by lightly dismissing every alleged case in the literature as an instance of faulty observation. Experienced aphasiologists find very occasionally (and it is necessary to emphasize the extreme infrequency) a patient whose power of verbal utterance is grossly impaired, and yet the understanding of verbal symbols seems to be intact; and, moreover, the power of communication by writing is retained to an unexpected degree.

When faced with such a problem it is important for the neurologist to be able to exclude certain sources of diagnostic error.

In the first place, the possibility must be borne in mind that the case might be one of gross dysarthria rather than dysphasia. Paralysis of the peripheral organs of articulation from disease of the ponto-medullary nuclei or from bilateral affection of the supranuclear pathways, would impair merely the instrumentalities of spoken speech. Clinical distinction may not be easy, and an analysis of extended speech-records may be necessary. A dysarthric patient will mispronounce every word, even though some phonemes may cause more trouble than others. The choice of words, the vocabulary utilized, the proper use of semantic units, and the grammatical construction might be expected to be correct in the case of dysarthria, while all these aspects will probably be impaired in the aphemic. A potential source of error exists, however. The dysarthric patient may have so much mechanical difficulty in the exteriorization of words, that he may exercise a verbal economy, sacrificing all the minor tools of grammar (articles, prepositions, conjunctions), retaining merely the 'full' words. There will result a syntactical disorder resembling a kind of telegrammatism. Such a truncated manner of speaking may be difficult to distinguish from the impoverished speech of an aphasiac.

Those cases of absolute mutism developing abruptly in the course of cerebral disease are almost certainly examples of anarthria and not of aphasia. The diagnosis is confirmed when it is found that the patient can express himself in writing, or by pointing to isolated letters of the alphabet so as to spell out messages. The autopathographic account written after his recovery by Sir Frederick Andrewes under the title 'On being bereft of speech' was not a case of an aphasia, but a total anarthria.

If after close examination it eventually becomes possible to conclude that the case is one of aphasia with dysarthria and not one of dysarthria alone, other considerations arise for scrutiny. The alleged ability to write normally needs investigation. Before deciding that this faculty is retained, it is necessary to examine with care a considerable amount of written material, embodying spontaneously inspired creative efforts. Such texts need to be analysed, and before they can be passed as normal it must be possible to exclude gross spatial disorders of penmanship; errors of spelling; incorrect word-selection and usage; verbal omissions, reduplication or reiterations; as well as contaminations of the text by inordinate use of words or phrases. Some of these features may be elusive and hence easily overlooked. The texts must be studied in the light of the patient's literary and educational background, and one must compare them with specimens executed prior to the illness before any conclusion can be reached as to whether the power of writing is, or is not, retained.

Having, perhaps, specifically confirmed that the putative aphemic patient is not a simple victim of dysarthria, and that the faculty of writing is as a matter of fact, intact, it will also be necessary to examine the implication that the patient's intellect is in no way impaired, particularly with regard to the understanding of verbal symbols. This may be quite a formidable task, involving a battery of tests both verbal and non-verbal in type. It will also entail an evaluation of the personality, and a searching comparison of pre-morbid with post-morbid behavioural patterns. Such a thorough-going analysis must surely have been rarely carried out in cases claimed to be an aphemia, and yet the onus of proof must nowadays lie at the doors of those who contend that aphemia exists as an entity in clinical neurology. Herein a search of the literature is revealing, for the purer the alleged type of motor aphasia, the less adequate have been the protocols.

One important complicating factor is apt to be overlooked in adjudicating upon every case of aphasia, and which becomes all the more significant in the case of so-called 'pure', partial defects of speech, e.g. alexia and aphemia. The pattern of a speech-affection in an aphasiac may be distorted by psychogenic factors which may elaborate one single modality of speech. In other words, hysterical features may embellish the clinical picture. Especially is this so when one is dealing with a simple-minded type of patient, highly suggestible, impressed by his new status as a cynosure of interest, and only too ready to oblige and assist the examining physician. Herein lies an important hazard of the interview-situation.

Perhaps it may eventually be possible to eliminate psychological factors in the evaluation of the case. There is still one other condition which may exist and dominate the picture of disordered enunciation of words, namely an articulatory apraxia. In a very mild aphasia, the act of writing may perhaps be affected scarcely at all, and then not for long, but the act of talking may be severely and persistently impaired by dint of an apraxia which is limited, or almost limited, to the articulatory organs. This idea may have occurred unwittingly to Broca himself, and to Bouillaud too, when they spoke of a 'disordered faculty of co-ordinating the movements necessary for articulate language'. Such statements were made decades before Liepmann's original description of apraxia.

Shortly after the abrupt onset of an aphasia, some patients may show not only a dysarthric type of dysphasia, but also an apraxic disorder in the execution of diverse movements within the oral region. This may be demonstrated visually by the use of a glossogram (Rey; de Morsier; Bay). Even clinical testing may show that the patient may fail to protrude the tongue on command (though he can automatically lick his lips). The patient with oral apraxia may be unable to push the tongue into one cheek or the other, or to wiggle it sideways, or to raise its tip. He may fail to purse up his lips to whistle or to kiss. Yawning and gargling may be impossible. Likewise there may occur an excessive contraction of the articulatory and respiratory actions. Occasionally during the vain efforts to speak, the patient may display spasmodic contraction of the head, body and limbs resulting in fatigue, and visible distress. Minor disturbances of swallowing may occur during the initial stages of the aphasia. Apraxia of the oral muscles may undergo resolution with the passage of time, and, as Bay has shown, a series of clinical stages may be identified during the restoration of function. Voluntary opening and shutting of the mouth is often the first act to reappear, followed by the baring of the teeth, puffing of the cheeks (both cheeks together at first, later one at a time), protrusion of the tongue, gargling, licking and smacking of the lips, clearing of the throat, and then clicking of the tongue. All these performances can take place better in a natural setting, i.e. automatically, than when serving as deliberate willed responses to the command of an examiner in a test-situation.

Whether these uncoordinated and undifferentiated disorders of innervation fall strictly speaking within the *cadre* of an apraxia in the precise sense of the word, is open to argument. Head would have said not. None the less the hypothesis of an articulatory apraxia can serve pragmatically to describe a special disorder of those limited motor-skills which involve the oral muscles. Nowadays we tend more and more to believe that a disturbance of articulatory 'motoricity', as the Germans say, occurs with many cases of aphasia, and produces important phonemic defects. They are not necessarily apraxic only, for they may entail merely a spasticity, or a weakness, or both.

Even when these oro-facial incoordinations have disappeared, minor defects may still occur within the domain of the motor-skills executed by the lips, tongue and palate. Dysarthria will then result and if continuing in severe form for an undue length of time, i.e. after other aspects of speech have returned to normal, the clinical picture of a severe and almost isolated articulatory apraxia results.

Articulatory apraxia, be it noted, can exist alone, that is without any impairment of symbolic formulation and expression. When this is the case, it probably represents the 'cortical dysarthria' of older writers, stemming from a limited unilateral lesion of the brain. Articulatory apraxia may however complicate an aphasia. In such an event, and when dysarthria dominates the clinical scene, we find what has been miscalled 'pure subcortical motor aphasia' or, by others, 'aphemia'.

It may be of interest to quote at this point a short series of statements made by Hughlings Jackson between 1861 and 1868 as indicating the maturation of his ideas.

> When my attention was first drawn to the class of cases I am discussing, I thought there was a fundamental distinction betwixt the mistakes of words and 'ataxy' of articulation—the mistakes of muscular movements. I used to suppose . . . that Broca's convolution was a sort of cerebellum for articulation . . . I soon concluded that the ataxy of articulation was a quasi-mental defect—an inability to combine muscular movements in a particular mental act. In a subsequent paper I remarked that 'It is hard to say where obviously motor symptoms ended, and mental ones began'. I have long believed that it is not only hard, but impossible, even using the words 'motor' and 'mental' in the popular sense. *I now think that the only differences in ataxy of articulation, mistakes of words, and disorder of ideas, are differences of 'compound degree.'*

Aphasia is more than a highest-level disorder of speech: it is also a disorder of language: that is, of communication. This statement presupposes a qualitative alteration in the processes of thought, especially in the mental mechanisms which occur immediately before the emission of speech and also during the extended act of speaking. A disorder of language transcends mere difficulties with speech for it also implies some upset in various non-verbal methods of communication, that is an 'asemasia'. Consequently there may be considerable reduction in the automatic or deliberate use of gesture; with difficulties in drawing, design, and plastic art; the handling and appreciation of music as well as mathematical symbols; and with the understanding or employment of various codes of communication such as shorthand or signalling, which may be seriously impaired.

But the most conspicuous defect in aphasic patients, is the faulty use or appreciation of verbal symbols. In so far as such symbols are conventional tools of thought, the pattern of the defect will depend to some extent upon the language-group to which the aphasic patient belongs. Thus the language habitually spoken by the person before his aphasia will have had its own linguistic idiosyncrasies including its syntax, its aesthetic properties, its store of phonemes or tamber-differences and its subtle yet indivisible bonds between sound and meaning. No two linguistic-groups are identical in these respects. 'Languages', as Goldstein truly said, 'differ not simply as to sounds or signs but they represent various attitudes towards the world, various fundamental types of world perspectives (*Weltansichten*)'. We have already made the point elsewhere that each person's manner of using his own language is individual and personal, never altogether shared with the rest of the community; and that it is something which reflects his total personality, in the same way as his handwriting or his pantomimic mannerisms.

These points illustrate the important part which linguistics, including phonetics and phonology, might in the future contribute to our understanding of aphasia. Nowadays a wider approach to the problem of aphasia obtains is witnessed in an interesting study by Grewel, wherein he pointed out that every language is made up of a polydimensional system of signs, comprising: (1) a system of distinctive sound-elements, or phonemes; (2) a system of words, or phonetic-semantic units; (3) a system of diversity in word-formation; (4) a system of diversity in sentence-formation; and (5) a system of accents (pitch, length, stress).

In cases of aphasia abnormalities relating to some or all or any of these systems can be identified. Although some of these features have been thoroughly studied, others have been largely neglected. Among the latter there is the question of the altered pronunciation met with in the fragmentary speech of aphasiacs,—what may be loosely called the disorders of articulation, or what Grewel would include under his terms 'aphonemia'; 'dysphonemia' and 'paraphonemia'.

The history of this vexed question of dysarthria and dysphasia entailed five distinct phases of orientation towards the problem. First of all was a long period when the two different kinds of speech-affection were confused. Then came a stage of sharp differentiation between the dysarthrias and the dysphasias. This was followed by a time when the two phenomena were once again con-fused. The next period was again one during which the two disorders were once more rigidly demarcated; and lastly there is the current conception whereby a re-alignment of ideas has taken place, correlating and associating the two affections.

These five modes of approach to the dysarthria-dysphasia problem may be discussed a little more closely. First there was the pre-aphasiological period which lasted through medical history up to the end of the eighteenth century. Loss of speech was not looked upon as a disordered operation of the mind, but to a paralysis, or 'dead palsy' of the tongue. Patients with speech-affections were subjected to local painful therapeutic essays with the object of revivifying the organs of speech. Treatment of this sort was meted out to Dr. Samuel Johnson and to William Harvey after their strokes.

The next period, when dysarthria and dysphasia were first differentiated, came about very gradually. One of the most forceful proponents was Hughlings Jackson, who distinguished articulatory difficulties due to paralysis of the tongue, lips or palate, from the dysphasias or true affections of speech. Jackson drew attention to the co-existence of difficulty of swallowing in the former group, namely the cases of the dysarthrias; while in regard to the latter group, made up of the dysphasiacs, he emphasized the fact that many of them not only could not speak properly, but they could not write correctly either. As a matter of fact Jackson tended to avoid the term aphasia, preferring to refer to disorders of expression. In this scission Hughlings Jackson was supported, oddly enough, by Bastian, who also said that the distinction between aphemia, as he chose to call it, and anarthria, depends upon the presence or absence of associated conditions, especially dysphagia and cranial nerve palsies.

The next stage, or the phase of confusion, dates from 1906 when Pierre Marie advanced the idea that one aspect of central disorder of speech was what he called 'anarthria'. He furthermore believed that anarthria was an integral part of the aphasia described by Broca. It must be remembered, of course, that Broca did not use the term aphasia but preferred to speak of 'aphemia'. Marie said that Broca's aphemia was really a compound of aphasia with anarthria. Anarthria is a term which never became popular in Great Britain, though, of course, we speak of 'dysarthria' for pure articulatory defects. However it still circulates in France, particularly in connection with the disordered pronunciation in aphasic disorders. Here it is probably synonymous with the so-called 'cortical dysarthria' of other European writers. Neurologists such as Henschen and Pick believed they could explain the co-existence of anarthria or articulatory defects in aphasic patients by supposing that the responsible lesion involved not only Broca's area, that is the foot of the third frontal convolution in the dominant hemisphere, but also a region sited more posteriorly, namely, the lower part of the pre-central gyrus. Reference has already been made to another conception which also developed and further complicated the issue. This dated from Liepmann's paper in 1900 upon apraxia. Regarding disorders of speech, Liepmann took up the attitude that many of the phenomena of motor aphasia could be fairly regarded as an 'articulatory dyspraxia'. This interesting and attractive notion was supported and even extended by other writers such as Ballet, Kleist, Wundt, and enthusiastically in this country by Kinnier Wilson. I have already referred to the recent work of de Morsier and Rey who sought by various instrumental methods to demonstrate that the disordered speech in patients with motor aphasia results from an apraxia of lip, tongue and palate. On the other hand there have been many opinions to the contrary. Liepmann himself by 1913 had retracted from his earlier views, and at that date his writings betrayed doubt as to the validity of what he had previously taught. This is interesting because Kinnier Wilson continued to support strongly the idea that motor aphasia is really an apraxia of articulation, or *l'apraxie d'élocution* as Wundt put it. Modern writers, especially those with organismic leanings, are sceptical about the simple, even naïve belief that motor aphasia can be correlated with an articulatory apraxia. Thus Weisenburg and McBride argued that a patient who is unable to emit a particular word, may nevertheless be able to place his articulatory organs in the correct posture. Head's views on this subject were expressed even more strongly. He emphasized that apraxia mainly consists in manifestations which are too extensive and indeed too different in nature to be reconciled with an aphasia. Nothing, he thought, was to be gained by attempting to regard executive disorders of language as high-grade disorders of movement. The words anarthria, verbal apraxia, and motor aphasia, were, in his opinion, merely descriptive terms for three different forms of abnormal speech, which could occur separately or in combination, and he felt there was no merit in classifying any form of aphasia as merely a variety of apraxia.

Of course this is not to say that apraxic disorders of articulation do not at times occur, which may also be coupled with aphasia. There is much evidence to that effect. From his experience of head injuries, Foix, who believed that an apraxia of the articulatory muscles often played an important role in contributing to the dysarthria of aphasic patients, ascribed this to a parietal cortico-subcortical lesion on the left side. Shortly after the 1939–1945 war, Nathan carefully described six patients with gunshot wounds of the skull in whom occurred facial dyspraxias, aphasias of various types, and also combinations of the two giving rise to an apraxic disorder of articulation. His first patient, for example, was quite unable to utter any word correctly. All consonantal sounds were impossible, though vowel sounds could be enunciated. For example, the word 'sister' was pronounced 'i—er'; so also was the word 'prisoner'. 'Yes' was articulated as 'eh'; 'no' as 'o'. Later the patient became able to enunciate a consonant in the middle of the word although not at the end or beginning. The other patients had similar but less intense forms of articulatory dysphasia.

The fourth historical phase in the history of this problem, namely a return to an attitude of distinction between the two disorders, began shortly after Marie's work. The chief exponent at that time was Dejerine who sharply disagreed with Marie upon all his ideas of aphasia. According to Dejerine distinction could be made between dysarthria (or anarthria) and aphasia, because in the former condition every sound would be mispronounced. As he put it 'l'aphasique ne sait plus parler; l'anarthrique ne *peut* plus parler'. The controversy became heated and even acrimonious, though after the passage of fifty-five years it now seems as if much of it was a mere dialectical quibble. Dejerine contended that Marie was merely re-describing a 'pure subcortical motor aphasia' and that anarthria should be restricted to an extreme degree of dysarthria due to paralysis of the muscles of phonation; Marie retorted that it all depended upon what was meant by 'paralysis', and whether this included states of dystonia and ataxia. After discussion he was prepared to concede that perhaps 'l'anarthrique ne *sait* plus parler' though somewhat illogically he went on to say that the anarthric patient has no intellectual defect, and no disorder of language. The dispute between the contestants was mainly over the site of the associated lesion, a problem which appears nowadays unimportant. Dejerine implicated a subcortical affection of the fibres emanating from the third frontal convolution on the left side. Marie looked for the pathological defect in or near the lenticular nucleus in either hemisphere. Others held still different views. Souques' demonstration of nine fatal cases did but little to decide the matter, for his cases showed diffuse changes in both situations.

We come now to the fifth stage, or the phase of re-alignment. As Goldstein stated, the difference between anarthria and motor aphasia is not always as clear as has been claimed, and to make a dogmatic distinction glosses over the complexity of the clinical phenomena. That articulatory disorders may occur in patients with aphasia of all types, whether receptive, expressive, or mixed, cannot be gainsaid. The closer our study of them the more conspicuous are the articulatory defects. Any sufficiently detailed case-records will bear eloquent witness to this opinion. Von Monakow described the speech in cases of motor aphasia as uncertain, monotonous, with defective intonation, slurred syllables and a tendency towards perseveration. In cases of sensory aphasia on the other hand, errors are found in false intonations and accent, monotony and disorders of rhythm.

Dr. Saloz's autobiographical account of his aphasic difficulties, made in retrospect of course, includes the following:

> . . . I often had the impression that I had the letter, syllable or word within my power but through a tempestuous cleavage another element would come and take its place and this would give to my speech a quality often incomprehensible and fantastic, and consequently an atmosphere of timidity and sadness. I never knew beforehand whether I would be able to express myself or not.'

What exactly are these articulatory disorders which are liable to occur in dysphasic persons?

First, the *rate of talking* may change with the onset of aphasia. As a rule the speech is retarded. Usually there is a bradylalia, that is a slowing up in a uniform manner but, at times, the retardation is irregular or jerky. This would seem to mirror the hesitancy of the pre-verbal thinking processes. However the chief trouble often seems to entail the emission of the beginning of a word, phrase or sentence. In this way there may arise a defect of speaking which closely resembles a stammer or stutter, with repetition of the initial sound. On the other hand an aphasiac's utterance is sometimes accelerated (tachylalia), more often in types of aphasia which are more receptive than expressive.

Changes in the *volume* of sound in spoken speech are rarely conspicuous, although not unknown. Subdued utterance is perhaps more usual than the opposite. I have, however, noticed in one Turkish aphasiac a habit of shouting when trying to express himself, and I was informed that such a phenomenon was by no means rare in that country. Possibly this noisiness represents a catastrophic reaction, whereby anger replaces the more usual effect of embarrassment at the failure to perform satisfactorily a difficult task.

The *melody of language* or what Monrad-Krohn liked to call 'the third element of speech' may also undergo interesting and important changes. Often it takes the form of monotony, as originally described by Brissaud, whose patient became incapable of adding emotional colouring to his words by way of the light and shade of accent and emphasis. Kinnier Wilson referred to a patient who had a left hemiplegia but no aphasia; there was however a loss of mimic movements and a curious alteration in the speech which had become shrill, monotonous and devoid of modulation. Another interesting upset in the melody of language was described by Monrad-Krohn under the term 'dysprody'. This comprises an alteration in the *chanson de parler*, whereby the aphasic patient whose vocabulary is not too restricted, nevertheless has changed the manner of speaking in such a way as to resemble a foreigner conversing with some difficulty in a language not his own. In Monrad-Krohn's case a Norwegian lady, convalescent from aphasia, spoke her native language with an intonation which others imagined to be German. As this event took place during the enemy occupation of Norway, considerable embarrassment was caused to the patient who found herself on all sides cold-shouldered.

Spoken Norwegian is a peculiarly musical or sing-song type of language. This raises the question as to what the pattern of an aphasia might happen to be in a patient who speaks one of the various tone-languages, such as the Sudanese Mende, or, even better, Chinese. In the latter, a mono-syllabic language made up of a mere four hundred and twenty homophones, alterations in mean-ing are brought about by tonal inflections, or different ways of proclaiming each particular monosyllable. The technical term is *Chêng* or 'musical note'. Formerly in the Peking dialect there were five such *Chêng* or tonal inflections; today there are only four, but so important are they that the meaning of a word depends as much upon the tonal inflection as the actual phonetic pattern of the monosyllable. What would happen in the case of a Chinese—or for that matter a Mende patient—who becomes aphasic? Would the tonal inflections be preserved or lost? With regard to the hypothetical case of aphasia in a Mende-speaking Sudanese I cannot answer. Prompted by my enquiries on this score, Professor Lyman of Peiping in association with his pupils Li and Hsu, found that in Chinese aphasiacs tonal inflections are usually retained correctly, however restricted the patient's vocabulary, provided only that the articulation of the available sounds is correct. If, however, dysarthria accompanies the aphasia, then according to Lyman *et al.*, the tonal inflections or *Chêng* are changed, distorted, and unrecognizable.

Strange to say, in the decrepit speech of aphasiacs it is often easy to pick up audible traces of a regional or provincial 'accent'. Indeed, there is evidence that after the onset of an aphasia, dialec-tical features may become exaggerated or perhaps merely re-emerge. (See Chapter 5, Section 8). This is certainly the case in Great Britain where a provincial accent carries certain social and educa-tional implications as well as mere topographical significance. Even in other linguistic communities dialect may become intensified, as shown in the case of certain polyglot aphasiacs. (Alajouanine, Pichot, Durand (1949), and others.) Goldstein offered an explanation in that dialect was to him much more 'concrete' . . . more 'passively emerging out of a situation' than was a cultured, correct diction.

A verbatim record of what an aphasic patient says shows a considerable number of distorted words, of instances of 'paraphasia'. It has been said that in cases of sensory aphasia, the defect is threefold: first, confusion in words, that is paraphasia; secondly, errors in grammatical construc-tion and word-order, a defect which has been called paragrammatism; and thirdly, disturbed word-finding. The last problem scarcely arises in this connection. The paraphasias can be divided into two groups: the 'literal' paraphasias where there is substitution of one consonantal sound for another; and 'verbal' paraphasias where one word replaces another. The new word need not necessarily be a dictionary word but may be a fragment of nonsense or gibberish: in other words a 'neologism'. These articulatory defects or paraphasias vary according to whether the patient is speaking spontaneously, repeating a phrase offered to him, or reading aloud. Thus it often happens that an aphasiac can repeat certain sounds which, however, he cannot emit spontaneously. Still further variability may be found: for example, a sound may be pronounced correctly in one situa-tion, or in one part of a sentence, whereas in another context or in another part of a sentence it may be enunciated imperfectly.

When paraphasia exists in severe form there results a gross speech disturbance which is often called 'jargon-aphasia' although the term is one which is not devoid of objection. Gibberish is perhaps a better word than jargon. The verbal type of paraphasia, in which one word replaces another, on analysis often shows interesting mechanisms. The substituted word may bear some relation to the word at fault. Thus the patient may say 'chair' instead of 'table'; 'bread' instead of 'butter'. Or the words may be of opposite meaning such as 'no' for 'yes'; 'fast' for 'slow'. Or the two words may be related somewhat in sound, for example, 'tissors' for 'scissors'. In such cases we are dealing more probably with a literal paraphasia. Sometimes the patient will combine a portion of one word with one which really belongs to a sentence yet to come. The mind hurries ahead as it were, and jumbles together portions of two or more key-phrases, so as to constitute a fantastic verbal *mélange*. Not infrequently a word or series of words keeps cropping up within the stream of talk in an unexpected fashion—a phenomenon sometimes spoken of as 'verbal intoxication'. We may mention incidentally that paragrammatism, a disorder in the syntax of an aphasic patient's utterance, is not a matter which constitutes an important defect in the English language. Paragrammatism was originally described in German-speaking aphasiacs and it comprised an upset in the inflexions, the suffices and prefices of speech. As English is not an inflected tongue, paragrammatism scarcely assumes the same importance as it does in German. More striking in English-speaking aphasiacs is the trick of leaving a sentence unfinished, or conversely, of omitting the beginnings of a phrase or sentence. These defects, called aposiopesis and prosiopesis respectively, are important phenomena in that they can be related to such differing aspects of language, as grammar, syntax, ideas and diction.

To illustrate the type of word-salad of a paraphasic patient, one may quote two verbatim records of what was actually said.[1] In reply to my request to tell me about his motor accident, the aphasiac declared:

I drove him when the straightway from he guards and place, I forget to talker, what, where the name of the police I told where the place there, we wert in on to the job with the crowbar I caught one lot of van, yes, one two,—the one man driver there, and another drag there, this one, and was bad up list of job himself, you see, well the other man called out t'us and drove on to the job what the van break, broke on the other, first of all, claimed away from it, well I was warred off on the top as I fall over it, cled off all the other one. I was just away from just by the van as I got up—then—and I didn't waited for long time within about I suppose er 13 hours 15 more like too long so we had to bathe, to bath to job more to, pay, to take us four more when I was with to . . . er . . . more word.

My second patient, to my enquiry as to the mode of onset of his illness, answered as follows:

Well, I will tell you as clearly as I can because it was not very clearly to me. Well, it was done out of, I was not in order and nothing happened to me at all because it was too . . . well, I was not careless, I was not able to give you the information because I was half ill, very, well, fairly ill you see, due to, what do you call it, I think . . . I was very well, I do not realise what it was at all, because I cannot realise what was happening, I think it was done out of your orders here, wasn't I, yes, I do not think you were equally with me at the time, I do not think I could account for it, it was simply . . . I was ill and it was not in a condition to account to you for the trouble I am afraid, sir, do you think you were at the time, I do not

---

[1] These statements were reproduced from tape-recordings by a stenographer without special skill in phonetics. This speech is set out as accurately as possible, as it would assail the ears of an English-speaking person, without recourse, however, to phonetic script.

hink you were, it was . . . who accounted for me at the time I think you were. I cannot actually tell you if I was at the time; was I in London actually, definitely, in my opening, in my . . . Oh, well, now if this is the case that accounts for the shole thing you see, because I was actually in the office at the time, but I cannot hold the position, my position, my position was out of order. I mean by this I was not ill, I got up on, let me see, let me see . . . I got as far as the office and then I had to call out because I could not carry on what has happened after that . . . It was, no I mean, as a little distance, whatever did not happen, I cannot understand how it was unaccounted for, not sufficiently accounted for, but it was very small, as you know. Actually, I think the, after the account, then something worse happened, a temporary arrangement and that was accounted for by . . . I think it was badly dealt with at the time . . .

Among the hypotheses which have been advanced to explain paraphasic errors, we may mention Wernicke's idea of a loss of sensory word-images. Kussmaul believed that the basic disturbance was one of attention. Piéron blamed an imperfect control of sensory over motor aspects, the sensory control normally including both acoustic and kinaesthetic factors. Pick, however, thought that incorrect division of attention played a role, and he said that distraction often provoked paraphasic errors even in normal people. But he considered that the essential cause of the defect in aphasic patients was a lack of inhibition. He also drew attention to an acceleration in the rate of speaking particularly in patients with sensory aphasia. These two defects, namely tachylalia and lack of inhibition, were apt to give rise to perseveration, whereby a word correctly emitted, immediately or after an interval, would continue to reappear in an incongruous fashion in such a way as to contaminate succeeding sentences. At this point reference may be made to another defect, of which traces may be detected in normal speech and even more so in aphasic utterances, namely the immoderate use of certain phrases, words, expressions, or even meaningless sounds with which the speaker decorates his articulate utterance. Thus phrases like 'in fact', 'actually', 'of course', 'you know', 'naturally', and 'if you know what I mean' often clutter up the speech of an aphasic person. They seem to serve as 'jumping-off words' or as 'fillers', that is, audible punctuation marks. Sometimes, however, we find not a recognizable phrase or word, but veritable gibberish. Monrad-Krohn referred to 'prosodic grunts'. For example, a patient described by Weisenburg and McBride, often interpolated the phrase '*say see essay*'. Thus, when he wanted to say 'Hullo' he would say '*Hullo-sh-see-say*;' 'Goodbye' would come out as '*Good-say see*'. We have already referred to another phenomenon. Thus a simple consonantal sound like, for example, the sibilant '*s*' which, emitted without difficulty, finds its way into the speech in an inappropriate fashion. A curious mannerism then arises, the letter '*s*' being tacked on to the end of nouns in an unnecessary and unexpected fashion, almost as though endowing them with plurality. In this way the patient might say 'Goodmornings doctors, I am better todays thankyous'. Another such defect is sometimes found in aphasic patients' utterances, namely, the overstressing of certain consonantal sounds. Thus during the stage of convalescence the 'r' might find itself trilled in an excessive fashion, or the 's' sound so exaggerated and stressed as to introduce a sort of hissing noise. This habit of interpolating meaningless fragments, like '*ta-ta*' or '*say-see-essay*' is reminiscent of some of the secret languages occasionally adopted by schoolboys and others. In French there are the pseudo-languages *javanais*, and also *ouchébemme*.

Among the few who have studied the phonetics of aphasia have been Alajouanine, Ombredane and Durand (1939). On the basis of a close observation of four aphasic subjects, using appropriate instrumental methods of recording, they concluded that it was possible to isolate in their cases a 'syndrome of phonetic disintegration'. Certain phonemes were found to be impossible (the aphonemia of Grewel); other phonemes suffered when occurring in sequence (the dysphonemia and the paraphonemia of Grewel). There seemed to be three types of fault which could occur singly or in combination, varying from one case to another. These disorders were spoken of as paralytic, dystonic, and apraxic. In their monograph the authors set out in detail the various types of phonetic change in a manner which does not lend itself to recapitulation here. This type of research is important and deserves to be repeated on a much greater scale. The findings as originally published are not altogether convincing, however. An analysis of only four patients, admittedly showing different types of aphasia and manifold phonetic changes, is scarcely enough. Though the authors stated that the phonetic alterations showed a 'homogeneity and a remarkable constancy' this is scarcely borne out by their protocols. From what we know today of the fluctuating behaviour of aphasiacs, it is unbelievable that the same speech performance should be uniformly maintained day after day, in all circumstances, for all semantic contexts and situations. The fragmentary speech of an aphasiac (and with it the phonetic qualities) notoriously varies according to whether the words are enunciated in conversation, or in reply to questions, or in the act of reading aloud. The performance differs also according to whether the words form part of inferior speech in the Jacksonian sense, or of propositionizing. The relationship of the aphasiac to his questioner; the mood; the degree of fatigue; the question of catastrophic reaction; all these constitute variables which modify considerably the performance of an aphasic patient.

Can the mechanism of any of these articulatory disorders in aphasiacs be explained? One possible way would be to use a linguistic approach. Some writers have sought to ascribe the changes in language from one district to another, and from one generation to the next, to a progressive and unrestrained slovenliness in utterance. This is the so-called 'ease' theory of linguistic change, also termed the 'principle of least effort' in talking. Professor Müller proclaimed that this principle of least effort constitutes a fundamental aspect of civilization; indeed he accused civilization of laziness, saying that sophisticated persons dispensed as far as possible with vigorous muscular movement. Certainly forceful articulatory movement seems to be necessary for some primitive articulations, and as one turns from the so-called primitive tongues to the speech of more civilized people we find what has been termed a progressive humanization of speech; that is, an avoidance of difficult guttural sounds and a preference for relatively easy sounds produced by the more forward part of the articulatory apparatus—the tip of the tongue, the front part of the palate and the lips. If this holds true in linguistics, can it be said to apply to the *modus operandi* of aphasia? It is doubtful. It is uncertain indeed, what actually distinguishes an easy sound from a difficult one. We have already mentioned that young children in primitive communities utter, in their stride as it were, with the utmost of ease, sounds which are enunciated with considerable trouble by adult members of other races. Can we truly say that one is a difficult sound and the other an easy sound? The context and total situation of the language have to be borne in mind. Certainly in any given language some sounds tend to be more difficult than others, in that they entail more forceful articulatory efforts, or perhaps a series—and maybe a protracted series—of muscular movements. Hence the 'tongue-twisters' to be found in any language. For example, the 'r' sound is almost universally regarded as a comparatively difficult sound, and a considerable number of normal people of various races mispronounce this sound in one way or another. (See a reference to the work of Tomás y Tomás, quoted in the footnote on p. 147). The sound spelt 'th' whether voiced or unvoiced, may also be regarded as difficult. So is the aspirate 'h'. Certain consonantal combinations are more laborious than isolated consonantal sounds. For example, it is more troublesome to say 'street' than 'reet' or 'treet' or 'steet'. In Russian a sound like '*shch*', as in the word *shchee*, obviously entails effort, and a succession of motor movements. Even a Frenchman finds some difficulty over words like *genre* or *Ingres*. Some evidence can be produced to support the suggestion that in aphasic patients there is a tendency to avoid difficult sounds, or to substitute an easy sound for a difficult one. Alajouanine, Ombredane and Durand would certainly agree. One of the earliest cases recorded, namely the aphasiac described by Broca a century ago, showed this phenomenon. His patient whose name was *Lelong* always spoke of himself as *Lelo*. For the numeral *trois* he would say *tois* thus evading the more tricky consonantal combination.

This hypothesis is not altogether convincing, however, and must not be pushed too far. Professor D. B. Fry's careful phonemic analysis of an elderly aphasiac of mine showed strikingly that the deterioration in his articulation bore no resemblance to the development of speech in childhood. (1959). Sometimes in paraphasic patients the substituted word is, if anything, more difficult to enunciate than the word which cannot be exteriorized—if indeed we are correct in using the expressions 'difficult' and 'easy'. More serious is the objection that sound-substitutions are irregular and inconstant in a given patient. At one moment he may emit a given consonantal sound correctly, a moment later he may fail entirely. In a single sentence he may use it correctly here and incorrectly there. Or he may read aloud using appropriate consonantal sounds but fail in his spontaneous speech. Or charged with emotion, the consonantal sound may be correctly enunciated, whereas during calm propositionizing the speech sound may seem to be beyond him. A particular sound proves as a rule to be unpronounceable in a given patient: he substitutes one which is within his power, but he has many alternatives and does not adhere to any one. This inconsistency, this paradoxical appearance or reappearance of sound-substitutions argues against any such rigid formula as Schultze's law of the minimal expenditure of energy.

A second hypothesis, which aims at explaining the articulatory disorders in aphasiacs, is based upon the development of speech in the child. Can it be that the dissolution of speech recapitulates in its clinical phenomena the stages taken by the child in its acquisition of speech? Such indeed is suggested at times. For example, we read A. F. Watts saying:

> . . . speech development in the child and in the race follows broadly the same lines, and in the second place the powers lost as a result of mental derangement disappear in the reverse order of their requirement just as in a stricken tree death appears in the newest twigs before it reaches the older branches.

Ombredane has devoted attention to this aspect of aphasia and he seems to have found certain similarities between the speech-defects in aphasiacs and the stages surmounted during a child's development of language. Thus, according to Ombredane, one of the commonest and earliest defects in the speech of an aphasic patient is the ability to distinguish the *liquidae* 'l' and 'r'. He also alleged that the uvular 'r' of the Parisians is a particularly difficult sound both for a French child to acquire and for an aphasiac to utter. On the other hand the sounds preserved best and longest in the speech of an aphasic patient are the vowel sound 'ah' and the consonantal sound 'm'. Indeed, Ombredane asserted that sounds articulated by the lips are retained better than any others. In the same way he believed that nasal vowel sounds disappear early from speech of a French aphasiac, just as they are mastered late by the French-speaking child. Interdental sounds are lost early, indeed earlier than are sibilants. Hence *this* might well be pronounced *ziss* both by the growing child and by the aphasic patient. Voiceless consonantal sounds are better enunciated than are voiced consonantal sounds. Anterior consonants are longer preserved than palatals. When Ombredane discussed substitutions, he alleged that velar occlusives are pronounced as /t/ or /d/. Affricative sounds are lost first and then fricative; aspirants tend to be replaced by explosives so that /f/ becomes /p/; and /s/ becomes /t/. Combinations of sounds are, as already mentioned, particularly difficult. But isolated sounds may prove to be more difficult to pronounce than the same consonantal sound occurring in the middle of a word. When pronounced in isolation as compared with in a series, words may be emitted either better or worse. The repetition of spoken speech may prove to be more correctly enunciated than when the same sound comes out spontaneously; very occasionally the opposite occurs.

Still another speculative idea put forward as conceivably able to explain the nature of articulatory defects in aphasic patients, is borrowed from linguistics, but is based not so much upon the evolution of speech in a child as the progressive changes which occur within a given language-group. This is the so-called process of sound-change or sound-law—the *Lautgesetz* devised originally by Leskien, and later elaborated by Rask and by Grimm. The notion is far-fetched and it appears most unlikely that the steps taken by evolving languages are similarly retrod by the aphasic patient during the dilapidation of his speech.

There is another argument which shows that nowadays one traces a less definite distinction between the semantic and phonetic aspects of speech. The phenomenon of stammering, for instance, has traditionally been regarded as a 'functional' disorder of diction, the aetiology of which is complex and debatable. *Bégaiment aphasique*, although first described by Pick in 1889, is still not sufficiently realized as an epiphenomenon of aphasia, following a focal lesion of the brain. In other words stammering may form part of a disorder of *speech*, rather than diction; indeed to be more precise, it may represent a disorder in the faculty of *language*. This observation at once presupposes a disorder of thought, or at least a modification in the manner of thinking. The diverse disorders in the written work of stammerers may also serve to underline that the disability is not wholly one of the act of talking but may perhaps be more fundamental, and involve the faculty of language.

A thought-speech disorder can also be traced in another alleged 'functional' disturbance of diction, namely that rapid and incoordinate method of speaking which goes under many terms: jabbering, *Poltern*, cluttering, associative aphasia, vocal ataxia, paraphrasia, battarysmus, *Bruddeln*, *Tumultus sermonis*, *brédouillement*, *paraphrasia praeceps*. Thanks to Kussmaul (1910), Gutzmann (1924), Fröschels (1925), Nadoleczny (1926), and Florensky (1933), we have a fairly clear clinical picture of this phenomenon and of the concomitant mental mechanisms. These latter present an interesting analogy with some of the disorders met with in the utterances of aphasic patients. Although it is dangerous to rely upon mere similarities, it is perhaps arguable that the paraphrasias of battarysmus are not only similar to some of the physiopathology of aphasia, but may even be identical as regards their production.

For example, the phenomenon of jabbering has been described by Chwatzeff thus:

> . . . words and sounds tumble from the lips at headlong speed; they become mixed up with each other; they are interchanged, swallowed, and not completed; often time is so short that the word may be completely unrecognizable. Cascades of words and sounds pour forth without pause for breath, until expiration is maximal. Speech becomes so rapid that the saliva is not swallowed but sprays from the lips of the patient while he is talking.

This description could apply quite well to many cases of so-called 'sensory' aphasia, or what Head would have termed 'syntactical aphasia'.

The disordered speech of battarysmus may be studied more closely: first, there is its remarkable rapidity (tachylalia). The intonation with which a word or phrase is uttered may not correspond with its meaning. Words and sentences are spoken so precipitantly that they are not pronounced clearly. Conscious attention may control the defect temporarily; hence jabberers speak better among strangers than in their home among friends. They also fare better when they read aloud. Words may crop up in wrong places within a sentence. Exaggerated pauses may also appear. But the torrent of words usually sweeps over the logical stopping-places which one would expect to encounter in a series of orderly speech-utterances. These pauses serve as a kind of punctuation, which indicates a break in the continuity of ideas. At other times the pauses emphasize the importance of a phrase just spoken or about to be spoken. Sometimes a misplacement occurs over longer speech-intervals. Thus a sentence may contain a word (or part of a word) which really belongs to the sentence which follows. Syllables, words, and even sentences may be not only dislocated, but even omitted altogether, as demonstrated by getting the patient to give an account of something which he has just read. A narrative of say ten or more sentences, then becomes condensed into three or four precipitant, explosive, and often barely intelligible phrases, in which detail is sacrificed on the altar of verbal economy.

Nor is this all. Lips and tongue may at times be observed to make frantic but silent movements, especially during the more protracted pauses. Furthermore, perseveration of words or of sentences is common.

In other words, the resemblances between the jabberer's speech and the speech of some aphasic patients is quite close. What of the underlying cerebral defect? Kussmaul attributed jabbering to an over-hasty method of speech and thought, coupled with a lack of mental concentration. Gutzmann believed that the *tempo* of thought was not necessarily accelerated, but that the explanation lay in a lack of coordination between the speed of thinking and the rate of motility of the muscles of articulation. Expressed differently, jabbering represents a 'word-ataxia'. Nadoleczny took the argument a little further. The errors made by the jabberer, what he called the 'pararthrias', represented for him the mode of speech of a person of hasty and excitable disposition, with inaccurate memory for word-forms, whose attention would be apt to become dissipated. Fröschel also discussed the normal relationships between thinking and speaking. For speech to proceed in orderly fashion, 'it is important that one concept shall not continuously be obscured by the aura of a following concept before the first has actually been translated into speech'. (Florensky). Normally the regulation of the psychomotor processes of speech (especially in its pre-verbal stages) is brought about through a special property of mental attentiveness which regulates thinking to suit the functional capacity of the motor organs of speech. This idea is much the same as Pick's concept of the normal inhibitory function in speech, exercised by the temporal lobe, and loss of which would release the uncontrolled logorrhoea of the sensory aphasiac.

Thus the analogy between the speech-defects in the jabberer and in sensory aphasiacs is deep. This may be true also for the mental mechanisms. In both conditions there is a disorder in the regulatory function of mental attentiveness, especially in its factor of distribution. This term refers to the faculty whereby one's attention is directed just so long and no longer upon a particular word-series, ranging ahead if necessary to cope with an idea of particular import or significance; choosing words rapidly and arranging them, discarding less appropriate terms in favour of *le mot juste*, putting the proper emphasis on those phrases which logically merit the stress. In the paraphrasia of the jabberer, just as in the paraphasia of the aphasiac, all these preverbal mental activities are at fault. The deliberate fixing of attention is too short to allow of the search for the right word, or to produce an orderly sequence of words; while undue preoccupation with one particular word may cause it to crop up incongruously and prematurely, or to perseverate.

If then we can discover suggestive evidence of a more profound disorder of language occurring in cases of alleged peripheral disabilities, e.g. stammering and cluttering, the opposite is also true. A most promising line of research would proceed from an investigation of the physical properties of the visible speech of aphasiacs through the medium of spectrography, as hinted in Chapter XV. Conspicuous changes will occur even in the absence of audible alterations in the mode of pronunciation on the part of the aphasiac.

Summary

(1) Many patients with aphasia show disorders of articulate speech which are both varied and variable in their character.

(2) Dysarthria and dysphasia, though often occurring in combination, are actually separate phenomena.

(3) Articulatory dyspraxia is also an independent entity, though it may co-exist with an aphasia and contribute to a defect of articulation.

(4) Appropriate spectrographic analysis of aphasic speech may reveal changes in the absence of obvious clinically detectable dysarthria.

(5) A further association is encountered in the fact that a disorder of symbolic thought is traceable behind some such cases of speech-defect as, for example, stammering and, more especially, battarysmus.

(6) To trace any rigid plan underlying the pattern of articulatory disorder in aphasic patients, is premature.

XVIII. THE NATURE AND CONTENT OF
APHASIC UTTERANCE

*Oh, the comfort, the inexpressible comfort of feeling safe with a person: having neither
to weigh thoughts nor measure words, but to pour them all out, joint as they are, chaff
and grain together, knowing that a faithful hand will take and sift them, keep what is
worth keeping, and then, with the breath of kindness, blow the rest away.*

George Eliot

. . . An uncommunicating communicator—a beastly bad thing to be.

Henry James

What do aphasic patients talk about? The question paraphrases the title of this particular section. Hitherto most writers have approached the subject from a rather different angle. They have dealt more with such questions as what an aphasiac is able to say and the manner in which he says it. In other words attention has been focussed upon the restriction of the vocabulary and the alterations in the grammatical construction; how the patient copes with particular test-situations in the hospital or clinic; and how the limited phrases available to the patient are articulated.

Allied to these matters are the cognate ones which concern written speech. But what is it that aphasiacs write about? The semantic content of their spontaneous efforts is a problem quite different from the ordinary study of the graphic errors demonstrated at the bedside when the patient writes to dictation, signs his name, or tries to copy. The question, then, of what it is that aphasiacs spontaneously talk and write about has rarely been raised.

Neurologists have studied the rules of aphasia which seem to determine which words are retained and which are lost. Verbal symbols and utterance obviously occupy various levels in the domain of language, some being vulnerable to the effects of brain-disease, others being more resistant. This comes out clearly in the history of the subject, described by Riese among others. First came the notion of superior (and most voluntary) levels of speech, as opposed to inferior (and most automatic) levels, the latter being better preserved in cases of aphasia. Hughlings Jackson, like Ribot, traced the laws of evolution and dissolution within the nervous system, whereby faculties acquired late in the phylogenetic or ontogenetic sense are peculiarly sensitive to disease-states, and are affected early. The same rules might well apply to language. According to Jackson, an aphasiac suffers a particular involvement of *propositionizing*, that is the assertive aspect of deliberate speech, and a relative sparing of emotional utterance. The latter is made up of affectively charged interjections, oaths and expletives: trite and well-worn

Based upon a lecture delivered at the centenary of St. Elizabeth's Hospital, Washington, D.C., and published in *Centennial Papers* 1956.

phrases low in propositional value: greetings: 'yes' and 'no', and so on. Baillarger, even earlier, contrasted voluntary and spontaneous speech in much the same connotation. Piaget, dealing with the development of speech in the child, distinguished egocentric from social usages. Goldstein held that an aphasiac, like all brain-damaged persons, shows a change in attitude from the conceptual or categorical towards one that is more concrete whereby in speech his ability to use abstractions is involved far more than concrete ideas. Alajouanine and Mozziconacci followed the same general ideas but preferred to use the terms 'intuitive thinking' (*la pensée imagée*) and 'formulated thought' (*la pensée formulée*): and they spoke of the *syndrome de dissociation automatico-volontaire* as the fundamental defect in aphasiacs.

Around these conceptions there has grown up a formidable literature, especially in the last 20 years, describing and analysing the halting and imperfect responses of the patient in the somewhat artificial environment of the medical interview. To add to the complexities it is now realized implicitly, though not always stated explicitly, that the aphasic patient's performance is characteristically erratic.

To classify spoken and written speech into a simple distinction between superior and inferior; intellectual and emotional; abstract and concrete, is nowadays not enough, especially when problems of speech-loss are entailed. It does no justice to the much more complex matter of the purposes and usages of speech, with its many ranks and hierarchies of linguistic attainment. This brings up a subject which will be discussed later in greater detail.

Normal persons vary considerably in their facility with language. Over and above the mere question of educational background, are a number of personal factors such as glibness or linguistic fluency, written or oral; size of vocabulary, and cultural level. Some persons display an enjoyment in words by reason of their melodic properties or their etymological ancestry. H. G. Wells, for example, said of Mr. Polly: '. . . words attracted him curiously, words rich in splendour, words rich in suggestions, and he loved a novel and a striking phrase. New words had terror and fascination for him'. Of Oscar Wilde it was said 'language was a vice with him. He took to it as a man might to drink. He was addicted rather than devoted to language'. Synaesthetic associations may conceivably play a part. Some of these aptitudes may have been professionally utilized, and may have determined and assisted the career of a preacher, politician, writer or poet. A few accomplished persons like to indulge in such verbal tricks as paradox, metaphor and wit, thereby producing in the reader or listener an impact which is startling, almost shocking. Others take pleasure in wisecracks and comebacks, plays upon words, puns, *double entendres*, and other verbal gymnastics. In this way there is built up an aspect of personality which includes these special habits of speech or linguistic usages. Such deeply rooted factors must surely go far in determining the pattern of the aphasia after a lesion of the brain.[1]

[1] Kenneth Tynan speaking of James Thurber said that he 'lived in a universe, an interior universe, entirely inhabited by words, which he would play with, dismember, anatomize, dissect, reassemble in strange and odd combinations. His mind was a seething kind of kaleidoscope of word forms, word shapes, abused words, misused words, neologisms, old coinages re-shaped. I remember him once calling me up in the middle of the night to tell me: "I've done it; I've invented the longest English sentence that spells the same forwards and backwards". I said: "What is it?" And he said: "A man, a plan, a canal-Panama". He was enormously proud of this sort of elaborate verbal architecture that was going on inside his brain.'

Plurilingualism, or polyglottism, is also involved in this problem. Three factors are entailed here each of which may influence the clinical manifestations of an aphasia. Of necessity, a polyglot patient possesses a particularly extended vocabulary. Secondly, he has had two or more competing systems of behaviour, each no doubt with differing affective significance. Thirdly, he had been constantly faced with the active process of translation, a task which entails something much more than an easy switch from one synonym to another, and which is a metalinguistic skill or accomplishment in itself.

Speech, therefore, is an important aspect of personality. Consequently we require information as to how the aphasic patient fares in the home, as opposed to his comportment within the highly artificial setting of the clinic. It behoves us to observe the day-to-day and hour-to-hour verbal and non-verbal activity of our patient. We should note how much of the twenty-four hours he spends in sleep; and also what exactly he does during his waking hours and what he tries to say. A continuous recording of the aphasiac's linguistic behaviour would be invaluable. We would like to know his verbal responses to every natural occasion, as opposed to the stimuli of a test-situation or medical interview. What are the circumstances which prompt the patient to speak? And what manner of diction does he employ when internal speech yields place to external speech, articulate or written?

Field studies show that ordinarily the aphasic patient is most of the time silent. He displays a poverty of speech. Rarely does he talk unless circumstances compel him to break silence, or try and reply to a direct question. He does not engage in conversational small-talk. This is particularly noticeable when he finds himself in the company of several people. The ensuing cross-talk presents particular difficulties and rarely does he interpolate or contribute to the general stream of conversation. The communication-net is all around him but he remains apart. He sits quietly in his chair looking dully upon the surrounding scene; as in a brown study. Sometimes he seems to be reading. A book or newspaper is open before him. But as Trousseau noted years ago, the pages may not be turned; indeed sometimes the book is held upside down. The patient is not really attending to the subject-matter; at the very most he is gazing vaguely at the illustrations though without full comprehension. Much of his waking time is devoted to the radio or television. These pursuits constitute a pleasurable type of reaction, but rarely if ever does the patient fully comprehend the content of what he hears or sees. In all probability he does not realize his short-comings in this respect, but a considerable experience of testing aphasiacs with story-telling pictures has shown two striking anomalies. First the average patient understands only a fraction of what lies behind the pictorial theme. Secondly the patient is quite unaware that something is eluding him and that his interpretation is inadequate.

Before making a content-analysis or content-assay of the nature of an aphasiac's utterance, it will be necessary to examine the problem of the content of speech as it applies to normal subjects of different social and educational class. Verbal utterance in a normal person may first of all be understood according to two main functional types of speech, namely communicative and expressive. The first of these represents speech as the medium for the transmission of ideas. The second function is not so much informative as emotive, and it concerns the expression of feelings. The purpose of such speech is not to convey the feelings of the speaker to others, but to allow the speaker an outlet for his emotional tension. Words may be uttered largely for the sheer pleasure deriving from their enunciation. This side of speech includes certain diverse and often forgotten aspects, such as the egocentric talk of children; ludic speech; song, poetry, and fine prose writings; much nonsense-talk, jingles, jokes, versification, and other examples of linguistic high spirits.

An even simpler terminology would be to divide speech into transitive and intransitive, the former corresponding roughly with communicative and the latter self-expressive. In communication-theory a distinction is sometimes made between 'mands' and 'tacts'. The former include requests, commands and demands; the latter are comments about the world.

When we apply this differentiation to the aphasiac, we can see at once that the difficulty he experiences in formulating phrases and sentences amounts to something like an enforced silence. Little or nothing is said unless ordained by sheer necessity. Much of the speech which emerges belongs to the group of mands, whereas tacts are largely in abeyance. Or, using the other classifications, communicative speech suffers more in aphasiacs than emotive; transitive more than intransitive.

In 1946 A. W. Morris distinguished four types of communication, namely (1) identifiers; (2) designators; (3) appraisors; and (4) prescriptors. This schema is actually of limited value whether it be applied to animal or to human vocalization.

Yet another division of speech recognizes four main modalities of utterances, namely: (1) declaratory (assertions); (2) interrogative; (3) imperative (orders); and (4) exclamatory. Some also add (5) aspirations (or wishes). The first three of these can be looked upon as mainly transitive, while the fourth is mainly intransitive. The fifth modality belongs to both categories.

Applying this classification to the residual speech of an aphasiac, it is found that interrogative and imperative utterance may persist, provided vocabulary is adequate, largely to fulfil the wishes and needs of the patient. Here too a certain amount of expressed aspiration may be included. Exclamatory utterances are largely retained, corresponding with Jackson's emotional utterance. Declaratory statement is the aspect of speech which suffers most, and an aphasiac rarely embarks upon speech belonging to this particular modality unless compelled to do so by sheer necessity, or in an attempt to respond to a direct question.

In normal persons, the range of transitive—that is, non-aphasic—types of speaking may be said to extend upwards from the simplest possible remarks of propositional value. Such statements may be in the nature of an assertion, a question or a request. In the simplest normal instance, the words entailed are few and syntax may suffer from an omission of the so-called 'logical words', that is to say, articles, prepositions, conjunctions, and indeed every word which is not pregnant with meaning. 'Empty' words are discarded, leaving 'full' words. As Schilder would have said, in such circumstances thought is 'word-near'. The result is a terse mannerism of speech, a phraseology enunciated in a telegrammatic fashion as exemplified by Dickens' Mr. Jingle. Such might represent the pattern of verbal behaviour in the case of a sick person with a paralytic or painful affliction of the organs of articulation. Only very exceptionally would this simple type of speech be met with in a perfectly normal person. The speech of many aphasiacs approximates to this kind of talk and may almost indeed be looked upon as an exaggeration of such a mannerism. This holds true both for the spontaneous writing of an aphasiac and for his spoken speech.

Reverting yet again to the verbal habits of normal people, we can recognize quite a different pattern of speech in the voluble chatter of the conversationalist who has but little information to impart. There is at times more than a hint of intransitivity, for one suspects that the listener does not always attend, but is awaiting his chance to butt in. 'Intoxicated by the exuberance of his own verbosity', the speaker is enjoying thoroughly what is little more than a monologue. In this kind of talk the syntax is anything but clipped or incisive, but is cluttered up with linguistic rags and tags, with clichés and well-worn phrases of little import. Strong intraverbal linkages predispose to an inordinate wordiness, poor in reference-function. Indeed, some of these verbal habits can be said to act as substitutes for thought. This sort of speech is perhaps the rule among children and also in primitive communities where noisy conversation seems to go on in a simultaneous and unin-hibited fashion. This is the 'phatic communion' of Malinowski.

Among aphasiacs, speech of this type is rare. The person who ordinarily talks in this manner will probably lose much of this habit of diction when he becomes a victim of cerebral disease. There will be a marked discrepancy between his pre-morbid volubility and his subsequent poverty of speech. There is, however, a striking exception. In many cases of what has usually been termed 'sensory' aphasia, the patient, far from being taciturn, may show the reverse phenomenon, and as long as he himself is holding the floor, he talks to excess. True, much of what he says is far from correct, being inaccurate in phraseology and in grammar. Perhaps many of his words consist in paraphasic errors which he probably does not realize. However, his stream of talk is promptly checked when a bystander interrupts with a question. At that point the aphasiac becomes embarrassed, hesitates, and gropes in his search for the appropriate term. No doubt, volubility was but a device for avoiding what Goldstein would have called a catastrophic reaction, and for maintaining a *milieu* which conforms with his own capacity.

This rather exceptional type of speech-affection merits closer attention. The free employment of neologisms and other paraphasic errors leads to a greater or lesser degree of unintelligibility: hence the term 'jargon aphasia'. Prosody is retained or even enhanced, so that there results a plausibility in the diction as if the aphasiac were using a foreign language. The patient gesticulates freely, being excitable and uninhibited in manner. As he talks he does not realize his speech-defect but when his words are played back to him on a tape-recorder he may register puzzlement, recognition here and there of a word correctly enunciated, and only rarely distress. The patient's attempts to write betray errors of the same kind. Comprehension of written speech is imperfect, and there is also a noteworthy defect in the understanding of the spoken speech of others. This latter is mainly due to a dysphonemia, or confusion of sounds which are somewhat similar in acoustic properties.

Another individual variant of speech in normal persons is that habit which prefers allusions to direct assertions; which refers to associations instead of the thing itself; which talks around and not about the point. Sentences may be unfinished, trailing off vaguely, leaving the listener mystified and uneasy. Speech of this kind would run the risk of failing in communicative function, were it not that it is usually adopted as a kind of private talk between close associates—initiates indeed. Allusive or predicative speech as it is called, includes the secret language of lovers, and the linguistic idiosyncracies of close-knit families. In its most exaggerated form it is to be found as we have already seen, in the esoteric language of young twins, especially when of sub-normal intelligence.

But allusive speech may also be the habitual peculiarity of a few, who employ it unwittingly on all occasions, with no desire either to cloak their thoughts or to arouse attention.

In states of aphasia this predicative tendency may become greatly intensified. Indeed the ordinary aphasic talk of one whose previous speech never did belong to this class may now display a large number of predicative characteristics. Nouns and verbs may be used according to their accessibility rather than their propriety. This may lend an air of elusiveness to the speech. Still more striking in aphasiacs is the involuntary use of the grammatical tricks of aposiopesis or of prosiopesis, that is a failure either to finish a sentence or to start one in the ordinary way. This feature, so common in aphasiacs, brings the resemblance to predicative speech closer still.

Reverting once again to personal habits of speech in non-aphasiacs, we may say that often the language of scientists and technologists illustrates a very high propositional or declaratory level. This is more particularly the case with written communication. Mindful of the imprecision of verbal symbols, scientists select their terms with care, using over and over again their limited repertoire of words, each with its strict definition. Style is deliberately and ruthlessly sacrificed, and terms which are redundant, inexact, vague, hyperbolical—what Walter Pater called surplusage —are drastically eschewed. The result is a text commendably full of communication-content and information, but dull, cold and austere. At the same peak of attainment belongs also the judicial summing-up in a Court of Law, where conflicting evidence is scrutinized and weighed, and ideas are tested in the crucible of logic.

This is the type of language which suffers severely after an aphasia. It is a style which contrasts markedly with the verbalization and writing of the average aphasiac. Moreover, fine prose-writing, which is ordinarily more evocative and less informative than the bald style of the scientist, suffers in an aphasia to a comparable degree.

Reference may be made to yet another linguistic usage in common experience. Speech and writing in some normal persons, which though ostensibly transitive and communicative in nature and purpose, fails to live up to their function, for they sadly lack clarity. The reader or listener is left puzzled, finding the subject-matter difficult and perplexing, but frequently it is the presentation which is to blame. Only too often the fault lies, not at the doors of the listener or reader, but with the exponent. Obscure speech may well be the index, not of abstruse subject-matter, but of unclear thinking, or of faulty technique in expounding the thesis, or of both. 'What is not clearly understood cannot be good French', applies to most other languages. In the same way imprecise talk is highly characteristic of aphasic utterance in cases where the vocabulary is not too drastically curtailed. This still applies, whether the former habits of talk were of this character, or not.

Within a very special *niche* we may place the phenomenon of wit. This comprises utterance and evocation indeed; but the reference-function is unusual in that it entails a deliberate upset or shattering of well-established intraverbal connections. To talk or write wittily is impossible without a high level of intelligence. Wit thus differs from humour, drollery, or clowning, which are not necessarily hall-marks of superior intellect. But wit does not necessarily imply the same lofty qualities of personality. As Wilkes said of Edmund Burke, 'Amidst all the brilliance of his imagination, and the exuberance of his wit, there is a strange want of *taste*. His oratory would sometimes make one suspect that he eats potatoes, and drinks whiskey'. Witty utterance combines both self-expression and communication, and hence it includes the two chief functions of speech, being at one and the same time, transitive and intransitive.

Language of this sort suffers severely in cases of aphasia, for an aphasiac is no longer capable of witty utterance. At any rate, he rarely displays his former propensities. A politician who had been under my close observation in hospital with a mild degree of aphasia at no time gave any inkling whatsoever of the fact that he had been notorious before his illness as the wittiest speaker in the House of Commons.

When one turns to the purely personal or intransitive employment of language in normal, non-aphasic subjects, we witness once again certain levels corresponding with different ranks and ratings in mentation.

Simplest of all these intransitive utterances is the babbling of the infant. In childhood the development of 'little speech' entails a large measure of egocentricity. The speech of some backward or psychotic children is mainly, if not entirely, autistic. Aphasic speech, in the same way, shows an increase in the elements of egocentricity, but a closer reversion to juvenile or infantile language is not common. This would be more characteristic of the dissolution of speech encountered in demented patients, as opposed to the true aphasias from focal lesions of the brain. It is also very suggestive of an hysterical disorder of speech.

Again, in the case of the normal adult, we may once more refer to phatic communion, which serves a double purpose, in that it participates in social behaviour while at the same time fulfilling a cathartic role. To a simpleton with his limited intellectual resources, silence is an embarrassment. Sound-stimuli in such a one's mentation fill an uncomfortable void, whether the noise emanates from a background of music, or is produced by whistling or idle chatter. Interjections also play a part, though it would be wrong to assume that they are all in the nature of expletives. Some are monosyllabic or abbreviated communications, and must therefore be looked upon as fragments of information. An interjectional pattern may be a highly individual thing, and may assume some of the properties of a mannerism or verbal tic. Interjections may thus be said to make up for their poor reference-function by their property of relieving a minor state of tension, like any other compulsive action.

As might be expected, interjections that are emotionally charged make up a great deal of the spontaneous speech of aphasiacs, but they do not appear in their spontaneous writings.

Reverting once more to the various levels of normal language, we may assert that poetry holds many examples of purely intransitive speech where communication of ideas scarcely arises. Simplest of these can be seen in nonsense verses of the hey-nonny type. Whether or not these jingles had their remote origin in genuine sense-words, their employment today can have no purpose other than melodic. As vehicles of information they fail, being little more than a *flatus vocis*. At the other end of the scale stands much of what is sometimes called 'modern poetry', so often incomprehensible to the ordinary reader. Words are used for other purposes, and communication is subordinate. But between these two extremes there lies the great *corpus* of poetry, representational, sonorous, with its highly selected phraseology.

Creative poetry is surely beyond the capacity of any aphasiac, and this statement probably applies to poetry of all grades and types. There are, of course, very little clinical data to support this opinion, for poets have not been conspicuous as victims of aphasia. Baudelaire's aphasia was, of course, so extreme as to be of no service in this argument. Professor Forel, however, was an amateur poet in addition to his many other interests, and it is clear from his own account that satisfactory versification was beyond his powers during the days of his speech-affection. A week after his stroke Forel composed a poem *Vom Gelehrten zum Gaga* but he was quite unable to keep to the metre, and he realized it. As Galsworthy put it . . . 'Rhythm thronged his head; words jostled to be joined together; he was on the verge of a poem'. At this point, however, the aphasiac undergoes a verbal block. This restraint in creative writing in aphasiacs will be treated in more detail, later.

To what extent does an aphasiac plan ahead and deal with notions of things to come? Some sort of answer is possible by noting how often he employs the future tense in his infrequent assertions. We recall that in some languages of primitive peoples, there is no grammatical construction to cope with conceptions of futurity. Spatial relationships may be expressed; occasionally there is a syntactical construction for referring to past events. But the idea of a future time is a difficult one and is beyond the imagination of primates, and even of young as well as primitive human subjects. Aphasiacs in their halting conversation are probably involved mainly with the past; only occasionally with the present; and rarely, if ever, with the future.

Thus we find the unhappy aphasiac, silent and lonely, an alien within a foreign and faintly hostile land. He dwells bewildered, amidst a confusion of symbols dimly understood. As often as not he is partially incapacitated and unable to fend for himself. Eager to make communion with others, to share their interests or enlist their aid, he meets a barricade which stands between his ill-formed notions and their expression. Should he succeed in fighting through, maybe he finds his words a grotesque parody of his will, made up of incoherencies and futile parrotings. Frustrated and bemused, he lapses into the security of his silence where he can face the simple things and actualities, leaving unexplored the world of generalities and ideas. He lives from hour to hour, with little thought for tomorrow, emmeshed in reverie upon the distant past, the satisfaction of his present needs or the awaiting of some immediate simple comfort.

XIX. APHASIA CONSIDERED AS A DISORDER
OF THE PREVERBITUM

Just take a look at the Corporal we all love. Do you know why Corporal Brook is mouthing like that and nothing's coming out? D'you know? Well, I'll tell you why. It's because he's got a blockage. Up here, in his nut.' Driscoll tapped his own head spitefully. 'Yes, no kidding. Up here. The poor sod is incapable of getting the next order out. He knows what it should be—he knows all right—but he can't say it. So he's stuck there. Like a bleeding goldfish.'

Leslie Thomas. The Virgin Soldiers

Intimately linked with the conception of an identity with language and thought, is the current idea that aphasia is a special type of disordered thinking. This view correlates with traditional views as to 'endophasy' or internal speech.

Bouillaud, and a little later Hughlings Jackson, were among the earliest to discuss the problem of the role of inner speech in aphasia. This however is a vague and unsatisfactory term, which has been used in at least three different senses: (1) unspoken speech, as when we silently move our lips while writing; (2) verbal formulation which precedes utterance; and (3) general processes of thought.

Jackson considered internal speech to be identical with uttered speech, except for the fact that it is silent. Writing can be regarded as the key to the nature of internal speech. First there comes what Jackson calls the *subject-proposition*. Next words become fitted to the proposition, so as to constitute internal speech to begin with, and then external speech. Internal speech and even external speech may accompany thought, but neither internal nor external speech are obligatory for the act of thinking to take place.

Later it was realized that thinking is a much more complicated problem and that it may not necessarily entail the use of images of any sort. In 1903 Binet said that thinking could not be reduced to a matter of images; thinking can take place without images, and in some cases images seem almost to interfere with thinking. They are independent and at times even antagonistic.

At about the same time appeared the work of the Würzburg school of philosophers (Marbe, Ach, Watt, Messer, Bühler, and Selz). Their attitude was that thinking entails special psychological states not realizable as images, not verbalized internally, but definable as an intellectual feeling, or an implicit knowledge. These ineffable processes of thought can be grouped together under the term *Bewusstseinanlagen* (attitudes of consciousness), an expression first used by Mayer and Orth in 1901.

Based upon an article appearing in the birthday volume in honour of the late Academician K. Henner of Prague.

235

Earlier still came Wernicke's belief that thinking comprised a special association-complex which he called the *Wortbegriff* (the idea, or conception, of a word). His original views were later modified by himself and also by others. Storch and Goldstein regarded the *Wortbegriff* as a special psycho-physical phenomenon, not definable in terms of motor or sensory speech-phenomena. According to Goldstein, inner speech may be defined as the totality of processes and experiences which occur when we seek to express our thoughts in external speech, or when we perceive heard sounds in language. Inner speech varies from time to time according to the circumstances in which talking occurs, for it stands in relation to non-language mental processes, and also to the external instrumentalities of speech. Thus speech may largely be determined by motor automatisms, and a lack of development of inner speech may be concealed by excessive talk and over-rapid speaking.

Using the terminology of modern theory, it can be said that a verbal habit may act as a substitute for thought.

The term 'inner speech' must be distinguished from the expression 'inner speech-form' originally employed by Von Humboldt to indicate the structure of a language, which he believed reflects the special way in which the speaker looks at the world, and grasps the world, corresponding with a specific world-perspective held by those sharing that same language. This idea may also apply to groups as well as individuals.

In 1885 Kussmaul was the first to focus attention upon the processes of thought which immediately precede the act of speaking or writing. This is what I would choose to call the *preverbitum*. According to Kussmaul, there occurs a series of stages in thought before its expression in speech, comprising (1) preparation; (2) internal diction; and (3) articulation. Pick expanded this same idea but considered that the preverbitum was even more elaborate, entailing the following stages: (1) intuitive thought; (2) structural thought; (3) the sentence schema; and (4) the choice of words. In 1925 Van Woerkoem regarded the preverbitum as made up as follows: (1) the conception of the whole idea; (2) analysis and synthesis in time and space; (3) sentence-schema; and (4) the choice of words. Van Woerkoem realized that the trouble in aphasiacs lay here, in a '. . . loss of geometric sense'.

The preverbitum may be defined as the complex silent thinking-processes which immediately precede exteriorization, either by way of spoken speech or as writing. It differs from inner speech in that it is of necessity formulated, disciplined and co-ordinated so as to serve usually as a communicative act. Unlike inner speech, it must proceed to the stage of conforming with accepted grammatical usages. Head also emphasized that speech, when examined introspectively, appears to be a progressive act though one stage merges smoothly with the next. Later Conrad (1954) spoke of the processes of thought which lead up to speech, as a 'pre-configuration' or *Vorgestalt*.

These ideas are probably far too rigid and schematic. The preverbitum may be regarded as varying considerably according to many different circumstances, such as, for example, the intellectual rank of the speaker; the type of thinking concerned at a particular moment; and thirdly, the medium of expression adopted, with particular reference to its speed.

The mere act of writing or speaking influences in a retrograde fashion the act of thinking. This is a specific property of the preverbitum, as opposed to inner speech. As Francis Bacon said 'Words exercise a reciprocal and reactionary power over the intellect'. According to Schopenhauer 'The real life of a thought only lasts until it reaches the borderline of words; there it petrifies, is dead thereafter, but imperishable, comparable to the fossils of animals and plants of prehistoric times'. This influence is shown by the common experience of the impromptu speaker or debater who starts to talk without knowing exactly what he is going to say, but who marshalls his ideas as he proceeds. It used to be said of the Prime Minister Charles James Fox that when speaking in the House of Commons he would find himself in the middle of a sentence, and then trust to Providence to rescue him. These ideas have already been expressed in Chapter XIII.

Much could be discussed on the topic of what has been called 'the grammar of thinking', which consists in a study of the syntax—if it can so be called—of verbal symbols when they crop up in the preverbitum. Hughlings Jackson referred to this procedure when he gave an example of the spoken sentence 'This blotting-paper is red'. As Jackson remarked . . . 'I had the ideas "blotting-paper" and "red" in my mind, and these roused the two words, automatically before the words could be put in propositional order'. Obviously it is not until the final stages of the preverbitum have been reached, that anything like a strict grammatical arrangement of words takes place. Prior to that stage, only key-words come to the fore, and subordinate parts of speech, articles, prepositions, conjunctions, find no place. The arrangement of the key-words within the preverbitum may perhaps be quite different from the order in which these words appear in the final spoken or written text. Can it be that there exists a logical syntax within the preverbitum, but quite different from that occurring in the accepted usage of speech? This idea is rather suggested by the sign-talk of deaf-mutes, who utilize and arrange their pantomimic signs in an order which may be foreign to that of the language of the *entourage*. Thus the deaf-mute, in order to express the sentence 'The dark handsome stranger, having got down from his horse, drank a glass of wine', would indicate by signs 'stranger—dark—handsome—horse—dismounted—drank'. This recalls the interesting problem of whether the structure of languages necessarily indicates the mode of thought. Thus, the Aryan group of languages where a regular subject-predicate type of construction is employed, is vastly different from the grammatical construction of languages found in Asia, Africa and North America. Are these differences fundamental, or even important? On the one hand we are reminded of the Sapir-Whorf hypothesis, or the 'principle of linguistic relativity', which states that differences in the structure of a language indicate underlying and far-reaching differences in thought and behaviour, with particular regard to such conceptions as space, time and causality. For example, in the Mende language the two sentences 'You *are* listening' 'You *were* listening' would require entirely different words for the pronoun '*you*', because to the Mende speaker, 'you' in the present time represents something quite different from 'you' as existed in the past. Again in many languages there are no expressions to indicate futurity. The syntax of English might be compared with Japanese. In the former we might say: 'Pleased to meet you'. A Japanese, however, would proclaim: 'Beginning-to honourable eyes to am-hanging'. Not all linguists, however, agree with the Sapir-Whorf hypothesis, considering differences in language-structure to be merely questions of metaphor. Thinking-processes may not be necessarily different, and to sustain the principle of linguistic relativity would be to make words our masters rather than our servants. The example of Finland may be quoted, where two vastly different languages are utilized almost interchangeably.

Inner speech in the sense of silent rumination, may at any time constitute a preverbitum and then find expression in written or spoken speech. In that event it goes through a stage of what is called 'predicative' thought. Indeed many people in their conversation have the habit of indulging almost entirely in a veritable predicative speech, that is to say a sort of allusive utterance where things are hinted at rather than expressed baldly. Or, instead of employing hints, predicative speech may proceed from one idea to another not directly, but obliquely, like a Knight's move on a chessboard. The obvious and immediate associated idea is omitted or by-passed, resulting in an unusual sequence of concepts. Often the train of reasoning appears illogical or frankly obscure, except to those who are appropriately alive to this idiosyncrasy on the part of the speaker. This is a verbal habit which runs the risk of not being understood except by intimates who are attuned to the same wavelength of predicative thinking as the speaker. In the case of written language, however, there is as a rule no trace of predicative tendencies, and this is one of the many differences between spoken and written language within a community. In the case of the English language these differences may well expand with time, rather than shrink, and generations hence spoken English may differ vastly from written English. Indeed it may not be going too far to suggest that written English might perhaps eventually be within the competency of the minority of English-speaking people and not the majority.

Interesting observations can be made on the differences between thinking and speaking in terms of time-factors. For example during the act of reading aloud, the eye travels ahead of the voice and maybe perceive several words in advance of the one which is being articulated. This can be demonstrated by the simple manoeuvre of suddenly switching off the light while a person is reading aloud: the speaker is able to continue to enunciate a number of words in the dark. That is to say, the difference in the eye/voice span is about five or six words, depending partly on the skill of the reader and partly on the subject-matter. Similarly the ear/pencil span can be shown in the manner in which a stenographer will hold in her memory a succession of words or even phrases which her pencil has not yet recorded. This span could amount to as many as fourteen words or even more.

Within the preverbitum there may be said to exist an inhibitory vigilant mechanism, possibly of a non-verbal character, which selects words to the exclusion of others which are less appropriate; inhibits over-free verbal associations; links words together in appropriate order according to the rules of convention, grammar, logic and perhaps euphony.

The notion of a preverbitum ties up in an interesting fashion with the anatomy of literary inspiration, and the methods of work employed by various writers of prose and poetry, or by orators. This is a fascinating subject which would repay further study. Comparatively few writers have analysed introspectively the stages which intervene between the creation of an idea and its final appearance in speech or writing. Exceptions must be made in the case of such poets as Spender, Mallarmé, Rilke, and MacNeice. Buhler has said 'Before words come to me I get a sense of rhythm, something like a time-schema. Before the words, I've had a sense of form, something into which the words as they appear can fit'. The preverbitum, in prose writers, may be much elongated.

Contemporary ideas regard aphasia not as a disorder of images but as a specific disorder of thinking in words. More specifically, one can look upon the various clinical variants of aphasia as disorders of the preverbitum lying at various psychological depths. Herein is a suggestive opportunity for another classification of the aphasias, more logical than most of the conventional attempts. Thus, most superficial of all would be those rare cases (if indeed they exist at all) of so-called aphemia, where the patient can understand and write, but cannot express himself at all in articulate speech. Of much firmer status are those comparatively common cases of mild aphasia where the patient is held up by an inability to supply the appropriate substantive by a deliberate willed effort of speech, e.g. when asked to name an object before him. Here exists a defect at a relatively superficial level, analogous to what Gautier called a severance of the golden thread which connects speech and thought. This is analogous of course with the common difficulty in recalling proper names. The intactness of the earlier stages of the preverbitum is shown by the fact that the speaker in groping for the word retains some nebulous and vague notion as to the physical appearance of the missing word—its probable length, initial letter and so on. Sometimes the clue is afforded by a synaesthetic association. As a rule the speaker recognizes the appropriate term as soon as he hears it or sees it in print before him. Characteristically, he will reject all inappropriate suggestions. As Louis Aragon said 'It was like not being able to think of a word. One knows how it goes more or less, and if there is an R in it, and how many syllables it has; one can even think of rhymes or equivalents for it. Ah! but the real word, the word that rings a bell, and is a song!'

Defects lying deeper within the preverbitum may be expected to give rise to a more profound aphasia entailing both motor and sensory components. This is what Goldstein called 'central aphasia'—an unfortunate term—and which is often characterized clinically by the uninhibited outpouring of a torrent of speech most of which is unintelligible.

No vigilant censor operates within the preverbitum, so that a word which comes to the surface of consciousness, leads at once to another word which is habitually linked thereto by dint of frequent cohabitation. This word is not suppressed, but in an incongruous fashion butts in and may continue to crop up inordinately so as to contaminate the speech which follows. Or, two words which form an appropriate part of the preverbitum, may unite in a grotesque fashion—the head of one and the tail of another, for example—like a fabulous monster.

Deepest of all within the preverbitum are those lesions which produce clinically a fundamental poverty of speech, whether or not characterized by recurrent utterance of speech-remnants.

XX. REGIONAL 'ACCENT', DEMOTIC
SPEECH, AND APHASIA

Nor, with all the resources of the mouth, can any one understand why no one language used more than a small part of those resources—the Arabs speaking deep in their throats, the Indians far back in the mouth, the German more forward, the Italian still further up front, and so forth—so that each language is somehow difficult for the speakers of every other language, so that if they can speak it only with an accent, as if each language had tried to be a secret code against the outside; and yet for all that, within each language every native speaker can understand all those who speak the same tongue, and yet distinguish the various accents of different regions where that language is spoken—the Northerner from the Southerner, the mountaineer from the plainsman, the city dweller from the farmer, and even in each city he can further sub-divide, recognizing the speech of this or that suburb?

Guy Endore

In this context, the term regional 'accent' means the method of talking which stamps the speaker as belonging to such and such a geographical area. Here 'accent' is used in a correct though popular sense as standing for a manner of pronunciation. It has been used in this context in the English language since 1600. But scientists have recently invested this word with a specific connotation, and to distinguish it from its technical employment within the metalanguage of phonetics (where accent refers to alterations in pitch level, duration or loudness of certain syllables within a word), 'accent' will be consistently printed between quotation marks.

Analysis reveals that at least four phenomena are entailed:

(a) A *dysphonemia*, or a distortion of some of the phonemes as compared with what is deemed correct usage for the country concerned. The standard is set by the way educated and cultured people speak their mother tongue. In Great Britain we speak of the 'Queen's English', or 'received pronunciation'. This is not necessarily the prerogative of the moneyed classes, for there also exist certain affected or 'refined' ways of mutilating phonemes which, to a student of language, are just as abnormal as any provincialism.

(b) A *dysprodia*, or alteration in the melodic pattern of a phrase or sentence which, in the case of the English language, at once stamps the speaker as hailing from, say, North America, or from Lancashire, Wales, Ireland, and so on. The foreigner when speaking English not infrequently carries over the specific melody, or *chanson de parler*, of his own native tongue, even though his vocabulary and grammar in English be impeccable.

Based upon a paper contributed to the *Livre Jubilaire* in honour of Dr. Ludo van Bogaert, 1962.

So much for the purely phonetic considerations of regional 'accent'. Other peculiarities can at times participate in what might be termed a regional manner of talking. Thus:

(c) Certain dialectical or provincial turns of phrase may obtrude into the diction (and even into the written speech) which are peculiar to the place of abode. Often these are really archaisms, or vestiges of out-moded expressions, surviving in the modern tongue.

And finally:

(d) There are, in English at any rate, subtle taboos concerning the choice of words. Certain terms or phrases, though grammatically correct, are avoided by upper class speakers for no logical reason. It is not a question of slang or colloquialisms, but simply whether or not a phrase is 'acceptable'. This is a hurdle which few foreigners overcome, for what is called 'U' and 'non-U' speech is not taught in text-books.[1] Many people speak their own language with perfect grammar and phonemic structure, oblivious of the fact that they are revealing their class by employing 'non-U' terms instead of 'U' terms. This highly selective use of the English language is something which is slowly and insensibly acquired by way of British public schools and in social intercourse.

It may be asked whether anything comparable with U and non-U speech exists in languages other than English. It would be strange indeed if it did not. Not so long ago discussion in the Press specifically referred to Russian in this connection. Several correspondents asserted that a type of U-Russian is spoken by aristocratic emigrés, and possibly also by the new privileged classes in the U.S.S.R.—writers, artists, politicians and physicists.

Few foreigners realize that a regional 'accent' carries with it, in England at any rate, a certain pejorative connotation. Not only does it indicate that the speaker has been brought up in a particular place—there is no harm in that—but it stamps him as belonging to a stratum of society where accents unfortunately flourish. This snobbish implication scarcely obtains in North America or on the continent of Europe, where a regional mode of pronunciation merely proclaims that the speaker does not come from the metropolis, and no question of social rank arises at all.

In England, a regional 'accent' is not socially acceptable. On the other hand, a faint Scottish method of talking, or even an Irish brogue, is tolerated, provided only that the prosodic qualities of the speaker's voice are musical and pleasing to the ear. A grating, raucous or cacophonous Scotch or Irish diction is not approved, any more than a Liverpudlian, Brummagen or Cockney 'accent'.

John Deane Potter expressed this state of affairs neatly when he wrote: 'Britain has created a mandarin class. And the entrance to it is guarded by the most craftily concealed traps in the world. They consist of five little sounds—the vowels of the English language. It is how you pronounce these tiny, constantly used sounds which may fix a gulf between you and some of the great prizes of life'.

As students of language we may regret this shibboleth but social prejudices are too strong. Possibly it was not always so, and we recall with some sympathy the words of Dr. Samuel Johnson: 'Good English is plain, easy and smooth in the mouth of an unaffected English gentleman.

---

[1] 'U' stands for upper class. The formula was invented by Miss Nancy Mitford inspired by a paper on 'Upper class English Usage' by Professor Alan Ross.

A studied and factitious pronunciation, which required perpetual constraint, is exceedingly disgusting. A small intermixture of provincial peculiarities may, perhaps, have an agreeable effect, as the notes of different birds concur in the harmony of the grove, and please more than if they were all exactly alike'.

The French being linguistically hypersensitive are said to resent hearing their language imperfectly spoken, even by well-intentioned foreigners. That is why so many English, including highly educated ones, are shy of speaking French to a Frenchman. This reluctance does not, however, preclude them from talking French to other foreigners.

In England, however, an alien 'accent' is quite in order, provided that it is spoken by a genuine foreigner. A French 'accent' is particularly attractive to English ears. But an Australian or a Yankee twang is all wrong. Oddly enough this prejudice does not extend to the mode of talking of an American from the deep South.

The foregoing remarks are made to show the odd linguistic prejudices, likes and dislikes, of the Englishman. They emphasize the fact that speech habits are closely bound up with the personality of the speaker. Talking is an important aspect of behaviour; it is therefore of interest to examine the relationship of 'accent' to aphasia. A two-fold problem is entailed here: (1) the integrity or otherwise of 'accent' within the speech-remnants of an aphasiac; and (2) the unexpected phenomenon whereby what appears to be a regional 'accent' emerges in a chronic or convalescent aphasiac.

A regional 'accent' is readily detected in the utterances of an aphasiac even though the scrappy relics of surviving speech be quite fragmentary. Nay more, the 'accent' may actually become exaggerated as compared with the pre-morbid way of speech. This applies both to the dysphonemic and the dysprodic elements. Thus the speech of a Welsh aphasiac may be limited to the affirmative particle: but he will continue to say 'yes, yes' (instead of 'yes') in the rapid, clipped and staccato fashion so typical of a Welsh intonation. This intensification of a regional 'accent' in aphasia is probably due to the removal of inhibitory factors as the result of disease. Henry Head would probably have implicated a loss of 'vigilance'. That this is so is supported by the experience of psychotherapy, where under amytal narcosis or under analysis a patient may lapse into methods of speaking which had previously been disciplined very nearly out of existence.

The following case-report suggests the re-appearance (or perhaps it was the development) of a regional 'accent' in the course of a traumatic neurosis.

Mrs. M. E., aged 49 years, was first examined by me on 21st June, 1958, on account of a post-traumatic syndrome which dated from a car-crash on 1st July, 1956. She sustained a compound fracture of the skull, but consciousness was lost for only a moment or two. Her symptoms were principally neurotic in character but a conspicuous feature was a curiously slow, syllabic and hesitant mode of speaking, with an excessive range of modulation, which was not wholly appropriate to the content of what she was saying. The impression she gave was that she was speaking with a Welsh 'accent', though she protested she had never before talked in that fashion. Although her speech-therapist ascribed her dysarthria to some local damage to the articulatory mechanism, the defect was almost certainly psychologically determined. The patient was born in Flintshire in Wales, but lived most of her life in Chester, a border town. Her husband was a Welshman. Considerable interest was aroused in the Press when her case went to the Law Courts, and the patient was twitted as claiming damages on account of the handicap of a Welsh 'accent'.

The following record illustrates the temporary re-emergence of a French intonation, in a bi-lingual Frenchwoman living in England:

Mrs. R., a hypotensive lady of 48 years, was referred to me in March, 1960, by Dr. R. S.

Nine days previously, while she was choosing wall-papers in a shop, her eyes seemed to go out of focus, and she felt lightheaded and curiously detached. She proceeded to an Oxford Street store where she found that while she knew what it was she wanted to say, she 'could think only in French'. Her speech, when it was emitted, was articulated with a French 'accent'. She feared she would be regarded as drunk, and she is sure that the shop assistant thought there was something peculiar about her. She went home by taxi, again experiencing difficulty in telling the driver her destination. At home she lay on the bed feeling very cold, and then fell asleep. The ringing of her telephone awoke her and as she answered she was conscious that her articulation was wrong, though by now it seemed to her more 'drunken' than French. For the rest of that day she had a dull headache, and all she 'could think of was French poetry'. The next day she felt rather elated and also dazed if she walked too far.

At examination no neurological abnormality could be found, but the systolic blood pressure was only 100. She admitted to having been recently subjected to unusual strain and worry.

The patient was French by birth, but had for many years resided in London. She regarded herself as 'practically bilingual' and ordinarily she spoke English without any trace of a foreign pronunciation.

In this patient, there had emerged a manner of talking which had probably been natural to her at one period of her linguistic development. The pathological process responsible was doubtless a minor degree of cerebrovascular insufficiency, though there is no firm clinical evidence as to the site of the transient ischaemia.

The third and fourth factors entailed in an accepted or received way of talking with the inhibition of dialectical and of non-U terms, may also be somewhat altered after an aphasia. Being more fundamental and more concrete than the later acquired refinements of speech these elements may re-emerge. They may be likened to the relative invulnerability of the mother-tongue in pluri-lingual aphasiacs.

It would be interesting to probe this matter more deeply in aphasiacs from countries where a highly organized dialect exists alongside the literary and more conventional tongue. Thus, aphasiacs in Switzerland might perhaps cope with *Bärndutsch*, *Schweizer-deutsch* or *Romanisch* better than with German or French; in Barcelona Catalonian phrases might become more evident after an aphasia, and in the Midi, aphasiacs might conceivably lapse into *Provençal*. Local neurologists ought to be able to throw light upon this question, and no doubt they will in time do so.

The next case is an unusual one for it exemplifies the appearance, rather than the re-appearance, of something closely akin to a regional 'accent' after a cerebrovascular catastrophe. In this case underlying personality factors may well have determined the particular type of 'accent' concerned.

In December 1957, Mrs. E. L., aged 37 years, right-handed, previously in good health, abruptly but in-completely lost consciousness. On the third day after this episode she was admitted under the care of Dr. A. M. G. Campbell to the Bristol Royal Hospital where she found herself paralysed down the left side and speechless. Both plantar responses were extensor in type. Originally she was unaware of her hemiplegia; as she gradually improved she began to wonder why she could not move her left arm. Later her speech slowly returned. At first she could utter nothing but her husband's name 'Bill'—which she articulated in an unusual fashion. Then she found herself able to say 'ta' (a provincialism meaning 'thank you'). Gradually her vocabulary increased and eventually returned to what had no doubt been the pre-morbid volume. Previously a 'beautiful' writer, she now found she could not write properly and she made many mistakes. Even a year later, her writing was somewhat impaired. In the early days after the stroke she found it hard to understand printed or written words, though she had always been able to comprehend what was said to her. Gradually her dyslexia improved.

As her spoken speech steadily returned, she began for the first time in her life to talk with a pronounced Welsh 'accent', a fact which she fully realized and resented. She could give no explanation for this manner of speech, for she was born and brought up in the West Country and had never visited Wales. No Welsh nurses or doctors had attended her in hospital. She had no close Welsh friends. At school none of her teachers had come from Wales. Once she had learned to sing a Welsh hymn (*Ar hyd y nos*) when she was in a choir competing at an Eisteddfod, but her singing mistress had been English.

Since her stroke she had undergone a considerable change in her personality—a fact confirmed by her sister. She had developed a bad habit of frequently swearing, a practice quite foreign to her nature. 'She does not mind in the slightest what she says, and is not at all shy or embarrassed'. The patient was fully aware of the alteration in her character, and she also imagined that she had undergone some physical deterioration. 'I have grown old, ugly, and fat' (which was not actually so).

When seen in December 1958 she showed a spastic left-sided hemiparesis with an extensor plantar response. Her speech was glib, grammatical and fluent. There was no groping for words and no paraphasic errors could be detected. She talked rather rapidly in a staccato and yet sing-song fashion which was highly reminiscent of a strong Welsh intonation. Indeed she could easily have passed as a Welshwoman. She was inordinately aware of her disabilities and was inclined to complain excessively of her vocal, paralytic and psychological anomalies.

The personal history was perhaps significant. This patient had married twice. She has always rather disliked Welsh people, and her first husband, whom she had divorced, was a Welshman. She asserted with vehemence, however, that he never at any time spoke like a Welshman. This latter observation should be taken with considerable reserve, for it is unlikely that she was of a sufficient cultural level even to detect that a person's manner of speaking was of a regional character.

The association of speech-loss with a left hemiplegia is interesting and it raises some doubt as to whether her initial difficulty in talking was due to an anarthria or to an aphasia. Unfortunately the hospital records do not clear up this question. However, the patient's retrospective statement made a year later to the effect that both reading and writing had been difficult, suggests strongly that a dysphasia must have been present, with or without dysarthria.

Such a case falls into the category of post-aphasic dysprodia, as first described by Monrad-Krohn. His original patient, already referred to on p. 218, a Norwegian lady, had sustained an apoplectic loss of speech during the enemy occupation of her country. As she recovered her powers of self-expression, her manner of speaking proved to have undergone a transformation. She had lost the natural prosodic qualities so characteristic of Norwegian speakers and these had been replaced by a 'foreign' type of intonation. Indeed, strangers assumed that she was a German, and she was embarrassed by the coldness displayed in shops and markets by her compatriots, who did not know who she was or what had befallen her.

This phenomenon of a seemingly foreign type of dysprodia after a stroke—even surviving into the convalescent stages of an aphasia—is probably commoner than generally imagined. Alajouanine and Lhermitte have put it on record that French aphasiacs often speak like a foreigner—English, German, or Belgian, in that order.

Yet another case of a putative Welsh 'accent' appearing in the course of an aphasia has been brought to my notice, though I never personally saw the patient. A very experienced logopaedist, Mrs. Van Thal, has described to me a woman of 56 years who had a cerebral accident in December 1953, causing an aphasia. Speech therapy was started in April 1954. Single words appeared first, and then phrases. By August a 'childish intonation' was noted. There was much literal paraphasia and many errors of syntax though the patient was now able to communicate with fair efficiency. By this time her intonation was high-pitched, sing-song and distinctly Welsh in its characteristics. The patient's 'in-laws' came from Wales (which she had visited a few times) but her husband did not talk like a Welshman.

Demotic speech

Demotic speech may happen to comprise a regional 'accent', but the two must be distinguished. The term refers to what may be called a plebeian or lowest class mode of spoken speech, as used in ordinary unselfconscious intercourse between social equals. By exercising particular care some demotic speakers can assume a more refined manner of diction when occasion demands, as when trying to impress a putative 'superior'. In English the features which betray demotic speech are, to begin with, a regional 'accent' with its hallmarks of dysphonemia, dysprodia, occasional use of dialect and of non-U terminology. The regional 'accent' is often associated with the dropping of the initial aspirate, or /h/ sound. Two, and possibly three other characteristics also appear. First the speaker may be guilty of frank errors of grammar. Secondly the speaker may indulge in malapropism or the misuse of unfamiliar terms, through dint of ignorance of their exact meaning. The third criterion of demotic speech lies in the inordinate employment of swearing, or diction which is socially inappropriate or unacceptable.

In the English language swearing is no straight-forward or simple phenomenon. It includes vituperative epithets of the most plangent sort, as well as various ejaculations of vivid affective colouring, many being of blasphemous derivation. As Hughlings Jackson said 'oaths had once an intellectual meaning; they expressed ideas, and were uttered with a definite intention. Curses have, in fact, formed an element in all religious services; but nowadays intentional swearing is obsolete; it has degenerated to meaningless swearing, which, like cadence and gesticulation, is but a kind of commentary of the emotions on the propositions of the intellect. Vulgar people insert an oath at the proper intervals of their speech as a sort of detonating comma, and thus they render forcible statements which might otherwise strike their hearers as commonplace'.

Then there is a very different kind of swearing, one which comprises the introduction of certain taboo words which are not necessarily uttered under emotional stress. In some circles they may even constitute terms of endearment, but ordinarily they are practically devoid of feeling-tone. Chiefly

they are used as omnibus expressions, being thus evidence of poverty rather than wealth of vocabulary. Most of these particular 'swear-words' are of a sexual or alvine connotation, though they
are usually employed wholly out of any such contexts. Such a speech-habit is an adolescent trait
being rare in the diction both of children and of the very mature. Swearing is common in Service
personnel, as Shakespeare observed. It is a stock-in-trade of the under-cover writers of graffiti.
Swearing, or 'bad language' as it is called, has been rated as 'poor man's poetry'.

Among the more notorious of these taboo words is one which etymologically refers to the sexual
act, but in such crudity as to be unacceptable in print, or at least until recently. English novelists
often camouflage the term as 'flipping' and the initiate at once interprets what he reads. But as an
item of demotic speech this word can mean almost anything. Often it is merely synonymous with
the adverb 'very' as in the phrase 'flipping hot weather'. Sometimes it stands for nothing much
more than a hyphen, a punctuation mark, as when a young soldier gave his age as 'twenty-
flipping-two'.

The genesis of swearing is uncertain and indeed there are probably several types, and several
origins. Among young adults it seems to serve as a badge of conformity, wherein it is considered
smart, even more racy than slang. In any event an over-indulgence in swearing betrays a linguistic
bankruptcy, and in such a verbal climate it flourishes best.

One interesting hypothesis traces the origin of this kind of swearing to a fundamental inter-sex
antagonism. A manifestation of this hostility is the holding up to ridicule of sexual partnerships.
Thus to quote W. L. Goodman:

> ... Does it (i.e. swearing) not lie rather in a very deep-rooted sexual antagonism between men and
> women? Ever since mankind first gathered together round the camp fire women must have had reasons
> of one sort or another to ward off the ceaseless importunities of men, and they in their turn had to conceal
> their motives, at least from eligible women, and pretend that the grapes were sour. The words are rarely
> used by women (and then with glaring incongruity) and only by men to men, which suggests an archetypal
> conspiracy seeking recognition in mutual verbal exhibitionism; where forbidden deeds and things are
> symbolically flaunted as short and brutal words, by men who instinctively feel them to be derogatory to
> ideas named in association with them. They are normally taboo for women, not because women are
> inherently less violent in speech, but because they are not in the plot.

This same theory would perhaps explain the marked difference between the swearing-habits of
the two sexes. Swearing is essentially a masculine penchant. When used by women—and many
lady novelists have lately succumbed to this departure from good taste—it usually constitutes a
pose and an artificial straining after sophistication. Rarely if ever are these taboo words used quite
correctly by women, either in writing or in talk.

And yet that strange hypertrophy of language known as Gilles de la Tourette's disease afflicts
females at least as often as males. Coprolalia of the coarsest type is the characteristic content of these
verbal tics. We witness here a linguistic perversion which transgresses the natural inhibitions of the
female sex.

The purpose of these remarks is to lead up to the inquiry how demotic speech behaves in cases of
aphasia. Being an aspect of inferior speech in the Baillarger-Jacksonian sense, it survives better than
superior speech, that is propositionizing, or symbolic formulation and expression. That element of

demotic speech made up of emotionally charged expletives is comparatively well retained in cases of aphasia. In some patients an oath or an interjection may form the sole item of speech, and may constitute a recurrent utterance. Thus the aphasic Baudelaire was powerless to emit anything except the truncated oath, *Cré nom!*

Hughlings Jackson was deeply interested in the capacity of aphasiacs to swear, and he also noted a persistence of what he called 'feminine oaths', e.g. 'dear me!' and 'bless my soul!' The all-purpose and shameful term euphuistically encoded as 'flipping' may also survive so as to occupy an undeserved role in an aphasiac's shrunken stock of words.

The survival of swearing in aphasic diction ties up with Dwight Whitney's theory of a natural and gradual evolution of normal speech from lowly levels to superior flights; from the designation of what is coarser, gross, more material—to the designation of what is finer, more abstract and more formal. Swearing clearly belongs to a more primitive, and therefore less vulnerable, stage of speech development.

Reference to the masculine as contrasted with feminine use of swearing raises the question whether the pattern of speech-loss is different in male aphasiacs as opposed to female. This intriguing but academic problem has been discussed more fully elsewhere. In that there exist in the English language terms favoured by males rather than females, and *vice versa*, we again witness an example of the dependence of manner of speech upon personality. Male aphasiacs will almost certainly employ a vocabulary which is different from that retained by a female patient. The comparative volubility of female versus male aphasiacs is quite another question, however.

XXI. CREATIVE WRITING BY APHASIACS

Pantagruel then throwed us on the deck whole handfuls of frozen words . . . of many colours, like those used in heraldry; some words gules (. . . jests and merry sayings), some vert, some azur, some black, some or (. . . fair words); and when we had somewhat warmed them between our hands, they melted like snow, and we really heard them, but could not understand them, for it was a barbarous gibberish. One of them only, that was pretty big . . . gave a sound much like that of chestnuts when they are thrown into the fire, without being first cut, which made us all start. . . . However, he threw three or four handfuls of them on the deck; among which I perceived some very sharp words, and some bloody words, which, the pilot said, used sometimes to go back and recoil to the place whence they came . . . we saw also some terrible words, and some others not very pleasant to the eye.

F. Rabelais

It is uncertain whether in the creation of a literary work the imagination and the sensibility are not interchangeable and whether the second, without disadvantage, cannot be substituted for the first just as people whose stomach is incapable of digesting entrust this function to their intestines. And innately sensitive man who has no imagination could, nevertheless, write admirable novels.

M. Proust

Chapter XVIII dealt with the question of a content-analysis of aphasic utterance; that is to say, a discussion of just what it is that an aphasiac talks about. It was concluded that, by and large, in an auspicious environment, an aphasiac remains relatively silent as though finding it distressing or difficult to embark upon the task of verbalization. Once silence is broken, however, the utterances seem, upon analysis, to include an undue proportion of interrogations, requests, and exclamations. Declarative utterances, that is propositionizing, are heard less often, unlike what obtains in normal circumstances among non-aphasiacs.

Furthermore, it can be submitted that the stylistic quality of the verbalization of aphasiacs rests at a relatively simple level. Some traces of speech in its role as the mirror of the subject's personality may, however, be still detected. The quality of wit is usually lacking from the speech of aphasiacs, however conspicuous it might have been in the past. Few aphasiacs, if any, can be expected to regain their pre-morbid brilliance in extemporaneous oratory, and lectures, sermons, and political harangues are likely to remain forever beyond the patient's capacity.

The chapter in question dealt mostly with the articulate utterances of aphasic patients, and less

Based upon an article which appeared in *Neurological Problems*. Ed. J. Choróbski (Jubilee Volume in honour of E. J. Herman). Pergamon Press, Oxford. 1967. p. 275.

with their written compositions. The very considerable differences, linguistic and personal, between the spoken and written forms of any language must obviously have an important bearing upon the pattern of aphasic production. In aphasiacs, written expressions are usually deranged at least as much as verbal utterances. Often the detriment goes deeper, and the disorder of writing may be much greater than that of the articulated speech. The slower and more deliberate *tempo* of the act of graphic expression goes only a little way towards overcoming the unpropitious factor of unfamiliarity. The relative artificiality of writing as a medium of self-expression, erects a barrier which the aphasiac with his verbal inertia surmounts only with difficulty. A content-analysis of a series of spontaneous writings of aphasiacs would probably show a preponderance of transitive over intransitive types. Written interjections and exclamations would, no doubt, be far less frequent than in spoken speech, as indeed is also the case in normal writing. Interrogations and requests would loom large; while declarations, if they occur at all, would be of an uncomplicated character, introspective, self-revealing and documentary.

An aphasiac's writings, whatever their theme, would probably display a relatively low level of literary attainment, being devoid of stylistic elegance, wit, sophistication, and verbal fastidiousness. The important linguistic and psychological study by Elvin and Oldfield (1951) demonstrated clearly the progress in essay-writing made by a university student who had been rendered aphasic from a skull-wound. The authors studied the steady improvement in speed, syntax and vocabulary, but did not concern themselves particularly with matters of style, or aesthetics.

At the highest level of written speech stands poetry, as evidence of inspired thinking. It represents the happiest consortium of thought and language with all its elusive-evocative, mellifluous and associational implications. Thus the French poet Paul Valéry (1934) discussed the problem of the search for *le mot juste*, one which would have to fulfil at least six conditions in order to fit into the literary framework. As he expressed his difficulties:

'Je cherche un mot un mot qui soit:
feminin
de deux syllabes
contenant E ou F
terminé par une muette et synonyme de brisure, désagrégation:
et pas savant, pas rare.
Six conditions—au moins.'

It is unlikely, therefore, on the face of it, that an aphasiac would ever be able to indulge again in serious writing of poetry, even though he may have written verse habitually before his loss of speech. Likewise it would seem safe to assume that an aphasiac who had never written verse before his illness, would not seek to direct his disordered speech-faculties along this particular channel. Hence the literature of aphasia and also of biography offers but few instances of poetry composed during a state of incomplete aphasia, or even after the recovery of speech function.

Baudelaire's aphasia, as already asserted, was so severe that all that remained of his genius was a recurrent utterance of an expletive and blasphemous character. As his friend Nadar exclaimed 'Les deux seuls mots qui puissent sortir des lèvres d'où avait jailli des plaintes immortelles. Oh,

17

l'horreur de cette fin lamentable, la crauté effrayante de Lui qui a frappé Baudelaire dans le verbe, ce sortisseur de gemmes de rubis, comme Il avait frappé Beethoven dans l'ouïe et Michel Ange dans la vue'.

Two other instances have already been quoted. The versatile Professor Forel was also an amateur poet, and it is clear from his own account that versification was beyond his powers during the days of his dysphasia. A week after his stroke, Forel attempted to compose a poem *Vom Gelehrten zum Gaga*, but he found himself unable to adhere to the desired metre.

In 1783, when Dr. Samuel Johnson was suddenly afflicted in the night with an aphasia, he became fearful that he would lose his understanding. In order to test the integrity of his faculties he composed and offered up a prayer to the Almighty in Latin verse. We are given to understand that the prayer was the following:

> 'Summe Pater, quodcumque tuum de corpore Numen
> Hoc statuat precibus Christus adesse velit:
> Ingenio parcas, nec sit mihi culpa rogasse,
> Qua solum petero parte, placere tibi'.

Johnson was not wholly satisfied with these lines, but he quite realized their imperfections. He lived another eighteen months, but although he regained his faculty of self-expression he was still a very sick man. His literary output did not altogether cease at this time. His nights were sleepless, and he would wile the time away by turning Greek epigrams into Latin. Many of these were published. During this same period Johnson also wrote a dedication to Burney's Commemoration of Handel. He also intended to write a preface to the posthumous collection of the works of John Scott, but never completed it. In November 1784 he translated into English verse Horace's ode *Diffugere nives, redeunt, jam gramina campis*. To construct an epitaph in Latin verse to David Garrick was, however, too much for him.

On 13th December, 1784 Johnson died from cardio-renal failure (see Chapter VIII).

A case-report published by Dreifuss (1961) is very significant in the context of this essay. Dreifuss's patient, a German-born American of 34 years, a fluent bilingual and a poet, developed a severe migraine at the age of 15 years. Attacks recurred every three months, and at the age of 16 he had his first episode of transient dysphasia. This lasted about four hours. However, from that time onwards he became aware of permanent high-level deterioration in his powers of expression. Previously he had written several poems, chiefly sonnets, which had been well received. Now he found himself occasionally at a loss for a word, and was compelled to cover up by resort to circum-locution. He became unable to compose poetry, and it was necessary for him to refuse an invitation to provide a piece of verse for his old school magazine. Difficulty in language-learning became obvious and persisted.

In the six following personally observed cases of aphasia, some measure of artistic and original execution was possible. The first five cases comprise examples where creative writing was attempted, while in the sixth instance musical composition was entailed. The seventh case was reported to me, but not personally studied.

Case 1. A male, aged 69, a Member of Parliament, presented himself at a neurological clinic complaining of

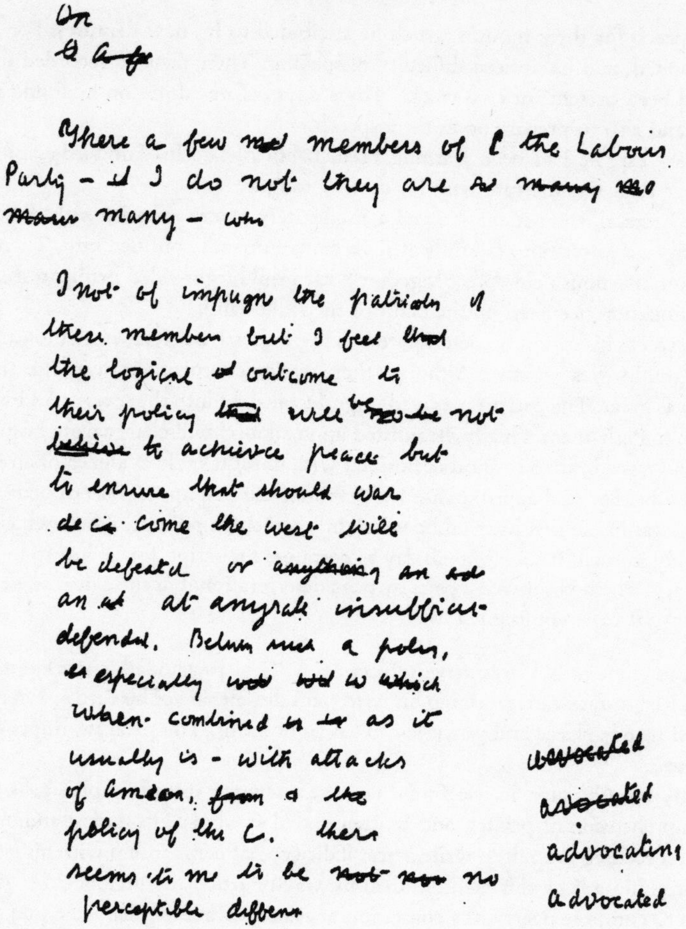

There are a few members of the Labour Party—I do not think they are many—who do not want Western Germany to be brought into the Western defensive system on any terms. They are now openly hoping that no German contingents can be embodied until the autumn of 1953, as they contend that, once Western Germany joins the European army, Germany will become another Korea. But South Korea was invaded because North Korea had a strong army and South Korea had not. The policy thus advocated would reproduce in Germany the very conditions that made the invasion of Korea possible. I do not, of course, impugn the patriotism of these members, but I do feel that the logical outcome of their policy will be, not to achieve peace, but to ensure that, should war come, the West will be defeated or, at any rate, insufficiently defended. Between such a policy, especially when combined, as it often is, with attacks on America, and the policy of the Communists, there seems to me to be no perceptible difference.

FIG. 8 (top) A sheet from the latter part of the manuscript (Case 1).

(bottom) The corrected version as eventually published (Case 1).

'stuttering' in his speech for three months which he attributed to his new dentures. For a month his hand-writing had deteriorated, and he noticed difficulty in spelling. These facts he recorded in his diary. Undue physical fatigue had been present for two weeks. Three days before admission he found it difficult to add a column of figures, and also to prepare notes for a speech.

For the past three years he had been learning French, but of late his knowledge of that language had deteriorated far more than was the case with his mother tongue.

On admission to hospital, the patient showed a moderately severe aphasia, with difficulty in expressing himself both verbally and in writing. Complicated verbal commands confused him. There was a right-sided upper quadrantic homonymous field defect together with a mild right-sided hemiparesis. Some impairment in two-point discrimination occurred on the palm of the right hand.

Over the ensuing weeks his condition deteriorated and a progressive defect was demonstrated in a succession of E.E.G's. Arteriography was negative. Although there was no complaint of headache, the clinical suspicion of a brain tumour was great. The patient betrayed imperfect insight into the severity of his case, and urged to be allowed to return to Parliament. Finally, he insisted upon taking his discharge from hospital after six weeks.

Six months later he was admitted to another hospital with unmistakable evidence of an infiltrating tumour in the left temporal lobe. He died approximately a year after the first appearance of neurological symptoms.

While the patient was in the first hospital he wrote in longhand a political article which was accepted and published by a weekly journal. It took him all day to compose the script, for he had to look up almost every word in the dictionary. The text showed a page by page deterioration, but the editor was able to assemble the material so as to make it coherent (see Fig. 8).

Case 2. An artistic, intelligent, but depressive subject aged 36, of psychopathic stock, attempted to commit suicide by means of barbiturates, after slashing his wrists and the left side of his throat. On recovering from his coma, he was found to be aphasic and powerless in his right limbs. The paralysis improved, but the speech impairment continued.

When seen twenty months later he was found to have a severe expressive aphasia, as well as a moderate disorder in the comprehension of printed and written verbal symbols. His undertsanding of spoken speech seemed to be intact. Teaching himself to write a neat italic type of penmanship with his left hand, he found it much easier to express himself by this medium than by way of articulate utterance. He also started to draw. Later still, he began to compose poetry of a contemporary and 'advanced' character, and one at least of these poems, written while he was still grossly aphasic, was published in a literary monthly. When asked why he preferred poetry to prose as a medium for his creative instincts the patient replied to the effect that 'prose was too difficult'.

Figure 9(a) shows one of these poems. At times the patient composed upon a typewriter, as shown in Figure 9(b).

Case 3. A schoolboy, aged 17, was admitted to hospital on account of a dysphasia. Three days before he had suddenly developed a severe headache while playing chess. He continued his game, but with reduced efficiency, and later on he was noticed to be confused and mumbling in his speech. Next morning headache was still present, though milder. He was now unable to name objects shown him, or to recall proper names; he could not tell the time aloud.

In hospital, a mixed type of speech loss was found, together with a right facial weakness. The tendon jerks were asymmetrical, but both plantars were flexor in type.

There was no sensory impairment by tactile inattention. B.P. 140/85. C.s.f. normal, with an initial pressure of 95.

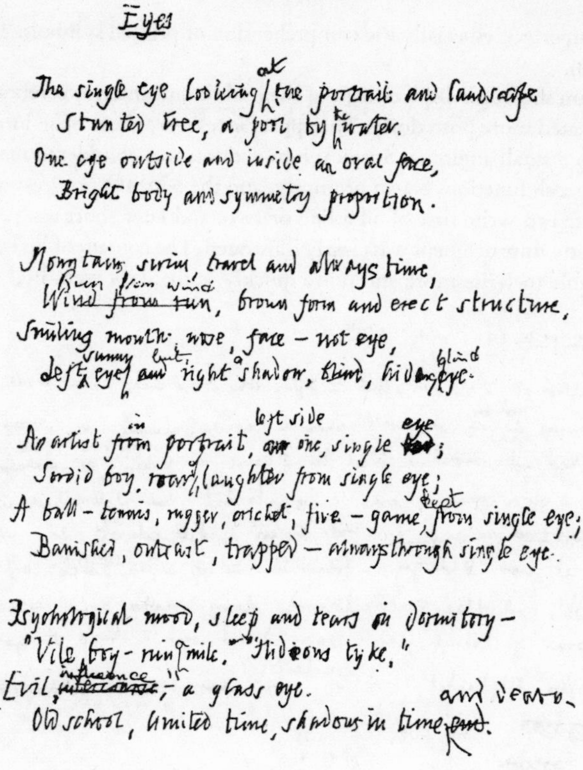

Eyes

The single eye looking at the portrait and landscape
Stunted tree, a pool by the water.
One eye outside and inside an oval face,
Bright body and symmetry proportion.

Mountain, swim, travel and always time,
Wind from sun, brown form and erect structure,
Smiling mouth, woe, face — not eye,
Left eye and right shadow, blind, hidden eye.

An artist from portrait, one one single eye;
Sordid boy roar, laughter from single eye;
A ball — tennis, rugger, cricket, five — game from single eye;
Banished, outcast, trapped — always through single eye.

Psychological mood, sleep and tears in dormitory —
"Vile boy — run smile," "Hideous tyke,"
Evil influence," a glass eye.   and tears.
Old school, limited time, shadows in time end.

(*a*)

To Sleep

                valley
he   the of stalk the azure rose of the twighlight,
Stanly twinin twinkling thousand stars — ars, leades,
Venus — a silent of earth, gallows of night.
Quiet, quiet night f the petals of a flower, open ros

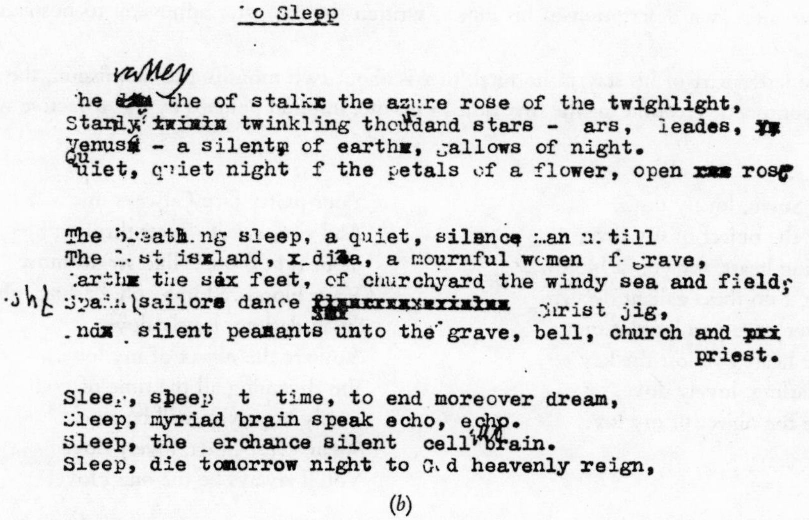

The breathing sleep, a quiet, silence man u till
The last island, india, a mournful women grave,
earth the six feet, of churchyard the windy sea and field
She Spain sailors dance   hrist jig,
  now silent peasants unto the grave, bell, church and pri
                                        priest.

Sleep, sleep t time, to end moreover dream,
Sleep, myriad brain speak echo, echo.
Sleep, the erchance silent cell brain.
Sleep, die tomorrow night to God heavenly reign,

(*b*)

FIG. 9 (*a*) Manuscript of a poem written by an aphasic patient (Case 2).
      (*b*) Poem written directly upon a typewriter (Case 2).

His speech was very imperfect, especially the comprehension of printed symbols. There was a gross degree of dysgraphia (see Fig 10).

A left carotid angiogram showed a displacement of the middle and anterior cerebral vessels together with a vascular abnormality situated more posteriorly. The appearances were those of an intracerebral temporal lobe haematoma secondary to a small angioma. Surgical intervention was considered inadvisable.

Improvement in the speech functions began promptly, and the patient's progress was actively encouraged. Each day he was instructed to write first of all a line or two, and later short essays upon themes of topical interest. In this way a steady improvement was clearly illustrated. The content of his composition even became humorous, and he was able to write more and more quickly as the days went by.

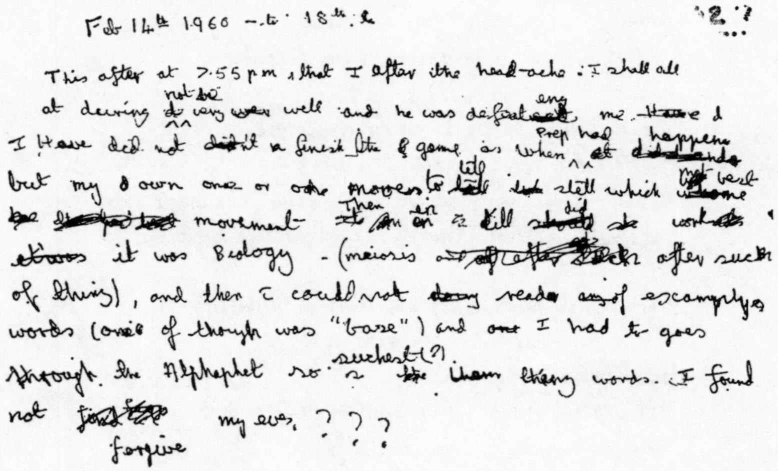

FIG. 10 Patient's own description of his illness, written the day after admission to hospital (Case 3).

During the latter part of his stay in hospital, that is about two months after admission, the patient even embarked upon poetic creation for the first time in his life, inspired perhaps by the attractive ward-maid in attendance.

Darling Susan, lovely dove,
You are the object of my love,
My pining heart, for you it bleeds,
For you, I do these gallant deeds;
But never once you look at me;
Of your heart I've lost the key
Susan darling, lovely dove,
You are the object of my love.

Your pretty face I always miss,
And also, sweet—your thrilling kiss
Your skin is pure, like virgin snow
Your blood-red lips—oh, darling, oh
Susan darling, lovely dove,
You are the object of my love,
I'm dreaming all the time of you
I only hope you will be true,
Susan sweet-heart, lovely dove
You'll always be the one I love.

Case 4. A woman, aged 53, was admitted to hospital unconscious. She was a chronic diabetic, a hypertensive arteriopath and an eccentric. She had been admitted in coma, and on recovery was found to be confused for

The Work in the Vinyard is Heavy But the Labours are few.

———————

```
I was in need of care and attention
So fate, has its way with with a Smile
It sent me to "Kings Collede" for treatment
And it has Been "Worth its While"
They took great ₤interest in my Case
May they Have Succes in all they do
An go on for ever, onward nee and upward
There work is very Sacred
To do the Masters "Will,"
May God Bless thier work for Humanty
The nurses who watch Night and Day
They are doing most Sacred Work for The Master
And Earn the Saviours "Well Done".
```

FIG. 11   Poem written by patient (Case 4) while still in hospital. The incorrect grammar and
spelling is to be noted, as well as the patient's own corrections.

some days, with a moderately severe 'nominal' aphasia. Her blood pressure measured 230/90, and she showed
signs of auricular fibrillation. Electroencephalography demonstrated a focus of abnormality, almost certainly
ischaemic, in the left anterior temporal region.

In hospital the patient steadily improved. She was persuaded to resume her former hobby of writing poems.
Her poetry was crude and immature, and dealt with themes of a pious and sentimental sort. Figure 11 illustrates
a verse which she wrote while convalescent in the hospital.

Case 5. A versatile man of 71 years; an architect-musician, poet and polyglot, was seen on account of a right
hemiplegia. He had been taken ill just a year previously, and since then a slight degree of improvement has
occurred. The distal segments of the right arm and leg were particularly affected. No sensory impairment was
demonstrable and the visual fields were full. The blood pressure measured 190/130. Speech had at one time
been affected, but within a week of the stroke the patient had begun to write with his left hand, and by the
tenth day was, once again, composing poetry of a naïve and facetious kind. The following verse represents one
of his writings after the stroke:

My buoyant nature bids me dance
And sing—though I'm no singer—
But what the hell am I to do
With one sound leg and a 'swinger'?
I cannot look symmetrical,
Intelligent or dapper;
Oh Lordie how I'm handicapped
With one good arm and a 'flapper'.

I would that you could listen to
My normal speech with wonder,
But now, alas, it sounds more like
Those 'ducks that die in thunder'.
As now I have a leg, arm, face
Like timber when the rot comes,
So willingly I offer you
The adjectival lot, chums!

The patient's speech was still imperfectly articulated, but the vocabulary was rich and the syntax correct.

There was some doubt about the nature of this patient's cerebral dominance. Although he proclaimed himself to be a right-handed subject, he had always been in the habit of using the left hand for certain activities
such as sharpening a pencil, using a hammer or a pair of scissors.

Case 6. A musician and orchestral conductor, aged 57, woke at 2 a.m. early in February 1961, unable to speak, or to move his right arm. He dropped off to sleep two hours later, and when he awoke for breakfast there was a mild weakness and dysaesthesia of the right limbs and moderate hesitancy of speech. Three days later another sudden exacerbation occurred, and lasted several hours. Two weeks later he had a third attack, and on 28th February a fourth and more serious episode took place. Two days after that he was admitted to hospital, alert but dysphasic. There was a mild degree of right hemiplegia. The blood pressure measured 200/130. An arteriogram showed no abnormalities. On 10th March the patient composed and orchestrated a piece of music (see Fig. 12a), a task which took him about two hours. The patient left hospital on 3rd April

FIG. 12(*a*) Musical composition which took two hours, i.e. about eight times longer than usual, and the patient was dissatisfied with the end result (Case 6).

1961, improved, though still unable to work. He could not play the piano or write music—although he said ... 'I have the music in me'. On 15th March, 1962 a right-sided focal convulsive seizure occurred lasting thirty minutes. His speech was lost for twelve hours. The degree of hemiplegia increased. On 19th March the patient had yet another attack, after which his arm became weaker still, and his speech worse than ever.

On re-admission to hospital, on 21st May, 1962, he still had a right hemiparesis, a dysphasia and a B.P. of 240/120. A further attempt was made to write a piece of music (with the left hand) (see Fig. 12b).

Ultra-sound examination revealed a definite shift of the falx cerebri to the right. On this account carotid arteriography was repeated and now demonstrated the presence of a left parietal meningioma. At operation, on 22nd June, a tumour the size of an orange was removed *in toto*.

FIG. 12(b) Piano score *Student Prince* 'Deep in my heart' written from memory with left hand (took about 1½ hours).

Following the operation the hemiparesis improved dramatically. The speech returned to normal and with it, the patient regained his ability to compose music (see Fig. 13).

He left hospital on 20th July, 1962.

Case 7. Miss V. A. Savage, speech therapist, very kindly sent me particulars of a patient who had been under her care on account of a severe expressive dysphasia with some defect in comprehension. The subject had been a handyman with a modest educational background. Before his stroke he had much enjoyed reading poetry and during his stage of convalescence it was suggested that he should try his hand at writing verse—though he had never done so before. Without assistance he wrote three little poems, one of them being as follows:

The Sun and the Flowers

All through the day the sun kisses the flowers
from the east and the south
and the west he throws kisses
such passionate kisses
not one flower he misses
larkspur and lupins
roses and lilies
peonies and pansies
wallflowers and gillies
antirrhinums and daisies
and love-lies-a-bleeding
rows of tall hollyhocks
flowering and seeding.

FIG. 13   An original composition. This work was carried out in about an hour (Case 6).

The foregoing seven cases illustrate the emergence of creative execution of prose, verse, musical composition, though at a relatively humble level. In Case 1 a professional politician managed to construct, and to get published, an article upon a subject germane to his political thinking, convictions, and prejudices. The level of argument was adequate, the syntax good and the vocabulary fairly rich, but a comparison of the written text with the final product, as printed, would have revealed how many adjustments had been needed at the editorial level.

The second and third patients both wrote verse at a time when they were still aphasic, and in each case this was a novel venture. The end-product was frankly jejune in Case 3. In Case 2 the effort was more ambitious. There was obviously an indication of emotion deeply felt, though not fully exteriorized. The vague and somewhat amorphous text conformed with the difficulties in communication, but the attempt was sufficiently in line with experimental *avant garde* verse to pass muster and to conceal the underlying aphasia.

The fourth and fifth patients had not been without experience in versification prior to the onset of aphasia; and after the speech impairment had improved, the patients went back to their literary pursuits. It is not possible to say whether there had been any change in the quality of the creative writing after the strokes, but of both patients it can be said that the post-aphasic poetic compositions were of a banal and wholly inferior character, entirely devoid of literary merit. But as Montaigne said: 'We have more poets than judges and interpreters of poetry. It is easier to write an indifferent poem than to understand a good one'.

In the sixth case, an aphasia temporarily produced a high level expressive amusia with a defective ability to compose, write down, and score a piece of music. This paralinguistic faculty improved as the speech defect grew less.

The question may be asked why it is that poetry is so rarely found in patients during or after recovery from an aphasia. The vast differences between the nature of the conventional writings of non-literary individuals, and that of verse, is of course fundamental. As a rule, people utilize written language for such mundane purposes as business correspondence and social or family letter-writing, and for little more. In such circumstances words are employed as counters to express straightforward ideas simply and clearly. The vocabulary entailed is comparatively sparse, syntax is direct, subject-matter is mainly concrete, and reference function obvious.

Poetry is quite different. A far greater vocabulary is called upon, and words may be employed which lie way beyond the range ordinarily in use. Words may crop up which are archaic, literary, and wholly unfamiliar, and yet in a particular context are not only appropriate but even indispensable. Euphony, and what Professor Pear calls 'euphasia', now plays an important role in the choice of terms, for poetry must appeal to the ear even more than to the eye. In order to set off a train of wide-ranging fancies, words may be selected purely for their allusive or evocative qualities. Obliquity of expression is frequent, and unorthodox syntax and unfamiliar tricks of word-order may be used with deliberation. Abstractions may replace concrete phraseology, though at other times concreteness in the form of metonymy, metaphor, or synecdoche may cleverly bypass the pedestrian generalization. The poet may juggle with the arts of alliteration, onomatopœia, rhythm, synaesthesia, harmony, hyperbole, and sound-symboly in order to suit his purpose, and it can be deemed certain that the final product emerges only after much labour and correction.

As W. R. Rodgers wrote: 'Words are tools for thinking. Like tools they can be jugged to a fine point, and are clearly capable of being used with fixed scientific precision. But since our world is one that moves, that exists in time and space and affect, our use of words must also have that moving quality; they must be not only fixed, but fluttering, which is why words have their restless tenses, and a line of poetry has never one meaning but many'. 'I would trust the maker of a dictionary to explain the meaning of one word, but not the meaning of two words', said a friend to Boswell who repeated the happy remark to Dr. Johnson, 'for words, like lovers, have the knack of conception, and left together are prone to forget themselves'.

Regarding prose-writing after an aphasia, we have available the careful study by Alajouanine (1956) upon the topic of artistic realization in cases of disordered self-expression. His series included the case of Ravel whose musical abilities were severely impaired, and also that of a well-known professional writer and stylist. The latter had sustained ten years previously an aphasia which at first was extremely severe being limited to a solitary recurring phrase. Improvement slowly developed but full restitution of function never took place. Creative literary work remained impossible, despite the relative integrity of aesthetic sense, judgement and memory. The permanent disturbance of literary technique was due to a Broca's aphasia, which, according to Alajouanine, . . . 'converted that delicate artist and subtle grammarian into an agrammatist'.

The whole process of *Geistesblitze* or literary inspiration is usually complex and lengthy, even though it varies from one writer to another. Various stylists have tried to explain the complicated gestation period which precedes the birth of their own particular art-forms, e.g. Stephen Spender, James Stephens, Edith Sitwell, Mallarmé, Edgar Allan Poe, Valéry, R. B. M. Nichols. In most instances there has been a prolonged stage of rumination, leading to tentative essays, in turn followed by embellishment; condensation or elaboration; improvement and correction. F. L. Lucas has told us that he could think of no constantly perfect stylist who had not laboured like an emmet. And, as to verse, Oscar Wilde well said '. . . how difficult it is to make the whole feet of poetry dance lightly among flowers without crushing them'.

Accomplished prose-writing occupies a place in literature not far removed from poetry. As to the subject of literary output after an aphasia, the same arguments obtain. Not one of the linguistic techniques of the poet or of the belletrist is within the capacity of an aphasiac. Even in the convalescent stages, or the allegedly recovered aphasiac, it seems doubtful whether the execution of highest level literary and poetic composition can be expected. The cases quoted in this article are exceptions to this dictum only in so far that each of the patients produced in an unexpected fashion, original pieces of writing. But five of the cases can be said to conform, in that the resulting literary creations were of an inferior quality, though the verse executed by the seventh patient was scarcely mediocre in rating.

By way of contrast to the usual experience of a loss of the highest flights of oratory, of literary composition, and of fine writing during and after an aphasia, one may refer to the interesting case reported by Riese (1949).

A very cultured and witty scientist developed Parkinson's disease, for the relief of which he submitted to a left frontal topectomy. Following this operation the patient was speechless for 3 days. Thereafter he regained his power of speech, but in a curious and limited fashion. His wit—so it was claimed—remained intact. Instead of simple statements, the patient now employed long-winded, technical expressions, and a veritable poetical or 'Shakespearean' mode of diction. ('Voluntary silence terminate'. 'Methinks the lady doth protest too much'. 'Scientific ineptitude'. 'Vituperative old man'. 'There but for the grace of God go I'.) Ordinarily the patient spoke very little and when he did, these verbal flamboyancies were articulated with even more monotony than before the operation. This mode of speaking lasted a few months, and then reverted to its former character, though the patient never became as fluent as he was before his operation.

Riese ascribed the peculiar type of speech during the three-month period of the dysphasia to the personality of the patient, his early intellectual training, his career and his personal philosophy. The new style of speech could be deemed a more figurative and more concrete form of thinking and expression. Subsequent pathological study showed that the critical area of speech was not involved, and Riese invoked a selective process of diaschisis.

It is evident that the patient had been actually relying upon verbal automatism and clichés in which an element of uninhibited facetiousness seems to have obtruded itself.

Although the literature of metalanguage has a great deal to say about the nature of poetry, there have been but few contributions of a neuro-psychological character. In striking isolation are the papers of Wilson (1954) and of Moore (1955). No one up to now has discussed fully the relationship of linguistic accomplishment with the phenomenology of aphasia. Wilson's discussion of poetic creativity is particularly rewarding in this connection. He believed that there were certain characteristics underlying the creative poet. His make-up combines strength (both vitality and ego-strength or integrative strength); a capacity for association and integration (of ideas and images—a generosity towards impressions and ability to encompass tensions); sensitivity (discriminant permeability); a desire for form and explication (linguistic facility or infatuation with words); and intelligence. It is in the last two respects that the poet is sensitive to the effects of brain damage, and it is because of these very factors that accomplished poetic writing is so far beyond the range of even the mildest aphasiac.

But with music the problem is different. The subject of the integrity or otherwise of musical ability—creative, executive, or appreciative—in the presence of dysphasia is a complicated one. Aphasia does not necessarily entail an amusia, as Luria, Tsvetkova and Futer have shown (1966). Their paper dealt with the case of Shabalin, composer and Director of the Moscow Conservatoire. Despite a severe dysphasia he continued to compose music and to superintend the work of his pupils. That his creative work was of a very high order is shown by the comment of Shostakovitch: '. . . Shabalin's Fifth Symphony is a brilliant creative work, filled with highest emotions, optimistic and full of life. This symphony, composed during his illness, is a creation of a great master'. Khrennikov too asserted 'We can only envy the brilliant creative activity of this outstanding man, who, in spite of his illness, created the brilliant Fifth Symphony, full of young feelings and wonderful melodies'.

XXII. DISORDERS OF WRITTEN SPEECH

It is obvious that all persons write in their own peculiar way, and that in all private letters everybody uses such characteristic forms as cannot be truly initiated by anybody else.
                                                                                                    Camillo Baldi 1622

The manner of writing can as far as it does not follow that of the schoolmaster, express something of natural temperament.

                                                                                                    Leibniz

Every single stroke of handwriting expresses a whole life.
                                                                                                    Okakura

Writing, or a means of expression, has to compete with talking. The talker need not rely wholly on what he says. He has the help of his mobile face and hands, and of his voice, with its variable pace, whereby he may insinuate fine shades of meaning, qualifying and strengthening at will, and clothing naked words with colour, and making dead words live.
                                                                                                    Max Beerbohm

Human communication fundamentally stems from articulate speech. Men deliberately commune with each other primarily by way of spoken speech but with gestural accompaniments to express emphasis or nuances. Language is therefore a 'living' entity, a flexible and delicate tool which differs from one user to another, and which is always undergoing change. That is to say new words and phrases develop; while novel turns of expression, new pronunciations, and subtle alterations in the meaning or associational context of words are constantly taking place. In this way language is forever subtly altering with the passage of time, as well as from one geographical region to another. Spoken language is consequently to be looked upon as an expression or a hall-mark of personality and of human behaviour.

To the communication theorist, a large amount of human speech is redundant, for conversationa utterances are apt to comprise words and phrases of meagre propositional value, but which serve as a means of securing a propitious bond between one speaker and another. That is, spoken language is commonly composed of long and elaborate phonemic patterns which are endowed with relatively small communicative content, and relatively poor in sematemes.

Ever since *homo sapiens vel loquens* appeared spoken speech, together with pantomime, has been the ordinary mode of expression, surplanting the simpler releaser systems peculiar to the lowlier orders of animal life.

At some considerably later period of prehistory, a few exceptional representatives began to record speech in a more permanent fashion, by devising symbols which should themselves indicate or stand for the commonly accepted verbal symbols. The probable steps in the evolution of a written form of language can be presumed. Doodling in the sand or scratching on rock-surfaces came first, and later led on to simple representational drawings. An interesting elaboration of these prehistoric cave-drawings was the depiction of human hands, and also of vertical strokes, the precise meaning of which is still obscure. Then came a technique of executing in miniature a series of drawings to stand for a connected idea. This art constituted the beginnings of pictograms. In due course the pictograms themselves became modified by dint of elision or simplification so as now to form ideograms. This process of stylization can be well observed in the transition from the antique into the conventional Chinese script. By a further gradual change, ideograms developed into syllabic writing (as in Japanese) where a simple character represents a combination of phonemes including consonants and vowels. An elaboration of syllabic writing is to be found in a language such as Sinhala where a character will perhaps represent a cluster of phonemes. Outside the main stream of development were the purely consonantal forms of graphic representations (e.g. Arabic and Hebrew), where vocalic phonemes were omitted or else were sketchily represented. Lastly came the orthodox Caucasian scripts in which the characters represent either consonants or vowels. A wholly logical alphabet is yet to be found, however, where a symbol stands specifically for a single phoneme with strict uniformity.

To aphasiologists, the important point is the comparatively late development of the act of writing and of interpreting written or printed symbols, and even today the power of manipulating written symbols actually remains a minority accomplishment.

The supreme merit of written as opposed to spoken speech lies in its property of preserving messages. The written word is therefore potentially a permanent record, one which can transcend the limits of time. For various reasons one may expect to encounter a number of differences, syntactic as well as semantic, between written and spoken speech. Written speech is usually found to be terser and more precise. On the whole it is more premeditated than articulate utterance, and indeed the thought which leads up to the act of writing (i.e. the preverbitum) may even become modified during the relatively slow process of expressing the idea on paper. Stricter rules of grammar and style apply to written speech: it is more logical, more polished, and more precise. The vocabulary utilized in writing is usually richer than that employed in spoken speech though exceptions may perhaps be found in the diction of eloquent and practised public speakers.

Hence the important differences which exist between the spoken and the written variants of every language, so that everyone can be regarded as a bilingual. In some instances, e.g. modern Greek and Turkish, the cleavage between the two modalities is considerable, the spoken variety of a tongue being often referred to as its vernacular. Even in English there are striking differences, although the educated individual who utilizes both with facility, may not realize this.

Certain compromise situations occur which occupy a position half-way between the written and the literary languages of a community. In the first place there is the example of popular journalism, which shuns much of the conservatism of the literary language, and descends more into the forum of the speaker. Secondly there is the prose employed by the playwright. This essentially records articulate speech as allegedly emitted from the lips of the actors. But the playwright, skilled though he be, often fails in his role as a simple mouthpiece. We suspect that some plays have been written more for the eye of a reader than for the ear of a play-goer. Even in the writings of so great an exponent as Bernard Shaw we find discrepancies. In a passage taken at random from *Mrs. Warren's Profession* we find the daughter declaiming the following words:

> Then where are our relatives—my father—our family friends? You claim the rights of a mother: the right to call me fool and child; to speak to me as no woman in authority over me at college dare speak to me: to dictate my way of life; and to force on me the acquaintance of a brute whom anyone can see to be the most vicious sort of London man about town. Before I give myself the trouble to resist such claims, I may as well find out whether they have any real existence.

Even allowing for the passage of half a century we cannot seriously accept those stilted phrases as spoken language. What would probably have been said in those particular circumstances, would be more like this:

> Then where are all our relations? Where's my father? And where are the friends of the family? You say that you're my mother and that you're responsible for me and that you've got the right to call me names like 'fool' and 'child'. Nobody at college would dream of talking to me like that, or telling me what I can do and what I can't: and make me go about with a swine who every one knows is the worst type of man about town. Before I go to the trouble of saying I won't, I might as well find out whether your claims are real or not.

An extreme form of vernacular is to be encountered in *dialect*, where differences in pronunciation, word-usage, and perhaps syntax are so great as to render the speech almost incomprehensible to those who are outside this community. Occasionally a dialect like *Schweizer Deutsch* receives some measure of cultural acceptance, and newspapers may be published in a written form of this idiolect. *Provençal* can claim to be something more than a dialect, for it is not confined to a particular geographical region.

Spoken speech possesses certain advantages over written speech as a medium of communication. By dint of various 'superfixes', such as changes in stress, pitch, and timing, and the use of semi-articulate transition-sounds, a wide range of meanings and shades of meaning can modify and amplify spoken speech. These embellishments are not indicated in written speech, though some slight attempts in that direction are made by the judicious use of punctuation marks, and also the more naïve resort to underlining and italics. Communication accordingly loses something of semantic value when it is committed to paper, even though advantages of a different sort occur.

It is tempting to look upon spoken and written speech as occupying two different levels within a linguistic hierarchy. In a Jacksonian sense, the execution and the interpretation of print represents a manipulation of 'symbols of symbols'. The use of articulate speech is, however, a simpler matter, and entails a primary symbol-system. Within the domain of language the one is 'higher' and the other is 'lower'. The superior level would be expected to prove more vulnerable to the influence of disease than the other. Hence in aphasia it might be surmised that written speech would by and large prove to be more seriously impaired than articulate utterance. On the whole, common experience bears out this notion.

That aphasiacs show an associated difficulty in the act of writing was however realized somewhat tardily. Prior to the nineteenth century only a few of the references to loss of speech from disease mentioned difficulties in writing. In 1798 Crichton referred to a man of 70 years whose speech suddenly became incomprehensible though fluent. What this patient wrote was just as faulty as what he spoke. Another early case was that published in 1829 by S. Jackson of Pennsylvania. The patient was suddenly affected with speechlessness, and when he was furnished with pen and paper he merely produced a meaningless scrawl . . . 'Didoes doe the doc'. Another early case was that described by Shapter in 1837. Marcé in 1856 is said to have afforded the first clearcut description. In his lectures on speech published in 1867 Trousseau quoted Lasègue's patient who experienced trouble with writing as well as with articulate utterance.

Hughlings Jackson's first paper on loss of speech, published in 1864, drew attention to the fact that speechless patients are unable to write properly and he gave two remarkable illustrations of disordered writing. (See Figs. 14(a) and (b)). In his later papers, Hughlings Jackson went into the

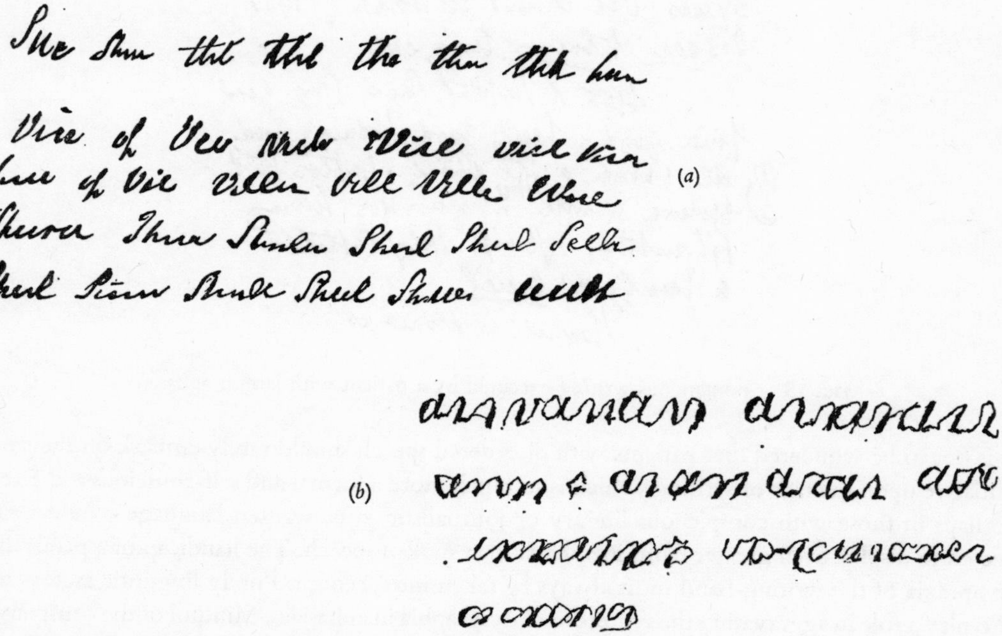

FIG. 14 (*a* and *b*) Two instances of dysgraphia with literal perseveration, as originally published by Hughlings Jackson.

problem more deeply. He utilized this associated disorder to differentiate a loss of speech from a purely articulatory disorder. An aphasiac, he said, might be able to sign his own name, or even to copy, but he could not express his ideas or write to dictation. Written words were, to Jackson, 'symbols of symbols'. We learn to write years after we have acquired words and also after we have acquired marks for these words. Writing is thus 'an acquirement of a double acquirement'.

The term 'agraphia' is usually ascribed to Benedickt (1865) and also to William Ogle who apparently used this same expression independently in 1867. The latter considered that two main types existed, namely the 'atactic' and the 'amnemonic', just as in the case of aphasia. At some later date the word 'dysgraphia' became introduced to connote degrees of writing-disorder short of total incapacity: this term is perhaps gaining in popularity.

Just as most aphasiacs display a certain reluctance to embark upon the act of speaking, so even more rarely do they spontaneously venture to express themselves in writing. This omission contrasts forcibly with the behaviour of a patient with anarthria due to bulbar palsy, who characteristically keeps handy a pencil and writing-pad, and is only too ready to use this means of communication.

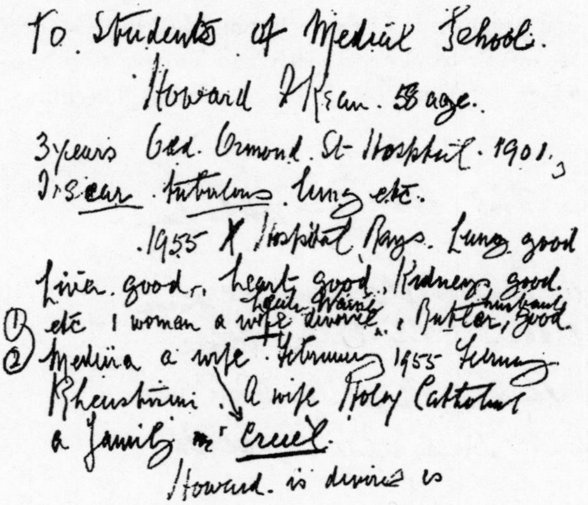

FIG. 15 Spontaneous writing executed by a patient with jargon aphasia.

It is not to be wondered that patients with disordered speech should rarely embark on their own initiative upon the task of writing, which is so much more a formal and self-conscious act. Except perhaps in those with conspicuous literary or journalistic gifts, written language would be expected to display even greater faults in aphasia than spoken speech. The handicap of a paralysis or an apraxia of the writing-hand must always be taken into account. Purely linguistic factors may also play a role in aggravating the symptom of dysgraphia in aphasiacs. Mindful of the conspicuous differences which we have referred to between the vernacular and the literary form of most languages, we realize that the former is considerably more 'automatic', and though poorer in utilized vocabulary, it is a more robust and useful medium of communication. In those tongues where the contrast between the two varieties is unusually great, the pattern of dysphasia is likely to differ widely according to whether articulate or written speech is concerned.

The paucity of spontaneous data in cases of agraphia calls for certain techniques of examination.

The various sources of evidence are not necessarily comparable as psychological tasks, for degrees of difficulty occur. Simplest of all is the signature. This occupies so special a place that its execution is hardly to be reckoned a proof of writing-ability. Many aphasic patients, although grossly crippled as to the ability to express ideas, can write to command their name in recognizable form with all the habitual idiosyncratic flourishes and twirls but it may well be found that the patients are quite incapable of writing anything else. The personal and individual qualities which are attached to the act of signing one's name mean that it is not much more than a motor automatism.

A slightly more difficult act, but still one which occupies a specific and limited place, is the execution of one's address. This task is facilitated if the command is given in the form . . .'write down your *name and address*'.

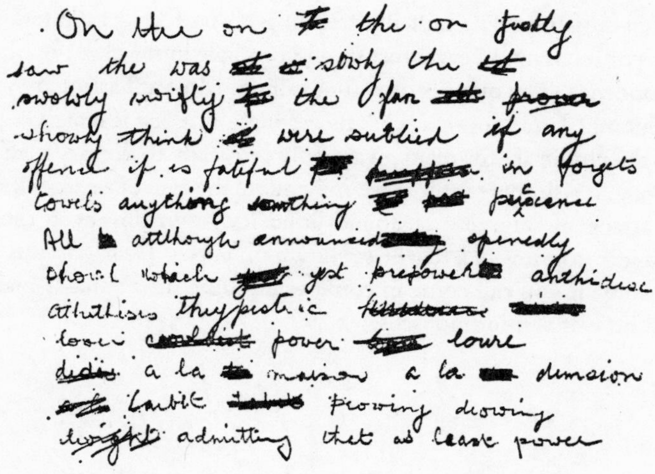

FIG. 16   Aphasic patient's description of his own illness.

Higher in the level of written performance, is the act of writing to dictation. Obviously the performance will depend in part upon the relative difficulty of the test-situation. Thus the speed of dictation, and the linguistic and syntactical nature of the text in question will very much influence the ease and correctness of the performance.

Yet another test of writing is the ability to copy a given text, whether it be printed or in script. Some aphasic patients utterly fail to carry out such a request. To this defect the term 'acopia' has at times been applied. Others succeed, but in diverse ways. For example, one patient may reproduce a text with faithful exactitude delineating precisely every graphic peculiarity of the model before him. Much the same would not be beyond the powers of a European who is asked to copy a paragraph of Chinese, Sinhala or Arabic. Understanding is lacking and the exercise is no more than a fragment of representational drawing. Other patients may be able to go further. Thus they can perhaps copy a piece of writing but in their own individual manner; or they may be able to convert a printed text into cursive writing, or *vice versa*.

Far more important as an index of writing-ability is the act of semi-spontaneous essay-writing. This is done by instructing the aphasic patient to write a few lines, or a paragraph, or a page, upon a set theme. Thus he may be told to pen a few sentences *à propos* of the weather; or a short account of his journey to the consulting room; or the clinical history of the course of his illness. If need be, the patient can be spared the embarrassment of supervision, and he may be left alone to carry out his exercise in his own time. He may be permitted to make as many corrections as he likes, but he should not be allowed to destroy unsatisfactory attempts. It would be useful if the examiner were to time with a stop-watch how long the patient took to write his little composition.

The product is usually a most revealing document and it should constitute an essential part of the test-procedure in every case of aphasia. There is an even more important piece of evidence however, though it is one which is often elusive. The aphasic patient may occasionally be noted to make a truly spontaneous attempt at writing—one which owes nothing to the prompting of the examiner or the test-situation. The best illustration is to be found in letters which the aphasiac writes to his friends or relatives. Every effort should be made in the clinic to obtain examples of an aphasiac's correspondence. The quest is often unavailing. Most aphasiacs are reluctant to write at all. If too dysgraphic, the letter never reaches its destination. Even if it arrives, it may never come to the attention of the physician, for relatives are only too ready to destroy such blatant evidence of linguistic dissolution. As a simple example we may quote the case of a surgeon described by Gee in 1902. During an attack of migraine he found difficulty in writing even though he spoke well enough. Attempting to compose a letter he set down on paper 'Dear you can. Pleae arue you can give to if you can some if you can come in come again some time aphasia again . . .' Here he left off, for he realized he was writing nonsense.

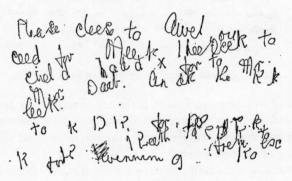

FIG. 17 Dysgraphic writing.

Two or three clinical matters of importance need to be mentioned. The patient whose right hand is often weak or awkward, should be encouraged to write both with the right hand and with the left, and the two specimens of writing should be compared. This is part of the procedure of examination, and questions of therapy are not implied. Secondly the examiner should be chary of testing the aphasiac's ability to write by first requesting him to execute his signature. A successful accomplishment might be followed by a perseveration which will block the execution of subsequent more elaborate pieces of writing. Thirdly an attempt should be made to secure a piece of composition or a letter written by the patient prior to his aphasia. One is thereby enabled to make a comparison of the penmanship and also the linguistic formula of the text.

All these various specimens of aphasic writing must be subjected to a critical analysis, and the diverse faults and errors noted and codified.

In the first place there are certain peculiar features belonging entirely to the category of disordered penmanship. Thus every gradation may be found, from a simple slovenliness to a veritable illegibility. Many of the individual characters of the writing may be retained so that, bad though it be, it is still identifiable as the handiwork of such and such a person. In some more advanced stages of dysgraphia, however, the authorship of the scrawl may no longer be recognizable, except perhaps to a forensic expert. Such items as size of the script (micro- and macrographia); shakiness; inconsistency of morphology; signs of too great or too little pressure upon the pen; exaggerated slope or even reversed direction of slant—all these are to be noted. On the whole the dysgraphic patient tends to write larger than was his pre-morbid practice. Even the alignment of the handwriting upon the paper; the width of the margins; and any deviations from the true horizontal are significant. Another factor, often overlooked, is the matter of speed with which the writing is executed. A previously fluent writer may now display hesitancies before committing pen to paper, and the act of writing may be performed with undue deliberation.

Scientific graphology, as practised in determining the authorship of documents, is rewarding in a study of the dysgraphic script of an aphasiac. Graphologists have up to now largely ignored the evidence of dysgraphia, just as aphasiologists have neglected graphology. If we are correct in believing that handwriting is a highly individual matter, personal, and specific, then the breakdown of this motor skill may well be open to analysis along graphological lines. It must be borne in mind, however, that the specific features of normal handwriting derive from maturity, becoming established only with age and experience. Dysgraphic appearances therefore are perhaps less important, or at any rate they are different, in the case of an educated adult aphasiac as opposed to a patient who is semi-illiterate or who is young in age.

One obvious characteristic of dysgraphic writing is that it almost always has been executed laboriously; hence it will show the hallmark of slow (as opposed to hurried) penmanship. Briefly, these will comprise a lack of smoothness; shakiness of the strokes; accurate placing of diacritics just above the appropriate letters, the dots themselves being circular in shape: an increasing veer towards the left, either with accurate vertical alignment, or with a progressive narrowing of the left-hand margin. The strokes at first are painstakingly executed, but later they tend to be clipped or curled, or they may be missing altogether. Frequently there occurs a change in direction after temporary breaks. Elaborate flourishes may be evident, and one can often detect signs of a subsequent touching-up of the script. The writing as a whole is 'narrow', the vertical components of each letter being greater than the horizontal. Finally one may notice 'breaks', i.e. places in the script where the patient has halted in his act of writing. The pen may, or may not, have been lifted from the paper during such periods of hesitancy. Important evidence of such pauses in the fluent act of expression on paper are constituted by the so-called 'probing dots'.

An unusual peculiarity in the script is sometimes seen whereby there occurs an excess in the number of strokes in an individual letter (e.g. m for n; nn for m; w for u). This may perhaps be regarded as the hallmark of an incipient dysgraphia. It is also sometimes seen in circumstances of intellectual fatigue (see Fig. 18, a–c) as well as in the handwriting of one who is under the influence of alcohol.

Faults in orthography belong to a different order of defect. Spelling mistakes may occur, both simple and bizarre, with omission of letters; literal rotations; or reduplications. Occasionally so complicated an irregularity may occur in the manner of spelling that no true system of defect can be discerned. At a still higher level, are the various grammatical and semantic disorders. Words may be omitted altogether. More often words are repeated, sometimes over and over again. A certain insight on the part of the writer may be displayed by the crossings out of redundant words; usually, however, not all of the graphic iterations are realized and corrected. Occasionally, there occurs a fantastic degree of verbal perseveration, with the same word cluttering up the text so that the underlying meaning is completely obscured.

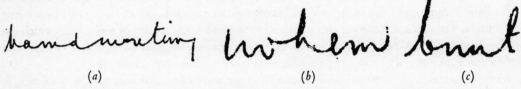

(*a*) (*b*) (*c*)

FIG. 18 (*a*, *b*, and *c*) Perseveration of loops in a condition of pre-dysgraphia.

Of course, it will be a great convenieuce & a treat! — Nice having
the flat all freshly done up — The inside of the front room door is
flush — (you know, quite plain, no ridges — Roy did all theirs at Dale View)
evidently the Houghtons did this one — Mr Sibley has done some of theirs
upstairs, & it is such an improvement — I suggested that the outer
sides of front room & bedroom doors be made likewise — Sid. all in
favour — So, altogether, I shall see quite a difference in the place.
The picture rail in f. room will be an improvement, I think;
it will dispose of the question, for the time being, of family pictures!
Sid. is sending some wallpaper patterns for f. & B. rooms for me to
choose from — (The Postal people are continuing their "work to rule"
& are going to ban overtime — so it will make matters still worse.)
Yesterday was wretchedly dull & wet; it poured with rain when I
went to post just before 12 o'c, at Griggs — & later. I wanted to catch that
collection but waited until then in case Sheila called in — Part of
Eva's fence, up by the Pyrsacanthus tree, has blown down & fallen on
Harrison's side! So I had to let Sheila know — I doubt if Roy can fix it.
Today has been fine & sunny & a nice little breeze. I washed a dust
sheet & some odds & ends, & altho' I didn't use the wringer, by 3.30
all were practically dry — (not hung out until 11.30) — the sun nicely on them.

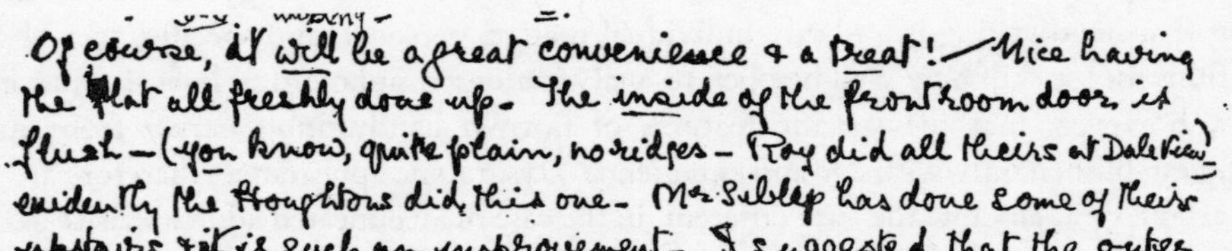

(*a*) before admission.

FIG. 19 (*a*) Progressive deterioration in the spontaneous letter-writing in a woman with a left temporal lobe glioma.

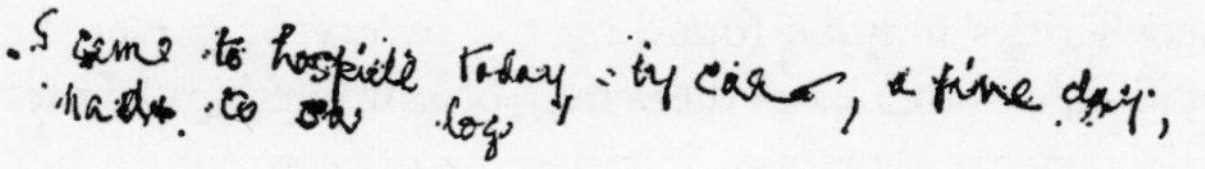

[handwritten letter]

(*b*) 25.4.62.

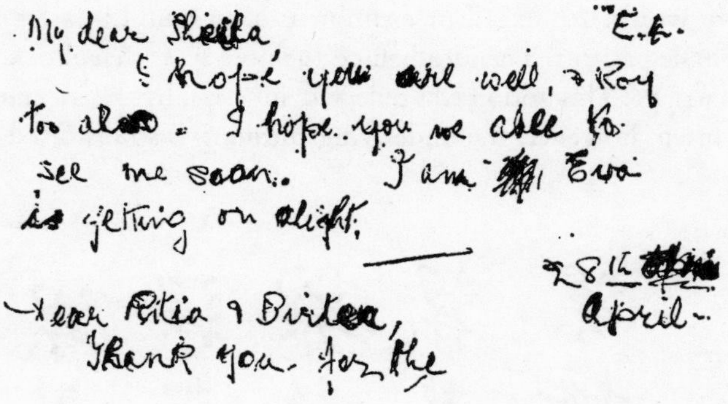

[handwritten letter]

(*c*) 27.4.62.

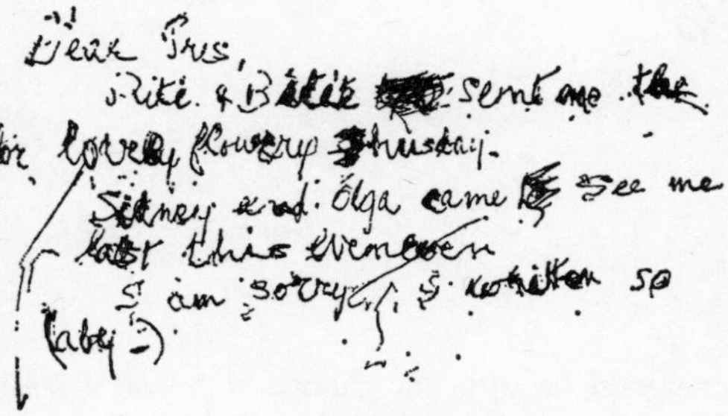

[handwritten letter]

(*d*) 29.4.62.

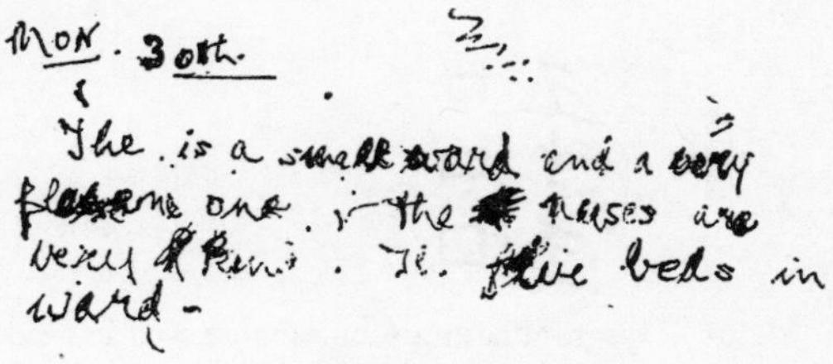

[handwritten letter]

(*e*) 30.4.62.

[handwritten letter]

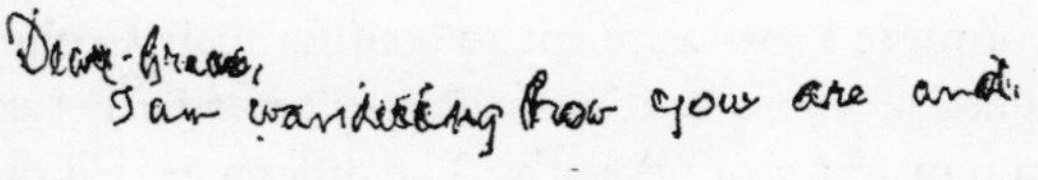

(*f*) 5.5.62.

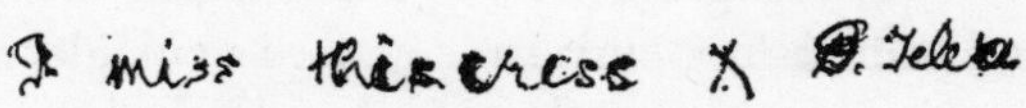

(*g*) 10.5.62.

FIG. 19 (*b–g*) Progressive deterioration in the spontaneous letter-writing in a woman with a left temporal lobe glioma.

Lastly there may be errors which transcend mere slips of orthography and which constitute real paragraphic defects. Meaningless words; wholly inappropriate words; fragments of written gibberish; all such peculiarities may be found by the observant reader. Some of the nonsense-words baffle interpretation; in other cases there may be glimmerings of meaning detectable, as in some contemporary neoteric writings. For instance the concept which lies behind a whole sentence or phrase may become compressed in its written expressive form and constitutes a neologism composed of the head of one word and the tail of another—words which had been linked with the dysphasiac's preverbitum; or else it may be made up of the first or accentuated syllable of a number of successive words. An excellent example can be found in a letter written by one of Foster Kennedy's aphasic patients. The idea behind the note was a telephone message to his wife *à propos* of a friend's marriage. This notion was reflected, in script, by the tricephalic word 'telwimar' (tel-wi-mar). More often, however, the underlying meaning is so distorted as to be elusive.

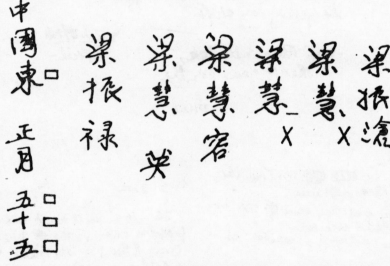

FIG. 20 Dysgraphia in a Chinese due to a left-sided temporal lobe astrocytic glioma. Note that words are missed out at places marked ×, and wrong words are written marked □, and wrong strokes marked —, indicating imperfect recall and recognition. (Courtesy of Gwe Ah Lang and Tan Khang Khoo. Proc. Alumn. Ass. Malaya 1958).

German dysgraphiacs—especially a generation or more ago—were apt to confuse their Gothic and Latin scripts. Luria has described a polyglot aphasiac whose writing in Russian was far better than in French, even though he spoke the latter tongue far more fluently. The difference tied up with the relatively illogical orthography of French as compared with Russian. Dysgraphia, like aphasia, has principally been studied in a few European languages. Some of the Asiatic tongues with their wholly different graphic structure would merit special attention. Thus the few cases of dysgraphia studied among the Japanese have shown a tendency for the *Kanji* or Chinese characters to be involved far less than the indigenous syllabic *Kano* script, probably because the former is far more concrete in nature. Dysgraphia in the Chinese might be expected to entail quite individual problems, for calligraphy is a highly skilled and respected activity among educated Chinese. Each ideogram in Chinese is made up of one or more of eight possible components, namely a dot, a hook, a long vertical stroke, a short horizontal one, and a leftward up-stroke, a rightward up-stroke, a leftward down-stroke and a rightward down-stroke. The precise execution of the strokes, in a fixed order, and accurately in the spatial relationship is a requisite. These specific features of Chinese writing require that particular attention be paid to certain defects in cases of dysgraphia. The literature upon this subject is not great and special mention must be made of papers by Lyman and Hsü, and of the courteous personal communications from Dr. Gwee Ah Leng.

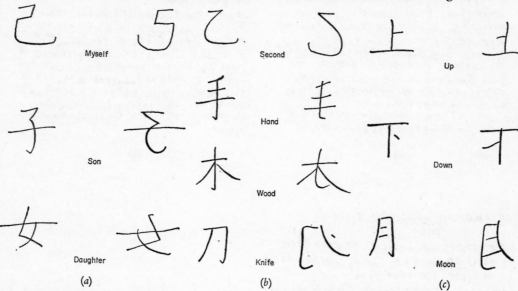

FIG. 21 Mirror-reversal in a Chinese skipper of an ocean-going fishing junk, based on Hong Kong. He was a literate individual with hypertension. Three weeks beforehand he had sustained a transient right-sided hemiparesis. The characters in the right-hand columns were drawn by the patient with his affected hand. On the left are shown the conventional Chinese characters. (Courtesy of Prof. A. J. S. McFadzean).

Among the possible dysgraphic defects in Chinese may be enumerated: (1) omission of component parts; (2) substitution of one symbol for another, involving either a part or the whole of the character; (3) mirror-reversals, complete or incomplete; (4) inaccurate spatial disposition of the constituents of a character; and (5) faulty brush-work (though this might not necessarily indicate a true aphasic disorder of writing). In addition to these rather obvious errors the writer may execute a character in an inaccurate fashion; that is to say, he may make the strokes in the wrong order. The resulting ideogram may appear normal enough, but its manner of construction was wrong.

Chinese dysgraphia may therefore at times be the result of a disorder of spatial thought rather

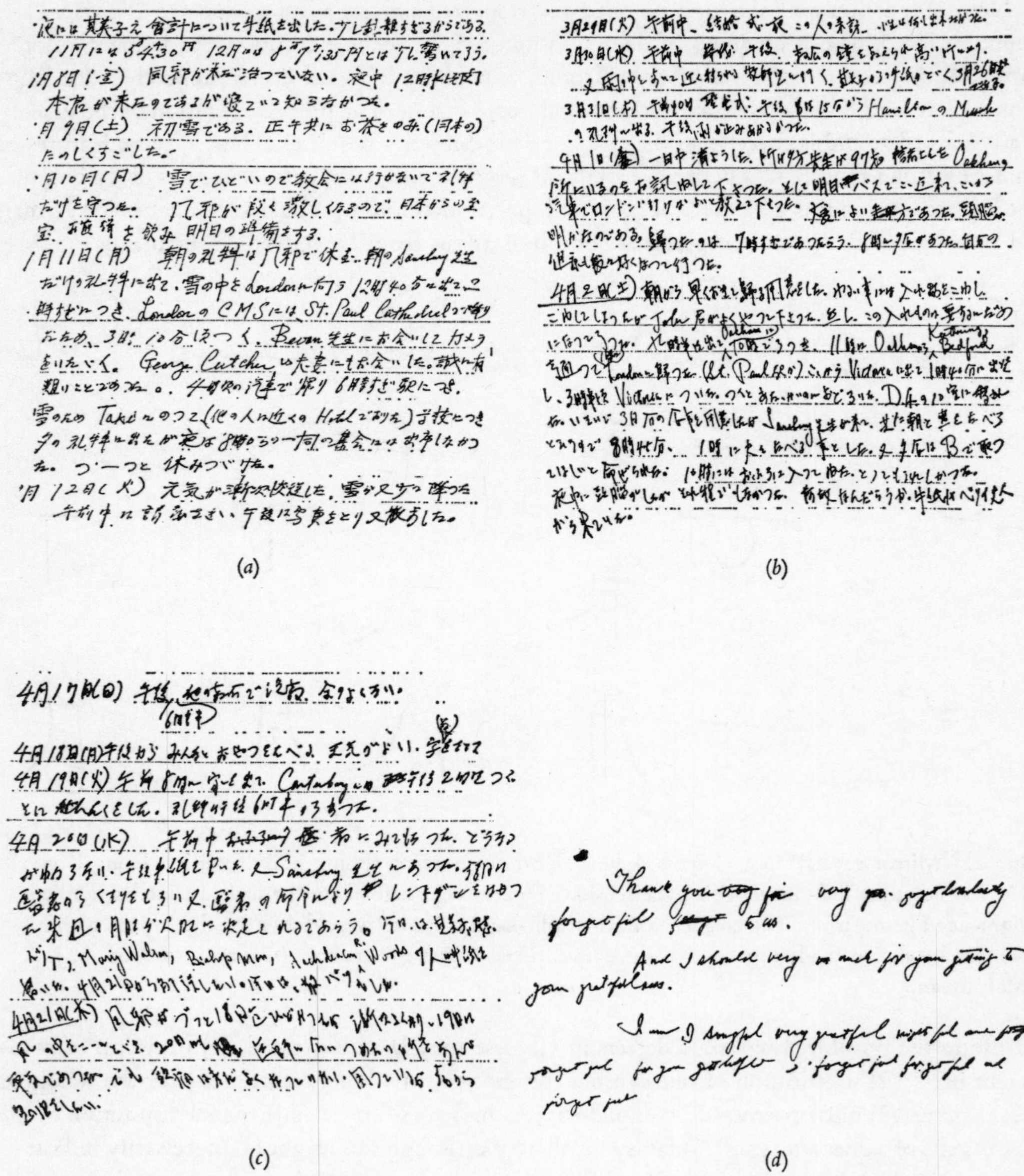

(a)

(b)

(c)

(d)

FIG. 22 (*a*) Progressive dysgraphia as illustrated by the diary of a Japanese professor with a left-sided brain tumour.

(*b* and *c*) Later entries in the patient's diary.

(*d*) Note written by same patient on admission to a London hospital.

than of an impairment of language. That is to say, a constructional apraxia of parietal origin may render it impossible for a Chinese patient to copy or to execute written or printed material, even though there be no aphasia. The responsible lesion may lie either within the dominant or the non-dominant hemisphere.

Something similar, though far less striking, may at times be encountered in cases of parietal disease among non-Chinese individuals. Again, either the dominant or the non-dominant hemisphere may be involved in such circumstances. It is indeed often possible to distinguish a *left* parietal dysgraphia from a *right* parietal dysgraphia, the latter being characterized by gross defects in spatial arrangements, often with an inordinately broad left-hand margin. The so-called 'Gerstmann syndrome' is usually regarded as comprising a dysgraphia without other defects in the realm of language, and has been conventionally correlated with a lesion of the supramarginal gyrus of the dominant half of the brain.

No discussion of dysgraphia would be complete without reference to some of the other instances of pathological writing, which reflect underlying unorthodoxies in thought or language. One of the least bizarre among these is a tendency towards *paligraphia*, or inordinate iteration within written composition. Although common in simple dysgraphia, it may also to some extent show itself in the writings of normal subjects. It may be a deliberate, indeed a studied, trick of literary composition. At a humbler level it may be found in popular journalism, as in the following example:

> They wore beards, they wore bowlers. They wore flat caps and berets. They wore trilbies. Some smiled, some frowned. Some seemed carried away in the pride and sadness of the great occasion. Some hobbled on sticks, and 23 of them were pushed in wheel-chairs.

It may also intrude into romantic writing intended for uncritical audiences. At times it forms part of experimental literary techniques, as in some of the poems of Aragon, or of Peguy. Paligraphia may be particularly evident in the uninhibited scribblings of the insane, especially schizophrenics. The problem of schizophrenic speech and its possible relationship with aphasia is discussed elsewhere. (See Chapter I). Suffice it to mention that inordinate iteration of graphic expression strongly suggests an underlying psychotic thought-disorder. One or two instances have been given in illustration in Chapter I.

Reverting to the problem of disordered writing as part of an aphasia, reference may be made to the rare cases of post-hemiplegic mirror-writing. In most cases the reversals are fragmentary, and as a rule they are executed with the left hand, the patient being dysphasic and paralysed on the right side. Rarely does there occur a consistent and elegant mirror-reversal of letters and words throughout the text. It is probably safe to conclude that the mirror-writing carried out by Leonardo da Vinci in his note-books was not a manifestation of dysphasia, even though there is evidence that he sustained a right hemiplegia towards the end of his life. Similarly, the remarkable example of post-hemiplegic mirror-writing illustrated in Fig. 23 was surely not a manifestation of aphasia, but clinical information about this particular case is lacking.

Reference may also be made to a case of reverse script which, as far as I can trace, is unique. The patient, an elderly arteriopath, had sustained a number of minor cerebro-vascular accidents. A

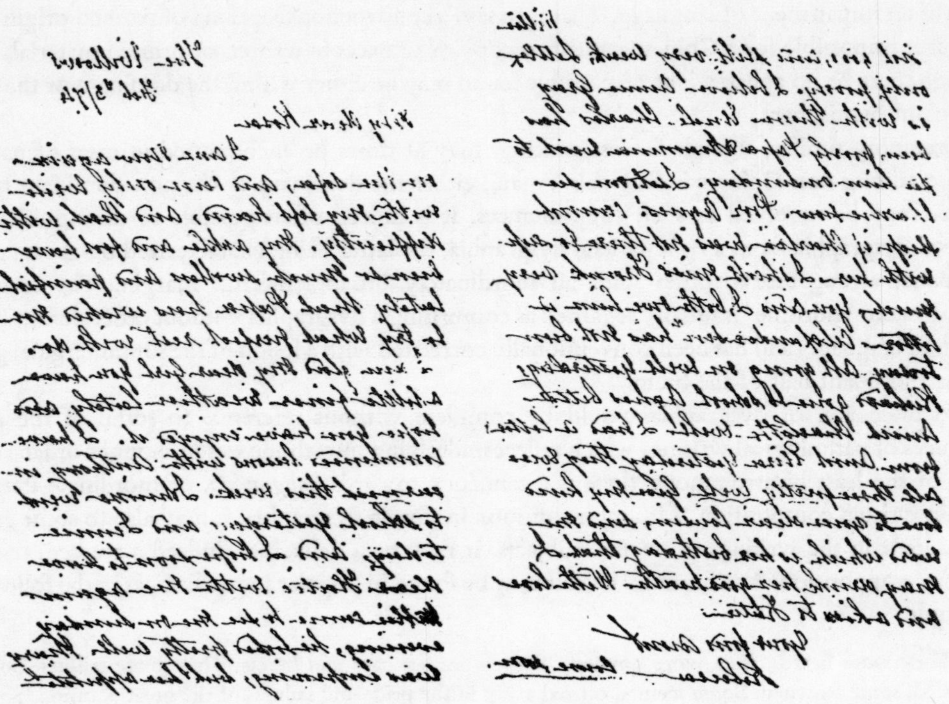

FIG. 23   Example of mirror-writing executed by an old lady suffering from a right hemiplegia (Critchley, *Mirror-writing*, 1928).

transient state of confusion had supervened at a time when she was trying to write a family letter. The result is illustrated below:

20/5/53

My dearest Kiddie and dear Lyrice,
    so you played
golf with the children today
at the C.C. I hope you enjoyed
your game.
    I am sure this holiday from
me will do you good—
the change from Basil and
Noreen certainly will—I
am sorry about Basil. Fancy
him going to Natal looking
for a job. You will have

to help him in the long run.
    He will find it difficult
wife a with job a get to
young that Vicky from returned just Have
us took about you wrote Hazel woman
proud herself does certainly Becky
very beautiful hotel a she lives in
car her pity a such. posh
her & in conked has has
Saturday on her left chauffeur
out drive a got even never We
                    her of

It is noteworthy that the second page of the text is made up of a reversed order of words, devoid of reversals or rotations.

Passing mention may be made of those rare cases of vertical writing (*Senkschrift*) though this peculiarity bears no real relationship with a disorder of language. In the same way the curious phenomenon of inverted writing is a freak occurrence which stems from a disordered visual perception rather than an acquired defect of speech.

From time to time various classifications of dysgraphia have been made, as for example by Ogle, Pitres, Wernicke, Forster, Goldstein, Pick, Henschen, Foix, Kleist, Lehmann-Facins, Nielsen, Victoria, Hrbk, Hécaen, Angelergues and Douzens, Leischner, and many others. It is doubtful whether effort of this kind is rewarding. Clinically an interesting but perhaps rather superficial distinction has at times been made between those aphasiacs who can read and interpret their faulty dysgraphic writings, and those who cannot. Travenec has applied the term 'passive cinaesthesio-lexia' to the latter group.

Finally reference must be made to the disordered writing executed by children and adolescents who are victims of specific dyslexia or congenital word-blindness. Quite inappropriately the term 'developmental dysgraphia' has occasionally been applied here, but without validity. Dysgraphia in the true sense of the word refers to the breakdown of a mature language-faculty. The errors in a dyslexic's writing to dictation or spontaneous composition is mainly a matter of faulty spelling coupled with imperfect execution of individual letters. Semantic and syntactic defects occupy a relatively minor role.

XXIII. TRUE ACQUIRED APHASIA AS OCCURRING IN CHILDHOOD

Thereupon would I flutter with my limbs, and sputter out some words, making some other few signs, like to my wishes, as well as I could; but could not get myself to be understood by them.

St. Augustine, Confessions

The literature upon the subject of speech disorders in childhood is particularly muddled. Manifestations of specific speech retardation, of defective articulation, stammering, dyslalia, the imperfect speech of the deaf or partially deaf, the halting speech performance of the mentally backward, and the loss of speech due to acquired brain disease are apt to be hopelessly confused. Moreover the nomenclature is unsatisfactory, for 'aphasia' when used in paediatrics seems to mean something quite different to the speech therapist than to the neurologist.

This Chapter deals solely with aphasia in the strict and precise sense of the word, that is to say, with a deterioration in language performance as the result of cerebral affections. Here the literature is meagre in the extreme and far from adequate, being descriptive rather than judicial. There is a need for a thoughtful, reasoned, and authoritative study of this interesting though difficult problem. In order not to muddy the waters still more, it would be best to omit altogether those problematical cases labelled 'congenital aphasia', which have been assumed to represent an inborn defect of comprehension or execution—congenital word-blindness, congenital auditory imperception, congenital dyscalculia, and the like. We are still so uncertain as to their precise aetiology that for the time being at any rate they might well be set aside.

There are a number of reasons why aphasia, *sensu strictu*, should be different in the child from that in the adult, not only as to its characters but more particularly as regards its essential nature. Guttmann's paper (1942) served rather to stress the points of similarity, and to gloss over the contrasting features.

Every aphasia represents an affection of the faculty of language, and, therefore, a disorder of thought. The problem of childhood aphasia must therefore entail a discussion of language in the child, and hence, of a child's processes of thinking. The very term 'aphasia in the *child*' is imprecise, for thought and language are vastly different in the second semester than in the first; in the second year of life than in infancy. Indeed during the whole pre-pubertal period, thought and language are faculties which are undergoing steady maturation. If these ever-expanding activities are ablated or disturbed, the resulting manifestation will vary in part according to the age at which the lesion

Based upon a Discussion on Speech Defects in Children, *Proc. Roy. Soc. Med.*, August 1950, **XLIII**, pp. 582–584. (Section of Neurology, pp. 38–40.)

appears. Aphasia in the school-child, in the youngster, in the toddler, and in the infant are problems of quite different nature.

In a child, speech is a new acquisition, and as with most recently evolved faculties, it is sensitive. Like an orchard blighted by a late frost, a child loses its speech easily, and he may show a taciturnity or even a mutism for a variety of reasons. In such cases there may be no focal disease of the brain but only a presumed thinly spread minor cerebral affection. This is exemplified in the poverty of speech in chorea. Speech may be lost even in disorders which do not directly involve the nervous system, e.g. in some febrile and toxi-infective states. But these affections of speech are not to be included among the true aphasias. Though vulnerable, speech in the child is also a highly resilient faculty. Hence a considerable restitution of function is always possible and speech may return to normal with little delay. Even in the aphasias due to focal brain damage, a permanent speech-defect is rare.

In the adult, language bears a relationship to thought which is quite unlike that occurring in early life. That is to say, the 'uses' or 'functions' of speech are not the same in the child as they are in the adult. In the grown-up, speech is largely (though not entirely) a means of conveying ideas and feelings to others. This is not so in the child. The transitive functions requiring the presence of a listener, are less obvious, and a child may talk aloud as a means of self-expression and as a form of play. To the young child speech is a newly acquired toy rather than a familiar instrument over which he has attained mastery. As Fowler Brooks (1939) put it, 'children do not use language chiefly to communicate, or to attain social ends, but to express personal power, to call attention to self-display, to command, request, and contradict'.

The various stages in the development of speech in the infant and young child have already been discussed in Chapter XII. A preliminary period of screaming (indicative of discomfort) leads on to a stage where both discomfort and comfort sounds are emitted. Then comes about a protracted phase of babbling in which the child makes sounds as a form of play. Thus he gains some degree of mastery over his phonetic utterance, and noises begin slowly to attain symbolic value. This is the beginning of baby-talk with its reduplications, its imperfect articulations, its primitive but developing syntax, its tussle with the difficult concept of shift-words, pronouns and generic terms. Gradually as the first two years slip by, the stage of 'little speech' is attained but in steadily evolving nature until around puberty. The evolution is not a smooth or gradual process, for as a child grows, his range of vocabulary from time to time seems to undergo temporary set-backs. Even at this comparatively late stage, 'much of his conversation may still be self-assertive. He asks questions, answers questions, argues, objects to suggestions, agrees to do things, and tells other children what to do or what not to do' (Fowler Brooks).

It must not be thought that these various stages—screaming, babbling, baby-talk—are clear-cut, well-defined levels like the stratifications of a Neapolitan ice. Indeed we know so little about the manifestations as well as the nature of childhood speech that any dogmatic discussion about speech pathology would be rash.

To probe deeper into the growth of speech in the child demands an enquiry into his thinking processes. The beginnings of awareness usher in a sort of autistic regime, which only very slowly, by a process of gradual socialization, leads to a mature type of 'thinking in words'. There is a lengthy intermediate period in which egocentric thought obtains, with a marked predominance of concrete over abstract ideas. Hence we find the vocal expression of these stages of thought in interjectional cries, in egocentric speech and finally in the newly attained adolescent speech, now grammatically and phonetically acceptable. As Vigotsky (1939) said, there is an interesting paradox in the child between the growth of speech and the growth of ideas. With regard to the former there is a progressive expansion in vocabulary; while on the semantic side the child starts from the whole, that is, from a meaningful complex, and only later does he begin to master the separate semantic units and the meaning of separate words. 'The semantic aspect develops from the whole to the particular, from sentence to word; the external aspect however, from the particular to the whole, from word to sentence'.

If then the semantic background of a childhood aphasia is complex, fluid and intangible, we must also admit that the same is true for the provocative lesion. Aphasia may arise in the child from a focal lesion of the brain or from one which is diffuse. The lesion may be static (e.g. embolism), regressive (e.g. trauma), or progressive (e.g. tumour). These are factors which must be taken into account when the resulting aphasia is studied. Focal, non-progressive lesions of the brain are rarely followed by a permanent speech-defect. How often do neurologists see a patient with a congenital or infantile hemiplegia who is also aphasic? The severest and most intractable cases of childhood aphasia are encountered in diseases where the lesion is diffuse rather than focal, progressive rather than stationary. Such conditions include Schilder's encephalitis, the cerebral lipidoses, the dementia praecocissima of Sancte de Sanctis, the juvenile dementia of Weygandt and Heller, and gargoylism. In such cases the dementing child may emit uncouth noises in an uninhibited fashion.

What of the clinical pattern of aphasia in the child? The literature affords but little information. The general impression is that aside from the basic similarities, there are some points of contrast with the adult varieties. The following clinical features distinguish the aphasias in early life:

Logorrhoea, or an uninhibited torrent of speech, is rare.
Jargon-aphasia is uncommon.
Simple *naming-defects*, as in anomia or amnesic aphasia, are not usual.
Dysarthria is common, but differs from that which accompanies aphasia in the adult, by reason of a dyslalia (amounting even to an idioglossia) representing an avoidance of difficult sounds and the substitution of easy ones.
Reduplications of simple sounds are common, as are speech-iterations. These latter may take the form of a word, a phrase, or neologism.
Syntactical defects are common, leading to a telegrammatic economy of speech—the 'para-grammar' of Fröschels.

It might be submitted quite tentatively that in children with aphasia there occurs something which approximates to Jackson's dissolution of a cerebral function, in a way which is less demonstrable in the adult. A recent faculty, still at a relatively simple stage, is disintegrating, and in so doing tends to slip down some of the steps which it has but lately ascended. This cannot be said of the adult with aphasia. But in a child we find a reversion to the syllabic reduplications of an earlier age, an off-loading of the more difficult and recent phonetic accomplishments, and an upset in grammar with a return to the almost exclusive use of nouns.

The typical impermanence of aphasia in the child, which has already been referred to, is witnessed in the rarity of speech-disorder in youngsters with a right-sided hemiparesis, even when it is clear from the clinical history that the lesion has dated from some time after the acquisition of speech. This resiliency extends well into the second or third decades of life, as evidence by the transient nature of the dysphasia in adolescents and young adults. Available data to support this contention are none too common however, and one turns to the evidence of spontaneous writings in default of recordings of articulate speech. One important contribution to the literature is to be found in the study by Elvin and Oldfield (1951) of the convalescent stages of a university student who had for a time lost his speech from a war wound. The head injury occurred when the patient was 23 years of age, namely in September 1944, and a right hemiplegia followed which lasted about 3 months, together with a complete and persisting right hemianopia. A year after being wounded the convalescent patient entered Oxford where he remained for 7 terms and was eventually placed in the second class of his honours examination. The authors made an interesting

TABLE 5 PROPORTIONAL ERRORS IN A SERIES OF ESSAYS

	Essay No. 1 October 1945	Essay No. 2 January 1946	Essay No. 3 May 1946	Essay No. 4 June 1946	Essay No. 5 October 1946	Essay No. 6 December 1946	Essay No. 7 January 1947	Essay No. 8 February 1947	Essay No. 9 January 1948	Total
Number of Words	1380	1495	2100	2200	2114	1605	1605	2537	1500	
Wrong Preposition	72	34	10	23	10	13	0	20	7	189
Ambiguous relation of Preposition	7	7	0	0	0	0	0	4	0	18
Number of Verb or pronoun wrong	22	7	0	18	24	6	13	20	14	124
Wrong tense of verb	7	7	0	0	0	6	6	0	0	26
Wrong form of verb	29	7	10	0	5	6	6	12	0	75
Wrong verb	7	7	10	0	14	6	25	8	7	84
Neologism	0	13	0	0	0	0	0	0	0	13
Omission of verb group	7	0	10	5	0	6	6	4	0	38
Minor omissions	22	0	5	14	18	6	0	20	0	85
Repetitions	7	7	5	0	5	6	0	0	0	30
Shift of grammatical form of idiom	—	13	0	5	5	6	13	8	0	50
Awkward expression making meaning indeterminate	72	67	19	9	10	6	0	4	14	201
Spelling errors	80	60	38	32	10	0	25	20	7	272
Totals	332	229	107	106	101	67	94	120	49	1205

Reproduced from *J. Neurol. Neurosurg. Psychiat.* 1951, **14 (n.s.)** 118. By permission of the authors and publisher.

19

analysis of the patient's written material, based upon two letters written 3 months after the trauma; 8 essays written between 13 and 31 months after the injury; two trial examination papers; and an essay written 6 months after he had taken his degree—that is 40 months after he had been wounded. These data were compared with an essay written in his last school-term, that is before he joined the army.

A linguistic analysis of the errors contained in 9 of these post-traumatic essays is shown in Table 5. (Essay No. 1 was written 13 months after the patient had been wounded, and No. 9, 40 months afterwards.) In Table 6 a comparative syntactical study of the patient's first and eighth essays is set out.

TABLE 6
VARIETY OF WORDS USED IN ESSAYS 1 (OCTOBER, 1945) AND 8 (FEBRUARY, 1947)

Part of speech	Essay No. 1 No. of different words	%	Essay No. 8 No. of different words	%	Absolute increase	%
Articles	3	—	3	—	0	0
Prepositions	19	5	22	4	3	16
Pronouns	11	3	15	3	4	36
Nouns (proper)	25	7	43	7	18	72
Nouns (common)	115	31	197	32	82	71
Verbs	70	19	95	16	25	36
Adjectives	77	21	160	25	83	108
Adverbs	33	9	52	9	19	58
Conjunctions	12	3	24	4	12	100
Total	365		611		246	67

Reproduced from *J. Neurol. Neurosurg. Psychiat.* 1951. **14 (n.s.)**,118. By permission of the authors and publisher.

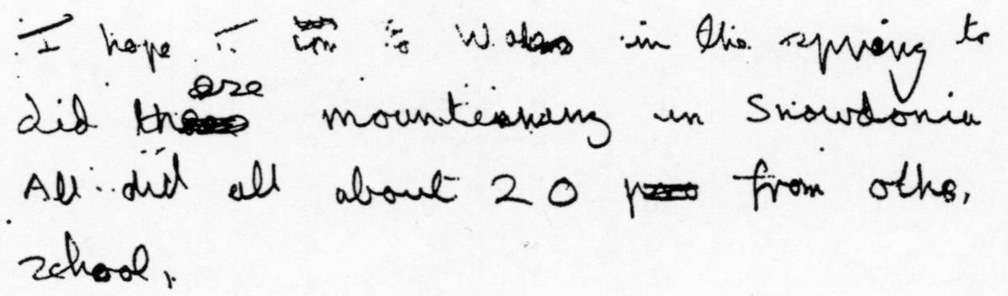

(a)

I hope I am to Wales in the sprĕng to did the̶s̶e̶ ere mountenning in Snowdonia

All did about 20 p̶r̶o̶ from other school

J. F. 19. 2. 60 .

(b)

FIG. 24

There was a 67 per cent augmentation in vocabulary, nouns and adjectives showing the greatest absolute and percentage increase. The relative parts of speech remained remarkably constant. Verbal repetitions decreased as well as the earlier tendency towards the use of vague, general, 'omnibus' terms. Conjunctions doubled in number over a period of 18 months, but for quite a lengthy period, prepositions tended to be incorrectly employed.

Further linguistic and semantic studies along these lines are sorely needed in aphasiological research, and a comparison of the rate of progress according to the age of the patient would be of particular interest.

In this connection the case may be quoted of a schoolboy of 17 years, who has been already referred to on pages 252–255. A sudden headache was followed by a mixed type of dysphasia and proved to be due to a spontaneous bleeding from a left-sided intracerebral angoma. The

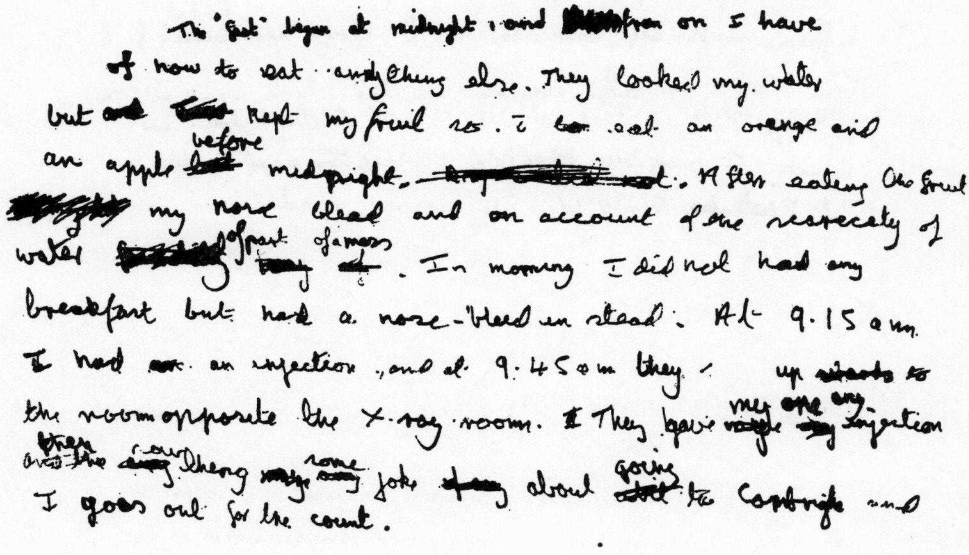

(a)

The "fast" begun at midnight, and ~~hhhh~~ from on I haveof now to eat anything else., They looked my water but ~~and few~~ kept my fruit so I ~~ee~~ eat an orange and an apple ~~but~~ midnight.
                                                                                                    before
~~Any did not.~~ After eating the fruit ~~Anyny~~ my nose blead and on account of the scarecety of
                    ed of part of a mess.
water ~~Anyny~~ ~~my of~~   In morning I did not had any breakfast but had a nose-bleed

in stead. At 9.15 a. m I had an injection, and at 9. 45 a m they.   up wards to the room opposite
                                          my one any   then   now   some   .   going
the X-ray room. ~~I~~ They gave ~~my~~ ~~any~~ injection ~~and the any~~ thing ~~Anyny~~ joke ~~Anyny~~ about ~~robit~~

to Cambridge and I goes out for the count.

J.F. 23.2.60

(b)

FIG. 25

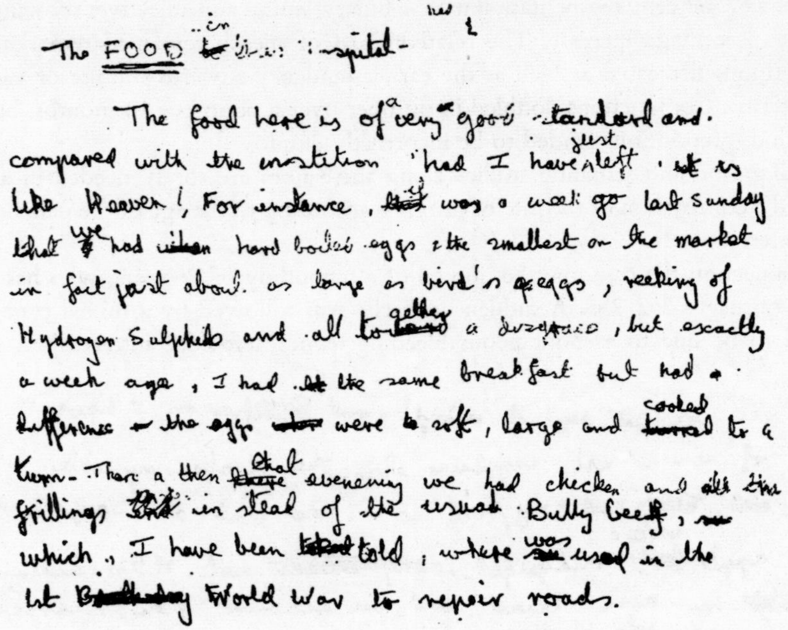

The FOOD ~~to this hospital~~ *in* ~~hospital~~

The food here is of very good ~~standard and~~ compared with the ~~institution~~ had I have *just* left, it is like Heaven! For instance, ~~this~~ was a week go last Sunday that ~~I~~ *we* had ~~when~~ hard boiled eggs & the smallest on the market in fact just about as large as bird's ~~a~~ eggs, reeking of Hydrogen Sulphide and all to~~gether~~ a disgrace, but exactly a week ago, I had ~~th~~ the same breakfast but had a difference - the eggs ~~too~~ were to soft, large and ~~turned~~ *cooked* to a turn. There a then ~~there~~ *that* evening we had chicken and ~~all the~~ frillings ~~that~~ in stead of the usual Bully beef, ~~or~~ which, I have been ~~told~~ told, where ~~was~~ used in the 1st ~~Birthday~~ World War to repair roads.

(a)

has

in
The FOOD ~~to~~ this Hospital.   i

                    a a
The food here is of very good standard and. compared with the instition
    just   *it*
had I have left, it is like Heaven!   For instance, ~~this~~ was a week go last
        we   *hard*
Sunday that~~I~~ had ~~when~~ boiled eggs, the smallest on the market in fact just
                                                    gether
about as large as bird's ~~a~~ eggs, reeking of Hydrogen Sulphide and all to~~ward~~

a disgrace, but exactly a week ago, I had ~~th~~ the same breakfast but had a
                                        cooked
lufference - the eggs ~~where~~ were ~~ta~~ soft, large and ~~turned~~ to a turn.
        that   *was*
There a then ~~there~~ evenening we had chicken and all the frillings ~~that~~ in stead
                                                            was
of the usuah Bully beed, ~~or~~ which, I have been ~~telled~~ told, where ~~eu~~ used

in the 1st ~~Birthday~~ World War to repair roads.

                                        J.F. 26-2-60.
(b)

FIG. 26

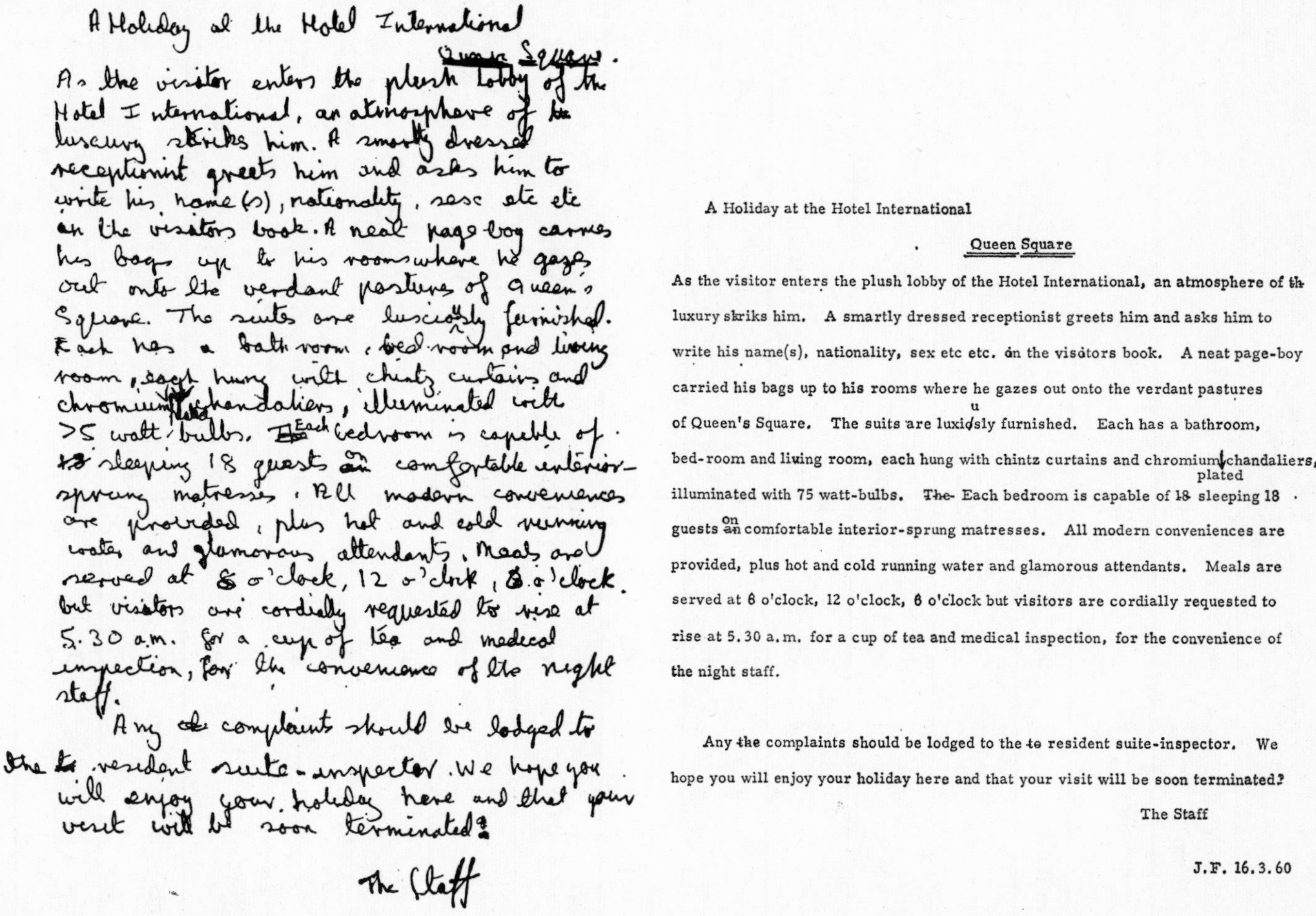

A Holiday at the Hotel International
Queen Square.

As the visitor enters the plush lobby of the Hotel International, an atmosphere of luxury strikes him. A smartly dressed receptionist greets him and asks him to write his name(s), nationality, sesc etc etc on the visitors book. A neat page-boy carries his bags up to his rooms where he gazes out onto the verdant pastures of Queen's Square. The suites are lusciously furnished. Each has a bath-room, bed-room and living room, each hung with chintz curtains and chromium chandaliers, illuminated with 75 watt-bulbs. Each bedroom is capable of sleeping 18 guests on comfortable interior-sprung matresses. All modern conveniences are provided, plus hot and cold running water and glamorous attendants. Meals are served at 8 o'clock, 12 o'clock, 8 o'clock. but visitors are cordially requested to rise at 5.30 a.m. for a cup of tea and medical inspection, for the convenience of the night staff.

Any complaint should be lodged to the resident suite-inspector. We hope you will enjoy your holiday here and that your visit will be soon terminated.

The Staff

(a)

A Holiday at the Hotel International

Queen Square

As the visitor enters the plush lobby of the Hotel International, an atmosphere of ~~th~~ luxury skriks him. A smartly dressed receptionist greets him and asks him to write his name(s), nationality, sex etc etc. on the visotors book. A neat page-boy carried his bags up to his rooms where he gazes out onto the verdant pastures of Queen's Square. The suits are luxi(u)sly furnished. Each has a bathroom, bed-room and living room, each hung with chintz curtains and chromium (plated) chandaliers, illuminated with 75 watt-bulbs. ~~The~~ Each bedroom is capable of ~~18~~ sleeping 18 guests ~~an~~ (on) comfortable interior-sprung matresses. All modern conveniences are provided, plus hot and cold running water and glamorous attendants. Meals are served at 6 o'clock, 12 o'clock, 6 o'clock but visitors are cordially requested to rise at 5.30 a.m. for a cup of tea and medical inspection, for the convenience of the night staff.

Any ~~the~~ complaints should be lodged to the ~~to~~ resident suite-inspector. We hope you will enjoy your holiday here and that your visit will be soon terminated?

The Staff

J.F. 16.3.60

(b)

FIG. 27

TABLE 7 (PERCENTAGES ARE TAKEN FROM THE TOKENS)

	Essay No. 1 6th day	Essay No. 2 10th Day	Essay No. 3 13th day	Essay No. 4 34th day
Total no. of words inc. erasures (*Tokens*)	25	140	143	188
No. of different words. (*Types*)	18	63	79	120
Type/Token Ratio	0·72	0·45	0·55	0·65
Nouns	7 28%	33 23·6%	31 21·6%	48 27·2%
Verbs	4 16%	15 10·7%	22 15·4%	28 14·9%
Pronouns	2 8%	12 8·7%	19 13·2%	14 7·3%
Adjectives	1 4%	2 1·43%	19 13·2%	21 11·2%
Adverbs	1 4%	11 8%	19 13·2%	3 1·6%
Prepositions	4 16%	18 13%	7 4·8%	24 13·6%
Articles	1 4%	11 8%	16 11·2%	17 9·0%
Conjunctions	—	7 5%	7 4·8%	5 2·6%
Erasures	2 8%	23 16·4%	16 11·2%	6 3·2%
Partial erasures	1 4%	1 0·7%	1 0·7%	—
Mis-spellings	4 16%	9 6·3%	3 2·1%	3 1·6%
Paragraphias	3 12%	—	—	—
Omissions	1 4%	8 5·6%	—	—

speech-impairment rapidly improved, his progress being clearly shown by his spontaneous writings. The patient was instructed to compose each day a short essay upon any topic he chose. At first his efforts showed extraordinary defects. The execution was slow and laboured, and the products were full of errors, words being omitted, misspelt, reiterated inordinately, and often replaced by neographisms. But improvement set in steadily, and many of his later essays were humorous, even witty. The compositions are illustrated in Figs. 24 to 27.

In Table 7, four of the essays are analysed according to the syntactical and linguistic properties. The increase in length of the compositions is shown as well as in the size of the vocabulary. The proportion of nouns and verbs remained fairly constant. Erasures, mis-spellings and omissions decreased. Verbal contamination and iterations were not conspicuous in any of the essays. Unfortunately the factor of speed of writing was not recorded in this patient's writing (nor was it in the Elvin-Oldfield case).

XXIV. TESTAMENTARY CAPACITY IN APHASIA

'My father lost the power of speech shortly before he died, and it was plain that he sought with all his might to tell me something. A year after his death I called up his phantom from the grave so that I might learn what I took to be a dying wish. The circumstances of the apparition are so similar to those I have just told you that it would only bore you if I repeated them. The only difference was that my father actually spoke.'
   'What did he say?' asked Susie.
   'He said solemnly: "Buy Ashantis, they are bound to go up."'

Somerset Maugham The Magician

There is an aphasiological problem in legal medicine which knocks importunately at the doors of clinical practice, cutting right through the tangled undergrowth of metaphysical and psychological argument, for it brings the neurologists right into the open forum of the jurist. Here meet the two disciplines of law and medicine. Whether communication be achieved or not depends in part upon the neurologist's sympathetic understanding of the problem.

The question in short concerns the testamentary competency of a dysphasic subject. At any moment, a neurologist may be confronted with this medico-legal *quodlibet* and even be required to declare and substantiate his opinions in a court of law. In such circumstances, it might transpire that a conflict of attitude develops between the neurological conception of what lies within the intellectual compass of a particular dysphasiac and the accepted prejudices of the lawyer. On the whole, the attorney inclines to take an over-simple view by merely ignoring the clinical difficulties.

The literature of both the law and neurology proves to be surprisingly unhelpful. The classic medical papers on this subject by du Saulle, Bramwell, and Edmunds were published between sixty and seventy years ago. My own earlier study dates from 1938. The contributions of Eliasberg are interesting but unconvincing. There has since been such progress in the study of aphasia, and there is so much more realization as to the complexities of the problem that the early papers can serve merely as signposts. We are now aware that disorder of speech is usually not an isolated feature but one which may be accompanied by a considerable change in mentality or behaviour. But for all our modern ideas, the practical problem of assessing an aphasiac's fitness to make a valid will is none the easier. We may bear in mind, however, that the appraisal of testamentary capacity is more likely to yield to a common-sense line of enquiry than to undue excursions into the philosophy of the schoolmen. This particular medico-legal problem is actually a duplex one. First, there is the question of *the validity of a will which has already been drawn up*. The aphasiac may die and leave a will which had been executed during his period of illness; the will may be contested, and

Based upon the Wartenberg Lecture delivered at the thirteenth annual meeting of the American Academy of Neurology, Detroit, 29th April, 1961, and published in *Neurology* 1961. **XI**, 749–754.

the neurologist may then be consulted as to the state of the man's mind at the time in question. The second problem arises *when an aphasic patient wishes to draw up a will or to add a codicil*. The doctor may then be asked whether his patient really is capable of intelligently advising or executing the drawing up of a will. In the former case, the will is produced as a *fait accompli* and nothing may have been known of its execution during the patient's lifetime. The neurologist may have only his notes and his recollections to support his opinions as to testamentary ability. In the latter case, the neurologist may have ample time to observe the mental state of his patient, with opportunities of obtaining second or third opinions in consultation. Moreover, he can ensure that he is present at the time of the signature to determine that the patient really does understand the precise nature of the testament and at that particular moment of time.

In either case, the neurologist may be called upon to uphold his viewpoint before a jury and to be subjected to cross-examination. Unwittingly, he may find himself in court not so much as a detached expert witness but almost a protagonist, taking an all-important part in supporting either plaintiff or defendant, and he might be set up counter to a neurologist on the other side of the dispute.

The question of capacity ultimately turns upon the integrity of the patient's mental state at the time of the signing of the will. The neurologist is confronted with the all too familiar question of whether aphasia *per se* entails an important detriment to a patient's cerebration, hindering intellectual operations to a significant degree. One does not need to stress the difficulties of carrying out reliable non-verbal intelligence tests. No two cases of aphasia are exactly alike, and the proportion of available to unavailable language ties up with the nature and quality of the patient's thinking. Certainly, in many cases of speech-defect, there does exist a definite affection of the general intellectual status, as well as obvious modifications in the total behaviour. In such, not only is there an impaired comprehension on the part of the patient of what he hears or what he sees before him in writing, but judgement, recollection, calculation, insight, and abstract thought are also severely deranged. There really occurs a minor dementia, in other words, and such patients are surely quite incapable of making a will.

It is often argued, however, that not all aphasiacs necessarily suffer a disorder of the internal process of thinking. There is available the evidence of those who have recovered from their aphasia and can recall in retrospect their state of mind when speech was still impaired. As already described, Dr. Samuel Johnson, when afflicted with aphasia, tested his sanity by composing and offering up a prayer in Latin verse. One of Foster Kennedy's patients, an eminent American statesman, was able to carry out his duties for half an hour after his stroke, thinking clearly about various topics, unaware of any mental disturbance; only later, when attempting to speak, did he discover his aphasia. Russell Brain's patient, a solicitor of 78 years, with paraphasia and syntactic and nominal defects, was nevertheless able to comprehend abstract legal questions put to him concerning the nature of a contract. Despite the welter of muddled phraseology, it was obvious that he was giving the correct replies. At one time, it would have been said that the aphasiacs who were most likely to preserve intact their processes of thought were those with a purely 'motor' or 'expressive' defect (with seemingly full appreciation of spoken and written speech) and especially those with 'amnestic aphasia' (where the main difficulty lies in naming persons or objects). Such patients are often regarded as capable of making a valid will. But the antinomy of 'motor' and 'sensory' types of aphasia has worn a little thin, thus adding to the present difficulties of coming to a medico-legal opinion.

Among the older aphasiologists, F. Bateman (1890) devoted a chapter in his monograph to this forensic problem. He quoted the case reported by Billod of a man who, despite an aphasia, continued to serve as mayor and municipal councillor with apparent efficiency. He used his left hand for the purpose of writing, and, while still aphasic, he drew up a holograph will which was subsequently upheld in a court of law. J. Collins, writing in 1898, answered the question on the basis of his classification of the aphasias into 'cortical' and 'sub-cortical' types. In his opinion patients belonging to the former category are ordinarily not capable of will-making, while those in the latter class, that is, of 'sub-cortical' aphasia, usually are capable of indulging in civil transactions. In the same year, Bastian, mindful of the difficulties of this problem, contented himself by merely enumerating types of cases in which the patient could not be expected to make a valid will. These comprised (1) cases of complete aphasia and agraphia; (2) cases in which complete word-deafness and word-blindness coexist; and (3) cases of 'total aphasia'. On the other hand, will-making might present no particular difficulty to patients with anarthria, 'aphemia', or 'pure word-blindness'.

Nowadays, these classifications and terminologies are virtually meaningless, and, in recognizing the complexities which underlie what would seem to be straightforward, we have actually increased our own difficulties.

In assessing testamentary capacity, one of the first tasks is to determine to what extent the patient understands printed and spoken language. The ability to say 'yes' and 'no' correctly is important but not crucial. An aphasiac need not necessarily be debarred from making a will when unable to say 'yes' or 'no', or when he says one of these while meaning the other. Much more important in such aphasic subjects is the ability to communicate by means of clear and unequivocal gestures. The patient may articulate 'no' when he means 'yes', but his vigorous nodding of the head should leave no doubt as to what he really desires to imply. Many aphasic patients can make intelligible signs and can themselves understand movements of gesture and pantomime, even though this particular type of nonverbal communication cannot be said to be wholly intact. In other words, restriction of vocabulary does not of itself preclude the patient from making a will.

What used to be called 'mixed sensori-motor' types of aphasia are the ones most likely to interfere with testamentary capacity. Those varieties in which the patient obviously does not understand what he hears and in which the speech has assumed the characters of 'jargon-aphasia' almost certainly debar the patient from making a will. One type of so-called sensory aphasia exists, however, in which testamentary capacity may possibly be intact, namely, the allegedly pure cases of alexia (word-blindness). Although the existence of any such type is nowadays regarded with some scepticism, neurologists will agree that a difficulty in comprehending written or printed matter can at times dominate the clinical picture. It is in just such a case that disturbance of mentation is minimal. Foster Kennedy and Alexander Wolf reported the case of an advocate who showed so little in the way of intellectual defect that he was able to plead a case in court eloquently, and yet he proved afterwards to have been alexic at the time. An older observation is that of the distinguished Dean of the Medical Faculty at Montpellier, Professor Lordat, who, on recovering from an alexic type of aphasia, wrote concerning his mental state, '. . . I did not experience any difficulty in the exercise of thought. Accustomed for so many years to literary studies, I congratulated myself on being able to arrange in my head the principal propositions of a lecture and on not finding any undue trouble in the alterations which I chose to introduce in the order of my ideas. The memory of events, principles, dogmas, abstract conceptions was as it had been during health'.

Just how convincing is the Professor's appraisal of his mentation is, I submit, open to doubt. I believe that autobiographical accounts of mental operations made in retrospect by recovered aphasiacs are not altogether reliable. Hindsight does not necessarily signify insight. The factors of unawareness of disability, or denial thereof, are subtle ever-present mechanisms. Like the notoriously fleeting memory of physical pain, the recognition of past confusion is imperfect. Organic repression of the nature and intensity of cerebral defect is both powerful and enduring.

When the will has already been made

The neurologist must realize that the law usually takes the attitude that the very existence of a testament is an important argument in itself, one where the burden of disproof is the responsibility of the plaintiff who challenges its validity. The document is assumed to be in order unless proved to the contrary. The existence of a testament implies that the testator knew at the time that he was making a will, that he was aware of the nature and extent of his property, and that he was cognisant of the natural recipients of his bounty. These were the propositions laid down in 1870 by Lord Chief Justice Cockburn. As Usden said in his valuable paper on *The Physician and Testamentary Capacity*, 'he should be prepared to accept the fact that all too often the courts neglect reputable medical testimony when it is contradictory to non-medical testimony. Case after case can be found where the court has paid absolutely no attention to the opinions of the experts because the behaviour of the testator as detailed by law witnesses pointed in the opposite direction'.

Accordingly, when a neurologist is asked to pass opinion in retrospect as to the state of mind of a deceased aphasiac at the time the will was signed, at least two separate factors should be considered: (1) the will itself and (2) the testator. Is the will itself an intrinsically plausible one? Or has the patient disinherited his wife and family and left his money to an unlikely charity or some attractive newcomer? These matters, though more within the province of the lawyer, may throw light upon the workings of the mind, and as such constitute important medical data. Is the will a simple one containing only one or two clauses, or is it an extremely long and complicated document? Obviously, the former might well have been within the capacity of the aphasiac while the latter certainly was not. Thus, an isolated piece of property or a modest sum of money distributed among a few likely recipients could be looked upon as the product of judgement of a simple and straightforward kind. But where the property is considerable and complex and the testatees numerous, a will to be competent would entail a conception of magnitude and of mental exercises entailing division and other arithmetical manipulations. Such intellectual analyses would be expected to suffer in all but the mildest cases of aphasia. Abstract attitudes of thought, like creative cerebration, are too remote for attainment in the face of speech-loss.

As to the testator, the neurologist will have to decide, from his notes or from his recollection of the case, not merely whether at the time in question the patient could have made simple affirmations or denials and in appropriate circumstances, but also whether his mind was clouded, whether he had been correctly orientated in all spheres, and whether he could understand what others were trying to convey to him. It must always be remembered that some fluctuation in the intensity of the symptoms is not unusual in cases of cerebral softening and that the patient may perhaps have been capable of making a will on one day and not on another, or even only at certain times of the day. Lastly, the neurologist must recall whether there had been any noteworthy aberration of conduct or behaviour during the aphasia.

The neurologist must also decide as to whether any gross or diffuse brain disease existed over and above the focal lesion responsible for the aphasia. Thus, cases in which there were evidences of diffuse cerebrovascular disease, or a history of multiple strokes, or faulty control over the sphincters should be regarded with grave suspicion from the standpoint of testamentary capacity. Although in itself advanced age is not regarded by the law as constituting testamentary incapacity, the combination of senility with aphasia should be held by the doctor as suspect. The nature of the concomitant neurological signs may be of importance. The association of a hemiplegia with such epiphenomena as apraxia, hemianaesthesia, and especially hemianopsia may be of serious import as indicating a particularly widespread destruction of brain-tissue.

Paralysis of the hand that holds the pen does not of itself render the aphasiac incapable of making valid will. As early as 1743, the Hanoverian law courts upheld a will made by means of signs by a citizen of Münden, who had been deprived of speech. The law, in England at least, has accepted such evidence as an affirming pressure of the hand, nodding, and graphic marks (*Hill* v. *Jeffs*, Judgement of Bargrave Deane J. 1913), even though neurologists today would look upon that particular decision with some dubiety. Where a testatrix commenced her signature but failed to complete it, the will was upheld, for it was ruled that she knew and approved the contents and meant to sign it (*Chalcraft* v. *Giles* 1948).

The law in England has taken cognisance of the unusual circumstance wherein a patient had discussed the disposal of his property and the general layout of his will and then suffered an aphasia. The testator could recollect that he had given instructions about his will but nothing more; he nevertheless believed that the will was executed in accordance with his wishes, and this limited degree of capacity was ruled valid (*Perera* v. *Perera* 1901).

When no will has yet been made

If the aphasic patient and his relatives are desirous for a testament to be executed *de novo*, a considerable responsibility falls upon the medical practitioner. He would be well advised not only to call in a colleague to assist but also a consultant and a lawyer. Here it is that the neurologist should take command of the situation. It is better that all relatives, friends, and servants should be excluded from the consultation. If the proceedings prove to be rather lengthy and tiring for the patient, one must not hesitate to order an adjournment. The phenomena of waning attention and also of extreme mental viscosity should be respected. Should the mental state be unsatisfactory at one particular time, it is possible that an improvement may occur within a few days, and all documents should be kept aside in readiness. In cases of aphasia due to cerebral tumour, temporary improvement can perhaps be obtained by means of hypertonic salt solution long enough to permit a valid testimony.

In a letter to the *British Medical Journal* (1962), Shribman set out the essential factors in deciding testamentary capacity:

'(1) does he understand the nature of the will;

(2) does he understand the effect of the will;

(3) does he appear to have reasonable knowledge of his estate, and has he any delusions thereon;

(4) has he the capacity to appreciate what dependants, relatives or friends, might reasonably be entitled to his bounty;

(5) has he any delusions *per se*, which would cause him to omit any person or persons as beneficiaries who otherwise might reasonably have been included;

(6) has he any delusions which would cause him to make a gift which he might not have made in the absence of such delusions;

(7) does he appear to understand the importance attached to his act;

(8) if the medical practitioner sees the draft of the will, do the requests appear to be reasonable; and

(9) can the testator repeat the instructions a week later.'

Having stated the problem in all its complexities the writer did not proceed to advise how these various pitfalls can be detected or surmounted.

In the case of an aphasiac—as opposed to a dement or a psychotic—certain precautions can be taken by the neurological consultant. The will should be as simple and brief as possible, clearly typed out so as to afford the minimum difficulty to the patient if he can still read. Where only one straightforward clause is concerned (for example, when the wife or a son is the sole beneficiary), it is not strictly essential that the testator should know the precise total value of his estate. This becomes imperative, however, if there are a great many beneficiaries, with specific conditions demanded and with certain residual legatees.

First, it must be clear to all that the patient is desirous of making a will, and every fragment of speech and movement of gesture on the part of the patient must be accurately noted and recorded. The patient is then asked which person or persons are desired as beneficiaries. Having obtained a reply, one would do well to repeat this question back to the patient to be certain that no paraphasic error in naming has been made. Furthermore one might also suggest one or two additional and unlikely names, noting whether the patient now gives evidence of dissent. Care must be taken, however, to avoid bewildering the patient with too many test-questions, for will-making before an assembly is a tiring ordeal for a sick and aphasic patient, who is in all probability overly suggestible. One must also watch for the occurrence of verbal perseveration, whereby the same answer might be given to a succession of questions, contrary to the patient's intention.

If the property concerned is a considerable one and a simple one-clause will is impractical, one may adopt the method employed with success by Edmunds and upheld by an English court of law (*Moore* v. *Moore* 1900). This has become known to the legal profession as the 'pack of cards' case. The physician, with the assistance of the patient's solicitor, prepared a large number of cards 5 × 4 in in size, upon which were printed in bold type various categories of property to be bequeathed, of functions to be performed, and of numerous persons including relations, friends, and charitable organizations. These were placed before the patient, who slowly and deliberately chose certain cards. These were then marked and fastened together. Thus, the patient was shown the card denoting the largest item and at the same time was asked, 'Whom do you give that to?' The patient then took the pack of cards containing the proper names and, after slowly turning them over, selected the one marked with the name of her brother. This procedure was then repeated until the property was disposed of. Thus, the doctor dealt the cards, the testatrix played them back, and the lawyer gathered the tricks. From the selected cards, the lawyer drew up an appropriate will in effective legal form. On the following day, the doctor and the solicitor read out the will slowly, and the patient signified concurrence clause by clause. A final assent was given, and the patient affixed her mark which was witnessed by both lawyer and doctor. On account of the magnitude of the estate, the will had to be 'proved in solemn form', that is, in open court. After the various witnesses had been examined and cross-examined, the President, Sir Francis Jeune, expressed himself satisfied with the validity of the will (*The Times*, 13th February, 1900). Such a procedure, which of course can only be adopted when the patient has no disorder in the comprehension of printed matter, is open to one serious objection, namely, the possibility that some desired legatee or charity might be forgotten and therefore omitted from the proffered collection of names.

Whatever technique is adopted, it should be the endeavour to probe sympathetically and patiently so as to ascertain the fundamental wishes of the subject.

When the will has been drawn up by the lawyer and typed, it must be read over slowly to the patient. All must be satisfied that he understands and agrees with the contents.

Lastly, the patient must sign the will or affix his mark, this signature (or its equivalent) being witnessed by two others who must sign in his presence. In English law, these witnesses should be told that the document signed is the patient's will. They need not include the medical men nor the lawyer, but they should be responsible persons, not domestic servants. They need not know the terms of the will, and they must not be beneficiaries or executors.

A combined 'private' report might well be drawn up by the practitioner, lawyer, and neurologist, read over and agreed, signed and witnessed, and safely filed along with the testament. The neurologist should preserve his copy against future contingencies.

Undue influence

When judging a patient's capacity to make a valid will, there is a third point which may arise over and above the problems of speech affection and intellectual capacity. It may be argued by the relatives and their legal advisers that the patient, by reason of his stroke, had lost full possession of his 'will-power', had developed unreasonable likes and dislikes, and had become susceptible to undue influence in drawing up his will. This is quite apart from the factor of suggestibility which a brain-damaged patient often shows especially in the course of a medical interview. Such a protest on the part of the family is to be expected when the terms of the will are surprising or disappointing. A disinherited wife or near relative may contest the validity of a will which names as beneficiary a comparative stranger or a charity. In at least one state, Louisiana, undue influence does not of itself invalidate a will, but, most states in North America and in English law, the factor of 'undue influence' is an important consideration in judging the validity of a will. The court might well seek the doctor's opinion, though of course the decision as to the validity will rest with the judge and jury. No more difficult task lies before a medical practitioner than to express an opinion on such a matter. It must be remembered that mere propinquity of relationship does not necessarily constitute a moral claim upon a testator's actions. The relatives may have been rapacious, the wife a shrew, and the sons and daughters ne'er-do-wells; the patient's action in willing his property to a nurse, friend, or servant who had shown him kindness, or to a charity with which he was in sympathy may not necessarily be evidence of an unsound mind. Fortunately for the practitioner's peace of mind, this dilemma is nowadays less likely to occur, for in England it is now impossible for a testator to leave his wife or next of kin entirely devoid of maintenance.

This vexed question of testamentary capacity in patients bereft of speech illustrates the fact that legal and neurological thought are somewhat out of alignment. The lawyer thinks in terms of full competency versus total incapacity. On our part, we believe that there exists a sort of spectrum of intellectual accomplishment in aphasiacs which makes it unrealistic to try to answer the lawyer's naïve enquiry as to whether a particular patient's will is or is not valid. Even among neurologists, there has been a subtle change in opinion. Today, I would say that fewer aphasiacs possess testamentary capacity than I thought was the case forty years ago, that is, when I first considered this problem. In aphasia, an absolute integrity of intellectual function is, I believe, the exception and not the rule. Many psychologists and neurologists think otherwise, however.

But obviously the problem is one which cannot be judged in isolation. When Hughlings Jackson was asked the same question, 'Can an aphasic patient make a will?', he gave the Delphic reply, 'Can a piece of string stretch across a room?' Today, we would give an answer in similar terms, but I would like to phrase my reply, 'Can this piece of string stretch across this room? Probably not'.

XXV. KINESICS; GESTURAL AND MIMIC LANGUAGE: AN ASPECT OF NON-VERBAL COMMUNICATION

> There's language in her eye, her cheek, her lips,
> Nay her foot speaks; her wanton spirit looks out
> At every joint and motive of her body.
> *William Shakespeare*

> Every little movement has a meaning of its own,
> Every little movement tells a tale.
> *Nineteenth Century Vaudeville Song*

> His cool, white flower-like hands had a curious charm. They moved, as he spoke, like music, and seemed to have a language of their own.
> *Oscar Wilde*

> The British Army Thumb . . . The good old British Thumb. Thumbs up lads, we're going off to war! Thumbs up, we'll beat the Germans, or the Bongos, or whoever it happens to be just now. Just keep those thumbs up. . . . He had seen photographs when he was a little boy of all those dreadful thumbs extended, each bent a little back, as they went to Flanders to be shot off by the Germans or lost in the mud. God knows how many thumbs there were lost in that mud. . . . Why did they do it always? Off they went again in the next war, those proud, confident mistaken digits. Thumbs up on the troop-ships, thumbs up in the tail turret of the bomber, thumbs up on the Arctic convoy. . . . Come on now, you on the stretchers, thumbs up all those who've still got 'em. Thumbs up! Thumbs up! . . . There was a little battle there and twenty thumbs were lying in caked mud graves. . . . fishes . . . ran in and out of the hulls of the dead battleships—Prince of Wales and Repulse—lying clearly in the sand of the ocean. They had been there since 1942 and they were full of dead thumbs.
> *Leslie Thomas. The Virgin Soldiers*

> Rien n'est jamais acquis à l'homme. Ni sa force, ni sa faiblesse, ni son coeur.
> Et quand il croit ouvrir ses bras son ombre est celle d'une croix.
> *L. Aragon*

Non-verbal forms of expression and communication are of considerable interest to aphasiologists. Birdwhistell has spoken of the gestural components of communication as 'kinesics'. Although he

Based upon *The Language of Gesture*, Arnold, London 1939, and also article in *Problems of Dynamic Neurology*. Ed. Halpern, Jerusalem, 1963.

erected an elaborate nomenclature—kines, kinesiologists, prekinesics, micro-kinesics, allokines, kinemes, kinology, kinics, kinemorpheme, among others—he never clearly defined the term kinesics, beyond calling it 'the study of units of gestural expression'. The author was also bold enough to hazard a system of annotating gestures by means of kinegraphs. Others, e.g. J. H. Mendelson *et al.* (1964) have utilized the term 'chereme' to stand for a unit of manual communication.

The silent panorama of gesture is an ubiquitous component of man's environment, though often taken for granted. It constitutes an important and even fundamental aspect of communication, for it can be, and often is, resorted to when verbal symbols are not feasible. Thus under the stress of a sudden upsurge of emotion, words may temporarily fail one, but this blocking of verbal expression does not inhibit the free play of gesticulation. The language of gesture remains available after disease of the organs of articulation has rendered them impotent, as in the mutism of advanced bulbar palsy. Most obvious of all there is the universally comprehended pantomime utilized by a stranger in a foreign land, the language of which is unfamiliar.

It is not surprising that the archaic and fundamental nature of gesture has tempted some philosophers of language to imagine that it might have been an actual 'ancestor' of speech. As described in an earlier chapter (Chapter IX) it has been alleged that somewhere between the highest primates and the lowliest representative of *homo sapiens* there once existed a race of man who mimed but did not speak. This notion of a prehistoric *homo alalus* is not seriously held nowadays. More probably mimetic movements as well as verbalization both grew up in concert, and blossomed side by side in symbolic elaboration. All the same it would be a mistake to brush aside the idea of a hierarchy in communicative systems, with gestures representing an elder brother of speech rather than an ancestor. The argument has been made and elaborated that miming and other silent phenomena play an important role in animal communication, which possibly transcends that of cries, calls and other sounds. Witness the language of the dance among bees; the elaborate avian displays; and the automatic motor expression of emotions among the mammalia including the anthropoids. A relationship between the visible and the audible forms of non-verbal communication in the subhominids appears to be direct rather than indirect.

The early philologists in their speculations as to the origin of language in man, for a time held a number of 'gestural' theories. In addition to Noiré's *yo-heave-ho* hypothesis there was the ontogenetic notion as to the audible intervention of a glottal stop. We are reminded too of the *click-click* hypothesis which seeks to find a correlation between the shape of the mouth, and the meaning of the issuing morphemes. These engaging ideas have been discussed in some detail in Chapter 9.

Classification

It becomes necessary to particularize the various types of expressive movements, for as a rule, terms such as gesture, gesticulation, and pantomime are used almost synonymously.

The principal division must be made between gestural movements which are carried out in silence, and those which accompany the act of speaking for reasons of emphasis. The first type was well illustrated by the silent films of some decades ago, and by various dance-sequences (Schehere-

20

zade for instance). When one person communicates with another by resorting wholly to bodily movements (as with a thumbs-up sign, a salute, a wave of the hand) we are again witnessing examples of pantomime. These signs, translated into Jackson's terminology, are in the main a form of propositionizing, in that they aim at stating, declaring or announcing an idea or a proposition.

In contrast to pantomime is 'gesticulation'. This word should be restricted to those gestural movements which *accompany* rather than *replace* speech. Thus in the fluttering of the hands of the excited conversationalist, and in the arm movements of the political speaker, orator, preacher or lecturer, we observe gesticulation in the true sense of the word. Here the motions serve a purpose ancillary to articulate speech. The message could pass quite well from sender to receiver even without the aid of gesticulation, but movement serves to drive home the point; to underline, or italicize the articulate utterance. If Jackson would have rated pantomime as propositionizing, he would doubtless have compared gesticulation with inferior or emotional speech.

Movements of pantomime and of gesticulation utilize the musculature of almost any part of the body, but principally the hands and forearms. More dramatic exponents may introduce movements of the shoulders, neck, head, trunk and even legs. There is however a set of mimic phenomena peculiar to the face, and here again one may discern at least two physiological categories or hierarchies. In the first place there is the gamut of facial grimaces—smiling, sneering, frowning, snarling—as well as a more subtle range of expressive movements, including a play of the lips, cheek, eyebrows and eyelids. All these interesting phenomena, the persuasive stock-in-trade of actors, teachers and advocates, can be spoken of as facial mimetic movements. These belong to the class of willed, deliberate, voluntary movements, susceptible to control, regulation or inhibition. None the less they may at times occupy a relatively lowly position in the range of volition, in that they may often seem but little voluntary, and largely automatic. That is to say they operate outside the conspectus of active attention, and in this way they may unwittingly betray the emotion behind the utterance. But at any moment awareness may be aroused, and the mimetic play may then be checked so as to mask the feelings. Or again, appropriate facial movements may be performed of such a kind as deliberately to deceive and mislead the audience.

Barzini in a critical vein asserted that among Italians reading facial expressions is an important art, to be learned in childhood, perhaps more important for survival than the art of reading print. Spoken words, he emphasized, may be sometimes at variance with the grimaces that accompany them: the words should then be overlooked: only the face counts. 'Italians are often disconcerted, unhappy and lonely in the north of Europe, and seldom know what is going on, surrounded as they are by blank faces on which little can be read and that little seldom exciting. They wrongly conclude that, as the people show no feelings, they have no feelings worth showing. The proverbial impassivity of the English is believed to be a definite proof of coldness and insensibility.'

Lastly there is a group of phenomena mainly concerning the face which are expressive in fact not in intent. There lie outside the range of voluntary activities for they are not only un-willed and non-deliberate, but they are also uncontrollable as a rule. Within this category belong pallor or flushing of the skin; outpouring of sweat; horripilation; dilatation of the pupils; lacrymation; and dryness of the mouth. Such phenomena, lying within the domain of the autonomic nervous system, are vestiges of more widespread appearances which Darwin studied as the expression of the emotions in animals, like lashing of the tail, arching of the spine, erection of the hairs of the pelt, baring of the teeth and drooling of saliva.

If a term is needed to cover the two foregoing classes of facial mimetic phenomena, we can, *faute de mieux*, speak of 'physiognomy', even though the strict and original meaning of this word referred to divination of character from facial delineaments.

Comparing for a moment the situation in man and animals, it can be asserted that pantomime is more elaborate and wide-ranged in man. It is true that domesticated animals sometimes execute a limited repertoire of silent movements apparently with communicative purpose—as when a dog stands by the front door in hopes of a run in the garden. Again, movements of gesticulation are to be identified among the various pantomimic displays of birds and mammals. The autonomic and non-voluntary movements betraying emotion are usually more conspicuous, and certainly morphologically more generalized, in animals than they are in man. But pure facial movements of expression, both deliberate and quasi-deliberate, are certainly better exemplified in man than in any other creature.

Common experience teaches that in man there is no real antagonism between spoken speech and the use of gesture. On the contrary, the two systems of motor expression and verbal communication seem to develop and flourish together. Thus talkative persons resort very freely to pantomime and to gesticulation, the head-water of language overflowing into every possible channel. This idea tallies with the observation that there are wide cultural and racial idiosyncrasies in this respect. In some countries the local people lavishly display gesture, and by and large these persons are relatively garrulous and volatile types. In comparison, some other races are both impassive and taciturn. So we find among the Celts, the Jews, the Latins and the Levantines, powerful talkers as well as mimes. By way of contrast stand the Nordic races, which combine in characteristic fashion a poverty of speech with an economy of gesture.

Besides these racial factors, considerations of a socio-cultural character also play a part. Thus an undue use of gesture is commonly frowned upon as vulgar, suggesting a certain lack of decorum or restraint. This attitude is not confined to the Anglo-Saxon peoples. Even in regions where talkers usually resort to ebullient gesticulation—as in Southern Italy, Sicily and Greece—the same canons of good taste obtain, and by and large the better educated use mimic movements relatively less.

This profusion of gestural movements proves attractive to some observers, but repugnant to others. Ruskin belonged to the latter group. As he wrote in 1845 . . . 'look at the talkers in the streets of Florence, being essentially unable to talk, they try to make lips of their fingers. How they poke, wave, flourish, point, jerk, shake fingers and fist at their antagonist . . . impersuasive and ineffectual as the shaking of tree branches in the wind'.

None the less one must admit that a modest amount of expressive movement is permissible, being both aesthetically pleasing and intellectually satisfying. Too great a paucity of mimetic play is apt to militate against a warmth or rapport during the process of communication. Hamlet's advice to the Players was very apt . . . 'Do not saw the air too much with your hand, thus—. Suit the action to the word and the word to the action, with this special observance, that you overstep not the modesty of nature'. In this instruction, Shakespeare was shrewd though not altogether original, for we find that centuries before, Cicero had ordained in his *De Oratore*: 'The action of the hand should not be too affected, but should follow the words rather than express them by mimicry'.

Oratory affords the opportunity of observing some of the most flamboyant examples of gesticulation. Here the cynic might even be tempted to trace a veritable inverse ratio between the semantic content of the diction and the total volume of gestural movements. Gesture betrays the affective violence of the message; perhaps sincerity is implied, though it does not necessarily follow; but it often conceals a sorry poverty of ideas. An experienced orator often gradually adopts certain gestural mannerisms which become idiosyncratic and personal, and though much employed, they take place largely outside the speaker's awareness—or at any rate only at its very fringe. Modern Press photography is very revealing on this point, and often unflattering. At the present time public speaking—political, ecclesiastical, didactic—is very much a self-taught contrivance, and bad habits of speech and gesture are easily picked up and perpetuated. A biographer—not with entire detachment—wrote of the Prime Minister Macmillan . . . 'as he grew older, his gestures became more eccentric: the shake of the head, the drooping of the mouth, the baring of the teeth, the pulling-in of the cheeks, the wobbling of the hand . . . the whole bag of tricks seemed in danger of taking over, so that his intellectual originality was constantly surprising'.

In classic times the situation was different, and for the Romans, Rhetoric along with Logic and Mathematics, formed the very basis of sound education. Each monograph upon the art of oratory contained detailed sections devoted to the proper use of gesture.

One of the most precise of these instructors was Quintilian. In his 'Institute of Oratory' he informed would-be advocates as to the manner in which they should deliver their speeches in the law courts. He counselled the orator not to push forward his trunk; not to walk about too much; never to turn his back upon the Judge; not to stamp the foot too often; and not to sway from side to side. It was permissible to draw back by degrees, but certainly not to leap back . . . 'an act ridiculous in the highest degree'. Quintilian considered that the public speaker might quite properly lean slightly towards the judge, but the practice of lurching over in the direction of the opposing advocates he deemed to be a breach of good manners. . . . 'and for a speaker to fall back among his friends to be supported in their arms—unless from real and evident fatigue—is foppish'.

According to Lucian the professional mime who made a gesticulatory error was guilty of a manual solecism.

Ordinarily the setting for expressive movements is simple social intercourse. A greater or lesser degree of gesticulation may properly embellish or adorn the verbal messages passed from one interlocutor to another. To a large extent such actions take place outside the awareness of both parties, but an on-looker may witness and appreciate to the full the wealth of mimic motility. Particularly is this the case when the verbal language employed is unfamiliar—or when distance renders the diction inaudible. In such circumstances the gesture lies wide open, as it were, for analysis.

Anyone observing the pantomime going on during a Southern European conversation-piece would shrewdly apprehend a great deal of the content of the 'message' passing from one to another. This is because so much of the gesture is self-explanatory, being imitative in nature, or else universally understood. In other words some of the gestures, albeit symbolic, are nevertheless made up of movements which are either innate, or else so fundamental as to constitute a veritable *lingua franca pantomimica*.

On the other hand the meaning of certain other gestures will elude most observers who do not share the particular language-system. Such mimic movements are not imitative, and hence they are not self-explanatory. They are symbolic, and the antecedent history of the symbol may be quite obscure.

It is unnecessary to specify more than a few examples. Take for instance the gestures (or fragments of pantomime) connoting approbation, appreciation or appraisal. In this context a variety of symbolic movements may be witnessed. A 'thumbs-up' sign may perhaps appropriately be given. Apposition of the thumb to the index finger, the forearm being lifted to the level of the face, the hand then being rocked forwards and back again, is another common sign. In some Latin countries it is the practice to pinch the cheek with a sort of rotary movement, and after that to flick the hand downwards and backwards. Or, the subject may ostentatiously kiss his apposed thumb and index finger. In Portuguese-speaking communities, the lobe of the ear is held and shaken; and extreme approval may be signalled by passing an arm right over the top of the head, so as to grasp and waggle the lobe of the opposite ear. Turkish or Greek conversationalists may smooth their chest with a downward stroking movement, using one hand or both. In some central American countries—Colombia for instance—the usual gesture is to draw downwards one lower eyelid with the index finger: in Italy this same gesture would generally connote slyness, cunning or deceit.

Barzini has much to say about the pantomimic habits of his countrymen. As he put it 'motorists no longer slow down and waste precious seconds to shout intelligible and elaborate insults to each other or to pedestrians, as they used to do . . . Now they merely extend one hand in the general direction of the person to whom they want to address a message, a hand with all fingers folded except the forefinger and little finger. It conveys the suggestion that the other man does, should or will shortly wear horns, in other words be cuckolded by his wife, fiancée or mistress'.

Passing reference may be made to the commonly encountered, semi-ritualistic gestures which are of uncertain origin, as for example, the military salute. The various forms of greeting traditional in different countries may have stemmed from what were originally purposive movements. Thus the ordinary handshake might once have been at one and the same time an indication that the host is unarmed, and also a search to ensure that the guest carries no weapon. Probably the same motive originally lay behind the back-slapping greetings of the American, whether it be the unimanual act seen in the United States or the bimanual and more theatrical gesture of the Latin Americans. Many would regard the *Namastis* or Hindu greeting—with the palms of the hands together and a slight inclination of the trunk—as being a more graceful, dignified and restrained gesture.

In a number of special circumstances a silent system of pantomime replaces altogether articulate speech as a medium of communication. These circumstances may be conveniently grouped along the following heads:

Occupational sign-languages

Sometimes it is necessary, or at least advisable, for one member of a trade or calling to signal to another, relying exclusively upon a series of gestures. Thus in some types of job the environment of noise is so great that spoken speech would be unavailing for the purpose of transmitting messages. For example, in a cotton-mill the operatives communicate with each other by way of a simple sign language. By contrast, there are other occupations where absolute silence is necessary, as for example, in a broadcasting studio: here again hand-signs are used instead of speech. At times it is not a matter of noise, nor yet of enforced silence, which renders speech inappropriate. The over-riding factor may be one of distance. Thus railway shunters may use crude arm-signs in order to signal instructions in a goods yard. The pilot of an air-liner communicates with the ground staff by way of signs rather than words. Stevedores loading ships are supervised by a foreman who directs the crane-driver merely by gestures. Secrecy is, on other occasions, the all-important factor which precludes speech and fosters the use of pantomime. This is met among Hatton Garden diamond merchants. So, also, in a casino, croupiers may signal to each other messages which would be indiscreet for all and sundry to hear. Best known of such circumstances, is at the race-course where bookmakers and their tic-tac men transmit information by means of the blower system ('the show').

Oriental literature

Signs formed an elaborate system of silent communication in the Middle and Far East, as described vividly in Penzer's *Ocean of Story* and Burton's translation of the *Arabian Nights*. One example may be taken, from the former source. The Mongolian Princess Naran signalled from her balcony to her lover below. She held up one finger and encircled it with her other hand; she then clasped her hands together and afterwards separated them. After that she placed two fingers together and with them pointed towards the palace. The upraised finger intended to convey the idea of a tree, and the encircling action, a wall. Clasping and unclasping the hands was an invitation to enter the flower garden, and the juxtaposition of two fingers was a sign that she would welcome a visit.

The Oriental Dance

Even at the present day, symbolic movements and postures of considerable complexity and of esoteric import, make up the grammar of the dance in the Far East. The oriental ballet differs from the occidental in being more restrained; it relies on unusual attitudes of the head and neck and on fantastic finger-twists, rather than upon wide-range movements of the trunk and extremities. In the East the dancer is more or less rooted to one spot while the Western dancer bounds, leaps and roams widely over the stage. These idiosignificant hand postures of the Eastern dance constitute a legacy direct from a remote past. In the West the conventional style is relatively recent, for in classic times the Graeco-Roman dance resembled that of the distant Orient. The Indian dance (Bharata, Natyam, Kathakale, Kathak, Manipuri) constitutes a most complex system of rigidly determined attitudes and movements, especially of the hands. The Abbinaya Darpana gives an almost encyclopaedic account of these gestures. Some of them symbolize the deeds of the gods or of famous overlords; others relate to the oceans, the rivers, the upper and lower worlds, various trees, animals, birds and fishes. Meaning encloses meaning, like a set of Chinese boxes, and some of the more obscure allusions are known only to initiates. A single example may be taken. In the *Udvistita-lapadura* posture, the hands are held before the chest, palms up, with fingers extended to the full. This attitude symbolizes husband; modest talk; the breasts; the open lotus; conversation; desire. It seeks to say 'I am beloved'. Its divine patron is *Sakti*.

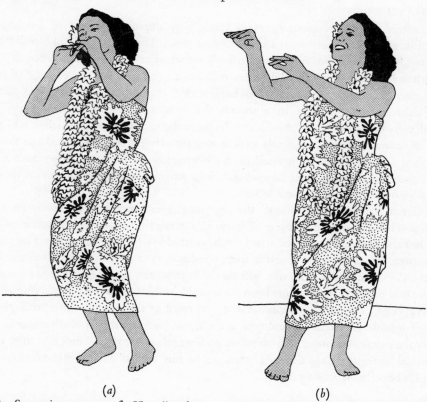

(a)   *(b)*

FIG. 28   Successive gestures of a Hawaiian dancer, symbolizing *Aloha*, meaning "good-bye for now beloved: come back again."

Almost as strictly regimented is the pantomime witnessed within the *No* plays of Japan, as well as the sleeve movements and gestures of the Chinese theatre. They differ from the Indian ballet in being wholly secular, for indeed the art of the Indian dance **is** believed to have been passed on to man from the Gods themselves.

Of simpler nature, and more easily comprehended by all and sundry, are the gestures made by dancers in Hawaii. (see Fig. 28)

Secret Societies

Hand-signs form an essential part of the ritual of those who share certain common religious, semi-religious or political interests. Obviously these signs constitute a tight-meshed yet limited kind of communication-network. The very essence is the transmission of messages incomprehensible to outsiders and understood only by a select few. The cult of secret societies is age-old and world-wide, and certain circumstances may cause it to flourish. China has been specially remarkable for its jealous socio-political brotherhoods, among which the *Hung* Society (or Heaven and Earth Community) is the best known.

Inter-racial sign-languages

In areas where despite propinquity races speak very different systems of language, sign-languages often establish themselves as a kind of *lingua franca*. This was the case in North America a century ago where the various indigenous tribes comprised at least 65 quite different linguistic families. When Indians belonging to different tribes came together for the purpose of barter or conference, sign-language was adopted. This has been the subject of study and documentation on the part of many ethnologists who have actually drawn up veritable lexicons.

Geographically far remote from the Amerindians are the various aboriginal tribes which live in the deserts of central Australia. Here too an elaborate sign-language is employed and this too has been described and set down by investigating anthropologists. Sign-languages have also been briefly mentioned as occurring in the Cameroons, in the Amazonian 'dumb villages', in the Aleutian Islands, and among the New Zealand Maoris.

Quite different circumstances attend the sign-languages employed in European monastic communities. Thus during the *summum silentium* in Benedictine monasteries, which follows the compline, and also at meal-times, articulate speech is forbidden, but manual gestures are permitted. The best known and at the same time the most consistent system of signs refers to the Trappist branch of the Cistercian order of monks. Within this community writing is forbidden, and spoken speech is allowed only at certain hours between a monk and his abbot. A complex sign-language has, however, been evolved which circumvents the spirit of the rule of silence, though not the letter. This pantomimic system as employed in the Cluny order in the eleventh century, was first recorded by the monk Bernardus, who depicted no fewer than 296 signs. Since that time a number of ecclesiastical historians have devoted attention to this subject, such as for example Herrgot (1726) and Dubois (1824) among others.

The sign-language of deaf-mutes

Most eloquent among the various sign-languages must be rated the gestural systems of deaf-mutes. Here the use of pantomime is almost obligatory in communication, as opposed to the occupational and other sign-languages where spoken speech is available in addition. In modern educational establishments deaf-mute pupils are instructed in reading, writing and in lip-reading, but where such facilities are not available resort must be had to gesture. The well-known art of finger-spelling or dactylography forms the bedrock of communication especially on the part of the normal person who wishes to transfer information to the deaf-mute. The communicative channel can also run the other way, that is from patient to interlocutor, though in practice perhaps this less often occurs.

Jermome Cardano (1501–1575) was probably the first to construct a sign-language to assist the deaf. At very much the same time the Benedictine monk Pedro Ponce de Leon (1520–1584) was also associated with this type of work, and Pereira also had the opportunity of working in concert with his deaf student Saboureaux de Fontenay, the godson of the duc de Chaulnes. de Leon's pupil Juan Pablo Bonet carried on with this work in Spain, to the wonderment of Sir Kenelm Digby.

The first English writer on the subject was the 'Chirosopher' John Bulwer, who wrote in 1644 *Chirologia*, and in 1648 '*Philocophus*, or The Deafe and Dumbe man's friend'. Sign-languages among the deaf were referred to by Mather in 1684. In 1692 La Fin advocated a silent language which might be executed by pointing towards various parts of the body (*b*. brow, *c*. cheek, *m*. mouth, etc.) As this sign-language applied only to the English tongue he later constructed another for use in Latin. La Fin's ideas never gained favour and in an anonymous pamphlet (*Digite Lingua*, London 1698) a return to finger-spelling was advocated. In 1694 Bishop Wilkins brought out his elaborate form of manual speech not necessarily restricted to the use of the deaf.

The modern history of the system of dactylography for deaf-mutes really starts from the work of the Jansenist Charles-Michel, the abbé de l'Epée (1712–1789) who stimulated by a meeting with Pereira, in 1755 opened in Paris a school for the education of the deaf and dumb. In 1791 the National Assembly assumed responsibility for the 'Institution nationale des Sourds Muets à Paris'. His *Dictionnaire général des signes* was completed by his successor Roch Ambroise Cucurron and the Abbé Sicard, and between them they elaborated the unimanual finger alphabet as practised in many European countries today. The Abbé Sicard collaborated also with the Revd. Thomas Hopkins Gallaudet (1787–1851), a visiting American who, with the help of Laurent Clerc, one of his pupils, opened the first school for the deaf in the United States in Hartford, Connecticut in 1817. Consequently the Parisian unimanual alphabet is also employed in North America today. Gallaudet afterwards married one of his deaf pupils, and they together opened a second institution in Washington D.C.

British instructors pursued an independent course however. Thomas Braidwood (1715–1806) had opened his school in Edinburgh in 1860 and for long he held a sort of monopoly of training and would not associate with the Paris school.[1] In this way a bimanual system of finger-spelling grew up independently and it is still in use in Great Britain, as well as Australia.

Over and above these methods of dactylology, all deaf-mutes possess another and lesser-known system of communication. This is a kind of pantomimic shorthand, whereby a single gesture signifies—not a letter—but a word, a phrase, or even a sentence. This 'natural sign-language' of the deaf and dumb as it is generally called, is largely unfamiliar to outsiders and indeed many are unaware of its very existence. The language is rarely committed to text-books nor is it taught in schools. Indeed in many educational establishments for the deaf it is deliberately frowned upon so that the art of lip-reading should not suffer. Except for a few obscure pamphlets there is practically no literature devoted to the subject. It seems to be handed on from one deaf-mute to another as a sort of tradition; or it may be picked up in their institutions or hostels. Possibly the Abbé de l'Epée

---

[1] Thomas Braidwood was visited in 1773 by Dr. Samuel Johnson, who described the school as a subject of philosophical curiosity . . . which no other city could show. The pupils, in Johnson's words, could 'hear with the eye'. In 1783 Braidwood moved his school from Edinburgh to Hackney, in London, and later to premises in the Old Kent Road.

incorporated fragments of this natural sign-language into his system or code of finger-spelling. The less instructed the deaf-mute, the greater the proportion of 'natural' signs, even though the total vocabulary be but small. The more deaf-mutes are in each others' company the greater the recourse to this natural sign-language. Deaf-mutes taken away from others similarly afflicted, and living in association with normal individuals, are less likely to use the natural sign-language to any extent, for it would be meaningless.

Most asylums for the deaf seem to possess their own private codes of symbols which may be incorporated within the more universal and natural sign-language. A deaf-mute as he grows up gradually achieves a rich and elastic symbolic system comprising natural signs, conventional symbols, facial mimicry, finger-spelling, and perhaps also lip-reading. He thus contrives to communicate freely all manner of propositions, including abstract ideas, shades of meaning and witticisms. Even very young deaf-mutes communicate freely with each other and the presence of this natural sign-language at an age prior to their receiving systematic instruction points to an 'instinctive' or at least a primitive type of symbolization.

This natural sign-language is economical and rapid so that it can be executed and comprehended about three times as fast as spoken speech. Moreover it is graceful and pleasing to the eye, and when an attractive facial mimicry accompanies the manual gestures, the result is eloquent indeed. One hesitates to support A. H. Payne, however, when he acclaimed it to be far more expressive, facile and beautiful than the English of Shakespeare and the Bible.

R. Tervoort 1953 apparently found that manual communication was effective only when gestures were accompanied by mouthing of the spoken word on the part of the gesturer, and by lip reading on the part of the observer. This observation is almost certainly incorrect, for it can be established that the deaf-mute's natural sign-language is 'international' and is comprehended by individuals irrespective of geographico-linguistic boundaries.

Although but little attention has as yet been devoted to this subject by neurologists, there are occasional references in general literature to this natural sign-language of deaf-mutes. For instance in Carson McCullers' *The Heart is a lonely Hunter* we read:

> In the dusk the two mutes walked slowly home together. At home, Singer was always talking to Antonapoulos. His hands shaped the words in a swift series of designs. His face was eager and his grey-green eyes sparkled brightly. With his thin, strong hands he told Antonapoulos all that had happened during the day.

Rabelais has afforded us the fullest description of the misunderstandings which may arise when one of the interlocutors is unaware of the other person's disability:

> Do you remember what happened at Rome two hundred and three score Years after the Foundation thereof? A young Roman Gentleman encountring by chance at the Foot of Mount Celion with a beautiful Latin Lady named Verona, who from her very cradle upwards had always been both deaf and dumb, very civilly asked her, (not without a Chironomatick Italianising of his Demand, with various Jectigation of his Fingers, and other Gesticulations, as yet customary amongst the Speakers of that Country) what Senators in her descent from the top of the Hill she had met with going up thither. For you are to conceive, that he knowing no more of her Deafness and Dumbness, was ignorant of both. She in the

Indian greeting (Namaste)

The natural gesture language of the deaf and dumb.
Sign indicating 'heaven'.

The natural gesture language of the deaf and dumb.
Sign indicating 'over there'.

Plate 9

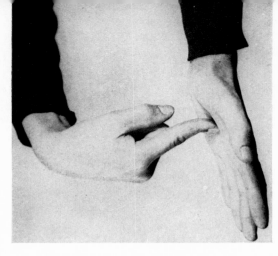

Excellent!

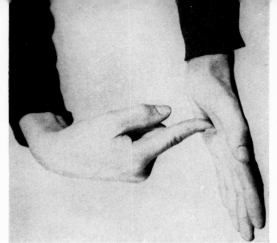

I insist

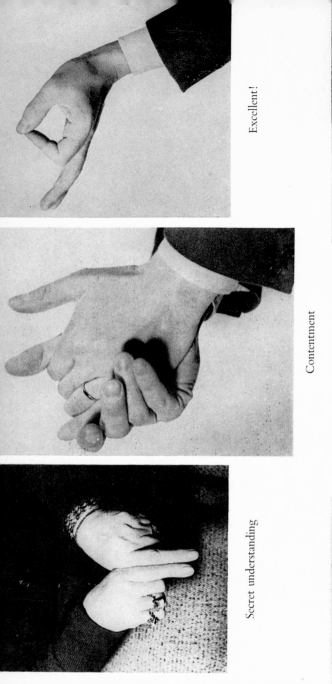

Contentment

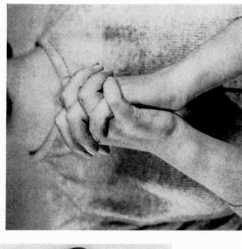

Please!

Secret understanding

What do you expect?

Approval

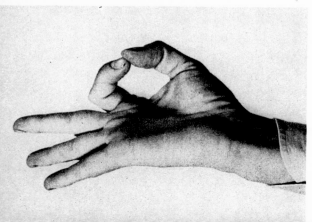

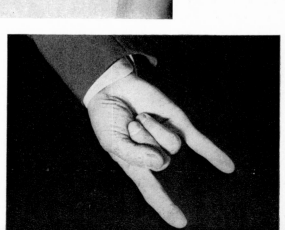

Against the evil eye

Plate 10

meantime, who neither heard nor understood so much as one word of what he had said, streight imagin'd, by all that she could apprehend in the lovely Gesture of his manual Signs, that what he then required of her was, what herself had a great mind to, even that which a Young Man doth naturally desire of a Woman. Then was it, that by Signs (which in all occurences of Venerial Love are incomparably more attractive, valid and efficacious than Words) she beckoned to him to come along with her to her House; which when he had done, she drew him aside to a privy Room, and then made a most lively alluring Sign unto him, to shew that the Game did please her. Whereupon, without any more Advertisement, or so much as the uttering of one Word on either side, they fell to, and bringuardised it lustily.

The Universal Symbol Language

There is also a universal and age-old language of symbolism which can be encountered in social intercourse, in art, heraldry, religion and the drama. Sometimes the original significance of the signs has become obscured, constituting what Bayley called the 'lost language of symbolism'. At other times the meaning is clear, being virtually the property of man's fundamental unconscious mind. Sometimes more than one meaning is attached to the sign, of which there may be one which is simple and one which is concealed. Before the introduction of printed language, graphic representations of a symbolic character were common, being comprehended even by the illiterate.

These stereotyped postures, especially those which involve the hand, are therefore to be found widely disseminated, particularly within the art museums of the world. They may be observed in statuary and bas-reliefs; carved on intaglios or on pottery; they may be seen engraved upon coins and medallions; and depicted in icons and paintings, especially among the primitives. Not infrequently they are reproduced as amulets and charms. A study of heraldry, of folk-lore, and of social anthropology will also afford its complement.

It will suffice to quote three of four obvious examples. Thus there is the sign of the open hand. As an emblem it often indicates power, authority or justice. It constitutes the gesture made by a Jew taking an oath in a law court, or a marriage ceremony. Painted in terra-cotta it may often be met with upon the outer walls of a house in the Mediterranean littoral. Even in the caves of the Aurignacian prehistory, a hand-imprint is often to be seen in among the wall-paintings of bison and reindeer. It constituted the standard of the Roman Legionaries. In heraldry the arms of every knight baronet in the United Kingdom comprise an augmentation of a human left-hand gules, borne on an escutcheon in the chief (or centre) of the shield. The brass ornaments of cart-horse harness often incorporate a hand-sign. Among North American Indians an open hand could be seen among their picture-writing, and it represented strength or mastery. To early Christians the hand symbolized God the Father. In India, a golden hand is the sign of labour and the fruits of the sun. Statues of Vishnu and also of Buddha sometimes show this manual gesture. In the Eleusinian mysteries it was the left hand that depicted justice, for it was endowed neither with skill nor with learning. Fashioned in brass, with a heart piercing the palm, an upraised hand was an emblem favoured by the early Friendly Societies.

A closed hand with the first two fingers extended, is a common sign of justice, but is even more frequently observed as a blessing and as such is a favoured gesture in primitive religious art. Occasionally the first two fingers are separated; less often still one finger is crossed over the other.

In the Orthodox church the fourth (or little) finger is also raised in benediction, the third finger alone flexed into the palm.

A fist with the first and fourth fingers extended constitutes the 'horns', or the *manu cornuta* of the Romans. Originally this sign represented the crescent moon of Diana. It may still be met with in Italy, where directed horizontally, it constitutes a charm against the evil eye. But when the horns point upwards, marital infidelity or cuckoldom is implied. An even more powerful protection against the *malocchio* consists in a fist with the thumb protruding between first and second fingers. This is the 'fig' or *manu in fica*, and fashioned in coral or some semiprecious stone, it is sold as an amulet in Brazil or Italy. It also carries a very pejorative implication of sexual impotency, and was known to the Romans as the *manus obscaena*.

The 'thumbs up' sign almost universally stands for appraisal, or approval. As such it can be traced at least as far back as the gladiatorial contests of Rome. In Poland this sign is made with the elbow abducted from the side so that the thumb points towards the breast. In the rites of Indian dancing an extended thumb symbolizes the phallus.

Further description of these various symbols would unnecessarily complicate the text, but it is perhaps in order to discuss shortly what might be termed the personification of the individual fingers. Thus in the early Christian church the thumb denoted God the Father; the third finger stood for Christ the Son, and the second finger represented the Holy Ghost. The pagans were much more down to earth. They associated each finger with purposes of the toilet. Hence *pollex* (thumb); the *index* (first finger used for scrubbing as well as pointing); the *impudicus* or *obscaenus*[1] (second finger for anal exploration); the *annulus* (third or ring finger); and the *auriculus* (or little finger, for inserting into the ear).

According to English folk-lore each finger has its own fancied personality as evidenced by the children's chant . . . 'This little pig went to market, etc. . . .'. This personification becomes even more elaborate in some British dialects. Thus we find in Scotland the thumb and fingers known as 'Black Barney; Lope Drake; Steal Corney; Runaway and little Canny Wanny who pays all'[2] Blind children who are being instructed in braille reading speak of their fingers as Tom Thumb, Peter pointer, Middleman tall, Ruby ring and Baby small. The same type of nomenclature may be encountered in other languages besides English. Thus German children may chant 'Dies ist der Daumen: Der schuettelt die Pflaumen; Der liest sie ein; Der traegt sie hein; und dieser klein schelm der isst sie ganz allein'. In Norwegian the fingers are known to children as 'Tommeltot, slikkepot, langemann, gullebrand and Little Peter Spillemann'.

There are also a number of manual-brachial postures rich in symbol content and widespread in significance. J. S. M. Ward described these as 'mantric signs' in that they are in themselves prayers or spells to be compared with the offering-up of prayers in a dead or esoteric language. Among these numerous mantric signs may be mentioned quite briefly, the signs of preservation; of

---

[1] Thus in Martial we read . . . 'ostendit digitum, *sed impudicum*, Alconti Dasioque Summachoque' (Epigrams VI. LXX) (He points his finger, and the insulting finger too, at Alion, Dasius and Summachus).

[2] Other variants are: 'The man who broke the barn, who stole the cow, who stood and saw, who ran awa', and wee periwinkle who paid for 'A'; 'The man who broke the barn, stole the corn, stood and saw, got none, and went pinkey-winkey all the way hom'; 'Tom Thumbkin, Bess Bumpkin, Will Wilkin, Long Linken, and Little Dicks; Tom Thumbkins, Bill Wilkins, Long Daniel, Bessie Borum, and the Little Boy that runs on before 'em'.

distress; of fidelity; of sacrifice; of horror; of destruction; of blessing; and many others. As Ward reported, these mantric signs can be observed in almost every form of pictorial art, in every age, and every clime. They have been designed on Egyptian papyri; engraved in stone and bronze; on seals; in terracotta figurines; on gold rings from Mycenae; on Grecian painted vases; Carthagenian lamps; ivory carvings; illuminated manuscripts; Cloisonné enamels; monumental brasses; pictures; tiles; stained glass; shields; beads; woven hangings; funeral vases. Perhaps they are best depicted in the religious paintings—primitive, mediaeval, renaissance—of Italy, Spain, France, and Germany. Even today these mantric signs are incorporated within the rituals of brotherhoods, and secret societies.

It is common knowledge that differences occur between individuals as regards the proclivity towards the use of gesture. Almost as widespread is the idea that communities differ one from another in this respect. The reason for such variation is open to debate. Many have been tempted to ascribe the differences to 'racial' factors without perhaps realizing how very complicated is the problem. The hypothesis of innate factors bound up with the question of race is one which has occasioned much loose thinking and considerable emotion on one side or the other. Few would deny that Mediterranean peoples indulge in gesture more than northern Europeans. Similarly Jews are commonly regarded as gesture-prone, as compared with Gentiles. Why this should be the case is less clear and it is indeed not known whether these differences always occur and have always occurred. The scope for personal prejudice is considerable.

In Germany during the thirties a number of ill-contrived pseudo-scientific ideas were formulated within the domain of anthropology, most of them of a pejorative character regarding those who were not of pure Nordic or Aryan stock. Thus as long ago as 1867, V. Hehn was contrasting the gestural patterns in Italians and Germans. He ascribed the differences to such factors as the massivity of the skeleton and the temperature of the blood. In 1903 A. Fouillée distinguished within each race an innate psycho-physiological character, and an acquired psycho-social one. The use of gesture, he believed, depends upon these two factors, the more important being the question of 'racial heredity'. K. Skraup, 1908, regarded five qualities as being important in determining bodily motion including gesture, namely intellect, occupation, temperament, culture and race. He even described a distinction between rural and urban dwellers in this respect. Of these many variables he regarded the most fundamental as that of intellectual status. In the same year A. Gehring spoke of a hierarchy of racial factors, within which are correlated the use of gesture. Thus while the thinking of the Graeco-Latin peoples is simple and unencumbered leading to liveliness of speech and movement, the Teutons are remarkable for their composure and taciturnity—characters which stem from the 'wealth and complexity of their thought'. An almost mystical conception was put forward in 1925 by O. Rutz who isolated four 'spiritual' types of mankind, which he termed spherical man, parabolic man, pyramidal man, and polygonic man. Each of these spiritual archetypes was looked upon as possessing its own peculiar gestural climate; and furthermore each was to be correlated with racial groups irrespective of social considerations.

At about the same time W. Berger became one of the first to bring into the problem anti-semitic prejudices. Jewish vivacity of speech and movement is, he said, due to a general expressive energy which Jews derive from their strong Asiatic strain. Berger, however, distinguishes between racial and national factors as applied to the Jew. F. Lenz (1927) also dealt with gesture as coupled with racial temperament, and he associated the Jews with Americans and modern Greeks as excelling not only in oratory, but also in a 'capacity for expressing thoughts and feelings by gesture and play of countenance'. In 1929 W. Boehle isolated three fundamental psychosomatic types—the affective, the motor, and the perceptive. These he correlated both with Kretschmer's classification, and also with Müller's trilogy of life-forces. Furthermore he associated them with racial groups, with skeletal characteristics, and with the volume and type of gesticulation.

H. Guenther has been described as the most emphatic protagonist of the notion of an intimate relationship between the practice of gesture, and race. According to this writer (1930) the 'Nordic' peoples are quiet and controlled. He had much to say about Jewish propensities in this field, and he aligned the type of gesture utilized by Jews and half-Jews with Mediterranean characteristics.

Rossell I. Vilar (1930) regarded race as being made up of a group of peoples possessing the same mentality and displaying the same gestures, both being independent of social-environmental factors. Neuville (1933) agreed and extended this viewpoint to the animal world. L. F. Clauss (1933) conceived that a certain rare intuitive capacity was needed to discern the typical racial core with its bodily expressions. Such intuition is superior to the processes of observation and comparison. The human body is a kind of stage, upon which the psycho-racial traits of the individual are manifested in voice, gesture and facial expression. In each bodily motion there is an 'expressive material' and an 'expressive style', both of which are racially determined. Each race has its characteristic body and soul, and each racial body-soul has its typical mode of expressive movement. Clauss identified six different types of mankind each with its own psychological features, and each with its distinct gestural modalities. 'Nordic gesture is restrained; it shuns the sweep away from the body; every movement that reaches out beyond the area actually necessary for the expression, strikes the Nordic man as uncontrolled, and, therefore, as unbecoming; the taciturnity of the Nordic soul reflects itself in its gestures; in contrast to that of the Mediterranean, the gestural movement of the Nordic does not playfully exhibit itself, but is confined to the essential. Bending of the knees or the trunk in gesticulation, as well as the lateral motions of the body are alien to the Nordic soul; as a speaker the Nordic always keeps an upright posture; expressive of his "Kraft" . . .' The gestures of the 'Phalic race' are described as spatially constrained like the movements of a fleeing chicken: 'Those of the Mediterranean are said to be playful and graceful; the Mediterranean soul requires and has a small, slender, cat-like body, fit for free motion; both its gestures and postures are theatrical. Just as the sounds of the Mediterranean languages swing and dance in contrast to the Germanic ones which have eliminated all sound that is not essentially meaningful, so the bodily language of the Mediterranean is a swinging and dancing of gestures . . . To the gestural style of the Orientaloid race belong the characteristics of explosiveness and lack of restraint. These are predetermined by the bodily structure of the race, which is flexible, excessively slender, and light . . . The Near Eastern race shows a tendency to bend the knees in gesticulation, to throw the trunk around, and to perform lateral gestures . . .'.[1]

L. A. Boettiger (1938) was also of the opinion that gesture and facial expression were far more

[1] This passage has been quoted practically verbatim from Efron's monograph, and this in turn has resorted freely to the original language employed by Clauss.

significant than the usual physical habitus. Like Clauss, he regarded a faculty of intuition as preferable to orthodox scientific techniques of anthropology.

In an effort to evaluate the respective importance of racial as opposed to cultural (environmental) factors D. Efron (1941) made an interesting study of the gestural behaviour in members of four contrasting communities. He chose a group of orthodox Jews living in New York; a number of Americanized Jews; some inhabitants of a 'little Italy' district; and a body of assimilated Italo-Americans. Each group was closely studied from the standpoint of gesture using careful techniques which included cinematography. The services of an illustrator were also enlisted. Out of a very considerable body of material, the findings were studied, analysed and then contrasted, one group with another. Efron made several interesting conclusions as to the pattern of bodily movements characteristic of Jews as opposed to Italians. His findings merit detailed quotation. According to his data the radius of the traditional Jewish gestures is somewhat confined, being close to the chest and face. Upper arm movement is rare. 'The eastern Ghetto Jew exhibits a tendency to gesticulate chiefly in the vertical and the frontal planes of his body . . . the Jew performs most of his movements in an up and down direction or in a direction towards the interlocutor . . . the Jewish gestures appear to involve more often a plan of *depth*, being more centripetal with regard to the body of the gesture. Rhetorically one might characterize the gesture of the traditional Jew as a gesture of address, that of the traditional Italian as a gesture of display.' The head plays a remarkable role in the gestures of the Jew . . . in a turtle-like fashion. Digital gestures are conspicuous but they are rarely descriptive. Often the speaker will move his finger rapidly as though typing or writing his ideas in the air. He rarely employs bilateral gesture, that is moving both arms simultaneously in mirror opposite movements. Jews are more apt to use the two arms in a sequential fashion whereby one arm makes a movement, and then the other follows suit; then a new gesture is made with the first arm, followed again by its partner ('ambulatory gesture' or 'gestural locomotion'). The tempo of Jewish gestures is quite irregular, and often jerky. A characteristic Jewish habit is that of touching or interfering with the body or clothing of the interlocutor. Occasionally he will display certain symbolic acts which involve touching his own face, nose, or chin with his hand. Jews, especially those of the traditional type, tend when in groups to stand huddled closely together. Indeed, so close may they be packed that manual gestures are hampered, permitting only lavish expressive movements of the head and shoulders. Inanimate objects are often picked up and used as a gesturing tool: this is well illustrated at meal-times when a fork may be brandished close before the face of the listener.

Efron proceeded to a consideration of the Italian mode of gesture. Compared with those of the Jews they are less spatially confined and more ample. The axis of movement is around the shoulder joint. Gestures of the head do not take place. As Van Veen also emphasized, the Italians, unlike the Jews, do not poke, grab or point in the face of the conversee. The greatest gestural 'promiscuity' is to be seen when the speaker perhaps touches the arm or knee of the interlocutor. Simultaneous gesturing on the part of two speakers does not occur. Unlike the Jews who pack themselves in tight clusters, a congregation of Italians stand at a little distance from one another, as if to allow plenty of play for their pantomime. Efron spoke of a preponderance of 'physiographic' over 'ideographic' forms of gesture, by which he meant—if one interprets correctly his rather involved text—that the Italian gesticulation is more concrete, representational and descriptive, while that of the Jew 'outlines the logical itineraries of the corresponding ideational processes'.

When Efron came to consider 'assimilated' or 'Americanized' groups of Jews and Italians he found interesting modifications of the 'traditional' patterns. In such circumstances, the Jew is freer and wider in the sweep of his gestures. Van Veen believed that this is due to his greater social freedom, and to the loss of his century-old sense of oppression and restraint. The Americanized Jew, he said, acquires the gestures which are more or less characteristic of the average American, namely, expository, indicative, and pictorial patterns of movement, using them with great freedom and abandon. Efron believed that the absence of gesture among the upper class sophisticated Jewish community in the States shows that Jews are not 'racially' inclined towards gesture. On the other hand the gestures of the Americanized Italian differ from those of the Italian migrant, in being 'less ample'. The Italian in the U.S.A., according to Van Veen, has not experienced any feeling of escape from centuries of oppression; at the same time he is embarrassed by the gestural voluminousness of his forebears.

Efron also made the point that a partially assimilated migrant may show in his system of gesticulation, expressive movements which belong to both his old and his new environments. Thus there appear what he called 'hybrid gestures', which are, he asserted, evidences of a 'gestural bilingualism'.

This writer concluded that gesture (or its absence) arises not so much from racial or biological forces, as from socio-psychological factors.

This monograph is an interesting field-study of gestural behaviour as seen in New York communities. It is regrettable that his work did not extend to an observation of gestures made by Italians in their own country and also of Jews in Israel. As far as the former group is concerned, Efron surely would have found that many of his points of distinction between Italian and Jewish gestures do not altogether apply.

XXVI. LANGUAGE, AND LOSS OF LANGUAGE, IN THE DEAF-MUTE

Incidentally, there are people who seem completely staggered when one talks about non-verbal referential processes—that is, wordless thinking; these people simply seem to have no ability to grasp the idea that a great deal of covert living—living that is not objectively observable but only inferable—can go on without the use of words. The brute fact is, as I see it, that most of living goes on that way. That does not in any sense reduce the enormous importance of the communicative tools—words and gestures.

Harry Stack Sullivan

How do the deaf and dumb communicate with each other? How do they manage to effect satisfactory reciprocal contact with the normal community? These problems have been partly answered in the previous chapter where sign-languages were discussed. The question goes deeper however and ties up with an enquiry into the thinking-processes in deaf-mutes.

Acquisition of speech by a normal child necessarily implies an adequate degree of auditory perception. To sort out and unscramble the surrounding confusion of noise is an important stage in development which should finally lead to an ability to detect meaning within a particular set of perceived sounds. A congenitally deaf child fails to receive environmental auditory stimuli, and hence he never attains the power to comprehend speech. Consequently a fundamental stage in language-development is by-passed. As a result, not only does the child never achieve the faculty of articulate speech, but of necessity he also suffers a hiatus in his intellectual maturation.

Aristotle proclaimed that of all the faculties, hearing was the one most essential for intelligence, though sight was the most important for the needs of animals. In the intellectual development of the maturing child the factor of language-training and learning is highly important. The efficiency of thought-processes expands according to the number of language-symbols which are available as tools for thought. Thus, as a deaf child learns finger-spelling and lip-reading, and still later, conventional reading and writing, its span of achievement increases materially.

A certain unorthodoxy in the thinking-processes of the deaf can be expected. The defect is a subtle one however, requiring close scrutiny for its detection. Whitney asserted . . . 'and who will dare to deny even to the uninstructed deaf-mute the possession of ideas, of cogitation, multitudinous and various, of power to combine observations and draw conclusions from them, of

Based upon an article in *Brain* 1938. **46**, 163 ('Aphasia' in a partial deaf-mute); the volume *The Language of Gesture*, Arnold, London 1939; a lecture on 'Thinking Processes in deaf-mutes' delivered at Hertford College, Oxford, on 5th September, 1951, and published in the 60th birthday volume dedicated to Academician A. Kreindler, Bucharest, 1960.

reasonings, of imaginings, of hopes? Who will say then, that he does not think, though his thinking faculty has not yet been trained and developed by the aid of a system of signs?' The writer obviously made light of any differences in mentation, but it is probable that as an academic linguist, his experience of deaf-mutes was limited. Those who have had day to day dealings with institutionalized deaf subjects, and psychologists who have undertaken specific research-projects into this problem, are usually cautious and more sceptical in their conclusions.

Thus, impressed by the extent to which language assists the development of intelligence and problem-solving, P. Oleron (1950) indicated two important points: first, that intelligence tests present a greater difficulty to children born deaf than to those with acquired deafness. Secondly, that deaf-mute children brought up among others similarly afflicted possess certain advantages over sporadic or isolated cases of deaf-mutism. His conclusions were based upon a series of 250 cases.

But a deaf-mute population necessarily includes a proportion of dullards and defectives. Even though many deaf-mutes are of normal or even high intellectual calibre, a survey might well show that the average intelligence quotient is lower in a community of deaf and dumb than of normals. Pre-natal disease may have been jointly responsible not only for deafness, but also mental retardation.

The term 'intelligence' is however one which lacks precision and is difficult to define. Agreement is still awaited as to just what is included herein. Among deaf-mutes the problem is not the quantitative level of intelligence so artificially estimated by psychometry, but its qualitative characters. Being deprived of one of the most important tools of thought, namely auditivo-articulatory speech-symbols, the congenitally deaf subject must surely be handicapped when it comes to silent rumination, browsing, emotional expression, creative thought, judgement, planning, and anticipation. All these aspects are ordinarily included within the comprehensive term 'thinking'.

We realize how much the mentation of ordinary people in ordinary circumstances depends upon language. The role is not exclusive however for we do not necessarily always think in words—or rather, in verbal symbols—as we have already discussed. Certainly, at times normal people can and do dispense with verbal symbols in their thought, but to what extent and how often this is so, is perhaps arguable. An even greater problem arises when one approaches pathological cases, as for example persons who have lost speech by reason of brain-disease. The vexed question as to the intellectual level of dysphasiacs has been already broached, and one recalls Henry Head's evaluation of this problem: 'It is not the "general intellectual capacity" which is primarily affected, but the mechanism by which certain aspects of mental activity are brought into play. Behaviour suffers in a specific manner; an action can be carried out in one way, but not in another. In so far as these procedures are necessary for the perfect exercise of mental aptitudes, "general intelligence" certainly suffers. For a man who, in the course of general conversation, is unable to express his thoughts, or comprehend the full significance of words and phrases, cannot move freely in the general field of ideas . . . The intellectual life of civilized man is so greatly dependent on speaking, reading and writing, that any restriction of these powers throws him back upon himself; . . . this "want of intelligence" is based primarily on some distinctive defect in a definite form of behaviour'.

Goldstein regarded the principal difficulty of a patient deprived of speech as an inability to cope with abstractions, i.e. with general ideas as opposed to the particular; with categories in contrast to concrete notions.

With deaf-mutes the premises are rather similar. Like the aphasiac, the deaf-mute lacks certain important components of his communicative armamentarium. Unlike the aphasiac, the deaf-mute never has had these tools within his possession. In the one a mature faculty has undergone a dissolution: in the other an innate component of the usual process of maturation is missing.

Evidence suggests that there is some qualitative aberration of thought in the congenitally deaf, comparable with that in the patient with an aphasia acquired in later life. The isolated case-report studied in a longitudinal dimension, and published in 1931 by G. Vermeylen, supports this view. M. Kuenberg (1930) carried out sorting tests in many deaf-mutes, with interesting results. At first her subjects would not attempt the task. Once their reluctance was overcome, they would start to arrange the articles, but never according to any system determined by one governing abstract idea. The system commonly adopted was one which was purely visual. Thereafter they could never switch to a fresh system of arrangement, always adhering to the original plan. These findings conformed with those made earlier by W. Frohn (1926), who found that deaf-mutes concentrate upon the particular, and that any relationship or association between objects, plays but a minor part in mentation. Similar expressions of opinion emerged from the studies reported by Heider and Heider (1940), McAndrew (1948), Temptin (1950) and Myklebust (1960).

These findings have been supported by the experience of observant teachers in institutions for deaf-mutes, where admittedly there may have been a material percentage of below-average inmates. But they have reported unequivocally that their pupils find it difficult to grasp conceptions of time, i.e. the past and the future. Certain grammatical components cannot readily be conveyed to deaf-mutes, such as for instance conjunctions and many prepositions. Words such as 'because' and 'why', and phrases like 'did you do so and so' are scarcely communicable. Business matters are difficult. Conceptions of right and wrong are hard to put across, especially when different time-factors are involved. Thus such a statement as 'you were very naughty last week, so you shan't go to the movies next Saturday' would be quite obscure to a deaf-mute.

As might be expected, the notion of 'noise' or 'sound' is as nebulous to a deaf-mute as 'colour' is to one born blind. And yet he can be made aware of sound by way of tactile appreciation of vibration. A hand laid upon a radio set will discover whether it is switched on or off. The pealing of church bells can be detected by manual contact with the outside wall of the belfry. During the war, deaf-mutes were always aware of air-raids, the sirens, the falling bombs, and the anti-aircraft gunfire.

Though speechless, deaf-mutes are not necessarily silent. When communicating with each other by dint of gesture, facial mimicry, and finger-spelling, they commonly utilize a variety of subdued chattering, grunting noises. That there is some measure of awareness is shown by the fact that when social circumstances ordain an atmosphere of silence, as in a church or at the cinema, these vocalizations cease. Nevertheless the deaf-mute does not inhibit the sounds which accompany certain bodily happenings, as shown by the noisy manner in which they eat, drink, cough, sneeze, vomit, and spit.

Research into the nature of dreaming in deaf-mutes would be rewarding as well as interesting. Unquestionably they dream and they may be observed to utter inarticulate cries in their sleep. The nature of their spectral imagery is uncertain however, though it seems likely that the dream-world is mainly visual, with perhaps haptic components. Mendelson, Siger and Solomon (1960), who studied the dreams of deaf-mutes, found that when an affective colouring is vivid, the dreamer may be noted to execute 'primitive' or 'home-made' signs. This is especially so when the dream entails elements of severe anxiety.

Communication as carried out by the deaf-mute in sign-language or in writing, is unorthodox by our standards. For example the process is relatively slow. Of considerable interest is the matter of syntax. The grammar of the gestural language is unlike that of spoken English. The conventional subject-predicate structure is replaced by something which resembles Chinese in many ways. Though the syntax is sometimes regarded as being more primitive and more childish, this is not altogether fair for it is more logical. Degand likened deaf-mute talk to *petit negre*. Thus, to indicate 'the bottle is empty' the appropriate sign would be *fini*. Deaf-mutes employ a bare minimum of words, as though writing an expensive telegram. Exact shades of meaning are not expressed clearly. A deaf-mute wishing to make the Lord's Prayer in sign-language would proceed thus: 'Father our . . . heaven . . . name Thy hallowed . . . Kingdom Thy come . . . will done . . . earth on, heaven in, as . . . bread give us daily . . . . trespass our forgive us . . . temptation lead not . . . evil deliver from . . . Kingdom, Power, Glory, Thine, for ever'. Other examples of deaf-mute telegrammatism are evidenced in: 'Man . . . dark . . . handsome . . . ride . . . walk' (for 'A dark handsome man rides and walks'); 'Hat . . . black . . . bring' (for 'bring me my black hat') or 'Hungry . . . cake . . . me . . . give' (for 'I am hungry, may I have some cake').

Referring to the grammar of the gestural language Marichelle said . . . 'that is why the deaf-mute is, and always will be, a foreigner as regards his native language, and indeed any other language he would like to study'.

With a normal individual some idea as to how he is thinking is betrayed when he indulges in the habit of talking to himself. This revealing act divulges just what is going on in the individual's mind at that particular moment, and it also tells us something of that person's mental imagery. So it is with the deaf and dumb. The deaf-mute often 'talks' to himself. That is to say in seeming solitude, he may be seen to make various grimaces or gestures, although he is addressing no audience. These are usually indicative of some feeling-tone or affect. Thus, a deaf-mute who has painfully stubbed his toe against an obstacle, may bang his two fists together making the sign 'bother!' Longer phrases, or even sentences, indicating not a sudden upsurge of emotion, but a deliberate proposition, may be observed in the sign-talk of a deaf-mute who believes he is alone. This is a common trick in the elderly or lonely deaf-mute. Helen Keller constantly 'talked' to herself unconsciously, using the manual alphabet. Her biographer wrote 'frequently when she is walking about in the hall or the verandah, one sees her hands given up to a startling pantomime, and the rapid movement of her fingers is like a fluttering of birds' wings'.

Observations such as these afford some inkling as to the nature of the symbols used by a deaf-mute in his imagery. Whitney believed that every deliberate thought in the mind of a deaf-mute is accompanied by an image of 'dactylic writhings'. In other words the deaf-mute thinks in finger-

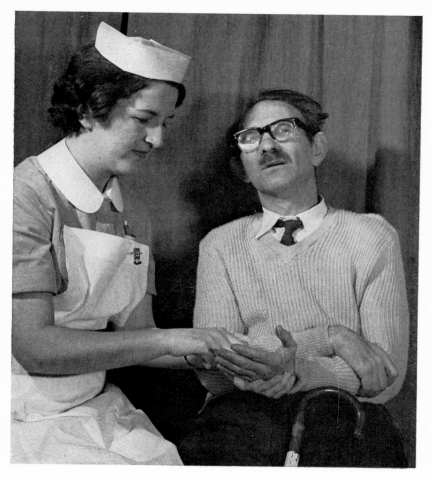

Tactile communication in the case of a deaf-blind patient.

Plate 11

twists. It would be of interest to discover whether minimal 'sub-vocal' activity can be demonstrated by electromyographic testing of the small muscles of the hands during the waking but completely relaxed state. Whitney referred to the Principal of an Asylum for the Deaf and Dumb whose thoughts could always be detected by the simple dodge of watching his hands. For as he cogitated, his fingers would involuntarily form the signs which were serving in his mind as symbols. If one is correct in assuming that the Principal was not himself deaf, then we must suspect that this manual trick was a habit he had picked up from his pupils.

Even before Whitney, Hughlings Jackson referred to this topic. 'When a deaf-mute is communicating with his fellows, there are strong discharges of cerebral motor nervous arrangements with accompanying vivid psychical states, actions; when he is thinking there are slight discharges of these nervous arrangements, and their accompanying psychical states, actions (so-called "ideas of movements") are faint; in the former case there are actual movements of muscles, in the latter, the discharges are too slight to produce actual movements. Suppose the deaf-mute were to lose both arms, he would try to move them, and would then I suppose have for himself vivid spectral pantomime during energizing of cerebral nervous arrangements representing the absent muscles of the limbs; the pantomimic actions arising during slighter discharges of these nervous arrangements, would serve in his mentation the same as when he was entire'.

Some years later, Bastian also became interested in this matter, and concluded that combined visual and kinaesthetic impressions constitute the 'thought-counters' of the deaf-mute.

It must be pointed out, however, that within the last decade there has been a change in attitude. Rosenstein (1960) for example could trace no significant differences in ability to abstract or generalize between deaf children and those with hearing. The author criticized earlier workers in this field on the grounds that the psychological tests employed were outside the linguistic capacity of the children. Farth (1961) agreed. Kates *et al.* (1961) (1962) tested conceptual attainments entailing only minimal verbal linguistic skills. Deaf subjects were compared with a younger hearing group matched for educational status, and also with an older hearing group matched for intellectual capacity. The authors found no differences between the deaf and the older hearing group in either rate of performance or conceptual attainment. The deaf subjects scored better than the younger hearing group with regard to speed. Again, when adequate communication was effected by means of sign-language, Putnam, Iscoe and Young (1962) found that a deaf population actually fared better than a control series of normals.

Such observations clash with the results of earlier work and also with the experience of those who operate within the deaf-mute communities. One must object that these more recent opinions are not altogether convincing.

It is surely fair to conclude that the deaf-mute is one who is potentially lame in his thinking as Hughlings Jackson said of aphasiacs, even though his intellectual level may be adequate. By dint of training and by the assiduous utilization of as many modalities of communication as is humanly possible, the lameness of thought is remedied more and more. The quality of the thinking-processes accords with the degree of attainment of language, a conception which is supported by the ideas propounded by that celebrated blind writer and historian P. Villey. Comparing and contrasting the relative handicaps of blindness and deafness, Professor Villey said: 'In manual work, the deaf man who sees, is superior to the blind man. From the intellectual point of view, I am convinced that the position of the blind man who hears, is preferable to that of the deaf man'.

And again . . . 'the faculty of hearing represents for a person the spontaneous, involuntary acquisition of language and, consequently, of a good share of human experience. It is, as a matter of fact, by means of language that our minds are elevated to the conception of general and abstract ideas. Our progress in the order of abstractions can only take place by means of parallel progress in the assimilation of language. Thanks to hearing, the mind of the child is, as it were, moulded from its earliest age by abstract ideas, and elaborated by the common conscience, which endeavours to invade and enrich it. That is not all. By the sense of hearing, no less than by that of sight, man is plunged into a world of sensations which stimulate him. He is enriched by them. Passive as he is supposed to be, he is snatched from his torpor and drawn into the common life. Constantly incited by the conversation of his parents, his brothers and his sisters, which brings him thus into the outer life, the blind child's mind cannot remain in inaction. There is no reason why it should become blind from idleness'.

A similar confrontation of the problems of the born-blind as opposed to the deaf-mute has been made by von Stockert (1952), though his conclusions were couched in an all too obscure terminology.

Arguments about the thought-processes of deaf-mutes with their accent upon their handicaps and short-comings are continually confronted with the contradiction afforded by Laura Bridgman and more particularly by Helen Keller. For example the latter asserted . . . 'I can remember the time before I learned to speak, and how I used to struggle to express my thoughts by means of the manual alphabet—how my thoughts used to beat against my finger-tips like little birds striving to gain their freedom, until one day Miss Fuller opened wide the prison-door and let them escape. I wonder if she remembers how eagerly and gladly they spread their wings and flew away. Of course, it was not easy at first to fly. The speech-wings were weak and broken, and had lost all the grace and beauty that had once been theirs'.

But Helen Keller was unique. Blind, deaf and mute, she constitutes an enigma to psychologists, a pinnacle of accomplishment, and a Galatea to the Pygmalion, Ann Sullivan Macy, her tutor. Why does Helen Keller stand out like a beacon against the background of others similarly deprived? Doubtless she had been endowed with a supernormal level of intelligence. She was aesthetically hypersensitive. In addition she had been blessed with vast Ego-strength—the will to surmount the highest obstacles. Her education became the life-work of her dedicated teacher. One wonders however whether some contrived element of stylistic artificiality has not perhaps crept in, fostered by those around her. As with most blind writers, Miss Keller's prose is rich in visualisms, replete with metaphors and similes which could only have been borrowed from the experience of others. Helen Keller's writings show these characteristics in profusion. When she wrote of her deep appreciation of music merely by dint of perceiving vibration through the world of touch, she must have been indulging in exaggeration. The intellectual and aesthetic discrimination between compositions by Schumann and say, Schubert, must surely have been outside her ken.

A normal infant reared *in vacuo* in an environment of enforced silence would never attain conventional speech. The congenitally deaf are at similar risk, and the growth of intelligence is to a large extent a product of environmental factors. The more propitious these factors, and the more richly endowed with signs and symbols, the better will be the end-product. The deaf child will learn from the proximity of other children and here the companionship of other deaf-mutes becomes all-important. In this fashion the little deaf-mute acquires its natural sign-language. The codified finger-spelling or dactylology is something it learns by dint of instruction usually at the hands of interpreters endowed with normal hearing. This additional accomplishment affords the deaf child a visa to a community whose speech it cannot hear, the significance of which it begins to grasp, none the less. But this is not enough. As Helen Keller wrote 'the deaf child who has only the sign-language of De l'Epée is an intellectual Philip Nolan [i.e. the author of 'The man without a Country'] an alien from all races and his thoughts of an Englishman, or a Frenchman, or a Spaniard. The Lord's Prayer in signs, is not the Lord's Prayer in English'.

Progress rapidly goes ahead when the deaf-mute child masters the art of reading and writing. For quite a while however the mode of expression on paper is unorthodox. It does not correspond with the pattern set by the language before him in print. Rather does it reflect the idiosyncrasies of the deaf-mutes processes of thought. Two examples may be given, selected at random from letters written by inmates of a Hostel for the Deaf.

(1)　From a woman aged 31 years.

Dear Friend Miss Jones,
　　I am going write a letter to you now I hope you are keeping well and alright now and I am. well and alright be happy now. We hare a new Television we were able to See the Lord Mayore Show on Thursday for One hour last night We saw the Memisial Service at the Albert Hall The kings and Queen were there, Them this morning We saw the Serrice at the Cens Caph. Where the king and Mr Churchill place the wraths. We all had fo bed and Supper Later yesterday night.
　　I can see pictures of Telension Serrice It is very nice good them and I like them very much.
　　We keeping them alwdy here Home It big Television Service brown light. It will be Soon Xmas One months in December.
　　I will send you Calendar and Xmas present for Xmas Which you would like it let me know?
I will write tell you about Pictures of Television Service anytime. We hare luck a new Television Serrice. Give my love to you and remsmber you now
　　With love from
　　　　Your friend Anne
　　　　　　Robertson　　xx
　　　x　　　　x
　x　　　x　　　x
　　　x　　　x

P.S.
I have a Biro pen from my friend Auntie Alice and She Send me for. my brithday Later
　　　　　　　　　　x　　　x　　　x　　　x
　　　　　　　　　x　　　x

(2) From a woman aged 66 years.

My Dear Dolly and Mary

Just a few lines leaves me I hope they are all quite well by now I am quite well now I am very sorry that Peggy have been not well long while Tom is still the same about Dr. Say she must rest all she can and she not to have any one to stay to make more work Tom was bad cough at times upset his heart I have heard from Emma yesterday morning she told me that she is much better her cough has gone also Winnie is keeping vell at Present she find the train Journey home at night rather tiring and cold she dont get home untill 7 o clock some evenings she has to go out so it dont give her much time for rest one good thing she do get saturday off other wise she is ok she is vah office in London she like work in London she is not Lodging at London she always go home with Pat every day Pat and Cecil are well Pat is busy these days Emma came back from John she cant go far because of the Hill and it is very bleak Watford Winnie and we was sorry we missed George Canning when he came Watford we had gone over to Stella Painter and he came and saw Pat I think he had so many Friends to go and see he had no time to come again when Emma go to Southend on sea again if Geage still has his Moctor car she will ask him to go and take me one day to see them Flossie sorry Ida has been ill I hope by now she is better I am very sorry that Yvonnes husband Jim is not well having trouble with his eyes and head now we have a new Televivian here now came last Thursday week and we were all able to see the Lord Mayor. Show going through London it was wonderful then last Saturday 11st week saw the King Queen at the Royal Albert Hall Memerial service last Sunday 12th we saw the service at the Censtaph the King and Mr. Churchhill put their wreath on it is very good to watch King going on I hope Annie Jill and family are all quite well by now with close lav to all and King Rd I will write to you again

Your loving sister in Law
Jennie B.

At some time or other the deaf-mute usually becomes instructed in the art of lip-reading. Teachers of the deaf are not in unanimity as to the emphasis which should be placed upon the so-called oral method of communication. Many teachers believe that it is of considerable utility, and that in order to concentrate upon this faculty the deaf child should abandon its natural system of signs. In institutions this is rarely achieved. Despite the direst penalties the deaf-mute children ordinarily resort to their natural signs as soon as the teacher is out of sight.

'The enthusiastic oral teacher will not permit a rival in the field of expression, and signs and gestures are banned, condemned and discouraged. Thus a feeling of frustration and negation is engendered when the child is forced back to the pure oral way, and we see the beginnings of conflict between oralism and the child's natural instincts. So often we find that from the outset the deaf child is a victim of this conflict between theory in education and natural tendencies.' (E. S. Greenaway).

The rôle of lip-reading has probably been exaggerated. It is one thing to follow the meaning of an instructor who uses in the class-room manual signs, accompanying each gesture with exaggerated movements of the lips and mouth, at the same time quietly articulating the words or phrase. But for a deaf-mute to attempt to follow the small range movements of the lips of an ordinary person not directly addressing the patient, is a task quite difficult and limited in scope. Out of sight, coder and decoder remain *incommunicado*.

The oral method of teaching the deaf also entails instructing the deaf-mute to make certain specific movements and then to phonate. But the end-result is unsatisfying. As E. S. Greenaway, Headmaster of the Doncaster Residential School for the Deaf, has pointed out, the deaf child who aspires to speak has to deal with a medium he will never appreciate at first hand. He will always lack the essential control in such a performance—hearing his own efforts. 'Very few deaf children ever attain a standard of speech appreciably near to the normal.'

The same inadequacies apply to lip-reading. Very little speech is visibly comprehensible on the lips, and the efficiency of this means of understanding the spoken word is low. It must be augmented by intelligent guess-work. The lip-reader needs to concentrate on the face of the speaker. Lip-reading requires an acquaintance with the language which may be beyond the deaf-mute's horizon. The educational task of the deaf-mute is twice or three times greater than that of the hearing child, as Greenaway pointed out.

Pathological cases

What would happen to a deaf-mute's ability to communicate, in the widest sense of the term, after a cerebral lesion, focal or diffuse? This is a matter of conjecture of great interest to aphasiologists. Would one discover an impairment in the deaf-mute's ability to employ dactylology; his natural system of signs; and his rudimentary oral speech? Furthermore, would he cease to comprehend the sign-language of others? Might the victim lose his ability to lip-read?

In other words can one imagine what one might designate an 'aphasia' in a deaf-mute?

If so, does it necessarily imply some generalized cerebral pathology? Or could it by chance follow a focal lesion? If so, where would be the probable location of such a lesion? Would it be co-terminos with the alleged speech-area in the normal individual with intact hearing?

Ninety years ago this problem was anticipated by Hughlings Jackson when he wrote 'No doubt, by disease of some part of the brain, the deaf-mute might lose his natural system of signs which are of some speech value to him'.

My own clinical experience has led to the conclusion that both 'motor' and 'sensory' types of aphasia' occur in deaf-mutes, and I have now had experience of five such cases. They have varied somewhat in clinical characters but all entailed subjects who had been deaf either since birth or shortly after; each had relied heavily or exclusively upon pantomime as a means of expression. In each case there occurred an impaired ability to communicate by gestures, associated with a greater or lesser degree of defective comprehension of the communicative efforts of others. In four of the cases there was an associated right hemiparesis, but in one the hemiplegia involved the left side, the patient being all the same a right-handed subject.

The first case on record, where Jackson's prescient prediction was confirmed, was published by J. Grasset in 1896. His paper was entitled *Aphasie de la main droite chez un sourd-muet*. An arteriopathic deaf-mute of 50 years gradually developed evidences of a cerebral softening. General intellectual level was lowered somewhat: memory and rate of comprehension had deteriorated, and the patient could no longer attend to his business. Nevertheless he was able to read with understanding, and to comprehend finger-talk in others. He was, however, unable to reply with the right-hand finger-alphabet but he could do so quite well with the left hand. Asked to spell out the alphabet he indicated 'A' with difficulty, and then with more difficulty 'B'. Further than that he could not go. However, when he switched to the left hand he found he was able to demonstrate the alphabet quickly and correctly. Shown printed words and told to spell them out dactylologically, he succeeded with his left hand but failed with his right. The patient also evinced a difficulty in writing. Some impairment of strength and co-ordination existed in the right upper limb, though insufficient in degree to account for the failure to write and to finger-spell.

The fact that Grasset's patient could carry out finger-spelling on one side but not the other indicates that the faculty of language was intact, though the means of exteriorization were faulty. Grasset would perhaps have been more accurate had he termed his case 'unilateral apraxia in a deaf-mute'.

In 1905 C. W. Burr described a case of 'loss of the sign-language in a deaf-mute from cerebral tumour and softening'. The lesion was probably in the frontal lobe.

My own first case was published in 1938 under the title 'aphasia in a partial deaf-mute'. The patient, a man of 42 years, gradually lost his hearing at 7 years of age. As his disability was steadily worsening he was taught the art of finger-spelling. At the age of 14, he was stone-deaf, and was admitted to an institution for deaf-mutes, where he remained 3 years. Finger-speech was discouraged and he was taught to lip-read. However, as soon as he left the residential school he relied chiefly on finger speech and manual signs for the purposes of communication.

Six weeks before I first saw this patient he sustained a stroke which caused a right-sided paralysis, and for 3 days a loss of what little articulate speech had previously been possible for him. The paralysis improved considerably over the next 4 weeks, and his speech also returned to some degree.

As soon as he was able to hold a pen, it was found that he could neither write nor perform simple arithmetical calculations. It was also discovered that he could no longer lip-read. For the first few days after the stroke he was quite unable to understand people trying to communicate with him in finger-spelling. In a few days, however, this ability returned, but he realized that he was unable to reply on his hands. His articulate speech was uttered only rarely, and it was considerably altered in character, being uncontrolled as to tone, too loud, dysarthric, and ungrammatical. He relied very little upon this channel of inter-communication.

Over the next two years I repeatedly saw the patient whose condition changed little if at all. Examination revealed a right-sided sensory deficit, and a slight weakness of the right half of the face and tongue. The reflexes were normal and symmetrical. There was no trace of apraxia.

Investigation of the patient's aphasia was carried out through the intermediary of a chaplain to the Institution for the Deaf and Dumb, who acted as interpreter.

The ability to lip-read was still very defective.

The patient was able to understand others talking on their hands to him.

When the patient attempted to finger-spell he perpetrated a large number of errors, chief among which were the following:

(a) confusion of vowels (e.g. /a/ instead of /e/);
(b) short telegrammatic phrases instead of sentences;

(c) defective syntax;

(d) inability to complete the alphabet in finger-spelling, or even the 5 vowels;

(e) slow, erratic, and jerky movements of the hands during the act of finger-spelling;

(f) omission of words;

(g) employment of wrong words.

Aside from these dactylographic defects, the patient was able to write, recognize colours, tell the time, build words from cards, type, and read with fair ability. Calculations were carried out with difficulty.

Since the publication of this case three other instances have been reported in the literature, namely by A. Leischner (1944); L. L. Tureen, E. A. Smolik and T. H. Tritt (1951); and by E. Douglass and J. C. Richardson (1959).

Leischner's patient developed a softening involving the left angular and supramarginal gyri which was confirmed at autopsy. At first a total loss of pantomimic speech resulted but later he improved so that he was able to make himself understood in sign-language, but only with considerable difficulty.

The case reported by Tureen *et al.* concerned a 43 year old congenitally deaf-mute who developed symptoms due to a haemorrhage into a left frontal glioblastoma. These were severe at first but after a few days some improvement occurred. It was then possible to demonstrate that though he could read print he could not understand sign-language, nor could he lip-read accurately. He had lost such minimal ability to speak as has been present beforehand. There was a reduced ability to execute finger-speech. Asked to make the signs for the alphabet he could proceed no further than /j/. He could not make known his thoughts or wishes either in writing, in finger-spelling; or by way of the universal or natural sign-language of deaf-mutes.

Douglass and Richardson's patient was a 21 year old female deaf-mute who developed a softening in the territory of the left middle cerebral artery. A right hemiplegia followed, so that she had to rely upon the left hand for dactylological expression. She developed some disturbance in the comprehension of printed material. Furthermore she was quite unable to understand finger-spelling or even the natural sign language of deaf-mutes. With her left hand she showed dysgraphia, an inability to finger-spell, or to perform the natural sign-language.

The foregoing cases of impaired sign-language all comprise patients who were linguistically deprived, being deaf-mutes. There is one other case on record of a rather different type. This concerned a brain-diseased patient who was not deaf, but who possessed the ability to utilize sign-language rather like a polyglot endowed with more than one symbol-system. The reason was because the patient—recorded by N. Reider (1941)—was a 32 year old male whose mother was a congenital deaf-mute. All the members of the family, including the patient, had learned to communicate by means of signs. Sign-language was indeed his 'mother-tongue', being acquired before both lip-reading and ordinary articulate speech. The patient's illness began with severe headaches, and after a series of four epileptic seizures, he became confused and disorientated, and speech was a matter of difficulty. During this period of dysphasia, the ability to communicate by way of signs was better preserved even though he made errors in finger-spelling. He also betrayed perseveration when communicating with his mother, indicating to her over and over again that he wanted to go home. The patient rapidly deteriorated. He lost all power of verbal speech but could continue to communicate with his hands. Twitchings of the right half of the face were almost continuously present. The patient died a month after the onset of the illness. Autopsy revealed suggestive evidences of a diffuse encephalitis, without any gross or focal abnormality.

The author emphasized the better and longer preservation of the earliest acquired language-modality, namely signs, together with the early involvement of the later endowment, namely speech.

Despite the experiences of the foregoing cases a number of questions remain unanswered. It appears as though many variables arise which are capable of influencing the final clinical picture. Such important factors as handedness, age, level of intelligence need to be taken into account. The picture may differ according to whether the patient was born deaf, or on the other hand, lost hearing in early childhood. Socio-domestic circumstances should be noted: is the deaf-mute an inmate in a residential institution for the deaf, or does he live at home? In the latter case, are there other deaf-mutes in his close entourage, or is he the sole victim? The educational status may be all-important especially as regards the degree to which the deaf-mute was in the habit of relying upon natural signs, figure-spelling, or lip-reading. Finally to what extent and with what freedom was he in touch with the world of the intellect by dint of reading and writing?

The cases on record are not uniform in respect to the impaired sign-language. Though one uses the metaphor 'aphasia' in this connection, at times it comes up for serious consideration whether the disability should not be regarded as an asemasia, or an apraxia, or even a so-called 'finger-agnosia' (whatever is entailed in that category).

XXVII. NON-ARTICULATE MODALITIES OF SPEECH, AND THEIR DISORDERS

And with it the sound of the drums—the everlasting drum . . . the fascinating, tedious, mysterious, maddening, attractive, symbolic, inevitable, everlasting, AFRICAN DRUM!

Morel, Nigeria

The chapter dealing with Kinesics (pp. 296–312), emphasizes that written and articulate speech are far from constituting the sole instruments for human communication. Pantomime and gesture are fundamental expedients whereby wittingly or unwittingly, man can transmit his ideas and feelings, and can moreover glean something of the content of the thoughts and emotions of others within view. A special aspect of gesture is represented by the numerous contrived accepted sign-languages.

But other modalities of language exist which possess reference function. These are often spoken of as examples of 'non-verbal communication'. The term is unacceptable, however, because many of these communicative systems are erected upon a basis of words, though these are neither uttered nor committed to graphic symbols. They are consequently 'verbal' in nature. For this reason the expression 'non-articulate modalities of speech' has been chosen. Some of these systems are intimately built into the user's socially orientated personality; others are adopted only on rare occasions and in special circumstances. It is tempting to suspect that these speech-surrogates are themselves vulnerable to the effects of brain-damage.

Braille reading

Perhaps the best known of these substitute systems of communication is represented by the Braille reading and printing as taught to the blind community and widely utilized by them. To what extent does braille become entrenched within the language faculty of the blind? And how do these learned skills react in states of brain disorder?

In the first place the physiology of tactile thought in the normal blind subject needs to be re-called. With a page of braille the sighted person senses with the pulp of his forefinger only a meaningless jumble of dots—and his tactile discrimination is by no means inferior to that of the blind subject. So also, the blind person who passes one of his non-reading fingers over the page of

Based upon a number of papers including "Tactile Thought with special reference to the Blind", *Brain*, 1953. **76**. 19–35; "Dyslexia in Braille Readers". *Bull. Johns Hopk. Hosp.*, 1962. **111**. 83–88; and "Aphasic disorders of signalling (constitutional and acquired) occurring in Naval Signalmen. *J. M. Sinai Hosp.*, 1942. **9**. 363–375.

braille cannot interpret the embossed signs that he feels. In other words, braille reading is a learned function of one limited part only, usually the index finger of one hand or the other; less often, of both hands. The blind student who by touch can interpret braille symbols at the rate of say, 60 words a minute, performs poorly, if at all, when he uses his thumb, or the 2nd, 3rd or 4th finger. And yet the threshold for tactile discrimination is not very different over the pulps or 'tactile rosettes' of all the fingers, whether one is speaking in terms of two points simultaneously applied, or of more than two points. Clearly some cerebral process is at work which transcends mere tactile discrimination as subserved by the parietal cortex.

A number of observations upon what might be termed the neurological aspects of braille reading may therefore be cited:

(1) The empirical invention of braille typology stands very near the limit of normal tactile discriminative powers. Each symbol, and there are 63 of them, is made up of one or more bosses within a 'cell' or cluster of six possible places. Only a few signs comprise one point; many are made up of 2, or 3, and some of 4 or 5 dots. Now 6 points happens to be the normal limit of the power of discriminating separate contacts at a single, synthetic, immobile contact. This takes place by a process of immediate subitizing of separate stimuli. Of course, if the exploring finger moves, synthetic touch becomes an analytic touch, and stimuli beyond the figure of 6 can slowly be appreciated. Louis Braille's empirical invention still further keeps within physiological capacities in that his embossed dots are set at a distance of either 2·5 mm or 3·0 mm apart; we remind ourselves that the minimum distance which constitutes the usual threshold of tactile discrimination over the pulp of the fingertips is about 2·0 mm. Each symbol, therefore, stands always just within the bounds of human achievement; but when one recalls that, in reading a page of braille, the blind person is sensing and interpreting about 2,000 to 2,500 embossed points a minute, the degree of accomplishment can be appreciated.

To illustrate the delicacy of the discriminatory powers called upon in braille reading, one may take the symbols standing for the consonants RS which are ⠗ ⠎ To the beginner who places his finger-tips upon this complex, the three vertical dots tend to merge into a sort of irregular linear impression, while the point farthest to the right, and the one most over to the left, are felt as distinct and separate elements. The tactile impression is rather vague, the intermediate elements being blurred; and the first symbol 'R' tends to be confused with the succeeding symbol 'S'. If the palpating finger is not held accurately in line with the long axis of the punctographic cell, the difficulties increase. As soon as the finger-tip is moved, however, and the beginner makes his exploratory touches across, up and down, and around the cell or adjacent cells, then simultaneous touch becomes successive touch, and the morphological arrangement of the dots becomes clearer. So eventually their symbolic identity is realized.

(2) The practised braillist is able to read with his master finger, rapidly and accurately, up to maybe 100 words a minute. He can still do so, even if a cloth is interposed between his finger and the page: or, indeed, even if he wears gloves and then reads through an intervening piece of material. In many blind persons, the master finger is exclusively one-sided though well-taught braillists should be able to read with either index finger. Even so, there is always a manual pre-

ference, the hand of choice reading faster than the other. In nearly three-quarters of bi-manual braille readers, the left hand is the one preferred. Ordinarily, the left forefinger hurries ahead and reads half of one line, which is then completed by the right finger, the left finger having already dropped down to the start of the next line of print. In other braille readers, one forefinger, say the left, marks the beginning of each line, leaving the other forefinger to act as interpreter. Yet another technique is for the right forefinger to sweep briskly across the page, interpreting the easy symbols, leaving the left forefinger to follow and to help identify unusual collections of symbols by means of swift small-range searching movements. In this case, the one finger is devoted to the 'service of recognition', and the other to the 'service of control'.

The blind person who relies upon one hand exclusively for braille reading may explain his difficulty when the other hand is tried, by saying that 'all the characters seem to be reversed'. And yet this same individual can probably identify a line of braille characters by moving his master finger in the opposite direction, that is from right to left. This act will be performed easily, although each symbol in turn must have appeared reversed to the horizontally moving finger.

The speed of braille reading is ordinarily increased by dint of skipping details and employing guesswork, based either on the initial letter, or on the length of the word, or on the context. A symbol-for-symbol interpretation is dispensed with, without detriment to the sense of the subject-matter. This process differs but little from the sighted person's ability to hoist in the meaning of a sentence as a whole without reading each individual letter or word.

(3) As the blind reader passes the finger-tips of his two hands over the page of braille type, it may often happen that actually the tips of several fingers are simultaneously touching the puncto-graphic symbols, but of these many finger-tips, only one is 'attending to' the nature and meaning of the symbols. The sense data from the other fingers are neglected, or disregarded: some might say 'repressed' or 'extinguished'. Other braille readers adopt a different technique and keep some or all of the non-reading finger-tips off the page. Possibly no two braille readers exploit exactly the same style. However, with most blind readers there are more cutaneous areas simultaneously stimulated than are essential for reading purposes. We can detect here two of the fundamentals of sensory patterning as described by Lashley, namely: (a) a selective emphasis of parts of a total mass of excitations into coherent and dominant patterns; and (b) selective pruning, that is, anticipatory sensitization of a receptive mechanism to specific patterns.

(4) Although it has been said that the pulp of one or more fingers 'learns' to read the meaning of braille symbols, the 'learning' process, of course, does not reside in the finger-tips, but in the cortex. Or, in any event, it is transcortical. The physiological mechanism behind an acquired sensorimotor co-ordination of this sort is still debatable. Some would imagine a firm concatenation of cortico-cortical neuronic linkages, a closed system of excitation, representing a sort of trail blazed by long practice. Others would think in terms of electrical fields set up by patterns of neural activity. Whether there occurs an actual morphological adaptation, such as an enlargement of certain cells or their processes, is uncertain and, I submit, improbable. Any hypothesis of engrams, schemata, traces or models necessitates an anatomical determination, in that cortical neurons activated by stimuli to the forefinger must form the basis of any mnemonic trace, or prepared pathway, or while the remainder of the cells are not concerned. This may be so; but

nevertheless, it must be realized that, after a relatively short further period of learning, other sets of cortical neurons can be sensitized so as to form comparable traces. In this way, the braillist who ordinarily reads with the pulp of one index finger may readily pick up the trick of learning to read braille with another finger, or with the thumb, or with his toes, or even with the tip of his nose, or his tongue.

This observation exemplifies two other fundamentals of patterning which Lashley described, viz.: (a) that of stimulus equivalence; whereby the effectiveness of a pattern within any receptor system for behaviour is determined by their proportions of some other generalized character, and not by the specific receptor or cortical cells excited; and (b) that temporal sequences and spatial patterns are interchangeable.

Transmissibility (or transformation) of the learned tactile effect is analogous to the ordinary experience in the visual sphere, whereby a common object—e.g. a dinner-plate—can be optically identified as such, even though it be rotated upon its axis, or tilted so as no longer to present itself as a circular object. The visual Gestalt is none the less accepted unhesitatingly by dint of a process of generalization, or abstraction. It is a commonplace that even a rat can be taught to recognize the symbol of triangularity and to select a three-sided figure (whatever its relational properties, that is, however orientated, and whatever its dimensions). Lashley's work shows that highly complicated powers of accurate discrimination of visual patterns can be attained by a rat.

Similar phenomena occur in the domain of ordinary stereognosis. At one end of the scale is the case of the adult who has grown up with an infantile hemiplegia. No sensory defect occurs except for the so-called 'virgin hand', or astereognosis from inexperience. At the other extreme is the normal stereognosic ability which is essentially a manual aptitude. But in certain conditions, this perceptual achievement can be acquired in other segments of the body. The sole of the foot, or the integument of the trunk—areas which ordinarily are not used as organs of sensory identification—can be trained to do so. Practice can bring about a remarkable degree of manipulative skill, coupled with stereognosic ability. When congenital dysplasia, or injury or disease at a very early age, deprives the subject of the use of the hands or upper limbs, the stumps, or perhaps the lower extremities, can acquire astonishing dexterity and sensitivity. This was well shown in a case of mine with acrocephalosyndactyly (Apert's syndrome) where a most exquisite degree of tactile discrimination was possible over the quite rudimentary stumps which constituted the upper limbs.

(5) Through practice, a skilled braillist ceases to pay attention to the constituent dots forming a punctographic cell; he identifies each symbol as a whole: a tactile Gestalt. This fact ties up with the question of the comparative legibility of the various braille signs. That some are easier to read than others is not surprising, but the principles determining legibility are still rather obscure. Bürklen has shown that the mere number of constituent dots is not all-important. For example, 'A', represented by one '•', and 'G', represented by four '::' are almost equally legible. Characters comprising simple geometrical shapes are more easily identified than those which are complex. Open characters, i.e. with dots far apart, are better read than comparable signs with their dots close together. Thus, ∴ ('U') is the sixth most legible sign, while ∶. ('H') is sixteenth. This observation is understandable if regarded as relative tasks in tactile discrimination. And yet, : ('B') is eleventh in order of legibility, while ⦂ ('K') is twenty-sixth, and .• ('I') is fourteenth, while •. ('AU') is

thirty-third. Obviously, some other factors are concerned in the question of legibility which are still obscure.

(6) Sensory perception is largely an appreciation of a change of state. Hence, a moving stimulus which fluctuates in intensity is felt more keenly than one of uniform magnitude. The effect of a moving stimulus can be achieved by passing the palpatory organ over an immobile object. Movements of touch not only produce a wider receptive target, but also a lowered threshold. These movements may be quite small in range and outside consciousness, but for all that they are powerful adjuvants to the exploratory act. Vibrations, or touch-twitchings as they are more often called (*Tastzuckungen*), are of importance in the tactile world both of the blind and of the agnosiac (as in the case described by Goldstein and Gelb). Blind people are perhaps more mobile and restless than sighted ones, for they are constantly adding to their knowledge of the environment by building up a storehouse of tactile and proprioceptive images. These movements may be so exaggerated as to constitute curious stereotyped tic-like mannerisms—'blindisms' as they are called. In braille reading, finger movements are extremely important. Although a stationary finger can eventually achieve recognition of an isolated symbol, a horizontal sweeping movement assists considerably in perception. When a series of embossed symbols are aligned so as to form words and phrases, a sweeping touch is essential for reading. In other words, a learned faculty is actually assisted by a mobile stimulus. The expert performs a horizontal movement which is uniform in direction, in speed and in pressure. When a less skilled braille reader meets an unfamiliar word, his stroking touch is halted for an instant; pressure upon the symbol increases; and the transverse motion of the finger is replaced by vertical zig-zag or circular movements of search (see Plate 12).

With practice, therefore, random finger movements are the first to be eliminated; and after them, the deliberate acts of search, leading to the behavioural parsimony of an unbroken, transverse sweep.

The rôle of movement in the act of recognition by touch alone is sometimes demonstrable in the different modes of behaviour according to levels of intelligence. The blind subject who is also a dullard may appear to utilize his stereognosic abilities well enough. But if he is given very intricate or unfamiliar objects to identify—say a medal or domino—he will rely more upon synthetic than upon analytic touch. He names the object promptly if at all, by guesswork seemingly, and usually his answers fall wide of the precision which might be expected. With a blind subject of high intelligence, the response is different. Still touching or holding an unfamiliar object, he hesitates to name it: he first explores the edges and surfaces rapidly yet methodically, and after a series of stroking and encircling touches, now exerting a gentle pressure, now measuring and weighing, he goes on to describe systematically the physical properties, or what Galen enumerated as 'tangible distinctions' (hardness and softness, viscosity, friability, lightness, heaviness, density, rarity, smoothness, roughness, thickness and thinness). Finally, he puts a name to it.

The rôle of motility in tactual perception is also illustrated in the case of two-dimensional stereognosis. An outline figure (e.g. a pastry-cutter in the shape of a heart, or ace of clubs), when placed in contact with the body-surface, is rarely felt save as an amorphous pressure. Even upon the palm of the hand, two-dimensional stereognosis scarcely ever evokes a sensitive or accurate perception. But if the figure be outlined upon the skin with a blunt point, then the chances of its

22

being recognized are greatly enhanced. Clearly, a pattern of evoked potentials fired off by a moving stimulus, is more significant than an identical pattern activated by manifold simultaneous stimuli. A more familiar example may be found, in some pathological states, in the phenomenon of tactile inattention, whereby two simultaneous contacts are felt only as one; whereas, if the two stimuli are applied asynchronously, they are felt as two, even though the interval between the two applications be quite short (i.e. one-fiftieth of a second).

(7) Braille reading is often said to be very tiring. Prolonged sessions lead to a generalized feeling of fatigue, but, in addition, a reduction has been described as occurring in the tactile sensibility of the finger-tip. As Javal wrote: '. . . when I have read much, the dots feel like wool to the right index finger, but, on the contrary, like points to the left'. This is what Diderot foresaw when he located the blind man's soul within the finger-tips ('the theatre of thought'), saying that, after profound thinking the digits would probably be as exhausted as the brain of a sighted person. The idea of an altered threshold following prolonged peripheral stimulation is an engaging one and probably was at the back of the minds of Stein and Weizsäcker when they introduced their doctrine of *Funktionswandel*. Bürklen found that such dulling of sensitivity was only slight and inconstant. In the case of older readers not in practice, the altered threshold could be charted by a curve with two peaks. With younger subjects in daily practice, no change in sensitivity could be demonstrated, even after six hours' reading. Of course, the results may be quite different in the case of braille learners.

(8) Braille reading and stereognosis, applied to unaccustomed test-objects, bring up the question of manual preference in the act of palpation. Most blind persons, as already said, prefer to use one hand rather than another for braille reading, and this hand has little to do with the question of ordinary cerebral dominance. Similarly, in his efforts to identify a difficult test-object, the normal blindfolded subject may display a manual preference, and he may often be observed to transfer, in his bewilderment, the puzzling object from one hand to another. With larger objects, the blind person (and also the blindfolded normal) will prefer to use both hands simultaneously, thereby gaining far more morphognosic data than with either hand separately or in succession.

(9) In the United States a modification of the British system known as Grade $1\frac{1}{2}$ Braille is usual and at one time there also existed a 'New York point', where the complex of the dots was orientated in a horizontal instead of a vertical manner.

It should not be forgotten that the braille systems of notation are actually the culmination of a number of other tactile codes, linear as well as punctuate, which were used until it was realized in the middle of the nineteenth century that the braille system was superior to all others. Before that there were the alphabets associated with the names of Moon, Fry, Lucas, Alston, Taylor, Gall, Lowther and Haüy, all of them entailing a tactile substitution for visual linguistic symbols. Doubtless there must have occurred up to a century ago cases of loss of competency in the manipulation of these forms of communication resulting from cerebral disease. None, however, was ever described and this can perhaps be explained by the inadequacy of any clear notion of acquired loss of language which existed up till then.

How far is this adventitious and very intricate system of communication sensitive to brain-disease? If vulnerability be admitted, and it is unreasonable to do otherwise, the additional problem arises as to whether any local area of the brain is of particular importance in maintaining this special coding system. Many years ago I was bold enough to predict that sometime in the future a case of tactile aphasia would be discovered in a blind braille reader. Such cases must surely have occurred in the past, perhaps not very infrequently, but unless specific enquiry is made, the loss of exquisite tactile skill entailed in touch-reading may remain unnoticed. Once indeed I specifically approached the National Institute for the Care of the Blinded for news of any braille reader who had lost this particular skill; the sole product of this enquiry was an elderly blind man who had developed a crippling rheumatoid arthritis which immobilized his interphalangeal joints.

Students of political biography may also recall that the Foreign Secretary, Earl Grey, late in life gradually lost his sight. He learned braille, but shortly before his death his 'reading finger' lost its cunning so as to preclude his comprehension of the tactile stimuli.

My prediction was actually confirmed in 1955 when Hoff, Gloning and Gloning in a paper dealing with the subject of alexia, acquired and congenital, referred briefly to the case of a blind person who had lost the faculty of touch-reading. Later in the same year, Gloning, Gloning, Weingarten and Berner published this particular case-report in some detail.

The patient was an intelligent ambidextrous man of 62 years. When he was 22 years old he was blinded by a bullet which entered through the left orbit. A tetraplegia followed but improved after two months; there were also some epileptic seizures over the ensuring two years. The patient learned to read braille fluently, using both index fingers either alone or in conjunction.

At the age of 57 the patient underwent a pneumonectomy for a bronchial carcinoma. Twelve months later he became troubled with headaches and an increasing clumsiness of the left hand. A little later the patient also experienced some hesitancy in word-finding. He now began to notice difficulty with braille reading. Though he could 'feel' the dots he could no longer interpret them. At the same time he found it impossible to type.

In the clinic the patient was seen to have an empty eye-socket on the left while the right eye was blind from optic atrophy. There was a mild left hemiparesis together with a cortical type of sensory affection, without, however, the slightest trace of astereognosis. A minor aphasic disturbance was present, but no dyspraxia. Right-left confusion existed as well as finger agnosia. No evidence of dyscalculia could be found, however.

The patient who for 38 years had never written anything more than his signature was still able to write his name. He found, however, trouble with braille writing, both spontaneously and to dictation: copying was better performed. He tended to confuse mirror-opposite characters like •. ('E') and .• ('I'). Little used letters such as ('X') and ('Y') were particularly puzzling.

When the patient tried to read braille characters he encountered considerable difficulties. No abnormality in the attitude and manoeuvring of the reading-fingers could be observed. As to literal symbols it transpired that the patient could feel the constitutent dots, describe their arrangement, and even copy them: he was, however, unable to interpret them. A few of the frequently occurring literal symbols remained within his competency, but not the more uncommon letters. The innate complexity of the symbol was a less potent source of error. He confused signs which are similar in their form (like 'Q' and 'ST'), or which are mirror-opposites ('E' and 'I'). The patient also tended to mistake the abbreviated shorthand symbol for the simple letter, e.g. he read *aber* instead of ' A '. Furthermore in the case of numerals he confused ' 5 ' and ' 9 '—symbols which are symmetrically opposite in conformation.

The tactile interpretation of words was much harder than letters. As he put it . . . 'Before, I could recognize a word just by putting my finger on it. It doesn't work any more'. He might guess at a word by dint of laboriously identifying the first two or three letters, but he often made mistakes. The longer the word the greater the handicap.

The patient's difficulties were even worse in attempting to read braille shorthand. His fingers would wander helplessly across the lines . . . 'It is just as if I had never learned to read', he complained.

Arteriography revealed a deformation in the parietal area on the right side, and at operation a metastatic growth a little larger than a walnut was removed from the right parietal lobe. Five weeks later the patient died. At autopsy another secondary growth was found in the region of the operculum parietale and the supramarginal and angular gyri of the left hemisphere.

Four years later, a second case of 'tactile alexia' was published, namely, by G. Simonyi and G. Palotas.

A 50 year old man, blind for eight years from retinitis pigmentosa, had been an intelligent art collector, who could identify and evaluate *objets d'art* partly by manual touch and partly by testing them with his teeth. He had often lectured upon such subjects as 'How does a blind person see?' An operation for lumbar sympathectomy was performed to relieve a peripheral arterial sclerosis. On regaining consciousness he found himself with a right hemiparesis, a hypaesthesia and a severe mixed aphasia.

The patient retained a lively repertoire of gestures and facial mimicry. He was able correctly to identify numbers and letters traced upon the palm of his left hand, but did so imperfectly with the right. Furthermore he could form an accurate mental conception of letters and also of their braille symbols.

Although the patient had learned to read and write braille for only seven years, he could read quite quickly and accurately immediately prior to his stroke. He ordinarily employed the four fingers of both hands, the right one being the leading and the left one the controlling hand. He had never been able to cope with braille stenography.

Following his stroke the patient found that he could make absolutely nothing of any of the braille symbols. Six months later, attempts were made to re-educate the patient, with moderate success. He was then helped to re-learn braille writing, using now the left hand only.

These two case-reports are alike in that they refer to blinded patients who, as the result of a brain lesion, lost their accomplishment of braille reading. One of these patients had lost his power of articulate speech in a mild degree; the other one severely so.

In the first of these cases, two metastatic growths were found, one in either parietal lobe. No post mortem verification occurred in the other case, but the lesion obviously lay within the left hemisphere, probably in the temporo-parietal region. The braille 'aphasia' in this case was clearly related, not to the right-sided sensory defect, but to the disorder within the sphere of language; for the tactile skill, which had previously been a bilateral endowment, became impaired in both hands. The first case is less straightforward. Bilateral lesions were found at autopsy and it is difficult in retrospect to determine which of the two metastases was of significance in determining the loss of the power to read braille. The authors seemed at first to infer that the lesion of the right parietal lobe was the more important in this connection. A further complicating factor lay in the fact that this blind patient was an ambidextrous subject, who had learned the art of tactile reading with the index fingers of each hand.

The authors of these two case-reports adopted rather different attitudes as to the nature of the disability which they described. Thus Gloning *et al.* believed that their patient had a mixed type of alexia. The loss of symbol function of the braille characters represented for them a parietal disorder of reading. They regarded the defect as lying within the ambit of a Gerstmann syndrome, traceable to a lesion within the region of the angular gyrus. In a blind person, the primary sensory field for reading is, in their opinion, not the visual sphere, but the hand-area within the post-central convolution. A transference of the act of reading takes place from the visual sphere into the tactile-kinaesthetic sphere. Consequently a lesion responsible for 'pure word-blindness' in a blind subject would be expected to lie quite near the primary sensory field in the parietal lobe. The left-sided lesion of the angular and supramarginal gyri was the more important finding, but it could not be ascertained whether the concomitant right-sided lesion had any influence upon the extent of the patient's alexia.

In the second case, namely the one recorded by Simonyi and Palotas, strict comparison between braille alexia and true verbal alexia did not seem to the authors to be justifiable. They considered that their patient represented an instance of typical aphasic alexia. Like Gloning *et al.* they also believed that in a blind subject the primary area of sensibility for braille reading is not the occipital cortex, but the post-central gyrus, a transposition having taken place from the visual to the tactile-kinaesthetic field. But unlike Gloning *et al.* they did not believe that an analogy exists between braille alexia and occipital alexia (or pure word-blindness).

Some of the differences of opinion would seem, in retrospect, to be rather in the nature of shadow-boxing. Notions of 'pure' alexia, and of localized speech centres within the brains of subjects whether blind or not, nowadays do not have the same allure as they did in nineteenth-century aphasiology. The two important case-reports, however, while not yet closing the chapter upon vulnerability of non-verbal systems of communication, have confirmed the prediction that a focal lesion of the brain would be capable of ablating the bimanual acquired skill of braille reading.

Signal techniques and their impairment in skilled signalmen

The traditional methods for the transmission and reception of messages across moderate or extreme distances without the intervention of spoken speech, comprise Morse telegraphy (entailing the use of a buzzer, or some other tapping-instrument), flashing-light signals, semaphore, and hoists of flags.

Telegraphy and flashing-light signals are both based upon the Morse alphabet of combinations of dots and dashes; the former, which is mainly an auditory method of communication, transcends all barriers of distance; the latter, a purely visual system, is limited by the range of vision, a matter of miles. Morse telegraphy as carried out by experts, may constitute a system of speech of great complexity and refinement. The operators may learn in time to recognize one another's 'touch'. By the use of abbreviations whereby single letters take the place of words, phrases or even sentences, and by other devices, it is possible to transmit with speed and with facility, shades of meaning, witticisms, innuendoes, and *doubles entendres*. It is also possible by other tactile tricks to register such feelings as amusement or annoyance. Thus when a telegraphist taps out ——··—— (MIM) he is indicating something in the nature of an appreciative chuckle. All these ideas are communicable, it should be noted, at a speed greater than spoken speech, resembling in this way the sign-language of deaf-mutes.

Employing the terminology of Hughlings Jackson, we look upon a spoken phrase as the symbol of an idea, and upon written words as 'symbols of symbols'. A certain combination of dots and dashes comes to mean something to the signaller and to 'stand for' a word or phrase: in this way we may speak of 'symbols of symbols of symbols'. But as facility is obtained after many years of professional telegraphy, the Morse speech probably assumes a physiological and psychological status as lofty as that of spoken or written speech; the Morse code then ceases to 'stand for' words, and becomes the direct medium of thought.

Thus some of the senior post-office telegraphists attain such ease in reading messages that they can undoubtedly 'receive' far more quickly than could be transmitted by ordinary key-board methods. At least one telegraphist has stated that it would be less trouble to take in the contents of a book if only he could sit back and listen to the reading matter being transmitted telegraphically; in this way he would spare himself the more onerous task of reading the print.

Flashlight signalling is taught in the signal schools of the Royal Navy almost to the exclusion of the 'buzzer' or auditory methods of conveying signals which are within the province of the telegraphist branch. The same Morse alphabet forms the basis, but the light signals differ from telegraphy in being slower. Nothing like the speed of telegraphy either in sending or receiving is ever attained. Moreover, Naval signalmen do not devote themselves to their job so intensively as the old-time post-office telegraphists, who used to remain at their instruments many hours a day, and every day. Nevertheless, a certain amount of 'individuality' becomes attached to the flashlight signalling of each experienced operator, and the identity of the sender can at times be recognized by an adept. Although flashlight signalling seems to be essentially a visual activity, it is questionable whether the mental image or engram is a purely visual one. The use of the hand in operating the lamp and the time-relationship of the dashes to the dots (one being three times as long-lasting as the other) introduces both kinaesthetic and temporal qualities to the problem.

Semaphore signalling is less elastic a medium than Morse telegraphy or flashlight. Its reception is a purely visual process, and the system is mainly an alphabetical one and hence relatively slow and unadaptable.

Hoists of signals are quite independent of the Morse alphabet. They utilize a series of coloured flags which may represent numerals, or letters. Words are made up of combinations of letter-flags, or else special flags may be shown. In this respect they are purely visual symbols, and the processes of learning, recall, and recognition must depend upon mechanisms more exclusively visual than in the case of flashlight signalling.

Signal-speech differs in one particular from spoken speech in that it is almost exclusively made up of propositional components. 'Inferior speech', 'emotional' or 'interjectional' forms of speech are almost entirely absent from messages transmitted by Morse code, semaphore, or hoists of flags. An exception can perhaps be cited in those rare cases of highly experienced telegraphists who can express emotional variations by way of their instrument.

The average young person finds no insurmountable difficulties in learning the techniques of signalling, provided sufficient time is devoted to practice under adequate supervision. In acquiring the art of Morse signalling, both with telegraph and with flashlamps, the student first masters and memorizes the alphabet and then practises sending and receiving. The speeds are then gradually increased as facility is acquired. At first, sending is found to be easier than receiving, and this usually remains the case until the signalman has become very experienced. Later, the reverse occurs. In this case, receiving becomes an almost 'passive' art requiring little or no call upon attention and but little mental effort. Sending never quite attains this same height of automatic activity, nor the same facility.

Signalling is learned far more readily by young adults and adolescents than by the elderly. It has become a practice in signal and telegraph schools to accept no candidates over the age of 30, owing to a greater slowness in gaining proficiency.

From time to time instructors at signal schools are said to come across new entries who seem never to master their subject, though young in years, educated, and intelligent. It seems as though the receiving of signals, whether by ear or by the eye, remains a matter of great difficulty, so that speed is never attained. To them, one letter seems to blend with the next and dots never appear very different from dashes. Frequently, these backward pupils are sent to the ophthalmic specialist, under the suspicion of some visual defect, though none is usually found. Just how often these difficult cases crop up within each batch of new entries is not known, and the impressions of different instructors vary considerably. Sometimes it is said that after many months, or even years, of perseverance, efficiency at reading Morse signals is attained quite suddenly. It is probable, however, that most of these backward pupils will be despaired of and rejected before that time.

Although these cases of inability to learn Morse are known, they have not been specifically described. The following case record is probably the first to draw attention to such a defect, occurring in a highly specialized manner in an intelligent young man.

Case 1. An Acting Petty Officer and Cadet Rating, aged 21, was referred for a neurological opinion on account of difficulty in learning Morse. He came of a distinguished Naval family which held an excellent Service record. The patient himself was an only surviving child, healthy and normal in physical development. There was no personal or family history of any similar defects; nor of left-handedness, or stammering. He attended a South Coast Secondary School where his record, though never a brilliant one, was up to the average. His attainments were patchy: he was ahead of his classmates in chemistry and mathematics. He was at his best in geometry, for which he won a prize. English and French were easily his worst subjects, especially the latter. His difficulty did not concern his grammar, but only the spelling. Nevertheless, the spelling defects, bad as they were, did not excite any particular comment in the school. He was able to read normally, but it is not known whether he learned this accomplishment at the usual age, or late. He left school at 15½ in Standard IV, where he was the same age as the other boys, in order to enter the Royal Navy. He went to H.M.S. 'St. Vincent' where he was immediately relegated to the Superior Grade. After a year he passed on to H.M.S.

'Iron Duke' for further training and then he was sent to H.M.S. 'Courageous' where he remained 2½ years. Afterwards he served in H.M.S. 'Dunedin', leaving to take a course ashore in order to qualify for advancement to Leading Torpedoman. These studies were interrupted when he was recommended for a special promotion course at H.M.S. 'St. Vincent' with the object of passing from the lower to the Quarterdeck. The confidential reports from the Captains had hitherto marked him out as above the average in intelligence, quickness and keenness. It was during this cadet-course that two main defects were noted, sufficiently severe and unusual to warrant medical reports. Briefly his instructors found that whereas he was adequate at all other subjects, he distinguished himself first by a proclivity for making bizarre spelling mistakes, and secondly by an inability to learn Morse signalling. The actual report of one of his officer instructors may be quoted: 'He is so anxious to prove himself keen that he trips over himself. He is extremely well-mannered and polite and outwardly humble about his shortcomings. He is smart in appearance, has an excellent bearing and speaks well. If integrity of character, loyalty and enthusiasm only were necessary he would be a commissioned officer; but his appalling lack of intelligence where clear and rapid thought are required—practical navigation, etc— quite rules out that possibility. He is an enigma. Undoubtedly keen and anxious to follow in the footsteps of his distinguished relatives, he shows knowledge and common sense in matters of seamanship. Yet in class he visibly cracks during a prolonged period of instruction and seems to lack the mental stamina required for lengthy concentration. He becomes dull and sleepy. When asked a question that requires logical thinking or is at all off the beaten track, his mind becomes a chaos of disordered thoughts, and his attempts at an answer are incoherently expressed and often rank nonsense. His confusion of thought has been manifest most particularly in his spelling, and in his reading of the Morse code made on buzzer or lamp. His spelling mistakes are not the usual ones of a normally bad speller. They are unique in that they consist of syllables transposed in a word or missed out altogether. Small words are often omitted and longer ones are deprived of the final letter. When reading the Morse code, even after eight months' daily practice, he cannot sort out the dots and dashes unless it is made very slowly.' When his course of instruction finished, he was recommended, not for a commission but for advancement to the rank of Warrant Officer, seamanship branch. He was at this stage transferred to the R.N.A. Hospital, Barrow Gurney, for a more complete examination in the Neuro-psychiatric Unit. There he was repeatedly seen and tested by the neuro-psychiatric specialists, Surgeon Lieutenant-Commanders D. Ross and E. W. Anderson, as well as by Surgeon Captain Desmond Curran, Consulting Psychiatrist to the Royal Navy, and by myself. Some of the points in the instructor's report could be substantiated though his comments upon general intellectual defects could not. He proved to be, if anything, somewhat above the average in intelligence. He was very good at mental arithmetic and accurately subtracted 7 serially from 100 in 40 seconds. He could repeat nine digits forwards and at least eight digits backwards. His responses to constructive thought tests were of superior grade. Asked the difference between 'character' and 'reputation' he at once replied: 'The character of a person is the educated instincts of that person; reputation is the opinion others have of him.' On the revised Stanford-Binet tests he also showed a superior grade of intelligence. Tests for constructional apraxia were carried out without error. He was not altogether accurate in his estimation of distances, though the defect was in no way striking. Numerous and repeated tests clearly demonstrated that there was no evidence of spatial disorientation. (This is important in view of the fact that the instructor had mentioned a tendency for him to confuse port and starboard while at the wheel.) No defects were found in reading printed or written matter, whether silently or aloud.

Neurological and physical examination proved negative. Exhaustive tests had already been made by the ophthalmic surgeon who had been consulted at the training establishment; no abnormalities had been revealed.

Examination indeed revealed only three types of disability, viz:

Difficulty in spelling. This took the form of rather unusual errors. They were outstanding in frequency even when compared with the common errors of his contemporaries. A study of the 'Journal' which he had to maintain each day showed that he would often omit letters or groups of letters. He would at times reverse syllables or diphthongs, e.g., he might write 'Britian' for 'Britain'. As a rule he could not correct the mistakes when they were pointed out to him; usually indeed he did not recognize that the word had been mis-spelled. It was also reported that on occasions he made similar reversals in speech, when excited. Thus in an extemporaneous debate he wanted to say '*writhing* in pain' but came out with '*withering* in pain'. This seemed, however, to have been purely an isolated occurrence, and no spoonerisms or reversals of this sort were ever noted in the hospital.

Defects in signalling. He proved to be good at semaphore and at hoists of signal-flags. He had always had considerable difficulty with Morse signals, especially in receiving messages. Although he had originally memorized the Morse alphabet within twenty minutes, he never became able to read Morse signals with ease or rapidity despite long practice. When he was tested with flashing lights, these defects were well demonstrated. He was able to send quite accurately, though slowly. When, however, he tried to interpret a message which someone else was sending with a flash lamp, he failed utterly. He explained his difficulty by saying that he was unable to distinguish between a dot and a dash, and that one symbol seemed to run into the next, especially if the signals were given quickly. There was no difficulty in translating a group of dashes and dots into the appropriate letter, once he had read them clearly. When tested with a buzzer the same defects seemed to be apparent. This form of signalling was of course comparatively strange to him as he had been taught by way of flash-lamp signals. He obviously found great difficulty in interpreting the sounds in terms of dots and he made far more errors than did a normal control subject who was ignorant of Morse signalling. At times he was apt to omit dashes or dots from the middle or end of a signal, and thus to read: ·–·–– as –·–; or – – – as – –

Defects in ciphering. It was also discovered that despite his skill at mental arithmetic, and his good visual memory, he made odd mistakes when instructed to write down on paper numbers which were dictated to him. Thus, when told to write down 'five million four hundred thousand and two' he put down: 5,40002. 'Three million, four hundred and five' was written as: 30,4005. These mistakes he seemed not to recognize; nor could he correct them when they were pointed out.

The case, therefore, is one where a small number of defects stood out against a background of intellectual normality. Despite the assertions of his instructor, that the cadet was slow in cerebration and incapable of clear and rapid thought, the contrary was the case. He actually proved to be somewhat above the average in general mental attainment. The instructor's faulty judgement may have been due to a misinterpretation of the existing defects; or to a failure to recognize their specificity. Or possibly he may have been misled by the presence of a mild neurotic reaction on the patient's part to the handicap of his special disability.

When the various disabilities are considered, it is found that they are actually closely comparable, and may well be regarded as aspects of one single underlying defect. Difficulty in spelling; difficulty in writing down long figures; and difficulty in recognizing the component parts of a set of Morse symbols are all instances of misspelling, whether of a series of letters, of numerals, or of dots and dashes. Thus the difficulty in correctly putting on paper a number running into six or seven figures, is really an instance of mis-spelled ciphering, and certainly not of acalculia. No error occurred when he was asked to write down a series of figures, or a number which did not extend beyond the tens of thousands. The real defect was revealed when he tried to put down on paper a verbal command which ran into millions, particularly when one or more noughts came into the middle. Thus 'five million and forty' would typically cause a difficulty in the correct disposition of the noughts and the commas. In this way the omission of one or more noughts, or the reversal of numeral combinations is comparable with the omission of letters in a word or the reversal of syllables and diphthongs. Similarly an inability to gauge correctly the exact number of dashes or dots in a given set, or to differentiate between the one and the other, is analogous to mis-spelling in Morse, as shown when he was asked to transcribe upon paper exactly what it was he thought he heard when listening to a telegraphic buzzer.

Every beginner experiences some difficulty in distinguishing dots from dashes, and in determining where one letter-combination ends and the next one begins. This temporo-spatial defect is of course bound up with the effort to recall the meaning of each symbolic combination, a task which may lag behind the rate of sending. The patient was still in the stage of regarding telegraphed speech as something built up of numerous small units, namely individual letters. When light-signals were employed, it was almost as though the dots were longer and the dashes were shorter than they should be, owing to a sort of 'halation' effect, mental rather than visual.

This difficulty in passing rapidly from one symbol to the next, recognizing quickly its visual or acoustic nature, and then promptly interpreting its meaning, is reminiscent of the difficulty which may be experienced by one, by no means ignorant of a language, who listens to a discourse in a foreign tongue. The isolated words are all familiar enough, but preoccupation with the need for accurate interpretation of each word in turn may slow up the process of interpretation of the phrases or sentence as a whole. The listener has not yet passed the stage of regarding the isolated word as the unit of speech.

Normal individuals learning the Morse code or a foreign tongue surmount these difficulties, however, as skill is achieved. In Jackson's terminology the activity may be said to pass from a highly voluntary to a less voluntary and more automatic one, and conscious effort at serial interpretation, symbol by symbol, is overcome. When the 'proposition' and not the word, far less the letter, becomes recognized as the unit of speech, then efficiency is attained, in linguistics, signalling, and telegraphy alike.

It is possible that certain personality traits might interfere with this advance from a laboured voluntary interpretation of one symbol after another into a facile recognition of a symbol or set of symbols as a whole. An ideational inertia could cause the subject to occupy himself exclusively with the meaning of the first symbol, and so by a process of perseveration, the other symbols become blocked. Such might be the explanation in part of the difficulty experienced by the elderly and the arteriosclerotic individual in learning new languages or Morse telegraphy. In other cases, an obsessional preoccupation with the visual or auditory image of the symbols might hold up the ready passage of attention from one symbol to the next.

In the patient described there was no evidence whatever that either of these psychological mechanisms were at work.

The 'spatial' characteristics of the Morse symbology raises the question whether the defect in the patient concerned might not be due to some innate disorder of spatial orientation, whether of a visual nature (visual disorientation) or of a personal character (disorder of corporeal awareness). This possibility seems to be supported by the instructor's statement that he was apt to confuse port and starboard and to be 'hopeless upon the Bridge'.

However, no such defect could be demonstrated, either in external or internal relationships. A large number of tests, both simple and elaborate, were devised to check up his left-right orientation and he was found to pass them without a single error. On scrutinizing his story, it proved that the instructor's impression was an erroneous one based upon a single mistake upon the Bridge, when the patient misheard the orders given him.

Although he was found to be inaccurate at times in his estimation of size and distance, especially when the dimensions concerned were great, the errors were not such as to distinguish the patient from the great majority of normal persons.

The possibility, too, that this particular defect was bound up with some psychomotor disability, such as a constructive apraxia, was rapidly disproved by appropriate testing.

The case in question almost certainly belongs to the category of the congenital dyslexias or instances of congenital word-blindness. That some degree of dyslexia existed at one time is suggested by the unusual spelling-mistakes which he did not recognize when confronted with them. One is clearly dealing with a type of symbolic dysgnosia or imperception, which also entailed difficulties in serial organization. In retrospect this diagnosis—or rather the label 'ex-dyslexia'—would seem the most satisfying. Though, later, the case was tentatively spoken of as an instance of 'congenital Gerstmann's syndrome', as a basis of a partly surmounted dyslexia, one nowadays hesitates to accept this form of speculation. His verbal speech was intact at the time of testing, despite the isolated instance when under emotional stress he said 'withering' for 'writhing'.

There is some similarity between this case of 'signal-aphasia' and certain varieties of receptive amusia. Flash-signals represent in the visual sphere a sort of melody or rhythm, which can be recognized in buzzer-signals just as in the rhythm of certain kinds of music. Although it must be rare for a patient to lose, as the result of a cerebral lesion, all traces of emotional appreciation of crude rhythmic music, nevertheless it is not unlikely that the higher, aesthetic and more intellectual understanding of tympany may be impaired as part of an amusia. Kleist described cases of this sort under the title 'pure melody deafness', which he defines as a lack of appreciation of intervals in their rhythmic structure as melodies. This defect, which he associated with a lesion of Brodmann's field 22, is in many ways comparable with the defect in signalling just described.

This personal case-report also agrees in many particulars with the one recorded by J. Spillane, also in 1942. Both have been erroneously ascribed to a 'congenital' type of Gerstmann's syndrome.

From the point of view of Naval recruitment, preselection and vocational tests, it might be important to determine how these signal aphasiacs might be detected quite early in their training. Unfortunately, there appears to be as yet no satisfactory means of doing so, though investigations to this end are worth while along such suggestive lines of inquiry as: consistency or inconsistency in educational attainment; proclivity towards unusual errors in spelling; left-right disorientation; incongruity between handedness and eyedness; unusual difficulty in comprehending spoken foreign languages; and the existence of musical rhythm-deafness. In particular an appropriate search for candidates who have been dyslexics would bring to light those who would be unsuitable candidates for the signal branch.

Acquired defects in the reception or transmission of signals

It would not be surprising to find that in cases of aphasia occurring in signalmen, the specialized professional activities would likewise become involved. This idea is supported by the existence of specific constitutional difficulties in signal learning, as illustrated by the foregoing case. Whether, in the acquired cases, the ability to transmit and to receive signals would be lost early or late in the development of the aphasia, is not yet known. Neither is it certain whether a defect in signalling can exist in pure form, that is, independent of any impairment in the execution or understanding of spoken and printed speech. The problem is comparable with that of aphasia in polyglots, and we are already aware that Pitrès' axiom upon this subject to the effect that the later acquired language always suffers most, is an over-simple generalization, often contradicted by the facts.

The following case report, although unsatisfactory in that it concerns a global dementia, nevertheless suggests that signal transmission can be impaired in the absence of verbal aphasia, and as part of an apraxia

Case 2. Signalman, Royal Fleet Reserve, aged 39 (12 years' service), suddenly noticed weakness and dysaesthesia in his right foot lasting about 15 minutes in all. Recovery was complete and maintained for the next five months, until one morning he complained of the same trouble in the right hand. The next day the pins and needles had gone from the hand but had involved the right foot. He continued with his duties and the symptoms cleared up within three weeks. Three months later the same symptoms recurred and for ten minutes there was a difficulty in 'getting his words out'. Again his symptoms cleared up and a fortnight later he was admitted to a Naval hospital. At this time his only complaint was slight headache, and he denied any affection of the extremities or of the speech. The report sent with him by the medical officer at his signal station indicated, however, that for three months he had been showing signs of increasing mental deterioration. It also stated that in the last two of his attacks, consciousness had been lost for a short while.

Examination at the time of admission revealed some weakness of the right side of the face and tongue, but no trace of paresis in the arms and legs though his hand and finger movements were clumsy. The pupils were unequal and irregular, the left one being inactive and the right one sluggish to light stimulation. All his tendon reflexes were brisk but equal on both sides of the body; both plantar responses were extensor in type. His memory proved to be much impaired. He gave the details of his history in a muddled fashion; his cerebration was slowed. Insight was defective and there were evidences of euphoria. *Speech* was slow, hesitating and dysarthric, but at no time did he misuse a word or fail to bring out the word he desired. His handwriting was executed in a laboured manner but there was no real agraphia.

Morse signalling. When asked to transmit the Morse alphabet first with his right and then with his left hand, it was apparent both subjectively and objectively that he was much more efficient with the left. With the right hand, his signalling was slow, hesitant, and irregular, and the dashes and dots were not clearly differentiated.

Examination of the cerebrospinal fluid revealed six cells; protein 40 mg per cent; increased globulin; Wassermann reaction, positive; Lange, 5555553210.

This patient was probably suffering from a Lissauer's type of general paralysis with focal syphilitic vascular lesions superimposed upon a diffusely spread cerebral disease-process. Although there was a history of a transient aphasic disturbance, there was no evidence while he was in the hospital of any speech affection other than a dysarthria. A difficulty in the transmission of Morse signals was clearly demonstrable, though this aspect of the case was not studied fully. The fact that this defect was of an executive nature, and that it affected the right hand only, suggests strongly an apraxic disorder rather than an aphasia. This belief is supported by the observation that he was clumsy and maladroit in such activities as fastening his pyjama-jacket.

The third case is of a different type, and is of interest in that the defect in signalling which was present was of the receptive (agnosic) variety rather than executive (apraxic); it was associated with a very clear-cut visual type of aphasia; and the signalling defect was far less intense than was the disordered impairment of printed speech. The third case shares with the second the same difficulty in correlating the clinical evidence with an isolated focus of cerebral disease.

Case 3. Chief Yeoman of Signals (Pensioner), aged 57. This patient had entered the Service at the age of 15 and served for twenty-four years in the signal branch in which he attained the highest possible rating. On going out, he became a customs official until his recall to the Colours in August 1939. His health had been excellent despite service in the China and West Africa stations. The family history was negative, except that a brother had died from epileptic fits in his fifties. He was in excellent health, working at a signal-station, until September 1940 when he accidentally tripped and fell down a flight of stairs in the black-out. He received no direct injuries but was generally 'shaken-up'. He returned to duty the next day, and did not report the accident. One week later, he began to notice some trouble with his vision. He frequently imagined he saw a shadow moving somewhere to his right but when he directed his gaze in that direction he would find that there was actually nothing there. A little later he remarked that he would have to turn his head well to the right in order to see objects clearly on that side. At about the same time he discovered that he was unable to read; although he could see the printed words distinctly he could not understand their meaning at all. In the same way, although he was able to write, he could not read what he had written, except from memory. After some time he lost his difficulty in seeing to the right, but there followed a similar defect in seeing objects to the left. The difficulty in reading improved a little, so that after some delay he might ultimately arrive at the meaning of the words, but he still experienced a considerable impairment in this direction. He reported these symptoms to a medical officer who discovered a left-sided hemianopia together with a well-marked dyslexia. He was admitted to a Royal Naval Hospital, where examination revealed a very intelligent elderly man with signs of a moderate arteriosclerosis. His radial and brachial arteries were palpable, and there was obvious though not advanced retinal vascular changes. Blood pressure was 185/105; heart rate was 60 per minute with occasional missed beats. Second aortic sound increased. Electrocardiogram normal.

Neurological examination showed no disorder of motor or sensory function. All tendon reflexes were present and equal; abdominal responses were obtained; plantar stimulation evoked a flexor response on each side. There was a left-sided homonymous hemianopia sparing the fixation point. The blind-spot was not enlarged; no scotomata were present. Visual acuity 6/6; 6/6 (with glasses); no defect of colour vision by Ishihara's tests.

Electroencephalogram: no abnormality in any area. Wassermann reaction, negative. Cerebrospinal fluid: normal. Radiogram of skull, normal.

Speech. His spontaneous speech was correct, fluent and well articulated. There was no defect in naming objects. The only unusual feature was a tendency to misname colours, although colour blindness did not exist. He understood fully and easily all that was said to him and he could carry out commands without the slightest trouble.

There was a very obvious difficulty in reading, although he had apparently improved a great deal in this respect before admission to hospital. He would read aloud accurately, but slowly and with hesitation. Now and then he would make a particularly long pause but ultimately he would arrive at the correct rendering. When questioned as to his difficulty he replied: 'I can see the words quite clearly, but I can only get the words out if I spell the first letter through from the beginning of the alphabet'. Thus he hesitated for a long time before the word 'five' and eventually he got it by saying to himself: 'A, B, C . . D, E, F . . five'. Small and large print were equally difficult and it made no difference if he read a word at a time, viewed through a small aperture in a sheet of paper.

He wrote fluently and neatly, with but few mis-spellings. The character of his hand-writing was not changed. Shown a specimen of his own script written some days previously he recognized it as his own, and read it correctly though slowly, just as in the case of print.

When shown pictures in an illustrated magazine, he recognized them as a whole and he could also identify the various details. It was very doubtful, however, whether he was aware of the ultimate significance, or the 'point' of a picture. Thus he did not seem to be able at once to realize the difference between a photograph and a comic drawing. It was obvious that he did not appreciate the point of the joke in a humorous drawing unless he could read the legend.

His power of map reading was defective. Thus shown a chart of the Mediterranean, he picked out Turkey in the top right-hand corner, but nothing else. Later he said that Malta was 'somewhere in the neighbour-hood' but when asked to point out its situation he put his finger in the middle of Greece. Shown a map of the British Isles, he hesitatingly indicated the position of Edinburgh, his home-town, but located Glasgow only a mile or two to the west.

His powers of calculation, of retaining digits and of comprehending the meaning of proverbs were all fairly good.

Recognition of naval signs and signals. (a) Ensigns. He was fairly good at identifying the various national flags, though he confused those of Norway and Sweden. He did not recognize the ensign of the U.S.S.R. (which he ascribed to Turkey) or of Spain. He may have been correct, however, when he explained that these two flags were 'since his time'.

(b) Ships' lights. He was fairly good at recognizing the meaning of conventional arrangements of ships' lights, though he made several errors. Thus he did not know the sign for a ship with two or more vessels in tow, though he knew the sign for a ship towing one vessel. He did not distinguish promptly the elementary distinction between the signals for a 'vessel at anchor' and a 'vessel under way'. He recognized neither the 'dredger sign' nor the 'pilot sign'.

(c) Hoists of signal-flags. He picked out the numerical and alphabetical flags, both in series and individually. He failed, however, to recognize a number of common symbols, such as the 'aeroplane'; 'affirmative'; 'blue affirmative'; 'aircraft carrier'; 'negative'; and 'battle cruiser' flags. He recognized more of the pendants but not the substitutes, until prompted. He identified the 'answering pendant' but not the 'interrogative'. He completely failed to read '1212' or 'Hannah' though both these signals are text-book hoists which every signalman learns early in training.

(d) He identified at once the flags shown by an Admiral, a Commodore and the Admiralty.

(e) Semaphore signals were imperfectly read, only in that he frequently failed to see the right-hand arm of the signaller on account of his hemianopia.

(f) Flashlight Morse signals. He was able with fair accuracy to interpret and write down a message flashed to him at a moderate speed (10 words per minute). When he was allowed to call out the interpretation (instead of writing it down) he improved still further.

(g) Tapping Morse signals were accurately and quickly interpreted.

(h) He was able to transmit Morse signals, both by flashlight and by tapping, with average speed and with accuracy.

In this case there developed after one or probably more than one vascular lesion, a left-sided hemianopia, as well as various agnosic defects concerned with the visual components of speech. These latter comprised chiefly: (1) an alexia, which later improved leaving a persisting difficulty and delay in the interpretation of written and printed symbols; (2) a defective appreciation of the ultimate significance of pictures, especially those which were impressionistic rather than representational; (3) impaired recognition of flag-symbols which should have been familiar by reason of his long professional contact with them; and (4) a minor degree of visuo-spatial disorientation, as shown by difficulties in map reading. These defects are enumerated in their approximate order of severity.

In contrast with these visuo-agnosic difficulties, his ability to interpret such a highly artificial system of speech substitutes as Morse flashlight signalling, was practically intact. It might have been imagined, especially in the light of Pitrès' 'law of regression', that such an achievement—elaborate in its nature, late in acquisition, subservient to verbal and printed speech—would have suffered more than verbalization after a cerebral lesion of such a type. An 'alexia for Morse signals' might well have occurred, greater in intensity than the 'literal alexia'.

This particular case-record is of interest, therefore. It suggests that both on physiological and anatomical grounds, speech and signals are not identically 'represented' in the cortex. There is a resemblance in this way to the faculties of music and speech, for a single lesion if large enough may ablate both accomplishments, whereas a small one may interfere with one or the other singly.

As mentioned earlier, the Morse system, even when learned and practised by purely visual methods, cannot be regarded as exclusively a visuo-psychic process. The assembling of dots and dashes in various combinations, with a strict ruling as to the relationships of a dot to a dash, entails both spatial and temporal mechanisms. This is further shown by the rigid conventions as to the length of interval between successive letters and between successive words. Furthermore when one recalls that in sending messages on a flash-lamp, the beam is regulated by rhythmic movements of the hand, it is clear that a sensori-motor or kinaesthetic element also takes part.

Hence a purely visuo-agnosic defect such as a literal alexia need not necessarily imply an 'agnosia' for such a complicated faculty as that of Morse signalling.

The recognition of signal hoists is an entirely different matter, lying entirely within the visual sphere. It would not be surprising, therefore, to find it suffering *pari passu* with a defective comprehension of pictures and of printed symbols, as indeed was the case in this patient.

It is unfortunate that this case in no way helps to establish the morbid anatomy of the condition. At least two lesions must have been present, one in either hemisphere. The history suggests that a lesion of the left optic radiations was followed by a right-sided homonymous hemianopia. This proved a transient defect, however, and was later followed by a hemianopia to the opposite side. Which of these two lesions was associated with the literal alexia, and with the impairment of code-flag reading, cannot be ascertained. Nor can it be gainsaid that in this particular patient, bilaterality of lesions may have been responsible for such signal-defects as existed. The association of alexia with hemianopia suggests the characteristic localization of a lesion within, or deep to, the angular gyrus. Here then is yet another point of interest in that the hemianopia was left-sided suggesting that the larger and more permanent lesion was in the right hemisphere.

Such clinical arguments as can be adduced in this case suggest that the lesions were both, or all, located within the visual or 'visuo-psychic' areas of the two hemispheres, (angular gyrus, optic radiations). There is no direct evidence that any lesions existed outside these zones, and this point may perhaps be correlated with the intactness of Morse signalling, which as has already been suggested, is not a purely visual performance. Electroencephalography unfortunately did not throw any light upon the clinico-anatomical problem, in that it failed to reveal any abnormality whatsoever.

The drum messages of Africa and Melanesia

Reporting after his journey across Africa from 1875 to 1877, H. M. Stanley wrote that members of the baEna tribe on the banks of the river Congo had a system of communication quite as effective as electric signals. 'Their huge drums by being struck in different parts convey language as clear to the initiated as vocal speech.'

The literature which deals with the topic of drum language is meagre, but especially valuable in this matter are the monographs of J. F. Carrington (1949), and of T. Stern (1957).

Talking drums are of two main types: (1) drums with skin tops. They are used in pairs, one giving a high note and the other a lower note; and (2) all-wooden drums, hollowed and through a longitudinal slit and with two lips, percussion of which elicits two distinct notes. Usually the higher note is spoken of as the 'male' voice and the lower one as the 'female'. In the case of the skin tambours one refers to male and female drums. The range of audibility is up to 7 miles at night-time and 5 miles by day. Although relaying of drum messages is theoretically possible over very long distances, in actual practice it is rare, on account of fundamental difficulties in linguistics.

The communicative property of drum beats is due to the important bitonal nature of most African tongues. What is effected is a simulation of a spoken message whereby an upper tone is expressed by percussion of a male drum, a low tone proceeding from a female drum. Thus in the Kele language the sentence 'the child has no father nor mother' (*wana ati la sango la nyango*) would read in drum talk 'HL. LH. L. HH. L. LH.' where 'H' represents the sound of the male and 'L' the sound of the female drum. The fact that a very large number of homotonic words exist in a particular language is a potential source of ambiguity. Thus the word for father (*sango*) is made up of a tonal pattern which comprises two equal high tones. At least 130 other words in the Kele language have a similar tonal pattern and, therefore, would share an identical drum sign. To make certain that the appropriate word or phrase is comprehended, resort is had (as in Chinese to a lesser extent) to the addition of explanatory or qualifying phrases. A few instances may be given from the Lokele language. To indicate a plantain the Lokele tribesman would utter the word *likondo*; but in drumming he would send the signal 'the plantain which is propped up high'. For 'manioc' the drum signal is 'manioc remains in deserted garden'. Again in Kele speech 'money' as transmitted by drums is expressed as 'the pieces of metal which arrange palavers'; and for a 'dead body'—'the corpse lying on its back on the clods of earth'.

Another device, familiar to information theorists, is to secure intelligibility by way of repetition. It has been said that in order to be understood the Duala may need to repeat each drum-figure as many as ten times (Betz).

Such practices go far to eliminate ambiguity. Sometimes drum 'words' are included which defy exact translation being probably in the nature of archaisms handed down by ancestral drummers but which have dropped out of the vernacular. There are other indications too that in a given territory the drum language is more 'conservative' than the spoken language.

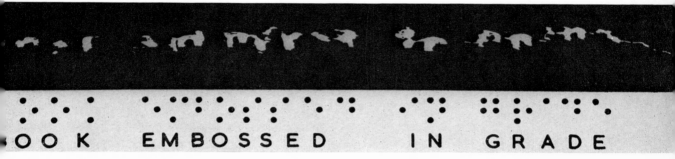

PROVE BENEFICIAL TO DR. HEWLETT JOHNSON (BRAILLE TRANSLATION)

Tracing of the touch-movements of the left index finger, of a male patient of 31 years, blind since the age of 5. He is reading the braille symbols depicted, and is slowed up when the finger reaches the rather unexpected term "Dr. Hewlett". The circumductory movements of exploration are well shown, but there is no record of the speed of the tracing nor of the varying degrees of pressure exerted by the reading finger. The patient was a particularly skilled and rapid braillist who always used the left hand for reading.

OO K   EMBOSSED   IN   GRADE

The touch-movements of a normal-sighted person who is not a braille reader, but who has memorized the visual form of the punctographic alphabet. Large braille type is used. There is no record of the varying pressures, nor of the very many errors made in trying to identify each symbol in turn. The time taken to read this line was from two to three minutes.

West African talking-drum signallers use two drums to produce a tone-and-rhythm code that mimics the tones and rhythms of human speech.

Plate 12

It is, therefore, obvious that the rigid dependence of the drum message upon the tonal properties of the dialect means that no elaborate *lingua franca percussiva* or transcontinental drum signal system is likely to occur. Exceptions to this statement probably occur in cases where emotional rather than propositional speech is being transmitted. Hilarity; festivity; threats; grief over bereavement —these are circumstances where appropriate drumming may well transcend linguistic barriers, and be transmitted and comprehended over very great distances.

The parallelism between drum signalling and articulate speech is illustrated by the fact that the drummer in transmitting a message often hums the appropriate phraseology quietly to himself. It has even been asserted that the village dogs can learn to recognize their names when sounded on a drum.

An interesting variant of African drum language is met with in the translation of the male-female rhythm back into vocal utterance, which in a simplified fashion is thus transmitted by dint of shouting. Thus, according to Carrington, the Lokele people shout *ki* (or *li* or *ti*) for the high note, and *kê* (or *lê* or *tê*) for the low. Thus in this shouted type of communication the term for a white man or European would be *kêlêkê kêliki kêlêkêlêkê* which represents the tonal pattern of the phrase *bosongo olimo ko nda lokonda*, which literally means 'red as copper, spirit from the forest'.

The elaborate nature of drum signalling demands long apprenticeship. That it enters intimately into the social life of the African is illustrated by the common practice of adding specific ancestral 'drum names' to the individual's patronym. It would seem probable, therefore, that such a system of communication as drum language would be sensitive to cerebral disease. In other words it is not difficult to imagine a veritable aphasia for drum signalling in an African (or Melanesian) as the result of brain damage. The lesion might either be focal or diffuse—it would be interesting to determine which: the functional loss might or might not be intimately bound up with impaired verbalization. Such cases have not been recorded, and in my visits to African neurological centres I have never encountered any instances. Nevertheless specific enquiry has yielded the impression that such cases have occurred though they have not been the subject of close study. In evaluating such alleged cases it would be important to include motor factors—paresis, ataxia, apraxia—which might simulate loss of language faculty.

Whistled languages

Another form of 'non-verbal' communication is of putative interest to aphasiologists, namely the 'whistling language'. This method of transmitting messages is uncommon and yet it is scattered geographically in an unexpected fashion. Whistling languages are to be found in parts of Mexico; in Caucasian Turkey; in the French Pyrenees; and in West Africa. The best known instance of a whistled talk is the so-called *Silbo* which can be heard in the Canary Islands, especially La Gomera. As local residents have informed me it is possible to transmit across long distances fairly elaborate messages which can be picked up and interpreted by those who are within ear-shot. Thus such a conversation as the following is perfectly feasible:

'Will you come with me to the cinema tonight?'
'Which cinema?'

'The Royal'.

'Very well'.

The normal carrying power is as far as 5 miles, if the *Silbador* is skilled and the weather conditions are propitious.

Of all the whistle languages *Silbo* is the one which has been most carefully studied, especially by A. Classé, though the Pyrenees system has been the subject of research by R. G. Busnel, A. Moles and M. Gilbert and by J. Parry. The Mazaleco whistles of Mexico were the subject of study by G. M. Cowan.

It has been stressed that *Silbo* is not to be considered as a code, but as a skeleton language, based upon the prosodic properties of the local spoken tongue. In short Silbo is nothing more than 'whistled Spanish'. The *Silbador* while whistling strives to articulate words as in speech. The diversity of tongue-movements produces differences in pitch. Classé has studied the phonetic *modus operandi* of the vocalic and consonantal phonemes of the Spanish language. The play of diversities in pitch and length produce an acoustic pattern which is identifiable by initiates. In La Gomera *Silbo* is learned by many children not long after the acquisition of speech. Learners begin to understand *Silbo* before they attempt to whistle themselves.

In the French Pyrenees, a very similar whistle language is to be heard in the village of Aas, located in the valley of Ossau.

As regards the technique of whistle talk it can be said that a digital method of whistling is the rule. As might be expected redundancy is an important factor in ensuring comprehensibility.

Most Gomeros are veritably bilingual, for the whistled form of communication constitutes nothing less than a second language. It is learned and practised by most of the inhabitants; it is acquired at an early age and like a spoken tongue the child's understanding antedates his power of execution. Indeed they may recognize their own name in *Silbo* before they can talk, in the same way as African dogs identify their names in drum-talk. Most Gomeros can converse in the *Silbo* by the age of 12. As in the case of spoken languages, there are dialects, as well as individual mannerisms. A *Silbador* can recognize his own whistles when taped just as he can discriminate the sender of various *Silbo* signals he hears. Though no doubt taking origin out of the nature of the peculiar geographical terrain and the need for intercommunication *à distance*, it flourished by dint of the specific phonemic and melodic features of the Spanish tongue and especially the local dialect. Like the Morse code in the case of experts, it can become a communicative medium of great elasticity and adaptability. A *Silbador* can crack jokes, as Classé noted when he heard his companion whistle ... 'Will you lend me your donkey because I want to ride to Santa Cruz tomorrow?' The waggishness turns on the fact that Santa Cruz stands on another island 7 hours away by sea. Classé also asserted that during the Spanish Civil War, Gomeros were employed at the front to transmit secret messages, until it was discovered that there were *Silbadors* on both sides.

The *Silbador* precedes his messages, just as in the case of the African drummer, with a preparatory signal. Ordinarily it is a whistled 'ah', which may be said to correspond with the interjected 'um', 'er' or 'now' of all too many public speakers. Even the imitative birds of the Canary Islands pick up *Silbo* and are heard to begin their song with the conventional 'ah'.

In other words *Silbo* is not to be looked upon as an outdoor parlour trick, but a real second language to the inhabitants of the Gomera. It follows, therefore, that it might well be sensitive to the same kind of morbid influences which will produce an aphasia. No such case has yet been reported, however, and neurologists in Las Palmas to whom I have talked have not been able to recall a case in point. Perhaps the possibility has not occurred to those who are not aphasiologically orientated.

Other forms of non-articulate communication

There are other media of communication in this connection, most if not all of which are sensitive to the aphasia-like deficits. Many years ago the case was recorded of a compositor who ceased to be able to assemble type upon his 'stick'. I have met with an acquired loss of skill in a teacher of shorthand at a secretarial college. The 'dysgraphia' in shorthand was much more obvious than the errors which were found in his written speech. An aphasia for stenotyping and also for straightforward typing are not unknown, though they are often masked in clinical practice by a more conspicuous disorder of spoken language. Some of these manual methods of communication entail elements of motricity, and would fall into the category of what Percival Bailey and Pierre Marie termed 'apractagnosia'.

XXVIII. THE NEUROLOGY OF PSYCHOTIC SPEECH

To discern all which symptoms (of melancholy) the better, Rhasis the Arabian makes three degrees of them. The first is falsa cogitatio, *false conceits and idle thoughts: to misconster and amplify, aggravating everything they conceive or fear; the second is* falso cogitata loqui, *to talk to themselves or to use inarticulate, incondite voices, speeches, obsolete gestures, and plainly to utter their minds and conceits of their hearts by their words and actions, as to laugh, weep, to be silent, not to sleep, eat their meat, etc.; the third is to put in practice that which they think or speak.*

Robert Burton, Anatomy of Melancholy

Speech has been called a socio-economic device for saving effort in the attainment of objectives (Whitehorn and Zipf 1943). One of its earliest and most fundamental purposes is to orientate the individual within the community. This socializing effect operates early in childhood, and in a phylogenetic sense it was perhaps one of the greatest factors in the origin of speech in primitive man. As maturity is slowly achieved in the individual as in the *genus*, the use of language becomes inextricably interwoven within the warp and woof of the organism, as exemplified not only by thinking processes, but also by the complicated structure of personality. The development of speech during the pre-hominoid stage synchronizes with the gradual elaboration of communal life; with cries and calls serving as a 'sound-tool'; and with the beginnings of delegation of labour. Thus language is primarily a vocal actualization of the tendency to see reality symbolically (Sapir). The same is true ontogenetically. As the child gradually acquires speech, the organization of his thinking slowly changes; it evolves by intricate steps from egocentric to socialized activity; and as he begins more and more to employ pronouns of the second and third person, he also utters fewer 'action words'. We readily agree with Fillmore Sanford (1942) that 'there are many indications that language is a vehicle of personality as well as of thought, for when a person speaks, he tells us not only about the world, but also, through both form and content, about himself'. The same author quoted Ben Jonson: 'Language most showeth a man; speak that I may see thee'.

Linguists go deeper, and from a study of man's various preferences, glossaries, and verbal habits, conclude that the choice and use of language is a highly individual accomplishment. This idea underlies Krechel's conception of *Spracherlebnis*, i.e. the personal or specific manner in which we experience and understand words. Each of us possesses his own private system of language—a specificity which might permit the identification of authorship if only linguistic techniques were adequate. Whether these personal traits reveal themselves better in one's natural spontaneous diction as Klages (1929) said, or in one's contrived, polished, and much corrected fine writing, is a matter of opinion. The link between language and personality may be even more ingrained, for,

Read at the Annual Meeting of the Royal Medico-Psychological Society, 3rd July, 1963, and published in *Brit. J. Psych.* 1964. **110**. 353–364.

according to the Whorf-Sapir hypothesis, the structure of a particular language is no accidental morphology, but bears some relationship with the mode of thinking, the prejudices and beliefs of the racial stock which uses that particular tongue.

Deviations of the inner mental life consequently betray themselves in an unorthodox use of language. Any considerable aberration of thought or of personality will be mirrored in the various levels of articulate speech—phonetic, phonemic, semantic, syntactic and pragmatic. In written language too, defects may be obvious, and being set out in a medium which is more permanent than the spoken word, lends itself better to linguistic analysis.

The effects of crude lesions of the dominant hemisphere within the area of speech-vulnerability are well known. Here we have the dysphasias in all their clinical diversity. The subtle, complex and less consistent deviations of speech which may be met with in many cases of dementia and of schizophrenia, and in some hysterics, also merit attention. The problem is an enormous one, and what one might term the neurology of psychotic speech forms a veritable *terra incognita*, a lush and uncharted jungle terrain.

Up to now this difficult topic has been approached from two main directions: the descriptive and the psychopathological. Scarcely any work has been done from the standpoint of linguistics. Aphasiological approaches have also been rare, perhaps because they may have been felt to be unrewarding.

In submitting the various psychotic patterns to aphasiological analysis, we are likely to find conspicuous differences between the phenomena of disturbed language as they show themselves in dements and as they occur in schizophrenes. That is true enough, but there is probably also a certain amount of overlap, at least as far as some of the more superficial features are concerned.

Let us first direct our attention to the dementias—conditions which imply mental derangement of organic nature. Here the correspondences and analogies with the dysphasias of local brain disease are likely to prove more germane than in most other psychoses.

In dementia, speech impairment essentially entails a poverty of speech due to inaccessibility of those different vocabularies which ordinarily we can utilize and which we may term the speaking vocabulary, the writing vocabulary, and the reading vocabulary. These terms refer respectively to the stock of words which we are in the habit of employing in conversation; to the larger one we draw on in written compositions; and to that even greater depository which also includes terms we recognize but rarely venture to use. With advancing mental inelasticity, bradyphrenia and memory-loss, the words utilized by the demented patient become severely restricted in conversation and to a somewhat lesser extent in letter writing. But the pre-morbid reading vocabulary suffers far less. This fact we indeed make use of in our psychometric assessment of intellectual falling off.

The difficulty in word finding differs however from the anomia of aphasiacs. The demented patient does not necessarily show any hesitancy in putting a name to an object presented to him, even though a faulty use of proper names is common enough. Paraphasic errors in naming do not occur; nor yet neologisms, substitutions and incapsulated or 'portmanteau' words. Neither does the patient seek to by-pass the elusive term by means of elaborate circumlocutions, as is so common with aphasiacs. But on the other hand the demented patient finds it difficult to retail a series of representatives of a generic class. For example it might be impossible for him to reel off the names of flowers, animals, vegetables, wines or foodstuffs, unless the specimens lie before him. His halting efforts may at times betray a serious lapse into a bald and concrete attitude, and the names he proffers may turn out to have some special connotation which facilitated their emission. Thus, asked to give a list of girls' names, a dement may painfully and slowly produce two or three examples, which, on enquiry, prove to be the names of some who dwell in close association, such as his wife, daughters, or grand-daughters.

Thus there grows up a barrier of silence which the patient is reluctant to break through. Prompted by a direct approach he may reply relevantly enough, but with an economy of diction which is almost telegrammatic. Here indeed is something akin to aphasic poverty of speech. The fragmentary utterances of the dement are capable of linguistic analysis. First of all, the content or semantic values of the speech are altered. Various classifications have been advanced to describe what takes place in the normal. The commonest grouping is into utterances which are (1) declarative; (2) interrogatory; (3) exclamatory; and (4) imperative. It can be demonstrated that the dement, like the aphasiac, rarely ventures upon declarations or propositions, unless to draw attention to some strident bodily need, e.g. hunger, thirst, or a full bladder. Even here the demented patient is in a graver plight than the aphasiac. On the other hand in their truncated utterances both aphasiacs and dements will resort to exclamations and demands, prompted by egocentric drives. Again, the aphasiac is less handicapped than the dement in this respect.

Another semantic classification of normal utterance speaks of 'mands' and 'tacts'; or using another terminology, transitive as opposed to intransitive utterances. Mands or transitive speech include requests and questions; tacts, or intransitive speech, comprise comments, statements, and animadversions. Applying this terminology to the dementias, we can say that tacts are rare, for mands constitute the bulk of the meagre pronouncements of the patient.

Another linguist (A. S. Diamond) has divided utterances into (1) requests for action (or commands); (2) statements; and (3) descriptive-statements. Analysing the content of spontaneous speech in dementia, we can say that only the first of these classes survives.

It is possible to study still closer the meagre sayings and writings of demented patients, especially from a statistico-linguistic angle. Thus an estimation of the token/type ratio may prove revealing, and may demonstrate mathematically the poverty of the available vocabulary, and the great tendency towards verbal iterations, perseverations, and contaminations. The same techniques are naturally applicable in aphasia, and the results are qualitatively the same, but perhaps more striking in cases of dementia.

Then again there is the verb/adjective ratio which may be found to deviate considerably from the normal pattern, and to show a change as in aphasia. Balken and Masserman (1940) found an upset in this ratio in the speech of neurotics. Again, in the spontaneous writings of dements such syntactical properties as sentence-length and differential punctuation counts, lend themselves to exact analysis.

As Allison has described, a patient with early dementia may preserve a façade of normalcy for quite a long time, by resort to a chatter of small talk. As time goes by, his repertoire of things to say becomes more limited and more stereotyped . . . 'more laced with clichés and set phrases'.

Pre-morbid sequential habits of speech may come to the surface more and more. Later the subject remains taciturn unless directly addressed. This social seclusion, be it noted, does not embarrass or perturb the patient.

There are two other verbal peculiarities which the dement may share with the aphasiac. In the course of conversation he will often resort to the grammatical use of aposiopesis, whereby a sentence is started but not finished. Again, he often resorts to vague generic terms to avoid a search for the appropriate noun or proper name. Hence there loom prominently such expressions as 'things' 'what's it's name' 'thingumybob' 'what d'you me call it'.

In more artificial and elenctic interviews where the discourse takes the form of question and answer, there may appear deviations from the normal which are far more subtle. Thus the patient may be able to answer well enough ordinary simple questions of a wholly concrete character. But if an enquiry is made which entails notions of a more abstract nature, the patient may be at a loss. Typically however he is not distressed thereby. Sometimes the patient interpolates little comments or asides which, though not wholly beside the point, are a trifle unexpected. For example, when shown a watch and asked what it is, the patient may reply to the effect that it is a timepiece—and then go on to say quite unasked for . . . 'and a very fine specimen too if I may say so, sir'. This is the phenomenon of 'gratuitous redundancy'. Again the patient's replies as to the identity of an object before him may be unorthodox in a different way. What he says cannot be written off as entirely inappropriate, but the patient gives a pseudo-description which is inadequate, unlikely, and often prolix. This is the phenomenon of 'regressive metonymy' first described by Mrs. Petrie in the case of leucotomized patients. In some ways it reminds one of the *Vorbeireden* met with in the Ganser syndrome. I have reason to believe that this may also represent the earliest stage of a developing jargon-aphasia, or in other words a minimal or incipient aphasia.

Phenomena of a perseveratory character are often discerned both in the spoken and in the written speech, and bear witness to the underlying ideational rigidity. In the early stages of a dementia this shows itself in the spontaneous letter writing, whereby a term—perhaps a slightly uncommon one—is introduced into the text quite congruously, but thereafter it keeps cropping up in a wholly inappropriate fashion. Aphasiologists speak of this verbal peculiarity as 'contamination', for it is familiar enough with local lesions of the brain. Still more striking is the reiteration of common words in the text, some of the errors being detected by the patient and elided, but not all of them. Even more bizarre, and outside the experience in aphasia, is a massive type of echographia which may show itself by a reply to a letter which constitutes an almost word-for-word transcription. Such a phenomenon is unlikely to come to light in ordinary everyday experience, but only in business houses where letters and copies of replies are filed and preserved. An astonishing example has been reproduced on pages 203–204, taken from the case of a young man with juvenile G.P.I. whose letter to his mother was an almost faithful reproduction of hers to him.

Echolalia is a phenomenon common to mental defect, schizophrenia, dementia and aphasia, in that order of frequency of occurrence. Echolalia or echo-reaction suggests a psychopathological complex which includes a defective recall of verbal symbols, coupled with extreme suggestibility, identification with the interlocutor, lack of insight, an impulse to maintain social contact in the way of speech (Stengel), and loss of supralinguistic inhibition.

Finally there are the verbal mannerisms in the speech (and less often in the writings) of patients with dementia. They are perhaps more often found in cases of Pick's disease or Alzheimer's disease, than in simple non-specific brain atrophy. Still more are they met with in the late secondary dementia which may follow a life-long mental defect, or a chronic schizophrenia. Such mannerisms are capable of a linguistic division:

(a) *Phonetic.* This type of peculiarity is illustrated in such features as an unduly high pitch of the voice during verbalization.

(b) *Phonemic.*[1] Several examples might be quoted. A patient in his diction may interpolate an /s/ or less often a /t/ sound in a frequent but quite unwarranted style. The final silent 'e' of the English tongue may be sounded as /ə/ in a somewhat affected manner. Thus 'wine' would be rendered as /wajnə/. Such a patient may also break down all diphthongs into their constituent vocalic phonemes. Thus 'soup' would be pronounced as /sow+əp/ and not /suwp/.

(c) *Prosodic.* Here the duration of a certain syllable (or word) may be unduly long, being extended to an inordinate degree while at the same time a very strong stress is laid upon that particular constitutent of speech.

(d) *Verbal.* Here certain words or phrases are emitted in a tic-like or compulsive fashion wholly out of context, and not necessarily in response to a bystander.

In this connection we recall the recurrent utterance of some aphasiacs who have available for communicative purposes only one word or phrase, maybe a piece of gibberish. But the functional rôle, namely that of communication, meagre though it be, distinguishes the recurrent utterance of the aphasiac from the verbigeration of the dement.

On the receptive side of speech, the conversation of others may not be entirely understood, especially if the semantic content is elaborate: or if the speaker talks too fast, or too softly; or if the message is masked by 'noise', e.g. the rivalry of other people chattering nearby. Written and printed texts may not be comprehended to the full, especially if they are at all obscure, or elusive or allusive in character. These receptive disorders are no different from those which obtain in aphasia, but it can be said that whilst so-called sensory aphasiacs may have a more or less intact sensorium, a demented patient with a comparable amount of receptive defect would probably be clouded as to his mentation, disorientated and severely bradyphrenic.

In the demented, communicative disorders often transcend the use of speech, and may embrace gestural systems. There may be a restriction of what has been called the kinesics of an individual, comprising thereby mimicry, mime, gesture and gesticulation. In severe cases this may be extreme. To such a state of total incommunicado the term 'asemasia' was applied many years ago.

Dysphasia or 'Dyslogia'

There is still more to be said regarding terminology. A precise term is needed to indicate disorders of language in cases of global dementia, i.e. where no focal disease of the brain can be said to

---

[1] One cannot resist drawing attention to the disturbing and idiosyncratic use of the word 'phoneme' by some psychiatrists. To students of language 'phoneme' is something in the nature of a sacred cow of respected pedigree. If not precisely defined, it is at least employed with due consistency. Psychiatrists should really devote themselves to the quest for some other means of indicating phantasms of the auditory nerve.

exist. Most medical men understand the term 'aphasia' as representing a state of communicative defect which is by definition, though not explicitly so, the expression of localized disease within the so-called speech 'centre'. In the opinion of many it would not be correct to apply this term to cases of dementia, unless of course the dementia happened to be an epiphenomenon of local disease of the brain. Even the terms 'latent aphasia' (Pichot 1955), or 'generalized aphasic difficulty' (Shakow, Dolkart and Goldman 1941) are not beyond criticism. 'Non-aphasic speech-impairment' is too clumsy and not self-explanatory. 'Pseudo-aphasia' might do; or alternatively 'alogia' or 'dyslogia'—were it not that these last two terms have been sequestrated by Kleist in quite another context.

Attempts have been made to isolate specific linguistic patterns among the demential speech-disorders according to aetiology and pathology. Allison (1962), for example, distinguished sharply between dementia due to global lesions, and dementia due to such focal disease as tumour or cerebrovascular accidents. Pichot (1955) separated the epileptic and the arteriopathic dementias from the senile varieties, and said that subclinical but nevertheless definite language-impairment may be found in the first two types. He applied the expression 'latent aphasia' here, and implicated a particular involvement of the temporal lobes in cases of arteriosclerosis and of epilepsy.

Whether it is of value to form such linguistic subgroups within the phenomena of demential speech impairment is, I submit, dubious. To a neurologist, it is perhaps the mixed clinical pictures which occasion the greatest difficulties in assessment. Two examples may be given. In the first place we may visualize a life-long mental defective who in his sixties, acquires a lesion of the dominant hemisphere, whether traumatic, ischaemic, or neoplastic. The ensuing picture of dysphasia is likely to be highly unconventional, and difficult to disentangle, particularly if no focal signs of neurological involvement happen to co-exist. The other type of case which is apt to cause diagnostic perplexity, concerns patients who have sustained non-progressive aphasia-producing lesions of the brain (e.g. apoplectic or traumatic) and thereafter begin to develop a superadded steadily advancing brain-atrophy. Or both types of clinical complexity may co-exist. One such case was under my care at the National Hospital referred from Friern Hospital through the kindness of Dr. Richard Hunter.

A middle-aged institutionalized patient had been known as a life-long eccentric, moody, hypochondriacal, anti-social, a prey to bouts of heavy drinking. At 55 years he suffered a fractured skull from a road accident which produced a right-sided weakness, sensory impairment and visual field defect, together with a serious and persisting dysphasia. Seen 5 years later the patient was found to have deteriorated intellectually and his speech was larded with an assortment of reiterated phrases of a type and purpose not typical of a simple organic defect. Air-studies revealed gross brain-atrophy much more marked in the region of the left temporal lobe. This case might be deemed to represent the picture of a dysphasia combined with a dyslogia.

Speech-disorders in schizophrenia

If, from an aphasiological point of view, the principal problem of speech-impairment in the dementias is one of terminology, the difficulties with schizophrenic speech-disorder are far greater.

Very tentatively Rümke and Nijam (1958) ventured the query whether the neologisms, confused speech and disturbed inter-human relationship found in schizophrenics could be regarded as an aphasia. 'Might the secret of schizophrenia', they asked, 'lie in a hitherto unknown high-level aphasic disturbance?'

Unlike what obtains in aphasia and in dementia, there is no true inaccessibility of vocabulary. The linguistic *quantum* is probably intact, but the utilization thereof may be gravely disordered. Resemblances there may be at times between the diction or writings of a schizophrenic and those of an aphasiac, but they must not be overstressed, and analogy must remain an analogy and nothing more. True it is, of course, that at one time some Continental neuro-psychiatrists like Schneider (1927), Fleischacker (1930) and Angyal (1958) were tempted to visualize a linguistic pathophysiology and even an underlying morbid anatomy as an explanation of the aphasia-like states in schizophrenes. Kleist speculated that there might be cortico-subcortical changes to account for the speech-impairment and he even attributed some of the iterative and perseveratory phenomena to lesions within the basal ganglia. These notions never received credence, and rightly so: Kleist in his neurological thinking had always been a deviationist and a materialist. The terms 'schizophasia' and 'schizographia', though misleading tokens of disordered physiology, may not be wholly unacceptable, for they are convenient descriptive labels which might be employed even more widely than Kraepelin and Teulié originally suggested.

The simplest attitude towards the diverse schizophrenic speech-disorders is to look upon them as a travesty of communication. The message breaks down, and ceases to constitute a conveyer of reference-function. This in turn is the product of the patient's gradual withdrawal from his environment. Despite certain superficial resemblances, the situation is basically nothing like that which is associated with speech-impairment in aphasia. The patient with aphasia fails in his communicative intent by virtue of an inaccessibility, if not indeed a loss, of verbal symbols in thought. In schizophrenia the thinking processes themselves are deranged but the verbal symbols are intact. The one represents a quantitative and the other a qualitative defect in endophasy or inner speech. This fundamental pre-linguistic distinction explains the difference between the clinical features in the two conditions.

The autism of the schizophrenic may be well shown in the frequency with which pronouns of the first person crop up in his speech and writings. In one letter of 1241 words a schizophrenic girl used the pronoun 'I' 87 times, and this easily ranked as the most frequent term. The runners-up were the articles 'the' and 'a' which appeared 43 and 33 times respectively. The pronoun 'my' also occurred 33 times and 'me' 20 times. By contrast 'you' occurred 11 times; 'your' 3, 'we' 3, 'him' 3, 'he' once and 'his' once. This count gave the incidence of 'I' as 6·2% (total pronouns of the first person = 11·2%). Fairbank it may be remembered found that 'I' constituted 8·4% of the spoken speech of schizophrenics, as compared with 5% in the telephone talk of ordinary people; 3·1% in the diction of college freshmen explaining proverbs; and 1·2% in commonplace written texts. In technical publications the incidence was found to be nil.

This heightened incidence of the first person singular is never encountered in cases of aphasia, either in their speech or in their writing.★

★ It is of interest to recall that the Bell Telephone Company once analysed a total of 100,000 words uttered in the course of telephone talks. No more than 30 different words made up 50% of the total (or 'tokens') while 70% comprised 100 different words (or 'types').

In aphasia there may be an extreme reduction of spoken and written speech, perhaps to the extent of a single recurring phrase, perhaps to a mere 'yes' or 'no'. Absolute mutism however does not occur, while in the schizophrene a total speechlessness may be found. The schizophrene though often displaying a verbal iteration does not struggle to emit a 'yes' and eventually come out with a 'no'. Nor will the schizophrene eke out his attenuated vocabulary by a play of gesture. In other words he is not one who is striving to communicate in the face of overwhelming difficulties.

Between the aphasiac and the schizophrenic interesting differences are to be observed in the total communicative set. The former is an anxious person who may be very aware of his defect (unless he be a jargon-aphasiac); he strives and strains to achieve mutual comprehension, betraying all the evidences of frustration when he fails. In vain he marshals every adventitious aid to intelligibility. The schizophrene, by contrast, may be aloof or negativistic. He may display 'advertance' by turning away from the one who seeks to converse with him. His voice may be hushed as if secretive, or it may sound artificial as in the so-called strangled speech (*Wügstimme*).

The similarities between schizophrenia and aphasia are less easy to distinguish when neologisms and jargon speech are concerned. The logorrhoeic schizophrene may emit a word-salad which apparently carries little if any reference-function. Schneider has identified such processes as fusion, derailment, omission and what he called 'drivelling', which go to make up a bizarre combination of telescoped ideas, word-monstrosities, echo-responses, irrelevancies, incoherences, nonsense words, and scattered verbal statements.

The neologisms of an aphasiac however are determined in part by a weakening of supra-linguistic inhibition or vigilance which permits an over liberal verbal association exteriorized in a medley of synonyms, antonyms, paraphonemic, metaphorical and metonymous substitutions, and telescoping of words. Another important factor may be present, which probably does not apply to schizophrenes: the sensory aphasiac has little or no self-criticism for he is largely unaware of the disordered nature of his utterance. Hence the often applied term 'anosognosic aphasia'. Moreover he may hotly deny that his speech is disordered and may project the defect of communication on to the stupidity of others. Again there may well be some acoustic perceptual defect like an audiometric scotoma, though this idea is rejected by some. Luria considers that there is an underlying tendency on the speaker's part to confuse phonemes of somewhat similar sound, e.g. the voiced /z/ /d/ with the unvoiced /s/ /t/. In other words an essential paraphonemia is hypothesized, a defect peculiar to paraphasia and foreign to the picture of schizophasia.

This is hardly the place to discuss the elaborate problem concerning the asyndetic thinking of schizophrenics in so far as it is responsible for the aberrations in verbalization. Enough has been said to show that the underlying mental mechanisms are quite different in schizophrenics as compared with aphasiacs, even though the verbal utterances are often similar.

The analogies of disturbed speech in psychotics and in aphasiacs may also be carried over into their writings. One striking difference may be stressed at the outset: aphasiacs are usually very reluctant to write, while schizophrenics often have a veritable *cacoëthes scribendi*. Consequently, genuine spontaneous writings are rare in the case of aphasiacs, though of course they may do their best to perform when directly requested by the physician.

Another difference between the writings of the psychotic and the aphasiac lies in the lay-out of the text upon the page. The schizophrenic likes to embellish his penmanship with ornate flourishes and elaborate capitals. He often writes vertically in the margins as well as along the lines. The page is barely large enough to contain all that he wishes to impart. Drawings may be inserted within the body of the text, not so much as illustrations, as extensions of what the patient wishes to express.

None of these peculiarities is to be seen in the painful attempts at letter writing made by the aphasiac. He clearly has a poverty of expression, and contents himself with a few lines placed either in the centre of the page or huddled along one edge.

Again, the verbal disorders of some schizophrenics may be strikingly dissociated as between speech and writing. Either may be severely disturbed, but in complete isolation. This is a phenomenon not met with in aphasia.

One obvious point of similarity however lies in the repetitiousness of the text in both conditions, as opposed to the ordinary verbal diversification of the normal subject. Words, phrases and word-clusters tend to show themselves over and over again, often quite incongruously. The aphasiac sometimes detects his error and makes erasures; but often not. Even when he makes corrections he usually overlooks the great majority of his repetitions.

Written compositions, whether executed by aphasiacs or by schizophrenics, are invaluable data for linguistic analysis, in that they are permanent records. They lack, however, the ephemeral paralinguistic overtones which are of such importance in human communication, but which are so difficult to transcribe.

If, for example, contrasting texts are reproduced—not in their original script but transcribed into conventional print—some of these linguistically significant features become evident.

There follow two letters written by aphasiacs, and one other, much longer, which was the work of a schizophrenic patient.

(1) Thank you ~~very~~ for very ~~yes~~ forget loss lastly forgetful ~~forget~~ to us.
   And I should very ~~ve~~ much for your getting to your gratefulness.
   I am I singful very grateful rightful and ~~forget~~ forgetful for your gettleftfed, forgetful forgetful and forgetful.

(2) Dear Doctor
   (~~Dear~~) I requirte it the took, I got not why ask when why then, I when you, my shall my you small my, why send sned say, send what why I when (~~when~~) I received her (~~she~~) she has have a cold, so let recusf the result. I have a resuft takes be to take hate from her from far.
   What change (~~cal~~) can (~~for~~) for you. What can I for me. All your the for the porter. Tell you your you ponten you will you go.

The foregoing examples differ in severity. The writer of the first letter was obviously struggling hard to communicate, but under such difficulties that the message she wished to impart did not come through. Some but not all of the contaminating words were crossed out; more of them passed unnoticed by the patient.

One instance of letter writing by a schizophrene may be reproduced.

(3) '. . . I like Titbits weekly. I like Titbits weekly too. I should like Titbits ordered weekly. I need jam, golden syrup or treacle, sugar. I fancy ham sandwiches and pork pies. Cook me a pork pie and I fancy sausage rools I want ham sandwiches. I want tomatoes and pickles and salt and sandwiches of corn beef and sandwiches of milk loaf and cucumber sandwiches. I want plain biscuits buttered, rusks, and cheese biscuits I want bread and cheese. I want Swiss roll and plain cake, I want pastries, jam tarts. I should like some of your pie you have for second course, some pastry. I want biscuits, fancy biscuits and fancy cakes. I want sweets, bull-seyes or cloves. I want rissols. I want rissols. I fancy fruit, do bring some oranges, apples, bananas, pears. Do brong some fruit, I get dry, oranges, I got tea for all next week from March 10th Sunday, all the week till Sunday March 17th. I shall want more tea March 17th Sunday. I want sugar I want jam, golden-syrup or treacle. I like plum jam. I like butter. It would be a treat. We only get margarine. I would like some butter. Bring some butter. I would kile a pot of cream from the dairy and some cherries with the cream. A pot of cream with cherries. Cream with cherries. I like chocolate roll with cream inside. Some nice cake Dundee cake and plain cake. I fancy tomatoes and sause, with bread and butter and salt. I like jam puffs and doe nuts. I like seedy cake, coco nut cake cocoanut cake. I want jam tarts, pastries I fancy pastries, bamberys I want a piece of rubber, a piece of India rubber. I like macaronis. I like macaroni's, macaroni's, pastry, a piece of rubber for my writing letters. Come soon, every week. Send Leslie this Sunday to visit me. Bring another lb. of tea soon, Leslie bring tea and sugar I want sugar and jam. Jam. Soon get me home by Easter I hope. Soon may I come home to you At Easter by my nirthday I hope to be home. I hope to be home soon, very soon. I like chocolate eclairs, I fancy chocolate eclairs. chocolate eclairs. Doenuts. I want doenuts. I do want some golden syrup a tin of golden syrup or treacle, jam. I fancy very much some fruit, oranges, apples, bananas. I want fancy cakes, ~~wrock cakes~~ rock cakes, bread pudding jam tarts, doenuts chocolate-eclairs, I would like a pot of honey. I would like some sandwiches of real butter. Ginger bread I like ginger biscuits fancy biscuits ginger breads. I want. I would like sandwiches of milk loaf and real butter. Soon get me home from the hospital want you, see the Committee about me coming home for Easter, my twenty fourth birthday. I trust you will have me home, very soon. I hope all is well at home, how is Father getting on. Never mind, there is hope, heaven will come, time heals all wounds, Rise again Glorious Greece and come the Hindoo Heavens, The Indian Heavens The Dear old times will come back. We shall see Heaven and Glory yet, come everlasting life and God. I want a new writing pad of note paper. . . .'

The schizophrenic patient expressed well enough her simple wants and feelings but the manner in which this was done betrays the underlying thought disorder, mild though it be.

All such specimens are capable of linguistic analysis. The texts of the three letters are analysed and compared with paragraphs taken from Hemingway and from Dr. Samuel Johnson, and also with two other letters written by an aphasiac and a schizophrene respectively. The following three tables show respectively (1) the type/token ratio; (2) the number of words intervening between one definite article and the next; and (3) the verb/adjective ratio.

The samples given are too small and the scatter of results obviously too wide for any conclusions to be drawn. The data are offered merely to demonstrate that linguistic analysis is possible of the writings of aphasic and psychotic patients, which, carried out on a bigger scale, might yield interesting results.

TABLE 8

	Total number of words 'Tokens'	Number of different words 'Types'	Type/Token Ratio 'T.T.R.'
Aphasiac (1)	39	11	0·28
(2)	42	21	0·50
(3)	89	45	0·50
Schizophrene (1)	1,241	331	0·26
Schizophrene (2)	79	52	0·65
Hemingway	167	51	0·30
Dr. S. Johnson (1)	168	90	0·53
(2)	127	80	0·65
(3)	266	170	0·64
(4)	298	185	0·62

TABLE 9   CARROLL'S INDEX OF DIVERSIFICATION

i.e. number of words from one 'the' to the next

Aphasiac (1)	4, 14, 2, 1, 2, 1.
(3)	40, 28, 1, 10+
Schizophrene (1)	3, 16, 6, 16, 11, 39, 10, 5, 19.
(2)	8, 52+
Hemingway	18, 40, 57, 5, 18+
Dr. S. Johnson's letter No. 846	6, 43, 26, 40, 2, 9, 7, 26, 20, 4, 53, 37+

Average=10—15 in normal written speech.

TABLE 10   VERB/ADJECTIVE RATIO

Aphasiac (1)	0·25
(2)	0·41
(3)	11·0
Schizophrene (1)	3·5
Schizophrene (2)	1·0
Hemingway	8·5
Dr. S. Johnson	2·0

Neoteric literature

Two other examples may be given of schizophrenic writings showing graphic perseveration (see Fig. 29).

Before leaving the subject of schizophrenic writing one can scarcely refrain from referring to something which is on the face of it at least, analogous, namely the unorthodoxies of obscure and reiterative writing as a deliberate art-form. Taking first the latter aspect, it is easy to find in *avant-garde* literature what might be called a studied jargon defiant of traditional syntax, as in the following examples:

The fall (bababadalgharaghtakamminarronnkonnbronntonnerronntuonnthunntrovarrhounawnskawntoohoohoordenenthurnuk!) of a once wallstrait oldparr is retaled early in bed and later on life down through all christian minstrelsy. The great fall of the offwall entailed at such short notice the pftjschute of Finnegan, erse solid man, that the humptyhillhead of himself prumptly sends an unquiring one well to the west in quest of his tumptytumtoes: and their upturnpikepointandplace is at the knock out in the park where oranges have been laid to rust upon the green since devlinsfirst loved livvy.

ich gehe nicht allein
ich gehe nicht allein
ich gehe nicht allein
ich gehe nicht allein
ich gehe nicht allein
ich gehe nicht allein
ich gehe nicht allein
ich gehe nicht allein
ich gehe   allein
ich gehe nicht allein
ich gehe nicht allein
ich gehe nicht allein
ich gehe nicht allein

As to obscure writing, there is the existentialist prose of Picasso.

25th March **XXXVI**
think evening Angelus to see you shattered in the glittering mirrorsplintering to the blow of a clog blowpipe to see you nailed upon the quivering pond which stands out and rolls itself up in a pill unfasten the hung naked body of the loved one of the festoon of months remove your hand your hands.

As an instance of contemporary verse a poem by Dylan Thomas may be selected almost at random:

Sir Morrow at his sponge
(The wound records)
The nurse of giants by the cut sea basin

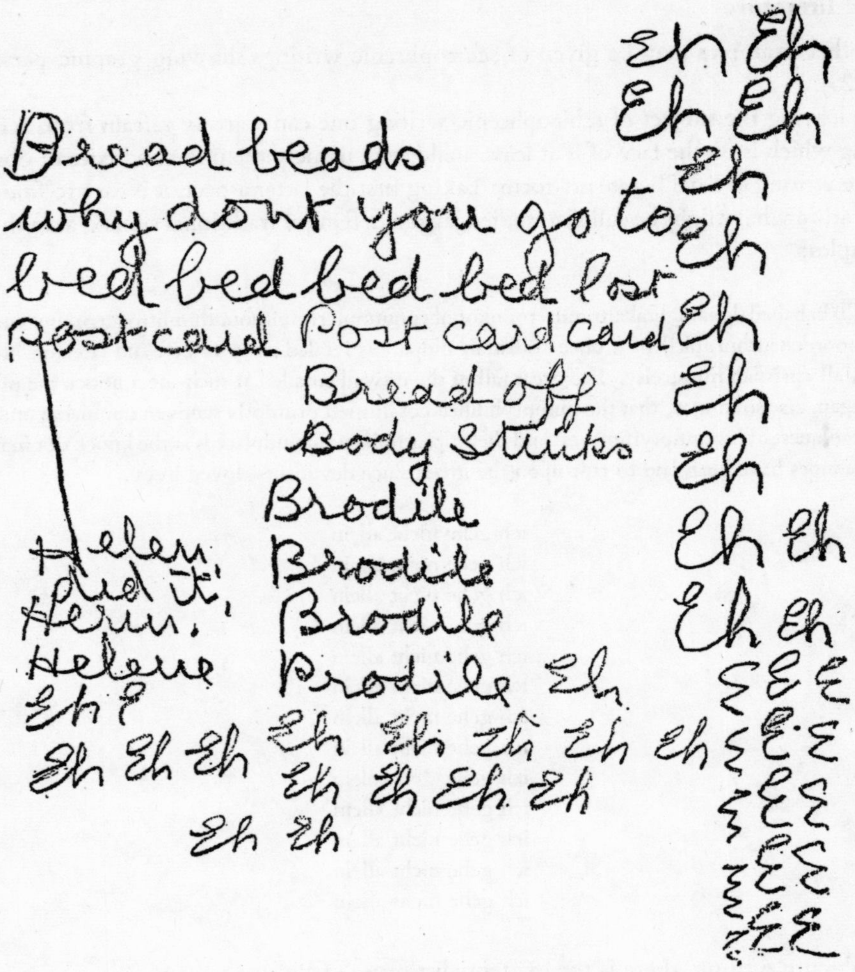

Bread beads
why dont you go toeh
bed bed bed bed lost
Post card Post card card
Bread off
Body Stinks
Brodile
Brodile
Brodile
Helen,
did it,
Henn,
Helene
Eh?
Eh Eh Eh
Brodile Eh
Eh Eh Eh Eh Eh
Eh Eh Eh Eh
Eh Eh

Eh Eh
Eh Eh
Eh Eh
Eh Eh
Eh Eh
Eh
Eh Eh
Eh
Eh
Eh Eh
Eh
Eh Eh
Eh
E E E E E E E E E E

```
UP SUNS LIGHTNINGS THUNDERS FOREVERS
UP WORLDS FOREVERS ALL UP TOGETHERS
UP IN MILLIONS MORE WORLDS SCENTS
UP SUNS LIGHTNINGS THUNDERS FOREVER WITH NO ENDS
UP IN MORE WORLDS COMMANDERS OF FIRE SCENTS
UP IN ALL WORLDS JUMPERS OVER SKIES
UP IN DADS SONS GIRLS MUMS THUNDERS FAMILIES HIGH
UP IN WORLDS OWN MADE PURE CIVILIZATIONS
UP IN COOLED UP SUNS LIGHTNINGS THUNDERS RELATIONS
UP IN MORE WORLDS CIVILIZATIONS


UP IN MORE WORLDS RAINBOWS
UP IN MORE WORLDS LILAC SCENTED CLOTHES
UP IN WORLDS SHAMROCK GREENS
UP IN MORE WORLDS BEST BEEN
```

FIG. 29 Psychotic speech: graphic perseveration

(Fog by his spring
Soaks up the sewing tides).
Tells you and you, my masters, as his strange
Man morrow blows through food.

Where does this type of writing belong in the Pantheon of literature? Let us quote the interpretation made by David Aivaz, a contemporary professional critic.

The transition from image to image is by means of the pun, the double meaning, the coined word, the composite word, the noun-verb, the pronoun with a double antecedent. And there is a larger machinery, verbal and syntactical: clauses that read both forward and backward; uneven images that are smoothed by incantatory rhythms, rhymes, word-patterns, verse-forms, by the use of commas in place of full-stop punctuation; cant, slang terms and formal, general abstract wording juxtaposed in image after image, so that the agitation of each becomes the repose of the group.

What does all this mean? The critic's words are metalinguistic, but the sense is not. Could these paragraphs be freely paraphrased, using the grammar of psychopathology? Thus a psychiatrist might well be tempted to speak of telescoping of ideas: agrammatism: klang-associations: idiosignificant and obscure allusions. This is perhaps another way of expressing the same opinions. Schneider's four-fold mechanisms of schizophrenic speech come to mind, namely fusion, derailment, omission and drivelling. There are also Piro's four fundamentals of psychotic speech, namely: semantic distortion, semantic dispersion, semantic dissolution, and enlargement of the semantic halo, whereby meaning is extended without restraint and language becomes ambiguous, vague and indeterminate.

Concerning another example of Dylan Thomas' verse, namely

If my head hurts a hair's foot
Pack back the downed bone. If the unpricked ball of my breath
Bump on a spout let the bubbles jump out

the opinions of two contrasting critics may be quoted, the one laudatory, the other sceptical. According to William York Tindall's views upon this poem . . . 'Occasion, theme, and feeling are of less interest than method. We are familiar with the process of conflicting images and with quarrels among words from incompatible areas. But here . . . are advances in rhythm and sound. Excellently sprung . . . the lines unsystematically display all the devices of Welsh sound: alliteration, assonance, dissonance, internal rhyme, and chiming vowels . . . Thomas was learning moreover that sentences need not begin with the beginning of a line or end with its ending. Beginning within the line has rhythmic importance . . .'.

To Henry Treece however this same poem was little more than a verbal compulsion, almost a psychopathic phenomenon, musical-rhythmic automatism, with a possibly unconscious sexual reference thrown in to emphasize the primitive source of the word-group.

The latter writer has boldly faced the problem by posing—and trying to answer—his own

24

question, '. . . is Dylan a fake?' Treece wrote: 'I feel that Dylan Thomas is extremely (and unconsciously) ill-balanced; yet, in the unbalance, lies much of his "charm" . . . His choking verbalisms, his fixations on certain threadbare or obscure epithets, his inability to resist inorganic alliterations, his wilful obscurity, his deafness to certain obviously poor rhymes, his preponderating rhythmic monotony, his careless use of words, the overstress or understress created by his rhetorical mechanisms, the overemphasized pathos and arrogance, the self-pity, the lack of humour, the poverty of historic background (reflected in his self-sufficiency), all these are evidence, and to spare, of a lack of maturity. But, unless such unbalance is known to the poet, it is less than just that he should be called a forger, and his works fakes'.

Perhaps in conclusion two points can be indicated where schizophrenic writing differs from much of this type of poetry. The one is clinical and compulsive: the other is compulsive too, but it may also at times prove lucrative. One is uninhibited and sincere, while the other may be redeemed by its much contrived euphony. Psychotic writing may or may not have been intended to be read: the other was written not only to be read but also to be declaimed.

This provocative subject could perhaps be clarified by a careful textual study of the works of poets who are well known to have been psychotic, as for example the pre- and post-morbid verse of the Swedish schizophrene Frøding.

XXIX. SPEECH AND SPEECH-LOSS IN RELATION TO THE FACTOR OF CEREBRAL DOMINANCE

Is the brain, which is notably double in structure, a double organ, 'seeming parted, but yet a union in partition'? Or is it a seeming whole made up actually of two organs? Have we, in fact, two brains as we have two eyes, two lungs, two kidneys? Or have we one brain as we have one body, built up of two similar halves?

Henry Maudsley, The Double Brain. *1889*

To understand this complex and still rather obscure topic, it is necessary to turn back the pages of neurological history, and to recapitulate the story which has been narrated in Chapter VI.

In the heart of the wine-growing region of Gard in the south of France, stands the quaint walled town of Sommières. There, at the turn of the eighteenth century, lived an obscure general practitioner, Dr. Marc Dax. It was he who, as the result of shrewd clinicopathological correlation, first realized that as far as language, at any rate, was concerned, the two cerebral hemispheres are not equipotential. In 1836, he delivered a short address upon this topic before the *Congrès Méridional*. The paper attracted no attention: it never appeared in print: the manuscript lay forgotten in a drawer long after his death the following year. Nearly 30 years later, and over a century ago, Paul Broca was slowly beginning to realize that every single one of his cases of aphemia was the result of a lesion of the left half of the brain. In 1865, he wrote a paper to that effect, which came to the notice of Gustave, the doctor son of Dr. Marc Dax, also in practice at Sommières. Dax junior wrote a tart letter to the medical press, claiming that Broca had deliberately ignored his father's pioneer work. Broca replied in a similar peevish vein, protesting that he had never even heard of Marc Dax or read any of his works; and that furthermore he had just discovered that no mention was ever made in the medical press of any paper by Dax. The son responded to this taunt by unearthing the original manuscript of the lecture given by his father in 1836, and he proceeded to reprint this paper and incorporate it within an article of his own in the *Gazette hebdomadaire* for 1865.

Such is the unusual story of the beginnings of our ideas as to the lateralization of certain cerebral functions to one hemisphere only. Though the conception rapidly gained acceptance, the two Doctors Dax themselves remained neglected figures. They became identified with national politics,

An elaboration of a chapter entitled 'Speech and speech-loss in relation to the Duality of the Brain, published *in Interhemispheric Relations and Cerebral Dominance*, ed. by V. B. Mountcastle (Johns Hopkins).

and the son was forced to give up his post at the local hospital, an appointment which he and his father held for 52 consecutive years.

Hughlings Jackson accepted the doctrine to the effect that the left hemisphere was principally concerned with speech, but with certain reservations. Mindful of the logical distinction between positive and negative consequences of disease, he ascribed the defects in self-expression to the left-brain lesion, while attributing the restricted utterance of an aphasiac to the operation of the intact hemisphere. Jackson spoke of the left half of the brain as the 'leading' hemisphere as regards the faculty of speech, regarding it as being concerned with creative aspects of language, while the right hemisphere was tied up with the 'automatic' use of words.

Jackson's views as to the modest role of the non-dominant hemisphere in the physiology of speech attracted little sympathetic attention. The more striking phenomenon of the correlation of language with the left hemisphere usurped the notice of all who were interested in aphasia. For a long time the matter rested thus, but early in the present century, neurologists began to enquire why it was that right-handedness, left cerebral dominance, and the lateralization of speech-endowment to the major hemisphere, should all three be associated in this peculiar fashion. The mere acquisition of superior motor skills by the right hand did not in itself appear enough to account for the importance of the left hemisphere *quâ* speech. The difference between the function of the two hemispheres was so much greater than the relatively smaller difference between the daily work of the two hands. Gradually the idea grew up that it was the acquisition of the art of writing with the right hand, an artificial and wholly assymetrical activity within the domain of language, which determined that the opposite hemisphere should achieve a special symbological importance. This view was first stated explicitly by Ernst Weber in 1904, who proclaimed that to explain the left-sided importance of the brain as regards speech, mere right-handedness was not enough. Right-handed children do not become aphasic after left-brained disease, unless old enough to have learned to write. Similarly, illiterate persons do not develop the same left-brained preponderance and therefore are liable to show little, if any, aphasia after disease of the left-brain. In other words, there was a greater likelihood of bilateral cerebral representation in the speech-functions of illiterates, and a relative immunity from speech-loss.

Although this notion is of course a naïve and gross over-simplification of the problem, it is one which cannot be completely brushed aside and forgotten.

Interest afterwards turned to the problem of cerebral dominance, and the inherent complexities of this apparently simple topic soon became evident. The difficulties in determining which was the dominant of the two halves of the brain became increasingly great, the closer the clinical scrutiny. The notion developed that there were degrees of dominance. Left-handedness and right-brain dominance no longer was regarded as a mirror-opposite variant of the normal state of affairs. Limited or feeble cerebral dominance; cross-laterality; correlation of inadequate dominance with cerebral immaturity; ambidexterity as a state of ambilevity, such were the topics which came up for discussion. These ideas profoundly influenced our interpretations of such clinical phenomena in sinistrals as aphasia, and also the effects of right parietal disease. A considerable amount of work has been done on the pattern of aphasia in left-handers, following lesions of either half of the brain. Data have been collected by such authors as Conrad, Subirana, Zangwill and his group, and many others. The exciting results are now well known, and need not be narrated here. Supplementing the clinical study of dominance, came the experimental techniques of Wada.

At the same time, there has grown up a tendency to focus some attention upon the minor hemisphere, and to posit a number of specific non-verbal properties to its pathology. The trend was, and still is, towards allocating certain neuropsychological endowments, some to the major hemisphere, and others to the minor. With increasing concentration of interest, this latter group seems to be steadily increasing in number, perhaps inordinately so.

The rôle of the minor hemisphere in such presumed major brain-activities as speech had meanwhile been somewhat overlooked. The position as expressed in 1935 by Weisenberg and McBride, might be taken as still representing conventional opinion. They wrote:

> The right brain, while not directly concerned in language in the right-handed individual, nevertheless is in a state of receptivity for language acquisition, the degree varying in accordance with the use of the left hand in writing. In addition, non-language functions and behaviour, which are almost always implicated in aphasia, have admittedly a bilateral cerebral basis. This is as far as we can go from the evidence obtained in this research. There is nothing to show that the right brain has any specific language function as indicated by Hughlings Jackson and some more recent investigators.

But can this opinion really be accepted as the final word in the problem? Quite apart from the question of left-handers and acquired disease, there is the rare appearance of aphasia after lesions in the right hemisphere in subjects who have shown no personal nor familial evidence of sinistrality whatsoever. The notion of 'ectopia' of the speech centres, from the left half of the brain to the right, has been argued on and off since the work of Bramwell in 1899, and the subject was ably discussed by Kurt Mendel in 1912. This phenomenon of genuine 'crossed aphasia' must be regarded as uncommon, and Penfield and Roberts gauged that less than one per cent of right-handed persons have some representation of speech in the right cerebral hemisphere. In 1955 Ettlinger, Jackson, and Zangwill discussed a series of sixteen such cases collected from the literature. The impression still exists that cases of 'crossed aphasia' are associated with some degree of familial sinistrality—the 'stock-brainedness' of Foster Kennedy. Nevertheless clinically convincing cases continued to be reported from time to time, as from K. Rothschild (1931); G. Marinesco, D. Grigoresco, and S. Axente (1938); J. M. Nielsen (1938); H. Goodglass and F. A. Quadfasel (1954); L. Roberts (1955); H. Hécaen and M. Piercy (1956); and T. Imura, K. Asakawa, S. Hotta, and S. Nihonmatsu.

Perhaps we still tend to overlook the possible rôle of the right half of the brain in the faculty of speech. Some aphasiologists, conspicuously Eisenson, are beginning to suspect that appropriate testing of a sufficiently searching character might well elicit defects within the sphere of language which are too subtle for ordinary routine techniques to bring to light. This idea may be accepted as yet another example of minimal dysphasia. Neuropsychologists need to pay closer attention to the linguistic capacities and incapacities of right-handed victims of right-brain disease. Already a number of suggestive clinical data can be mentioned in this context:

(1) Disordered articulation is a common and striking sequel of disease of the minor hemisphere, though it may be transient. Of course, dysarthria of this kind is to be regarded as a manifestation

of a disorder of the act of speaking rather than of language. But if the dysarthria is severe, a poverty of speech will result which mimics closely an aphasia and may cause difficulties in bedside diagnosis, even at the hands of very experienced neurologists. In so far as gross dysarthria hampers or hinders articulate self-expression, it can be looked upon as a disorder in the act of communication.

(2) Creative literary work, demanding a particularly high level of performance, may, I submit, be noticeably affected in such circumstances. Examples of this phenomenon in professional writers who have been afflicted with disease of the minor hemisphere are not rare in clinical practice. A journalist with a right frontal glioma showed this phenomenon particularly well. His regular contributions to his paper deteriorated in a gross dysgraphic fashion, but returned to normal after the growth had been removed. In this man's case there was no evidence whatsoever of sinistrality.

(3) Appropriate techniques may reveal hesitancies or actual blocking in word-finding. The patient surmounts the naming-difficulty by resorting to very unusual circumlocutions whereby approximate pseudo-synonyms emerge,and odd explanations and circumstantial comments are gratuitously offered. This phenomenon, which differs somewhat from the orthodox verbal behaviour of a patient with anomia, is the same 'gratuitous redundancy' which we have already referred to more than once as a feature of incipient or minimal dysphasia.

(4) Again, special techniques such as tachistoscopy, for example, may demonstrate inordinate delays in the visual identification of verbal symbols by the patient. A similar retardation may be noted in the auditory perception of speech.

(5) Right-brain disease may perhaps lead to difficulties in the learning of novel linguistic material.

(6) One may also mention the interesting phenomenon described by Nathanson, Bergman, and Gordon in 1952, associated with lesions of the non-dominant parietal lobe. Here the patient shows a variety of hesitancies and inaccuracies of speech, but only when the present disability is the topic under discussion. This phenomenon resembles Weinstein's 'non-aphasic disorders of naming'.

(7) Difficulties in the full understanding of the ultimate meaning of pictorial matter is a common phenomenon of all types of brain-disease, and some are already tending to associate this defect more specifically with lesions of the minor hemisphere. Pictorial material may be deemed a far cry from speech, but both can be looked upon as modalities of symbolic formulation and handling.

Eisenson has continued his interest in linguistic disorders arising after lesions of the non-dominant half of the brain. Employing a battery of verbal tasks that encompass a wider range of difficulty than is ordinarily employed, he found that patients with right cerebral damage performed less well than did the controls (1962). Another curious finding was that reported by Anasta-sopoulos (1959) who found that a lesion of the minor temporal lobe was followed by a logorrhoea on the part of the patient coupled with a reluctance to listen to the speech of others.

Penfield's experimental work may be quoted, whereby the contrasting phenomenon of either vocalization or else temporary interference with speech can be secured by electrical stimulation either of the dominant or the non-dominant hemisphere, but the relationship of these findings in the context of normal language-function is still obscure.

The foregoing phenomena, it may be noted, are mainly intensifications of what may occur as temporary difficulties under physiological conditions. In this way it accords with the findings of Howes and Geschwind, who have demonstrated by statistical methods than an aphasia merely represents a random disturbance of the processes underlying the production of normal language.

This notion may be extended so as to embrace a conception of a spectrum of speech-defect depending upon the intrinsic difficulty of the test situation. Such a continuum may be regarded as ranging from the 'normal' subject at one extreme, through the linguistic pattern of non-dominant hemisphere-defect, to culminate at the other limit, in a frank aphasia from disease of the dominant half of the brain.

XXX. THE CITY OF YES AND THE CITY OF NO

My nerves are strained like wires between the city of No and the city of Yes.
Yevgeny Yevtushenko

To walk in my own way and be alone . . . to cock my hat where I choose—at a word,
a 'yes', a 'no'.

Cyrano de Bergerac

The everlasting no, *the everlasting* yea.
T. Carlyle

Two of the most intriguing words in any language are those which stand for 'yes' and 'no'. This statement refers of course to the *spoken* language of a country, for 'yes' and 'no' are essentially fragments of conversational speech. They play a lesser rôle in written language, save in that very special branch of literature which records, or aspires to record, spoken speech: namely, playwriting, and the depicting of conversation in novels.

In all tongues 'yes' and 'no' are fascinating subjects for study by dint of their phonetic structure; their etymology; their functions as items in speech. These two words seem to occupy a special psycholinguistic rôle, for one encounters only too often an almost superstitious avoidance by recourse to synonyms, circumlocutions, contrary statements, or even gesture.

As already emphasized, 'yes' and 'no' belong more to the spoken speech than to the written or literary forms of a language. The considerable liberties which are taken testify clearly to the fact that a spoken language is essentially a growing thing, while written language is far more conservative, and tends to remain more stable. Consequently there is always a gap or discrepancy between the written and the spoken forms of any living language, including English; a gap which will perhaps tend to widen in the course of time rather than to shrink. Particularly is this so by reason of the pervading influence of the telephone, radio, television, and tape-recorders. Generations hence it may even be the exception rather than the rule to find individuals who can read and write. But 'yes' and 'no' or their equivalents will always be with us.

Let us now examine the rôle played in speech by these terms 'yes' and 'no'. What exactly do they mean? Or to avoid that ambiguous term 'meaning', what do they indicate? . . . what is their function?

In the first place, and most obviously of course, they act as affirmations or denials, often in direct response to a direct question, one which requires a direct reply—a confirmation or a refutation. 'Yes' or 'no' then supply a monosyllabic completion of the subject at issue. 'Are you hungry?' . . . 'Yes'. 'Have you finished your work?' . . . 'No'.

Based upon a paper published in *Perspect. Biol. Med.* 1961. **5**. 101–121.

In the English language, a special problem is set up by the negative form of enquiry. A question containing the adverb 'not', ordinarily though quite illogically, leads to the reply 'no' instead of 'yes'. Hence the amusement which used to attend the music hall song 'Yes, we have no bananas!' and yet this wording is more apposite than the conventional 'No, etc.'. One suspects that cross-examining lawyers sometimes resort to a complicated and confusing series of quick-fire negative questions, with the deliberate intention of shaking a witness's confidence. It is not altogether surprising to find that simpler primitive communities speaking pidgin-English rather than the accepted form of the tongue, use the negative reply to the negative question in order to indicate concurrence. Even in Japanese the same practice obtains. To the question 'Won't he come?' (*kimasen ka*) the reply would be, 'Yes, he won't come' (*hai kimasen*), whereas we, quite simply, would say, 'No'.

But the questions are in themselves even more complicated things. Not all of them are bald requests for information. Some are purely rhetorical. Others are not so much in the nature of an enquiry as an invitation, even a subtle seduction. This being so, there is entailed something more than an inescapable 'yes' or 'no'. There is a place for a term more subtle and less compromising. There ought to be a word to express a *qualified* 'yes' and a *qualified* 'no'. As a conventional gambit we could also usefully employ an ambiguous phrase . . . something like *forse che si, forse che non*. . . . preferably expressed in a monosyllable if that were possible. There is a need for the expression of individual personality-traits, for we can identify 'yes-men' and also 'no-men' . . . and more significant, perhaps, their feminine counterparts.

Lady Lewisham wrote in her autobiography:

> My mother always divided human beings into Yes-People and No-People. We regard ourselves as Yes-People. No-People are those who are cautious, hesitate, wonder whether it's done or not, and never do a thing. . . . There are far too many women who have the leisure who live utterly empty lives, just slopping around the shops and cinemas, living absolutely at second-hand not *doing* anything. They simply aren't Yes-People.

Eric Linklater put this point even more neatly:

> Juan . . . had a talent for acquiescence . . . There are people whose temper expresses itself naturally in 'No', that graceless and obstructionary plug of a word; and there are others whose eager nature must always find release in the runnel of a fluent 'yes'.—Negative and affirmative created He them.—And because 'No' will timeously stop a leak, they that use it see nothing but virtue in it, forgetting that what will prevent wine from running out, must also withhold men from drinking. But 'Yes', that wasteful syllable, that running tap of a word, will carry those who utter it, as if on a pleasant stream, through rich and various country. It is a bridge that leaps over stagnation, a sky-sail to catch wind in the doldrums. It is a passport to adventure, birdlime for experience, a knife for the great oyster of the world and the pearls or the poison that hide within. 'Yes' is the lover's word, for peril and for bliss, and 'No' the miser's and the word the barren womb has said. The trumpet, sounding for the charge, cries 'Yes'; and the key in the rusty lock speaks 'No'. They are an opening or a shutting; creation or criticism; life—or in all probability, a very much longer life. Juan said 'Yes' by nature, and had in consequence enjoyed many delightful experiences and several disastrous ones.

If 'yes' is the lover's word, as Linklater alleged, we understand why the French refer to marriage as *le grand oui* or 'The great I will'; and also why William Sansom spoke of 'the pillow-sweet sound of humanity's favourite word—yes'.

So-called advanced writers are apt to play tricks with the affirmative particle, especially in the context of sexual themes. We recall what James Joyce wrote about Mrs. Marion Bloom, '. . . yes and my heart was going like mad and yes I said yes I will yes . . .'

If we admit that there are personality-types which we can dub yes-men and no-men, so also we can point to certain communities which belong to 'yes-land' or 'no-land'. Thus, according to Tyler, some primitive tribes derived their names from the expressions employed for either 'yes' or 'no'. For example the Gureang, Kamilaroi, Kogai, Wolaroi, Wailwun and Wiratheroi peoples were named respectively after *gure*, *kamil*, *ko*, *wol*, *wail*, *wira*, all of which meant 'no'. *Pica*, meaning 'yes', gave its name to the Pikambul tribe. The Cocatapuyas of Brazil were so called after *tapuya* 'a man' and *coca* 'no'. Best known of all, however, are the two adjacent districts of early France, known as Languedoc (*langue d'oc*) and Langedoil (*langue d'oïl*) after their choice of the Latin approximate equivalents for 'yes', namely *hoc* and *hoc illud*.

Nor is that all. Dante divided the European languages of Latin origin into three idioms, which were characterized by the specific terms for affirmation, *oc*, *oïl* and *si* (. . . *nam alii oc, alii oïl, alii si, affirmando loquntur, ut putu Hispani, Franci, et Latini*. The *lingua d'oco* was looked upon as celebrated for its poets.

The employment of 'yes' and 'no' as 'qualified' assertions has already been mentioned. This is in keeping with one of the many facets of language-function. Speech is not always a simple communicative act. Its purpose need not necessarily convey information. Speech sometimes, deliberately or not, serves to conceal information, to distort it, and to wrap up ideas and feelings so as to make them unintelligible to others. At times the positive intention is to mislead. Actually we do not even require to await W. S. Gilbert's Utopia, where he looked forward to meeting

> A marvellous Philologist who'll undertake to show
> That 'yes' is but another, and a neater form of 'no'.

Victor Hugo had the same idea in mind when writing *Dans la bouche d'une femme*, '*non'n'est que le frère aîné de 'oui'* (A woman's 'no' is nothing more than the elder brother of 'yes').

Less dynamic is the diplomatic or ambiguous use of 'yes' and 'no' and the emergence of the tantalizing and at times exciting expression 'perhaps', the equivalent in Queen's English of the American archaism 'maybe'. Women are adepts at the adroit handling of this verbal weapon. 'Perhaps' is essentially a feminine word, one which is less often on the lips of the male, who has none of the coy prowess as a linguistic skirmisher in the warfare between the sexes. Language-engineers may well direct their attention to the coining of new words and phrases to sort out difficult situations. We need a word for 'perhaps-yes' and another for 'perhaps-no'. As is commonly said: 'If a lady says "no" she means "maybe"; if she says "maybe" she means "yes", and if she says "yes" she's no lady'. In this cynical wisecrack we also find indications of verbal taboo, or the superstitious avoidance of a term, a phenomenon to which later reference will be made.

Around this theme a Danish play has been written, namely J. L. Heibert's '*Nei*' (No). Here the heroine who has given her word to her guardian never to say 'yes' manages successfully to achieve a love affair, and to carry it to its appropriate conclusion.

One of the subtler techniques in language is the judicious employment of silence as an aspect of communication. Although this negative form of speech can be made to stand for almost anything, in practice it usually is found to be affirmative in function. Silence, as we all know, gives consent. Or, to quote Han Suyin, 'Abdullah answered neither "yes" nor "no" . . . which meant yes'.

'Yes' and 'no' may serve not only as assertions and negations, but also as questions. The skilful employment of 'yes?' and of 'no?' may constitute a verbal shorthand within which a whole sentence or even a paragraph chock-full of sentences may be condensed. We recall the fallacy which grammarians used to hold, namely that the unit of language is a word. As a matter of fact, a word is rarely so—though the use of 'yes' or 'no' as questions constitute a brilliant exception.

In this connection 'yes?' is the more useful term, for it may also signify . . . 'what do you want?' It is more tightly packed with meaning than the interrogative 'no?'. 'No?' rather suggests a proposition already posed, already common to speaker and listener, already turned down by one party. 'No?' is therefore more rhetorical than 'yes?', for it implies that a reply has already been given. 'No?' merely asks for confirmation.

In some respects, just as in some languages, 'yes' is a stronger word than 'no'. Thus there may be a symbol which stands for affirmation, while negation is expressed by this same symbol plus a qualifying prefix or suffix. So we find in Chinese *shu*= yes: *po-shu*= (no-yes)=no. This usage is carried over into pidgin-English where *can-do* means 'yes' and *no-cando* stands for 'no'. Someone has said that the Chinese remained slaves for 5,000 years because they had no word for no; but of course this is linguistically not quite accurate.

The opposite would seemingly apply to the language of the Pima Indians of Arizona, where 'no' is *ha* and 'yes' is *ha-o*. Like in modern Maya 'no' is *ma* and 'yes' is *malo*.

Then there is the exclamatory or interjectional use of 'yes' and 'no'. In this case it is 'no!' which crops up in speech more often than 'yes!'. 'No!' indicates amazement, astonishment, surprise, often a little tinged with malice. 'Have you heard the latest? Brown's wife has left him! . . .' 'No!' I refer—be it said—to the English language, for in other languages the usage may be different.

But there is another common use of 'yes' and 'no' in the conversational employment of all languages. Here the function can perhaps be looked upon as interjectional or exclamatory, but very feebly so. Furthermore, 'yes' and 'no' now carry a light burden of reference-function or significance. Though not propositions in the Jacksonian sense, they are not entirely emotionally-charged expletives. They serve a function. I have in mind the use in animated conversation of 'yes' and 'no' as interpolations by the one-who-is-mainly-listening, into the stream of utterances of the one-who-is-doing-most-of-the-talking. To study this phenomenon most satisfactorily all that is needed is to note carefully the verbal behaviour of someone telephoning. Most of the time, he—or should it be she?—is listening to a sound-track which you as an onlooker cannot hear. All that is audible is the interpolation 'yes . . . yes . . . oh! yes . . . yes . . . no! . . . no! . . . yes' with every nuance of intonation and stress available in the melody of speech. 'Yes' and 'no' have no direct function here as simple affirmations or negations. Their real purpose is to express a state of pleasure in agreement. Thus they serve as intimacy signals which maintain a warm relationship or co-operation between speaker and listener. Hence they belong to the group of what are called 'recurrent modifiers'. They also serve as purveyors of secondary information. A message is received: it is understood. That it really is understood is shown—not by its being repeated back to the sender—that would cost too much in words and time, but by resort to the affirmative particle. The simple monosyllable 'yes' serves just as well.

In the same way, among the Maya Indians of Yucatan it was deemed a hallmark of courtesy to utter a soft affirmative sound in the throat, while listening to what an elder has to say.

These recurring modifiers, particularly 'yes', to a lesser extent 'no', thus maintain a conversation. Perhaps inordinately so, as any man waiting outside a telephone booth can testify. Alice found this, too, when she tried to talk to her cat: 'If you would only purr for 'yes' and mew for 'no', or any rule of that sort . . . one could keep up a conversation! But how can you talk with a person if they always say the same thing?'

'Yes' as a recurring modifier may at times be replaced by a synonym. (This phenomenon of alternatives to 'yes' and 'no' will be met with a little later.) The synonym most often used is a simple vowel-sound, a rather ugly one. I refer to the common interpolation of 'ah' which in a dictionary may mean nothing at all and yet it is full of function, for it serves to oil the wheels of conversation. This inelegant usage is often found in South American Spanish. I have heard it on the lips of Poles, and it occurs, too, in Chinese. Witness what Ernest Gann said: '. . . Hank thought that he had never been able to use the Chinese "ah" in just the right way, an exhaltation of breath that became both punctuation and signal of understanding. It was as if two people in a conversation had individual radios. The one receiving would send out a flow of "ah's" saying "I am listening . . . I still hear you . . . We have not lost communication . . . Continue sending". The "ah" was more of a staccato grunt than a word. It leaped quickly from the lips when properly done and had infinite variations of tone and emphasis'.

In this setting the Chinese *ah* lies half-way between the Englishman's use of 'yes' and 'no' as audible punctuation marks, and the elaborate employment of actual 'punctuation words' such as we find characteristically in Malay, and also among the Mayas.

James Barlow in his novel *The Patriots* has referred to another type of modifier. '. . . It was difficult to be talkative in the face of Mr. Webster's monologue. The other man was a nodder; he nodded his head at frequent intervals and said "Um" or "Mm, Mm", which were variants of the word "yes".' Here we see the common use of an audible gesture—a 'prosodic grunt' as Monrad-Krohn would have said—in the whorp and woof of conversation.

Earliest appearances of 'yes' and 'no'

Both these words develop early in childhood speech. According to Jespersen a normal child enunciates 'no' before it can say 'yes'; and at a little later age, when both terms are available, 'no' comes out more often than 'yes'. This may cause surprise, for it might be argued that acceptance is easier than resistance or rejection; that it is simpler to agree with a proposition put forward in verbal symbols, rather than to listen to it, turn it over in the mind, and then decide upon a policy of rejection. Hence the weaker word 'yes' might be expected to slip out more readily, more often, and at an earlier age than the stronger word 'no'. Soviet psychologists, like O. K. Tikhomirov, and A. R. Luria, have found that young children respond to affirmative commands ('Pick it up') at an earlier age than to proscriptions, or inhibitory commands ('*Don't* pick it up'). There may be other considerations, however. The very young child often resents any interference with its activities or repose, and shows it unmistakably by a protest, one which may take the form of an interruption of silence by way of a scream, or a tantrum; or if older and more sophisticated, an unequivocal 'no'. This phase of negativism may antedate the more mature state of affairs in which acceptance or acquiescence also finds a place. Even deaf children and also victims of congenital auditory imperception indulge in infantile babbling. A little later they too acquire 'yes' and 'no', but again, the latter term appears first.

R. A. Spitz has devoted a great deal of attention to the earliest appearance of the particles in the ontogency of speech. Using psychodynamic and somewhat involved terminology, he wrote 'the acquisition of the "no" is the indicator of a new level of autonomy, of the awareness of the "other" and of the awareness of the self; it is the beginning of a restructuration of mentation on a higher level of complexity; it initiates an extensive ego development, in the framework of which the dominance of the reality principle over the pleasure principle becomes increasingly established'.

The retention of 'yes' and 'no' in aphasic utterance

When we examine closely the curtailed vocabulary of a patient affected with aphasia, we are struck by the tenacity with which the terms 'yes' and 'no' are retained. This statement remains true despite the notorious inconsistency of an aphasiac's verbal performance. He may talk more one day than another; more one moment than the next. With one interlocutor he fares better, with another he wilts. Some topics of conversation will expand the available vocabulary. Emotional factors and fatigue act as intrinsic influences.

Hughlings Jackson distinguished superior and inferior levels of speech, the former comprising propositions or declaratory utterances, the latter including emotionally charged speech and trite well-worn phrases poor in reference-function. This latter type of utterance is far better retained in aphasia. Thus the patient may have little speech available except such feminine oaths as 'oh dear!' 'bless my soul!', 'botheration!'—or full-blooded expletives; or 'thank you', 'please', 'goodbye', and, very characteristically, 'yes' and 'no'.

The use of 'yes' and 'no' by a severely aphasic patient may represent two very different levels of attainment. In that 'yes' may in a particular context indicate 'it is so' the aphasiac may be said to be *speaking*; that is, emitting a proposition. But in other cases, the aphasiac merely *utters* the words 'yes' and 'no'; he does not *speak with* them. In such instances, the words are of interjectional value only, being used by speechless patients as vehicles for the variation of vocal tones by which emotion may be exhibited.

The aphasiac may not always apply the words 'yes' and 'no' as he would wish. Thus he may say 'no' when he means to say 'yes'; or *vice versa*. He does not always notice his error. If he does, he corrects himself: that is, if he can, for in some cases he fails however much he tries. Or he may register distress and exasperation.

There are some aphasiacs who can say only one of these terms, that is 'yes' but not 'no'; or perhaps it is the other way round. Again it would be interesting to determine whether 'no' or 'yes' is more often retained in such cases of aphasia, but there is not yet enough evidence available to expand this topic. From Henschen's figures it would appear as though 'yes' survived better than 'no'. In Chapter VIII the topic of Dr. Samuel Johnson's aphasia was discussed. On the very day that he sustained his vascular accident, he wrote . . . 'I perceived myself almost totally deprived of speech. My organs were so obstructed that I could say "no" but could scarcely say "yes" . . .' That Dr. Johnson should have found 'no' easier to emit than 'yes' somehow does not surprise us: it conforms with what we recall of his cantankerous, rumbustious pigheadedness.

In these rare and fascinating cases of aphasia with recurrent utterance, 'yes' and 'no' may constitute the sole items of speech utilizable. The 'yes' and the 'no' will each be applied correctly enough, but when it comes to the expression of any other idea or feeling, then either 'yes' or 'no' will emerge in an uninhibited manner. Here again, the aphasiac may realize his error, or he may not. If he does, then he may utilize one or other of these two words to express quite a variety of ideas, by dint of varying the tones with which the words are spoken, and by resort to facial mimicry.

More typical patients with aphasia have a considerably shrunken store of words with 'yes' or 'no' proving elusive. That is to say these two words may be emitted, but only in an automatic fashion, and not when they should appear as a deliberate evocation. Thus when asked a question which ordinarily requires a 'no' in reply, the patient may be at a loss. But a moment earlier he may have used the word 'no' quite correctly. A moment later he uses it again. But on both occasions his 'no' was sandwiched among a series of other words which swept it along as it were. Or the patient may be made to say the elusive word by the device of charging it with emotional content. One of Jackson's patients tried over and over again to say the word 'no' but without avail. Finally, and in some distress, he blurted out: 'I can't say "no", sir!'

In the same way the aphasiac unable to use 'yes' as a deliberate assertion, or 'no' as a denial, can perhaps employ these same terms as recurring modifiers, tossed into the stream of someone else's flow of words. In this rôle they are less voluntary and more automatic; inferior rather than superior speech.

Synonyms for 'yes' and 'no'

In most languages and particularly in their spoken forms, 'yes' and 'no' crop up very frequently, but still more often under a number of disguises. Some of the alternative forms are ephemeral and belong more to the domain of slang than accepted usage. They form part of the smart talk of youngsters, particularly those who are members of a select or small community. A few of these synonyms catch on and become incorporated within the storehouse of the language; others soon wither and die.

Why should it be that in popular speech 'yes' and 'no' are so often distorted, transfigured, or avoided? One reason is bound up with the factor of frequent employment. Repetition is thereby avoided and variation introduced. But that cannot be the sole explanation. Another factor is the need to tack on a qualifying word so as to express shades of meaning to the simple assertive or nugatory term. A third reason is one which belongs within the realm of social anthropology. A naked 'yes' and more particularly, a bald 'no' is often felt to be somewhat crude, a little offensive, too down to earth to conform with the canons of courtesy. It needs to be toned down a little, or wrapped up, or softened—whichever metaphor pleases most. In any case there is a linguistic taboo in many languages, one which is often beyond the competency of a foreigner.

Correct idiomatic use of these two little words testifies to a facility in a spoken language. Many foreigners spend a lifetime in an English-speaking country but still employ these terms awkwardly and inappropriately. The Devil is said once to have dwelt in the Basque country and at the end of two years all he succeeded in learning were the local equivalents for 'yes' and 'no'. Even then he probably did not always employ them correctly.

Fourthly the personal or individual employment of alternatives to 'yes' and 'no' may be influenced by dialectual considerations, or even by the use of professional jargon on occasions. Examples of these synonyms for 'yes' and 'no' may be given under the following categories:

Vernacular, slang or *popular alternatives*: 'You bet' . . . 'I'll say' . . . 'You're telling me' . . . 'How right you are' . . . 'O.K.' . . . 'Oke' . . . 'Okey doke' . . . 'Righto' . . . 'Righteo' . . . 'Not 'arf' . . . 'No kidding'. These are alternatives for 'yes', some of them of North American origin. Indeed even in serious American speech, 'yes' is rare: 'yep' has probably not been heard very much since the turn of the century. 'Eeyah' is characteristically heard in the State of Maine. 'Ye-ah' finds a place, but perhaps only among the older generation. This may really be a modifica-tion of the German or Jewish *Ja* . . . an instance of Teutonic influence in North American culture and language. 'Oh yeah?' has a special rhetorical connotation of its very own.

As alternatives to 'no' we find 'nope' (perhaps a little corny nowadays), 'no fear' . . . 'not on your life' . . . 'don't make me laugh' . . . 'shucks' . . . 'am I hell!' . . . 'not in these trousers' . . . or simply 'not in these'.

Adjectival or *qualifying forms:* To replace the affirmative particle we can use: 'of course', 'certainly', 'no doubt, 'without doubt', 'definitely', 'indubitably', 'naturally', 'surely', 'sure', etc. Instead of 'no' we may employ: 'never', 'not likely', 'certainly not', 'oh no!', 'oh dear no!', etc.

Avoidance of bald or crude forms: Here we find such polite, almost honorific expressions as 'Yes, please', 'Yes, thank you', or better still . . . 'yes' with the repetition of the verb within the question, e.g. 'Have you finished your day's work?' . . . 'Yes, I have'. 'Yes', with the attachment of the interlocutor's name, or rank, or title is another example: 'Yes, sir', 'Yes, Mr. Brown', 'Yes, doctor'. Where we require a negative particle, politeness enjoins the use of such expressions as 'No, thank you', 'Not at all', 'No, I haven't'—or better—'No, not yet'. Again, the additional attachment of names or titles constitutes good form in speech.

'Yea' and 'nay'

The English language, notoriously rich as to its vocabulary, possesses certain monosyllabic alternatives to the ordinary 'yes' and 'no'. These are available over and above the numerous qualifying phrases already discussed. They are, however, to some extent archaic, and when intro-duced into current speech they smack somewhat of pedantry, or a deliberate attitudizing, like an actor in a charade. This is unfortunate. Thus we have the forms 'ay' (or 'aye') and other expressions which resemble them phonetically; and also the 'yea'—a genuine antique which regrettably does not appear in modern speech. In opposition to these two affirmatives there stands the alternative negative form, namely 'nay'.

'Ay' is of great antiquity and it lingers on today in certain well-defined circumstances. In the first place it survives in the jargon of the Royal Navy, especially in its reduplicated form. Properly used it indicates not so much an assertion as an intimation that an order is received, understood, and will be promptly executed. To the Commander's 'Splice the mainbrace' would come the appropriate 'Ay, ay, sir'.

Even today the word 'ay' is employed as a substantive indicating an abstract state of acquiescence, and also a generic term for those who acquiesce, e.g. 'The ayes have it'.

'Ay' is also widely used in provincial English in place of the more conventional 'yes'. *The English Dialect Dictionary* (1898) listed numerous modifications, including *ai, aay, aey, eigh, ey, ei, eea, eeah, a aw, hey, hei, hi, oi, wyah,* and *weyer*. Some of these are today sheer curiosities of speech. But others are commonplace still. For example the 'ay' of the Lowland Scot and of the North-Countryman is well known to every Londoner who hears it around him on Cup Final Saturdays. In rural Somerset there exists another form, highly characteristic but probably in a state of rapid elimination; this is a prolonged but flat 'a' sound, resembling nothing so much as the bleating of a local sheep.

But to all these affirmatives, the opposite negative term is nowdays 'no', not 'nay'. 'Nay' is still heard today as a fossilized fragment of dialect, but it is much rarer than 'ay'.

'Yea' is now obsolete. Of respectable antiquity it first appeared in written English about a thousand years ago, and it can be found in the writings of Bede. As a part of spoken speech it was surely much older. In Biblical language we characteristically find 'yea' and 'nay' rather than 'aye' or 'yes', or 'no'. Thus we read 'Swear not . . . but let your yea be yea; and your nay, nay; lest ye fall into condemnation'. (James V. 12). Also: 'But let your communication be yea, yea; nay, nay: for whatsoever is more than these cometh of evil' (Matt. V. 37). Here we have direct translation from the Greek *ou* and *nai*. Elsewhere in the Bible we find the terms 'yea' and 'nay' in slightly different connotation, and as translations of different and more precise terms in the Greek and Hebrew texts (e.g. *aph, aphki, illur, gam, alla, e, menounge, al, lo,* and *ouchi*). The date of appearance of the Revised Version is, of course, significant in determining the choice of the terms 'yea' and 'nay'.

Our modern 'yes' certainly derives from 'yea', and there are two ideas as to its precise origin. Some believe it represents *yea seva*, meaning 'yea, even so'; more likely, however, it stems from a fusion of *yea* with *si*, which is the third person singular present subjunctive of *beon*, to be. 'Yes' thus indicates 'yea, it is'. Originally spelt *yese, yise,* or *yyse*, it is to be found in written form as early as A.D. 1,000, when it was used by Aelfric. For centuries, 'aye', 'yea', and 'yes' were all in currency, but the indications for their use were different. 'Yes' was more emphatic than either 'yea' or 'aye'. 'Yes' was employed as an answer to a question containing a negative particle: otherwise the appropriate expression would have been 'aye' or 'yea'.

The older form for 'no' was 'nay' (with such variants as *nei, nai, naei, nayy, nayl, nail* and *na*).

'Nay' was certainly present in the literary language as early as 1225. 'Nay' and 'no' were contemporaries, but as in the case of 'yea' and 'yes' they were not used interchangeably. This is well shown in Thomas More's *Confutation of Tindale* which was written in 1557. 'Nay' was weaker than 'no', just as 'yea' was not so emphatic as 'yes'. If the appropriate question contained a negative particle then 'no' was to be used; if not, then 'nay' was the correct term.

'Yea' and 'nay' were therefore antithetic. So we find the Quakers dubbed 'yea and nay men' as early as 1656. Occasional exceptions occur, however. Euphony and rhyme may over-ride, and so determine the choice of words, as in Shakespeare's lines written in 1588:

> Taffeta phrases, silken terms precise,
>   Three-piled hyperboles, spruce affectation,
> Figures pedantical; these summer-flies
>   Have blown me full of maggot ostentation:
> I do forswear them; and I here protest,
>   By this white glove—how white the hand God knows!
> —Henceforth my wooing mind shall be expressed
> *In Russet yeas and honest kersey noes*[1]

Yet another old usage of 'nay' is seen in 'nay-word' meaning a pass-word. In the *Merry Wives of Windsor* we read . . . 'we have a nay-word how to know each other'.

The English language is the poorer for shedding those alternative terms by which one can express a more emphatic assertion or negation. Nowadays we have to rely upon qualifying phrases. Some other languages have retained their variables, e.g. the French *oui*, *oui-da*, *ouiché* and *si*; the Italian *si* and *gia*. The Danish *jo* is firmer than *ja*. In Norwegian there are *jei* and *nei* with the slightly stronger alternatives *jeida* and *neida*. *Jeisso* implies an element of surprise. After a negative question one may use *jo*. In Portuguese there are at least two forms, namely *se* and *é* (meaning 'it is'), while as a recurrent modifier during a telephone conversation the common interpolation is '*sei*'(= I know). Arabic has *aiwa* to connote a strong 'yes', *na'am* for a polite 'yes' and *ae* for ordinary purposes. The modern Greek says *ne* for 'yes', but *malista* when emphasis is intended.

Many Germans whose complaisance blinds them to their linguistic shortcomings, are fond of the assertive interjection 'Of course'. They are quite oblivious to the semantic overtones of an almost derisory sort which this phrase possesses. Their teachers have misled them by proclaiming 'Of course' to be the correct rendering of the enthusiastic *Jawohl* affirmative.

'Thank-you–yes', or 'Thank-you–no'

A subtle linguistic practice which differs from one language to another is the use of 'thank you' as implying either assertion or negation. This implication may mystify and even embarrass one who is not proficient in a foreign tongue. At the dinner-table a second helping is proffered: 'thank you' would indicate 'yes' in England and in Norway, but 'no' in France and in Brazil. The implicit idea to an Englishman would be 'Yes, please; and *thank you* for asking me', while to a Frenchman it would be '*Thank you* for asking me but I would rather not have any more'. The

---

[1] The adjectives 'russet' and 'kersey' are textile metaphors indicating 'simple', 'lowly', 'unostentatious'.

French usage can certainly claim traditional support, for in Latin the expression *benigne* connotes 'thank you—No'. A foreign student often feels the need for two expressions at his command to save him social embarrassment, namely a *merci-oui* and a *merci-non*, or if in Portugal an *Obregado-se* as well as an *Obregado-não*. *Takk* in Norwegian really implies *Ja-takk*. How much better it would be if such a hyphenated word really existed, and also for that matter a *nei-takk* or even a *neida-takk*. *Efharisto* in modern Greek means 'thank you', and 'yes' is implied, while in Arabic *ashkurek* implies 'no'. Language-engineers might well devote some attention here, and start to fashion some new and more meaningful particles.

The alternative is to leave the language very much alone, and to ensure that words mean just what they set out to mean—nothing more, nothing less. 'Thank you' should then stand for 'thank you' only, and imply neither yes nor no.

In German there is that interesting all-purpose word *bitte* which seems to mean not only 'please', in the sense of the Italian *per favore*, but also at times a 'thank you' (*merci*, *prego*); it can be used as a sort of 'yes' and 'no'; or as a 'don't mention it', or 'not at all'. In this way a satisfactory and quite protracted conversation can be erected upon a scaffolding of bows and smiles and the use of *bitte*. This word *bitte* must surely be early on the lips of the German infant, and no doubt it is a hardy vestige in the truncated vocabulary of a German aphasiac.

Reduplicated 'yes' and 'no'

In some languages, including English, emphasis is achieved by repetition. A Norwegian may affirm *Ja-ja* or even *Ja-ja-ja*. A German does likewise. A Dutchman tends to modify the vowel of the first syllable and to say *Je-ja* as a stronger form of *Ja*. *Oui-oui* is commonly heard in France, more so indeed than *si*. Perhaps the repetition is indicative of petulance or astonishment rather than emphatic assertion. The clue lies in the intonation or the manner of utterance, for cadence, as Herbert Spencer said, is the involuntary commentary on the emotions of the intellect.

For some mysterious reason in Great Britain 'yes-yes' is typical of the English spoken by the Welsh, and not necessarily for the sake of emphasis. It can survive as such in aphasic utterance; and where a speech-afflicted Englishman would painfully evoke a 'yes', a Welsh aphasiac would come out with 'yes-yes'.

But 'no-no' is rare in Wales. Perhaps it is rarer, too, in the diction of spoken English than is 'yes-yes', but here again it may be a purely personal matter. After all, speech is but an aspect of behaviour, and just as we have 'yes-men' and 'no-men' so too we may run up against their colleagues the 'yes-yes men' and the 'no-no men'.

I suppose *nein-nein* would stand in contrast to *ja-ja* in Germany, and no doubt the same idea finds expression in the spoken speech all over the world.

Except, of course, those languages where terms for 'yes' and 'no' do not occur, or at any rate are rarely employed. The Irish, for example, usually repeat the verb introduced in the question, with or without a negative adverb. This is so although perfectly good terms for 'yes' and 'no' exist in Erse, namely *yead* (yes) and *ni* (no). The Irishman carries over his linguistic habits when speaking English even though he may not know a word of his native language. Thus to the question 'Are you feeling better?' the Irishman will reply, 'I am', or 'I am not' as the case may be: 'Will you have the same again?' . . . 'I will'.

This is to go one stage further than the more common, and older, linguistic trick of saying, 'Yes, I am' or 'No, I am not'. Not only was this the practice in Anglo-Saxon England, but it is to be found today in the pidgin-English of Samoa and Fiji.

The same lack of clear-cut words of 'yes' and 'no' is also to be found in the Manx and Cornish languages, where in the same manner the verb is repeated with or without the adverbial 'not' (e.g. Manx: *Nailt?* (will you?); *Naillym* (yes) *cha naillym* (no); Cornish: *Parys ough-why?* (are you ready?); *Of*=I am or yes; *Nag of*=I am not or no).

It would be interesting to observe whether 'yes' and 'no' loom as large in the speech of an Irish aphasiac as in the case of an Englishman. Probably not. Probably too, the clumsier practice of repeating the key verb will not be found either. Perhaps aphasia is a more crippling affliction in an Irishman . . .

In some ways Japanese resembles Erse, at least as far as the avoidance of terms for 'yes' and 'no' is concerned. The Japanese language contains no crisp or unequivocal adverbial expression. The word *iie* is used to denote an indignant denial. The words *he, hei* and *hai*, though often translated as 'yes', are really nothing more than crude signals indicating the reception and comprehension of signals. Ordinarily a Japanese repeats the verb, in the same way as an Irishman. Thus for 'yes' he would say 'that is so', i.e. *so da* or, more politely, *so desu*; or still more politely *sayo de gozaimasu*.

Some linguistic generalizations: 'yes' and 'no' as monosyllables

In every language in which there are clear-cut terms for 'yes' and 'no' these can be expected to crop up in the vernacular with very great frequency. Therefore they might be expected to show themselves as short words, probably monosyllables, poor in consonants and especially in awkward consonantal clusters. Broadly speaking this is the case; and yet exceptions occur. Thus the Finno-Ugric tongues flaunt the conventions, as usual. So we find: *Kyllö, Igem,* and *Evet* for 'yes'. As a rule and in most languages the words for 'no' are shorter or briefer than the words for 'yes'.

Latin merits special attention. It seems strange that this great linguistic ancestor should be so lacking in a clear-cut unequivocal term to connote 'yes'. Even 'no' is identified with difficulty—the terms *imo, immo, multo modo,* and *minime* finding a place. As for 'yes', we find *ita, sic, maxime admodum, oppido, certe, sane,* and *plane*. Perhaps the commonest or at any rate the simplest terms were *non* and *etiam* ('*aut etiam aut non repondere*' Cicero).

Phonetic properties of 'no'

It is interesting that in many languages of the world the term connoting negation commences with one of the nasal consonants and more especially the letter 'n'—*non* (French); *nu* (Rumanian); *no* (Spanish, Italian); *não* (Portuguese); *nàni* or *noun* (Provençal); *neen* or *nee* (Dutch); *nein* (German); *nej* (Swedish); *nei* (Norwegian, Icelandic); *nie* (Polish); *na* (Romanisch); *ne* (Czech); *nyet* (Russian); *nem* (Hungarian); *ne* (Lithuanian, Lettish); *na, nage, nae* (Welsh); *nä* (Sinhala); *nahim* (Hindi); *na* (Persian); *may* (Harari). Even in ancient Egyptian (middle period) the adverb was *nn* (the vowel is of course problematical) or *n*. In the Vest-jydsk dialect of Danish a 'no' is expressed by a nasalized (*ng*)*ai*, coupled with a screwing up of the nose—another example of an audible gesture in spoken speech.

The English and the Spaniards both say 'no', but the pronunciation is different. Continentals use the pure phoneme *o*, while in the U.K. and the U.S.A., a brief terminal semi-vowel sound—a faint 'w'—is tacked on to the end, so that 'no' is enunciated something like 'no(w)'.

Some linguists read particular significance into this prevalence of the *n* or *m* sounds, as supporting the theory of an origin of the word in a particular gesture, e.g. an audible accompaniment of a negatory closure of the lips.

But there are a few exceptions even in Western European tongues. In Albanian we find *jo* meaning, oddly enough, 'no' and not 'yes'. The Turks say *hayir* or *yok*; the Finns use the term *ei*. In Arabic we find *la*, and in modern Greek *ochi*. In Malay *tidak*. The Japanese say *iie*, that is when they do not use *sukoshi mo*, or *chitto mo*. It would be foolish, however, to limit our enquiries to European or even the Aryan group of languages. The vast wonderland of African tongues—and dialects—repay exploration. Thus the Bantu and semi-Bantu languages contain scores of linguistic groups. Among them we find some examples where nasal consonantal monosyllables indicate 'no', e.g. *nga*, *n-taive*, *nedda*, *mbai*, *n-kiw*, *ndawa*, *nw*, *nuna*, *ndala*, *ndema*, *nale*, *nda*, *nanena*, *ndagile*, *n-dww*, *mma*, *ne*, *nya*, *nyonyw*, *nanta*. But these are actually in the minority and are outnumbered by a diversity of other terms, some of them being quite complicated. What, for example, can one make of *ceke*, *cei*, *oya*, *leka*, *āā*, *tawi*, *ta yaya*, *tindi*, *awnanga*, *pu*, *aca*, *tiww*, *iii*, *haiya*, *dzi*, *si-oyw*, *ote*, *ode*, *ehe*, *chw̄ū*, *kaka*, *ahāā*, *siw*, *ebu*, *si*, *bule*, *sibfw̄*, *asima*, *bakw̄*, *fuww̄*, *lika*, *yai*, *ta*, *te*, *tau*, *yw̄*, *cara*, *lietu*, *kiimw̄*, *saye*, *ke*, *akipale*, *tayu*, *i-ai*, *isi*, *ohina*, *ye*, *itè*, *ete*, *aiwa*, *pe*, and *patlu*? We go on to recall *sega* (Fijian), *hapana* (Swahili), *Awulla* (Australian aboriginal), *es* (Basque). All are synonyms for 'no'. Among some of the Amerindian tongues diverse terms are met with to indicate negation. Thus we find *há* (Pima), *da* (Apache), *totá* or *t'aadoo* (Navaho), and *peya* (Papago). Of special interest is the Zulu representative of the Bantu family, where 'no' is expressed by *ċa*: here the initial consonant is actually a dental click, and not a palatal explosive.

Phonetic properties of 'yes'

The linguistic equivalents of 'yes' do not show quite the same phonetic consistency as in the case of 'no'. Nevertheless, where at least Western European languages are concerned there is a certain correspondence with the occurrence of the half-vowel sound Y. Thus *Ja* occurs in Swedish, Dutch, German, Lettish and even Malay. In Iceland it is spelt *Ja* and is pronounced *Yow* to rhyme with cow. The Chinese say *Yu* in reply to a sentence containing the verb to have. In Welsh we find *ie*. Next in frequency come the various vowel sounds—*ano* (Czech); *āā* (Vest-jydsk Danish); *igem* (Hungarian); *evet* (Turkish); *oes* (Welsh); *ovu* or *o* (Sinhala); *aiwa* (Egyptian Arabic); and *hai* (Japanese), '*ii* (Iraqi Arabic), *oh* in Navaho, *í* or *áy* (Harari), and *co* in Fiji. Somewhat unexpected in *na'am* which to a Baghdadi means 'yes', and *ndio* which in Swahili also stands for 'yes'; and whatever can we make of the Hawaiian language where the word 'yes' is—*mirabile dictu-no*,[1] just as in Greek *nai* (rhyming with day) means 'yes'.

---

[1] There are other words, of course, e.g. *ae* = 'yes' and *aole* = 'no'.

The Abipones of South America have three terms for 'yes'—*hee* by men and youths, *haa* by women, while old men give a grunt. All say *yna* for 'no'.

An unexpected distortion of the word 'yes' is heard at times in Devonshire. The initial semi-vocal sound is glossed over, if not indeed omitted, and the sibilant is exaggerated. Thus we get a variety of hissing sounds to denote concurrence, such as 'yesss' or even 'esss'. Nay, more. Not infrequently the Devonian merely gives an audible indrawing of air through the teeth so as to form an inverted hissing sound reminiscent of the honorific noises emitted by a Japanese. This is almost the only instance of an inspiratory sound in spoken English. It is for this reason that their neighbours speak of the Devonians as 'wind-suckers'.

I have heard something similar in Northern Albania. In Sweden an inspiratory 'yow' or 'you' is met with among young women, indicating a shy 'yes'.

Pantomimic 'yes' and 'no'

A traveller, they say, can tour the world and make do with a nod or a shake of the head as the sum-total of his system of communication. True, a nod will be understood as affirmative from pole to pole, just as a side-to-side turn of the head will be taken as 'no'. But the language of gesture is even richer and more complex. Numerous other pantomimic movements exist, of more local usage. Gesture-variants for 'no' will be found to outnumber those for 'yes'.

For example in Ceylon and in Southern India, affirmation is expressed not by a nod, but by a sideways waggle of the head upon the neck, a gesture which may strike the uninitiated Occidental as a grudging or deprecating commentary. A rapid side-to-side shake of the head, almost a quivering, may connote 'yes' in Albania.

Gestures for 'no' are usually manual. A sideways shake of the forefinger is found in the Mediterranean countries. In Florence the whole forearm, hand and index finger may be moved back and forth in a lateral direction, all in a piece. A Spaniard may give a stately abductive sweep of the arm as if dismissing something unworthy. A Greek expresses 'no' by brushing one hand against the other in a brief washing movement: here the implication is 'no—no more'; 'not any longer'; 'it is finished'. A Sikh bends back his wrist and extends the whole arm, just as though he were thrusting away something unpleasant.

Most interesting of all is the Levantine 'no' which consists in a backward toss of the head, often accompanied by semi-closure of the eyelids and a quiet click of the tongue. There is a colloquial and abbreviated form which comprises merely a rapid up and down movement of the eyelids. In Bulgaria a sharp jerk of the head means 'no' while the same gesture carried out slowly, signifies 'yes'.

In ancient Egyptian hieroglyphs *nn* (or 'no') was symbolically depicted by arms raised to a right angle, with palms upwards.

The origins of these gestures are of interest. Many of them are stylized and abbreviated fragments of a more complicated piece of pantomime. Thus the Levantine gesture for 'no' is perhaps a curtailed act of recoil from some distasteful object or proposition. The conventional shake of the head for 'no' is merely a cut-down action of shaking off from the shoulders the birds of ill-omen. The Greek bimanual gesture is a repetition *in parvo* of the symbolism of Pontius Pilate. Nodding of the head in assent can be looked upon as a miniature movement of submissive bowing, or humble obeisance.

Psycho-analysts have their own ways of thinking, of course; notions which for them are certainties. The horizontal turning of the head is ascribed to an infantile gesture of recoil from the maternal breast.

Nor are they put out by the existence of what they call 'deviant' semantic gestures for yes and no. In their own peculiar jargon they refer to the 'dynamics which result in the first concept formation'. With more words than sense they have said 'these include the use of aggressive cathexis for mental operations and the attachment of aggressive charges to a device used in object relations, resulting in the replacement of action, destructive or otherwise, by communication. This formulation holds equally true in those cultures which do not use the head-shaking 'no' or the head-nodding "yes".'

Perhaps the very phonemic patterns are but audible gestures and the characteristic *n* and *m* sounds of negation may be no more than the sound-track which accompanies a disapproving pursing of the lips. In this connection we remember, too, that in Sicily negation is often expressed by a sound resembling T-T-T. Nor let us forget the vulgar audible gesture indicative of disgusted negation whereby the speaker holds his nose and emits some such sound as 'phooey'.

How about the artificial sign-languages? Deaf-mutes possess more than one system of gestures: an empirical one based on finger-spelling, and a more natural one which is internationally understood—a *lingua franca pantomimica*. Amerindians, like Australian bushmen, also have a code of signs. In monastic communities where silence is ordained some of the time (as among the Benedictines) or all the time (as among the Trappists), signs are freely used as a form of communication. Then there are the sign-languages of secret societies. Students of the byways of language realize that through all these quite diverse systems of signs there runs a thread of common comprehensibility. This testifies to the very fundamental nature of gesture as a modality of speech. As Marmontel wrote: 'Pantomime speaks to the eyes a more powerful language than that of words. It is even more impassioned than eloquence, and no speech can equal its warmth and force'. Besides the conventional nods and shakes of the head, hand movements are used for 'yes' and 'no'. A turning over of the palm means 'no' to a deaf-mute as much as to an American Indian; while a simple flexion of the forefinger held alongside the head, denotes 'yes'.

Nearer home and more familiar are the audible gestures of North American custom, which may well have been borrowed from some of the Indian tongues. A grunting sound which may be approximately recorded as uh-uh is in common currency for 'yes'. But the visiting innocent must bear well in mind that uh-uh can also mean 'maybe'. Furthermore, it can also stand for 'no'. The precise shade of meaning is expressed by dint of variations in intonation, just as it is in the Chinese language. Let a local linguist explain in technical language '. . . the usual *uh-uh* of negation has higher vowel-like resonance, with internal (and often initial) glottal closure; it may or may not be accompanied by closed-lip or open-lip nasalization. The *uh-uh* of affirmation is just like the negation except for glottal continuant internally instead of glottal closure' (G. L. Trager).

In this ambivalence we therefore witness another illustration of the Spanish proverb which says: *Entre el Si y el No de la mujer no me atreveria yo a poner una punta de alfiler* ('Between a woman's 'yes' and 'no', there is not room for a pin to go').

XXXI. TOTAL SPEECHLESSNESS

> *'Di bene fecerunt, inopis me quodque pusilli*
> *Finxerunt animi, raro et perpauca loquentis.'*
> Horace. Sat. I. 4. 17.

> *Silence is the unbearable repartee.*
> G. K. Chesterton

> *Silence is said to be golden, but the best fools the world has ever produced had nothing to*
> *say on the subject.*
>
> J. Billings

> *Blessed is the man, who having nothing to say, abstains from giving wordy evidence of the fact.*
> G. Eliot

> *Half the world is composed of people who have something to say and can't, and the*
> *other half who have nothing to say and keep on saying it.*
>
> Robert Frost

Who could possibly forget Anatole France's *Comédie de celui qui épousa une femme muette*? Léonard, High Court Judge, has married Catherine who, he discovers, has never spoken in her life. In his dismay he eventually consults a distinguished physician, who in turn calls in two apothecaries and a surgeon. By dint of an operation carried out with a monstrous armamentarium of instruments, Catherine speaks. Her first words were 'fetch me my mirror', and thereafter, to her husband's consternation, she chatters and chatters incessantly. Her stream of rapid vapid small-talk, mainly about sex, clothes, and cooking—in that order—drives him to frantic despair. No longer can he concentrate upon his legal work. In desperation he begs the surgeon to return. To check his wife's logorrhoea is an impossibility, he is told. The only feasible solution would be to render the husband deaf—which, it was emphasized, would in no way incapacitate him in his judicial sphere. The operation is done, and the curtain falls upon a scene of harmony restored.

In clinical practice such a state of absolute speechlessness, or *aphasia totalis* as it is sometimes called, would be a rare but highly interesting phenomenon. To unravel the explanation, it would be imperative at the outset to make a sharp distinction between those cases where fully matured speech had become ablated, and those where speech had never developed. The former constitute somewhat of a curiosity in clinical medicine. Possibly the most usual explanation lies outside organic neurology, for most acquired cases of mutism are instances of hysteria. In such cases it is

Based upon a paper contributed to the Birthday Volume dedicated to Professor Gozzano, Rome, 1967, and on a paper read at the Anglo-German Neurological Meeting in London, 2nd May, 1968.

traditional to teach that purely psychological mechanisms are operative, and yet there are arguments to suggest that a conversion hysteria behaves almost as though it were utilizing physiological patterns in an unexpected fashion. For example, hysterics with a hemiparesis may also show an affection of articulate speech, but only when the dominant hand is the one which is out of action. The impaired speech may then take the form of a stammer, or a dysphonia, or a complete mutism. On the other hand, hysterical hemiplegia involving the non-dominant limb is not as a rule associated with disordered speech. In organically determined cases an absolute aphasic mutism is not found except possibly as a transient manifestation immediately after an abrupt stroke. For practical purpose indeed, the 'aphasia totalis' referred to by the linguist Roman Jakobson is a mythical entity. However, in some instances of cerebrovascular disease a total loss of articulate utterance may be encountered. Such cases prove eventually to be examples of an *anarthria totalis*, the responsible lesion being usually located within the brain-stem. Such patients can be distinguished from very severe aphasiacs by dint of various clinical inconsistencies. First, the patient's sensorium may be absolutely clear, without any demonstrable confusion, disorientation, dyscalculia, or severe memory-loss. Secondly the faculty of language is intact except for the loss of articulate utterance. Thus the patient can express himself in writing, and not even the most searching linguistic analysis will reveal any trace of a minimal dysgraphia. Furthermore, the anarthric patient often resorts to such manoeuvres for expressing himself as picking out from a toy alphabet the letters which go to form the words he seeks. Cases of this sort have from time to time been erroneously regarded and even reported as examples of an aphasia where the intellect has been preserved untarnished. The autopathographic account by Sir Frederick Andrewes—*On being bereft of speech*—is probably an example where anarthria was mistaken for aphasia.

A combination of dysphonia with a striking poverty of speech may also be found in advanced cases of Parkinsonism. Particularly is this so after bilateral thalamotomy, and speech disorder of this kind must be regarded as a hazard of repeated stereotactic interventions. The disorder of articulation and phonation may ultimately amount to a veritable speechlessness.

In addition, neurologists not infrequently encounter patients who momentarily lose their power of articulate utterance though, strictly speaking, they are by no means deprived of the faculty of language. Something like this may be observed in some victims of migraine and also of epilepsy. In the latter circumstances, an arrest of speech may replace a seizure and constitute an epileptic equivalent, or else it may follow an attack. Furthermore there is the clinical phenomenon of 'sleep-paralysis' or 'waking-paralysis' associated with narcolepsy. This consists in a temporary incapacity of speech and movement despite a clear sensorium. A personally observed patient with narcolepsy, introspective and intelligent, proclaimed that on such occasions he would be quite unable to move or speak until someone intervened to rouse him. Otherwise such a state of helplessness would endure for as long as ten minutes. During this time he would be incapable of articulation. Nevertheless his comprehension was intact, and verbal symbols were utilized in his silent thinking-processes with complete facility.

Where the language function is a recent acquisition—as in a child—we may expect to find a certain vulnerability. This is often met with in paediatric practice. A severely ill child may show a progressive taciturnity which may eventually constitute a complete speechlessness. This may be so even when the central nervous system is not primarily involved. In thinly-spread affections, such as for example an acute chorea, a dwindling and dissolution of speech may proceed to a complete but temporary mutism. With graver disorders like the progressive encephalopathies and the severer types of encephalitis, a state of progressive dementia is associated with a complete ablation of speech.

Delay in the development of speech in the child is a not uncommon phenomenon, and several possible explanations arise. Thus the child may be otherwise normal both physically and mentally as borne out by subsequent follow-up studies. There exists a simple speech retardation and nothing else. When speech eventually develops it may fall into one of several patterns:

(1) speech may at long last develop, in a slow but steady manner, word by word;

(2) the same may be true, but the emerging speech is found to be imperfectly articulated. Here the speechlessness yields through dyslalia to an eventual state of articulatory normalcy; or

(3) the child, who has been a source of worry to its parents through its failure to talk, may suddenly break silence by emitting, not a halting word in isolation, but a whole sentence with elaborate vocabulary and syntax. Thereafter the patient continues to talk with ease and even prolixity.

As the philologically minded Guy Endore wrote in his novel *Umweg bei Nacht* . . . 'Wie schnell entdecken doch Kinder diese wunderbare innere Welt, in der sie allmachtig sind! Wer lehrt sie die verbluffende Kunst, mit Symbolen zu manipulieren?'* To continue the quotation, but lapsing into the English tongue . . . 'So that from the tenderest age they can sit down as masters at the keyboard of the ten billion cells of their brains and tease the various microscopic nerve endings into producing endless simulacra of reality? Endless variations on whatever melody they love best?'

'As soon as they know words as the symbols for things, they realise that they have a magic instrument within them by which, by the mere calling up of the right word, they can bring to their minds the image of the things they crave. Broca's area in the brain's frontal lobe, so the anatomists tell us, is the keyboard of the magic instrument.'

Apart from these specific cases of delayed maturation of speech, there are various pathological instances of mutism. The two commonest reasons for failure to talk are (1) deafness and (2) mental defect. Or the two may be combined. In cases of mental defect, the speech when it appears may be so distorted as to be incomprehensible to most adults. Particularly is this so in cases of twinning associated with oligophrenia. When speech comes it may be unintelligible to others, though mutually comprehended. Such a phenomenon constitutes a striking example of the 'secret language' of childhood.

This is exemplified in the case of the uniovular twin brothers G.G. whom I first saw when they were 11 years of age. They were restless phenyl-pyruvic oligophrenics with a mental age of 3. In hospital they 'spoke' very little, and displayed indifference to requests or questions. Most of their time was spent in playful wrestling or fighting, like a couple of high-spirited puppies.

---

* 'How quick children are to discover this wonderful inner world where they are all powerful! Who teaches them this amazing art of manipulating symbols?'

They were re-admitted 4 years later, by which time they were far less hyperkinetic. To some extent they responded to the speech of others. It was almost impossible to understand what they said, and yet their sounds were certainly communicative and not merely verbal play. This was demonstrated by placing the twins in a room, with a tape-recorder concealed. Obviously one twin would articulate, while the other listened and then replied, showing that their utterances were mutually comprehensible, though not to others.

Indeed their first 'word'—intelligible to all around—came later, and comprised the coarse all-purpose interjection 'bugger'!

Another alleged cause of failure to develop speech in childhood is the entity described as 'congenital motor aphasia', or better, as a 'congenital alogia'. Here the conception is of an isolated specific partial disorder in speech-attainment comparable with developmental dyslexia and perhaps also with congenital auditory imperception. Personally I cannot recall having seen such a case where one could confidently exclude other possible explanations, e.g. deafness—partial or complete; intellectual subnormality; hysteria; autism. It is perhaps significant too that in adult neurological practice such cases do not seem to appear. In other words the status of this condition must be for the time being held as suspect.

Two rather unusual cases of delayed development of speech may be quoted:

Case P.O'S. male, aged 18 years. Having acquired speech late he was conspicuous by reason of his taciturnity. Gradually he spoke less and less and by the age of 10 years his talk was reduced to a word or two, and this only when he was at home. Outside the family circle, and at school, he was completely silent. He was intelligent, however, and did well at his lessons. His reading and writing were fluent and accurate; he learned to play the flute. There was no evidence of deafness or of articulatory apraxia. His performance I.Q. (W.I.S.C.) was 131. In 1963 he was thoroughly investigated at the National Hospital, Queen Square. At first he could not be persuaded to open his mouth; or to whistle; or blow out a lighted match; or say 'Ah'; or accept and eat a biscuit. In hospital he used his mouth in the ordinary way for eating and drinking. During his sleep he was often observed to talk aloud and clearly: one could identify the actual words and phrases he used. Attempts to make him talk under hypnosis and under sodium amytal were quite unsuccessful. Dr. Craike, under whose care the patient was, kept him under observation, and up to 1968 saw him on 79 occasions. Although the patient is said to speak at home, he was never heard to do so during any medical interview.

This case obviously belongs to the cadre of a psychologically determined elective mutism.

Case S.R. female, aged 12 years, had never learned to speak, and had always experienced difficulty in swallowing. Clinical examination revealed a nervous, hyperactive child of defective stature and weight, with a cranial circumference of only 19½ inches. She communicated freely by dint of a repertoire of grunting noises, and by means of gesture. There was a left-sided cataract with bilateral hypermetropia. The masseters and temporalis muscles were poorly developed. Continual grimacing and athetoid movements of the face and tongue were to be seen. Palatal elevation on phonation was through a small range (she was unable to blow her nose). Despite her appearance of alertness her I.Q. proved on formal testing to be no more than 40 (though this may well have been an under-estimate), giving her a mental age of 5 years (as contrasted with her chronological age of nearly 13).

In this case a diagnosis was made of a congenital supranuclear bulbar palsy, associated with mental subnormality.

Finally we are confronted with those very rare instances met with in adulthood of a life-long speechlessness. Here the most likely explanation is not an aphasia, but rather an hysteria.

Two examples may be given:

(1) A 17 year old coloured girl was admitted to hospital in Charleston, South Carolina, on account of a state of mutism dating from birth. Except for occasional crude vocalizations, the girl had never uttered a sound. Otherwise the patient's development had been normal and the motor milestones had been reached and passed at the usual age. She was not unintelligent and had attended the 7th grade at a school for non-whites, by dint of writing her answers to the teachers' questions. She could go shopping, displaying a written list of goods required, and she would make no errors in calculating the change. Careful audiometric testing revealed absolutely no hearing-defect. The girl would express her wishes and feelings by way of gestures, mimicry, and at times by a repertoire of sounds such as cries and grunts. Neurological examination was entirely negative. The facies was rather blank and devoid of animation—but this apparently is often noticed in country negroes when translated to a hospital environment. Even under the intravenous administration of sodium amytal there resulted neither vocalisation nor phonation: nor did her expressionless facies show any alteration.

This patient was followed up 12 years later. It was found that her parents had died some years before, and that she had been brought up in a remote part of the country by an aged and ailing grandmother. Although she remained withdrawn she began to speak normally some months after she left hospital.

The explanation of this girl's speechlessness is uncertain. A primitive type of hysteria occurring in circumstances of social deprivation in a coloured unsophisticate seems the most probable suggestion.[1]

The second case is even more interesting and unusual:

(2) A married young woman of 25 years, a factory-worker, was referred to me by Dr. Nelson-Jones on account of speechlessness which had been present for 20 years. Speech had developed in a normal way. At the age of 5 years she underwent a tonsillectomy. About the same time she became greatly frightened by an enemy air-raid. She also became upset when her father was posted overseas in the Army. At this point she lost her speech. When 7 or 8 years of age she was taken to a faith-healer, who got her to say a few words. Following this seance, she lapsed into a silence which she maintained until I saw her in 1962. She communicated by dint of finger-spelling. She could not whistle or yawn. The noise made when coughing, laughing, sneezing, weeping, was extremely subdued. In her sleep she had been noted at times to make moaning noises. She could grunt. Whenever she hurt herself she would emit a quiet 'shsh' as an interjection. She had a pet budgerigar at home to which she would sometimes make little sounds.

Despite her mutism, the patient got through school, took and held down a job in a factory, met and was courted by a young man, whom, in due course, she married. He pronounced his wife as being calm in disposition, and he was not greatly concerned by her state of speechlessness.

Examination showed a state of mild hypothyroidism (for which she was having appropriate treatment). She displayed a general hypomimia, in that her facial emotional movements and her manual gestures were both infrequent in appearance and small in amplitude. Through a very restricted range, she would nod for 'yes' and move her head sideways for 'no'. When wishing to convey a 'thank you' and a 'good-bye' she would make minimal movement of the lips, in utter silence. Asked to blow out a lighted match; to say 'ah'; and to give a cough, she did so but the sounds emitted were extremely quiet in tone.

There was a mild degree of auditory impairment in the left ear.

[1] For notes of this case I am indebted to the courtesy of Dr. Rhett Talbert, M.D.

The patient refused to enter hospital for treatment, though she continued to attend Dr. Nelson-Jones's out-patient clinic periodically.

It was obvious that hers was a very abnormal over-protected life. She and her husband lived in his mother's house. The patient did scarcely any housework, and no cooking at all.

By the end of 1963, she still would not volunteer any speech-sounds. Occasionally, when asked a question, she would give a whispered reply. However, by August 1967 she had lost this faculty and she had reverted to a complete mutism. She refused to enter hospital or to submit to psychiatric treatment.

It is difficult to avoid concluding that this was an hysterical picture, and it seemed that her marital status had simply exacerbated the disability.

The final sentence brings to mind a number of possible repercussions in a mute young woman recently married. What if a baby should complicate the scene? Would the maternal silence include the ordinary vocal demonstrations of tenderness, the cooing sounds of comfort directed towards the fretful infant? Incontrovertibly the child's acquisition of speech would be severely handicapped in such circumstances. But even earlier. Does a state of speechlessness involve the inarticulate cries of love-play and sexual transport?

These last ideas bring up for consideration the whole problem of interjectional utterances, those non-verbal yet vocal exclamations of affective upsurge. What is their linguistic rank or rating, and how do they behave in states of pathology?

In English-speaking communities certain interjectional noises are conventionally uttered and understood. Thus, cries of pleasure include such sounds as 'ah!' or 'mm!'. As indices of pain we meet 'oo!', 'ow!', 'oh!', and 'ah!'. Annoyance is betrayed by the phoneme /t/ which may be reiterated.

It is tempting to imagine that these phenomena are innate or instinctive. If so, one might expect them to be retained in clinical states of speechlessness whether due to an aphasia, anarthria, or hysteria. However, the matter is not so straight-forward. Multilingual students are well aware that the acoustic pattern of interjectional behaviour is anything but uniform and certainly does not transcend racio-linguistic barriers. Thus in such a cognate tongue as Icelandic 'ak' would stand for 'alas!' A Dutchman in pain might exclaim 'o wee' or 'och', and in a state of delighted surprise 'hoezie' or 'heisa'. Turning to languages further remote in pattern, we find an expression of grief in Russian 'och' or 'gore', whereas the Hungarian would utter 'jaj', the Turk 'vah', 'meded' or 'yaziklar olsun', and the Greek 'alloimono'. In a language like Japanese—so different in structure from the European subject-predicate pattern—we find an elaborate system of interjections. Thus we have as representing a cry of pain 'aita'; 'ara' denotes joy or surprise; 'domo' indicates puzzlement or surprise, and 'oya' a sign of great astonishment.

The diversity of these interjectional patterns argues against an innate or instinctive basis. There is a greater probability of an underlying quasi-communicative factor. This would upgrade the status of exclamatory noises so that they might be said to constitute speech although of a lowly rank.

To do this would imply that in pathological states of mutism, whether organically determined or psychogenic, interjections would also be lost.

There is one final and interesting point for consideration, one which concerns yet another instance of inferior speech. I refer to the noises which are emitted by man in his communication with domesticated animals. Whether a person is addressing a calling a kitten or a pet dog, he emits a series of conventional noises. More complicated are the sounds uttered as calls or commands to working animals, horses, plough-oxen, hunting dogs, elephants, and so on. In different countries, quite different calls are met with to indicate 'stop', 'go', 'go back', 'faster', 'slower', 'turn right', 'turn left', and so on. The lack of a uniform world-wide pattern indicates again that these sounds are an aspect of speech, rather than instinctive cries. In other words, they too might be expected to suffer in pathological conditions involving language. Nevertheless they will be retained far better than propositional or superior speech. In this connection we recall the second case, where the long-standing hysterical mute was able to communicate after a fashion with her pet budgerigar. I well remember the extent to which a very severe aphasiac who could scarcely express himself intelligibly, temporarily improved when he was suddenly confronted with a friendly poodle puppy.

Obviously these off-beat aspects of language-pathology deserve a deeper and trans-cultural study by aphasiologists.

BIBLIOGRAPHY

It would be unwieldy and unbalanced to append a complete list of volumes and articles referred to in this collection of essays. Any reader, sufficiently interested to trace a source, could refer to the original papers indicated in the footnote to each chapter.

It was considered useful, however, to append a brief list of selected works which might prove of interest. Not all of them are necessarily referred to in the text. Most of these volumes contain bibliographies:

Aphasia

Papers on Aphasia, delivered at the VII International Congress of Neurology, Rome 1961. Excerpta Medica. International Congress Series No. 38. Amsterdam 1961.

Th. *Alajouanine* and P. *Mozziconacci* 'L'Aphasie et la Désintégration fonctionnelle du Langage.' 1947.

Th. *Alajouanine*. 'L'Aphasie et le langage pathologique.' Ballière, Paris, 1968.

J. Alves *Garcia*. 'Les Troubles du Langage.' Masson, Paris, 1951.

J. *González Cruchaga* 'El Sindrome Afasico' Editorial Andres Bello Santiago de Chile, 1969.

R. *Husson*, J. *Barbizet*, J. *Cauhépé*, P. *Debray*, P. *Laget*, and A. *Sauvageot*. 'Mécanismes cerebraux du langage oral et structure des Langues.' Masson, Paris, 1968.

A. *Kreindler* and A. *Fradis*. 'Performance in Aphasia.' Gauthier-Villars, Paris, 1965.

A. R. *Luria*. 'Role of speech in the regulation of normal and abnormal behaviour.' Pergamon Press, Oxford, 1961.

A. R. *Luria*. 'Higher cortical functions in Man.' Tavistock Publications, London, 1966.

R. C. *Oldfield* and J. C. *Marshall* (Editors). 'Language.' Penguin Books, Harmondsworth, 1968.

C. E. *Osgood* and M. M. *Miron*. (Editors). 'Approaches to the Study of Aphasia.' University of Illinois Press, 1963.

D. M. *Rioch* and E. A. *Weinstein* (Editors). 'Disorders of Communication.' Research Publication No. XLII. (Assoc. Res. Nerv. Ment. Dis., 1962). Williams and Wilkins Co., Baltimore, 1964.

W. *Ritchie Russell* and M. L. E. *Espir*. 'Traumatic Aphasia.' Oxford University Press, 1961.

A. V. S. *de Rueck* and M. *O'Connor* (Editors). Ciba Foundation Symposium on 'Disorders of Language.' Churchill, London, 1964.

V. *Soriano* (Editor). International Journal of Neurology. Issue devoted to 'Aphasia.' 1964, *4*, Nos. 3–4.

H. *Schuell*. 'Differential diagnosis of aphasia with the Minnesota Test.' University of Minnesota Press.

H. *Schuell*, J. J. *Jenkins*, and E. *Jimenez-Pabon*. 'Aphasia in adults.' Hoeber Medical Division, N.Y., 1964.

R. *Tissot*. 'Neuropsychologie de l'Aphasie.' Masson, Paris, 1966.

Linguistics

D. E. *Broadbent*. 'Perception and Communication.' Scientific Book Guild, London, 1961.

C. *Cherry*. 'On human communication.' Technical Press, Massachusetts Institute of Technology and Wiley, New York, 1957.

C. F. *Hockett*. 'A course in modern linguistics.' Macmillan Co., New York, 1959.

G. A. *Miller*. 'Language and communication.' McGraw-Hill, New York, 1963.

S. *Saporta* (Editor). 'Psycholinguistics.' Holt, Rinehart and Winston, New York, 1961.

General

P. *Chauchard*. 'Le Langage et la Pensée.' Presses Universitaires, Paris, 1962.

V. B. *Mountcastle* (Editor). 'Interhemispheric relations and cerebral dominance.' Johns Hopkins Press, Baltimore, 1962.

E. *Renan*. 'De l'origine de langage' (1848). Oeuvres complètes. Tome VIII. Calmann-Levy, Paris, 1958.

E. *Sapir*. 'Culture, Language and Personality.' University of California Press, 1958.

L. S. *Vygotsky*. 'Thought and Language.' Massachusetts Institute of Technology Press, and Wiley, New York, 1962.

INDEX